CONCISE FRENCH AND ENGLISH DICTIONARY

Here at last is the dictionary (complete with an alphabetical list of some of the more important idioms and phrases) that one can safely put in the hands of the beginner.

Journal of Education

TEACH YOURSELF BOOKS

CONCISE
FRENCH & ENGLISH
DICTIONARY

French—English/
English—French

TEACH YOURSELF BOOKS
Hodder and Stoughton

First published 1946
Revised edition 1972
Second impression 1973
Third impression 1973
Fourth impression 1976

Copyright © 1972 edition
Hodder and Stoughton Ltd.

ISBN 0 340 05784 X

Printed in Great Britain
for Hodder and Stoughton Paperbacks, a division of Hodder
and Stoughton Ltd, Mill Road, Dunton Green, Sevenoaks,
Kent by Hazell Watson & Viney Ltd, Aylesbury, Bucks

FOREWORD

THE object of this Dictionary is to provide a handy guide to the French and English languages in which the user will find the essentials needed for reading, writing, speaking and translating. It does not claim to be exhaustive ; indeed no dictionary can make that claim since, however up-to-date and comprehensive it may have been when compiled, new words have certainly come into being since it issued from the press.

Language is constantly in flux both as regards grammar and vocabulary, and all the lexicographer can do is to include only such neologisms as seem to have real vitality. He is faced here with a grave difficulty, since neologisms—especially those born in wartime and those of a slangy nature—sometimes die rapidly and sometimes have a remarkably sturdy life. What is one to do with a word like *décade* which came to be used during the late war for " tobacco ration," i.e. the amount allowed for ten days? It has been omitted as it has probably disappeared. On the other hand such a word as *démarreur*, " self-starter," has evidently earned its place as a permanent acquisition of the language and it, together with similar modern words, has been included.

The French-English section contains some 15,000 words, the English-French over 20,000, and the Dictionary, since a proper selection has been made, covers a range of vocabulary wide enough to meet all one's needs for reading books and news-papers, for correspondence, for translating, and for the give-and-take of everyday life and conversation. But it is a dic-tionary and not an encyclopædia, and you must not ask from it services which it cannot render.

It contains a reasonable amount of familiar and even slang words, since French, like English, is largely spiced with slang ; but it keeps its slang within proper bounds and, without being unduly prim, excludes words which might give offence.

You have in this handy volume that slips so snugly into your pocket, not only a far-flung vocabulary in both French and Eng-lish, but also a complete list of those headaches of schooldays, the Irregular Verbs, with lists of Christian and Geographical names, the French weights and measures, and a neat selection of French Idioms and Phrases well worth your leaning by heart.

Space has been saved by excluding some adverbs formed by adding *-ment* to the feminine of the adjective and by not printing the feminine of nouns and adjectives if it is the same as the masculine or merely adds *-e*. The various meanings of a word are shown by an explanatory word or remark in brackets after the translation, e.g. *try*, essayer (attempt) ; faire l'épreuve de (test) ; juger (an accused). It has, of course, been possible to give only the most usual meanings of some words, but it will nevertheless be found that with this Dictionary and the use of the context, together with some common sense, there is little that cannot be successfully tackled.

ABBREVIATIONS

Very few abbreviations have been used, and these scarcely require explanation.

Some of those to be found are :

v.t.	= transitive verb
v.i.	= intransitive verb
v.r.	= reflexive verb
v. imp.	= impersonal verb

adj.	= adjective	
adv.	= adverb	
prep.	= preposition	Used, as a rule, only when the omission might cause ambiguity.
conj.	= conjunction	
interj.	= interjection	
subst.	= noun *or* substantive	

In addition, *fig.* = figurative, *coll.* = colloquial, *fam.* = familiar, are also to be found.

The gender of a noun is indicated by *m.* = masculine, *f.* = feminine. When both genders are given, the sign *m.* (*f.*) indicates the respective forms, e.g. tuteur(-trice) *m.* (*f.*).

CONTENTS

ACKNOWLEDGMENTS

The Publishers gratefully acknowledge the special services in the preparation of this dictionary of Major H. E. Husey, Mr. Norman Scarlyn Wilson, Mr. P. G. Wilson and Mr. E. S. Jenkins.

The Publishers also express their appreciation to Messrs. Burgess and Bowes Ltd. for the use of certain of their copyright material.

A FRENCH-ENGLISH DICTIONARY

*N.B.—An asterisk * indicates that the word in question also appears in the section of idioms and phrases that follows the main body of the dictionary.*

A

* à, (*prep.*) to; in; at; on

abaissant, (*adj.*) degrading, lowering

abaisse, *f.* undercrust; dough

abaisser, *v.t.* to lower, pull down, humble; s'-, *v.r.* to slope; - jusqu'à, to stoop to, condescend to

abalourdir, *v.t.* to make stupid or dull

abandon, *m.* unrestraint; désertion; surrender.

abandonner, *v.t.* to forsake, give up; - la partie, to throw up the sponge (*fam.*)

abandonné, profligate; abandoned; deserted

abasourdir, *v.t.* to stun, dumbfound

abâtardir, *v.t.* to debase

abat(t)is, *m.* demolition; slaughter (of game, cattle); giblets

abat-jour, *m. inv.* lamp-shade

abattage, *m.* demolition, felling

abattant, *m.* flap (of counter, etc.)

abattement, *m.* dejection

abattoir, *m.* slaughter-house

abattre, *v.t.* to pull down, knock down, slaughter; s'-, *v.r.* to abate; to crash down

abattu, dejected, despondent

abbaye, *f.* abbey

abbé, *m.* abbot; monsieur l'abbé, your Reverence, Father, general designation of a (Roman Catholic) priest

abbesse, *f.* abbess

abcès, *m.* abscess; gathering

abdication, *f.* abdication

abdiquer, *v.t.* to abdicate, renounce

abdomen, *m.* abdomen

abécédaire, *m.* primer; spelling-book.

abée, *f.* sluice, mill-dam

abeille, *f.* bee; - mère, queen bee

abêtir, *v.t.* to make stupid; *v.i.* (or *v.r.*) to grow stupid

abhorrer, *v.t.* to loathe

abîme, *m.* abyss, chasm

abîmer, *v.t.* to overthrow, engulf, damage; s'-, *v.r.* to get spoiled; - la santé, to injure one's health

abject, (*adj.*) mean, base, abject

abjuration, *f.* abjuration

abjurer, *v.t.* to abjure, retract

ablatif, *m.* and (*adj.*) ablative (case)

ablette, *f.* bleak, whitebait

ablution, *f.* ablution, washing

abnégation, *f.* abnegation; self-denial

aboi, *m.* bark (of dogs), baying; aux abois, at bay, in desperate straits

aboiement, *m.* barking

abolir, *v.t.* to abolish

abominable, (*adj.*) abominable; (of weather) wretched

abomination, *f.* abomination; avoir en -, to loathe

abominer, *v.t.* to abhor, loathe

abondamment, (*adv.*) abundantly; copiously

abondance, *f.* abundance; plenty

abonder (en), *v.i.* to abound (in)

abonnement, *m.* subscription (to a paper, etc.); season ticket *abonner, v.t. to subscribe; s'- (à), v.r. to become a subscriber (to)

abord, m. access; manner of approach or addressing ; d'-, at first, straightway

abordable, (adj.) accessible

aborder, v.i. to approach, accost; v.t. to land, to collide with

aborigène, m. or (adj.) aboriginal

abortif-(ive), (adj.) abortive

aboucher, v.t. to bring together

abouler, v.t. to fork out (fam.)

aboutir (à), v.i. to border (upon), end (in), lead (to)

aboyer, v.i. to bark

aboyeur, m. barker; dun; chien -, dog given to barking

abréger, v.t. to abridge, shorten

abrégé, m. précis, abstract, epitome

abreuver, v.t. to water (horses, etc.); to soak, saturate

abreuvoir, m. water-trough, horse-pond

abréviation, f. abbreviation, shortening

abri, m. shelter

abricot, m. apricot

abricotier, m. apricot tree

abriter, v.t. to shelter, shield ; s'-, v.r. to take shelter

abrivent, m. windbreak

abrogation, f. abrogation, repeal

abroger, v.t. to abrogate, repeal

abrupt, (adj.) sheer: abrupt; blunt (of speech, etc.); -ement (adv.)

abrutir, v.t. to stupefy, besot; s'-, v.r. to become besotted

abrutissant, (adj.) stupefying; deadly dull

abrutissement, m. brutishness; degradation

absence, f. absence; avoir des absences (d'esprit), to have fits of absent-mindedness

absent, (adj.) absent, wanting; s'absenter, v.r. to absent oneself

absenteisme, m. absenteeism

abside, f. apse

absinthe, f. absinth; s'absinther, v.r. to take absinth(e)

absolu, (adj.) absolute; utter; positive

absolument, (adv.) absolutely; - défendu, strictly forbidden

absolution, f. absolution; acquittal

absorber, v.t. to absorb, engross

absorption, f. absorption

absoudre, v.t. to absolve, pardon

(s')abstenir (de), v.r. to abstain, refrain (from)

abstention, f. abstention

abstinence, f. abstinence, fasting

abstraction, f. abstraction; faire - de, to disregard, leave out of account

abstraire, v.t. to abstract; s'-, v.r. (dans), to bury oneself in

abstrait, (adj.) abstracted, inattentive, absent-minded, abstract (of ideas, etc.)

abstrus, (adj.) abstruse

absurde, (adj.) absurd, nonsensical

absurdité, f. absurdity

abus, m. abuse; error; misuse

abuser, v.i. to deceive; - de, to impose upon, take unfair advantage of

abusif(-ive), (adj.) improper; abusive

acacia, m. acacia

académicien, m. academician

académie, f. academy; - de musique, music school

académique, (adj.) academic(al)

acajou, m. mahogany

acanthe, f. acanthus

acariâtre, (adj.) bad-tempered, shrewish

accablant, (adj.) overpowering, crushing

accablement, m. dejection

accabler, v.t. to overwhelm ; accablé (de), overwhelmed (with); worn out (with)

accalmie, f. lull

accaparer, v.t. to corner, monopolise

accéder (à), v.i. to accede (to); comply (with); have access (to)

accélérateur, m. accelerator

accélération, f. acceleration

accélérer, v.t. to accelerate, speed up

accent, *m.* accent, tone

accentuation, *f.* accentuation

accentuer, *v.t.* to stress, accentuate, emphasise ; **s'accentuer,** *v.r.* to become (more) marked

acceptation, *f.* acceptance

accepter, *v.t.* to accept

acception, *f.* acceptation, sense, meaning

accès, *m.* access, approach; attack, fit

accessible, *(adj.)* accessible, approachable

accession, *f.* accession

accessit, *m.* honourable mention, second prize

accessoire, *m.* accessory; "props"; **garantie -,** collateral security

accident, *m.* accident; irregularity (of ground, etc.)

accidenté, *(adj.)* eventful; uneven

acclamation, *f.* acclamation, cheering

acclamer, *v.t.* to applaud, cheer

acclimatation, *f.* acclimatisation; **le Jardin d'Acclimatation,** the Zoo (in the Bois de Boulogne)

acclimater, *v.t.* to acclimatise

accointance, *f.* dealings; intimacy (nearly always implying bad company)

accolade, *f.* embrace; accolade; brace (printing and music); **recevoir l'-,** to be knighted

accommodant, *(adj.)* accommodating, easy-going

accommodation, *f.* adaptation, conversion

accommodement, *m.* arrangement, agreement; **entrer en - avec,** to come to terms with

*accommoder, *v.t.* to settle; to attire; to adapt

accompagnement, *m.* accompaniment

accompagner, *v.t.* to accompany

accomplir, *v.t.* to accomplish, achieve, complete

accomplissement, *m.* accomplishment, performance, carrying out

accord, *m.* agreement; **d'accord!** agreed! **être d'-,** to be in tune (music), to agree

accordéon, *m.* accordion; (of car) folding hood

accorder, *v.t.* to grant, concede; to bestow; **s'accorder,** *v.r.* (avec), to tally (with), to agree

accordeur, *m.* tuner (of instruments)

accort, *(adj.)* trim, vivacious

accoster, *v.t.* to accost, go up to; to draw alongside (ship)

accouchement, *m.* confinement, lying in

accoucher (de), *v.i.* to give birth (to)

s'accouder (sur), *v.r.* to lean one's elbows (on)

accoudoir, *m.* elbow-rest

accouplement, *m.* coupling (machinery); pairing, mating

accoupler, *v.t.* to couple

accourcir, *v.t.* to shorten, abridge

accourcissement, *m.* shortening, shrinking

accourir, *v.i.* to run, hasten (up)

accoutrer (de), *v.t.* to equip; *(fam.)* to rig out (in)

accoutumer, *v.t.* to accustom; **s'-,** *v.r.* to get used (to)

accréditer, *v.t.* to accredit, give countenance

accrédité, *m.* accredited agent or representative

accroc, *m.* tear, rent; hitch

accroche-cœur, *m.* kiss-curl

accrocher, *v.t.* to hook, hang up; **s'accrocher,** *v.r.* (à), to cling to

accroire, (faire - à qn.) *v.t.* to make (someone) believe

accroissement, *m.* growth, increase

accroître, *v.t.* to increase, add to

s'accroupir, *v.r.* to squat

accueil, *m.* reception, welcome

accueillir, *v.t.* to greet, welcome

accumulateur, *m.* accumulator

accumuler, *v.t.* to accumulate; to hoard

accusateur, *m.* accuser; *(adj.)* accusing

accuser, *v.t.* to accuse; to indicate

accusé de réception, *m.* acknowledgment of receipt

acerbe, *(adj.)* sharp, harsh

acérer, *v.t.* to steel, to sharpen

acétique, *(adj.)* acetic

acétylène, *m.* acetylene

achalandé, *(adj.)* having custom (of shops, etc.)

acharnement, *m.* eagerness, desperation (esp. of work, etc.)

achat, *m.* purchase

acheminement, *m.* step, preliminary measure

acheminer, *v.t.* to despatch, forward; s'acheminer (vers), *v.r.* to wend one's way (towards)

*acheter, *v.t.* to buy

acheteur(-euse), *m.* (*f.*) buyer, purchaser

achèvement, *m.* finishing, completion

achever, *v.t.* to finish, conclude, round off

achevé, *(adj.)* accomplished; arrant

achromatique, *(adj.)* achromatic, free from colour

acide, *m.* acid; *(adj.)* acid, tart, sour

acier, *m.* steel; - inoxydable, stainless steel

aciérie, *f.* steel-works

acompte, *m.* instalment, payment on account

à-côté, *m.* an aside

à-coup, *m.* jerk, jolt

acoustique, *f.* acoustics

acquéreur(-euse), *m.* (*f.*) purchaser

acquérir, *v.t.* to acquire, secure

acquiescer (à), *v.i.* to acquiesce (in), assent (to)

acquisition, *f.* acquisition

acquit, *m.* discharge; receipt; pour -, paid

acquittement, *m.* acquittal, discharge

âcre, *(adj.)* acrid, pungent

acrimonie, *f.* acrimony

acrobate, *m.* (*f.*) acrobat

acrostiche, *m.* acrostic

acte, *m.* act, action; deed, document

acteur(-rice), *m.* (*f.*) actor (actress)

*action, *f.* action; lawsuit; share (Stock Exchange)

actionnaire, *m.* shareholder

activer, *v.t.* to stir up, stimulate

activité, *f.* activity; marché sans -, dull (flat) market

actuaire, *m.* actuary

actualité, *f.* actuality; event of the moment; film d'-, newsreel, topical film

actuel(le), *(adj.)* real; present

actuellement, *(adv.)* at the (present) moment

adage, *m.* proverb, saying

adaptateur, *m.* adapter, converter

adaptation, *f.* adaptation, adjustment

adapter, *v.t.* to adapt, adjust

addition, *f.* addition; bill (restaurant)

additionner, *v.t.* to add up, tot up

adénoïde, *(adj.)* adenoidal; végétations adénoïdes, adenoids

adhérent, *m.* adherent, supporter

adhérer, *v.i.* to adhere, stick

adhésion, *f.* adhesion

adieu, *m.* farewell, good-bye; faire ses adieux à, to say good-bye to, bid farewell to

adjacent, *(adj.)* adjacent, adjoining

adjoindre, *v.t.* to associate

adjoint, *m.* associate, assistant; - (au maire), deputy mayor

adjudant, *m.* company sergeant-major; - chef, regimental s.m.

adjudication, *f.* adjudication, award; mettre qch. en -, to put something up for auction

adjugé! Gone! Sold!

adjuger, *v.t.* to award; (at sales) to knock down

adjurer, *v.t.* to adjure, conjure

admettre, *v.t.* to admit; to grant

administration, *f.* administration; Government service; entrer dans l'-, to become a civil servant

administrer, *v.t.* to administer, govern, manage

admirable, *(adj.)* admirable
-ment, *(adv.)* admirably, capit-
ally

admirateur(-trice), *m. (f.)* admirer; *(adj.)* admiring

admiration, *f.* admiration; faire
l'- de, to arouse the admiration
of

admissible, *(adj.)* allowable, eligible

admission, *f.* admission, admittance, intake *(tech.)*

admonestation, *f.* admonition

admonester, *v.t.* to admonish,
reprimand

adolescence, *f.* adolescence, youth

adolescent, *m.* youth; *(adj.)*
youthful, adolescent

s'adoniser, *v.r.* to smarten oneself up *(fam.)*

s'adonner (à), *v.r.* to devote oneself (to), become addicted (to)

adopté(e), *m. (f.)* adopted child

adopter, *v.t.* to adopt, take up

adorable, *(adj.)*, charming

adorateur(-trice), *m. (f.)* adorer,
worshipper

adosser, *v.t.* to lean (something
against); s'- au mur, to lean
against the wall

adoucir, *v.t.* to soften, sweeten,
assuage

adresse, *f.* address, destination;
dexterity

adresser, *v.t.* to address; s'- à,
v.r. to apply to

adroit, *(adj.)* adroit, skilful

adulateur(-trice), *m. (f.)* flatterer; *(adj.)* flattering

adulation, *f.* adulation, fawning

adulte, *m. (f.)* adult; *(adj.)* adult,
grown up

adultère, *m.* adultery; *(m.* or *f.)*
adulterer, adulteress

adultérer, *v.t.* to adulterate

advenir, *v.i.* (used impersonally),
to chance, happen

adversaire, *m.* adversary, enemy

adverse, *(adj.)* adverse; opposing

adversité, *f.* adversity, misfortune

aérage, *m.* airing, ventilation

aérer, *v.t.* to air, ventilate

aérien(ne), *(adj.)* aerial; raid -
air-raid

aérolithe, *m.* aerolite, meteorite

aéronaute, *m.* aeronaut

aéronautique, *f.* aeronautics;
(adj.) aeronautical

aéroport, *m.* airport

aéroporté, *(adj.)* air-borne

aérostat, *m.* airship, balloon

affabilité, *f.* affability, graciousness

affable, *(adj.)* affable, gracious

affadir, *v.t.* to make cloying,
tasteless

affadissement, *m.* insipidity;
nausea

affaiblir, *v.t.* to weaken; s'affaiblir, *v.r.* to grow weak

*affaire, *f.* affair, business

affairé, *(adj.)* busy

affaissement, *m.* collapse; dejection

s'affaisser, *v.r.* to sink, fall in

affamer, *v.t.* to starve

affectation, *f.* affectation

affecter, *v.t.* to affect; (military,
etc.) to detail, to post

affection, *f.* fondness, affection

affectionner, *v.t.* to have a liking,
fondness, for

affectueux(-euse), *(adj.)* affectionate, fond (of)

affermer, *v.t.* to farm, lease

affermir, *v.t.* to strengthen,
harden

afféterie, *f.* affectation, affected
manner

affiche, *f.* bill, poster

afficher, *v.t.* to display; " défense d'-," " Stick no bills ";
s'afficher, *v.r.* to show off, attract attention to oneself

afficheur, *m.* bill-sticker

affiler, *v.t.* to sharpen, to set

affilier (à), *v.t.* to affiliate (with)

affiner, *v.t.* to refine

affinité, *f.* affinity

affirmatif(-ve), *(adj.* and *m.)* affirmative; signe -, nod

affirmer, *v.t.* to affirm, declare

affleurer, *v.t.* to level, to make
flush

affliction, *f.* affliction, sorrow

affliger (de), *v.t.* to afflict (with); to pain

affluence, *f.* flow; plenty, concourse; **heures d'-**, "rush" hours; **- de visiteurs**, great number, throng of visitors

affluent, *m.* tributary

affolement, *m.* panic

affoler, *v.t.* to madden, drive crazy; to bewitch, infatuate

affranchir, *v.t.* to emancipate; to pay the postage on, to prepay

affranchissement, *m.* liberation; postage, prepayment

affréter, *v.t.* to charter (of ships)

affreux(-euse), *(adj.)* frightful, horrible

affront, *m.* insult, indignity

affronter, *v.t.* to insult; to confront, face

affubler, *v.t.* to dress, rig out (usually disparaging)

affût, *m.* gun carriage; hiding place; **être à l'- de**, to lie in wait for

affûtage, *m.* set of tools, sharpening

affûter, *v.t.* to whet, sharpen

afin de, in order to

afin que *(with subjunctive)*, in order that, so that

africain, *(adj.)* African

agaçant, *(adj.)* annoying

agacer, *v.t.* to annoy, irritate

agate, *f.* agate

***âge**, *m.* age

âgé, *(adj.)* old, aged; **- de cinq ans**, five years old

agence, *f.* agency, office, bureau

agenda, *m.* memorandum-book, diary

s'agenouiller, *v.r.* to kneel down

agent, *m.* agent; **- de police**, policeman; **- de location**, estate agent

agglomérer, *v.t.* to agglomerate

agglutiner, *v.t.* to agglutinate

aggraver, *v.t.* to aggravate, worsen; **s'-**, *v.r.* to grow worse

agile, *(adj.)* agile, nimble

agiotage, *m.* stock-jobbing

agioteur, *m.* jobber, speculator

agir, *v.i.* to act, act upon; il

s'agit de, the question is to, it is a matter of

agissant, *(adj.)* active, busy

agitateur(-trice), *m.* *(f.)* agitator

agitation, *f.* agitation; unrest; roughness (of sea)

agiter, *v.t.* to agitate; to shake; wave, wag

agneau, *m.* lamb

agnelet, *m.* lambkin

agonie, *f.* agony; death-throes

agonisant, *(adj.)* dying, at the point of death; *(noun)* dying person

agrafe, *f.* buckle, clasp

agrafer, *v.t.* to buckle, fasten by a hook, etc.

agraire, *(adj.)* agrarian

agrandir, *v.t.* to enlarge, increase; to elevate (mind or spirit)

agrandissement, *m.* increase; advancement; enlargement

agréable, *(adj.)* agreeable, pleasant, nice

agréer, *v.t.* to approve (of); to accept

agrégation, *f.* aggregation; competitive examination for teaching post at a *lycée*

agrément, *m.* pleasure; (plural) trimmings, amenities

agrès, *m. pl.* rigging, tackle.

agresseur, *m.* aggressor

agressif(-ve), *(adj.)* aggressive

agression, *f.* aggression

agricole, *(adj.)* agricultural

agriffer, *v.t.* to clutch (at), grab

aguerrir, *v.t.* to inure to war; **aguerri**, seasoned (of troops)

aguets (aux), *m. pl.* on the watch, on the look-out

aguichant, *(adj.)* *(fam.)* seductive, provocative (glance, etc.)

ahurir, *v.t.* to astound, dumbfound

aide, *m.* helper, assistant; *f.* help, aid; **venir en - à**, to come to the help of

aider, *v.t.* to help, assist

aïeul, *m.* grandfather, ancestor

aigle, *m.* *(f.)* eagle

aiglefin, *m.* haddock

aigre, (*adj.*) sour, sharp; **tourner à l'-,** to turn sour; **-ment,** (*adv.*)

aigrette, *f.* tuft, crest; aigrette

aigreur, *f.* sourness, tartness

aigrir, *v.t.* to embitter; to sour

aigu (*fem.* **aiguë**), (*adj.*) pointed, sharp; acute

aiguière, *f.* ewer

aiguille, *f.* needle; hand (of watch, etc.); **- a tricoter,** knitting-needle; **- aimantée,** magnetic needle

aiguillette, *f.* shoulder-knot

aiguilleur, *m.* pointsman (rail)

aiguillon, *m.* prick, sting; goad

aiguillonner, *v.t.* to goad, prod

aiguiser, *v.t.* to sharpen

ail, *m.* garlic

aile, *f.* wing (of bird, plane, building or car); **ailé,** winged

aileron, *m.* pinion; aileron; fin

aillade, *f.* garlic sauce

ailleurs, (*adv.*) elsewhere; **d'-,** besides

aimable, (*adj.*) pleasant, kind

aimant, *m.* magnet

aimanter, *v.t.* to magnetise

aimer, *v.t.* to like, care for, love; **- mieux,** to prefer

aîné, (*adj.*) elder (of two); eldest; Risler aîné (Daudet), Risler senior

aînesse, *f.* primogeniture

ainsi, (*adv.*) thus, so; **- de suite,** and so on; **- soit-il,** amen; **- que,** as well as

*air, *m.* air; appearance, look; song

airain, *m.* bronze, brass

aire, *f.* area; threshing-floor; eyrie

airelle, *f.* bilberry

ais, *m.* board, plank

aisance, *f.* ease; **être dans l'-,** to be well off; **cabinet d'-s,** water-closet

*aise, *f.* ease, comfort

aise, (*adj.*) (usually with **bien**), (very) glad

aisé, (*adj.*) easy; well-to-do

aisselle, *f.* armpit

ajonc, *m.* furze

ajour, *m.* opening (to let in light)

ajournement, *m.* adjournment

ajourner, *v.t.* to adjourn, postpone

ajouter, *v.t.* to add, to add up

ajustement, *m.* adjustment, settlement

ajuster, *v.t.* to adjust, put in order; to settle (affairs, differences, etc.)

alambic, *m.* (chem.) alembic, still

alarme, *f.* alarm; **sonner l'-,** to give the alarm; **tirer le signal d'-,** to pull the communication cord (railway)

alarmer, *v.t.* to alarm, frighten

albâtre, *m.* alabaster

album, *m.* album

albumine, *f.* albumen

alcali, *m.* alkali

alchimie, *f.* alchemy

alcool, *m.* alcohol; **- à brûler,** methylated spirit

alcôve, *f.* recess, alcove

alentours, *m. pl.* vicinity, surroundings

alerte, *f.* alarm, warning; (*adj.*) alert, brisk

alerter, *v.t.* to give the alarm to

aléser, *v.t.* to bore, drill (of metals, etc.)

alexandrin, alexandrine; **vers -,** alexandrine (a twelve-syllable line in poetry, much used in France in the seventeenth and eighteenth centuries)

alezan, *m.* (or *adj.*) chestnut (horse)

algarade, *f.* abuse; escapade

algèbre, *f.* algebra

algérien(ne), (*adj.*) Algerian

algue, *f.* seaweed

aliéniste, *m.* mental specialist

aliéner, *v.t.* to alienate, estrange; **un aliéné,** madman; **asile d'aliénés,** lunatic asylum

alignement, *m.* alignment; row

aligner, *v.t.* to draw up in line, to mark out

aliment, *m.* food

alimentation, *f.* feeding, nourishment

alimenter, *v.t.* to feed, supply

alinéa, *m.* paragraph; indented line (new paragraph)

alité, (*adj.*) confined to bed, laid up

s'aliter, *v.r.* to take to one's bed

alizé, *m.* trade-wind

allaiter, *v.t.* to suckle

allécher, *v.t.* to allure, entice

allée, *f.* lane, avenue; going

alléger, *v.t.* to ease, alleviate; (of ships) to lighten

allégorie, *f.* allegory

allégorique, (*adj.*) allegorical

allègre, (*adj.*) cheerful, brisk

allégresse, joy, cheerfulness

alléguer, *v.t.* to allege

allemand, German

*****aller,** *v.i.* to go; to suit; **s'en -,** *v.r.* to go away

alliage, *m.* alloy

alliance, *f.* alliance, marriage; wedding-ring

allié(e), (*noun* or *adj.*) ally, allied

allier, *v.t.* to ally, to alloy

allô, Hullo! (telephone, etc.)

allocution, *f.* speech; **prononcer une -,** to deliver a speech, address

allonger, *v.t.* to lengthen; to eke out; **- une gifle,** to slap, deal a blow; **s'allonger,** *v.r.* to grow longer

allumer, *v.t.* to light; to inflame, excite

allumette, *f.* match; **- suédoise,** safety match; **frotter une -,** to strike a match

allumeur, *m.* lighter; lamp-lighter

allure, *f.* pace, bearing, gait

allusion, *f.* allusion; **faire - à,** to refer to

almanach, *m.* almanac

aloès, *m.* aloe(s)

aloi, *m.* quality, standard; **de bon -,** genuine

alors, (*adv.*) then, at that time

alose, *f.* shad

alouette, *f.* lark

alourdir, *v.t.* to make dull, stupid

aloyau, *m.* sirloin

Alpes, *f. pl.* the Alps; **une alpe,** a mountain

alpestre, alpin (*adj.*) Alpine

alphabet, *m.* alphabet; primer

alphabétique, (*adj.*) alphabetical

alsacien(-enne), (*adj.*) Alsatian

altérant, (*adj.*) causing thirst

altération, *f.* change (for the worse)

altercation, *f.* dispute

altéré, (*adj.*) thirsty, haggard, drawn

altérer, *v.t.* to change (for the worse); to impair (of health); to adulterate (of food)

alternatif(-ve), (*adj.*) alternat(iv)e, alternating

alterner, *v.i.* to alternate, take turns

Altesse, *f.* Highness

altier, (*adj.*) haughty

altitude, *f.* height; **prendre de l'-,** to climb (aviation)

alun, *m.* alum

alvéole, *m.* socket, cavity

amabilité, *f.* kindness, amiability

amadou, *m.* tinder, touchwood

amadouer, *v.t.* to wheedle

s'amaigrir, *v.r.* to grow thin

amalgame, *m.* amalgam

amande, *f.* almond

amandier, *m.* almond tree

amant(e), *m.* (*f.*) lover

amarrage, *m.* mooring, berth

amarrer, *v.t.* to moor, make fast

amas, *m.* heap

amasser, *v.t.* to pile up, amass

amateur, *m.* amateur; lover (of something)

amazone, *f.* Amazon; horse-woman; riding-habit

ambassade, *f.* embassy

ambassadeur, *m.* ambassador

ambiance, *f.* surroundings

ambigu (*fem.* **ambiguë**), (*adj.*) ambiguous; (*m.*) mixture, medley

ambitieux(-euse), (*adj.*) ambitious

ambition, *f.* ambition

ambitionner, *v.t.* to covet (something)

ambre, *m.* amber

ambulance, *f.* ambulance

ambulant, (*adj.*) itinerant

âme, *f.* soul, spirit; bore (of gun)

amélioration, *f.* improvement, change (for the better)

améliorer, *v.t.* to improve; **s'-,** *v.r.* to get better aménager, v.t. to fit up, fit out

amende, f. fine; **frapper qn. d'une -**, to fine someone; **- honorable**, apology

amendement, m. amendment

amener, v.t. to lead, bring (someone)

amer(-ère), (adj.) bitter; (m.) bitters, gall

américain, (adj.) American

amerrir, v.i. to alight, land on the sea (aviation)

amerrissage, m. landing (on water)

amertume, f. bitterness

améthyste, f. amethyst

ameublement, m. furniture, furnishing

ameutement, m. mob, gathering

ami(e), m. (f.) friend; **petite -**, lover, mistress; (adj.) friendly, kindly

amical, (adj.) friendly

amidon, m. starch

amidonner, v.t. to starch

amincir, v.t. to thin, fine down

amiral, m. admiral

amirauté, f. Admiralty. (N.B.— The French Admiralty is the *Ministère de la Marine*)

amitié, f. friendship, friendliness; **se lier d'- avec**, to form a friendship with; **faites mes amitiés à**, remember me to

ammoniaque, m. ammonia

amnistie, f. amnesty

amnistier, v.t. to amnesty, pardon

amoindrir, v.t. to lessen, reduce; v.i. to grow less

amollir, v.t. to soften

s'amollir, v.r. to grow soft, weak

amonceler, v.t. to heap up

amoncellement, m. heap, pile

amont, m. head waters (of river); **en -**, upstream; **en - de**, above

amorce, f. bait; priming, detonator

amortir, v.t. to deaden, muffle; to redeem, pay off

amortissable, (adj.) redeemable

amortissement, m. redemption; **fonds d'-**, sinking fund

amortisseur, m. shock-absorber

amour, m. (often *fem.* in plural) love; Cupid; **mariage d'-**, love match; **- propre**, self-respect, self-conceit

amourette, f. (passing) love affair

amoureux(-euse), (adj.) amorous, loving; **être - de**, to be in love with; m. (f.) lover

amovible, (adj.) removable

ampère, m. ampere

amphibie, m. amphibian; (adj.) amphibious; **opération -**, combined operation

amphithéâtre, m. amphitheatre

ample, (adj.) ample, roomy

ampleur, f. fullness, copiousness

amplificateur, m. amplifier

amplifier, v.t. to amplify, magnify

ampoule, f. bulb (electric); blister; phial

amputer, v.t. to amputate

amulette, f. amulet, charm

amusement, m. recreation, pastime

amuser, v.t. to amuse, entertain; **s'amuser (bien)**, v.r. to enjoy oneself, have a good time

amygdale, f. tonsil

an, m. year; **avoir cinq ans**, to be five years old; **le jour de l'an**, New Year's Day

anachorète, m. anchorite, hermit

analogie, f. analogy

analogue, (adj.) analogous, similar

analyser, v.t. to analyse

ananas, m. pineapple

anarchie, f. anarchy

anarchiste, m. anarchist (also adj.)

anathématiser, v.t. to anathematise, curse

anatomie, f. anatomy

anatomique, (adj.) anatomical

ancêtre, m. or f. ancestor (-tress), forebear

anchois, m. anchovy

ancien(ne), (adj.) ancient, old, senior, former, ex-.

ancillaire, (adj.) ancillary, subordinate

ancrage, m. anchorage

ancre, *f.* anchor; jeter (lever) l'-, to drop (weigh) anchor

andalou(se), (*adj.*) Andalusian

âne(-esse), *m.* (*f.*) ass, donkey

anéantir, *v.t.* to destroy, annihilate; anéanti, exhausted

anéantissement, *m.* annihilation; prostration

anecdote, *f.* anecdote

anémique, (*adj.*) anæmic

ânerie, *f.* stupidity; foolish action (or remark)

anesthésier, *v.t.* to anæsthetise

anfractuosité, *f.* unevenness (of surface), windings (of road—gen. plural)

ange, *m.* angel; - gardien, guardian angel; faiseuse d'anges, abortionist; être aux anges, to be overjoyed, in the seventh heaven

angélique, (*adj.*) angelic; (*f.*) angelica

angine, *f.* sore throat; - de poitrine, angina pectoris

anglais, (*adj.*) English; l'Anglais(e) Englishman (-woman); filer à l'anglaise, to take French leave

angle, *m.* angle, corner

anglican(e), (*adj.*) and *m.* or *f.* Anglican

anglicisme, *m.* anglicism, English idiom

anglophile(-phobe), (*adj.* and *m.* or *f.*) pro- (anti-) English

angoisse, *f.* anguish, pang

anguille, *f.* eel

angulaire, (*adj.*) angular; pierre -, corner stone

anguleux(-euse), (*adj.*) bony, many-cornered

ânier, *m.* donkey-driver

aniline, *f.* aniline

animal, *m.* animal; brute; (*adj.*) animal

animer, *v.t.* to animate, prompt; to enliven; animé, lively, spirited

animosité, *f.* animosity, spite

anis, *m.* anise

anneau, *m.* ring; link (of chain); ringlet

année, *f.* year. (Usually a particular year, an having a more general sense)

annexe, *f.* annex

annexer, *v.t.* to annex, append; pièces annexées, enclosures

anniversaire, *m.* anniversary

annonce, *f.* announcement; advertisement; - de spectacle, playbill

annoncer, *v.t.* to announce; to herald; se faire -, to give in one's name (one's card)

annonceur, *m.* announcer, advertiser

annonciation, *f.* Annunciation; fête de l'-, Lady Day

annotation, *f.* annotation, note

annoter, *v.t.* to annotate

annuaire, *m.* year book

annuel(le), (*adj.*) annual, yearly

annuité, *f.* annuity

annulaire, *m.* ring-finger, third finger

annuler, *v.t.* to annul, rescind, cancel

anoblir, *v.t.* to ennoble (e.g. to raise to noble rank)

anodin, *m.* anodyne, palliative; (*adj.*) anodyne, mild

anomal, (*adj.*) anomalous

ânon, *m.* ass's foal

ânonner, *v.t.* to mumble, deliver (a speech) hesitantly, to hum and haw

anonymat, *m.* anonymity

anonyme, (*adj.*) anonymous; société -, joint stock (limited liability) company

anormal, (*adj.*) abnormal, exceptional

anse, *f.* handle; bay (geographical)

antagoniste, *m.* antagonist; (*adj.*) antagonistic

antan (d'), (*archaic*) of yester year

antarctique, antarctic

antécédent, (*adj.*) antecedent, previous; (*m.*) antecedent; (*plural*) antecedents, past (career, etc.)

antenne, *f.* antenna; aerial (wireless)

antérieur, (*adj.*) anterior, previous

anthropoïde, (*adj.*) and *m.* (*f.*) anthropoid (ape)

anthropophage, *m.* cannibal; (*adj.*) man-eating

anti-aérien(ne), (*adj.*) anti-aircraft; **défense passive anti-aérienne,** A.R.P. (Civil Defence)

antichambre, *f.* anti-chamber; **faire -,** to hang about in the waiting-room (i.e. before seeing some important person)

antichoc, (*adj., inv.*) shock-proof

anticipation, *f.* anticipation; **par -,** in advance, beforehand

anticiper, *v.t.* to anticipate

antidater, *v.t.* to ante-date

antidérapant, (*adj.*) non-skid

antidote, *m.* antidote

antipathie, *f.* antipathy, aversion

antipathique, (*adj.*) unlikable

antiquaire, *m.* antiquary

antique, (*adj.*) antique, ancient

antiquité, *f.* antiquity; **magasin d'antiquités,** antique shop

antiseptique, (*adj.* and *m.*) antiseptic

antithèse, *f.* antithesis

antre, *m.* cave; den

anxiété, *f.* anxiety

anxieux(-euse), (*adj.*) anxious, uneasy

aorte, *f.* aorta

août, *m.* August

apache, *m.* hooligan, rough

apaiser, *v.t.* to appease, calm; to allay

apanage, *m.* appanage

aparté, *m.* aside (theat.), stage-whisper

apathique, (*adj.*) apathetic

apercevoir, *v.t.* to perceive, catch sight of

aperçu, *m.* sketch, summary; glimpse

apéritif, *m.* appetizer, cocktail

apeuré, (*adj.*) scared, frightened

apiculteur, *m.* bee-keeper, apiarist

apitoyer, *v.t.* to move to pity

aplanir, *v.t.* to level, plane

aplatir, *v.t.* to flatten, hammer down; **s'aplatir,** *v.r.* to go flat (of

tyres); **- par terre,** to lie flat on the ground

aplomb, *m.* uprightness; self-assurance, poise

apogée, *m.* apogee, zenith

apologie, *f.* defence, justification

apoplexie, *f.* apoplexy

apostat, *m.* apostate, renegade

apostolique, (*adj.*) apostolic

apothéose, *f.* apotheosis

apothicaire, *m.* apothecary

apôtre, *m.* apostle; **faire le bon -,** to put on a saintly air

apparaître, *v.i.* to appear, become visible (or apparent)

apparat, *m.* pomp, display

appareil, *m.* apparatus, appliance, machine; **- photographique,** camera

appareiller, *v.t.* to fit up; *v.i.* to get under way (nautical)

apparence, *f.* appearance, semblance; **selon toute -,** to all appearances

apparent, (*adj.*) apparent (but not real); evident

apparenté (bien), (*adj.*) (well) connected

apparition, *f.* appearance; apparition

appartement, *m.* flat, set of rooms

appartenir, *v.i.* to belong; (impersonal) to behove

appas, *m. pl.* charm, attraction

appât, *m.* bait, lure

appauvrir, *v.t.* to impoverish

appel, *m.* appeal, call; **- d'incendie,** fire alarm; **faire - à qn.,** to appeal to someone; **cour d'-,** court of appeal

***appeler,** *v.t.* to call; **s'appeler,** *v.r.* to be called, named

appendice, *m.* appendix (of book, or anatomical)

appendicite, *f.* appendicitis

appétissant, (*adj.*) appetising, tempting

appétit, *m.* appetite; **manger de bon -,** to eat with relish, heartily

applaudir, *v.t.* to applaud; **s'- (de),** *v.r.* to congratulate oneself (on)

applaudissement, *m.* (generally plural), applause

application, *f.* application, applying; diligence

applique, *f.* wall-bracket; appliqué lace, etc.

appliquer, *v.t.* to apply; to administer; **appliqué,** studious

appoint, *m.* balance (i.e. cash remaining over)

appointements, *m. pl.* salary

apport, *m.* (initial) share; **- de capitaux,** contribution of capital

apporter, *v.t.* to bring, convey

apposer, *v.t.* to affix (poster, signature, etc.)

appréciation, *f.* appreciation; valuation; rise in value

apprécier, *v.t.* to appreciate; to appraise

appréhender, *v.t.* to dread, apprehend, arrest

appréhension, *f.* apprehension; **- au corps,** arrest

***apprendre,** *v.t.* to learn, teach

apprenti, *m.* apprentice

apprentissage, *m.* apprenticeship; **faire son - (chez),** to serve one's apprenticeship (with)

apprêter, *v.t.* to prepare; to dress (of food); to finish (of fabrics, etc.)

apprivoiser, *v.t.* to tame; **La Mégère apprivoisée,** *The Taming of the Shrew*

approbateur(-trice), *(adj.)* approving; *m. (f.)* approver

approbation, *f.* approval

approchant (de), *(adj.)* approximating (to)

approche, *f.* approach

approcher, *v.t.* to bring near; *v.i.* to approach; *v.r.* **s'approcher (de),** to come near, approach

approfondir, *v.t.* to deepen; **faire une étude approfondie de,** to make a thorough study (of)

appropriation, *f.* appropriation; **- de fonds,** embezzlement

approprier, *v.t.* to appropriate; to adapt

approuver, *v.t.* to approve, sanction

approvisionnement, *m.* supplying, victualling

approvisionner (de), *v.t.* to supply, provision (with)

approximatif(-ve), *(adj.)* approximate, rough

appui, *m.* prop, support; **- de fenêtre,** window-ledge; **à hauteur d'-,** breast-high

appuyer, *v.t.* to lean, support

âpre, rough, harsh

***après,** *(prep.)* after; *(adv.)* afterwards

après-demain, *m.* day after to-morrow

après-midi, *m.* or *f.* afternoon

apte, *(adj.)* fit, suited

aptitude (à, pour), *f.* (natural) gift, aptitude (for)

aquarelle, *f.* water-colour

aqueduc, *m.* aqueduct

aqueux(-euse), *(adj.)* watery

aquilin, *(adj.)* aquiline; Roman (of nose)

aquilon, *m.* north wind

arabe, *(adj.)* Arab; Arabian; Arabic

arachide, *f.* pea-nut

araignée, *f.* spider; **avoir une - au plafond,** to have a screw loose, be off one's head

arbalète, *f.* cross-bow

arbitrage, *m.* arbitration, arbitrament

arbitraire, *(adj.)* arbitrary

arbitre, *m.* arbiter, arbitrator; referee, umpire; **libre -,** freewill

arborer, *v.t.* to hoist (flags, etc.)

arbre, *m.* tree; **- fruitier,** fruit tree; **- moteur,** driving-shaft

arbrisseau, *m.* shrub

arbuste, *m.* shrub, bush

arc, *m.* bow; arch; arc; **- arc-en-ciel,** rainbow

arc-boutant, *m.* flying-buttress

arc-bouter, *v.t.* to buttress, shore up

archange, *m.* archangel

arche, *f.* ark; arch (of bridge)

archéologue, *m.* archæologist

archet, *m.* bow (of violin)

archevêché, *m.* archbishopric

archevêque, *m.* archbishop

archiduc, *m.* archduke
archipel, *m.* archipelago
architecte, *m.* architect
architecture, *f.* architecture
archives, *f. pl.* archives; **Les Archives,** The Public Record Office
archiviste, *m.* archivist; filing-clerk
arçon, *m.* saddle-bow
arctique, Arctic
ardent, *(adj.)* eager, passionate; burning, blazing
ardeur, *f.* zeal, eagerness; heat
ardoise, *f.* slate
ardu, *(adj.)* steep; arduous, difficult
are, *m.* unit of measurement (100 square metres)
arène, *f.* arena; *(pl.)* sands
aréole, *f.* halo, nimbus
arête, *f.* fish-bone; mountain-ridge, watershed
*****argent,** *m.* money; silver
argenterie, *f.* silver-plate
argentin, *(adj.)* silvery (sound, etc.); Argentine
argile, *f.* clay
argot, *m.* slang
arguer, *v.i.* to argue; *v.t.* to infer, assert
argument, *m.* argument; synopsis (of play, etc.)
aride, *(adj.)* dry, barren
aristocrate, *m.* *(f.)* aristocrat
aristocratie, *f.* aristocracy
aristocratique, *(adj.)* aristocratic
arithmétique, *f.* arithmetic
arlequin, *m.* harlequin
arlésien(-ne), *(adj.)* Arlesian; of Arles
armateur, *m.* ship-owner, fitter-out (of ships)
arme, *f.* weapon, arm; - **à feu,** fire-arm; **faire des armes,** to fence; **passer l'- à gauche** *(fam.),* to peg out, go west
armée, *f.* army; - **de l'Air,** Air Force; - **du Salut,** Salvation Army
armement, *m.* arming; equipment; *(plural)* armaments

armer, *v.t.* to fit out, arm; **béton armé,** reinforced concrete
armistice, *m.* armistice
armoire, *f.* cupboard, wardrobe
armoiries, *f. pl.* (coat of) arms
armure, *f.* armour, armour-plating
armurier, *m.* gunsmith
aromatique, *(adj.)* aromatic
arome, *m.* aroma
arpent, *m.* acre (French, i.e. about 1½ acres English)
arpenter, *v.t.* to survey, measure (land); to stride about
*****arracher,** *v.t.* to tear, tear up; pull out (tooth)
arrangement, *m.* arrangement
*****arranger,** *v.t.* to arrange; to settle
arrestation, *f.* arrest; **mettre qn. en -,** to arrest someone, take someone into custody
arrêt, *m.* stop; decree; - **facultatif (obligatoire)** — trams, etc., stop here by request (must stop here)
arrêter, *v.t.* to stop, arrest; **s'arrêter,** *v.r.* to stop, come to a stop
arrhes, *f. pl.* earnest-money
arrière, *(adv.)* backwards, back; *noun, m.* rear, stern, back (football); **lanterne -,** tail-light; **faire marche -,** to back; **en -,** in arrears; **aller en -,** to back, go astern
arriéré, *(adj.)* backward, behind the times
arrière-goût, *m.* after-taste
arrière-pensée, *f.* ulterior motive, mental reservation
arrière-petit-fils, *m.* great-grandson
arrière-plan, *m.* background, up-stage
arrimer, *v.t.* to stow cargo
arrimeur, *m.* stevedore
arrivage, *m.* consignment, delivery
arrivée, *f.* arrival, coming
*****arriver,** *v.i.* to arrive; to happen
arriviste, *m.* *(f.)* pusher, go-getter

arrogant, (*adj.*) arrogant

s'arroger, *v.r.* to arrogate (to oneself)

arrondir, *v.t.* to round, round off

arrondissement, *m.* district (of Paris); subdivision of a French department

arrosage, *m.* irrigation, watering

arroser, *v.t.* to water, sprinkle; to dilute with water; to wet

arrosoir, *m.* watering-can, sprinkler

arsenal, *m.* arsenal

arsenic, *m.* arsenic

art, *m.* art; skill; **beaux arts,** fine arts

artère, *f.* artery

artésien(ne), (*adj.*) artesian; of Artois

artichaut, *m.* artichoke

article, *m.* article; **- de fond,** leading article; **articles de Paris,** fancy goods

articulation, *f.* articulation; joint

articuler, *v.t.* to pronounce clearly; to connect by joints

artifice, *m.* artifice, stratagem; **tirer un feu d'-,** to let off fireworks

artificiel(le), (*adj.*) artificial, false

artillerie, *f.* artillery; **- de campagne,** field artillery

artilleur, *m.* artilleryman, gunner

artimon, *m.* mizzen

artisan, *m.* artisan, (skilled) workman

artiste, *m.* (*f.*) artist, performer

artistique, (*adj.*) artistic

as, *m.* ace (of cards); expert pilot, first-rate player

asbeste, *m.* asbestos

ascendant, *m.* ascendant, ascendancy

ascenseur, *m.* lift elevator

ascension, *f.* ascent; **Fête de l'-,** Ascension Day

ascensionniste, *m.* (*f.*) mountain-climber, balloonist

ascétique, (*adj.*) ascetic

aseptique, (*adj.*) aseptic

asiatique, (*adj.*) Asiatic

asile, *m.* refuge, shelter; **salle d'-,** infant school; **- des pauvres,** workhouse

aspect, *m.* aspect, sight; point of view

asperge, *f.* asparagus

asperger, *v.t.* to sprinkle (with water)

asphalte, *m.* asphalt

asphyxier, *v.t.* to suffocate; **to gas** (war)

aspic, *m.* asp; aspic

aspirant (à), *m.* candidate (for), aspirant (to); midshipman

aspirateur (électrique), *m.* vacuum-cleaner

aspiration, *f.* aspiration, craving; inhaling; suction

aspirer, *v.t.* to breathe in, suck in; to aspirate; *v.i.* **- à,** to aspire to

aspirine, *f.* aspirin

assaillir, *v.t.* to assail, attack

assainir, *v.t.* to cleanse, improve (sanitation, atmosphere, etc.)

assainissement, *m.* cleaning

assaisonner, *v.t.* to season

assassin, *m.* murderer; (*adj.*) murderous; bewitching

assassinat, *m.* murder, assassination

assassiner, *v.t.* to murder; (*fam.*) to bore (to death)

assaut, *m.* assault, attack; **troupes d'-,** shock troops

assemblage, *m.* gathering; assembling (of machine parts, etc.)

assemblée, *f.* assembly, meeting

assembler, *v.t.* to call together, fit together; to muster (crew, etc.)

asséner, *v.t.* to deal, strike (a blow)

assentiment, *m.* assent; **signe d'-,** nod

asseoir, *v.t.* to establish, lay; (*fam.*) to snub; **s'asseoir,** *v.r.* to sit down; **assis,** seated, sitting

assermenter, *v.t.* to swear in

asservir, *v.t.* to enslave

asservissement, *m.* subjection

*****assez,** (*adv.*) enough, sufficient(ly); fairly, tolerably

assidu, (*adj.*) assiduous, persevering

assidûment, (*adv.*) assiduously

assiéger, *v.t.* to besiege

assiette, *f.* plate; position, situation

assignation, *f.* transfer (of shares, etc.); appointment, rendezvous

assigner, *v.t.* to assign, fix; to summon (to court of law)

assise, *f.* layer, bed-plate, foundation; **les assises,** sittings (of court), Assizes

assistance, *f.* audience, spectators; help, aid; **prêter - à,** to help, assist

assistant, *m.* bystander, onlooker

assister (à), *v.i.* to be present (at); *v.t.* to help

association, *f.* association, company

associé, *m.* partner

associer, *v.t.* to associate, connect; **s'associer à,** *v.r.* to associate with, go into partnership with

assombrir, *v.t.* to darken, obscure; **s'-,** *v.r.* to grow dark, become gloomy

assommant, (*adj.*) tedious; overwhelming

assommer, *v.t.* to fell, knock senseless; (*fam.*) to bore

assommoir, *m.* bludgeon, poleaxe; low tavern, " dive "

assomption, *f.* assumption

assortiment, *m.* assortment; matching

assortir, *v.t.* to assort, match; to stock

s'assoupir, *v.r.* to doze off

assourdir, *v.t.* to deafen; to muffle, deaden

assouvir, *v.t.* to sate, satiate, appease

assujettir, *v.t.* to subdue, subjugate; to fasten

assurance, *f.* assurance; insurance; **- sur la vie,** life insurance

assurément, (*adv.*) undoubtedly, certainly

assurer, *v.t.* to assure; to ensure;

to insure; **assuré,** confident, sure, safe

astérisque, *m.* asterisk

asthme, *m.* asthma

astiquer, *v.t.* to polish (leather, metal)

astre, *m.* star

astreindre, *v.t.* to compel

astrologue, *m.* astrologer

astronaute, *m.* astronaut, space-traveller

astronome, *m.* astronomer

astucieux, (*adj.*) artful, wily

atelier, *m.* workroom; studio; workroom staff

athée, *m.* (and *adj.*) atheist; atheistic

athlète, *m.* athlete

athlétique, (*adj.*) athletic

Atlantique, *m.* Atlantic ocean; (*adj.*) Atlantic

atmosphère, *f.* atmosphere

atmosphérique, (*adj.*) atmospheric

atome, *m.* atom

atours, *m.* (and *pl.*) finery

atout, *m.* trump; **jouer -,** to play a trump

âtre, *m.* hearth, fireplace

atroce, (*adj.*) atrocious

atrocité, *f.* atrocity

s'attabler, *v.r.* to sit down to table

attache, *f.* fastening, clip; leash

attaché, attached, devoted; *m.* attaché (diplomatic)

attachement, *m.* attachment, fondness

attacher, *v.t.* to attach; to tie up, fasten

attaque, *f.* attack; **- de nerfs,** hysterics; **- directe,** direct drive (mech.); **lancer une -,** to launch an attack

attaquer, *v.t.* to attack, set upon

s'attarder, *v.r.* to stay (up, out) late, to linger

atteindre, *v.t.* to reach, attain, hit; **être atteint de,** to be wounded by, attacked by (disease, etc.)

atteinte, *f.* reach; blow, hit.

attelage, *m.* coupling (railway); team (horses, etc.)

atteler, *v.t.* to harness, put to

attenant (à), *(adj.)* adjoining

*attendre, *v.t.* to wait (for); s'-, *v.r.* to expect; en attendant, in the meanwhile

attendrir, *v.t.* to soften, move to pity; s'-, *v.r.* to be softened, moved to tears

attendu, *(prep.)* considering; - que, seeing that

attentat, *m.* (criminal) attempt

attente, *f.* waiting, expectation; dans l'- de vous lire sous peu, awaiting your prompt reply; salle d'-, waiting-room

attentif(-ve), *(adj.)* attentive, careful

attention, *f.* attention; faire -, to pay attention; Attention! look out!

atténuer, *v.t.* to attenuate; to extenuate; to tone down

atterrement, *m.* consternation

atterrer, *v.t.* to overwhelm, dismay

atterrir, *v.i.* to sight land; to run ashore; to land (a plane)

atterrissage, *m.* landfall, landing; terrain d'-, landing-ground

attester, *v.t.* to attest, bear (call to) witness

attiédir, *v.t.* to cool

attifer, *v.t.* to dress up, trick up (usually disparaging)

attique, *m.* attic (architectural); *(adj.)* Attic, Athenian

attirail, *m.* apparatus, gear

attirer, *v.t.* to attract, draw

attiser, *v.t.* to poke, stir up

attraction, *f.* attraction, attractiveness

attrait, *m.* attraction, inducement, appeal

attraper, *v.t.* to catch, seize

attribuer, *v.t.* to ascribe, impute; to allot; s'- quelquechose, to claim, arrogate something to oneself

attribut, *m.* attribute; predicate

attribution, *f.* allocation; function

attrister, *v.t.* to grieve, sadden

attroupement, *m.* mob, crowd

attrouper, *v.t.* to gather, get together

aubaine, *f.* windfall, godsend

aube, *f.* dawn; blade (of turbine, fan, etc.)

aubépine, *f.* hawthorn

auberge, *f.* inn

aubergiste, *m.* (*f.*) inn-keeper

aucun, *(pron.)* anyone, (with implied or expressed negative) no one; any, not any

audace, *f.* boldness, audacity

audacieux(-euse), *(adj.)* bold, daring; impudent

au-dessous, *(adv.)* below, under(neath); - de *(prep.)*, below, under

au-dessus, *(adv.)* above, over; - de *(prep.)*, above, over

au-delà, *(adv.)* beyond; - de *(prep.)*, beyond

audience, *f.* hearing, session, audience

auditeur, *m.* hearer, listener (to speech, wireless, etc.)

audition, *f.* audition, hearing

auditoire, *m.* auditorium; audience, congregation

auge, *f.* trough

auget, *m.* trough; bucket (of water-wheel, etc.)

augmentation, *f.* increase, rise

augmenter, *v.t.* and *v.i.* to increase, rise

augure, *m.* omen, augury; augur

auguste, *(adj.)* august; sacred

aujourd'hui, *(adv.)* to-day, nowadays

aumône, *f.* alms; faire l'- à, to give alms to

aumônier, *m.* almoner; - militaire, chaplain, padre

aune, *m.* alder; *f.* ell

auparavant, *(adv.)* before(hand)

*auprès, *(adv.)* close to, hard by

auréole, *f.* halo, glory

auriculaire, *m.* little finger; *(adj.)* auricular

auriste, *m.* ear specialist

aurore, *f.* dawn, daybreak

ausculter, *v.t.* to sound (a patient)

auspice, *m.* omen; (*plural*) auspices, patronage

aussi, so, as; also; therefore

aussitôt, (*adv.*) immediately, at once; - que, as soon as

austère, (*adj.*) austere, severe

austral, (*adj.*) austral, southern

*autant, (*adv.*) as much, as many

autel, *m.* altar; (*fig.*) the Church; maître -, high altar

auteur, *m.* writer, author

authentique, (*adj.*) authentic, genuine

auto, *f.* car (colloquial)

autobus, *m.* motor-bus

autocar, *m.* motor-coach

autocrate, *m.* autocrat; (*adj.*) autocratic

autodémarreur, *m.* self-starter

autographe, *m.* autograph; (*adj.*) autographic

automate, *m.* automaton

automatique, (*adj.*) automatic

automne, *m.* autumn; en -, in autumn

automobile, *f.* motor-car, car; (*adj.*) self-propelling

automobilisme, *m.* motoring

autorisation, *f.* authorisation, permit, licence

autoriser, *v.t.* to authorise, empower

autoritaire, (*adj.*) dictatorial, overbearing

autorité, *f.* authority

autour, *adv.* about, round; (*prep.*) - de, round, about

*autre, other

autrefois, (*adv.*) formerly

autrement, (*adv.*) otherwise

autrichien(ne), (*adj.*) Austrian

autruche, *f.* ostrich

autrui, (*pron. indef.*) others, other people

auvent, *m.* pent-house; dashboard (of cars)

auxiliaire, *m.* assistant; (*adj.*) auxiliary

aval, *m.* lower part of stream; en -, downstream

avaler, *v.t.* to swallow, devour

avance, *f.* advance

avancement, *m.* putting-forward; promotion

*avancer, *v.t.* to advance; *v.s.* to be ahead of time

avanie, *f.* insult, affront

*avant, *m.* bow (ship); forward (football); (*adv.* and *prep.*) before

avantage, *m.* advantage

avantageux, (*adj.*) advantageous, favourable

avant-bras, *m.* forearm

avant-dernier, last but one

avant-hier, (*adv.*) the day before yesterday

avant-propos, *m.* foreword, preface

avant-scène, *f.* apron (of stage); loge d'avant-scène, stage box.

avare, *m.* miser; (*adj.*) avaricious

avarice, *f.* avarice

avarie, *f.* damage

avarier, *v.t.* to damage, spoil

avec, (*prep.*) with

avenant, (*adj.*) handsome, comely

avènement, *m.* accession

avenir, *m.* future; à l'-, in future, henceforth

Avent, *m.* Advent (ecclesiastical)

aventure, *f.* adventure; chance; dire la bonne -, to tell fortunes

aventurer, *v.tr.* to venture, risk

aventurier(-ère), *m.* (*f.*) adventurer(-ess), sharper

avenue, *f.* avenue, drive

averse, *f.* shower

aversion, *f.* aversion, dislike

avertir, *v.t.* to warn, notify

avertissement, *m.* warning, notice

avertisseur, *m.* motor horn; alarm signal; call-boy (theat.)

aveu, *m.* confession; consent

aveugle, (*adj.*) blind

aveuglement, *m.* blindness; infatuation

aveuglément, (*adv.*) blindly

aveugler, *v.t.* to blind, dazzle

aviateur(-trice), *m.* (*f.*) airman-(-woman), aviator

aviation, *f.* aviation

avide, (*adj.*) greedy, eager

avilir, *v.t.* to debase

avilissement, *m.* degradation, depreciation

aviné, *(adj.)* drunk(en)

avion, *m.* aeroplane; - de combat, fighter; - de bombardement, bomber; - de reconnaissance, reconnaissance plane; - de chasse, fighter, pursuit plane; par -, by air-mail

aviron, *m.* oar; rowing

*avis, *m.* opinion; advice; notice

avisé, *(adj.)* prudent

aviser, *v.t.* to perceive, catch a glimpse of; s'aviser de, to take it into one's head to

avocat, *m.* barrister, advocate

avoine, *f.* oats

*avoir, *v.t.* to have; to get

avoisiner, *v.t.* to be close to, adjoin

avorter, *v.i.* to miscarry

avoué, *m.* attorney, solicitor

avouer, *v.t.* to confess, acknowledge

avril, *m.* April; donner un poisson d'avril à, to make an April fool of

axe, *m.* axis; axle

axiome, *m.* axiom

azote, *m.* nitrogen

azur, *(adj.)* azure, blue; Côte d'-, Riviera

azyme, *(adj.)* unleavened

B

baba, *m.* rum cake, baba

babil, *m.* chattering; twittering

babillard, *(adj.)* babbling, talkative; *m.* chatterbox

babiller, *v.i.* to prattle, chatter

bâbord, *m.* port (side)

babouin, *m.* baboon

babouines, *f. pl.* lips, chops

bac, *m.* ferry(-boat)

baccalauréat, *m.* school leaving examination

bachelier, *m.* bachelor (of law, etc.). B ès Lettres (Sciences). One who has successfully taken the school leaving examination.

bachot, *m.* wherry; *(fam.)* =

baccalauréat; une boîte (un four) à bachot, a crammer's establishment for this exam.

bacille, *m.* bacillus

bâcler, *v.t.* to bar, bolt; *(fam.)* to scamp, botch (work, etc.)

bactérie, *f.* bacterium, microbe

badaud, *m.* stroller, saunterer

baderne, *f.* mat, fender (nautical); vieille -, old fogey

badigeonner, *v.t.* to whitewash

badinage, *m.* trifling, jesting

badine, *f.* switch, cane

badiner, *v.i.* or *t.* to trifle, banter

bagage, *m.* baggage; - littéraire, an author's total output; (in *pl.*) luggage; - à main, hand luggage

bagarre, *f.* scuffle, brawl

bagatelle, *f.* trifle

bagne, *m.* prison, hulks

bague, *f.* ring

baguette, *f.* rod, wand; mener qn. à la -, to rule someone with a rod of iron

bah! rubbish! bosh! *(scorn)*; you don't mean it! *(surprise)*

bahut, *m.* (antique) chest, trunk; cupboard

baie, *f.* bay, bight; berry; fenêtre en -, bay (bow) window

baigner, *v.t.* to bathe, wash; se -, to take a bath, bathe

baigneur(-euse), *m. (f.)* bather

baignoire, *f.* bath (tub); ground floor box (behind the theatre pit)

bail, *m,* lease

bâiller, *v.i.* to yawn

bailli, *m.* bailiff

bâillon, *m.* gag

bâillonner, *v.t.* to gag

bain, *m.* bath; bain de mer, watering-place, seaside resort; salle de bains, bathroom

baïonnette, *f.* bayonet; - au canon! fix bayonets!

baiser, *v.t.* to kiss.   (N.B.— embrasser is a more prudent word to use); *m.* a kiss

baisse, *f.* ebb; fall (in prices, etc.)

baisser, *v.t.* to lower; *v.i.* to be on the decline, to be getting low; le - du rideau, the fall of the curtain

baissier, *m.* bear (Stock Exchange)

bal, *m.* ball, dance; **- costumé,** fancy dress ball

baladeuse, *f.* trailer (car, etc.)

balafre, *f.* gash, scar

balai, *m.* broom; **- mécanique,** carpet-sweeper

balance, *f.* balance, scales; **- à bascule,** weigh-bridge

balancer, *v.t.* to balance, poise; *v.i.* to swing, to waver (in indecision)

balancier, *m.* pendulum; beam

balayer, *v.t.* to sweep, scour

balayeur (de rues), *m.* crossing-sweeper; **balayeuse,** *f.* carpet-sweeper

balbutier, *v.t.* and *v.i.* to stammer

balcon, *m.* balcony; circle (theatre)

baleine, *f.* whale(bone)

baleinier, *m.* whaler

balise, *f.* beacon; **- flottante,** buoy

balistique, *(adj.)* and *f.* ballistic(s)

baliverne, *f.* (usually plural) nonsense, rubbish

ballade, *f.* ballad, ballade (poem)

ballant, *(adj.)* dangling

balle, *f.* ball; bullet; bale; *(slang)* franc; **à l'épreuve des balles,** bullet-proof; **- de golf,** golf-ball

ballon, *m.* balloon; football; **- d'essai,** trial balloon, feeler''

ballottage, *m.* voting

ballotter, *v.t.* to toss about

balnéaire, *(adj.)* pertaining to baths; **station -,** watering-place, spa

balte, *(adj.)* Baltic

balustrade, *f.* railing

bambin, *m.* babe, tot

bambou, *m.* bamboo

ban, *m.* banishment; *(pl.)* banns of marriage

banal, *(adj.)* commonplace, vulgar

banane, *f.* banana

bananier, *m.* banana tree

banc, *m.* bench; bank (sand, etc.); **- des prévenus,** dock; **- de**

roches (d'huîtres), reef (oyster bed)

bancal, *(adj.)* bandy-legged

bandage, *m.* bandage; tyre

bande, *f.* band, party, gang; strip; **envoyer sous -,** to send (in wrapper) by post

bandeau, *m.* bandage, head-band

bander, *v.t.* to bandage, bind; to tighten; **se bander,** *v.r.* to band together

bandit, *m.* bandit; ruffian

bandoulière, *f.* shoulder-belt (-strap)

banlieue, *f.* suburbs, outskirts

bannière, *f.* banner

bannir, *v.t.* to banish, exile

banque, *f.* bank, banking (financial); **billet de -,** bank-note

banqueroute, *f.* bankruptcy; **faire -,** to go bankrupt

banquet, *m.* banquet, feast

banquette, *f.* seat (railway carriage, etc.)

banquier, *m.* banker

baptême, *m.* baptism; **nom de -,** Christian name

baptiser, *v.t.* to baptise, christen

baptistère, *m.* baptistry

baquet, *m.* tub; bucket-seat (of car)

bar, *m.* (public) bar

baragouiner, *v.t.* and *v.i.* to talk gibberish, to jabber

baraque, *f.* hut, hutment; booth

barbare, *(adj.)* barbarous, barbaric; *m.,* barbarian

barbaresque, *(adj.)* Berber

barbe, *f.* beard; **faire la - à qn.,** to shave someone; **quelle -!** what a bore (pest)!

barbelé, *(adj.)* barbed; **fil de fer -,** barbed wire

barbier, *m.* barber

barbon, *m.* greybeard, dotard

barbouiller, *v.t.* to daub; to smear

barbu, *(adj.)* bearded

barbue, *f.* brill

barème, *m.* ready-reckoner; **- graphique,** graph

baril, *m.* barrel, keg

barioler, *v.t.* to speckle; **bariolé,** gaudy

baromètre, *m.* barometer

baron(ne), *m.* (*f.*) baron (baroness)

baroque, (*adj.*) baroque; quaint, odd

barque, *f.* boat; **- de pêcheur,** fishing-smack

barrage, *m.* dam(ming); (*mil.*) barrage

barre, *f.* bar, rod; helm

barreau, *m.* small bar, prison bar; **être admis au -,** to be called to the bar

barrer, *v.t.* to fasten (strengthen) with bars; to bar (the way, etc.)

barrière, *f.* barrier; toll gate; starting-point (turf)

barrique, *f.* hogshead, cask

baryton, (*adj.*) and *m.* baritone

*****bas,** (*adj.*) low; deep; mean, base

bas, *m.* lower part; stocking

basalte, *m.* basalt

basané, tanned, sunburnt

bas-bleu, *m.* blue-stocking

bascule, *f.* see-saw; **chaise à -,** rocking-chair

basculer, *v.t.* and *v.i.* to rock, tip (up)

base, *f.* base; basis

baser, *v.t.* to base, ground

basilique, *f.* basilica

basque, *f.* tail of coat

basque (*adj.* and *subst.*) Basque

basse-cour, *f.* farmyard

bassesse, *f.* baseness; mean action

bassin, *m.* basin; dock; (ornamental) pond, lake

basson, *m.* bassoon(ist)

baste, (*int.*) enough! avast!

bastingage, *m.* bulwarks

bastion, *m.* bastion

bât, *m.* pack-saddle

bataille, *f.* battle; **donner (livrer) - à,** to give battle to, engage in battle with; **- rangée,** pitched battle

batailler (contre), *v.i.* to battle (with, against)

bataillon, *m.* battalion

bâtard, *m.* and (*adj.*) bastard; illegitimate; **chien -,** mongrel

bateau, *m.* boat, vessel; **- à**

vapeur (voiles), steamer (sailing-boat); **- de pêche (de sauvetage),** fishing- (life-) boat

batelier, *m.* boatman

bâtiment, *m.* building; ship, vessel; **- marchand,** merchant ship

bâtir, *v.t.* to build, construct; to tack (with thread)

bâtisse, *f.* masonry, ramshackle

batiste, *f.* cambric [house

bâton, *m.* stick, staff; **travailler (parler) à bâtons rompus,** to work (talk) in a desultory manner

bâtonner, *v.t.* to beat, cudgel

battage, *m.* beating; threshing

battant, *m.* leaf, flap (of table, counter); **porte à deux battants,** double, folding door; **porte battante,** swing door

battement, *m.* beating; clapping

batterie, *f.* battery (military or electric); **- de rechange,** refill for torch; **- de cuisine,** kitchen utensils

batteur, *m.* beater, thresher; **la batteuse,** threshing machine

battre, *v.t.* and *v.i.* to beat, thrash; to thresh; **- la campagne,** to beat (scour) the country; **- les cartes,** to shuffle; **se battre,** *v.r.* to fight

baudet, *m.* donkey

baume, *m.* balm, balsam

bavard, (*adj.*) talkative, garrulous

bavarder, *v.i.* to chatter, gossip

bave, *f.* froth, slaver

baver, *v.i.* to slaver, drivel, dribble

bavette, *f.* bib

béant, (*adj.*) wide-open, gaping

béat, (*adj.*) sanctimonious; complacent

béatifier, *v.t.* to beatify

*****beau,** beautiful, fair, fine

beaucoup, (*adv.*) much, many, a great deal; **de -,** by far; **- de,** much, many

beau-fils, *m.* stepson

beau-frère, *m.* brother-in-law

beau-père, *m.* stepfather, father-in-law

beaupré, *m.* bowsprit

beauté, *f.* beauty

bébé, *m.* baby

bec, *m.* beak, bill; **- de gaz,** gas-burner; **- de plume,** nib; **blanc-bec,** simpleton, green-horn; **avoir le - salé,** to be always thirsty, fond of the bottle

bécane *f.* (*coll.*) bike, bicycle

bécarre, *m.* natural (in music)

bécasse, *f.* woodcock

bécassine, *f.* snipe

bêche, *f.* spade; **- de mer,** sea-slug, trepang

becqueter, *v.t.* to peck at; (*slang*) to kiss

bedaine, *f.* paunch

bedeau, *m.* beadle; verger

beffroi, *m.* belfry

bégayer, *v.t.* and *v.i.* to stammer, stutter

bègue, *m.* stammerer; (*adj.*) stammering

bégueule, *f.* prude; (*adj.*) prudish

béguin, *m.* hood, bonnet; fancy, infatuation; **avoir un - pour,** to have a crush on

beignet, *m.* fritter

bêler, *v.i.* to bleat

belette, *f.* weasel

belge, (*adj.*) Belgian

bélier, *m.* ram

belle, *see* **beau**

belle-fille, *f.* stepdaughter; daughter-in-law

belle-mère, *f.* stepmother; mother-in-law

belle-sœur, *f.* sister-in-law

belles-lettres, *f. pl.* humanities, belles-lettres

belligérant, *m.* and (*adj.*) belligerent

belliqueux, (*adj.*) bellicose, warlike

bémol, *m.* flat (in music)

bénéfice, *m.* profit; benefit; bene-fice, living (church)

benêt, *m.* booby; (*adj.*) stupid

bénin(-igne), (*adj.*) benign, mild, kindly

bénir, *v.t.* to bless; to consecrate; **pain bénit,** consecrated bread;

(**que**) **Dieu vous bénisse,** God bless you!

bénitier, *m.* holy-water stoop

béquille, *f.* crutch; sprag (motoring)

berceau, *m.* cradle

bercer, *v.t.* to rock, to lull

berceuse, *f.* rocking-chair; lull-aby

béret, *m.* beret

berge, *f.* bank, rampart

berger, *m.* shepherd; **bergère,** *f.* shepherdess; easy-chair

bergeronnette, *f.* wagtail

berline, *f.* limousine (car)

berlue, *f.* dimness, falsity of vision; **avoir la -,** to be blind to the facts

berner, *v.t.* to toss in a blanket; to chaff, hoax

bernique, (*int.*) (*fam.*) Nothing doing! It's no go!

besace, *f.* (beggar's) sack, wallet

bésicles, *f. pl.* spectacles, goggles

besogne, *f.* work, task, job of work

besogneux, (*adj.*) needy

besoin, *m.* need, want, require-ment; **pas - de dire,** needless to say; **avoir - de,** to have need of

bestial, (*adj.*) beastly, brutish

bestiaux, *m. pl.* beasts, cattle

bêta(sse), (*adj.*) and *m.* (*f.*) stupid, blockhead

bétail, *m.* cattle

bête, *f.* beast, animal; fool; **faire la -,** to act like a fool; (*adj.*) stupid; **- noire,** pet aversion

bêtise, *f.* stupidity; trifle; **faire des bêtises,** to play the fool

béton (de ciment), *m.* concrete; **└ armé,** ferro-concrete; **béton-nière,** *f.* concrete-mixer

betterave, *f.* beetroot; sugar-beet

beugler, *v.i.* and *v.t.* to low, bellow; to bawl

beurre, *m.* butter; **rond de -,** pat of butter

beurrée, *f.* slice of bread and butter

beurrer, *v.t.* to butter

beurrier, *m.* butter-dish

bévue, *f.* blunder; " howler "

biais, *m.* slant, bias (bowls); **en -,** askew, aslant

bibelot, *m.* curio, knick-knack

biberon, *m.* tippler, toper; feeding-bottle

Bible, *f.* Bible

bibliographe, *m.* bibliographer

bibliothécaire, *m.* librarian

bibliothèque, *f.* library; bookcase

biche, *f.* doe, hind

bicoque, *f.* hovel, shanty

bicyclette, *f.* bicycle; **aller à -,** to bicycle, to ride a bicycle

bidet, *m.* nag; bidet

bidon, *m.* tin, can; **- à essence,** petrol-tin; **- de secours,** spare tin (can)

bidonville, *f.* shanty-town

bielle, *f.* connecting-rod

***bien,** (*adv.*) well, good, very; *m.* goods, property; **bien-être,** *m.* well-being; **bien-fonds,** *m.* real estate; **- que,** (*conj.*) although

bienfait, *m.* benefit, kindness

bienfaiteur(-trice), *m.* (*f.*) benefactor(-tress)

bienheureux(-euse), (*adj.*) happy; blessed

bienséance, *f.* propriety, decency

bienvenu, (*adj.*) welcome

bière, *f.* beer; coffin; **- blonde,** pale ale

biffer, *v.t.* to cross out, strike out

bifteck, *m.* beefsteak

bifurcation, *f.* road-fork

bifurquer, *v.t.* and *v.i.* to fork, branch off

bigame, (*adj.*) bigamous; *m.* bigamist

bigamie, *f.* bigamy

bigarrer, *v.t.* to variegate, mottle

bigre! (*int.*) By Jove!

bijou, *m.* jewel

bijouterie, *f.* jewellery; jeweller's shop; **bijoutier,** *m.* jeweller

bilan, *m.* balance-sheet

bilatéral, (*adj.*) bilateral

bile, *f.* bile, gall; anger

bilieux(-euse), (*adj.*) bilious; testy

billard, *m.* billiard-table (room), (game of) billiards

bille, *f.* billiard-ball; marble; billet (of timber)

billet, *m.* note; ticket; **- doux,** love-letter; **- simple,** single ticket; **- d'aller et retour,** return ticket; **- de faveur,** free ticket; **- de banque,** bank-note

billot, *m.* block (of wood); executioner's block

bimensuel(le), (*adj.*) fortnightly

bimoteur, (*adj.*) and *m.* twin-engined (aircraft)

binocle, *m.* pince-nez

biographe, *m.* biographer; **biographie,** *f.* biography; **biographique,** (*adj.*) biographical

biplace, *m.* and (*adj.*) two-seater

biplan, *m.* biplane

bis, twice; encore; **douze bis,** 12a (to avoid use of 13)

bisaïeul, *m.* great-grandfather

biscotte, *f.* rusk

biscuit, *m.* biscuit; biscuit-ware (in pottery, etc.)

bise, *f.* north wind

biseau, *m.* bevel; **biseauter,** *v.t.* to bevel

bisque, *f.* crab soup; bisque, odds (in sport)

bissac, *m.* (double) wallet, bag

bissecter, *v.t.* to bisect; **bissecteur (bissectrice),** (*adj.*) bisecting (line, etc.)

bisser, *v.t.* to encore (song, etc.)

(année) bissextile, *f.* leap year

bistouri, *m.* lancet, surgeon's knife

bistro(t), *m.* wine-shop, public-house

bitume, *m.* pitch, tar, bitumen; **bitumineux,** (*adj.*) bituminous

bivouac, *m.* (bivac), *m.* bivouac; **bivouaquer,** *v.i.* to bivouac

bizarre, (*adj.*) odd, strange

blafard, (*adj.*) pale, wan

blague, *f.* pouch; **- à tabac,** tobacco-pouch; humbug; **quelle -!** What a joke! **sans -,** really? honest Injun? **blaguer,** *v.i.* to tell lies, hoax, tease; **blagueur,** *m.* wag, story-teller

blaireau, *m.* badger; shaving-brush

blâme, *m.* blame, disapprobation

blâmer, *v.t.* to blame, censure

blanc, (*adj.*) white; **nuit blanche,** sleepless night; **- comme un linge,** (as) white as a sheet; (*noun, m.*) white (of eyes), bull's eye (of target); **chèque en -,** blank cheque; **- d'œuf,** white of egg; **- de chaux,** whitewash

blanchâtre, (*adj.*) whitish

blanchir, *v.t.* to whiten, bleach

blanchissage, *m.* washing, white-washing

blanchisserie, *f.* laundry

blanchisseuse, *f.* washerwoman

blanquette, *f.* stewed veal

blasé, (*adj.*) bored, satiated (to the point of indifference)

blason, *m.* coat of arms

blasphème, *m.* blasphemy; **blasphémer,** *v.t.* and *v.i.* to blaspheme; **blasphémateur,** blasphemer, blasphemous

blatte, *f.* cockroach

blé, *m.* corn; **manger son - en herbe,** to live on one's capital, to spend one's money in advance

blême, (*adj.*) livid, pale; **blêmir,** *v.i.* to turn pale

blesser, *v.t.* to wound, hurt; to offend

blessure, *f.* wound, injury

blet(te), (*adj.*) over-ripe, sleepy

bleu, (*adj.*) blue; **peur bleue,** blue funk; **- clair (foncé),** light (dark) blue; **un petit -,** express letter (in Paris); **conte -,** fairy tale

bleuâtre, (*adj.*) bluish

blindé, (*adj.*) armoured; **auto blindée,** armoured car

bloc, *m.* block, lump; coalition (of political parties); **-notes,** (writing) pad; **- de cuisine,** kitchen unit

blocus, *m.* blockade; **faire le - de,** to blockade

blond, (*adj.*) light, fair

bloquer, *v.t.* to block (up); to clamp (of machinery); to blockade

(se) blottir, *v.r.* to squat, crouch

blouse, *f.* overall, smock-frock

bluet, *m.* cornflower

bobine, *f.* bobbin, spool, reel; coil

bocage, *m.* grove, coppice

bocal, *m.* jar, bottle

bock, *m.* glass of beer

bœuf, *m.* ox, bullock; beef

bohémien(ne), (*adj.*) and *m.* (*f.*) Bohemian; gipsy

boire, *v.t.* to drink; to soak up (in); **- à petits coups,** to sip; **- d'un seul trait (coup),** to swallow at one gulp

*****bois,** *m.* wood, forest; -de lit, bedstead; **gravure sur -,** wood-cut; **boiserie,** *f.* panelling

boisson, *f.* beverage, drink

boîte, *f.* box; **- aux lettres,** letter-box; **- d'allumettes,** matchbox; **- des vitesses,** gear-box; **- (de nuit),** night-club

boiter, *v.i.* to limp, walk lame

boiteux, (*adj.*) lame

boîtier, *m.* case

bol, *m.* bowl, basin; bolus

bolchéviste, (*adj.*) and *m.* (*f.*) Bolshevist

bombardement, *m.* bombardment, shelling; **avion de -,** bomber

bombarder, *v.t.* to shell, bombard; **bombardier,** *m.* bomber (man or plane)

bombe, *f.* bomb; **- incendiaire,** incendiary bomb; **- à retardement,** delayed-action bomb; **à l'épreuve des bombes,** bomb-proof; **- glacée,** ice-pudding; **être en -,** to be on the spree

bomber, *v.t.* to throw out, swell (the chest, etc.); **bombé,** convex, bulging

*****bon,** (*adj.*) good, honest, right, nice; **un - à rien,** good for nothing; **un - de poste,** postal order; **un - au porteur,** bearer bond

bonasse, (*adj.*) simple-minded, silly

bonbon, *m.* sweet(meat)

bonbonnière, *f.* sweetmeat box; neat little dwelling

bond, *m.* bound, leap, bounce; **faire faux - à qn.,** to fail to keep an appointment with someone

bondé, (*adj.*) chock full; **salle bondée,** packed house (theatre)

bondir, *v.i.* to leap, bound, bounce (of ball, etc.)

bonheur, *m.* good fortune, luck; **par -,** luckily; **faire qc. au petit -,** to do something without serious thought, haphazard

bonhomie, *f.* good nature, kindliness

bonhomme, *m.* good, simple fellow; **aller son petit - de chemin,** to jog along quietly

boni, *m.* bonus, balance in hand

boniment, *m.* (showman's) patter; clap-trap

bonjour, *m.* good day; **souhaiter (dire) le - à,** to greet, say good day to

bonne, *f.* maid-servant; **- à tout faire,** maid of all work, general servant

bonnet, *m.* cap; **c'est - blanc et blanc -,** it's six of one and half a dozen of the other

bonneterie, *f.* hosiery

bonsoir, *m.* good evening

bonté, *f.* goodness, kindness; **ayez la - de,** be so kind as to . . .

bord, *m.* edge, rim, side; **au - de la mer,** at the seaside; **à - de,** on board, aboard

bordeaux, *m.* Bordeaux (wine); **- rouge,** claret

bordée, *f.* broadside, volley; **- de bâbord (tribord),** port (starboard) watch

border (de), *v.t.* to border, edge (with)

bordereau, *m.* memorandum, schedule

bordure, *f.* border, edging, frame

boréal, *(adj.)* north, northern

borgne, *(adj.)* one-eyed, blind in one eye; **cabaret -,** dubious, shady tavern

borne, *f.* boundary-stone, limit; **dépasser les bornes,** to go too far

borner, *v.t.* to mark, form the boundary of; to limit; **se borner (à),** *v.r.* to confine oneself (to); **borné,** limited, restricted (of view, outlook, etc.)

bosquet, *m.* grove, thicket

bosse, *f.* hump, bump, boss; **avoir la - de,** to have a gift for, be good at

bosseler, *v.t.* to emboss

bossu, *(adj.)* hunchback(-ed), humped

bot (pied), *(adj.)* club (foot-ed)

botanique, *(adj.)* botanical; *f.* botany

botte, *f.* bunch, truss; (high) boot; **à propos de bottes,** suddenly, without rhyme or reason (without reference to anything previously said)

se botter, *v.r.* to put on one's boots (shoes); **le chat botté,** Puss in Boots

bottier, *m.* boot (shoe) maker

bottine, *f.* (half) boot

bouc, *m.* he-goat; **- émissaire,** scapegoat

boucan, *m.* row, rumpus, shindy (*fam.*)

*bouche, *f.* mouth

bouchée, *f.* mouthful

boucher, *v.t.* to stop up, plug

boucher, *m.* butcher; **boucherie,** *f.* butcher's shop (trade), butchery (slaughter)

bouche-trou, *m.* stop-gap, makeshift

bouchon, *m.* stopper, cork, wisp of straw; **- de contact,** wall-plug (electric)

boucle, *f.* buckle, loop; curl, ringlet

boucler, *v.t.* to buckle, fasten; to curl (of hair); **- une affaire,** to settle, clinch a deal (*fam.*)

bouclier, *m.* buckler, shield

bouddhiste, *(adj.)* Buddhist

bouder, *v.i.* to sulk; **bouderie,** *f.* sulkiness, sulks

boudin, *m.* black-pudding; **- d'air,** inner tube (of tyre)

boue, *f.* mud, mire

bouée, *f.* buoy; **- de sauvetage,** lifebuoy

boueur, *m.* dustman, scavenger

boueux, *(adj.)* muddy, miry

bouffée, *f.* puff, whiff

bouffer, *v.i.* and *v.t.* to puff (out); (*fam.*) to guzzle; **bouffant,**

puffed, baggy; **opéra bouffe,** comic opera

bouffi, (adj.) bloated, swollen

bouffon, m. clown, buffoon, jester; (adj.) farcical

bouffonnerie, f. clowning, antics

bouge, m. slum, den; bilge

bougeoir, m. candlestick

bouger, v.i. to stir, budge, move

bougie, f. candle; **- d'allumage,** sparking plug

bouillabaisse, f. bouillabaisse, a sort of fish-soup, a speciality of Provence

bouillir, v.i. to boil; **faire - qc.,** to boil something

bouilloire, f. kettle

bouillon, m. bubble; broth

bouillonner, v.i. to bubble, seethe

boulanger, m. baker

boulangerie, f. baking; bakery

boule, f. ball; hot water bottle; **partie de boules,** game of bowls

bouleau, m. birch tree

bouledogue, m. bulldog

boulet, m. cannon-ball

boulette, f. pellet; rissole; **faire une -,** to make a blunder, drop a brick

boulevard, m. boulevard; rampart; **boulevardier,** m. man about town

bouleverser, v.t. to upset, throw into confusion

boulle, m. buhl (furniture)

boulon, m. bolt, pin

boulonner, v.t. to bolt

boulotter, v.i. to jog along, get along quite nicely; (fam.) to eat

bouquet, m. bunch of flowers, bouquet; aroma; **ça, c'est le -!** That takes the biscuit, puts the lid on it l.

bouquetière, f. flower girl

bouquin, m. old book

bouquiniste, m. dealer in second-hand books

bourbe, f. mud, mire

bourdon, m. drone; great bell; bumble-bee

bourdonnement, m. humming, buzzing

bourdonner, v.i. to hum, buzz

bourg, m. market town, borough

bourgeois, m. citizen, townsman, person of middle class; **petit -,** small tradesman (etc.); Philistine; (adj.) middle-class

bourgeoisie, f. middle class

bourgeon, m. bud; pimple

Bourgogne, f. Burgundy (province); m. Burgundy (wine)

bourrage, m. stuffing, padding; cramming; **- de crâne,** eyewash, balderdash

bourrasque, f. squall

bourre, f. wad; flock, cotton-waste

bourreau, m. executioner, hangman

bourreler, v.t. to torment

bourrelet, m. pad, cushion; flange

bourrelier, m. harness-maker

bourrer, v.t. to stuff, pad; to tamp; to fill (a pipe)

bourrique, f. she-ass, donkey; dunce

bourru, (adj.) morose, surly

bourse, f. purse, pouch; scholarship; **la Bourse,** the Stock Exchange; **la - du Travail,** Labour Exchange

boursier, m. exhibitioner, holder of scholarship

boursouflé, (adj.) swollen, bloated; turgid

bousculer, v.t. to jostle

bousiller, v.t. to bungle, botch (a piece of work)

boussole, f. compass

*bout, m. end; extremity; fag-end

boutade, f. whim; flash of wit

bouteille, f. bottle; **- isolante,** vacuum flask

boutique, f. shop; **parler -,** to talk shop

boutiquier, m. shopkeeper

bouton, m. bud; button, knob; pimple; **un - de sonnerie,** a bell-push; **- de col,** collar-stud

boutonner, v.i. to bud; v.t. to button (up)

boutonnière, f. buttonhole; rosette (of an order, decoration, etc.)

bouvier, m. drover, cattle-man

bouvreuil, *m.* bullfinch
boxe, *f.* boxing
boxer, *v.i.* and *v.t.* to box;
boxeur, *m.* boxer
boyau, *m.* gut; hose-pipe; (communication) trench
boycotter, *v.t.* to boycott
bracelet, *m.* bracelet, bangle
braconner, *v.i.* and *v.t.* to poach;
braconnier, *m.* poacher
braillard, *m.* bawler, brawler;
(*adj.*) bawling, noisy
brailler, *v.i.* to bawl, shout; to brawl
braire, *v.i.* to bray
braise, *f.* embers
braiser, *v.t.* to braise
brancard, *m.* stretcher; **brancardier,** *m.* stretcher-bearer
branche, *f.* branch, bough; **avoir de la -,** to look distinguished
brandir, *v.t.* to brandish, flourish
branle, *m.* oscillation; **mettre qch. en -,** to set something going
braquer, *v.t.* to aim, point, direct (gun, gaze, etc.)
bras, *m.* arm; **- dessus, - dessous,** arm-in-arm; **en - de chemise,** in one's shirt sleeves; **avoir les - rompus,** to be dead tired
brasier, *m.* brazier
brasse, *f.* fathom; stroke (in swimming)
brassée, *f.* armful
brasser, *v.t.* to brace; to brew, mix; to hatch (a plot)
brasserie, *f.* brewery; saloon, saloon-restaurant
brasseur, *m.* brewer
brassière, *f.* bust bodice
bravade, *f.* bravado, bluster
brave, (*adj.*) brave, bold; **un homme -,** a courageous man; **un - homme,** an honest, decent fellow
braver, *v.t.* to brave, defy
bravo, *m.* bravo, cheer; hired assassin
bravoure, *f.* bravery
brebis, *f.* ewe, sheep
brèche, *f.* breach, gap; notch
bredouiller, *v.i.* to mumble, stammer; **revenir bredouille,** to come back empty-handed
bref, brève (*adj.*) brief, short; (*adv.*) briefly, in a word
brelan, *m.* gaming-house
breloque, *f.* trinket, charm
brème, *f.* bream
bretelle, *f.* shoulder-strap, sling; (*pl.*) braces
bretteur, *m.* swash-buckler, swordsman
breuvage, *m.* beverage, drink
brevet, *m.* warrant, certificate; **- de pilotage,** pilot's certificate, "wings"
breveté, *m.* patentee; (*adj.*) certificated
bréviaire, *m.* breviary
bribes, *f. pl.* scraps, fragments
bric-à-brac, *m.* odds and ends
brick, *m.* brig
bricoler, *v.i.* to do odd jobs
bride, *f.* bridle; tie (mech.); **lâcher la - à un cheval,** to give a horse his head; **lâcher la - à sa fureur,** to give free rein to one's anger
brider, *v.t.* to bridle, curb, check
bridge, *m.* bridge; **- aux enchères,** auction bridge; **- contrat,** contract bridge; **faire un -,** to have a game of bridge
brièvement, (*adv.*) briefly, concisely
brièveté, *f.* brevity
brigade, *f.* brigade; squad, gang
brigadier, *m.* corporal (of cavalry or police); foreman
brigand, *m.* brigand, robber
brigue, *f.* intrigue
briguer, *v.t.* to solicit, canvass
brillant, (*adj.*) brilliant, glittering; *m.* brilliance, brightness
briller, *v.i.* to shine, sparkle
brin, *m.* blade, sprig, shoot; fragment; **un - de vent,** a breath of wind
brioche, *f.* brioche, bun; blunder (*fam.*)
brique, *f.* brick
briquet, *m.* tinder-box; (cigarette) lighter
brisant, *m.* breaker; reef
brise, *f.* breeze; **brise-tout,** *m.*

or *f.* person who breaks everything; **brise-vent**, *m.* windscreen; **brise-lames**, *m.* breakwater, groyne

briser, *v.t.* to break, shatter; **brisé de fatigue**, tired out, exhausted

britannique, (*adj.*) British

broc, *m.* pitcher, jug

brocanteur, *m.* second-hand dealer

brocart, *m.* brocade

broche, *f.* brooch; pin, skewer

brocher, *v.t.* to stitch; **livre broché**, paper-bound book

brochet, *m.* pike (fish)

brochure, *f.* pamphlet, booklet

brodequin, *m.* laced boot; buskin; the comic " sock " worn by actors in ancient times

broder, *v.t.* to embroider; **brodeur(-euse)**, *m.* (*f.*) embroiderer(-ess)

broderie, *f.* embroidery

bromure, *m.* bromide

broncher, *v.i.* to shy, stumble; to flinch

bronchite, *f.* bronchitis

bronze, *m.* bronze

bronzer, *v.t.* to bronze, brown, **se -**, *v.r.* to get suntanned

brosse, *f.* brush; **- à dents (cheveux)**, tooth (hair) brush

brosser, *v.t.* to brush; **brosseur**, *m.* batman; scene-painter

brouette, *f.* wheelbarrow

brouhaha, *m.* hubbub

brouillard, *m.* fog, mist; wastebook; **faire du -**, to be foggy

brouiller, *v.t.* to mix, jumble; **se - avec**, *v.r.* to fall out with, quarrel with; **un œuf brouillé**, scrambled egg

brouillon, *m.* rough copy, draft

broussaille, *f.* brushwood, undergrowth

brouter, *v.t.* to browse on

broyer, *v.t.* to pulverise, grind (to dust)

bru, *f.* daughter-in-law

bruine, *f.* drizzle

bruire, *v.i.* to rustle, murmur

bruit, *m.* noise, din; rumour

brûler, *v.i.* and *v.t.* to burn; to scorch, be on fire; **- une étape**, to pass a halting place without stopping; **se - la cervelle**, to blow out one's brains; **brûleur**, *m.* gas-burner

brumaire, *m.* second month of French Republican year (October–November)

brume, *f.* mist, fog; **brumeux**, (*adj.*) foggy

brun, (*adj.*) brown, dusky; **brunâtre**, (*adj.*) brownish

brunette, *f.* girl of dark hair

brunir, *v.t.* to brown, burnish

brusque, (*adj.*) abrupt, sharp

brut, (*adj.*) rough, raw; gross

brutal, (*adj.*) brutal, savage

brutaliser, *v.t.* to ill-treat, bully

brutalité, *f.* brutality, savagery

bruyant, (*adj.*) noisy, boisterous

bruyère, *f.* heather; **coq de -**, grouse; **pipe en bruyère**, briar pipe

buanderie, *f.* wash-house

bûche, *f.* log; blockhead

bûcher, *m.* funeral pyre, pile of faggots; *v.t.* and *v.i.* to swot (for an examination)

bûcheron, *m.* wood-cutter, lumber-jack

bucolique, (*adj.*) bucolic, pastoral

budget, *m.* budget

buée, *f.* vapour, steam

buffet, *m.* refreshment room, sideboard, buffet

buffle, *m.* buffalo

buis, *m.* box-tree (-wood)

buisson, *m.* bush, thicket; **faire l'école buissonnière**, to play truant

bulbe, *m.* (*f.*) bulb; **bulbeux**, (*adj.*) bulbed, bulbous

bulle, *f.* bubble; (papal) bull

bulletin, *m.* bulletin, report, ticket

buraliste, *m.* clerk

bureau, *m.* office; writing-desk, bureau; **- de location**, box-office; **- de tabac**, tobacconist's shop

bureaucrate, *m.* bureaucrat; **bureaucratie**, *f.* bureaucracy

burette, *f.* oil-can
burin, *m.* graver; **buriner,** *v.t.* to engrave
burlesque, *(adj.)* burlesque, ludicrous
buste, *m.* bust
but, *m.* object, aim, goal, target
butanier, *m.* tanker *(naut.)*
buter, *v.i.* to knock, strike (against); **se buter,** *v.r.* to prop oneself, come up (against)
butin, *m.* spoil, booty
butoir, *m.* buffer, stop
butor, *m.* bittern; dolt
butte, *f.* hillock, knoll; **en - à,** exposed to
buvable, *(adj.)* drinkable
buvard, *m.* blotter; **papier -,** blotting-paper
buvette, *f.* refreshment bar
buveur, *m.* toper, drinker
byzantin, *(adj.)* Byzantine

C

*ça, *(pron.)* that, this, it
çà, *(adv.)* hither; **çà et là,** hither and thither, here and there
cabale, *f.* cabal, clique, intrigue
cabaler, *v.i.* to cabal, intrigue
cabalistique, *(adj.)* cabalistic
caban, *m.* oilskins, pilot-coat
cabane, *f.* hut, (log) cabin
cabaret, *m.* tavern, eating-house, (intimate) restaurant
cabaretier(-ère), *m. (f.)* tavern-, inn-keeper
cabas, *m.* shopping-basket
cabestan, *m.* capstan, windlass
cabillaud, *m.* fresh cod
cabine, *f.* cabin; **- de luxe,** state-room; **- de signaux,** signal-box
cabinet, *m.* office, closet; cabinet (political); **- de toilette,** dressing-room; **- (d'aisance),** water-closet, W.C.; **chef de -,** principal private secretary
câble, *m.* cable, rope
câbler, *v.t.* to cable; to connect up (apparatus, etc.)
câblogramme, *m.* cable(gram)
cabotage, *m.* coast-wise trade

cabotin(e), *m. (f.)* strolling player, barn-stormer
se cabrer, *v.r.* to rear, jib
cabriole, *f.* caper; **faire des -s,** to cut capers
cabriolet, *m.* gig, cabriolet
cacahouette, *f.* pea-nut
cacao, *m.* cocoa
cacatoès, *m.* cockatoo
cachalot, *m.* cachalot, sperm-whale
cache, *f.* hiding-place (for things); **cache-cache,** hide and seek; **cache-nez,** *m. (inv.)* muffler; **cache-col,** *m.* man's scarf
cacher, *v.t.* to hide, conceal; **se - à qn.** *v.r.* to hide from someone
cachet, *m.* stamp, seal; cachet (pharmaceutical); **lettre de -,** order of arbitrary imprisonment, under the royal seal
cacheter, *v.t.* to seal (up); **cire à -,** sealing-wax
cachette, *f.* hiding-place (for person)
cachot, *m.* dungeon, cell
cadastre, *m.* cadastral survey
cadavéreux, *(adj.)* cadaverous
cadavre, *m.* corpse, carcase
cadeau, *m.* present; **en -,** as a present
cadenas, *m.* padlock
cadence, *f.* rhythm, cadence
cadencé, *(adj.)* rhythmical
cadet(te), *(adj.)* younger, junior; *m.* (golf) caddie
cadran, *m.* dial; **- solaire,** sun-dial
cadre, *m.* frame(work); limits; (military) skeleton of unit; **avoir passé par les -s,** to have risen from the ranks
caduc *(f.* **caduque),** *(adj.)* decaying, decrepit
cafard, *m.* cockroach; sneak, tell-tale (school); **avoir le -,** to be depressed, fed up, " browned off ''
café, *m.* café; coffee; **- crème** (or **au lait),** white coffee; **- noir** (or **nature),** black coffee; **café complet,** Continental breakfast
cafetier, *m.* café proprietor

cafetière, *f.* coffee-pot

cage, *f.* cage, (lift) shaft

cagot, *(adj.)* canting, sanctimonious

cahier, *m.* exercise book

cahin-caha, *(adv.)* so-so; **aller -,** to jog along quietly, to be in only moderately good health

cahoter, *v.t.* and *v.i.* to jolt, shake

cahoteux, *(adj.)* bumpy (of roads)

caille, *f.* quail

cailler, *v.t.* and *v.i.* to clot, curdle

caillou, *m.* pebble, boulder

caillouter, *v.t.* to pave, metal (a road)

caisse, *f.* cash-box, pay-desk; (packing) case; **payer à la -,** to pay at the desk; **- d'épargne,** savings bank; **grosse -,** big drum; **faire la -,** to balance, check up one's cash

caissier(-ère), *m.* (*f.*) cashier

caisson, *m.* ammunition waggon; locker

cajoler, *v.t.* to coax, wheedle

cal (*pl.* cals), *m.* callosity

calamité, *f.* calamity, disaster

calandre, *f.* mangle, roller

calandrer, *v.t.* to press, mangle

calcaire, *m.* limestone; *(adj.)* chalky

calciner, *v.t.* to calcine; **être calciné,** to be burnt to death

calcul, *m.* calculation, arithmetic; **faux -,** miscalculation; **règle à -,** slide rule

calculer, *v.t.* to calculate, reckon; **calculé,** premeditated

cale, *f.* hold (of ship); chock, wedge; **- sèche,** dry-dock

calèche, *f.* open carriage, barouche

caleçon, *m.* (pair of) pants

calembour, *m.* pun

calendrier, *m.* calendar, almanac

calepin, *m.* note-book

caler, *v.t.* to wedge, prop up; to stall (of engines); **c'est un homme calé,** to be a man of means; **être très calé en** (sur) **qch.,** to be well up in something

calfater, *v.t.* to caulk

calfeutrer, *v.t.* to stop up chinks

calibre, *m.* calibre, bore (of gun)

calice, *m.* chalice; calyx

calicot, *m.* calicot

califourchon (à), astride; **se mettre - sur,** to bestride

câlin, *(adj.)* winning, caressing

câliner, *v.t.* to caress, wheedle

calleux, *(adj.)* callous, horny

calmant, *(adj.)* calming; *m.* sedative

calme, *(adj.)* calm; *m.* calmness, equanimity

calmer, *v.t.* to calm, soothe, allay

calomniateur(-trice), *m.* (*f.*) slanderer; *(adj.)* libellous, slanderous

calomnie, *f.* calumny, slander

calomnier, *v.t.* to slander, libel

calorie, *f.* calorie

calorifère, *m.* central-heating apparatus; stove

calorifuge, *(adj.)* heat-proof

calorimètre, *m.* calorimeter

calotte, *f.* skull-cap; priests, clergy (depreciatory); box on the ears (*fam.*)

calquer (sur), *v.t.* to trace (from), make a tracing (of)

calvados, *m.* cider-brandy (from the *département* of that name)

Calvaire, *m.* Calvary

calvitie, *f.* baldness

camarade, *m.* and *f.* comrade, mate

camaraderie, *f.* comradeship, coterie, set

cambrer, *v.t.* to camber; to arch (of foot); **se cambrer,** *v.r.* to brace oneself; draw oneself up

cambriolage, *m.* housebreaking, burgling

cambrioler, *v.t.* to break into, burgle

cambrioleur(-euse), *m.* (*f.*) burglar, housebreaker

came, *f.* cam; **arbre à cames,** camshaft

camée, *m.* cameo

camelot, *m.* newsvendor; street hawker

camera, *f.* cine-camera

camion, *m.* lorry

camionnage, *m.* haulage

camionneur, *m.* lorry (truck) driver; vanman

camisole (de force), *f.* straight-jacket

camp, *m.* camp; asseoir (lever) le -, to pitch (strike) camp; ficher le -, (*fam.*) to clear out, " beetle off "

campagnard, *m.* countryman, rustic; (*adj.*) rustic

campagne, *f.* country (as opposed to town); campaign; battre la -, to scour the country

camper, *v.i.* to, encamp; *v.t.* to put (men) under canvas; se -, *v.r.* to pitch one's camp; to plant oneself

camphre, *m.* camphor

camphré, (*adj.*) camphorated

camus, (*adj.*) snub-nosed; *m.* snub-nose

canadien, (*adj.*) Canadian

canaille, *f.* mob, riff-raff; scoundrel

canal, *m.* canal; duct; channel (of river, etc.)

canaliser, *v.t.* to canalise; to put in mains, pipes, etc.

canapé, *m.* sofa, couch

canard, *m.* duck; false news or rumour; hoax

canarder, *v.t.* to shoot from ambush, snipe

canari, *m.* canary

cancan, *m.* cancan (dance); tittle-tattle; faire des cancans, to gossip (ill-naturedly)

cancer, *m.* cancer; the Crab (astronom.)

cancéreux(-euse), (*adj.*) cancerous; *m.* (*f.*) sufferer from cancer

candélabre, *m.* (branched) candlestick

candeur, *f.* artlessness

candidat, *m.* candidate, applicant

candide, (*adj.*) ingenuous, artless

cane, *f.* duck (as opposed to drake)

caneton, *m.* duckling

canevas, *m.* canvas; outline (of play, picture, etc.)

caniche, *m.* and *f.* poodle ·

caniculaire, (*adj.*) sultry; les jours caniculaires, dog-days

canif, *m.* penknife

canin, (*adj.*) canine

canne, *f.* cane, walking-stick; - à sucre, sugar-cane; - à pêche, fishing rod

cannelle, *f.* cinnamon; tap, faucet

cannelure, *f.* groove, slot; fluting (architect).

canon, *m.* cannon, gun; barrel (of rifle, key, etc.); canon; rule

canonique, (*adj.*) canonical

canoniser, *v.t.* to canonise

canonnier, *m.* gunner

canonnière, *f.* gunboat

canot, *m.* (open) boat

canotage, *m.* rowing; faire du -, to row, go in for rowing

canotier, *m.* oarsman; straw-hat

cantatrice, *f.* (professional) singer

cantine, *f.* canteen

cantique, *m.* canticle, hymn

canton, *m.* canton, district

cantonade, *f.* wings (theatre)

cantonner, *v.t.* to divide up (into districts, etc.); to quarter, billet (of troops)

cantonnier, *m.* roadman; ganger (railways)

caoutchouc, *m.* (india)rubber; mackintosh

cap, *m.* cape, headland; bow (of ship); mettre le - sur, to lay a course for, steer for

capable, (*adj.*) able, capable

capacité, *f.* capacity, ability

cape, *f.* cape, cloak; rire sous -, to laugh up one's sleeve

capillaire, (*adj.*) capillary

capitaine, *m.* captain

capital, (*adj.*) capital; essential; *m.* capital (finance)

capitale, *f.* capital, chief town; capital letter

capitaliste, *m.* and *f.* capitalist

capiteux(-euse), (*adj.*) heady, strong

capitulation, *f.* capitulation, surrender

capituler, *v.i.* to capitulate

caporal, *m.* corporal; French tobacco

capot, *m.* bonnet, casing, cowling

capote, *f.* hood (of car, etc.); overcoat

capoter, *v.i.* to capsize, overturn

caprice, *m.* caprice, whim

capricieux(-euse), *(adj.)* capricious, temperamental

capsule, *f.* capsule

captieux(-euse), *(adj.)* specious, captious

captif(-ive), *(adj.)* and *m.* *(f.)* captive

captiver, *v.t.* to captivate, charm

captivité, *f.* captivity

capturer, *v.t.* to capture, seize

capuchon, *m.* hood; cap

capucin(e), *m.* Capuchin monk or friar; *(f.)* nun

caquet, *m.* cackle

caqueter, *v.i.* to cackle, chatter

car, *(conj.)* for, because

car, *m.* (tram) car; often used for autocar, motor-coach

carabine, *f.* carbine

caracoler, *v.i.* to prance (horse-riding)

caractère, *m.* character; nature; **avoir bon -,** to be good-natured

caractéristique, *(adj.)* and *f.* characteristic

carafe, *f.* decanter, water-bottle

caramel, *m.* caramel, burnt sugar

carapace, *f.* shell (tortoise, etc.)

carat, *m.* carat; **de l'or à quatorze carats,** 14-carat gold

caravane, *f.* caravan

carbonate (de soude), *m.* carbonate (of soda)

carbone, *m.* carbon

carboniser, *v.t.* to char, carbonise; **être carbonisé,** to be (accidentally) burnt to death

carburant, *m.* motor-fuel

carburateur, *m.* carburettor

carbure, *m.* carbide

carcasse, *f.* carcase, framework

cardiaque, *(adj.)* and *m.* *(f.)* cardiac (patient)

cardinal, *(adj.)* and *m.* cardinal

carême, *m.* Lent; **faire -,** to fast

carénage, *m.* careening (of ship); stream-lining (car, etc.)

caresse, *f.* caress

caresser, *v.t.* to caress, fondle, stroke

cargaison, *f.* cargo, freight

cargo, *m.* cargo-boat, freighter; tramp steamer

caricature, *f.* caricature

caricaturer, *v.t.* to caricature, take off

caricaturiste, *m.* caricaturist

carie, *f.* decay; blight

carillon, *m.* chimes, peal of bells

carillonner, *v.i.* to chime, to ring bells

carillonneur, *m.* bell-ringer

carlingue, *f.* fuselage (of plane)

carme, *(adj.)* and *m.* Carmelite (friar)

carmin, *m.* carmine

carnage, *m.* slaughter

carnassier, *(adj.)* flesh-eating; *m.* carnivore

carnassière, *f.* game-bag

carnaval, *(pl. -s)* *m.* carnival

carnet, *m.* note-book, booklet; **- de chèques,** cheque-book; **- de bal,** dance programme

carotte, *f.* carrot; *(coll.)* trick, hoax; **tirer une - à qn.,** to wheedle money out of someone (by telling a lie)

carotter, *v.i.* and *v.t.* *(coll.)* to wangle; to get by fraud

carpe, *f.* carp (fish); **faire des yeux de - pâmée,** to show the whites of one's eyes

carquois, *m.* quiver (archery)

carré, *m.* square; *(adj.)* square; **partie carrée,** a party of two men and two women (applied to pleasure outings, etc.)

carreau, *m.* (small) square tile (of floor, not roof); diamonds (at cards); **rester sur le carreau,** to be killed on the spot, (or) to be left for dead on the ground

carrefour, *m.* cross-roads; place where several roads meet

carreler, *v.t.* to tile, pave (a floor); to draw squares

carrément, squarely, straightforwardly, bluntly

carrer, *v.t.* to square (number, etc.)

carrière, *f.* quarry; career; **donner libre - a,** to give rein (scope) to

carrosse, *m.* coach

carrosserie, *f.* coach-building, coachwork; body (of car)

carrousel, *m.* tournament; merry-go-round

carrure, *f.* breadth of shoulder

cartable, *m.* writing-pad, satchel

*****carte,** *f.* map; card; playing card; **- postale,** post card; **- routière,** road map

cartel, *m.* cartel, trust, combine; wall-clock

cartilage, *m.* cartilage

cartographe, *m.* map-maker, cartographer

cartographie, *f.* mapping

carton, *m.* cardboard; cardboard-box; cartoon; **- de bureau,** filing-case

cartonner, *v.t.* to bind books (in stiff cover, " boards ")

cartouche, *f.* cartridge; scroll, cartouche

*****cas,** *m.* case

casanier, *(adj.)* stay at home, home-loving

casaque, *f.* coat (livery); jacket

cascade, *f.* waterfall

cascader, *v.i.* to lead a fast life *(coll.)*

case, *f.* hut, cabin; pigeon-hole; square (of chess-board)

caser, *v.t.* to put away; **- des papiers,** to file papers; **caser qn.** to find a job for someone; **se -,** *v.r.* to find a job, to settle down

caserne, *f.* barracks

casier, *m.* set of pigeon-holes

casque, *m.* helmet; **- blindé,** crash-helmet

cassation, *f.* quashing, setting aside; **cour de -,** court of appeal

casse, *f.* cassia; damage, breakage; **il y aura de la -,** *(fam.)* there's going to be trouble

casse-cou, *m.* reckless fellow; death-trap

casse-croûte, *m.* *(invar.)* snack,

quick lunch (bar)

casse-noisette, *m.* *(invar.)* nutcrackers

*****casser,** *v.t.* to break; **cassé,** worn out (esp. of voices)

casserole, *f.* saucepan, stewpan

casse-tête, *m.* *(invar.)* tomahawk; puzzle

cassette, *f.* casket; money-box

cassis, *m.* black-currant; black-currant liqueur

cassure, *f.* break, fracture

castor, *m.* beaver

casuel, *m.* perquisites (i.e. tips, etc.); *(adj.)* fortuitous

cataclysme, *m.* cataclysm, disaster

catacombes, *f. pl.* catacombs

catalogue, *m.* catalogue, list

cataplasme, *m.* poultice, plaster

cataracte, *f.* cataract

catarrhe, *m.* catarrh

catastrophe, *f.* catastrophe, disaster

catéchiser, *v.t.* to catechise

catéchisme, *m.* catechism

catégorie, *f.* category

catégorique, *(adj.)* categorical, unequivocal

cathédrale, *f.* cathedral

cathode, *f.* cathode

catholicisme, *m.* (Roman) Catholicism

catholique, *(adj.)* Catholic; *m.* and *f.* (Roman) Catholic

cauchemar, *m.* nightmare

cause, *f.* cause; lawsuit; **et pour -,** and for a very good reason; **en connaissance de -,** with full knowledge of the action; **être chargé d'une cause,** to hold a brief

causer, *v.t.* to cause; *v.i.* **- (avec)** to chat, converse (with, to)

causerie, *f.* talk, chat

causeur(-euse), *(adj.)* talkative; *m.* *(f.)* conversationalist, talker

caustique, *(adj.)* caustic, biting; *m.* caustic

cauteleux(-euse), *(adj.)* crafty, cunning

cautériser, *v.t.* to cauterise

caution, *f.* security, guarantee; **se porter - pour qn.,** to go bail for, stand surety for, someone

cavalerie, f. cavalry

cavalier(-ère), m. (f.) rider, horse-man (-woman); m. partner, escort (to lady); knight (at chess); (adj.) off-hand, unceremonious

cave, f. cellar

caveau, m. small cellar; (burial) vault

caver, v.t. to hollow out; to stake, put up money (at cards)

caverne, f. cave, cavern

caverneux(euse), (adj.) cavernous, hollow

caviar, m. caviare

cavité, f. cavity

ce (pron.) it; (dem. adj.) this

ceci, this

cécité, f. blindness

céder, v.t. to yield, surrender; v.i. to yield, give way; - à la tentation, to yield to temptation; il m'a cédé sa part, he handed over (gave up) his share to me

cédille, f. cedilla

cédrat, m. citron

cèdre, m. cedar

cédule, f. schedule

ceindre, v.t. to encircle, gird (on)

ceinture, f. girdle, belt; chemin de fer de -, inner circle railway; - de sécurité, safety belt

ceinturer, v.t. to tackle (at Rugby football)

*****cela** (ça), that

célèbre, (adj.) celebrated, famous

célébrer, v.t. to celebrate; to solemnise; to praise

célébrité, f. celebrity

celer (à), v.t. to conceal (from)

céleri, m. celery

célérité, f. celerity, swiftness

céleste, (adj.) celestial, heavenly

célibat, m. celibacy

célibataire, m. and f. bachelor, spinster

cellier, m. store-room, store-cupboard

cellule, f. cell

celte, m. and f. Celt

celtique, (adj.) Celtic

cendre, f. ashes, cinders; **mercredi des cendres,** Ash Wednesday

cendré, (adj.) ash-grey

cendreux(-euse), (adj.) ashy, gritty

cendrier, m. ash-bin; ash-tray (for cigarette ends)

Cendrillon, f. Cinderella

cène, f. the Last Supper

cénotaphe, m. cenotaph

censé, (adj.) supposed, reputed

censeur, m. censor; censurer, critic

censure, f. censure, blame; censorship

censurer, v.t. to censor; to censure, find fault with

cent, a hundred; **je vous le donne en cent,** I give you a hundred guesses (I bet you'll never guess); **faire les cent pas,** to be on sentry-go (also used of street walkers); **dix pour cent,** ten per cent.

centaine, f. (about) a hundred; **quelques centaines d'hommes,** some hundreds of men

centaure, m. centaur

centenaire, m. and f. centenarian

centième, (adj.) hundredth; m. hundredth part

centigrade, (adj.) centigrade

centigramme, m. centigramme

centime, m. centime (1/100 of a franc)

centimètre, m. centimetre (about ⅖ of an inch)

central, (adj.) central, principal

centraliser, v.t. to centralise

centre, m. centre, middle

centrer, v.t. to centre

centrifuge, (adj.) centrifugal

cep (de vigne), m. vine(-stock)

cependant, (adv.) meanwhile; (conj.) yet, still, for all that

céramique, (adj.) ceramic; f. ceramics, (art of) pottery

cerceau, m. hoop

cercle, m. circle, club

cercler, v.t. to encircle, hoop

cercueil, m. coffin

céréale, *f.* (usually **plantes céréales**) cereals

cérébral, *(adj.)* cerebral, of the brain

cérémonie, *f.* ceremony; **visite de -**, state (or formal) visit; **faire des cérémonies**, to stand on ceremony

cerf, *m.* stag; **cerf-volant**, *m.* kite

cerise, *f.* cherry

cerisier, *m.* cherry-tree, (-wood)

cerner, *v.t.* to encircle, surround; to invest (a city, etc.)

certain, *(adj.)* certain, sure; **d'un - âge**, elderly

certes, *(adv.)* to be sure!

certificat, *m.* certificate

certifier, *v.t.* to attest, certify

certitude, *f.* certainty

cerveau, *m.* brain, intelligence; **rhume de -**, cold in the head; **un - brûlé**, hare-brained fellow

cervelas, *m.* saveloy

cervelle, *f.* brain(s) (considered anatomically); **se brûler la -**, to blow one's brains out

cesse, *f.* cease, pause; **sans -**, incessantly

cesser, *v.i.* and *v.t.* to cease, leave off

cession, *f.* transfer

chabot, *m.* chub

chacal, *(pl. -s)*, *m.* jackal

chacun(e), *(pron.)* each, each one, everyone

chagrin, *m.* grief, sorrow

chagrin, *m.* shagreen; **La Peau de -**, (Balzac) *The Wild Ass's Skin*

chagriner, *v.t.* to grieve; to vex

chahut, *m.* (*fam.*) row, rumpus

chaîne, *f.* chain; warp (textiles); network, channel (T.V.)

chaînon, *m.* link (of chain)

chair, *f.* flesh; **- de poule**, gooseflesh; **être bien en -**, to be plump, well-covered

chaire, *f.* pulpit; (professorial) chair; desk, rostrum

chaise, *f.* chair; **- percée**, nightcommode; **- de poste**, postchaise; **chaise-longue**, couch

chaland, *m.* barge, lighter; customer, buyer

châle, *m.* shawl

chalet, *m.* (Swiss) chalet, cottage; **- de nécessité**, public convenience

chaleur, *f.* heat, warmth; zeal

chaleureux(-euse), *(adj.)* warm, cordial

chaloupe, *f.* launch

chalumeau, *m.* straw (for drinking); blow-pipe

chalut, *m.* trawl-net

chalutier, *m.* trawler (man or boat)

chamailler, *v.t.* to squabble

chambellan, *m.* chamberlain

chambre, *f.* room, bedroom; **- à un (deux) lit(s)**, single (double) room; **- des Députés**, Chamber of Deputies (French House of Commons); **faire une -**, to clean, "do" a room; **- d'explosion**, combustion-chamber; **- d'ami**, spare room

chameau, *m.* camel; shunting-engine; **ce - de —**, that hog (swine) of a —

chamelier, *m.* camel-driver

chamois, *m.* chamois; **peau de -**, shammy- (wash-) leather

champ, *m.* field; **prendre la clef des champs**, to decamp; **champ d'aviation (de foire)**, flying (fair) ground

Champagne, *f.* Champagne (province); *m.* champagne (wine)

champêtre, *(adj.)* rustic; **garde -**, *m.* country policeman

champignon, *m.* mushroom

champion(ne), *m. (f.)* champion

championnat, *m.* championship

chance, *f.* luck, fortune; chance; **pas de -!** no luck!

chanceler, *v.i.* to stagger, totter

chancelier, *m.* chancellor

chancellerie, *f.* chancellery

chanceux(-euse), *(adj.)* uncertain, risky

Chandeleur, *f.* Candlemas

chandelier, *m.* candlestick; candle-maker

chandelle, *f.* candle; taper; **le jeu ne vaut pas la -**, it's not worth while, not worth doing change, *m.* exchange; **cours du -**, rate of exchange; **bureau de -**, foreign exchange office

changeant, (*adj.*) variable, fickle

changement, *m.* change, alteration; **- de vitesse**, changing of gear

changer, *v.t.* to change, alter; to exchange; *v.i.* to change, suffer a change; **- de place (mains)**, to change places (hands)

changeur, *m.* money-changer

chanoine, *m.* canon (eccles.)

chanson, *f.* song, ditty; (*pl.*) rubbish, nonsense

chansonnier(-ère), *m.* (*f.*) song-writer; *m.* song-book

chant, *m.* singing, song, chant

chantage, *m.* extortion (of money), blackmail

chanter, *v.t.* to sing, to crow; **qu'est-ce que vous me chantez là?** what yarn (what rubbish) is it that you're spinning (telling) me?

chanteur, *m.* singer

chantier, *m.* workshop, ship-building yard; cask-stand

chantre, *m.* chanter, chorister

chanvre, *m.* hemp

chaos, *m.* chaos

chapeau, *m.* hat; cap (i.e. cover); **- haut de forme**, top-hat

chapelet, *m.* rosary, beads

chapelier, *m.* hatter

chapelle, *f.* chapel, side-chapel

chapellerie, *f.* hat trade, hat shop

chaperon, *m.* hood; chaperon; **le petit - rouge**, Little Red Riding Hood

chapiteau, *m.* capital (architectural)

chapitre, *m.* chapter

chapon, *m.* capon

chaque, (*adj.*) each, every

char, *m.* waggon; **- (d'assaut)**, tank (military)

charbon, *m.* coal; carbuncle; smut (disease in cereals); **- de bois**, charcoal

charbonner, *v.t.* to carbonise, to char

charbonnier, *m.* charcoal-burner; coal merchant; collier (ship)

charcuterie, *f.* pork-butcher's shop; pig meat

chardon, *m.* thistle

chardonneret, *m.* goldfinch

charge, *f.* load; charge (i.e. attack, expense, or accusation)

chargement, *m.* cargo, freight; lading, loading

*charger, *v.t.* to charge; to load; to register

chariot, *m.* waggon; carriage (of typewriter)

charitable, (*adj.*) charitable

charité, *f.* charity; **faire la - à**, to give alms to

charivari, *m.* discordant music; din

charlatan, *m.* quack, charlatan

charme, *m.* charm; spell

charmer, *v.t.* to charm, delight, bewitch

charnel(le), (*adj.*) carnal, sensual

charnier, *m.* charnel-house

charnière, *f.* hinge

charnu, (*adj.*) fleshy, plump

charpente, *f.* framework (usually of timber)

charpentier, *m.* carpenter, joiner

charpie, *f.* lint

charretier, *m.* carter, carrier

charrette, *f.* cart; **- à bras**, barrow

charron, *m.* wheelwright

charrue, *f.* plough

charte, *f.* charter

chartreux(-euse), (*adj.*) Carthusian; *f.* chartreuse (liqueur)

chas, *m.* eye (of needle)

chasse, *f.* hunt, hunting, chase; **- à courre**, stag-hunting

chasse-mouches, *m.* (*invar.*) fly-swatter

châsse, *f.* shrine, reliquary

chasser, *v.t.* to chase, hunt, to drive out, expel; *v.i.* to hunt; to skid (of car); to drag (anchor)

chasseur, *m.* hunter, huntsman; page-boy; " buttons "; rifleman, light-infantryman; fighter (plane or pilot)

châssis, *m.* frame, under-carriage;
- **de fenêtre,** window sash

chaste, *(adj.)* chaste, pure

chasteté, *f.* chastity, purity

chat(te), *m.* *(f.)* cat; also term of
endearment

châtaigne, *f.* chestnut

châtaignier, *m.* chestnut tree

châtain, *(adj.)* chestnut-brown,
nut-brown

château *m.* castle; **châteaux en
Espagne,** castles in the air

châteaubriant, *m.* rump-steak,
grilled steak

châtelain, *m.* lord of manor;
governor of castle

châtelaine, *f.* lady of manor;
châtelaine (keys)

chat-huant, *m.* brown owl

châtier, *v.t.* to punish, chastise,
chasten

châtiment, *m.* punishment,
chastisement

chaton, *m.* kitten; catkin (botanical)

chatouiller, *v.t.* to tickle

chatouilleux(-euse), *(adj.)* ticklish; touchy

chatoyer, *v.i.* to glisten, shimmer

châtrer, *v.t.* to castrate

chaud, *(adj.)* hot, warm; **avoir -,**
to be warm (of person); **faire -,**
to be warm (of weather)

chaudière, *f.* boiler, copper

chaudron, *m.* cauldron

chaudronnier, *m.* boiler-maker,
brazier

chauffage, *m.* heating, warming;
- **central,** central heating

chauffe, *f.* stoking, firing;
chambre de -, stoke-hold

chauffer, *v.t.* to warm, heat,
stoke; to air (of linen)

chauffeur(-euse), *m.* *(f.)* stoker,
fireman,chauffeur;*(fam.)*crammer

chaufour, *m.* lime-kiln

chaume, *m.* thatch, stubble

chaumière, *f.* (thatched) cottage

chaussée, *f.* causeway, roadway

chausser, *v.t.* to put on (shoes,
etc.); **bien chaussé,** well-shod

chausses, *f. pl.* hose, breeches

chaussette, *f.* sock; **supporte-**

chaussettes, *m.* *pl.* sock-sus-
penders

chaussure, *f.* footwear, boots
and shoes

chauve, *(adj.)* bald

chauve-souris, *f.* bat (zoology)

chauvinisme, *m.* chauvinism,
jingoism

chaux, *f.* lime; - **vive,** quicklime; **blanchir à la -,** to whitewash

chavirer, *v.i.* to capsize, turn
turtle; *v.t.* to turn (something)
upside down

chef, *m.* head, chief, leader; - **de
cuisine,** chef; - **de gare,**
stationmaster; - **de train,** guard;
- **de cabinet,** principal private
secretary

chef-d'œuvre, *m.* masterpiece

chef-lieu, *m.* chief town (of a
French department)

*****chemin,** *m.* way, road; - **faisant,**
on the way; **à moitié -,** half-
way; - **de fer,** railway; **se
mettre en -,** to set off; **grand -,**
highway

chemineau, *m.* tramp

cheminée, *f.* chimney, fireplace,
funnel (railway engine, steamer)

cheminer, *v.i.* to walk, proceed

cheminot, *m.* railwayman

chemise, *f.* shirt, chemise
(women), jacket, casing; **en
bras de -,** in one's shirt-sleeves

chemisier, *m.* shirt-maker

chênaie, *f.* grove of oaks

chenal, *m.* channel

chenapan, *m.* rogue, vagabond

chêne, *m.* oak

chenet, *m.* andiron, fire-dog

chenil, *m.* dog-kennel

chenille, *f.* caterpillar

chèque, *m.* cheque; - **barré,**
crossed cheque; - **repas,** meal
voucher

cher (chère), *(adj.)* dear, beloved; expensive; **la vie chère,**
high cost of living

chercher, *v.t.* to seek, look for;
aller -, to go and fetch

chercheur(-euse), *m.* *(f.)* investi-
gator, researcher

chère, *f.* fare, cheer; **faire bonne -,** to live well, do oneself well

chérir, *v.t.* to cherish, love dearly

cherté, *f.* dearness, costliness

chérubin, *m.* cherub

chétif(-ve), *(adj.)* sickly, puny, paltry

cheval, *m.* horse; **- de course (trait),** race- (draught-) horse; **aller à -,** to ride; **cheval-vapeur,** horse-power

chevaleresque, *(adj.)* knightly, chivalrous

chevalerie, *f.* knighthood

chevalet, *m.* easel, trestle

chevalier, *m.* knight, horseman; **- d'industrie,** sharper, adventurer

chevaucher, *v.i.* and *v.t.* to ride, to overlap

chevelu, *(adj.)* hairy; **cuir -,** scalp

chevelure, *f.* (head of) hair

chevet, *m.* head of bed; **livre de -,** bedside book

cheveu, *m.* (a single) hair

cheville, *f.* peg; ankle; padding (in literature)

chèvre, *f.* she-goat; derrick

chevreau, *m.* kid

chèvrefeuille, *m.* honeysuckle

chevreuil, *m.* roe-deer

chevrier(-ère), *m.* (*f.*) goat-herd

chevron, *m.* rafter; chevron

chevrotant, *(adj.)* tremulous

chez *(prep.)*; **- moi (mon oncle),** at my (my uncle's) house (*or* home *or* shop); **- les Chinois,** among the Chinese

chic, *m.* smartness, stylishness *(adj. invar.* in *fem., var.* in *pl.)* smart, stylish; **avoir du chic,** to have style

chicane, *f.* chicanery, pettifogging

chicaner, *v.i.* to quibble

chiche, *(adj.)* stingy

chicorée, *f.* chicory

chien(ne), *m.* (*f.*) dog (bitch), **entre - et loup,** in the twilight

chiendent, *m.* couch-grass

chiffe, *f.* rag

chiffon, *m.* rag, scrap (of paper); chiffon

chiffonner, *v.t.* to rumple, crumple

chiffonnier, *m.* rag (and bone) man; small chest of drawers

chiffre, *m.* number, figure, numeral, cipher

chiffrer, *v.i.* to calculate; *v.t.* to number (pages), to code

chimère, *f.* chimera

chimie, *f.* chemistry

chimique, *(adj.)* chemical

chimiste, *m.* chemist (in scientific sense)

chinois(e), *(adj.)* Chinese

chiper, *v.t.* to filch, scrounge

chipoter, *v.i.* to trifle; *v.t.* to nibble (at)

chiquenaude, *f.* fillip

chiquer, *v.t.* to chew (of tobacco)

chiromancien(ne), *m.* (*f.*) palmist

chirurgie, *f.* surgery

chirurgien(ne), *m.* (*f.*) surgeon

chlore, *m.* chlorine

chloroforme, *m.* chloroform

choc, *m.* shock, impact

chocolat, *m.* chocolate; *(adj. invar.)* chocolate-coloured

chœur, *m.* chorus; choir

choir, *v.i.* (with *être*) to fall

choisir, *v.t.* to choose, select

choix, *m.* choice, selection; **article de -,** choice article; **"au - "** (i.e. at customer's choice of articles all at one price)

choléra, *m.* cholera

chômage, *m.* unemployment

chômer, *v.i.* and *v.t.* to be out of work; to stay away from work

chômeur, *m.* unemployed workman

chope, *f.* beer-mug

choquer, *v.t.* to shock, knock; **être choqué de,** to be shocked at

chose, *f.* thing; **faire les choses à demi,** to do things by halves; **Monsieur Chose,** Mr. So-and-so

chou, *m.* cabbage; **chou-fleur,** cauliflower; **- de Bruxelles,** Brussels sprout; **mon petit chou,** my dear, darling

choucas, *m.* jackdaw

choucroute, *f.* sauerkraut

chouette, *f.* owl; (*adj.* and *interjection invar.*) fine, first-rate

choyer, *v.t.* to pet, coddle

chrétien(ne), (*adj.*) and *m.* (*f.*) Christian

christianisme, *m.* Christianity

chrome, *m.* chromium

chronique, *f.* chronicle, news; (*adj.*) chronic

chroniqueur, *m.* chronicler, reporter

chronomètre, *m.* chronometer

chrysalide, *f.* chrysalis

chuchoter, *v.i.* to whisper

chut ! (*interj.*) hush!

chute, *f.* fall, downfall

ci, (*adv.*) here; **celui-ci,** this one, the latter; **ci-gît,** here lies; **ci-après,** hereafter; **ci-dessus,** aforesaid; **ci-inclus,** enclosed (herewith)

cible, *f.* target

ciboire, *m.* pyx

ciboulette, *f.* chives

cicatrice, *f.* scar

cicatriser, *v.i.* and *v.t.* to heal (up); to scar (over)

cidre, *m.* cider

ciel, (*pl.* **ciels** or **cieux**) *m.* sky, heaven; **- de lit,** tester (of bed)

cierge, *m.* wax-candle, taper

cigale, *f.* grasshopper

cigare, *m.* cigar

cigarette, *f.* cigarette

cigogne, *f.* stork

cil, *m.* eyelash

cilice, *m.* hair-shirt

ciller, *v.t.* to blink, wink

cime, *f.* summit, tree-top

ciment, *m.* cement; **béton de -,** concrete

cimenter, *v.t.* to cement

cimetière, *m.* cemetery

cinabre, *m.* cinnabar

cinéaste, *m.* film-producer, scenario-writer

cinéma, *m.* cinema, picture-palace

cinématographique, (*adj.*) cinematographic

cingler, *v.t.* to lash; *v.i.* to sail along

cinq, (*adj.* and *m. invar.*) five

cinquantaine, *f.* about fifty

cinquante, (*adj.*) fifty

cintre, *m.* arch; (*pl.*) flies (above stage)

cintrer, *v.t.* to bend, arch

cipaye, (*adj.*) and *m.* Sepoy

cirage, *m.* waxing, polishing; blacking (of boots)

circoncire, *v.t.* to circumcise

circonférence, *f.* circumference, perimeter

circonflexe, (*adj.*) circumflex (accent)

circonscription, *f.* division, district, constituency

circonstance, *f.* circumstance; **en pareille -,** in such a case

circonvenir, *v.t.* to circumvent

circuit, *m.* circuit, lap

circulaire, (*adj.*) and *m.* circular

circulation, *f.* circulation (of blood); unobstructed movement of traffic

circuler, *v.i.* to circulate, go round; **circulez !** keep moving!

cire, *f.* wax; **- à cacheter,** sealing-wax

cirer, *v.t.* to wax, polish; **toile cirée,** oilcloth

cireur, *m.* shoe-black; polisher

cirque, *m.* circus

cisaille, *f.* shears; parings

ciseau, *m.* chisel; (*pl.*) shears, scissors

ciseler, *v.t.* to engrave, chisel

citadelle, *f.* citadel

citadin, *m.* citizen, townsman

citation, *f.* quotation; mention (in despatches)

cité, *f.* city; **cité-jardin,** garden-city

citer, *v.t.* to quote, cite, mention (in despatches)

citoyen(ne), *m.* (*f.*) citizen(ess)

citron, *m.* lemon

citronnier, *m.* lemon (citron) tree

citrouille, *f.* pumpkin

civet de lièvre, *m.* jugged hare

civière, *f.* stretcher, bier

civil, (*adj.*) civil; *m.* civilian; **en -,** in mufti

civilisation, *f.* civilisation

civiliser, *v.t.* to civilise
civilité, *f.* civility; (*pl.*) compliments
claie, *f.* hurdle, fence
clair, (*adj.*) clear, manifest; bright, unclouded, light; - **de lune**, moonlight; **y voir -**, to see clearly; understand
clairet(te), (*adj.*) light-red, pale
clairière, *f.* clearing, glade
clairon, *m.* bugle; bugler
clairsemé, (*adj.*) sparse, scattered, thinly sown
clairvoyance, *f.* perspicacity; second sight
clameur, *f.* clamour, outcry
clampin, *m.* laggard
clandestin, (*adj.*) clandestine; underground (resistance, etc.)
clapet, *m.* valve
clapoter, *v.i.* to lap, plash (of water)
claque, *f.* slap; hired applauders (in French theatres); *m.* opera-hat
claquer, *v.i.* to clap, bang; (*coll.*) to die, " crack "; *v.t.* to smack, slap; crack (whip, etc.)
clarifier, *v.t.* to clarify
clarine, *f.* cow- (sheep-) bell
clarinette, *f.* clarinet; also player thereof
clarté, *f.* clearness, clarity, light, transparency; **à la - de la lune**, by the light of the moon
classe, *f.* class; form; **billet de première -**, first-class ticket; (**salle de**) -, classroom; **faire ses classes**, to be at school; **la rentrée des classes**, the beginning of term
classement, *m.* classification, rating
classer, *v.t.* to classify; to file (papers)
classique, (*adj.*) classic, classical; **les classiques**, the classics
clause, *f.* clause
clavecin, *m.* harpsichord
clavette, *f.* key, key-bolt
clavicule, *f.* clavicle, collar-bone
clavier, *m.* keyboard
clé (clef), *f.* key; **fermer à clé**, to lock; **clef anglaise**, monkey-wrench; **roman à clef**, novel introducing real people under fictitious names
clématite, *f.* clematis
clémence, *f.* clemency, mercy
clément, (*adj.*) merciful, lenient
cleptomane, *m.* and *f.* kleptomaniac
clerc, *m.* clerk, cleric, learned man
clergé, *m.* clergy
cliché, *m.* negative (in photography); hackneyed phrase
clicher, *v.t.* to stereotype
client, *m.* client, patient, customer, visitor (at hotel)
clientèle, *f.* customers; practice (of a doctor or lawyer); goodwill
cligner, *v.t.* and *v.i.* to blink, screw up one's eyes; - **de l'œil à**, to wink at
clignoter, *v.i.* to twinkle, flicker
climat, *m.* climate, clime
clin d'œil, *m.* wink; **en un -**, in a twinkling
clinique, *f.* clinic, surgery; (*adj.*) clinical
clinquant, *m.* tinsel; glitter
clique, *f.* gang, set
cliqueter, *v.i.* to chink, clink, clank
cliquetis, *m.* clink, clanking, clashing
clisser, *v.t.* to cover bottles with a wicker case
cloaque, *m.* cesspool, sink of iniquity
cloche, *f.* bell; blister
clocher, *m.* belfry, bell-tower, steeple
clocher, *v.i.* to hobble, limp
clocheton, *m.* bell-turret
clochette, *f.* hand-bell
cloison, *f.* partition, bulkhead; - **étanche**, watertight bulkhead
cloître, *m.* cloister, monastery, convent
cloîtrer, *v.t.* to cloister; **se cloîtrer**, *v.r.* to enter a convent or monastery
clopin-clopant, (*adv.*) haltingly; **aller - -**, to hobble along
clopiner, *v.i.* to hobble

cloporte, *m.* woodlouse

clore, *v.t.* to close, enclose

clos, (*adj.*) closed; *m.* enclosure; - (de vigne), vineyard; à huis -, behind closed doors, *in camera*

clôture, *f.* closure, closing (of theatre, etc.); end (of sitting); enclosure

clou, *m.* nail; carbuncle; star turn (*theat.*); un vieux -, an old crock (vehicle, etc.)

clouer, *v.t.* to nail (up), pin down; cloué à son lit, bed-ridden

clouter, *v.t.* to stud; passage clouté, pedestrian crossing

club, *m.* club (political, etc.)

coaguler, *v.t.* to coagulate, congeal; se -, *v.r.* to curdle, congeal

(se) coaliser, *v.r.* to form a coalition, band together

coalition, *f.* coalition, union

coasser, *v.i.* to croak (of frog)

cobaye, *m.* guinea-pig

cobra, *m.* cobra

cocagne, *f.* feast; pays de -, land of plenty

cocaïne, *f.* cocaine

cocarde, *f.* cockade

cocasse, (*adj.*) funny, droll

coche, *m.* (stage-)coach; *f.* nick, notch

cocher, *m.* coachman, driver; porte-cochère, carriage entrance, main gate

cochon, *m.* pig, hog; - d'Inde, guinea-pig; (*adj.*) des histoires cochonnes, "risky" (bawdy) stories (*fam.*)

cochonnerie, *f.* nastiness, filthiness; low trick

cocotier, *m.* coconut palm; noix de coco, coconut

cocotte, *f.* hen; light woman

cocu, *m.* cuckold

code, *m.* code (of law, etc.); - de la route, highway code

*cœur, *m.* heart, middle, centre; courage; hearts (at cards)

coffre, *m.* chest, box, coffer; coffre-fort, safe, strong-box

coffret, *m.* small box

cognac, *m.* cognac, brandy

cognée, *f* axe, hatchet

cogner, *v.t.* to knock (in), hammer (in); *v.i.* to bump (against)

cohérence, *f.* coherence

cohérent, (*adj.*) coherent

cohéritier(-ère), *m.* (*f.*) co-heir (-heiress)

cohue, *f.* mob, throng

coi (coite), (*adj.*) quiet, tranquil; rester -, to keep quiet

coiffe, *f.* head-dress, cap (of peasant women, etc.)

coiffer, *v.t.* to cover (the head); coiffer Sainte-Catherine, to be twenty-five and single; se -, *v.r.* to put on one's hat, do one's hair

coiffeur(-euse), *m.* (*f.*) hairdresser

coiffure, (*f.*) style of hairdressing; head-dress; salon de -, hairdressing establishment

coin, *m.* corner, wedge; place de - face à la machine, corner seat facing the engine

coincer, *v.i.* and *refl.* to jam (of machinery, etc.)

coïncidence, *f.* coïncidence

coïncider (avec), *v.i.* to coincide (with)

col, *m.* neck; mountain pass; collar; faux -, detachable collar (of shirt, etc.)

colère, *f.* anger; se mettre (être) en -, to get (be) angry

colérique, (*adj.*) choleric, irascible

colibri, *m.* humming-bird

colifichet, *m.* bauble, trinket

colimaçon, *m.* snail

colin-maillard, *m.* blindman's buff

colique, *f.* colic, "gripes"

colis, *m.* package, parcel, piece of luggage; - postal, postal packet

collaborateur(-trice), *m.* (*f.*) collaborator, collaborationist

collaboration, *f.* collaboration

collaborer (avec), *v.i.* to collaborate (with)

collage, *m.* gluing, pasting

collant, (*adj.*) sticky; tight(-fitting)

collation, *f.* collation (of documents); light meal

colle, *f.* paste, size; **- forte,** glue; **- de poisson,** isinglass

collecteur(-trice), *m.* (*f.*) collector

collectif(-ive), (*adj.*) collective

collection, *f.* collecting; collection

collectionner, *v.t.* to collect (stamps, etc.)

collège, *m.* college; **- électoral,** electoral body (or college)

collégien(ne), *m.* (*f.*) school-boy (-girl)

collègue, *m.* (*f.*) colleague, fellow-worker

coller (à), *v.t.* to paste, stick (on, to); **robe qui colle,** tight-fitting dress

collerette, *f.* collar, tucker

collet, *m.* collar (of coat, etc.); **elle était très - monté,** she was very stiff and starchy (prim and proper)

colleur (d'affiches), *m.* bill-sticker

collier, *m.* necklet, necklace; **donner un coup de -,** make an effort; collar (mechanics, etc.)

colline, *f.* hill

collision, *f.* collision

colloque, *m.* conversation, colloquy

colombe, *f.* dove

colombier, *m.* dove-cote, pigeon-house

colon, *m.* colonist; farmer

colonel, *m.* colonel

colonial, (*adj.*) colonial

colonie, *f.* colony, settlement

coloniser, *v.t.* to colonise

colonne, *f.* column; **- verté-brale,** spinal column; **cin-quième -,** fifth column

colophane, *f.* rosin

coloration, *f.* colouring, colour

colorer, *v.t.* to colour, stain

colorier, *v.t.* to lay colour on; **colorié à la main,** hand-coloured

coloris, *m.* colouring, tint

colossal, (*adj.*) gigantic, huge

colosse, *m.* colossus

colporter, *v.t.* to peddle, hawk

colporteur(-euse), *m.* (*f.*) pedlar

colza, *m.* colza, rape

coma, *m.* coma

combat, *m.* combat, fight; *hors de combat,* disabled; **livrer combat à,** give battle to; **- à out-rance,** fight to a finish

combattant, *m.* combatant; **ancien -,** ex-service man

combattre, *v.t.* and *v.i.* to fight (against), combat

combien, (*adv.*) how much, how many; **- de temps,** how long; **- de fois,** how many times

combinaison, *f.* combination; scheme, cunning device

combiner, *v.t.* to combine, unite; **se - avec,** *v.r.* to combine with

comble, *m.* top, summit; **c'est le -!** that's the limit, that beats everything; **de fond en -,** from top to bottom, utterly; **pour - de malheur,** as a crowning misfortune

combler, *v.t.* to load, fill, fill up

combustible, (*adj.*) combustible; *m.* fuel

comédie, *f.* comedy, play; **- de mœurs,** comedy of manners

comédien(ne), *m.* (*f.*) player, actor (actress)

comestible, *m.* article of food; (*adj.*) edible

comète, *f.* comet

comique, (*adj.*) comic, comical; *m.* comic actor

comité, *m.* committee, board

commandant, *m.* commander, major; **- en chef,** commander-in-chief

commande, *f.* order; **fait sur -,** made to order; **levier de -,** control lever, control

commandement, *m.* command, commandment

commander, *v.t.* to command, order; to give an order (restaur-ant, etc.); to be in command of

commanditaire, *m.* sleeping-partner

commanditer, *v.t.* to finance

*comme, (*adv.*) how, as; (*conj.*) as

commémorer, *v.t.* to commemor-ate

commençant(e), *m.* (*f.*) beginner

commencement, *m.* beginning, outset

commencer (à, de), *v.t.* and *v.i.* to begin (to), to start; **il commença par rire,** he began by laughing

comment, (*adv.*) how? what! why!

commentaire, *m.* commentary, comment; - **des nouvelles,** news commentary

commenter, *v.t.* to comment

commérage, *m.* (malicious) gossip

commerçant, *m.* merchant, tradesman; (*adj.*) commercial, mercantile

commerce, *m.* commerce, trade, business; - **en gros (détail),** wholesale (retail) trade; **rompre (tout)** - **avec,** to break off all dealings (relations) with

commercial, (*adj.*) commercial

commère, *f.* gossip, goodwife; **les Joyeuses Commères de Windsor,** *The Merry Wives of Windsor*

commettre, *v.t.* to commit; to entrust (to one's charge)

commis, *m.* clerk, assistant; - **voyageur,** commercial traveller

commissaire, *m.* commissary, commissioner; - **de police,** superintendent of police

commissariat, *m.* commissionership, office, police station

commission, *f.* commission; committee; message; **faire une** -, to run an errand

commissionnaire, *m.* agent; porter; **petit** -, errand-boy

commode, (*adj.*) convenient, comfortable; **peu** -, awkward; *f.* chest of drawers

commodité, *f.* comfort, convenience

commotion, *f.* commotion, shock, concussion

commuer (en), *v.t.* to commute (to)

commun, (*adj.*) common, usual; *m.* the generality, common run (of people); **le sens** -, common

sense; **d'un** - **accord,** with one accord

communal, (*adj.*) communal; **école communale,** elementary school

communauté, *f.* community

commune, *f.* parish, commune; **la Chambre des Communes,** the House of Commons

communication, *f.* communication; **mettre en** -, to connect up; **vous avez la** -, you are through (on telephone); **couper la** -, to ring off

communion, *f.* communion

communiquer, *v.t.* to communicate, impart; *v.i.* to communicate (of rooms, etc.)

communiqué, *m.* official statement, communiqué

communiste, *m.* (*f.*) Communist

commutateur, *m.* commutator, switch

compact, (*adj.*) compact, solid

compagne, *f.* companion, mate (*fem.* of **compagnon**)

compagnie, *f.* company; **et Cie,** and Co.; **fausser** - **à,** to give the slip to

compagnon, *m.* comrade, companion; journeyman

comparable (à), (*adj.*) comparable (with)

comparaison, *f.* comparison

comparaître, *v.i.* to appear (particularly before a judge or magistrate)

comparer (à), *v.t.* to compare (with)

comparse, *m.* supernumerary, " extra " (in film studio, etc.)

compartiment, *m.* compartment (railway carriage), division

comparution, *f.* appearance (before the court)

compas, *m.* pair of compasses; scale

compassé, (*adj.*) formal, stiff, exact

compassion, *f.* compassion, pity; **avoir** - **de,** to take pity on

compatible (avec), (*adj.*) compatible (with)

compatriote, *m.* and *f.* compatriot, fellow-countryman (-woman)
compendieux(-euse), *(adj.)* compendious
compensateur, *m.* compensator
compensation, *f.* compensation, adjustment
compenser, *v.t.* to compensate, make up for, adjust
compère, *m.* godfather, confederate; *(coll.)* comrade; announcer (in theatrical revue, etc.)
compétence, *f.* competence, competency, jurisdiction
compétent, *(adj.)* competent
compétiteur(-trice), *m.* *(f.)* competitor
compilation, *f.* compilation
complaire, *v.i.* to please, to humour
complaisance, *f.* complaisance, kindness, self-satisfaction
complaisant, *(adj.)* obliging, complacent
complément, *m.* complement
complémentaire, *(adj.)* complementary
complet(-ète), *(adj.)* complete, full (of bus, theatre); **au grand complet,** at full strength; *m.* suit (of clothes)
compléter, *v.t.* to complete
complexe, *(adj.)* complex, intricate; *m.* complex
complexité, *f.* complexity
complication, *f.* complication, intricacy
complice, *m.* and *f.* accomplice; *(adj.)* accessory
complicité, *f.* complicity; **agir de - avec,** to act in collusion with
compliment, *m.* compliment; *(pl.)* (kind) regards
complimenter (de, sur), *v.t.* to compliment, congratulate (on)
compliquer, *v.t.* to complicate
complot, *m.* plot, conspiracy
comploter, *v.t.* to plot, scheme
comporter, *v.t.* to allow (of), to comprise; **cette idée comporte certains avantages,** this idea has certain advantages attached

to it; **se comporter,** *v.r.* to behave
composer, *v.t.* to compose, make up, settle; **se - de,** *v.r.* to consist of; **composé,** composed, composite, compound
compositeur(-trice), *m.* *(f.)* composer, compositor
composition, *f.* composition, compound, arrangement; **entrer en - avec,** to come to terms with
compote, *f.* compote (of fruit, etc.)
compotier, *m.* fruit dish
compréhensif(-ive), *(adj.)* comprehensive, intelligent
compréhension, *f.* understanding
comprendre, *v.t.* to include, to understand; **vin compris,** wine included (i.e. in over-all charge); **je n'y comprends rien,** I can make nothing of it
compresse, *f.* compress
compresseur, *m.* compressor
compression, *f.* compression
comprimé, *m.* lozenge, tablet
comprimer, *v.t.* to compress; **air comprimé,** compressed air
compromettre, *v.t.* and *v.i.* to compromise
comptabilité, *f.* book-keeping, accountancy
comptable, *m.* book-keeper, accountant; *(adj.)* accountable
comptant, *m.* cash; **vendre au -,** to sell for cash; *(adj.)* **argent -,** ready money
***compte,** *m.* account, reckoning
***compter,** *v.t.* to count, number; to intend
compteur, *m.* meter, calculating machine; **- de stationnement,** parking meter
comptoir, *m.* counter; **garçon de -,** bartender
computer, *v.t.* to compute
comte(sse), *m.* *(f.)* Count(ess)
comté, *m.* county
concasser, *v.t.* to pound, crush (stones, etc.)
concave, *(adj.)* concave
concéder, *v.t.* to concede, grant
concentration, *f.* concentration

concentrer, *v.t.* to concentrate

conception, *f.* conception

concernant, (*prep.*) concerning, respecting

concerner, *v.t.* to concern, affect

concert, *m.* concert, harmony; **salle de -,** concert hall

concerter, *v.t.* to concert, plan; **se - avec,** *v.r.* to connive with

concession, *f.* concession

concessionnaire, *m.* concessionary, holder of licence (for selling something)

concevoir, *v.t.* to conceive, imagine; **ainsi conçu,** worded as follows

concierge, *m.* (*f.*) caretaker, porter (portress)

concile, *m.* council

conciliabule, *m.* confabulation

concilier, *v.t.* to conciliate, reconcile

concis, (*adj.*) concise

concision, *f.* concision, brevity

citoyen(ne), *m.* (*f.*) fellow-citizen (-ess)

concluant, (*adj.*) conclusive

conclure, *v.t.* to conclude, infer; to end; to clinch

conclusion, *f.* conclusion, decision

concombre, *m.* cucumber

concordat, *m.* concordat, agreement

concorde, *f.* concord, harmony

concorder (avec), *v.i.* to agree (with), to tally

concourir, *v.i.* to converge; to co-operate; to compete

concours, *m.* concourse; competition; assistance

concret(-ète), (*adj.*) concrete, solid

concurrence, *f.* concurrence; rivalry; **faire - à,** to compete with (against)

concurrent(e), *m.* (*f.*) competitor, rival, candidate

concussion, *f.* extortion (of money)

condamnation, *f.* condemnation, judgment; **prononcer -,** to pass sentence

condamner, *v.t.* to condemn,

convict; **- à mort,** to sentence to death

condensateur, *m.* condenser

condenser, *v.t.* to condense

condescendre (à), *v.i.* to condescend (to)

condisciple, *m.* school-fellow

condition, *f.* condition, state; (*pl.*) terms, conditions; **sans -,** unconditional; **à - que,** on condition that

conditionnel(le), (*adj.*) conditional; *m.* conditional (mood)

conditionner, *v.t.* to condition

condoléance, *f.* condolence

conducteur(-trice), *m.* (*f.*) driver (*not* conductor) of tram, etc., guide; **- souple,** flex; (*adj.*) conducting, transmitting

conduire, *v.t.* to conduct, lead, drive (car, etc.); to run (a house); **se -,** *v.r.* to conduct oneself, behave

conduit, *m.* conduit, pipe; **- principal,** main

conduite, *f.* behaviour; management, direction; driving (car); **mauvaise -,** ill-behaviour, loose living; **- intérieure,** saloon (car)

cône, *m.* cone

confection, *f.* making (roads, goods); ready-made clothes

confectionner, *v.t.* to manufacture, make (up)

confédération, *f.* confederacy

confédérer, *v.t.* to confederate, unite

conférence, *f.* conference; lecture

conférencier, *m.* lecturer

conférer, *v.t.* to compare, to award; *v.i.* to confer, discuss

confesse, *f.* confession (to a priest)

confesser, *v.t.* to confess, own up

confesseur, *m.* confessor

confession, *f.* confession (of faith)

confessional, *m.* confessional-box

confiance, *f.* confidence; **homme de -,** trustworthy, reliable man

confiant, (*adj.*) confident; confiding

confidence, *f.* confidence (i.e. something told in confidence)

confidentiel(le), *(adj.)* confidential

confier, *v.t.* to entrust; to impart

configuration, *f.* configuration, lie of the land

confire, *v.t.* to preserve (fruit, etc.)

confirmation, *f.* confirmation, corroboration

confirmer, *v.t.* to confirm (report, etc.)

confiscation, *f.* confiscation, seizure

confiserie, *f.* confectioner's shop; confectionery, preserves

confiseur(-euse), *m.* (*f.*) confectioner, sweet seller (*or* maker)

confisquer, *v.t.* to confiscate, impound

confitures, *f. pl.* jam, preserves

conflit, *m.* conflict

confluent, *m.* junction (of rivers)

confondre, *v.t.* to confuse; to confound, baffle; to mingle; **se confondre,** *v.r.* to blend, intermingle; to be profuse in

conformation, *f.* conformation

conforme (à), *(adj.)* conformable (to), consistent (with)

conformément (à), *(adv.)* in conformity, accordance (with)

conformer, *v.t.* to form, conform; **se - à,** *v.r.* to conform (to), comply (with)

conformité, *f.* conformity, agreement

confort, *m.* comfort; **tout - moderne,** every modern convenience (hotel, etc.)

confortable, *(adj.)* comfortable

confrère, *m.* colleague, fellow-member

confrérie, *f.* brotherhood, confraternity

confronter, *v.t.* to confront

confus, *(adj.)* confused, jumbled

confusion, *f.* confusion; embarrassment; muddle

congé, *m.* leave; **un jour de -,** a day off; **donner - à,** to dismiss (an employee)

congédier, *v.t.* to dismiss, discharge, pay off

congeler, *v.t.* to congeal, freeze

congénital, *(adj.)* congenital

congestion, *f.* congestion ; **pulmonaire,** pneumonia

congestionner, *v.t.* to congest

congrégation, *f.* congregation

congrès, *m.* congress

congru, *(adj.)* adequate

conifère, *(adj.)* coniferous; *m.* conifer

conique, *(adj.)* conic(al), cone-shaped

conjecture, *f.* conjecture, surmise

conjoindre, *v.t.* to unite, join (in marriage)

conjointement, *(adv.)* conjointly, jointly

conjonctif(-ive), *(adj.)* conjunctive

conjonction, *f.* conjunction

conjoncture, *f.* conjuncture

conjugaison, *f.* conjugation

conjugal, *(adj.)* conjugal; **vie conjugale,** married life

conjuguer, *v.t.* to conjugate

conjuration, *f.* conspiracy, plot; incantation

conjuré(e), *m.* (*f.*) conspirator

conjurer, *v.t.* and *v.i.* to plot; to ward off; to urge

*****connaissance,** *f.* knowledge; acquaintance; consciousness

connaissement, *m.* bill of lading

connaisseur(-euse), *m.* (*f.*) expert, connoisseur

*****connaître,** *v.t.* to know, to be acquainted with

connexion, *f.* connection

connivence, *f.* connivance

conquérant, *m.* conqueror; *(adj.)* conquering

conquérir, *v.t.* to conquer

conquête, *f.* conquest, acquisition; **faire la - de,** to gain the affection, win the heart, of

consacrer, *v.t.* to consecrate, dedicate

conscience, *f.* conscience; consciousness, awareness; conscientiousness

CON

consciencieux(-euse), *(adj.)* conscientious
conscription, *f.* conscription
conscrit, *m.* conscript
consécration, *f.* consecration, dedication
consécutif(-ive), *(adj.)* consecutive
conseil, *m.* counsel; council; **demander - à,** to seek advice from
conseiller, *v.t.* to advise, counsel; *m.* counsellor; **- municipal,** town councillor
consentement, *m.* consent
consentir (à), *v.i.* to consent, agree (to)
conséquence, *f.* consequence, result; **en -,** consequently
conséquent, *(adj.)* following, consequent (on); **par -,** consequently
conservateur(-trice), *m.* *(f.)* guardian, curator; *(adj.)* conservative, preservative
conservation, *f.* conserving, conservation, preservation
conservatoire, *m.* academy (of music, etc.)
conserve, *f.* preserve, pickle; convoy (nautical)
conserver, *v.t.* to preserve, keep, maintain
considérable, *(adj.)* considerable
considération, *f.* consideration; reason; respect
considérer, *v.t.* to consider, deem; **à tout -,** all things considered
consignation, *f.* consignment
consigne, *f.* orders (esp. to sentry); password; left-luggage office
consistance, *f.* consistence, consistency
consister (en), *v.i.* to consist (of)
consolation, *f.* consolation, comfort
console, *f.* console (kind of table); bracket
consoler, *v.t.* to console, solace
consolider, *v.t.* to consolidate
consommateur(-trice), *m.* *(f.)* consumer; customer (in café, etc.)

consommation, *f.* consummation, accomplishment; drink (taken in café, etc.)
consommé, *m.* clear soup
consommer, *v.t.* to consume; to consummate
consonne, *f.* consonant
consorts, *m.* *pl.* associates (in ill-doing)
consoude, *f.* comfrey
conspirateur(-trice), *m.* *(f.)* conspirator
conspiration, *f.* conspiracy
conspirer (contre), *v.i.* to conspire (against)
conspuer, *v.t.* to scorn, run down, boo
constance, *f.* constancy
constant, *(adj.)* constant, firm
constater, *v.t.* to state; to ascertain
constellation, *f.* constellation
consternation, *f.* consternation, dismay
consterner, *v.t.* to dismay
constipation, *f.* constipation
constiper, *v.t.* to constipate
constituant, *m.* constituent, component; *(adj.)* constituent
constituer, *v.t.* to constitute, set up
constitution, *f.* constitution; composition
constitutionnel(le), *(adj.)* constitutional
constructeur, *m.* constructor
constructif(-ive), *(adj.)* constructive
construction, *f.* construction; edifice; building
construire, *v.t.* to build, construct, erect
consul, *m.* consul
consulaire, *(adj.)* consular
consulat, *m.* consulate
consultatif(-ive), *(adj.)* consultative, advisory
consultation, *f.* consultation; opinion
consulter, *v.t.* to consult, take the opinion of
consumer, *v.t.* to consume, use up

contact, *m.* contact, touch; **établir (rompre) le -,** to switch on (off)

contagieux(-euse), *(adj.)* contagious, noxious

contagion, *f.* contagion

contaminer, *v.t.* to contaminate, infect

conte, *m.* story, tale; **- de fées,** fairy-tale

contemplateur(-trice), *m.* *(f.)* contemplator

contemplation, *f.* contemplation

contempler, *v.t.* to contemplate, behold; to meditate

contemporain(e), *(adj.)* contemporary; *m.* *(f.)* contemporary

contenance, *f.* countenance; **faire bonne -,** to show a bold front, put a good face on a matter

contenir, *v.t.* to contain; to restrain

content, *(adj.)* content, pleased, satisfied

contentement, *m.* contentment

contenter, *v.t.* to content, gratify

contentieux(-euse), *(adj.)* contentious

contenu, *m.* contents; *(adj.)* restrained, reserved

conter, *v.t.* to tell, relate; **en - de belles,** to take someone in

contestable, *(adj.)* debatable, questionable

contestation, *f.* dispute

contester, *v.t.* and *v.i.* to contest, dispute

conteur, *m.* narrator, story-teller

contigu(-uë), *(adj.)* contiguous, adjoining

continence, *f.* continence, continency

continent, *m.* continent; *(adj.)* continent (i.e. chaste)

continental, *(adj.)* continental

continu, *(adj.)* continuous

continuel(le), *(adj.)* continual

continuer (à, de), *v.i.* to continue (to); *v.t.* to continue, carry on

contour, *m.* contour-line; outline

contourner, *v.t.* to trace the outline of; to skirt

contracter, *v.t.* to contract, incur; to draw together

contraction, *f.* contraction

contradiction, *f.* contradiction

contradictoire, *(adj.)* contradictory, conflicting

contraindre, *v.t.* to constrain, compel

contrainte, *f.* constraint, compulsion

contraire, *(adj.)* contrary, opposite, adverse; **au -,** on the contrary

contrarier, *v.t.* to oppose, annoy, thwart

contrariété, *f.* annoyance, vexation

contraste, *m.* contrast

contraster, *v.t.* and *v.i.* to contrast

contrat, *m.* contract, agreement; **- de mariage,** marriage settlement

contravention, *f.* infringement, breach of regulation; **dresser une - à,** to take someone's name (i.e. possible prosecution to follow)

contre, *(adv.* and *prep.)* against; *m.* **le pour et le -,** the pros and cons

contre-amiral, *m.* rear-admiral

contre-attaque (monter une -), to launch a counter-attack

contrebande, *f.* contraband (goods); smuggling

contrebandier, *m.* smuggler

contre-cœur (à), reluctantly

contre-coup, *m.* rebound, recoil, repercussion

contredire, *v.t.* to contradict

contrée, *f.* region, country

contrefaire, *v.t.* to forge; to feign

contrefait, *(adj.)* counterfeit, spurious; deformed

contremaître, *m.* foreman; petty officer

contremander, *v.t.* to countermand, cancel

contrepoids, *m.* counterpoise; counterbalance

contre-poison, *m.* antidote

contresens, *m.* misinterpretation, misconstruction; **à -,** in the wrong (*or* opposite) direction

contretemps, *m.* mishap, untoward event

contre-torpilleur, *m.* (torpedo-boat) destroyer

contrevenir (à), *v.t.* to contravene

contrevent, *m.* outside shutter (of window)

contribuable, *m.* and *f.* tax-payer

contribuer(à), *v.i.* to contribute (to)

contribution, *f.* contribution; tax; **percevoir une -,** to collect a tax

contrit, (*adj.*) penitent, contrite

contrôle, *m.* control, check; auditing; **- des naissances,** birth-control

contrôler, *v.i.* to inspect, check, audit

contrôleur, *m.* controller, inspector; ticket-collector

controverse, *f.* controversy

controverser, *v.t.* to controvert, to debate

contumace, *f.* contumacy; **condamner par -,** to sentence in absence; (*adj.*) contumacious

contusion, *f.* bruise

contusionner, *v.t.* to bruise

convaincre, *v.t.* to convince; to convict

convalescence, *f.* convalescence

convalescent(e), *m.* (*f.*) convalescent person; (*adj.*) convalescent

convenable, (*adj.*) becoming, befitting, seemly

convenance, *f.* propriety; suitability; **mariage de -,** marriage of convenience; **observer (braver) les convenances,** to respect (flout) convention

convenir, *v.i.* to suit; to agree; to acknowledge; **si cela vous convient,** if that suits you, is agreeable to you; **l'heure convenue,** the appointed time

convention, *f.* convention; agreement; covenant

conventionnel(le), (*adj.*) conventional

converger, *v.i.* to converge

conversation, *f.* conversation; **engager la - avec,** to get into conversation with

conversion, *f.* conversion

convertir, *v.t.* to convert

convertisseur, *m.* converter, transformer

convexe, (*adj.*) convex

conviction, *f.* conviction

convier, *v.t.* to invite; to urge

convive, *m.* and *f.* guest (at meal)

convocation, *f.* convocation; summons

convoi, *m.* convoy; train (rail); **- funèbre,** funeral procession

convoiter, *v.t.* to covet

convoitise, *f.* covetousness

convoquer, *v.t.* to convoke, convene

convulsif(-ive), (*adj.*) convulsive

convulsion, *f.* convulsion

coopératif(-ve), (*adj.*) co-operative; and *f.* co-op(erative) store

coopération, *f.* co-operation

coopérer (avec), *v.i.* to co-operate (with)

copain, *m.* (*coll.*) mate, " pal "

copeau, *m.* shaving (of wood)

copie, *f.* copy, reproduction

copier, *v.t.* to copy, reproduce

copieux(-euse), (*adj.*) copious, hearty

coq, *m.* cock; **coq de bruyère,** grouse; **- d'Inde,** turkey-cock

coque, *f.* hull (of ship); shell (of egg); **œuf à la -,** boiled egg

coquelicot, *m.* (wild) poppy

coqueluche, *f.* whooping-cough

coquet(te), (*adj.*) coquettish, stylish, trim; *f.* coquette, flirt

coqueter, *v.i.* to flirt

coquetier, *m.* egg-cup

coquetterie, *f.* coquetry, affectation; smartness

coquillage, *m.* shell-fish; shell

coquille, *f.* shell (of snail, etc.)

coquin(e), *m.* (*f.*) rogue, rascal

cor, *m.* horn; corn (on foot)

corail, *m.* coral

corbeau, *m.* raven; corbel (*arch.*)

corbeille, *f.* basket; flower-bed

corbillard, *m.* hearse

cordage, *m.* rope; (*pl.*) ropes, rigging

corde, *f.* cord, line; hangman's rope; **instrument à cordes,** stringed instrument

cordeau, *m.* string, line

cordelier(-ère), *m.* (*f.*) Franciscan friar (nun)

cordelle, *f.* tow-line

corder, *v.t.* to cord, to string

cordial, (*adj.*) cordial, hearty; *m.* cordial, restorative

cordialité, *f.* cordiality, heartiness

cordier, *m.* rope-maker, rope-merchant

cordon, *m.* string, strand; cordon (of police); **- bleu,** first-rate cook; blue ribbon (of order, etc.); **- de soulier,** shoe-lace; **- (de la porte),** door-pull (used by concierge to open door to residents or callers)

cordonnier, *m.* boot- (shoe-) maker

coriace, (*adj.*) tough

cormier, *m.* service tree

corne, *f.* horn (of animal *or* motor-car); **- de brume,** fog-horn

cornée, *f.* cornea (of eye)

cornemuse, *f.* bagpipes

corner, *v.t.* to sound the horn, hoot; to trumpet, to wheeze

cornet, *m.* trumpet; **- à piston,** cornet

cornette, *f.* mob-cap; cornet (obsolete military rank)

corniche, *f.* cornice, ledge

cornichon, *m.* gherkin

cornouaillais, (*adj.*) Cornish

cornouiller, *m.* cornel tree

cornu, (*adj.*) horned

cornue, *f.* retort (chemical)

corollaire, *m.* corollary

corporation, *f.* corporation, guild

corporel(le), (*adj.*) corporal; corporeal

*corps, *m.* body; dead body; main body, frame; **- d'armée,** army corps

corpulence, *f.* corpulence, obesity

corpulent, (*adj.*) stout, corpulent

corpuscule, *m.* corpuscle

correct, (*adj.*) correct, proper

correction, *f.* correction; correctness; punishment

correspondance, *f.* correspondence; intercourse; connection

correspondant (à), (*adj.*) corresponding (to, with); **train -,** a connection (railway)

correspondre, *v.i.* to tally (with); **- avec,** to write letters to

corridor, *m.* corridor, passage

corriger, *v.t.* to correct (mistakes, exercises); to punish

corroboration, *f.* corroboration

corroborer, *v.t.* to corroborate

corroder, *v.t.* to corrode, eat away

corrompre, *v.t.* to corrupt, bribe

corrosif(-ive), (*adj.*) corrosive; *m.* corrosive

corrosion, *f.* corrosion

corroyeur, *m.* currier

corrupteur(-trice), *m.* (*f.*) corrupter, suborner; (*adj.*) corrupting

corruption, *f.* corruption, bribery; tainting

corsage, *m.* bust (of women); bodice

corsaire, *m.* corsair, privateer

corse, (*adj.*) Corsican

corset, *m.* corset, stays

corsetier(-ère), *m.* (*f.*) corset-maker

cortège, *m.* train, retinue

corvée, *f.* forced labour; drudgery; fatigue (military)

coryza, *m.* cold in the head

cosaque, *m.* Cossack

cosmétique, (*adj.*) and *m.* cosmetic

cosmopolite, *m.* and *f.* cosmopolite; (*adj.*) cosmopolitan

cosse, *f.* husk, pod

cossu, (*adj.*) well-to-do

costume, *m.* costume, dress, suit

costumer, *v.t.* to dress (someone) (up); **se - en,** to dress up as

costumier(-ère), *m.* (*f.*) costumier

cote, *f.* number, quota; price-list, quotation (of shares, etc.)

côte, *f.* slope (of hill); coast, shore; rib

*côté, *m.* side; du - de, in the direction of; de l'autre -, on the other side, on the other hand

coteau, *m.* hillside, hillock

côtelette, *f.* cutlet

coter, *v.t.* to number; to classify; to quote (shares)

coterie, *f.* set, clique

cotier(-ère), (*adj.*) coastwise, coasting; *m.* coasting-vessel

cotillon, *m.* cotillion; petticoat (*archaic*)

cotisation, *f.* quota, assessment

cotiser, *v.t.* to rate; se -, to club together, subscribe

coton, *m.* cotton, cotton-wool; - poudre, gun-cotton

cotonnade, *f.* cotton-cloth; (*pl.*) cotton goods

cotonnier(-ère), *m.* (*f.*) cotton-worker; (*m*) cotton-plant

côtoyer, *v.t.* to hug the coast

cotret, *m.* faggot, stick of wood

cotte, *f.* short skirt, petticoat; - de mailles, coat of mail

cou, *m.* neck (creature *or* bottle); prendre ses jambes à son -, to take to one's heels; tendre le -, to crane one's neck; cou-de-pied, instep

couchant, *m.* sunset, waning; le -, the west

couche, *f.* bed, couch; child-bed; layer, seam; fausse -, miscarriage

coucher, *v.t.* to put to bed, to set down; *v.i.* - chez, to sleep at, have a room at; se -, *v.r.* to go to bed, to lie down, to set (of the sun)

couchette, *f.* cot (of child); berth (on train or ship)

coucou, *m.* cuckoo; cuckoo-clock

coude, *m.* elbow; crank; bend (of road); un coup de -, a nudge with the elbow; jouer des coudes, to elbow one's way

coudée, *f.* cubit

coudoyer, *v.t.* to elbow, to jostle

coudre, *v.t.* to sew, stitch; machine à -, sewing-machine

coudrier, *m.* hazel tree

couenne, *f.* rind (of bacon)

coulage, *m.* leakage; scuttling, sinking (of ship)

couler, *v.t.* to sink, scuttle a ship; *v.i.* to go to the bottom, founder; to flow (of water), to leak (of cask, etc.)

couleur, *f.* colour, tint; complexion; (*pl.*) colours (of flag)

couleuvre, *f.* adder, snake

coulis, *m.* jelly; draught (through vent)

coulisse, *f.* groove; (*pl.*) the wings (stage); porte à -, sliding door

couloir, *m.* corridor, lobby, passage-way; filter

*coup, *m.* knock, blow, stroke; tout à -, suddenly; du premier -, at the first shot (attempt); - de pied, kick; - de soleil, sunstroke; - de téléphone, telephone call; - de main, (1) helping hand, (2) surprise attack

coupable, (*adj.*) guilty, culpable; *m.* (*f.*) culprit

coupant, *m.* cutting-edge; (*adj.*) sharp, cutting

coupe, *f.* cup; cutting, cut (dress, cards, hair)

coupe-fil, *m. inv.* wire-cutters

coupée, *f.* gangway

coupe-gorge, *m.* cut-throat; death-trap

coupe-papier, *m.* paper-knife

*couper, *v.t.* to cut, cut off, interrupt; to adulterate wine with water

couperose, *f.* acne

coupeur(-euse), *m.* (*f.*) cutter (of clothes)

couple, *m.* pair, couple; *f.* brace

coupler, *v.t.* to couple, connect

couplet, *m.* verse (of song)

coupole, *f.* cupola

coupon, *m.* coupon, voucher; portion cut off or detached; (*pl.*) remnants (at sales, etc.)

coupure, *f.* cut, gash, piece cut out

cour, *f.* court, courtyard; faire la - à, to woo, pay court to courage, *m.* courage, valour

courageux(-euse), (*adj.*) brave, courageous

couramment, (*adv.*) readily, generally, fluently

courant, *m.* current; (*adj.*) running, current; eau courante, running water (in bedroom); le deux courant, the 2nd inst. (i.e. of present month); courant d'air, draught; prix courant, price list; être au courant de..., to be in the know, to know all about

courbature, *f.* stiffness, tiredness

courbe, *f.* curve; (*adj.*) curved

courber, *v.t.* to bend, curve; *v.i.* to sag; se -, to stoop

courbure, *f.* curvature, bend; camber (of road)

coureur(-euse), *m.* (*f.*) runner, wanderer; - de routes, tramp

courge, *f.* gourd

courir, *v.i.* to run, to race; *v.t.* to run (risk, etc.), to chase, to gad about

courlieu (*or* courlis), *m.* curlew

couronne, *f.* crown, coronet, wreath

couronnement, *m.* coronation (of king), top-piece, coping (of wall)

couronner, *v.t.* to crown, to cap; to award a wreath(i.e. of laurels)

courrier, *m.* courier, messenger; post, mail-boat; par retour du -, by return of post

courroie, *f.* strap, belt

courroucer, *v.t.* to anger, irritate

courroux, *m.* anger, wrath

cours, *m.* course, path; quotation (of prices); - du change, rate of exchange

course, *f.* run, running, race; errand; faire des courses, to go out shopping, to run errands; champ de courses, racecourse

coursier, *m.* charger, war-horse

court, (*adj.*) short; à - d'argent, short of money; (*adv.*) short; *m.* court (tennis)

courtage, *m.* brokerage

courtier, *m.* broker, jobber

courtisan, *m.* courtier

courtisane, *f.* courtesan

courtois, (*adj.*) courteous, courtly

courtoisie, *f.* courtesy, politeness

couru, (*adj.*) sought after, popular

cousin(e), *m.* (*f.*) cousin; - germain(e), first cousin

coussin, *m.* cushion

coussinet, *m.* pad; - à billes, ball-bearing

coût, *m.* cost

couteau, *m.* knife; - (de table), table-knife

coutelas, *m.* cutlass

coutelier, *m.* cutler

coutellerie, *f.* cutlery (i.e. knives and forks); cutler's shop (or trade)

*coûter, *v.i.* to cost; - cher (peu), to be expensive (cheap)

coûteux(-euse), (*adj.*) costly, dear

coutre, *m.* coulter (of plough)

coutume, *f.* custom, habit

coutumier(-ère), (*adj.*) customary

couture, *f.* seam; needlework

couturière, *f.* seamstress, needle-woman, dressmaker

couvée, *f.* brood, clutch

couvent, *m.* convent, nunnery

couver, *v.t.* to hatch (eggs, plot, etc.), to sit on (eggs)

couvercle, *m.* lid, cover

couvert, *m.* cover, place at table; cover-charge (in restaurant); sous le - de, under cover of; mettre (ôter) le -, to lay (clear) the table

couverture, *f.* covering, blanket; - de lit, bedspread

couvre-chef, *m.* head-gear

couvre-feu, *m.* curfew

couvre-lit, *m.* coverlet

couvre-plat, *m.* dish-cover

couvreur, *m.* roofer

couvrir (de), *v.t.* to cover (with); se -, to put on one's hat; be overcast (of weather)

crabe, *m.* crab

crachat, *m.* spit, spittle

cracher, *v.i.* to spit; *v.t.* to spit out, spit forth; to fork out (money)

crachoir, *m.* spittoon

craie, *f.* chalk

craindre, *v.t.* to fear, be afraid of

crainte, *f.* fear, dread; **de - que ... ne** (with subjunctive), for fear that (lest)

craintif(-ive), *(adj.)* timid

cramoisi, *(adj.)* crimson

crampe, *f.* cramp

crampon, *m.* climbing-iron, stud (of boot sole)

cramponner, *v.t.* to clamp, to cramp; **se - à,** to clutch, hold on to

cran, *m.* notch, cog; **avoir du -,** to have courage (" guts ")

crâne, *m.* skull, brain-pan; *(adj.)* swaggering; **bourrer le - à,** to stuff someone up with false notions

crânerie, *f.* swagger, swank; pluck

crapaud, *m.* toad

crapule, *f.* debauchery, lewdness

crapuleux(-euse), *(adj.)* debauched, lewd, dissolute

craquelin, *m.* cracknel

craquer, *v.i.* to crack, crunch, crackle

crasse, *(adj.)* gross; *f.* squalor, dirt; dross

crasseux(-euse), *(adj.)* dirty, filthy, squalid

cratère, *m.* crater, shell-hole

cravache, *f.* hunting-crop

cravate, *f.* scarf, necktie

crayeux(-euse), *(adj.)* chalky

crayon, *m.* pencil; pencil-drawing

crayonner, *v.t.* to make a pencil sketch; to jot down

créance, *f.* belief, credit, credence; debt

créancier(-ère), *m.* *(f.)* creditor

créateur(-trice), *m.* *(f.)* creator, maker; *(adj.)* creative

création, *f.* creation, founding

créature, *f.* creature

crécelle, *f.* rattle (i.e. hand-rattle)

crèche, *f.* manger, crib; public day-nursery

crédence, *f.* credence table *(eccles.)*; sideboard

crédibilité, *f.* credibility

crédit, *m.* credit (repute); credit (in financial sense); **vendre à -,** to sell on credit; **le Crédit Lyonnais** (a well-known bank)

créditer, *v.t.* to credit (someone's account)

créditeur(-trice), *m.* *(f.)* creditor

crédule, *(adj.)* credulous

crédulité, *f.* credulity, credulousness

créer, *v.t.* to create

crémaillère, *f.* pot-hanger; **pendre la -,** to give a house-warming; **chemin de fer à -,** rack and pinion (mountain) railway

crémation, *f.* cremation

crème, *f.* cream, custard

crémer, *v.t.* to cremate; *v.i.* to cream

crémier(-ère), *m.* *(f.)* dairy-man (-woman)

crémerie, *f.* milkshop, dairy; small restaurant

crémone, *f.* window-fastener

créneau, *m.* battlement(s) (gen. used in plural)

créneler, *v.t.* to indent, notch

créosote, *f.* creosote

crêpe, *f.* pancake; *m.* crape, mourning band; **- de Chine,** crêpe de Chine

crépir, *v.t.* to rough-cast (wall)

crépiter, *v.i.* to crackle, to sputter

crépuscule, *m.* twilight, gloaming

cresson, *m.* cress

crête, *f.* crest (of bird, hill, wave)

crétin, *m.* cretin, idiot

cretonne, *f.* cretonne

creuser, *v.t.* to excavate, hollow out

creuset, m. crucible, melting-pot

creux(-euse), *(adj.)* hollow; **chemin -,** sunken road; *m.* hollow (of hand)

crevaison, *f.* puncture (of tyre); bursting

crevasse, *f.* crevasse, crevice

crève-cœur, *m.* heart-break; acute disappointment

crever, v.i. to burst; (coll.) to die, peg out; v.t. to burst, puncture

crevette, f. shrimp, prawn

cri, m. cry, shriek, squeal; **le dernier -,** the latest fashion

criailler, v.i. to bawl; to nag

criard(e), m. (f.) squaller, scold; (adj.) crying, screaming; loud (colour)

crible, m. sieve, riddle

cribler, v.t. to sift, riddle; **criblé de dettes,** up to the eyes in debt; **criblé de balles,** riddled with bullets

cric, m. jack (for lifting, etc.)

cricket, m. cricket (game)

cri-cri, m. cricket (insect); chirping (of cricket)

criée, f. auction

crier, v.i. to cry, scream, cry out; to shout; v.t. to shout (orders, wares, etc.)

crieur(-euse), m. (f.) crier, shouter

crime, m. crime

criminel(le), (adj.) guilty, criminal; m. (f.) criminal, felon

:rin, m. horse-hair; **à tous crins,** out and out, thorough-going (blackguard, etc.)

crinière, f. mane (of horse)

criquet, m. locust, cricket

crise, f. crisis; fit, attack; **- de nerfs,** fit of hysterics

crisper, v.t. to contract, contort, clench

crisser, v.t. and v.i. to grate, rasp, squeak

cristal, m. crystal; **- taillé,** cut glass

cristalliser, v.t. and v.i. to crystallise

critérium, m. criterion

critique, (adj.) critical; crucial; m. critic; f. criticism, censure

critiquer, v.t. to criticise; to censure

croasser, v.i. to caw (of rooks, etc.)

croate, (adj.) Croatian

croc, m. hook; fang, tusk

crochet, m. hook; **- à boutons,** buttonhook; **faire un -,** to turn aside from one's path; (pl.) brackets (in printing)

crocheter, v.t. to crochet; to pick (a lock)

crochu, (adj.) hooked; crooked

crocodile, m. crocodile

***croire,** v.t. to believe, to think; **- aux fantômes,** to believe in ghosts; **- en Dieu,** to believe, have faith, in God

croisade, f. crusade

croisée, f. crossing; transept; window

croiser, v.t. to cross; to pass (someone coming towards you); v.i. to cruise; **mots croisés,** crosswords (puzzle); **un croisé,** a crusader

croiseur, m. cruiser

croisière, f. cruise

croissance, f. growth

croissant, (adj.) growing, rising; m. crescent (of moon); bread-roll (of horse-shoe shape)

croître, v.i. to grow, increase

croix, f. cross; **la Croix Rouge,** the Red Cross; **la Croix de Guerre,** the Military Cross; **faire le signe de la -,** to cross oneself

croquant, (adj.) crisp; m. gristle

croque-mitaine, m. bogy (man)

croque-mort, m. undertaker's man, mute

croquer, v.t. to munch, crunch; **être joli à -,** to be as pretty as a picture

croquet, m. crisp biscuit; croquet (game)

croquis, m. sketch

crosse, f. butt (of rifle); crook, crozier (of bishop)

crotte, f. mud, dirt; dung

crotter, v.t. to soil, dirty

croulement, m. collapse (of building, empire, etc.)

crouler, v.i. to totter, crumble, tumble down; **faire - la salle,** to bring the house down (with applause)

croupe, f. crupper, rump; **monter en -,** to ride pillion croupier, *m.* croupier (at roulette table, etc.)

croupir, *v.i.* to stagnate; to wallow

croûte, *f.* crust; casser une -, to have a bite, a snack

croûton, *m.* piece of crust

croyable, (*adj.*) credible

croyance, *f.* belief

croyant(e), (*adj.*) believing; *m.* (*f.*) believer (gen. in God)

cru, (*adj.*) raw, crude, coarse; *m.* wine-growing district; vin du - (*or* du pays), local wine

cruauté, *f.* cruelty

cruche, *f.* pitcher, jug; (*coll.*) blockhead

crucifier, *v.t.* to crucify

crucifix, *m.* crucifix

crucifixion, *f.* crucifixion

crue, *f.* rising, swelling; la - de la Seine, the Seine floods

cruel(le), (*adj.*) cruel

crypte, *f.* crypt

cubain, (*adj.*) Cuban

cube, (*adj.*) cubic; *m.* cube

cueillage, *m.* picking, gathering (of fruit, etc.)

cueillir, *v.t.* to gather, pick (flowers, fruit, etc.)

cuiller *or* cuillère, *f.* spoon; scoop

cuillerée, *f.* spoonful

cuir, *m.* hide; leather; - chevelu, scalp; - à rasoir, razor-strop

cuirasse, *f.* cuirass, breast-plate; armour

cuirassé, (*adj.*) armoured, armour-plated; *m.* battleship (or other heavily protected warship)

cuirassement, *m.* armour-plating

cuirasser, *v.t.* to plate with armour; se -, to steel oneself

cuire, *v.i.* and *v.t.* to cook; to smart (of eyes); cuit à point, done to a turn; trop cuit, over-done; - quelquechose au four, to roast something; faire - un gigot de mouton, to cook a leg of mutton

cuisant, (*adj.*) smarting (of pain); stinging (of cold); bitter (of disappointment)

cuisine, *f.* kitchen; cook's galley;

cookery; art of cooking; "bonne - bourgeoise," " good plain cooking "

cuisinier(-ère), *m.* (*f.*) cook; cuisinière à gaz, gas-cooker

cuisse, *f.* thigh; leg (of chicken)

cuisson, *f.* cooking; sensation of pain (*or* of burning)

cuivre, *m.* copper; - jaune, brass

cuivrer, *v.t.* to copper, cover with copper

cul, *m.* bottom, backside, stern

culasse, *f.* breech (of gun)

culbute, *f.* somersault, " cropper "

culbuter, *v.i.* to turn a somersault; *v.t.* to overthrow

cul-de-jatte, *m.* cripple

cul-de-sac, *m.* blind alley

culée, *f.* abutment (of bridge)

culer, *v.i.* to go backwards

culminer, *v.i.* to culminate

culot, *m.* (*coll.*) nerve, self-assurance

culotte, *f.* breeches, pair of breeches; (*coll.*) avoir une -, to get drunk

culpabilité, *f.* culpability, guilt

culte, *m.* cult, worship; form of worship

cultivateur, *m.* farmer, cultivator

cultiver, *v.t.* to cultivate, till, raise

culture, *f.* cultivation; culture (of mind or bacteria)

cumuler, *v.t.* to hold several offices, be a pluralist

cunéiforme, (*adj.*) cuneiform

cupide, (*adj.*) greedy

cupidité, *f.* cupidity, greed

Cupidon, *m.* Cupid

curateur(-trice), *m.* (*f.*) guardian, trustee

cure, *f.* care, cure; residence of *curé*

curé, *m.* parish priest (*not* curate)

cure-dents, *m.* toothpick

curieux(euse), (*adj.*) curious; interested; peculiar; *m.* (*f.*) a sight-seer, interested bystander

curiosité, *f.* curiosity; curio; peculiarity

cursif(-ive), (*adj.*) cursive; cursory

curviligne, (*adj.*) curvilinear

cuspide, _f._ cusp
cutané, (_adj._) cutaneous, of the skin
cuticule, _f._ cuticle, skin
cuve, _f._ vat, tub
cuvée, _f._ tubful, vàtful
cuver, _v.i._ and _v.t._ to ferment (of wine); - son vin, to sleep off one's drink
cuvette, _f._ wash-basin; basin
cycle, _m._ cycle (of history); (bi)cycle
cyclisme, _m._ cycling
cycliste, _m._ (_f._) cyclist
cyclo-moteur, _m._ moped
cygne, _m._ swan
cylindre, _m._ cylinder; roller
cylindrique, (_adj._) cylindrical
cymbale, _m._ cymbal
cynique, (_adj._) cynical; brazen; _m._ cynic
cynisme, _m._ cynicism; shamelessness
cyprès, _m._ cypress
cypriote, (_adj._) Cypriot
czar(ine), _m._ (_f._) Tsar, Tsarina

D

dactylo(graphe), _m._ and _f._ typist
dada, _m._ hobby-horse
dadais, _m._ booby
dague, _f._ dirk, dagger
daigner, _v.t._ to deign, condescend
daim, _m._ deer, buck
dais, _m._ canopy
dallage, _m._ flagstone paving
dalle, _f._ flagstone
daller, _v.t._ to pave with flagstones
damas, _m._ damask (linen); Damascus blade; damson
dame, _f._ lady; married lady; queen. (cards, chess); rowlock; jeu de dames (game of draughts)
dame! (_interj._) rather, well; dame! c'est juste, well, you see, it is right
damier, _m._ chess-(draught-) board
damnation, _f._ damnation
damné, (_adj._) damned (person); âme damnée, tool, catspaw

damner, _v.t._ to damn
dancing, _m._ dance-hall
dandin, _m._ simpleton
(se) dandiner, _v.i._ to strut, to waddle
danger, _m._ danger, risk, hazard; affronter les dangers, to face the risks; être en - (de), to be in danger (of)
dangereux(-euse), dangerous
danois, _m._ Dane; Great Dane (dog); (_adj._) Danish
*dans, (_prep._) in, within; into; with; during
danse, _f._ dance, dancing
danser, _v.i._ to dance
danseur(-euse), _f._ dancer
dard, _m._ dart, sting; forked tongue (of snake)
darder, _v.t._ to hurl; spear or harpoon; dart (beams)
*date, _f._ date (time)
*dater, _v.t._ to date (a letter)
datte, _f._ date (fruit)
dattier, _m._ date tree
daube, _f._ stew
dauber, _v.t._ to stew, braise
dauphin, _m._ dolphin; Dauphin (eldest son of French king)
davantage, more, any more; any further; any longer
*de (_prep._) of; out of; made of, composed of; from; by, with; concerning; about
dé, _m._ die; thimble; dice
débâcle, _f._ breaking up (of ice); (_fig._) downfall, collapse
déballage, _m._ unpacking; show (of goods at low prices)
déballer, _v.t._ to unpack
débandade, _f._ stampede; à la -, helter-skelter
débander, _v.t._ to disband; relax, unbandage
débarbouiller, _v.t._ to wash, to cleanse
débarcadère, _m._ (arrival) platform; landing-stage
débarder, to unload (wood, etc.)
débardeur, _m._ stevedore, docker
débarquement, _m._ landing; disembarkment (troops, etc.)

débarquer, v.t. to land, unload; v.i. to disembark, detrain

débarras, m. riddance; **chambre de -**, lumber-room

débarrasser, v.t. to rid; to free; disencumber

débarrer, v.t. to unbar

débat, m. debate (Parliament); pleadings (legal); dispute, altercation

débattre, v.t. to debate, discuss; se -, v.r. to struggle

débauche, f. debauch; debauchery; lewdness

débauché, m. a rake, dissolute person

débaucher, v.t. to lead astray; to debauch; se -, v.r. to go astray

débile, (adj.) weak, feeble

débilité, f. debility, weakness

débine, f. (fam.) poverty

débineur(-euse), m. slanderer

débit, m. sale; retail shop; debit; delivery (of oratory); **- de tabac**, tobacconist's shop

débitant, m. retailer

débiter, v.t. to retail; to supply (electricity, gas); to debit; to deliver (speech, etc.)

débiteur, debtor

déblai, m. cutting; excavation

déblayer, v.t. to clear away

déboire, m after-taste, (fig.) vexation, rebuff

déboiser, v.t. to clear of trees

débonnaire, (adj.) good-natured; compliant

débordement, m. overflowing; dissipation

déborder, v.i. to overflow; to project, jut out; **débordé de travail**, snowed under with work

(se) débotter, v.r. to take one's boots off

débouché, m. outlet, issue; (fig.) opening

déboucher, v.t. to uncork; to open; v.i. to emerge, debouch

déboucler, v.t. to unbuckle

debours, m. (usu. pl.) (out-of-pocket) expenses

débourser, v.t. to disburse, spend

debout, upright; standing

déboutonner, v.t. to unbutton

débrayer, v.t. to disconnect; (motoring) to declutch

débris, m. pl. remains; ruins; wreck

débrouiller, v.t. to disentangle; se -, v.r. to get out of a difficulty

début, m. beginning; first appearance

débuter, v.i. to begin; to make one's first appearance

deçà, (adv.) on this side (of)

décadence, f. decline, decay

décamper, v.i. to decamp; (fig.) to bolt

décapiter, v.t. to behead

décarburer, v.t. to decarbonise

décéder, v.i. to decease, to die

déceler, v.t. to disclose, reveal

décembre, m. December

décence, f. decency

décent, (adj.) decent

déception, f. deception; disappointment

décerner, v.t. to award

décès, m. demise, death, decease

décevoir, to dupe; to disappoint

déchaîner, to unchain, unbind, let loose; to give vent to (passions, fury)

décharge, f. unloading, discharge; relief, exoneration

décharger, v.t. to unload, to discharge

décharné, (adj.) emaciated

(se) déchausser, v.r. to pull one's shoes off

déchéance, f. forfeiture; disgrace

déchet, m. waste, loss

déchiffrer, v.t. to decipher

déchiqueter, v.t. to slash; to cut into long pieces

déchirer, v.t. to tear, to rend; **- en morceaux**, to tear to pieces

déchirure, f. rent, tear

déchu, (adj.) fallen (from position of honour, etc.)

décider (de), v.t. to decide, to determine (to); se - à, v.r. to make up one's mind (to)

décimale, f. decimal

décimer, v.t. to decimate, to thin out

décisif, (adj.) decisive

décision, f. decision; resolution; final issue

déclamation, f. elocution; harangue

déclamer, v.t. and v.i. to declaim; (fam.) to spout

déclaration, f. declaration; proclamation; disclosure; schedule (law, bankruptcy)

déclancher, v.t. to launch; to unlatch; - une offensive, to launch an offensive

*__déclarer,__ v.t. declare, make known

déclassé, (adj.) degraded

déclin, m. decline; ebb

déclinaison, f. declension

décliner, v.t. to refuse, decline (invitation); (legal) refuse to recognise jurisdiction

déclivité, f. slope

déclouer, v.t. to unnail

décollage, m. take-off (of aeroplane)

décoller, v.t. to unglue, unpaste; v.i. to take off (of aeroplane)

décolleté, (adj.) low-necked (of dress)

décolorer, v.t. to discolour, fade

décoloration, discoloration

décombres, m. pl. rubbish, débris

décommander, v.t. to countermand (an order)

décomposer, v.t. to decompose; to distort (face)

décomposition, f. decomposition, putrefaction

décompte, m. deduction, abatement

décompter, v.t. to discount; (fig.) to be disappointed

déconcerter, v.t. to disconcert, to put out; baffle

déconfit, (adj.) discomfited, nonplussed

déconseiller, v.t. to dissuade; - qn. de faire qch., to advise someone against doing something

déconsidérer, v.t. to bring into disrepute, discredit

déconvenue, f. failure, discomfiture

décor, m. setting; arrangement of stage; decoration (of house)

décoration, f. medal; ribbon or star of an order; decoration (of house)

décorer, v.t. adorn; do up (a house); to decorate (a person)

découcher, v.i. to sleep out, away from home

découdre, v.t. to unstitch, to unpick

découpler, v.t. to uncouple

décourager, v.t. to discourage

décousu, (adj.) unstitched (of hem); scrappy (conversation); incoherent

découverte, f. discovery

découvrir, v.t. to discover; uncover; unmask (something)

décrasser, v.t. to clean, scour

décrépit, (adj.) senile; dilapidated

décret, m. decree; order

décréter, v.t. to enact (law)

décret-loi, m. Order in Council

décrier, v.t. to decry

décrire, v.t. to describe (a sight, etc.)

décrocher, v.t. to unhook; take down

décroissance, f. decrease

décroître, v.i. to diminish; decrease

décrotter, v.t. to clean (boots); to scrape

décrotteur, m. shoe-black; " boots "

décrue, f. fall (of a river)

dédaigner, v.t. to scorn, disdain

dédaigneux, (adj.) disdainful

dédain, m. scorn, disdain

dédale, m. maze, labyrinth (of streets)

*__dedans,__ (adv.) inside, within; m. interior

dédicace, f. consecration; dedication

dédier, v.t. to consecrate (a building)

(se) dédire, v.r. to take back what one has said; to retract (a statement)

dédommagement, m. indemnity; damages; compensation

dédommager, v.t. to indemnify

déduire, *v.t.* to infer, deduce; to take off; allow (5 per cent., etc.)

déesse, *f.* goddess

défaillance, *f.* lapse (moral or physical); fainting fit

défaillir, *v.i.* to become feeble; to faint

défaire, *v.t.* to undo; untie (a parcel); to cancel, to annul (agreement, treaty); to rid

défaite, *f.* defeat

défalquer, *v.t.* to deduct (sum from total)

*****défaut,** *m.* want, lack (of something); shortcoming, defect; (legal) default

défavorable, *(adj.)* unfavourable

défectueux, *(adj.)* defective, unsound

défendeur(-eresse), *m.* *(f.)* defendant (legal)

*****défendre,** *v.t.* to defend (prisoner, etc.); to stand up for, to protect; to forbid; **se -,** *v.r.* to defend oneself

*****défense,** *f.* defence; prohibition

défenses, *f. pl.* tusks (elephant, boar)

défenseur, *m.* defender; supporter

défensif, *(adj.)* defensive

déférence, *f.* respect, deference

déférer, *v.t.* to submit, refer (case to court); to confer, bestow

déferler, *v.t.* to shake out (flag, sail); *v.i.* to break into foam

défi, *m.* challenge; defiance

défiance, *f.* mistrust, distrust

défiant, *(adj.)* distrustful

déficit, *m.* deficit, shortage

défier, *v.t.* to challenge; **se -,** *v.r.* to distrust

défigurer, *v.t.* to disfigure; to distort (the truth); deface (statue)

défilé, *m.* defile, gorge; *(mil.)* march past

défiler, *v.t.* to unstring, unthread; *v.i.* to march past

défini, *(adj.)* definite

définir, *v.t.* to define

définitif, *(adj.)* final (resolution); permanent

définition, *f.* definition

déflation, *f.* deflation (of currency, etc.)

défleurir, *v.i.* to lose blossoms (tree, etc.)

défoncer, *v.t.* to break, stave in

déformer, *v.t.* to deform, distort

défraîchi, *(adj.)* faded (flowers); soiled (shop goods)

défrayer, *v.t.* defray, pay (expenses)

défricher, *v.t.* to clear (ground)

défunt, *(adj.)* deceased, late.

dégager, *v.t.* to redeem (pledge); to clear (road traffic); to free; **se -,** *v.r.* to extricate oneself; to be given off (gas, etc.)

dégarnir, *v.t.* to strip, dismantle (room)

dégarni, *(adj.)* empty; stripped; depleted

dégât, *m.* damage

dégel, *m.* thaw

dégeler, *v.t.* and *v.i.* to thaw

dégénérer, *v.i.* to degenerate

dégénéré(e), *m.* *(f.)* and *(adj.)* degenerate

dégingandé, *(adj.)* ungainly

dégivrer, *v.t.* to defrost, de-ice

dégonfler, *v.t.* to deflate (balloon, etc.); to reduce (swelling); **se -,** *v.r.* to subside; collapse; *(slang)* to climb down

dégorger, *v.t.* disgorge; *v.i.* to overflow (stream, gutter, etc.)

dégourdir, *v.t.* to revive; to remove stiffness

dégourdi, *(adj.)* sharp, cute; wide-awake

dégoût, *m.* disgust

dégoûter, *v.t.* to disgust

dégoutter, *v.i.* to drip, trickle down

dégradation, *f.* degradation (*mil.*); loss of civil rights; degradation (moral)

dégrader, *v.t.* to degrade (from rank); **se -,** to lower oneself

dégrafer, *v.t.* to unhook, unfasten

dégraisser, *v.t.* to skim; clean

degré, *m.* degree (heat); step (of ladder, stair)

dégringolade, *f.* tumble (downstairs); collapse of prices; down-fall (of government or financial house)

dégringoler, v.t. and v.i. to tumble down; come clattering down

dégriser, v.t. to sober

déguenillé, (adj.) ragged, in tatters

déguerpir, v.i. to move out (tenant); to clear out, decamp

déguisement, m. disguise; dis-simulation

déguiser, v.t. to disguise

dégustation, f. tasting (wines, etc.)

déguster, v.t. to taste, sample

***dehors,** (adv.) out, outside; m. outside, exterior

déjà, (adv.) already; previously, before

déjeuner, m. lunch; **petit -,** breakfast

déjeuner, v.i. to lunch

déjouer, v.t. to thwart; to baffle

delà, beyond

délabré, (adj.) out of repair; tumble-down (house)

délabrer, to dilapidate; ruin (house, fortune)

délai, m. delay; **dans le plus bref -,** as soon as possible

délaisser, v.t. to forsake, desert, abandon

délassement, m. relaxation

(se) délasser, to rest, to take some rest

délateur, m. informer

délayement, m. diluting

délecter, v.t. to delight

délégation, f delegation (of authority)

délégué, m. delegate (at meeting); deputy (but *not* Parliament)

délibération, f. discussion, de-bate; reflection

délibérer, v.i. to deliberate; to take counsel

délibéré, (adj.) deliberate; de-termined

délicat, (adj.) delicate; dainty (dish, etc.); scrupulous, nice (feelings)

délicatesse, f. delicacy; refine-ment

délice, m. delight; f. pl. delights

délicieux(-euse), (adj.) delicious

délié, (adj.) loose; nimble, sharp (wit)

délier, v.t. untie; release

délirant, (adj.) delirious

délire, m. delirium, frenzy

délirer, v.i. to rave in delirium

délit, m. offence; misdemeanour

délivrance, f. deliverance; rescue; release

délivrer, v.t. to deliver; to rescue (a prisoner)

déloger, v.i. to remove (to another place); to get away; to drive out

déloyal, (adj.) disloyal, false, un-faithful

déluge, m. flood, deluge

demain, (adv. and m.) to-morrow; **à -,** good-bye till to-morrow

demande, f. request, petition, application; question, enquiry

***demander,** v.t. to ask, ask for; **se -,** v.r. to wonder

demandeur(-eresse), m. (f.) plaintiff

démangeaison, f. itching

***démarche,** f. gait, step, walk

démarrer, v.t. to unmoor; to start a car

démarreur, m. self-starter (car)

démasquer, v.t. to unmask

démêlé, m. dispute

démêler, v.t. to unravel, disen-tangle

démembrer, v.t. to dismember

déménagement, m. removal; moving (house, furniture)

déménager, v.t. to move house

démence, f. insanity

(se) démener, v.r. to struggle; to stir oneself

démenti, m. denial, contradiction

démentir, v.t. to give the lie to; **se -,** v.r. to contradict oneself

démesuré, (adj.) excessive; im-moderate

démettre, v.t. to dismiss; to dis-locate (a joint); **se -,** v.r. to re-sign (office, position)

démeublement, m. removal of furniture; stripping a house démeubler, *v.t.* to remove furniture from a house

demeurant (au), (*adv. phrase*) after all, all the same

demeure, *f.* dwelling-place; abode

demeurer (*être*), *v.i.* to remain; to stay; stop in a place

demeurer (*avoir*), *v.i.* to live, reside

*demi, half. (N.B.—In most compounds *demi* remains invariable, the second component taking the plural)

démission, *f.* resignation; il est démissionnaire, he is resigning (has resigned) his position

démocrate, *m.* democrat

démocratie, *f.* democracy

démocratique, (*adj.*) democratic

demoiselle, single woman; young lady

démolir, *v.t.* to demolish, pull down (house)

démolition, *f.* demolition

démon, *m.* demon, fiend; little imp (child)

démonétiser, *v.t.* to withdraw, call in coinage

démonstration, *f.* demonstration; (*mil.*) show of force

démonter, *v.t.* to dismount, unseat; to take to pieces

démontrer, *v.t.* to prove, show, demonstrate

*démordre, *v.i.* to let go one's hold; to desist

dénatalité, *f.* fall in birth-rate

dénaturé, (*adj.*) unnatural; hard-hearted (parent)

dénaturer, *v.t.* to disfigure, distort (facts)

dénégation, *f.* denial

dénicher, *v.t.* to find out; dislodge; unearth

denier, *m.* a small coin, farthing or penny; denier (hosiery)

dénier, *v.t.* to deny; disclaim responsibility

dénigrer, *v.t.* to disparage; to run down (somebody or something)

dénombrement, *m.* census of population

dénominateur, *m.* denominator

dénommer, *v.t.* to denominate, name

dénoncer, *v.t.* to denounce; inform against; to expose (vice, etc.)

dénoter, *v.t.* to denote, show (energy, contempt, etc.)

dénouement, *m.* outcome, ending

dénouer, *v.t.* to undo (knot); untie; untangle

denrée, *f.* commodity; foodstuff

densité, *f.* density

*dent, *f.* tooth

denté, (*adj.*) toothed, cogged (wheel)

denteler, *v.t.* to notch

dentelle, *f.* lace

dentifrice, *m.* tooth-paste

dentiste, *m.* dentist

dentition, *f.* cutting the teeth; dentition

dénuder, *v.t.* to denude, lay bare

dénuement, *m.* penury, destitution

dépannage, *m.* (on the spot) repairs (to car)

dépanner, *v.t.* to repair (broken down engine)

dépaqueter, *v.t.* to unpack (goods, etc.)

départ, *m.* departure

département, *m.* department (administrative); sub-division (of France)

départir, *v.t.* to divide (property); deal out (favours)

*dépasser, *v.t.* to go beyond; overreach; surpass; overtake

dépayser, *v.t.* to remove someone (from usual surroundings); to bewilder

dépecer, *v.t.* to cut up

dépêche, *f.* despatch (official); telegram

dépêcher, *v.t.* to despatch; se -, *v.r.* to make haste

dépeindre, *v.t.* to describe; portray

dépendance, *f.* dependence; dependency (of a country); outbuildings

dépendant, (*adj.*) dependent

dépendre (de), *v.i.* to depend (on).

dépens, *m. pl.* cost, expense

dépense, *f.* expenditure, outlay (of money)

dépenser, *v.t.* to spend

dépensier(-ère), *(adj.)* extravagant; *m. (f.)* spendthrift

dépensier, *m.* dispenser (of hospital)

dépérir, *v.i.* to decay, dwindle

dépérissement, *m.* decay

dépeuplement, *m.* depopulation

dépeupler, *v.t.* to depopulate (a country); to thin (a wood)

dépilatoire, *(adj.)* and *m.* depilatory

dépister, *v.t.* to track down game; *(fam.)* to outwit (police)

dépit, *m.* spite, resentment; **en - de**, in spite (defiance) of

dépiter, *v.t.* to vex

déplacement, *m.* displacement; transfer (of official or person)

déplacer, *v.t.* to displace, shift (an object); to take the place (of someone); **se -**, *v.r.* to move about, to travel

déplacé, *(adj.)* out of its place; ill-timed; uncalled for (remark)

déplaire, *v.i.* to displease, offend

déplaisant, *(adj.)* disagreeable, displeasing

déplaisir, *m.* displeasure, annoyance

déplier, *v.t.* to unfold, spread out

déplorable, *(adj.)* deplorable

déplorer, *v.t.* to deplore, lament

déployer, *v.t.* *(mil.)* to deploy troops; to spread; to display (goods)

dépolir, *v.t.* to dull (surface)

déportation, *f.* deportation (of alien); transportation (convict)

déporter, *v.t.* to deport (alien); transport (convict)

déposer, *v.t.* to deposit; set down; depose (king, etc.); *(legal)* to give evidence

déposition, *f.* evidence, statement

déposséder, *v.t.* to dispossess

dépôt, *m.* deposit; handing in (of telegram); store, warehouse;

sediment; **en -**, in trust, in bond; **- de bagages**, cloakroom for luggage at station

dépouille, *f.* skin, hide (taken from animal); spoils, booty; **- (mortelle)**, mortal remains

dépouiller, *v.t.* to strip, despoil

dépourvu, *(adj.)* destitute, short (of); **au -**, taken unawares

dépraver, *v.t.* to deprave

dépréciation, *f.* depreciation; fall (in currency); wear and tear

déprédation, *f.* misappropriation

dépression, *f.* dejection, depression (moral); dip (in ground)

déprimé, *(adj.)* depressed; low (in spirits); flat (market)

déprimer, *v.t.* to depress

depuis, *(prep.)* (of time) since, for; (of time and place) from

dépuratif, *m.* cleansing (of blood)

député, *m.* deputy (Parliament); delegate

députer, *v.t.* to depute (someone)

déraciner, *v.t.* to uproot; eradicate

déraillement, *m.* running off the rails

dérailler, *v.i.* to jump the rails (railway); derail

déraisonnable, *(adj.)* unreasonable, irrational

déraisonner, *v.i.* to talk nonsense

dérangement, *m.* disturbance, trouble; derangement

déranger, *v.t.* to disturb, to trouble; to upset (plans); **se -**, *v.r.* to move, stir

déraper, *v.i.* to skid

derechef, *(adv.)* a second time; yet again

déréglé, *(adj.)* out of order; disordered (mind)

dérégler, *v.t.* to upset, disorder (habits)

dérider, *v.t.* to smooth out, unwrinkle

dérision, *f.* mockery

dérisoire, *(adj.)* ridiculous, laughable; absurdly low (price)

dériver, *v.t.* to divert; to derive from; to unrivet; *v.i.* to drift

dernier(-ère), (*adj.* and *subst.*) last, latest

dérobée (à la), stealthily, on the sly

dérober, *v.t.* to steal; **se -**, *v.r.* to steal away, to escape

dérouler, *v.t.* to unroll, unfold

déroute, *f.* rout, full flight

dérouter, *v.t.* to lead astray

derrière, *m.* behind, backside

derrière (*prep.*) behind, at the back

dès, (*prep.*) from, since

dès (que), as soon as

désabuser, *v.t.* to undeceive

désaccord, *m.* disunion, disagreement

désaccorder, *v.t.* to put out of tune

désaccoutumer, *v.t.* to get out of the habit (of doing something)

désaffection, *f.* disaffection (towards someone)

désaffectionner, *v.t.* to disaffect (followers, members of a political party)

désagréable, (*adj.*) disagreeable, unpleasant

désagrément, *m.* discomfort; source of annoyance

(se) désaltérer, *v.r.* to quench one's thirst

désappointer, *v.t.* to disappoint

désapprobation, *f.* disapproval

désapprouver, *v.t.* to disapprove of

désarçonner, *v.t.* to unseat (a rider); to dumbfound

désarmement, *m.* disarmament

désarmer, *v.t.* to disarm

désarroi, *m.* disorder, disarray

désastre, *m.* disaster

désastreux(-euse), (*adj.*) disastrous

désavantage, *m.* drawback, disadvantage

désavouer, *v.t.* to repudiate, disclaim

désaxé, (*adj.*) eccentric

desceller, *v.t.* to unseal

descendant, *m.* descendant (of old family)

descendre (*être*), *v.i.* to come down; go down; descend; to put up at (hotel)

descendre (*avoir*), *v.t.* to go down (the street, hill, steps); to carry down; to bring down

descente, *f.* descent

descente, *f.* (de lit) bedside rug

descriptif(-ive), (*adj.*) descriptive

description, *f.* description

désemballage, *m.* unpacking

désembarquer, *v.t.* to put ashore, disembark; unship goods

désemparé, (*adj.*) crippled; (*fig.*) all at sea

désemparer, *v.t.* to disable (a ship)

désemplir, *v.t.* to half-empty

désenchanter, *v.t.* to disenchant; to disillusion

désenfler, *v.t.* to reduce the swelling; *v.i.* to go down (tyre, etc.)

désengager, *v.t.* to free from an obligation; to take out of pawn

désenivrer, *v.t.* to sober

désert, *m.* desert

désert, (*adj.*) deserted (place); lonely (spot)

déserteur, *m.* deserter

déserter, *v.t.* to desert; to go over to the enemy

désespéré, (*adj.*) desperate; hopeless

désespérer, *v.i.* to despair; to lose hope; to despair of

désespoir, *m.* despair

déshabiller, *v.t.* to undress; **se -**, *v.r.* to take off one's clothes

déshabillé, *m.* boudoir wrap; **en -**, in undress

déshabituer, *v.t.* to disaccustom (someone to something)

déshériter, *v.t.* to disinherit

déshonneur, *m.* disgrace, dishonour

déshonorant, (*adj.*) discreditable

déshonorer, *v.t.* to dishonour, to disgrace

désignation, *f.* designation; pointing out (indication); description of (goods)

désigner, *v.t.* to designate, show

désillusion, *f.* disillusion

désillusionner, *v.t.* to undeceive; disillusion

désinfecter, *v.t.* to disinfect

désintéressé, *(adj.)* not involved; unprejudiced; unselfish (of motive)

désinvolte, *(adj.)* easy, free; unembarrassed, unselfconscious

désinvolture, *f.* free and easy manner; offhand manner; unselfconsciousness

désir, *m.* desire

désirable, *(adj.)* desirable

désirer, *v.t.* to desire, want

désireux(-euse), *(adj.)* desirous, eager, anxious

(se) désister, *v.r.* to desist

désobéir, *v.i.* to disobey

désobéissance, *f.* disobedience

désobéissant, *(adj.)* disobedient

désobligeance, *f.* disagreeableness; unkindness (towards someone)

désobligeant, *(adj.)* disobliging; ungracious

désœuvré, *(adj.)* unoccupied (of persons); *(fam.)* at a loose end

désolé, *(adj.)* desolate, dreary (region), grieved, very sorry

désoler, *v.t.* to desolate; to distress, grieve

désopilant, *(adj.)* extremely funny; droll

désordonné, *(adj.)* ill-regulated (life); untidy (person or house)

désordre, *m.* disorder; confusion

désorganisation, *f.* disorganisation

désorganiser, *v.t.* to disorganise

désorienter, *v.t.* to lose one's bearings; to bewilder

désorienté, *(adj.)* puzzled; at a loss

désormais, *(adv.)* from now on

despote, *m.* despot

dessaisir, *v.t.* to dispossess (somebody of something)

dessécher, *v.t.* to dry up (ground, river, etc.); to drain; to wither

dessein, *m.* design; plan, scheme

desseller, *v.t.* to unsaddle

desserrer, *v.t.* to loosen (a screw); unscrew (a nut); to unclench (a fist)

dessert, *m.* dessert

desservir, *v.t.* to clear away (the table); to do a bad turn

dessin, *m.* drawing

dessinateur, *m.* sketcher, drawer; draughtsman; designer (dress, etc.)

dessiner, *v.t.* to draw, to sketch

dessouder, *v.t.* to unsolder

*dessous, *(adv.)* and *m.* under(neath), below, beneath; underpart

*dessus, *(adv.)* and *m.* above, over; top

destin, *m.* destiny, fate

destinataire, *m.* and *f.* addressee (of parcel, letter); consignee (goods); payee

*destination, *f.* destination

destinée, *f.* destiny

destiner, *v.t.* to destine; to doom

destituer, *v.t.* to dismiss, discharge; to remove from office

destitution, *f.* dismissal (from office)

destruction, *f.* destruction

désuétude, *f.* disuse

désunion, *f.* disunion (of people); disconnection (of parts)

désunir, *v.t.* to divide (people); to disjoin

détachement, *m.* detachment; indifference

détacher, *v.t.* to unloosen, detach; unfasten; uncouple (truck)

détail, *m.* retail; detail

détaillant, *m.* retailer

détailler, *v.t.* to divide, cut up; to retail goods; to detail

détaler, *v.i.* to take oneself off; decamp

détecteur, *m.* detector (mine, elec., etc.)

détective, *m.* detective

déteindre, *v.t.* to take the colour out of; *v.i.* to lose colour, fade

détendre, *v.t.* to slacken, relax; se -, *v.r.* to become slack; to relax

détenir, *v.t.* to detain, hold

détente, *f.* relaxation, loosening; easing of political tension détention, f. holding (of securities); imprisonment

détenu, m. prisoner

détériorer, v.t. to make worse; to damage, spoil

déterminé, (adj.) determined, resolute; particular; specific

déterminer, v.t. to determine; to fix, settle

déterrer, v.t. to dig up; discover

détestable, (adj.) detestable

détester, v.t. to detest; hate

détirer, v.t. to stretch (cloth, etc.)

détisser, v.t. to unweave

détonation, f. detonation; report (firearm)

détour, m. deviation; roundabout way

détourner, v.t. to turn aside; to embezzle

détracteur(-trice), m. (f.) disparager

détraqué, m. and (adj.) crazy, daft (person)

détraquer, v.t. to put out of order; to throw out of gear

détremper, v.t. to soak; dilute

détresse, f. distress; grief

détriment, m. detriment, loss; prejudice (of)

détroit, m. straits (geog.)

détromper, v.t. to undeceive

détrôner, v.t. to dethrone

détrousser, v.t. to rob, to rifle (safe, pockets)

détruire, v.t. to destroy; ruin

*dette, f. debt

deuil, m. mourning; bereavement; se mettre en -, to go into mourning

deux, (adj.) and m. two

deuxième, (adj.) second

deux-points, colon (typ.)

dévaliser, v.t. to rob, plunder

dévalorisation, f. devaluation

devancer, v.t. to precede; to leave (the others) behind

*devant, (prep.) before, in front of (someone, something); m. front, forepart

devanture, f. shop-front; frontage of building; shop-window

dévaster, v.t. to lay waste

dévastation, f. devastation

déveine, f. (run of) bad luck

développement, m. development (of body, etc.)

développer, v.t. to develop (general); to work out a plan (project)

*devenir, v.n. to become; to grow into

dévergondage, m. profligacy, licentiousness

déverser, v.t. to slope, slant; to pour, dump

déversoir, m. weir, sluice

dévêtir, v.t. to undress, divest (garment)

déviation, f. deviation (from); variation of compass

dévider, v.t. to reel off (thread), unwind

dévier, v.t. to deviate, swerve

devin, m. soothsayer

deviner, v.t. to guess

dévisager, v.t. to stare at

devise, f. motto; (finance) currency

deviser, v.i. to gossip, chat

dévisser, v.t. to unscrew

dévoiler, v.t. to unveil

*devoir, v.t. to have to; be obliged to (moral obligation); to owe (something to somebody)

*devoir, m. duty; exercise, task

dévorer, v.t. to devour

dévot, m. religious person; faux -, hypocrite

dévotion, f. piety

dévouement, m. devotion (self-); self-sacrifice; devotion to duty

dévouer, v.t. to devote, sacrifice; se -, v.r. to devote oneself

dévoyer, v.t. to mislead; to lead astray

dextérité, f. skill

diabète, m. diabetes

*diable, m. devil; railway porter's truck

diablerie, f. devilry; mischievousness, fun

diabolique, (adj.) diabolical

diacre, m. deacon (eccles.)

diadème, m. diadem

diagnostic, m. diagnosis

dialecte, *m.* dialect

dialogue, *m.* dialogue

diamant, *m.* diamond

diamétral(-aux), *m.* diametrical

diamètre, *m.* diameter

diane, *f.* reveille (*mil.*)

diantre! (*interj.*) the deuce!

diapason, *m.* pitch (*mus.*); tuning fork

diaphane, (*adj.*) diaphanous; translucent

diaphragme, *m.* diaphragm (*med.*)

diarrhée, *f.* diarrhœa

dictateur, *m.* dictator

dictature, *f.* dictatorship

dictée, *f.* dictation

dicter, *v.t.* to dictate

diction, *f.* delivery (speech, etc.)

dictionnaire, *m.* dictionary; - de géographie, gazetteer

diète, *f.* diet

Dieu, *m.* God

diffamation, *f.* slander, libel

diffamatoire, (*adj.*) defamatory, slander-(libel-)ous

diffamer, *v.t.* to slander

différence, *f.* difference; à la - de, unlike, contrary to

différend, *m.* difference (dispute), disagreement

différent, (*adj.*) different

différer, *v.t.* to defer, postpone judgment; to differ

difficile, (*adj.*) difficult

difficilement, (*adv.*) with difficulty

difficulté, *f.* difficulty

difforme, (*adj.*) deformed, misshapen

difformité, *f.* deformity

diffuser, *v.t.* to diffuse (light, heat)

diffusion, *f.* diffusion (light, etc.), broadcasting (news, etc.)

digérer, *v.t.* to digest; assimilate; to put up with, stomach

digestion, *f.* digestion

digital(-aux), *m.* and (*adj.*) digital (nerve)

digitale, *f.* digitalis (*med.*); foxglove

digitaline, *f.* digitalin (*med.*)

digne, (*adj.*) worthy; dignified

dignitaire, *m.* dignitary

dignité, *f.* dignity

digression, *f.* digression

digue, *f.* dike *or* dam; embankment (river, canal); breakwater, jetty; sea wall

dilapider, *v.t.* to squander

dilatation, *f.* expansion; distension (stomach)

dilater, *v.t.* dilate, expand

dilemme, *m.* dilemma

dilettante, *m.* amateur, dilettante

diligence, *f.* diligence; industry; haste, despatch; stage-coach

dimanche, *m.* Sunday

dîme, *f.* tithe

dimension, *f.* dimension, size

diminuer, *v.t.* to lessen; diminish; reduce; to shorten; to abate (fever)

diminutif, (*adj.*) diminutive

diminution, *f.* lessening; reduction, lowering (of price)

dinde, *f.* turkey-hen

dindon, *m.* turkey-cock

dîner, *m.* dinner; *v.i.* to dine

dingue, (*adj.*) (*fam.*) cracked, daft

diocèse, *m.* diocese

diphtérie, *f.* diphtheria

diplomate, *m.* diplomat

diplomatie, *f.* diplomacy

diplomatique, (*adj.*) diplomatic

diplôme, *m.* diploma

*dire, *v.t.* to say, to tell

direct, direct, straight

directement, (*adv.*) directly

directeur(-trice), *m.* (*f.*) director; manager; headmaster; governor or warden (of prison)

directif, (*adj.*) directing, guiding

directives, *f. pl.* broad lines (of policy); general lines

diriger, *v.t.* to direct, manage

discernement, *m.* discernment

discerner, *v.t.* to discern, distinguish

discipline, *f.* discipline

discipliner, *v.t.* to discipline

discontinuation, *f.* discontinuation

discontinuer, *v.t.* and *v.i.* to discontinue

disconvenir, *v.i.* to be unsuited to; to deny

discordance, *f.* discordance (sounds); clashing (colours); disagreement (evidence)

discordant, *(adj.)* discordant; jarring

discorde, *f.* dissension, discord; **semer la -,** to make (foment) trouble

discourir, *v.i.* to discourse

discours, *m.* talk; speech, address

discréditer, *v.t.* to discredit

discret(-ète), *(adj.)* discreet, cautious

discrétion, *f.* discretion; prudence

discussion, *f.* discussion, debate

discutable, *(adj.)* debatable

discuter, *v.t.* to discuss, debate; to question (something)

disert, *(adj.)* eloquent

disette, *f.* scarcity, dearth

diseur, *m.* réciter; **diseur(-euse) de bonne aventure,** fortune-teller

disgrâce, *f.* disfavour, disgrace

disgracié, *(adj.)* out of favour

disgracier, *v.t.* to dismiss from favour

disgracieux, *(adj.)* uncouth, awkward

disjoindre, *v.t.* disjoin, sever; **se -,** *v.r.* to come apart

disloquer, *v.t.* to dislocate; to put out of joint (limb); **se -,** *v.r.* to break up

disparaître, *v.i.* to disappear

disparate, *(adj.)* dissimilar, ill-matched, ill-assorted

disparition, *f.* disappearance; vanishing

dispendieux, *(adj.)* expensive

dispensation, *f.* dispensation; distribution of favours

dispense, *f.* exemption (from)

dispenser, *v.t.* to exempt, excuse; to dispense (medicine, etc.)

disperser, *v.t.* to disperse, scatter

disponibilité, *f.* availability (capital); available funds; *(mil.)* **être en -,** to be unattached, on half pay

disponible, *(adj.)* available; at someone's disposal; **l'actif -,** liquid assets

dispos, *(adj.)* fit, well

disposer, *v.t.* to dispose; arrange; set out; to have at one's disposal

dispositif, *m.* apparatus, gadget

disposition, *f.* arrangement; disposal; frame of mind, humour

disproportion, *f.* disproportion

disproportionné, *(adj.)* out of proportion

disputable, *(adj.)* debatable

dispute, *f.* dispute; quarrel

disputer, *v.t.* and *v.i.* to dispute, argue; to discuss something; **se -,** *v.r.* to quarrel

disque, *m.* disk, disc, (gramophone) record

dissemblable, *(adj.)* dissimilar

dissension, *f.* dissension; discord

dissimulation, *f.* dissimulation, deceit

dissimuler, *v.t.* to conceal

dissipateur, *m.* spendthrift

dissiper, *v.t.* to dissipate; squander

dissolu, *(adj.)* dissolute

dissoudre, *v.t.* to dissolve; **se -,** *v.r.* to melt; to break up (of a meeting, etc.)

dissuader, *v.t.* to dissuade

distance, *f.* distance, interval

distancer, *v.t.* to outdistance, to outrun

distant, *(adj.)* distant; stand-offish

distendre, *v.t.* to distend; to strain (a muscle)

distillateur, *m.* distiller

distiller, *v.t.* to distil; to condense (water)

distillerie, *f.* distillery

distinct, *(adj.)* distinct, separate from; clear

distinctif, *(adj.)* characteristic; distinguishing (sign)

distinction, *f.* distinction; honour

distingué, *(adj.)* distinguished; eminent; well-bred, smart

distinguer, *v.t.* to distinguish; to mark; **se -,** *v.r.* to distinguish oneself

distorsion, *f.* distortion (of limb, of vision)

distraction, *f.* division, separation; inattention; amusement

distraire, *v.t.* to separate; to misappropriate (funds, etc.); to amuse, divert

distrait, *(adj.)* inattentive

distribuer, *v.t.* to distribute; to issue, give out; to deliver letters

distributeur, *m.* distributor; penny-in-the-slot-machine; - d'-essence, petrol pump

distribution, *f.* distribution; issue (of rations); delivery (letters); prize-giving (schools); - des rôles, cast(ing) of a play

district, *m.* district; region

diurne, *(adj.)* daily; diurnal (motion)

divaguer, *v.i.* to wander; to digress; wander away from the point

divan, *m.* divan, couch

divers, *(adj.)* changing; varying; different, varied, diverse

diversité, *f.* diversity

divertir, *v.t.* to entertain, amuse; embezzle

divertissement, *m.* entertainment, amusement; misappropriation of funds

divette, *f.* star (music, light opera)

divin, *(adj.)* divine; holy

divinité, *f.* divinity; deity (god, goddess)

diviser, *v.t.* to divide, separate

division, *f.* division (general use); branch; department (administrative) ; *(mil.)* division

divorce, *m.* divorce

dix, *m.* and *(adj.),* ten

dizaine, *f.* ten (about); half a score

docile, *(adj.)* docile; submissive; tractable (animal)

dock, *m.* dock (naval)

docteur, *m.* doctor (general usage); - ès lettres, Doctor of Literature; - en droit, Doctor of Laws; - en médecine, M.D.

doctoral, *(adj.)* pompous; heavy (manner); grandiloquent

doctrine, *f.* doctrine

document, *m.* document

documentaire, *(adj.)* documentary

documenter, *v.t.* to document

dodo, *m.* sleep; faire -, to go to bye-bye; take a nap

dodu, *(adj.)* plump

dogmatique, *(adj.)* dogmatic

dogmatiser, *v.i.* to dogmatise

dogme, *m.* dogma

dogue, *m.* large watch-dog; - anglais, mastiff

*doigt, *m.* finger

doit, *m.* debit, liability

doléances, *f. pl.* complaints; whining

dolmen, *m.* druidical stone

domaine, *m.* domain; field, scope; estate; (with *public* or *état*) public property

dôme, *m.* dome, cupola; vault (of the heavens)

domestique, *(adv.)* tame; domestic (animal, life); *m.* and *f.* servant, menial

domestiquer, *v.t.* to domesticate (an animal)

domicile, *m.* residence, abode; sans -, no fixed abode; à -, at one's private house

domicilié, *(adj.)* settled, domiciled

dominance, *f.* sway; preponderance, predominance

dominant, *(adj.)* dominant; ruling (power), prevailing

domination, *f.* domination, rule

dominer, *v.i.* to rule, hold sway over; *v.t.* dominate, rise above

dominicale (l'oraison), the Lord's Prayer

dommage, *m.* damage, injury; quel - ! what a pity!

domptable, *(adj.)* tameable

dompter, *v.t.* to tame

dompteur, *m.* tamer

don, *m.* gift, giving

donation, *f.* donation, gift

*donc, *(conj.)* therefore, consequently

donnée, *f.* fundamental idea, notion

données, *f. pl.* data

*donner, *v.t.* to give; to deal (cards)

donneur, *m.* giver; dealer (at cards)

dont (*rel. pron.*) from (by, with) whom or which; whose (used for de qui, duquel, desquels, etc.)

dorénavant, (*adv.*) henceforth, from now on

dorer, *v.t.* to gild; to glaze (pastry), to brown (meat, etc.)

dorloter, *v.t.* to fondle

dormeur, *m.* sleeper

*dormir, *v.i.* to sleep; to be asleep

dortoir, *m.* dormitory; sleeping quarters

dorure, *f.* gilding; glazing (cakes, etc.), browning (meat)

*dos, *m.* back

dose, *f.* amount, proportion; dose of medicine

dossier, *m.* file; documents; record (of prisoner, person); back (of seat)

dot, *f.* dowry

doter, *v.t.* to dower; to endow (hospital)

douaire, *m.* jointure (of widow, etc.); marriage settlement

douairière, *f.* dowager

douane, *f.* customs (examination and administration); custom-house

douanier, *m.* customs officer

double, (*adj.*) double

doubler, *v.t.* to double; to line (a coat)

doublure, *f.* lining

doucement, (*adv.*) softly, gently, slowly

doucereux(-euse), (*adj.*) sweet-ish, sickly (taste)

douceur, *f.* sweetness (honey, sugar, perfume); softness (sound); gentleness (of charac-ter); pleasant thing (of life)

douche, *f.* shower bath

doucher, *v.t.* to douche (*med.*)

doué, (*adj.*) talented

douer, *v.t.* to endow

douille, *f.* socket, (bulb) holder (elec.)

douillet(te), (*adj.*) soft, downy; soft (over-delicate, fearful of pain)

douleur, *f.* pain; grief

douloureux(-euse), (*adj.*) pain-ful, sore; aching; sad, distressing

doute, *m.* doubt, uncertainty; sans -, doubtless

douter, *v.i.* to doubt; se -, *v.r.* to suspect, conjecture

douteux(-euse), (*adj.*) doubtful

doux (douce), (*adj.*) sweet; soft; mild

douzaine, *f.* dozen

douze, (*num. adj.*) twelve

doyen(ne), *m.* dean (*eccles.*); doyen (diplomatic corps); senior

dragée, *f.* sugar almond; sugar pill (*pharm.*)

dragon. *m.* dragon; dragoon (*mil.*)

drague, *f.* dredge(r)

draguer, *v.t.* to dredge (river, etc.)

dragueur, *m.* dredger; - de mines, mine-sweeper

drain, *m.* drain-pipe

drainer, *v.t.* to drain (soil; also med.)

dramatique, (*adj.*) dramatic

dramatiser, *v.t.* to dramatise

dramaturge, *m.* playwright

drame, *m.* drama; sensational affair

drap, *m.* cloth; être dans de jolis draps, to be in a fine mess (awkward fix)

drapeau, *m.* flag; regimental colour

draper, *v.t.* to drape, hang, cover

draperie, *f.* drapery

drapier, *m.* draper

drelin, *m.* tinkle

dresser, *v.t.* to erect, set up; to lay (a table); to pitch (tent, etc.); to draw up (contract, balance-sheet); to train animal; se -, *v.r.* to rise, stand up; to rise up (in protest)

dressoir, *m.* sideboard, dresser

drogue, *f.* drug; chemical

droguer, *v.t.* to dope; to physic (a person); faire - qn., to keep someone waiting; se -, *v.r.* to take drugs

droguiste, *m.* drysalter

droit, *m.* right (civil rights); tax, duty; copyright; as tax or duty used with various words, e.g. *droits d'auteur, droits de port* (harbour dues)

droit, (*adj.*) straight, upright; right

droiture, *f.* uprightness

drôle, (*adj.*) funny, droll, odd

drôle(sse), *m.* (*f.*) scamp, rascal (hussy)

drôlerie, *f.* drollery; jest

dromadaire, *m.* dromedary

droppage, *m.* drop(ping) by parachute

dru, (*adj.*) thick-set, strong; dense (undergrowth)

druide, *m.* druid

dû, *m.* due (right)

duc, *m.* duke

duchesse, *f.* duchess

duel, *m.* duel

dûment, duly; in due form

dune, *f.* dune (sand-hill), down

duo, *m.* duet (*mus.*)

dupe, *f.* dupe

duperie, *f.* deception; trickery

duplicata, *m.* duplicate

duplicité, *f.* deceit, double-dealing

dur, (*adj.*) hard; tough (meat, wood); cruel (nature)

durable, (*adj.*) lasting

durant, (*prep.*) during

durcir, *v.t.* to harden

durée, *f.* duration; life; wear; lasting quality

durer, *v.i.* to last, continue

dureté, *f.* hardness; roughness, toughness (of meat, etc.); harshness

duvet, *m.* down (young bird, etc.)

dynamique, (*adj.*) dynamic

dynamique, *f.* dynamics (*math.*)

dynamite, *f.* dynamite

dynamo, *f.* dynamo

dynastie, *f.* dynasty

dysenterie, *f.* dysentery

dyspepsie, *f.* dyspepsia

E

*eau, *f.* water

ébahir, *v.t.* to astound, flabbergast; s'- de, *v.r.* to be dumbfounded at

ébahissement, amazement

ébarber, *v.t.* to trim; to scrape

ébats, *m. pl.* frolic, revels

(s')ébattre *v.r.* to gambol, frolic

ébauche, *f.* rough sketch

ébaucher, *v.t.* to sketch out, to outline (plan or picture)

ébauchoir, *m.* roughing chisel

ébène, *f.* ebony

ébénier, ebony tree

ébéniste, *m.* cabinet maker

éblouir, *v.t.* to dazzle

éblouissement, *m.* dazzling; giddiness

éboulement, falling in; caving in (of wall)

(s')ébouler, *v.r.* to fall in, to cave in

éboulis, *m.* mass of fallen earth

ébouriffer, *v.t.* to ruffle, tousle; to amaze

ébrancher, *v.t.* to lop off (branches)

ébranlement, *m.* shaking; shock; unhinging (of mind)

ébranler, *v.t.* to shake; to move; to disturb

ébrécher, *v.t.* to notch; to make a notch in

ébrouement, *m.* snorting (of horse)

ébrouer, *v.i.* to snort

ébruiter, *v.t.* to make known; to noise abroad

écaille, *f.* scale (of fish); shell (of oyster); flake; chip of marble

écailler, *v.t.* to scale; to open (oyster)

écale, *f.* shell, pod (of peas)

écaler, *v.t.* to shell (peas)

écarlate, (*adj.*) scarlet

écarquiller, *v.t.* to open the eyes wide; to straddle (legs)

écart, *m.* distance apart, stepping aside; à l'-, on one side, aside

écarté, (*adj.*) isolated, lonely, secluded

écarter, *v.t.* to separate, to part (fingers, branches); draw aside (curtains); to brush aside; to discard (cards); s'-, *v.r.* to move aside; to step aside; to make way for

ecclésiastique, *m.* an ecclesiastic, clergyman; (*adj.*) ecclesiastical

écervelé, (*adj.*) scatter-brained; thoughtless

échafaud, *m.* scaffolding; scaffold

échafaudage, *m.* scaffolding; erection of scaffolding

échalote, *f.* shallot

échancrure, *f.* notch in wood; opening (garment); indentation (coast line)

échange, *m.* exchange (of ideas); exchange (barter); **libre -,** free trade

échanger, *v.t.* to exchange (general and commercial)

échantillon, *m.* sample; pattern

échantillonner, *v.t.* to sample (wines, etc.); to prepare samples

échappement, *m.,* escape, leakage (of gas); exhaust, release (steam)

*échapper, *v.i.* to escape (the consequences of something); **s'-,** *v.r.* to escape; to break, escape (from prison)

écharpe, *f.* scarf, sash, sling (for limbs)

échasse, *f.* stilt

échauder, *v.t.* to scald

échaudure, *f.* scald

échauffement, *m.* heating (bearings); overheating (the body)

échauffer, *v.t.* to warm, to heat

échauffourée, *f.* scuffle; clash (street mobs)

échéance, *f.* date (of payment); maturity (bill); expiration (of tenancy)

échéant, (*adj.*) falling due; **le cas - que,** should it happen that, should it arise that

échec, *m.* check (at chess); check, defeat; **- et mat,** checkmate

échelle, *f.* ladder; scale (of plan, map); ladder (in stockings)

échelon, *m.* rung (of ladder); (military formation) échelon

échelonner, *v.t.* to space out (objects); to dispose troops in échelon

écheveau, *m.* skein (of yarn, wool)

échevelé, (*adj.*) dishevelled

échevin, *m.* sheriff

échine, *f.* spine, backbone; chine (of animals)

échiquier, *m.* chess-board; the exchequer

écho, *m.* echo

échoir (*être*), *v.i.* to fall due, to mature

échoppe, *f.* booth, street stall; graver

échouer, *v.i.* to run aground; to ground; to fail, miscarry (plan)

échu (from *échoir*), due

éclabousser, *v.t.* to splash, to spatter (with mud)

éclair, *m.* lightning, flash of lightning

éclairage, *m.* lighting; illumination

éclaircie, *f.* break, opening (in clouds); clearing (in forest)

éclaircir, *v.t.* to clear (up); to lighten; **s'-,** *v.r.* to clear up (weather)

éclaircissement, *m.* clearing up

éclairer, *v.t.* to light, to enlighten

éclaireur, *m.* scout

éclat, *m.* splinter, chip; burst (of shell); flash (light)

éclatant, (*adj.*) bursting; glittering, sparkling; brilliant (success, etc.)

éclater, *v.t.* to burst (tyre, etc.); to fly into pieces (glass); **- de rire,** to burst out laughing

éclipse, *f.* eclipse

éclipser, *v.t.* to eclipse; to obscure (light)

éclisse, *f.* splint (*surg.*)

éclopé, (*adj.*) lame

éclore (*être*), *v.i.* to hatch out; be hatched; to open out (flowers)

écluse, *f.* sluice, lock

éclusier, *m.* lock-keeper

écœurant, (*adj.*) disgusting, loathsome

écœurer, *v.t.* to disgust; to sicken

*école, *f.* school

écolier(-ère), *m.* (*f.*) scholar; schoolboy (girl)

éconduire, *v.t.* to show out, get rid of (politely)

économat, *m.* stewardship; treasurership

économe, *m.* bursar (of a college); steward, housekeeper

économe, (*adj.*) economical

économie, *f.* economy, management; savings (in *pl.*)

économique, (*adj.*) economic (problem); inexpensive

économiser, *v.t.* to save, economise

écorce, *f.* bark, peel

écorcher, *v.t.* to graze, rub off (skin); to flay

écorchure, *f.* scratch, graze; abrasion

écorner, *v.t.* to dehorn (an animal); to dog-ear (a book)

écossais(e), *m.* (*f.*) Scot, Scots-man(woman) and (*adj.*) Scottish, Scotch

écot, *m.* share, quota; score, reckoning

écoulé, (*adj.*) ultimo

écoulement, *m.* flow; discharge (of liquid)

(s')écouler, *v.r.* to flow out; to pass; elapse (of time)

écoute, *f.* listening-place; être à l'-, to be listening in

écouter, *v.t.* to listen to; to pay attention (to someone)

écoutez! look here! I say

écoutille, *f.* hatchway (*naut.*)

écran, *m.* screen (cinema); mettre à l'-, to film, make a film of

écrasant, (*adj.*) crushing (weight, defeat)

écraser, *v.t.* to crush; to flatten out

écrémer, *v.t.* to skim (milk)

écrevisse, *f.* crayfish

(s')écrier, *v.r.* to cry out, exclaim

écrin, *m.* case (jewel)

écrire, *v.t.* to write

écrit, (*adj.*) and *m.* written (word); writing

écriteau(x), *m.* placard, bill, notice

écriture, *f.* handwriting; (*fig.*) Scripture

écrivailler, *v.i.* (*fam.*) to scribble (i.e. penny-a-line journalism)

écrivain, *m.* author, writer

écrou, *m.* nut

écrouelles, *f. pl.* scrofula

écrouer, *v.t.* to commit to prison; (*fam.*) to run in

écroulement, *m.* collapse; ruin; downfall (of hopes)

(s')écrouler, *v.r.* to collapse, fall in, tumble down

écru, (*adj.*) raw, unbleached (materials)

écu, *m.* shield; piece of money, a crown

écueil, *m.* rock, reef

écuelle, *f.* bowl, basin

éculer, *v.t.* to wear down at heel (shoes)

écume, *f.* froth, scum

écumer, *v.t.* to scum, skim (soup, etc.)

écumeux, (*adj.*) foamy, frothy; scummy

écurer, *v.t.* to scour

écureuil, *m.* squirrel

écurie, *f.* stable

écusson, *m.* coat-of-arms, escutcheon

écuyer, *m.* a squire; equerry; horseman

édenté, (*adj.*) toothless

édifice, *m.* edifice; building

édifier, *v.t.* to erect (church, etc.); to edify

édit, *m.* edict

éditer, *v.t.* to publish; to edit

éditeur, *m.* publisher, editor (of text, *not* of newspaper)

édition, *f.* edition, issue, impression (of work)

édredon, *m.* eiderdown

éducation, *f.* education, bringing up; keeping (of bees)

éduquer, *v.t.* to bring up, educate a child

effacer, *v.t.* to efface, obliterate, erase; s'-, *v.r.* to stand aside; to fade, wear away

effarement, *m.* fright, alarm

effarer, *v.t.* to frighten, to scare, alarm

effaroucher, *v.t.* to scare away, startle

effectif, (*adj.*) effective, efficacious; m. effective (force), total strength

effectuer, v.t. to effect, carry out, accomplish

efféminé, (adj.) effeminate, unmanly

effervescent, (adj.) effervescent

effet, m. effect, result; (commerce) negotiable instrument; **effets** (pl.) bills (to pay, or negotiable); **effets mobiliers,** personal effects; **en -,** indeed

(s')effeuiller, v.r. to shed (leaves, petals)

efficace, (adj.) efficacious; effective

efficacité, f. efficiency

effigie, f. effigy

effilé, (adj.) frayed, fringed (material); slim, tapering

effilocher, v.t. to fray (material)

effleurer, v.t. to touch, stroke lightly; to skim the surface (of the water)

effondrer, v.t. to break in, stave in; **s'-,** v.r. to fall in, cave in; to slump (prices); to collapse (government)

(s')efforcer (de), v.r. to strive, to do one's utmost (to)

effort, m. effort, exertion

effraction, f. breaking in, burglary

effraie, f. barn owl, screech owl

effrayant, (adj.) terrifying, frightful

effrayer, v.t. to frighten, scare, startle; **s'-** v.r. to be or get frightened

effréné(e), (adj.) unbridled, unrestrained

effriter, v.t. to exhaust (land); disintegrate; **s'-,** v.r. to become exhausted; to crumble to dust

effroi, m. fright, terror

effronté(e), (adj.) impudent, bold

effronterie, f. impudence, insolence, effrontery

effroyable, (adj.) frightful, fearful, dreadful

effusion, f. effusion; outpouring; **- de sang,** hæmorrhage; bloodshed

*égal (égaux), (adj.) equal; all,

the same, indifferent; level, even

égaler, v.t. to equal

égaliser, v.t. to equalise, adjust (pressure)

égalité, f. equality; evenness, regularity; deuce (tennis); **- à rien,** love all

*égard, m. consideration, respect

égaré, (adj.) strayed, misguided

égarement, m. mislaying (of object); miscarriage (of letter); bewilderment

égarer, v.t. to lead (someone) astray; to misguide (someone); to bewilder; **s'-,** v.r. to lose one's way

égayer, v.t. to cheer up (sick person); to divert, amuse (someone)

églantine, f. wild rose (dog rose)

église, f. church

égoïste, m. and f. selfish person; (adj.) selfish

égoïsme, m. selfishness

égorger, v.t. to cut the throat

(s')égosiller, v.r. to bawl, yell; to talk oneself hoarse

égout, m. sink; sewer

égoutter, v.t. and v.i. to drain; to drip

égratigner, v.t. to scratch

égratignure, f. scratch

égrener, v.t. to shell (peas)

éhonté, shameless; unblushing

éjaculer, v.i. to ejaculate

élaborer, v.t. to elaborate

élan, m. impulse; bound, dash; moose, elk

élancé, (adj.) tall, slender, slim

(s')élancer, v.r. to dash forward, to bound forward; to make a spring (at)

élargir, v.t. to widen; to enlarge, extend (ideas, etc.)

élasticité, f. elasticity

élastique, m. elastic; (adj.) elastic

électeur(-trice), m. (f.) elector

électricien, m. electrician

électricité, f. electricity; (fam.) **donner l'-,** to switch on the light

électriser, *v.t.* to electrify (substance or person)

électrocution, *f.* electrocution

électron, *m.* electron

élégant, *(adj.)* elegant

élégance, *f.* elegance

élégie, *f.* elegy

élément, *m.* element

élémentaire, *(adj.)* elementary

élevage, *m.* breeding; raising

élévation, *f.* elevation, lifting; height; promotion, preferment

élève *m.* and *f.* pupil

élevé, *(adj.)* high; educated

élever, *v.t.* to elevate, raise; to bring up (child)

élevure, *f.* pimple, blister

éligible, *(adj.)* eligible

élire, *v.t.* to elect, to choose

élite, *f.* elite; flower, pick of

élite (d'), *(adj.)* select

éloge, *m.* eulogy, praise (deserved)

éloignement, *m.* removal, putting away; estrangement; distance, remoteness

éloigner, *v.t.* to remove; estrange; **s'-,** *v.r.* to move off, retire, withdraw

éloquence, *f.* eloquence

éloquent, *(adj.)* eloquent

émail, *m.* enamel

émailler, *v.t.* to enamel

émanciper, *v.t.* to emancipate; **s'-,** *v.r.* to free oneself from

émaner, *v.i.* to emanate, proceed from

emballage, *m.* packing, wrapping

emballer, *v.t.* to pack up; to wrap up; *(fig.)* to excite; to arouse enthusiasm; *v.r. (fam.)* to be carried away (by excitement)

embarcadère, *m.* landing-stage; quay, wharf; departure platform (railway)

embarcation, *f.* boat (ship's boat)

embarquement, *m.* embarking (passengers); shipment (of goods)

embarquer, *v.t.* to embark (passengers); to ship goods; **s'-,** *v.r.* to get into (a train, plane, ship)

embarras, *m.* encumbrance, obstruction; impediment in speech

embarrassant, *(adj.)* embarrassing; awkward; cumbrous; perplexing

embarrasser, *v.t.* to embarrass; to hamper; to encumber

embaucher, *v.t.* to engage; to take on. to sign on (workmen)

embaumer, *v.t.* to embalm, to scent

embellir, *v.t.* to embellish

embellissement, *m.* embellishment

embêtant, *(adj.)* vexing, annoying

embêtement, *m.* worry, anxiety; bother

embêter, *v.t. (fam.)* to annoy, bother

emblée (d'), *(adv. phrase)* at the first onset

emblème, *m.* emblem

emboîtage, *m.* packing in cases

emboîter, *v.t.* to encase; **- le pas (à),** to fall into step (with)

embonpoint, *m.* stoutness

embouchure, *f.* mouth (of river)

(s')embourber, *v.r.* to stick (get stuck) in the mud

embouteillage, *m.* bottling; bottle-neck; traffic-block

embouteiller, *v.t.* to bottle up, block up

embranchement, *m.* branch line

(s')embrancher, *v.r.* to branch off

embraser, *v.t.* to set on fire; to set ablaze

embrasser, *v.t.* to embrace; to kiss; to comprise

embrayer, *v.i.* to let in the clutch (aut.)

embrocher, *v.t.* to spit, run through (with skewer, etc.)

embrouiller, *v.t.* to confuse; tangle up; to muddle

embrumé, *(adj.)* foggy, misty

embrun, *m.* spray

embuscade, *f.* ambush, ambuscade

embusqué, *m.* shirker from active service

(s')embusquer, *v.r.* to lie in ambush; to shirk

émeraude, *f.* emerald

émerger, *v.i.* to emerge

émeri, *m.* emery

émérite, (adj.) superannuated; emeritus (professor); practised, experienced

émerveiller, v.t. to astonish; s'- (de), to wonder, marvel (at)

émetteur, m.transmitter(W.Tel.)

émettre, v.t. to emit, utter

émeute, f. riot

émietter, v.t. to crumble

émigrant, (adj.) and m. emigrant

émigration, f. emigration

émigré, m. exile

émigrer, v.i. to emigrate

éminence, f. eminence; rising ground; superiority

éminent, (adj.) eminent

émissaire, m. emissary; bouc -, scapegoat

émission, f. emission; poste d'-, transmitting station

emmagasiner, v.t. to warehouse (goods), store; to store up (energy, etc.)

emmancher, v.t. to fix, fit together; fit handle to

emménager, v.t. to move into (house), install

emmener, v.t. to lead away, take away

emmitoufler, v.t. to muffle up

émoi, m. emotion, agitation

émotion, f. emotion, thrill

émoudre, v.t. to grind

émousser, v.t. to blunt, to dull

émouvoir, to move; to stir up; s'-, v.r. to become excited

empailler, v.t. to pack in straw

empaqueter, to pack up; to make into a parcel

(s')emparer, v.r. to take possession; to seize hold of

empâter, to make sticky; to cram (goose, fowl)

empêcher,v.t.to prevent, to hinder

*(s')empêcher, v.r. to refrain from (always used in the negative)

empereur, m. emperor

empeser, v.t. to starch

empester, u.t. to infect; to stink

empêtrer, v.t. to entangle

emphase, f. bombast

emphatique, (adj.) emphatic; affected, bombastic

empierrer, v.t. to stone, macadamise (road)

empiéter, v.i. to encroach upon, to trespass

empiler, v.t. to pile up

empire, m. empire; sovereign authority; dominion over

empirer, v.i. to worsen, v.t. to make worse

emplacement, m. emplacement

emplâtre, m. plaster (medical)

emplette, f. purchase

emplir, v.t. to fill up

emploi, m. employment, use; occupation

employé(e), m. (f.) employee

employer, v.t. to use; to employ (workman, etc.)

emplumer, v.t. to feather (something)

empocher, v.t. to pocket (money); - un coup, to receive a blow

empoigner, v.t. to grasp, seize, grab

empoisonner, v.t. to poison

emporté, hot-headed; quick-tempered

emporter, v.t. to carry away, take away; l'- sur, to prevail over, get the better of; s'-, v.r. to lose one's temper

empourprer, v.t. to tinge with crimson; s'-, v.r. to turn crimson

empreinte, f. impression, stamp (but not postage)

empressé, (adj.) eager, ready

empressement, m. eagerness, readiness, alacrity

(s')empresser, v.r. to hurry, hasten (to do something)

emprisonnement, m. imprisonment

emprisonner, v.t. to imprison

emprunt, m. loan

emprunté, assumed, false (name, etc.); embarrassed (air)

emprunter, (à), v.t. to borrow (from)

ému, (adj.) (from verb émouvoir) moved, agitated

en, (prep.) in, into (place), in (time)

*en, (pron.) (used partitively) some, any of it, of them

encablure, *f.* cable's length

encadrer, *v.t.* to frame (picture)

encaisse, *f.* cash in hand

encaisser, *v.t.* to collect (cash, bills, etc.); to pack in cases

encaisseur, *m.* collector (of bills, cash, etc.) payee

enceinte, *f.* surrounding wall; enclosure

enceinte, *(adj. f.)* pregnant

encens, *m.* incense

encenser, *v.t.* to incense; flatter

encensoir, *m.* censer

encercler, *v.t.* to encircle, to close in

enchaîner, *v.t.* to chain up (dog, etc.); to link up, connect

enchantement, *m.* enchantment, magic

enchanter, *v.t.* to enchant, bewitch; to charm, delight

enchanté (de qch.), to be delighted (with something)

enchère, *f.* bidding at auction; vente à l'-, public auction

enchérir, *v.t.* to put up the price; to make a higher bid

enchérissement, *m.* rise, increase (in price, etc.)

enchevêtrer, *v.t.* to mix up, confuse, tangle

enclin, *(adj.)* disposed, inclined

enclos, *m.* enclosure; ring-fence

enclume, *f.* anvil

encoignure, *f.* corner, angle (of room, etc.)

encoller, *v.t.* to gum, to paste; to size

encolure, *f.* neck and shoulders

encombrant, *(adj.)* cumbersome, clumsy

encombre, *m.* hindrance

encombrement, *m.* litter (of things); congestion (traffic)

encombrer, *v.t.* to encumber; to block up (streets)

encontre (à l'-), against, contrary to

encore, *(adv.)* still; yet, more, again

encouragement, *m.* encouragement

encourager, *v.t.* to encourage; hearten (someone)

encrasser, *v.t.* to soil, to make greasy

encre, *f.* ink

encrier, *m.* inkstand

encyclopédie, *f.* encyclopædia

(s')endetter, *v.r.* to get into debt

endiablé, reckless, possessed

endimancher, *v.t.* to dress up in Sunday clothes; also **s'-,** *v.r.*

endolori, *(adj.)* aching

(s')endolorir, *v.r.* to become painful

endommager, *v.t.* to damage, injure

endormi, *(adj.)* asleep, sleeping

(s')endormir, *v.r.* to fall asleep

endos(sement), *m.* endorsement (on cheque, etc.)

endosser, *v.t.* to endorse; to put on (clothes)

endroit, *m.* place, spot; right side (of material)

enduire, *v.t.* to smear, to coat

enduit, *m.* layer

endurci, *(adj.)* hardened; callous, hard

endurcir, *v.t.* to harden

endurer, *v.t.* to endure, suffer

énergique, *(adj.)* energetic (persons); strong (measures)

énervant, *(adj.)* enervating; aggravating

énervement, *m.* irritation

énerver, *v.t.* to enervate; to get on someone's nerves

enfance, *f.* childhood

enfant, *m.* and *f.* child (boy or girl)

enfantement, *m.* childbirth

enfanter, *v.t.* to bear a child

enfantin, *(adj.)* infantile

enfer, *m.* hell

enfermer, *v.t.* to shut in; to shut up (something or somebody) to enclose; to surround

enfiler, *v.t.* to thread (needle); to string beads; to go along (a street); to pull on, draw on (stockings); *(mil.)* to rake (with gunfire)

enfin, *(adj.)* finally, lastly; in fact, in a word; *(interj.)* at last!

enflammer, *v.t.* to inflame; to ignite; to set on fire; to excite

enflé, (adj.) swollen

enfler, v.t. to swell

enflure, f. swelling (limb, face, etc.)

enfoncé, (adj.) smashed in; sunken, deep-set (eyes)

enfoncer, v.t. to drive in (nail, etc.); to break, burst in a door

enfourcher, v.t. to bestride

enfreindre, v.t. to infringe

(s')enfuir, v.r. to escape; to flee

enfumé, (adj.) smoky; smoked

engagement, m. engagement

engager, v.t. to engage; to pledge, pawn; to take on (workmen); to begin, open (conversation, negotiations); s'-, v.r. to undertake; to bind oneself (to something)

engelure, f. chilblain

engendrer, v.t. to beget (child); to breed (disease)

engin, m. engine, machine; device

englober, v.t. to include

engloutir, v.t. to swallow up

engorger, v.t. to choke up, to block up; to stop up

engouffrer, v.t. to engulf

engourdir, v.t. to benumb

engrais, m. manure; fertiliser

engraisser, v.t. to fatten; to manure (land); v.i. to get fat

engrenage, m. gearing, throwing into gear (machinery, etc.)

engueuler, v.t. (slang) to abuse; to give someone a telling off

enhardir, v.t. to embolden

énigmatique, (adj.) enigmatic

énigme, f. riddle; enigma

enivrer, v.t. to intoxicate; inebriate; to elate

enjamber, v.t. to stride, step over; v.i. to walk with long strides

enjeu, m. stake (gambling)

enjoindre, v.t. to enjoin (silence)

enjôler, v.t. to coax, wheedle; to humbug

enjoliver, v.t. beautify; (fam.) to embroider (a story)

enjoué, (adj.) playful; cheerful

enlacer, v.t. to interlace, entwine; to hug (someone)

enlaidir, v.i. to grow ugly

enlèvement, m. removal; abduction

enlever, v.t. to remove, carry away, take away; to carry off; to take down (curtains, etc.); s'-, v.r. to come off; to rise; to flare up (persons)

enliasser, v.t. to tie papers (into bundles)

enluminer, v.t. to illuminate; to colour (maps, etc.)

ennemi, m. enemy

ennoblir, v.t. to ennoble

ennui, m. worry, anxiety; boredom, tediousness

ennuyant, (adj.) annoying, vexing, tedious

ennuyer, v.t. to annoy, worry, vex; to bore (somebody); s'-, v.r. to be bored

ennuyeux(-euse), (adj.) dull; irksome

énoncé, m. statement of facts

énoncer, v.t. to state (opinion)

(s')enorgueillir, v.r. to become proud, elated

énorme, (adj.) enormous, huge

énormément, (adv.) enormously, hugely

énormité, f. enormity; heinousness (of crime, conduct)

(s')enquérir, v.r. to enquire

enquête, f. enquiry, investigation

enquêter, v.i. to hold an enquiry

enragé(e), (adj.) mad (dog); out and out (opinions)

enrager, v.t. to enrage, madden; to excite (somebody)

enrayer, v.t. to brake; to lock (wheel); to check (disease)

enregistrer, v.t. to register, to record

(s')enrhumer, v.r. to catch a cold; to take cold

enrichir, v.t. to enrich; to make somebody rich; s'-, v.r. to grow rich; to make money

enrôler, v.t. to enrol; (mil.) to enlist

enroué, (adj.) hoarse, husky (voice)

enrouement, m. hoarseness

(s')**enrouer**, *v.r.* to become hoarse

enrouler, *v.t.* to roll up, wrap up

ensanglanter, *v.t.* to cover, stain with blood

enseigne, *f.* sign; signboard (shop, public house); (*mil.*) ensign; *m.* sub-lieutenant (*navy*)

enseignement, *m.* teaching; education; instruction

enseigner, *v.t.* to teach; to show, point out

*****ensemble**, (*adv.*) together.

*****ensemble**, *m.* the whole; general effect

ensemencer, *v.t.* to sow (seed)

enserrer, *v.t.* to enclose (something)

ensevelir, *v.t.* to bury (someone, a corpse)

ensevelissement, *m.* burial

ensoleillé, (*adj.*) sunny

ensorceler, *v.t.* to bewitch

ensuite, (*adv.*) then; in the next place, afterwards; well? what then?

(s')**ensuivre**, *v.r.* to follow, ensue, result. Used in 3rd person only

entacher, *v.t.* to taint; tarnish; to besmirch, sully someone's good name

entaille, *f.* gash, notch

entailler, *v.t.* to notch, nick; to gash, cut

entame, *f.* first cut (of bread, etc.)

entamer, *v.t.* to cut into; to begin, start (conversation, etc.)

entasser, *v.t.* to heap up; accumulate; to pack, crowd, cram (people, cattle)

entendre, *v.t.* to hear; to mean, intend; understand, expect; s'-, *v.r.* to agree; to understand one another

entendu (**bien**), of course

entente, *f.* understanding; agreement, (with *double* = double meaning)

enterrement, *m.* funeral

enterrer, *v.t.* to bury

entêtement, *m.* obstinacy

entêté, (*adj.*) obstinate; headstrong

enthousiasme, *m.* enthusiasm, rapture

enthousiasmer, *v.t.* to fire with enthusiasm, to render enthusiastic

enthousiaste, *m.* and *f.* enthusiast

entier(-**ère**), (*adj.*) entire, whole

entièrement, (*adv.*) entirely

entonner, *v.t.* to intone

entonnoir, *m.* funnel; shell-hole, crater

entorse, *f.* sprain

entortiller, *v.t.* to twist, to wind; to wheedle, coax; s'-, *v.r.* to get entangled in something

entourage, *m.* surroundings (of place); set, circle (of friends); environment

entourer, *v.t.* to surround

entr'acte, *m.* interval (theatrical); interlude

(s')**entr'aider**, *v.r.* to help one another

entrailles, *f. pl.* bowels, entrails

entrain, *m.* spirits (good); liveliness

entraînement, *m.* training, coaching (a team, etc.); enthusiasm

entraîner, *v.t.* to drag, draw along; to carry away; to sweep a person off his feet; to involve

entraîneur, *m.* trainer, coach

entrant, (*adj.*) incoming, ingoing

entraver, *v.t.* to shackle, fetter; hinder

*****entre**, (*prep.*) between

entre, (used for reciprocity, as s'**entre-tuer**, to kill one another)

entre-baillé, half open; ajar

entrée, *f.* entry, entrance; admission

entrefaites (**sur ces**), meanwhile

entrefilet, *m.* paragraph; short article (newspaper)

entremêler, *v.t.* to intermingle, intermix

entremets, *m.* side-dish; sweet (as course)

(s')**entremettre**, *v.r.* to interpose, intervene

entremise, *f.* intervention; mediation

entrepont, *m.* between-decks

entrepôt, *m.* warehouse, store

entreprendre, *v.t.* to undertake

entrepreneur(-euse), *m.* (*f.*) contractor

entreprise, *f.* undertaking

*entrer (with *être*), to enter; to come in, to go in

entresol, *m.* mezzanine floor; rooms between first and second floors

entretenir, *v.t.* to maintain, keep up; to support (family); s'-, *v.r.* to talk, converse with; (*sport*) to keep fit

entretien, *m.* upkeep, maintenance; support (of family); conversation

entrevoir, *v.t.* to catch a glimpse of

entrevue, *f.* interview

entr'ouvrir, *v.t.* to half open

enture, *f.* incision, cut

énumérer, *v.t.* to enumerate

envahir, *v.t.* to invade, to over-run (a country)

envahisseur, *m.* invader

enveloppe, *f.* envelope; wrapping (of parcel); outer cover of tyre

envelopper, *v.t.* to envelop, to wrap up (something or somebody)

envenimer, *v.t.* to envenom, poison (wound, etc.); to irritate, aggravate; s'-, *v.r.* to fester, suppurate

envergure, *f* spread, span

envers, *m.* wrong side, back of material

envers, (*prep.*) towards, to

envi (à l'), in emulation

*envie, *f.* desire, longing

envier, *v.t.* to envy; to covet; to hanker after

envieux(-euse), (*adj.*) envious (of)

environ, (*adv.*) about

environner, *v.t.* to surround

environs, *m. pl.* surroundings, outskirts, neighbourhood

envisager, *v.t.* to consider, contemplate (possibility)

envoi, *m.* sending, despatch, consignment

envol, *m.* taking-off (aeroplane); flight, take-off

(s')envoler, *v.r.* to fly away (birds, etc.); to take off (aeroplane)

envoyé, *m.* envoy, representative

envoyer, *v.t.* to send, to despatch (telegram, etc.)

envoyeur(-euse), *m.* (*f.*) sender

épais, (*adj.*) thick; heavy (fog)

épaisseur, *f.* thickness; density (foliage)

épaissir, *v.t.* to thicken

épanchement, *m.* effusion; overflow (of liquid)

épanouir, *v.t.* to cause to open out (flowers); s'-, *v.r.* to open out, to bloom; to beam (face)

épanouissement, *m.* blossoming; cheerfulness

épargne, *f.* economy, thrift; caisse d'-, *f.* savings bank

épargner, *v.t.* to save, economise; to spare

éparpiller, *v.t.* to scatter

épars, (*adj.*) scattered

éparvin, *m.* spavin (of horse)

épatant, (*adj.*) wonderful, amazing; (*fam.*) topping

épater, *v.t.* to astound, amaze, flabbergast

épaule, *f.* shoulder

épaulement, *m.* breastwork, earthwork

épave, *f.* wreck (*naut.*); derelict; waif

épée, *f.* sword

épeler, *v.t.* to spell

éperdu, (*adj.*) distracted, bewildered

éperdument, (*adv.*) distractedly, madly

éperon, *m.* spur

épervier, *m.* sparrow-hawk

éphémère, (*adj.*) ephemeral, transitory

éphémère, *m.* may-fly

épi, *m.* ear (of grain); spike of flower

épice, *f.* spice; pain d'-, gingerbread

épicé, (*adj.*) highly spiced

épicerie, f. grocery
épicier, m. grocer
épidémie, f. epidemic
épiderme, m. epidermis
épier, v.t. to watch, to spy on
épigramme, f. epigram
épilepsie, f. epilepsy
épileptique, epileptic
épinards, m. pl. spinach
épine, f. thorn
épineux(-euse), (adj.) thorny;
prickly; ticklish (matter, business)
épingle, (f.) pin; - de nourrice, safety-pin
épingler, v.t. to pin; to fasten
with a pin
Épiphanie, f. Epiphany; Twelfth
Night
épique, (adj.) epic
épiscopal, (adj.) episcopal
épisode, m. episode
épisser, v.t. to splice (rope)
épistolaire, (adj.) epistolary
épitaphe, f. epitaph
épître, f. epistle, letter
éploré, (adj.) tearful, weeping
éplucher, v.t. to clean, pick (salad
or wool); to peel (potatoes); to
sift (a question, etc.)
éponge, f. sponge
éponger, v.t. to sponge
épopée, f. epic (poem)
époque, f. era, age, epoch
épouse, f. wife, spouse
épouser, v.t. to marry, wed; to
adopt (a cause, doctrine)
épousseter, v.t. to dust (furniture)
épouvantable, (adj.) dreadful,
appalling; frightful
épouvantail, m. scarecrow
épouvante, f. fright, terror
épouvanter, v.t. to terrify; to
frighten
époux, m. husband
épreindre, v.t. to squeeze out
(juice)
(s')éprendre, v.r. to fall in love
*épreuve, f. proof, test, trial;
print (photo)
épreuve (à l'), on trial
épris, (adj.) enamoured (of somebody or something)

éprouver, v.t. to try, to test
(somebody or something); to
feel, experience
épuisé, (adj.) exhausted, worn out
épuisement, m. exhaustion;
breakdown (nervous)
épuiser, v.t. to exhaust; to
drain, empty (well), to wear out;
s'-, v.r. to become exhausted
épuration, f. purifying, purging
(morals, town of bad characters)
épurer, v.t. to purify
équanimité, f. equanimity
équateur, m. equator
équerrer, v.t. to square (carpentry), to bevel
équestre, (adj.) equestrian
équilibre, m. equilibrium
équipage, m. equipment; crew
(of ship, aeroplane)
équipe, f. gang of workmen;
team, side (sport)
équipement, m. equipment
équiper, v.t. to equip; to fit out
équitable, (adj.) equitable
équitation, f. horsemanship
équité, f. equity
équivalent, m. and (adj.) equivalent
équivaloir, v.i. to be equivalent
to, equal in value to (conjugated
like valoir)
équivoque, (adj.) ambiguous;
equivocal; questionable (conduct)
équivoquer, v.i. to quibble
érable, m. maple tree
éraflure, f. slight scratch
ère, f. era, epoch
érection, setting up; erection
éreintant, (adj.) exhausting,
back-breaking (work, etc.)
éreinter, v.t. to exhaust; to tire
out; to smash up (car, etc.)
ergoter, v.i. to cavil (at), to
quibble
ériger, v.t. to erect; to set up, raise
ermitage, m. hermitage
éroder, v.t. to eat away
érotique, (adj.) erotic; amatory
(poem)
errant, (adj.) roaming, wandering
erratum, m. misprint; (pl.) des
errata

errer, *v.i.* to wander about, to roam

erreur, *f.* error, mistake

erroné, *(adj.)* erroneous, mistaken

érudit, *m.* scholar; *(adj.)* learned

éruption, *f.* eruption

érysipèle, *m.* erysipelas

ès (contraction for en les, in the); licencié ès arts, B.A.

escabeau, *m.* wooden stool

escadre, *f.* squadron (of ships)

escadrille, *f.* flotilla *(navy)*; flight *(air force)*

escadron, *m.* squadron *(mil.)* and *(av.)*

escalader, *v.t.* to scale, climb (wall)

escale, *f.* calling place; port

escalier, *m.* staircase, flight of stairs; flight of steps (exterior); - tournant *or* en vis, winding, spiral stair; - de service, back-stairs

escamotage, *m.* sleight of hand, conjuring

escamoter, *v.t.* to conjure away; to whisk away; to make something vanish; *(fam.)* to sneak, filch

escapade, *f.* prank; escapade

escarbille, *f.* clinkers, ashes

escarbot, *m.* beetle

escargot, *m.* snail

escarmouche, *f.* skirmish

escarpé, *(adj.)* steep, sheer

escarpin, *m.* pump (shoe)

escarpolette, *f.* swing

esclavage, *m.* slavery; bondage

esclave, *m.* and *f.* slave

escompte, *m.* discount, rebate

escompter, *v.t.* to discount (a bill); to anticipate

escorte, *f.* escort; convoy *(naval)*

escorter, *v.t.* to escort

escouade, *f.* squad, gang (of workmen)

escrime, *f.* fencing

(s')escrimer, *v.r.* to endeavour; make an effort to accomplish something

escroc, *m.* swindler; sharper; crook

escroquerie, *f.* swindle

espace, *m.* space; distance, interval; interval of time

espadon, *m.* swordfish; sword

espagnol(e), *(adj.)* Spanish

espagnolette, *f.* fastener (of window)

espalier, *m.* espalier (tree or wall)

*espèce, *f.* species, kind, sort

espèces, *f. pl.* specie, cash, coin

espérance, *f.* hope

espérer, *v.t.* to hope, expect

espiègle, *(adj.)* mischievous, roguish; waggish

espièglerie, *f.* mischievousness, roguishness; prank

espion(ne), *m. (f.)* spy

espionnage, *m.* espionage, spying

espionner, *v.t.* to spy

espoir, *m.* hope

esprit, *m. (theolog.)* spirit; Saint-Esprit, the Holy Ghost

esprit, *m.* spirit, mind; character, disposition, wit; plein d'-, full of wit, witty

esprit de vin (sel), spirits of wine (salts)

esquif, *m.* skiff

esquisse, *f.* sketch; draft, outline

esquisser, *v.t.* to sketch; outline (portrait or plan)

esquiver, *v.t.* to evade, or dodge (blow); s'-, *v.r.* to slip away, off; to make oneself scarce

essai, *m.* trial, testing; attempt; essay *(lit.)*; try (rugby)

essaim, *m.* swarm (of bees, etc.)

essaimer, *v.i.* to swarm (bees)

essayer, *v.t.* to try, test (machine); to try on (suit, clothes); to try, attempt, endeavour

essence, *f.* petrol; essence, extract; gist of the matter

essentiel, *(adj.)* essential

essentiellement, *(adv.)* essentially

essieu, *m.* axle (wheel)

essor, *m.* soaring, flight; prendre son -, to soar, to take wing

essouffler, *v.t.* to wind (person or horse); s'-, *v.r.* to get out of breath, to get puffed

essuie-main, *m.* towel (hand)

essuyer, *v.t.* to wipe; to suffer (reverse, blow)

est, *m.* east

estafette, *f.* courier; (*mil.*) despatch rider

estafilade, *f.* gash, slash (in face); tear (in clothing)

estaminet, *m.* public house; tavern; tap-room

estampe, *f.* print, engraving; stamping machine, puncher

estamper, *v.t.* to print, engrave; to stamp

estampiller, *v.t.* to stamp; to mark

esthétique, (*adj.*) æsthetic

estimable, (*adj.*) estimable

estimation, *f.* estimation; appraising; valuing

estime, *f.* esteem, regard

estimer, *v.t.* to esteem; to value, to rate

estival, (*adj.*) summer

*estomac, *m.* stomach

estomaquer, *v.t.* to take one's breath away; to stagger, astound

estrade, *f.* platform, stage

estropier, *v.t.* to cripple, lame

estuaire, *m.* estuary

esturgeon, *m.* sturgeon

et (*conj.*) and; et . . . et, both

étable, *f.* cow-shed, house; cattle-shed

établi, *m.* work-bench

établir, *v.t.* to establish, settle; to set up (agency, business); to establish, prove; to draw up (plan); prescribe, lay down

établissement, *m.* establishment; settlement; institution; proving (facts)

étage, *m.* storey (floor, building)

étagère, *f.* whatnot, set of shelves

étai, *m.* stay; prop

étain, *m.* tin, pewter

étalage, *m.* display, show of goods; window-dressing; (*fam.*) show-off

étaler, *v.t.* to display goods; to set out goods; to expose; to flaunt (one's wealth)

étalon, *m.* stallion; standard; - d'or, gold standard

étamer, *v.t.* to tin; to plate

étameur, *m.* tinsmith

étamine, *f.* coarse muslin; strainer

étanche, (*adj.*) water-tight

étancher, *v.t.* to stop; quench; staunch

étançon, *m.* stanchion

étang, *m.* pond

étape, *f.* stage; (*mil.*) halting place

*état, *m.* state; condition

état-major, *m.* staff (*mil.*)

étau, *m.* vice, screw-vice

étayer, *v.t.* to prop up, shore up (timber, etc.)

été, *m.* summer

éteindre, *v.t.* to put out, extinguish; to turn off (electric light); s'-, *v.r.* to go out (fire, light); to fade, grow dim; to die down (sound); to become extinct

étendard, *m.* standard, colours (*mil.*)

étendoir, *m.* clothes-line, drying place

étendre, *v.t.* to stretch, spread out; to stretch out; s'-, *v.r.* to stretch out; lie at full length

étendu(e), (*adj.*) extensive (knowledge); far-reaching (in influence); wide (space)

étendue, *f.* extent; stretch

éternel(le), (*adj.*) eternal

éterniser, *v.t.* to perpetuate

éternuer, *v.i.* to sneeze

éthique, *f.* ethics; (*adj.*) ethical

étinceler, *v.* to sparkle, glitter, flash

étincelle, *f.* sparkle; glitter

étincellement, *m.* sparkling, glittering, scintillation

étique, (*adj.*) emaciated

étiqueter, *v.t.* to label

étiquette, *f.* label; etiquette, formality

étirer, *v.t.* to stretch; to draw out

étoffe, *f.* stuff, cloth, material

étoile, *f.* star; fate, destiny

étoilé, (*adj.*) starry

étonnement, *m.* astonishment, amazement, wonder

étonner, *v.t.* to astonish, to amaze, to startle; s'-, *v.r.* to be astonished; to wonder

étouffant, suffocating, stuffy, close

étouffement, *m.* suffocation, asphyxiation

étouffer, *v.t.* to suffocate, to stifle, choke, smother

étoupe, *f.* tow, oakum

étourderie, *f.* giddiness; thoughtlessness

étourdi(e), *(adj.)* giddy, heedless, thoughtless

étourdir, *v.t.* to stun, to deafen, to daze; to make giddy

étourneau, *m.* starling; a feather-brain

étrange, *(adj.)* strange, odd, queer, extraordinary

étranger(-ère), *m.* *(f.)* stranger; foreigner; outsider

étranger (à), irrelevant; outlandish; foreign

étranger (à l'), abroad

étrangler, *v.t.* to strangle, choke

étrangleur(-euse), *m.* *(f.)* strangler, garotter

étrave, *f.* stem *(naut.)*

être, *m.* being; existence; individual

être, *(v. auxiliary)* to be, to exist

être (with *prep.* à), to belong to; to be at or in

être (with *prep.* en), to be in, to be dressed in (mourning, etc.)

étrécir, *v.t.* to narrow; to take in (clothes); s'-, *v.r.* to become narrower; to contract

étreindre, *v.t.* to bind, to clasp, hug; to impede

étreinte, *f.* embrace, hug; grasp, grip

étrenne, *f.* (generally in plural), New Year's (or other) gift

étrier, *m.* stirrup

étriller, *v.t.* to curry; *(slang)* to thrash, to dress somebody down; to fleece (someone)

étriqué, *(adj.)* skimpy, tight

étroit, *(adj.)* strait, narrow, tight; confined, limited; strict, rigorous

étroitement, narrowly, tightly; closely, intimately

étude, *f.* study (intellect); acquirements, attainments; solicitor's office

étudiant(-e), *m.* *(f.)* student; undergraduate

étudier, *v.t.* to study; to read; to study (observe)

étui, *m.* case, box

étuve, *f.* hot-room, sweating-room; oven; drying place

étymologie, *f.* etymology

évacuation, *f.* evacuation

évacuer, *v.t.* to evacuate (general usage); to evacuate, withdraw (wounded)

(s')évader, *v.r.* to make one's escape

évaluation, *f.* valuation, appraisement

évaluer, *v.t.* to value, appraise (property, etc.); to assess damages

évangélique, *(adj.)* evangelical, protestant

évangéliste, *m.* evangelist

évangile, *m.* gospel

(s')évanouir, *v.r.* to faint, swoon; to vanish

évanouissement, *m.* swoon, faint, vanishing

évaporé, *(adj.)* flighty, irresponsible

évaporer, *v.t.* to evaporate; to grow heedless

évasé, wide, bell-mouthed

évaser, *v.t.* to widen out, to make bell-shaped

évasif(-ive), *(adj.)* evasive

évasion, *f.* evasion, escape

évêché, *m.* bishopric; bishop's palace

éveil, *m.* awakening; warning, hint; alarm

éveillé, *(adj.)* wide awake; lively, sharp, intelligent

éveiller, *v.t.* to awake; to wake somebody up

événement, *m.* event; occurrence, issue, result

éventail, *m.* fan

éventer, *v.t.* to air; to expose to the air; *(fig.)* to get wind of something; to get the scent of (hounds)

éventrer, *v.t.* to rip up; disembowel; to gut (fish)

éventualité, *f.* contingency; eventuality

éventuellement, (*adv.*) possibly

évêque, *m.* bishop

évidence, *f.* obviousness, plainness, clearness

évident, (*adj.*) evident

évier, *m.* sink (scullery)

évincer, *v.t.* to evict, eject (tenant); to supplant

éviter, *v.t.* to avoid, to shun

évolution, *f.* evolution; development

évoquer, *v.t.* to evoke, to call forth, conjure up

exact, (*adj.*) exact; accurate, correct (calculation); true; **c'est exact,** it is true

exactitude, *f.* exactness, exactitude, correctness, punctuality

exagérer, *v.t.* to exaggerate; overstate, overrate (qualities);

exalter, *v.t.* to exalt; to excite; **s'-,** *v.r.* to grow enthusiastic (over something)

exalté, *m.* excitable person

exalté, (*adj.*) uplifted, hot-headed

examen, *m.* examination; investigation, survey, overhaul; **passer un -,** to take (sit for) an examination; **être reçu (refusé) à un -,** to pass (fail) an examination

examinateur, *m.* examiner

examiner, *v.t.* to examine; to investigate; to survey

exaspérer, *v.t.* to exasperate, provoke, aggravate

exaucer, *v.t.* to hear, grant (desires)

excédant, (*adj.*) exceeding, excess

excédent, *m.* surplus

excéder, *v.t.* to exceed; go beyond (limit); to wear, tire out

excellence, *f.* excellence; excellency; **par -,** above all (superiority)

excellent, (*adj.*) excellent; delightful

exceller, *v.i.* to excel

excentricité, *f.* eccentricity

excentrique, (*adj.*) eccentric, odd

excepté, (*adj.*) excepted

excepter, *v.t.* to except, exclude

exception, *f.* exception

exceptionnel(le), (*adj.*) exceptional, out of the ordinary

excès, *m.* excess; abuse; intemperate; **à l'-,** immoderately

excessif(-ive), (*adj.*) excessive

exciter, *v.t* to excite; to arouse, stir up; to animate, inflame; **s'-,** *v.r.* to get worked up, get excited

exclamation, *f.* exclamation

(s')exclamer, *v.r.* to exclaim; cry out, protest

exclure, *v.t.* to exclude, shut out, leave out

exclusif(-ive), (*adj.*) exclusive

exclusion, *f.* exclusion (from); debarring

excursion, *f.* excursion, tour

excuse, *f.* excuse; **faire des excuses,** to apologise

excuser, *v.t.* to make excuses for; to excuse, pardon; **s'-,** *v.r.* to apologise

exeat, *m.* pass, leave (to go out)

exécrable, (*adj.*) extremely bad (taste), abominable

exécrer, *v.t.* to execrate, to loathe, detest

exécuter, *v.t.* to execute; to carry out (plan); to perform (promise, orders); to put to death

exécuteur(-trice), *m.* executor (legal, wills); hangman

exécution, *f.* execution, performance, carrying out (plans, etc.)

exécutoire, *m.* writ (of execution)

exemplaire, (*adj.*) exemplary

exemplaire, *m.* sample, specimen of work; copy (book, etc.)

exemple, *m.* example; lesson, warning; **par -,** for instance, indeed

exempt, (*adj.*) exempt, free (from)

exempter, *v.t.* to exempt, to excuse (from)

exercé, (*adj.*) practised, experienced

exercer, *v.t.* to exercise; to practise (profession); to drill (*mil.*); to exert, make use of (force, etc.)

exercice, *m.* exercise (general

use); use (of power); carrying out (functions, duties)

exhalaison, f. exhalation, vapour

exhaler, v.t. to exhale; to vent (one's wrath on)

exhausser, v.t. to raise, to increase, make higher

exhiber, v.t. to exhibit; present, show; produce

exhibition, f. exhibition, display

exhorter, v.t. to exhort

exhumer, v.t. to disinter

exigeant, (adj.) exacting; hard to please

exigence, f. unreasonable demand; exigency

exiger, v.t. to exact; demand, require

exigu (ë), (adj.) scanty, very small

exil, m. exile, banishment

exilé(e), m. (f.) exile

exiler, v.t. to exile, banish; s'-, v.r. to go into exile

existence, f. existence, life

exister, v.i. to exist, to be in existence

exorbitant, (adj.) excessive, outrageous (price, demand)

exotique, (adj.) exotic

expansion, f. expansion; (fig.) expansiveness

(s')expatrier, v.r. to leave one's country

expédient, (adj.) expedient; m. expedient

expédier, v.t. to forward, send

expéditeur, m. sender; shipper

expédition, f. despatch; shipment; copy (legal)

expérience, f. experience; experiment, test

expert, m. expert; valuer

expertise, f. valuation; estimate (by experts)

expier, v.t. to expiate (crime); atone for

expirer, v.i. to expire; to come to an end; to run out (lease); to die

explication, f. explanation

expliquer, v.t. to explain, make clear; to account for

exploit, m. exploit

exploitation, f. working; exploitation

exploiter, v.t. to exploit; to work; to take advantage of

explorateur, m. explorer

exploration, f. exploration

explorer, v.t. to explore; investigate, search

explosif, m. and (adj.) explosive

explosion, f. explosion

exportation, f. exportation, export

exporter, v.t. to export

exposé, m. statement, account, report

exposer, v.t. to expose (to view), to display; to show, exhibit; to explain; expose (somebody, hypocrite, etc.)

exposition, f. exhibition, show (goods, cattle, etc.)

exprès, (adv.) purposely, on purpose

express, m. express (train)

expression, f. expression; expressiveness; utterance; voicing (opinion); show (of feelings)

exprimer, v.t. to express; to squeeze out

expropriation, f. expropriation; forced purchase

exproprier, v.t. to expropriate (property, etc.)

expulser, v.t. to expel, eject, drive out

exquis, (adj.) exquisite, delightful

extase, f. ecstasy; rapture

extension, f. extension, strain, stretching; extent

exténué, (adj.) tired, worn out

exténuer, v.t. to emaciate, waste (the body); to exhaust

extérieur, (adj.) exterior, outer, external

extérieur, m. exterior, outside of building; à l'-, abroad; foreign countries; outside, out of doors

extérieurement, (adv.) outwardly, externally

exterminer, v.t. to exterminate, destroy; to wipe out

externat, m. day school; post of

dresser (or medical student) in hospital

externe, *m.* and *f.* day scholar; non-resident medical student in a hospital

extinction, *f.* extinction; quenching (of fire)

extirper, *v.t.* to extirpate

extorquer, *v.t.* to extort, to wring or wrest from

extorsion, *f.* extortion

extra, *m.* extra, something extra

extraction, *f.* extraction; descent, birth; drawing of a tooth

extradition, *f.* extradition

extraire, *v.t.* to extract, to pull out

extrait, *m.* extract; certificate, certified copy (from a register)

extraordinaire, (*adj.*) extraordinary; unusual

extravagance, *f.* extravagance; folly (of action)

extravagant, (*adj.*) extravagant, foolish, wild (spending); unreasonable (demand)

extrême, (*adj.*) extreme; farthest; utmost (point); intense (cold); drastic (measure); l'- Orient, the Far East

extrémité, *f.* extremity; last degree (misery, etc.)

extraverti(e), (*adj.*) extrovert

exubérance, *f.* exuberance; superabundance

exultation, *f.* exultation

exulter, *v.i.* to exult, rejoice

F

f.a.b. (franco à bord), free on board, f.o.b.

fable, *f.* fable; story

fabliau *m.* short story

fabricant, *m.* manufacturer

fabricateur, *m.* fabricator; forger, coiner

fabrication, *f.* manufacture; making

fabrique, *f.* making, manufacture, factory

fabriquer, *v.t.* to manufacture

fabuleux(-euse), (*adj.*) fabulous; incredible; prodigious

façade, *f.* front, frontage; (*fig.*) appearance

face, *f.* face, countenance; surface; side of a coin; faire -, to face (danger, etc.); en - de, opposite

facétie, *f.* joke, jest

facétieux(-euse), (*adj.*) facetious

fâché, (*adj.*) angry, sorry; displeased

fâcher, *v.t.* to vex, grieve; to anger; to make somebody angry; se -, *v.r.* to get angry; to lose one's temper

fâcheux(-euse), (*adj.*) troublesome, vexatious, regrettable

facile, (*adj.*) easy; ready, quick

facilité, *f.* easiness (of work, etc.); ease (accomplishment of task); talent, aptitude, facility

faciliter, *v.t.* to facilitate; to make easier, easy; to promote (progress of somebody, something

*façon, *f.* making, fashioning; make, workmanship; manner; way

faconde, *f.* fluency of speech, loquacity

façonner, *v.t.* to work, to make up, to shape, to fashion

factage, *m.* carriage, goods delivery

facteur, *m.* postman; commission agent; porter, carrier of parcels; factor (*maths.*)

factice, (*adj.*) factitious, unnatural; artificial

faction, *f.* faction; duty; sentry; être de -, to be on sentry-go

factionnaire, *m.* sentry, sentinel

facture, *f.* invoice, bill; workmanship, get up

facultatif(-ive), (*adj.*) optional; arrêt-, stop by request (bus, etc.)

faculté, *f.* option, right, faculty; Faculty (members of a profession or calling)

fadaise, *f.* silly remark, nonsense

fade, (*adj.*) insipid, tasteless (food)

fagot, *m.* faggot; bundle of wood, firewood; bundle of clothes

fagoter, *v.t.* to dress without taste; to be dowdy

faible, (*adj.*) feeble; weak; faint (voice, etc.)

faiblesse, *f.* weakness; failing; fainting fit

faiblir, *v.i.* to weaken; to grow weaker

faïence, *f.* earthenware; crockery

faïencier, *m.* dealer in earthenware, crockery

failli, *m.* bankrupt

faillir, *v.i.* to fail

faillir (used with *infinit.*), e.g. **j'ai failli être écrasé,** I was nearly run over; **j'ai failli manquer le train,** I nearly missed the train

faillite, *f.* bankruptcy; **faire -,** to go bankrupt

faim, *f.* hunger

fainéant, *m.* idler, loafer, sluggard

fainéant, (*adj.*) lazy, idle

*****faire,** *v.t.* to make; to do; to create; construct, perform (duties); prosecute (studies); transact (see **faire,** under idioms and expressions).

*****(se) faire,** *v.r.* to become

faire-part, *m. inv.* announcement (birth, marriage, etc.)

faisan, *m.* pheasant

faisandé, (*adj.*) high, gamy (meat)

faisceau, *m.* bundle of sticks, etc.

faiseur, *m.* maker, doer; (*slang*) bluffer, humbug

fait, *m.* fact, act; **en - de,** in point of fact; **tout à fait,** quite

faîte, *m.* top, summit (tree, etc.)

faix, *m.* burden, load

falaise, *f.* cliff

*****falloir,** (*imp. verb*) to be necessary; to be lacking; to be in need; to be obligatory

falot, *m.* lantern

falsification, *f.* forgery (documents); falsification (accounts); adulteration (of food)

falsifier, *v.t.* to falsify, tamper with; to fake (document); to adulterate (food)

famé, (*adj.*) repute; **mal (bien)- ,** of ill (good) repute

famélique, (*adj.*) half-starved; *m.* starveling

fameux(-euse), (*adj.*) famous

familial, (*adj.*) family (life, etc.)

familiariser, *v.t.* to familiarise; **se -,** *v.r.* to make oneself familiar with

familiarité, *f.* familiarity

familier(-ère), *m.* domestic (belonging to the family); familiar

famille, *f.* family; household

famine, *f.* famine

fanatique, (*adj.*) fanatical; *m.* or *f.* fanatic

faner, *v.t.* to toss, make (hay); to make fade; **se -,** *v.r.* to droop, wither (flowers, etc.)

fanfare, *f.* flourish of trumpets

fange, *f.* mire, filth, mud

fangeux(-euse), miry, muddy; filthy (mind)

fanon, *m.* dewlap (cattle)

fantaisie, *f.* imagination, fancy; freakish notion; **articles de -,** fancy goods

fantasmagorique, (*adj.*) weird, fantastic

fantasque, (*adj.*) odd, whimsical (person); fantastic (idea)

fantassin, *m.* foot soldier, infantryman

fantoche, *m.* puppet

fantôme, *m.* phantom, ghost, spectre

faon, *m.* fawn

faquin, *m.* cad, rascal

farce, *f.* stuffing, force meat; farce, practical joke, prank

farceur(-euse), *m.* (*f.*) practical joker; a wag

farcir, *v.t.* to cram, to stuff

fard, *m.* make-up, paint, rouge

fardeau, *m.* burden, load

farder, *v.t.* to rouge, to make up (the face)

faribole, *f.* idle story; stuff and nonsense

farine, *f.* flour; meal; **- d'avoine,** oatmeal

fariné, (*adj.*) floury; covered with flour

farineux(-euse), farinaceous, mealy (potatoes)

farouche, (*adj.*) wild, savage; unsociable; shy

fascicule, *m.* bunch, cluster; instalment, part

fascination, *f.* fascination; charm

fasciner, *v.t.* to charm, fascinate, bewitch

fasciste, *m.* (*f.*) and (*adj.*) Fascist

faste, *m.* pomp, ostentation, display

fastueux(-euse), (*adj.*) pompous, showy, ostentatious

fat, *m.* fop, coxcomb; (*adj.*) conceited, foppish

fatal, (*pl.* -als) (*adj.*) fatal, disastrous; inevitable; mortal (wound, etc.)

fatalisme, *m.* fatalism

fataliste, *m.* and *f.* fatalist

fatalité, *f.* fatality

fatigant, (*adj.*) tiring, fatiguing; tedious

fatigue, *f.* fatigue, tiredness, weariness

fatiguer, *v.t.* to tire, fatigue; **se -,** *v.r.* to become tired; to tire (oneself)

fatras, *m.* rubbish, lumber; jumble (ideas)

fatuité, *f.* fatuity, self-satisfaction

faubourg, *m.* suburb, outskirt (of town)

faubourien(ne), (*adj.*) suburban; *m.* suburbanite

fauché, (*adj.*) (*slang*) broke to the wide; cleaned out

faucher, *v.t.* to mow, cut, reap

faucheuse, *f.* mowing machine

faucille, *f.* sickle

faucon, *m.* falcon

faufiler, *v.t.* to slip in; **se -,** *v.r.* to intrude; to sneak (in, out); to edge in or out of a place

faussaire, *m.* and *f.* forger

fausser, *v.t.* to falsify (the truth); to alter (the facts)

fausseté, *f.* falseness; falsehood, untruth

faute, *f.* fault; mistake, error; **- de,** (for) lack of; **sans -,** without fail

fauteuil, *m.* arm-chair; stall (in theatre)

fautif(-ive), (*adj.*) faulty

fauve, (*adj.*) fawn-coloured; tawny; fallow (deer)

fauve, *m.* (in *pl.*) wild beasts (esp. lions, tigers, big cat tribe)

***faux(-sse),** (*adj.*) false; untrue; not genuine

faux, *m.* forgery (*legal*)

faux, *f.* scythe

faux-col, *m.* (stand-up) collar, (detachable) collar

faux-filet, *m.* sirloin of beef

faux-fuyant, *m.* subterfuge

faveur, *f.* favour; silk ribbon

favorable, (*adj.*) favourable

favori(te), (*adj.*) favourite

favoris, *m. pl.* side-whiskers

favoriser, *v.t.* to favour; to befriend; aid, assist; to be partial to

fébrifuge, *m.* febrifuge (*med.*)

fébrile, (*adj.*) febrile; feverish (preparations)

fécond, (*adj.*) fertile; fecund; prolific

fécondité, *f.* fruitfulness; fecundity; fertility (land)

féconder, *v.t.* to fertilise; fecundate

fécule, *f.* starch

fédéré, (*adj.*) federated

fée, *f.* fairy

féerie, *f.* fairy scenes, fairyland

féerique, (*adj.*) enchanting; fairylike

feindre, *v.t.* to feign, to sham, to pretend

feinte, *f.* feint, sham, pretence, make-believe

fêler, *v.t.* to crack

félicitation, *f.* congratulation

félicité, *f.* intense happiness, bliss, felicity

féliciter, *v.t.* to congratulate

félonie, *f.* felony, treason

fêlure, *f.* crack, fissure

femelle, *f.* female (of animals; to use *femelle* in regard to persons amounts to an insult)

féminin(e), (*adj.*) feminine

femme, *f.* woman, wife; **- de ménage,** charwoman, housekeeper; **- de journée,** daily help; **- de chambre,** housemaid, chambermaid; **sage-femme,** *f.* midwife

fenaison, *f.* hay harvest; hay-making

fendiller, *v.t.* to crack, to split; **se -,** *v.r.* to crack, to chip, to chap

fendoir, *m.* cleaver

fendre, *v.t.* to cleave; to split (wood)

***fenêtre,** *f.* window; **porte-fenêtre,** *f.* french window; **- à guillotine,** sash window

fente, *f.* split, crack, chink, cleft, fissure, slot, cranny

féodal(-aux), *(adj.)* feudal

féodalité, *f.* feudalism

fer, *m.* iron; **- de fonte,** cast iron; **- forgé,** wrought iron; **- à cheval,** horseshoe; **- à repasser,** flat-iron; **- en tôle,** sheet iron

fer-blanc, *m.* tin-plate

ferblanterie, *f.* tin ware, tin trade

ferblantier, *m.* tinsmith

(fer-de-)lance, *m.* (poisonous reptile) fer-de-lance

férir, *v.t.* to strike; **sans coup -,** without striking a blow

ferme, *f.* farm

ferme, *(adj.)* firm, steady (market)

ferme ça ! or la - !, shut up !(*fam.*)

fermé, *(adj.)* closed (door, etc.)

ferment, *m.* leaven

fermentation, *f.* fermentation

fermer, *v.t.* to shut, to shut up, to stop up, to lock, to fasten; to clench (fist); to turn off (water, gas, etc.); **se -,** *v.r.* to close, to shut

fermeté, *f.* firmness; resolution (with firmness)

fermeture, *f.* shutting, closing; fastening; closing down (of business, etc.); lock-out (works, etc.)

fermier(-ère), *m.* *(f.)* farmer; tenant of farm

fermoir, *m.* clasp, snap (of a bag or book)

féroce, *(adj.)* ferocious, savage, wild

férocité, *f.* ferocity, ferociousness

ferraille, *f.* scrap-iron

ferrant, (maréchal -), *m.* farrier, shoeing-smith

ferré, *(adj.)* iron-shod; **route ferrée,** metalled road; **voie ferrée,** railway track

ferronnier, *m.* iron worker; iron-monger

ferrugineux(-euse), ferruginous, chalybeate

fertile, *(adj.)* fertile, fruitful (in)

fertilisation, *f.* fertilisation

fertiliser, *v.t.* to fertilise

fertilité, *f.* fertility; fruitfulness

férule, *f.* ferule; cane (schoolmaster's)

fervent, *(adj.)* fervent, earnest, ardent

ferveur, *f.* earnestness; fervour

fesse, *f.* buttock

fessée, *f.* a good spanking

fesser, *v.t.* to spank

festin, *m.* feast; banquet

festoiement, *m.* feasting

feston, *m.* festoon, garland

festoyer, *v.t.* to regale, to feast; *v.i.* to carouse

fête, *f.* feast, festival; **c'est aujourd'hui ma -,** it's my birthday; **jour de -,** feast day, holiday; **en -,** in holiday mood; **souhaiter la -,** wish somebody happy returns

fête-dieu, *f.* Corpus Christi

fêter, *v.t.* to keep a day as a holiday; to keep a saint's day

fétiche, *m.* mascot

fétu, *m.* straw

***feu,** *m.* fire; **coup de -,** (gun-) shot

feu, *(adj.)* late, deceased (when used between article and noun is variable : **le feu mari, la feue femme,** etc.)

feuillage, *m.* foliage

feuille, *f.* leaf; sheet (of paper); newspaper (small)

feuillet, *m.* leaf (of book)

feuilleter, *v.t.* to turn over the pages of a book

feuilleton, *m.* serial story (in newspaper)

feutre, *m.* felt; felt hat

fève, *f.* bean

février, *m.* February

fiacre, *m.* cab; hackney coach

fiançailles, *f. pl.* betrothal, engagement

fiancé, *m.* betrothed (bridegroom)

fiancée, *f.* betrothed (bride)

(se) fiancer, *v.r.* to become engaged

fiasco, *m.* failure

fibre, *f.* fibre

fibreux(-euse), fibrous

ficeler, *v.t.* to tie with (string, etc.), to do up (parcel)

ficelle, *f.* string, twine; packthread

fiche, *f.* slip of paper, memorandum slip, voucher, card of membership; ticket; - **policière,** registration form (hotel)

ficher, *v.t.* to drive in, to thrust

fiche(r), (*slang*) (- **un coup**) to give a blow; **fichez-moi la paix,** shut up; **fichez le camp,** get out; hop it; scram!; (**je m'en) fiche! I** don't care a hoot!

fichtre! hang it! the deuce

fichu, *m.* neckerchief; (*adj.*) lost, done for; **mal -,** badly turned out

fiction, *f.* fiction

fidèle, (*adj.*) faithful, loyal, staunch (friend)

fidélité, *f.* fidelity, faithfulness

fief, *m.* fief, fee

fiel, *m.* gall (of animal)

fiente, *f.* dung

fier (fière), (*adj.*) proud, haughty

(se) fier (à), *v.r.* to trust (someone)

fierté, *f.* pride, haughtiness

fièvre, *f.* fever; **avoir la -,** to be feverish; to have a temperature

fiévreux, feverish

figue, *f.* fig

figuier, *m.* fig tree

figurant(e), *m.* (*f.*) walker-on; supernumerary (film, etc.)

figure, *f.* figure, form, shape, image; face, countenance (of humans)

figurer, *v.t.* to represent; *v.i.* to appear, to figure; **se -,** *v.r.* to imagine

***fil,** *m.* thread; wire; **sans-fil,** wireless

filament, *m.* filament

filante (étoile), *f.* shooting star

filateur, *m.* spinner (textile trade); informer (police)

filature, *f.* spinning; shadowing (by police)

file, *f.* file (of soldiers, etc.)

filer, *v.t.* to spin; (*slang*) to make off, to buzz off

filet, *m.* net; string; fillet (of beef, etc.)

fileur, *m.* spinner

filial, (*adj.*) (*pl.* **als** *or* **aux**) filial

filiale, *f.* subsidiary company

filigrane, *m.* filigree

fille, *f.* daughter, girl; **vieille -,** spinster, old maid; **jeune -,** *f.* young girl; unmarried young woman

fillette, *f.* quite young girl

filleul(e), *m.* (*f.*) godchild

film, *m.* film; **tourner un -,** to make (or to act in) a film

filon, *m.* vein, seam, lode (of ore)

filou, *m.* sharper, trickster

fils, *m.* son

filtre, *m.* filter

filtrer, *v.t.* to filter, to strain

***fin,** *f.* end, close, termination; aim, object, purpose

fin(e), (*adj.*) fine; refined; delicate; nice; slender; thin; keen

final, (*adj.*) final, ultimate, last

finance, *f.* finance, treasury

finances, *f. pl.* cash, resources, money

financier(-ère), (*adj.*) financial; *m.* financier; **marché financier,** money market

finaud, (*adj.*) cunning, wily

finesse, *f.* fineness; good quality; shrewdness; cunning

fini, (*adj.*) finished, ended, over; finite

finir, *v.t.* to finish, end

fiole, *f.* phial, flask

firmament, *m.* firmament, sky

fisc, *m.* Treasury, Exchequer, the Inland Revenue

fission, *f.* fission (nuclear, etc.)

fissure, *f.* fissure, cleft (in rock)

fiston, *m.* (*fam.*) youngster, son

fixation, *f.* fixing (date, etc.); assessment, rating

fixe, (*adj.*) fixed, firm; regular (salary); settled, set

fixer, *v.t.* to fix; to determine; to fix (photography)

flacon, *m.* bottle; flask; flagon

flageolet, *m.* small kidney bean; flageolet (*mus.*)

flagorner, *v.t.* to flatter, fawn upon

flagornerie, *f.* flattery, toadyism

flagrant, (*adj.*) flagrant, glaring (injustice); **(pris) en - délit,** (caught) red-handed

flair, *m.* scent (of dogs, etc.), nose; **avoir du -,** to have a gift, a flair for

flairer, *v.t.* to scent, smell (out), nose out

flambant, (*adj.*) flaming, blazing

flambé, (*slang*) done for; lost

flamber, *v.i.* to flame, blaze; to singe

flamme, *f.* flame

flammèche, *f.* spark

flanc, *m.* flank, side

flanelle, *f.* flannel

flâner, *v.i.* to lounge, to saunter

flâneur, *m.* idler; lounger

flanquer, *v.t.* to flank; to chuck (out), pitch out; **- à qn. un coup de pied,** to fetch someone a kick

flaque, *f.* puddle, pool

flasque, (*adj.*) flaccid, flabby

flatter, *v.t.* to stroke, to smooth, to pat, to caress; to flatter; **se -,** *v.r.* to flatter oneself

flatterie, *f.* flattery, adulation

flatteur(-euse), (*adj.*) flattering; *m.* (*f.*) flatterer, sycophant

fléau, *m.* scourge, pest; flail (*agric.*)

flèche, *f.* arrow; spire (of church)

fléchir, *v.t.* to bend; to give way, to sag

flegmatique, (*adj.*) phlegmatic; calm

flegme, *m.* phlegm; (*fig.*) lack of enthusiasm

flétan, *m.* halibut

flétrir, *v.t.* to fade, wither up; to brand, stigmatise; to stain, sully. **se -,** *v.r.* to wither

fleur, *f.* flower; bloom (of youth); choice, pick (of a nation); **à - de,** on a level with, on the surface of

fleuraison, *f.* flowering (season)

fleurer, *v.i.* to smell, to be sweet-smelling

fleuret, *m.* foil (fencing)

fleuri, (*adj.*) in bloom; in flower

fleurir, *v.i.* to flower, to blossom

fleuriste, *m.* and *f.* florist

fleuron, *m.* flower-shaped jewel, ornament; finial (*arch.*)

fleuve, *m.* river (large)

flexibilité, *f.* flexibility, pliability

flexible, (*adj.*) flexible, pliable

flibot, *m.* flat-bottomed boat

flibustier, *m.* pirate, freebooter; cheat, rascal

flic, *m.*(*slang*) policeman, detective

flirter, *v.i.* to flirt

flocon, *m.* flake (snow); tuft, flock of wool

floconneux(-euse), (*adj.*) fleecy

floraison, *f.* blossoming, flower time

floral(-aux), floral

florissant, (*adj.*) flourishing

flot, *m.* wave; (*fig.*) flood, surge, tide, flood-tide; **à -,** afloat

flotte, *f.* fleet

flotter, *v.i.* to float; to wave; to waver; to hesitate

flottille, *f.* flotilla

fluet(te), (*adj.*) slender, thin

fluide, *m.* fluid

flûte, *f.* flute; long roll (of bread)

flûter, *v.i.* to play the flute; (*slang*) to tipple

flûtiste, *m.* flute-player

flux, *m.* flow (of blood)

fluxion, *f.* inflammation

foi, *f.* faith; **mauvaise -,** bad faith, dishonesty

foie, *m.* liver; **huile de - de morue,** cod-liver oil

foin, *m.* hay

foire, *f.* fair; (*slang*) diarrhœa

fois, *f.* time, occasion; **une -,** once

foison, *f.* abundance, plenty, surfeit (of compliments, etc.)

foisonner (de), *v.i.* to abound (in)

folâtre, (*adj.*) playful, frisky

folichon, (adj.) frolicsome, larky
folichonner, v.i. to play about, to lark, to rag
folie, f. folly; madness; insanity; faire des folies, to squander money, to behave foolishly
follement, (adv.) madly
fomentation, f. fomentation
fomenter, v.t. to foment (sedition, etc.); to stir up (trouble)
foncé, (adj.) dark, deep; bleu -, dark blue
foncier(-ière), (adj.) landed (property); fundamental
fonction, f. function; office
fonctionnaire, m. functionary, official, civil servant
fond, m. background; bottom (well, etc.); depth; à -, thoroughly
fondant, (adj.) melting; m. bonbon, sweet
fondateur(-trice), m. (f.) founder
fondation, f. foundation
fondé de pouvoir, m. proxy; power of attorney
fondement, m. foundation; base; (endowed) institution
fonder, v.t. to found, lay the foundation of; to start, set up (a business)
fonderie, f. foundry
fondeur, m. founder (metal)
fondre, v.t. and v.i. to melt (snow, etc.); to smelt (ore); to cast; to dissolve, melt (sugar, etc.); - en larmes, to burst into tears
fondrière, f. quagmire, bog; hollow (in ground)
fonds, m. landed estate; funds; - de commerce, goodwill of business; - de roulement, working capital
fontaine, f. fountain; spring; source, well; cistern
fonte, f. melting; smelting; thawing (snow); cast-iron
forage, m. drilling; boring
forain, (adj.) foreign; from outside; marchand -, pedlar; stallholder at a fair
forban, m. pirate
forçat, m. convict

*force, f. strength, force; might, rigour; - armée, armed forces; the military
forcé, (adj.) forced; compulsory
forcément, necessarily, inevitably
forcené, m. madman; (adj.) frenzied
forcer, v.t. to force; break open; to compel; se -, v.r. to overstrain oneself; to compel oneself to do something
forer, v.t. to drill, to bore
forestier, m. forester, forest-ranger; (adj.) pertaining to forests
forêt, f. forest
foret, m. drill; gimlet; borer
forfait, m. crime (grave); - contract; job work; acheter à -, to buy outright
forfanterie, f. boasting; bragging
forge, f. forge; smithy; black-smith's shop
forger, v.t. to forge; (fig.) to forge, coin; to fabricate, invent
forgeron, m. blacksmith
forgeur, m. forger, coiner of words (N.B.—faussaire is the word usually employed for forgeur meaning someone who forges a signature)
(se) formaliser, v.r. to take offence, take exception to
formalité, f. formality, form
format, m. size, shape (of book, paper)
forme, f. form, shape, figure; aspect; etiquette
formé, (adj.) formed, full grown, mature
formel(le), (adj.) formal; express; explicit
former, v.t. to form, to shape; to fashion; to create; constitute; se -, v.r. to take shape; to improve oneself
formidable, (adj.) formidable, dreadful; c'est -, it's terrific!
formulaire, m. formulation, for-mulary
formule, f. formula; prescription
fors, (prep.) except, but (rarely used)

fort, (adj.) strong; powerful, robust, vigorous

fort, (adv.) (used as a superlative) very; very much; highly

fort, m. fort, stronghold, fortress; a powerful, strong man

fortement, (adv.) strongly, vigorously, much

forteresse, f. fortress, stronghold

fortifiant, (adj.) strengthening, fortifying, invigorating

fortification, f. fortification

fortifier, v.t. to fortify; to strengthen; to invigorate

fortin, m. small fort

fortuit, (adj.) fortuitous, casual

fortune, f. fortune, chance, luck; wealth, property

fortuné, (adj.) fortunate, lucky, happy

fosse, f. hole in ground, pit; grave

fossé, m. ditch, moat

fossette, f. dimple

fossoyeur, m. grave-digger

fou (fol, folle), (adj.) mad, foolish, insane, senseless; wild, rash; **rendre -,** to drive mad

foudre, f. thunderbolt, lightning

foudroyant, (adj.) terrible, crushing; withering

foudroyer, v.t. to strike with lightning; to crush; to confound

fouet, m. whip; lash

fouetter, v.t. to whip, to spank; to flog, lash (person, animal, etc.); to beat (eggs); to whip cream

fouettée, f. whipping, spanking

fougère, f. fern, bracken

fougue, f. ardour, dash, spirit

fougueux(-euse), (adj.) fiery, ardent, impetuous

fouille, f. digging, excavation

fouiller, v.t. to dig, excavate; - quelqu'un, to search somebody; to fumble; - dans les poches, to grope, search in one's pockets

fouillis, m. jumble, muddle

fouine, f. marten, weasel

foulard, m. foulard, silk; scarf; silk handkerchief

foule, f. crowd; throng of people; pressing, crushing

fouler, v.t. to crush, crumple; to trample down (grass, etc.)

foulure, f. sprain or wrench

four, m. oven (kitchen, etc.); kiln

fourbe, (adj.) knavish, rascally; m. rascal, knave

fourberie, f. cheating, swindle

fourbir, v.t. to rub up; furbish

fourbu, (adj.) dead-beat (person); foundered; broken down (horse)

fourche, f. fork (hay fork, pitch fork); **la route fait -,** the road forks

fourchette, f. fork (table use)

fourchon, m. prong (of a fork); fork of a tree

fourchu, (adj.) forked (road)

fourchure, f. fork, bifurcation

fourgon, m. wagon (railway), van

fourmi, f. ant

fourmilier, m. ant-eater

fourmilière, f. ant-hill

fourmillement, m. swarming; pricking sensation; pins and needles

fourmiller, v.i. to swarm; to teem (with life, movement)

fournaise, f. furnace; (fig.) hot place

fourneau, m. furnace (of boiler, etc.); - à gaz, gas cooker

fournée, f. batch

fournir, v.t. to complete; to supply; furnish (details); provide

fournisseur, m. supplier, caterer

fourniture, f. supply, providing

fournitures, f. pl. supplies, requisites

fourrage, m. forage, fodder

fourrager, v.i. to forage

fourreau, m. scabbard, sheath

fourrer, v.t. to stuff, or cram (in one's pockets, etc.); - le nez dans, to thrust, shove one's nose into something

fourreur, m. furrier

fourrure, f. fur

fourvoyer, v.t. to lead astray; se-, v.r. to go astray, to lose one's way

foyer, m. hearth; home; grate, focus

frac, m. dress-coat

fracas, *m.* din, uproar

fracasser, *v.t.* to crash, shatter; smash to pieces

fraction, *f.* fraction; fractional part

fracture, *f.* fracture of bone, etc.; breaking, forcing (of door)

fragile, *(adj.)* fragile; brittle; frail, delicate (health)

fragilité, *f.* fragility; delicacy of health

fragment, *m.* fragment; chip (stone, etc.)

fragmentaire, *(adj.)* fragmentary

fraîcheur, *f.* freshness, coolness; chilliness

fraîchir, *v.i.* to grow colder

frais (fraîche), *(adj.)* fresh; cool (wind)

*frais, *m. pl.* expenses, cost

fraise, *f.* strawberry; ruff

fraisier, *m.* strawberry plant

framboise, *f.* raspberry

framboisier, *m.* raspberry bush

franc, *m.* franc

franc (franche), *(adj.)* free; frank, open, candid

Français(e), French, Frenchman (woman)

(les) Français, *m. pl.* the French

(le) français, *m.* the French language

franchement, *(adv.)* frankly, freely, candidly

franchir, *v.t.* to clear (an obstacle), to jump over; to cross; to pass through

franchise, *f.* frankness, candour

franc-maçon, *m.* freemason

franc-maçonnerie, *f.* freemasonry

franco, *(adv.)* carriage paid; - à bord, free on board (f.o.b.)

frange, *f.* fringe

frappant, *(adj.)* striking (likeness, etc.)

*frapper, *v.t.* to strike; to hit; to strike (medal, etc.); to mint (coins); to type (letter); to ice (wine)

fraternel(le), *(adj.)* fraternal, brotherly

fraternité, *f.* brotherhood, fraternity

fraude, *f.* fraud, deception; smuggling; fraudulence; deceit; passer en -, to smuggle something through

frauder, *v.t.* to defraud; cheat; swindle

fraudeur, *m.* swindler; smuggler

frayer, *v.t.* to scrape, rub; to clear a way, path

frayeur, *f.* fright; fear, dread

fredaine, *f.* prank, escapade

fredonner, *v.t.* to hum (a tune)

frein, *m.* brake; bit, bridle; mettre le -, to put on the brake

frelatage, *m.* adulteration (of food)

frelater, *v.t.* to adulterate (food)

frêle, *(adj.)* frail, weak

frelon, *m.* hornet

freluche, *f.* tuft (silk, of tassel)

frémir, *v.i.* to shudder; to tremble, quake; to rustle (leaves)

frémissement, *m.* shudder; quivering

frêne, *m.* ash tree

frénésie, *f.* frenzy, madness

frénétique, frantic, frenzied

fréquent, *(adj.)* frequent

fréquentation, *f.* frequentation, frequenting

fréquenter, *v.t.* to frequent; to visit often

frère, *m.* brother

fresque, *f.* fresco

fret, *m.* freight; chartering

fréter, *v.t.* to freight; to charter (a ship)

frétiller, *v.i.* to frisk (be lively); to wriggle

fretin, *m.* small fish, fry; rubbish

friand, *(adj.)* fond (of good things)

friandise, *f.* dainty, delicacy, titbit

fricassée, *f.* fricassee

friche, *f.* waste, fallow land

friction, *f.* rubbing, chafing (limbs); (dry) shampoo

frigorifier, *v.t.* to refrigerate

frileux(-euse), *(adj.)* chilly; sensitive to the cold

frimas, *m.* hoar frost, rime

fringant, (*adj.*) brisk, lively, frisky (horse) ; dashing

friper, *v.t.* to crumple, to crush (a dress)

friperie, *f.* rubbish; old clothes, second-hand clothes

fripier, *m.* dealer in old clothes

fripon(ne), *m.* (*f.*) rogue, rascal

fripon, (*adj.*) roguish, rascally

friponner, *v.t.* to cheat, to pilfer

fripouille, *f.* rascal, rotter, bad hat

frire, *v.t.* to fry

frise, *f.* frieze

frisé, (*adj.*) curly (hair)

friser, *v.t.* to curl, to wave

frisson, *m.* shiver (from cold)

frissonner, *v.i.* to shiver, shudder

frit, (*adj.*) (from verb *frire*) fried; pommes frites, fried potatoes

friture, *f.* frying; fry of fish

frivole, (*adj.*) frivolous, shallow

frivolité, *f.* frivolity; trifle

froc, *m.* frock, gown

*froid, (*adj.*) cold

froideur, *f.* coldness (temperature); chilliness (of manner)

froisser, *v.t.* to rumple; to hurt (the feelings) ; se -, *v.r.* to take offence

frôler, *v.t.* to touch lightly; to rub, graze ; - la mort, to be near death's door

fromage, *m.* cheese

froment, *m.* wheat

froncer, *v.t.* to wrinkle, pucker ; - les sourcils, to frown; to knit the brow

fronde, *f.* sling; catapult

front, *m.* forehead; brow; front

frontal(-aux), (*adj.*) frontal, front

frontière, *f.* frontier, border

frontispice, *m.* title page; frontispiece

frotter, *v.t.* to rub; to rub up, polish; to scrub; se - (contre), *v.r.* to rub (against something)

frotteur(-euse), *m.* (*f.*) floor polisher, floor-scrubber

frottoir, *m.* rubber, polisher

frou-frou, *m.* rustling; swish (of silk, etc.)

fructueux(-euse), (*adj.*) fruitful, profitable

frugal, (*adj.*) frugal

frugalité, *f.* frugality

fruit, *m.* fruit

fruitier, (*adj.*) fruit-bearing; *m.* fruiterer

fruste, (*adj.*) defaced, worn (coin); rough (style, manners)

frustrer, *v.t.* to frustrate; disappoint

fugitif(-ive), (*adj.*) fugitive; *m.* (*f.*) fugitive, runaway

fugue, *f.* escapade; flight; fugue (*mus.*)

fuir, *v.i.* to flee, fly away, run away; to recede (horizon)

fuite, *f.* flight

fumée, *f.* smoke

fumer, *v.i.* to smoke; to steam ; *v.t.* to manure (land)

fumet, *m.* flavour

fumeur, *m.* smoker (of tobacco)

fumeux(-euse), (*adj.*) smoky

fumier, *m.* manure, dung (heap)

fumiste, *m.* stove-setter; wag, practical joker; humbug

fumoir, *m.* smoking-room

funèbre, (*adj.*) funeral (ceremony); funereal

funérailles, *f. pl.* obsequies

funeste, (*adj.*) fatal, deadly

funiculaire, *m.* cable railway

furet, *m.* ferret

fureter, *v.i.* to ferret; nose about, pry (into)

fureur, *f.* fury, rage, wrath

furibond, (*adj.*) furious; full of fury

furie, *f.* fury, termagant

furoncle, *m.* boil (*med.*)

furtif(-ive), (*adj.*) furtive, stealthy

fuseau, *m.* spindle

fusée, *f.* fuse; rocket

fuselage, *m.* fuselage (*aviation*); body; frame

fusil, *m.* steel (for sharpening); gun (rifle, but *not* cannon); coup de -, gunshot, rifle-shot

fusillade, *f.* rifle fire, fusillade

fusiller, *v.t.* to shoot down; to execute by shooting

fusion, *f.* fusion, melting

fustiger, *v.t.* to beat, thrash (not often used now)

fût, *m.* stock (of rifle, etc.); shaft (chimney); cask

futaie, *f.* forest (of old trees)

futaille, *f.* cask, tun (of wine)

futaine, *f.* fustian (textile)

futé, *(adj.)* sly, smart, astute

futile, *(adj.)* futile, trifling

futur, *(adj.)* future

futur(e), *m.* *(f.)* intended (bride, etc.)

fuyard, *m.* fugitive; runaway

G

gabare, *f.* lighter, barge; drag-net

gabarit, *m.* model; mould

gabelou, *m.* customs officer (used in a sense of depreciation)

gâche, *f.* staple; wall hook; trowel

gâcher, *v.t.* to mix (mortar, etc.); to spoil, to waste

gâchette, *f.* catch (of a lock); trigger

gaffe, *f.* boat-hook; *(coll.)* a blunder, bloomer; **faire une -,** to put one's foot in it

gaffer, *v.t.* to hook; to blunder; to drop a brick

gage, *m.* pawn, pledge; deposit, security

gager, *v.t.* to bet, wager; to hire, pay; to pledge

gages, *m. pl.* wages

gageure, *f.* bet, wager

gagnant, *(adj.)* winning; *m.* winner

gagne-pain, *m.* livelihood; bread-winner

gagne-petit, *m.* cut-price stores; knife-grinder

gagner, *v.t.* to gain, to earn, to get; to make (money); to win; to reach (an objective)

gai, *(adj.)* gay, merry, bright

gaiement (gaîment), *(adv.)* cheerfully, gaily, merrily

gaieté, *f.* gaiety, merriment, brightness; cheerfulness

gaillard, *m.* strapping fellow; jovial fellow

gaillarde, *f.* a buxom girl or woman

gaillard(e), *(adj.)* brisk, hearty, jovial, fit, healthy, buxom

gain, *m.* gain, profit, benefit

gaine, *f.* sheath, case; corset (dress)

gainer, *v.t.* to sheath, to case; to clothe tightly

gala, *m.* gala; festive occasion

galamment, *(adv.)* courteously; with great politeness (*not* gallantly used in ordinary sense of bravery)

galant, *(adj.)* civil, courteous (to ladies); courtly

galanterie, *f.* politeness (to ladies); *(pl.)* love affairs, intrigues

gale, *f.* itch; mange (dogs)

galère, *f.* galley; convict ship

galerie, *f.* gallery

galérien, *m.* galley-slave; convict

galet, *m.* pebble, pebble stone, shingle (beach)

galetas, *m.* attic, garret; hovel

galeux(-euse), itchy; mangy

galimatias, *m.* balderdash, gibberish; bombast

gallicisme, *m.* French turn of phrase

gallois(e), *(adj.)* Welsh

galoche, *f.* clog

galon, *m.* braid; officer's gold braid on sleeve; N.C.O.'s stripes

galop, *m.* gallop

galopade, *f.* canter; galloping

galoper, *v.i.* to gallop

galopin(e), *m.* *(f.)* errand-boy (girl); young scamp

galvaniser, *v.t.* to galvanise

gambade, *f.* gambol, leap; **faire des gambades,** to cut capers

gamelle, *f.* bowl, tin can; (*naval* and *mil.*) mess-tin

gamin(e), *m.* *(f.)* street-boy (girl); youngster, young girl

gamma, *m.* gamma (*Greek Alph.*) **rayons -,** gamma rays (*atom phys.*)

gamme, *f.* scale (*mus.*); range, series

gammée (croix), *f.* swastika

ganache, *f.* lower jaw (of person); jowl (of animal); blockhead

gangrène, *f.* gangrene

ganse, *f.* braid; piping

gant, *m.* glove

ganter, *v.t.* to glove; **se -,** *v.r.* to put on one's gloves

gantier(-ère), *m.* (*f.*) glover glove-maker

garage, *m.* shunting, side-tracking (railway); basin (canal); garage; storage (cars, etc.)

garagiste, *m.* garage-keeper

garant, *m.* guarantee, guarantor

garantie, *f.* guarantee; pledge of execution (of contract, etc.); guarantee (of quality)

garantir, *v.t.* to warrant; to guarantee

garçon, *m.* boy; lad; young man; bachelor; servant; waiter (in restaurant, etc.)

garçonne, *f.* boyish, mannish girl

garçonnière, *f* bachelor's (or spinster's) establishment

garde, *m.* guard; keeper; **- champêtre,** country policeman

*****garde,** *f.* care, custody, guardianship; **la -,** the Guards

garde-à-vous! attention!

garde-barrière, *m.* and *f.* gatekeeper (level crossing)

garde-chasse, *m.* gamekeeper

garde-côte, *m.* coastguard; coast defence vessel

garde-feu, *m.* fireman (in a building); fender

garde-magasin, *m.* storekeeper

garde-malade, *m.* male nurse; *f.* sick-nurse

garde-manger, *m.* larder, pantry; meat-safe

garde-meuble, *m.* furniture warehouse, repository

garde-robe, *f.* wardrobe

garder, *v.t.* to keep, preserve; to guard, to protect, to watch over; **se -,** *v.r.* to beware; to protect oneself

gardien(ne), *m.* (*f.*) guardian, keeper; caretaker (of public buildings); **- de la paix,** policeman

gare! (*interj.*) look out!

gare, *f.* railway station; **- de triage,** marshalling yard; **- maritime,** *f.* harbour station; **- de bifurcation,** *f.* junction

garenne, *f.* warren (rabbits, etc.)

garer, *v.t.* to shunt (train); to dock (vessel); to garage (car); to park (car); **se -,** *v.r.* to get out of the way

gargariser, *v.t.* to gargle

gargote, *f.* cheap eating house

garnement, *m.* a scamp, rogue (generally used with **mauvais**)

garni, (*adj.*) filled; provided (with); furnished

garnir, *v.t.* to furnish; to provide; to fit out; to decorate; to trim (dress); to line (coat); to fill; to cover; to garnish (*culinary*)

garnison, *f.* garrison

garniture, *f.* fittings; appointments; ornaments; trimming; lining (of coat, etc.); dressing (*culinary*)

garrot, *m.* tourniquet (*surg.*); garrotting

garrotter, *v.t.* to strangle; to tie down, pinion

gars, *m.* young fellow; lad

gaspiller, *v.t.* to waste, to squander

gâteau, *m.* cake; open tart

gâter, *v.t.* to spoil; to pamper, spoil (child)

gauche, (*adj.*) left (hand, etc.); awkward, clumsy; left wing (in politics)

gauchement, (*adj.*) awkwardly; clumsily

gaucher(-ère), *m.* (*f.*) left-handed person

gaucherie, *f.* awkwardness; clumsiness

gaudriole, *f.* broad joke

gaufre, *f.* waffle, wafer (*culinary*)

gaufrer, *v.t.* to emboss

gaufrette, *f* wafer biscuit

gaule, *f.* switch, small stick

gaulois(e), *m.* (*f.*) gallic

gaver, *v.t.* to cram, to stuff with food; to feed forcibly

gavroche, *m.* ragamuffin; street arab

gaz, *m.* gas; - **asphyxiant,** *m.* poison gas; **usine à -,** gasworks

gaze, *f.* gauze

gazette, *f.* gazette; newspaper

gazeux(-euse), *(adj.)* gaseous

gazomètre, *m.* gasometer

gazon, *m.* turf; grass, sward

gazouiller, *v.i.* to twitter, to warble

geai, *m.* jay

géant, *m.* giant

geignard, *(adj.)* fretful

geindre, *v.i.* to whimper, to whine

gel, *m.* frost, freezing

gelée, *f.* frost; jelly; - **blanche,** hoar frost

geler, *v.t.* to freeze; *v.i.* to become frozen

gémir, *v.i.* to groan, to moan

gémissement, *m.* groan, groaning; moan

gemme, *f.* gem

gencive, *f.* gum (in mouth)

gendre, *m.* son-in-law

gêne, *f.* discomfort, embarrassment; financial straits

gêner, *v.t.* to constrict; to cramp; to hinder; to inconvenience; to embarrass

général(-aux), *(adj.)* general; *m.* general (*mil.*)

généraliser, *v.t.* to generalise

génération, *f.* generation

générer, *v.t.* to engender; to generate

généreux(-euse), *(adj.)* generous; liberal; open-handed

générosité, *f.* generosity

genêt, *m.* broom, furze

génie, *m.* spirit; genius; engineering

genièvre, *m.* juniper; gin

génisse, *f.* heifer

genou, *m.* knee

genouillère, *f.* knee-piece

genre, *m.* genus, species; kind; manner; sort; fashion; taste

gens, *m.* and *f. pl.* (when an adjective comes before **gens** it is feminine, when after, mascu-

line), people, folk, persons, men and women

gentil(le), *(adj.)* pretty, nice; pleasing

gentilhomme, *m.* nobleman; man of good birth

gentillesse, *f.* graciousness, amiability; kindness

gentiment, *(adv.)* nicely; prettily

géographe, *m.* geographer

géographie, *f.* geography

géologie, *f.* geology

géologue, *m.* geologist

géométrie, *f.* geometry

gérance, *f.* management (of business, etc.); managership

gérant, *m.* manager; director

gérante, *f.* manageress

gerbe, *f.* sheaf (of corn)

gerce, *f.* crack, fissure; chap (in skin); clothes moth; wood louse

gercer, *v.t.* to chap the hands; to crack (wood)

gerçure, *f.* crack, cleft; flaw (in wood); chap (hand)

gérer, *v.t.* to manage; to run (a business)

germain(e), *(adj.)* Germanic; cousin -, first cousin

germanisme, *m.* germanism; German phrase or idiom

germe, *m.* germ, seed, bud; shoot, sprout

germer, *v.i.* to germinate, to sprout, to shoot

gésir, *v.i.* to lie (only used in certain forms, and but rarely); **ci-gît,** here lies (somebody in grave)

geste, *m.* gesture, motion; sign; *f.* heroic exploit

gestion, *f.* management, administration

gibet, *m.* gallows

gibier, *m.* game

giboulée, *f.* shower; - **de mars,** April shower

gibus, *m.* opera hat

gifle, *f.* slap (in face); smack

gifler, *v.t.* to slap (the face); to smack

gigantesque, *(adj.)* gigantic; tremendous, colossal

gigot, *m.* leg of mutton

gilet, *m.* waistcoat; vest

gin, *m.* gin (drink)

gingembre, *m.* ginger

girafe, *f.* giraffe

girofle, *m.* clove

giroflée, *f.* stock, gilliflower; wallflower

giron, *m.* lap

girouette, *f.* weather-cock

gîte, *m.* home; resting place

givre, *m.* hoar frost

givré, *(adj.)* frosted, rimy

glace, *f.* ice; ice-cream; plate-glass, window, mirror

glacé, *(adj.)* icy, cold, frozen, iced; glazed (paper, etc.)

glacer, *v.t.* to freeze, to ice; to chill; to glaze

glacial, *(adj.)* icy; cold

glacier, *m.* glacier

glacière, *f.* refrigerator; ice chest

glaçon, *m.* icicle; ice floe

glaïeul, *m.* gladiolus; iris

glaire, *f.* white of egg; glair (viscid substance)

glaise, *f.* clay, loam

glaive, *m.* sword; blade

gland, *m.* acorn; tassel

glande, *f.* gland

glaner, *v.t.* to glean

glaneur(-euse), *m.* (*f.*) gleaner

glapir, *v.i.* to yap; to yelp

glapissement, *m.* yapping; yelping

glas, *m.* knell

glissade, *f.* slip, slide; sliding

glissant, *(adj.)* slippery

glisser, *v.i.* to slip, to slide (on ice), to skid

glisseur, *m.* glider (*aviation*)

glissoire, *f.* slide (on ice, etc.)

global(-aux), *(adj.)* total

globe, *m.* globe; sphere; globe for lamp

gloire, *f.* glory; honour

gloriette, *f.* summer-house

glorieux(-euse), *(adj.)* glorious

glorifier, *v.t.* to glorify; **se -,** *v.r.* to boast

glose, *f.* comment; marginal note

glossaire, *m.* glossary; dictionary

glousser, *v.i.* to cluck (hen); to gobble (turkey)

glouton, *m.* glutton; *(adj.)* gluttonous

glu, *f.* bird-lime

gluant, *(adj.)* sticky

glutineux(-euse), glutinous

glycérine, *f.* glycerine

gobelet, *m.* goblet

gobe-mouches, *m.* fly-catcher; simpleton

go (tout de -), all of a sudden, easily

gober, *v.t.* to gulp, to swallow

godailler, *v.i.* to tipple; to pub-crawl

godet, *m.* small cup, mug

godiche, *m.* and *f.* simpleton; lout

goéland, *m.* sea-gull

goélette, *f.* schooner

goémon, *m.* sea-weed

gogo (à), galore

goguenard, *(adj.)* mocking, jeering

goguenarder, *v.i.* to jeer, to sneer, to banter

goinfrerie, *f.* gluttony

golf, *m.* golf

golfe, *m.* gulf

gomme, *f.* gum; **- à effacer,** indiarubber; **- à mâcher,** chewing-gum

gommeux(-euse), *(adj.)* gummy; *m.* a " swell," dandy

gond, *m.* hinge (of door)

gondole, *f.* gondola

gonflement, *m.* swelling; blowing up, pumping up (tyres)

gonflé, *(adj.)* swollen; inflated (tyre); distended

gonfler, *v.t.* to swell; to pump up, blow up (tyres); to distend

goret, *m.* little pig; porker

gorge, *f.* throat, neck; bosom, bust (of a woman)

gorgée, *f.* mouthful, draught (wine, etc.)

gosier, *m.* throat; gullet

gosse, *m.* and *f.* youngster; kid (child)

gothique, *(adj.)* Gothic

gouache, *f.* painting in gouache

gouailler, *v.t.* to chaff

goudron, *m.* tar

goudronner, *v.t.* to tar

gouffre, *m.* gulf; pit; abyss; whirlpool; vortex

goujat, *m.* blackguard

goujon, *m.* gudgeon

goulot, *m.* neck (of bottle)

goulu, (*adj.*) greedy; gluttonous

goupillon, *m.* brush; holy water sprinkler

gourde, *f.* gourd, flask

gourgandine, *f.* prostitute

gourmade, *f.* cuff, a slap

gourmand, (*adj.*) greedy; gluttonous

gourmand(e), *m.* (*f.*) glutton

gourmandise, *f.* greed, greediness

gourme, *f.* .strangles; impetigo (*med.*)

gourmer, *v.t.* to punch, to cuff; to curb

gourmet, *m.* epicure

gousse, *f.* pod, shell, husk

gousset, *m.* arm-pit; gusset

goût, *m.* taste (sense of); flavour; taste; style. manner

goûter, *m.* a snack between meals; afternoon meal for school-children; afternoon tea

goûter, *v.t.* to taste; to relish

*****goutte,** *f.* drop (of liquid); a nip or dram (liquor); gout

gouttière, *f.* gutter; spout, rain-pipe

goutteux(-euse), gouty

gouvernail, *m.* rudder, helm; (*aviation*) elevator

gouvernante, *f.* housekeeper (to bachelor), governess

gouvernement, *m.* government (in general sense)

gouverner, *v.t.* to govern; to steer

gouverneur, *m.* governor (of province, colony, etc.)

grabat, *m.* pallet; litter of straw

*****grâce,** *f.* grace, gracefulness; charm; thanks; **coup de -,** finishing stroke; **de - !** for pity's sake! **de bonne -,** willingly; **faire - à qn.,** to let somebody off (something)

gracieux(-euse), (*adj.*) gracious (manner); graceful (figure, etc.); **à titre -,** gratis

gracieusement, (*adv.*) gracefully; graciously; kindly

grade, *m.* grade; rank; degree (university)

gradin, *m.* step; tier (of seats, etc.)

graduel(le), (*adj.*) gradual

graduer, *v.t.* to graduate (measures) (not used in sense of to graduate from a university)

grain, *m.* grain (corn); particle (dust); berry; bead (necklace, rosary); spot (beauty spot); squall

graine, *f.* seed (of plants); egg (silkworms)

graisse, *f.* grease, fat

graisser, *v.t.* to grease; oil, lubricate; to grease, soil (clothes)

graisseux(-euse), greasy, oily

grammaire, *f.* grammar

gramme, *m.* gram(me), (measure, $\frac{1}{1000}$ of kilogramme)

grand, (*adj.*) great; large; tall; big

grand'chose, (used with **pas**) not much

grand-duc, *m.* grand duke

grand'mère, *f.* grandmother

grand-père, *m.* grandfather

grand'route, *f.* highway

grandement, grandly, nobly

grandeur, *f.* size; height (of tree, etc.)

grandiose, (*adj.*) imposing

grandir, *v.i.* to grow, to grow tall, to increase

grange, *f.* barn

granit, *m.* granite

graphique, (*adj.*) graphic; *m.* graph, diagram

grappe, *f.* bunch, cluster (of grapes, etc.)

grappin, *m.* grapnel, hook

gras(se), (*adj.*) fat (of meat); **fat** (general sense, tissue, etc.)

grasseyer, *v.i.* to speak thickly; to roll the " r's ".

grassouillet(te), (*adj.*) chubby

gratification, *f.* gratuity, bonus

gratin, (used with **au**) cooked with cheese or crumbs

gratis, (*adv.*) gratis; free of charge

gratitude, *f.* gratitude, thankfulness

gratte-ciel, *m.* sky-scraper

gratter, *v.t.* to scrape, scratch

grattoir, *m.* scraper, scratching knife, eraser

gratuit(e), (*adj.*) gratuitous, free

gratuité, *f.* gratuitousness (*not* gratuity)

gravats, *m. pl.* rubbish

grave, (*adj.*) grave, serious, solemn; severe; weighty (opinion, etc.)

graver, *v.t.* to engrave; to imprint, impress; to cut, to carve; - à l'eau forte, to etch

graveur, *m.* engraver

gravier, *m.* gravel

gravir, *v.t.* to climb; to scale, to ascend

gravité, *f.* gravity, seriousness; solemnity, weight, importance

gravure, *f.* engraving

gré, *m.* will; bon - mal -, willy-nilly; savoir - à qn. de, to be grateful to someone for

grec(que), (*adj.*) Greek; *m.* a sharper

gredin, *m.* scoundrel, rogue

greffe, *f.* grafting (trees)

greffe, *m.* record office, registry

greffier, *m.* clerk of the court; registrar; recorder

grège, (*adj.*) raw (refers only to silk)

grêle, (*adj.*) slender, slim, thin; shrill (voice)

grêle, *f.* hail; hailstorm

grêler, *v.* (*imper.*) to hail

grêlon, *m.* hailstone

grelot, *m.* small bell

grelotter, *v.i.* to shiver (with cold); to jingle, ring

grenade, *f.* pomegranate; grenade, bomb (generally hand, e.g. Mills bomb)

grenat, *m.* garnet; colour of garnet (red)

grenier, *m.* loft; garret; granary

grenouille, *f.* frog

grès, *m.* sandstone; stoneware

grésil, *m.* sleet

grésiller, *v.i.* to sizzle, crackle; (*imp.*) to sleet

grève, *f.* beach, strand; strike (industrial, etc.); faire la perlée, to go slow, ca'canny

grever, *v.t.* to mortgage, to encumber with debt

gréviste, *m.* (*f.*) striker

gribouille, *m.* simpleton

gribouiller, *v.t.* and *v.i.* to scrawl, scribble

grief, *m.* injury, wrong; grievance

grièvement, (*adj.*) grievously, sorely; gravely; badly (hurt)

griffade, *f.* clawing; scratching

griffe, *f.* claw; talon; scratch

griffer, *v.t.* to claw; to scratch

griffonnage, *m.* scrawl, scribble

griffonner, *v.t.* to scrawl, scribble

grignon, *m.* hard crust of bread

grignoter, *v.t.* to gnaw; to nibble

gril, *m.* gridiron

grillade, *f.* grilling; a grill (steak, etc.); broiling, broil

grille, *f.* grate; grating; railing

grille-pain, *m.* toaster

griller, *v.t.* to grill, to broil, to toast (bread)

grillon, *m.* cricket (insect)

grimace, *f.* grimace, grimacing

grimaud, (*adj.*) cross, peevish, ill-tempered

grime, *m.* old man, old fogey

grimoire, *m.* incomprehensible nonsense; scrawl

grimpant, (*adj.*) climbing; twining (plants); *m.* a creeper; (*slang*) trousers

grimper, *v.t.* to climb, to clamber up

grincer, *v.t.* to gnash (the teeth), to grate

grincheux(-euse), (*adj.*) ill-tempered, surly, crabbed

griotte, *f.* cherry (morella)

grippe, *f.* influenza

grippe-sou, *m.* money-grubber

gripper, *v.t.* to clutch, to seize; to pounce on

gris, (*adj.*) grey; grey-haired; raw, dull (weather); tipsy

grisaille, *f.* grizzled wig; hair partly grey; greyness

grisailler, *v.i.* to turn, go grey

grisâtre, (*adj.*) greyish

griser, *v.t.* to give a grey tint to; to make tipsy; se-, *v.r.* to get tipsy

grisonnant, (adj.) hair turning grey

grisonner, v.i. to grow grey

grisou, m. fire-damp (in mine, etc.)

grive, f. thrush

grivelé, (adj.) speckled

grivois, (adj.) merry; obscene; broad (story)

grog, m. grog

grognard, m. grumbler; growler

grognard, (adj.) grumbling

grognement, m. grunt, grunting; snarl, groan

grogner, v.i. to grunt; to snarl, to grumble; to groan

grogneur(-euse), m. (f.) grumbler

groin, m. snout (of a pig)

grommeler, v.i. to mutter; to grumble

grondant, (adj.) scolding

grondement, m. rumble(ing), growling

gronder, v.t. to scold; to reprimand; v.i. growl

grondeur(-euse), (adj.) and m. (f.) grumbler, grumbling

gros(se), big, large, stout, corpulent; thick; coarse; considerable; main part; pregnant; rough (voice); **en -,** wholesale

groseille, f. currant; **-à maquereau,** f. gooseberry

groseillier, m. gooseberry bush

grosse, f. gross (12 dozen); engrossed draft, copy

grossesse, f. pregnancy

grosseur, f. size, bulk; bigness, largeness

grossier(-ère), (adj.) coarse, rude

grossièreté, f. rudeness; incivility; coarseness

grossir, v.t. and v.i. to grow bigger; increase; to swell, to swell out; to augment

grotte, f. grotto

grouillant, (adj.) swarming; crawling; stirring

grouiller, v.i. to swarm; to crawl; to be alive (with); to rumble (used of the intestines)

groupe, m. group; clump (of trees)

groupement, m. grouping; coupling (mech.)

grouper, v.i. to group; **se -,** v.r. to form groups

gruau, m. young crane (bird); small crane (for lifting); groats

grue, f. crane (bird); crane for lifting; prostitute

grumeleux(-euse), clotted; lumpy

gruyère, m. cheese (gruyère, a Swiss cheese)

gué, m. ford (of river)

guenille, f. rag; rags; tatters

guenon, f. she-ape or monkey; fright, very ugly woman

guêpe, f. wasp

guère, (adv.) not much, but little; hardly, scarcely

guéridon, m. small table; round table; stand

guérir, v.t. to heal; to cure; **se -,** v.r. to be recovered (from); to recover one's health; to be cured

guérison, f. cure, recovery, healing

guérite, f. sentry box; turret, watch tower

guerre, f. war; warfare; hostilities; struggle (against disease, etc.)

guerrier, m. warrior, veteran; (adj.) warlike

guerroyer, v.i. to war, to make war

guet, m. watch, watching

guet-apens, m. ambush; ambuscade

guêtre, f. gaiter; legging; spat

guetter, v.t. to lie in wait for; to watch for; to be on the look-out for

gueule, f. mouth, jaw (of animals); mouth of persons (only used as insult); wide opening; (fam.) **ta gueule!** shut up!

gueuler, v.i. to bawl, to yell, to shout

gueux(-euse), m. (f.) tramp; loafer, beggar; scoundrel

gui, m. mistletoe

guichet, m. wicket-gate; ticket window; counter (in post office)

guide, *m.* guide; guide-book; handbook; *f.* rein

guider, *v.t.* to guide; to lead

guidon, *m.* handle-bar (of bicycle); pennant (*mil.*); broad pennant (*naval*)

guigne, *f.* sweet cherry; (*slang*) bad luck

guignol, *m.* Punch and Judy Show

guillaume, *m.* rabbet-plane

guillemet, *m.* inverted comma

guilleret, (*adj.*) brisk, sprightly

guillotine, *f.* guillotine

guindé(e), *adj.* stilted

guindeau, *m.* windlass

guingan, *m.* gingham

guinguette, *f.* small suburban tavern (with garden); roadside inn

guirlande, *f.* garland; wreath

*guise, *f.* manner, way, guise

guitare, *f.* guitar

gustation, *f.* tasting

gymnase, *m.* gymnasium

gymnastique, *f.* gymnastics

gymnote, *m.* electric eel

gynécée, *m.* women's apartments in a house (rarely used)

gynécologie, *f.* gynæcology (*surg.*)

gypaète, *m.* vulture

gypse, *m.* gypsum; plaster of Paris

gyroscope, *m.* gyroscope

H

Words beginning with "aspirate" h are shown °h—

habile, (*adj.*) clever, skilful, cunning, smart

habileté, *f.* ability, skill, skilfulness; cleverness, smartness

habillé, (*adj.*) dressed

habillement, *m.* clothing; dressing; dress, clothes; - **complet,** a suit of clothes (usually referred to as **un complet**)

habiller, *v.t.* to dress; to equip; to clothe; **s'-,** *v.r.* to dress, to put on one's clothes

habit, *m.* costume, dress; coat; - **de soirée,** dress-coat

habitable, (*adj.*) habitable

habitant(e), *m.* (*f.*) inhabitant;

resident, dweller; inmate (of house)

habitation, *f.* habitation; dwelling

habiter, *v.t.* to inhabit, to dwell in, to live in (a place); *v.i.* to live, reside

habits, *m. pl.* clothes

*habitude, *f.* habit, custom, practice, use

habitué(e), *m.* (*f.*) frequenter; regular customer

habituel(le), (*adj.*) usual, customary

habituer, *v.t.* to accustom, habituate; **s'-** (à), *v.r.* to get used (to), to get accustomed (to)

°hâbler, *v.i.* to boast, to brag

°hache, *f.* axe, hatchet

°hacher, *v.t.* to chop up, to hash (meat); to hack up

°hachette, *f.* hatchet

°hachis, *m.* mince (meat)

°hagard, (*adj.*) haggard; drawn

°haie, *f.* hedge; fence; hurdle

°haillon, *m.* rag

°haillons, *m. pl.* rags and tatters

°haine, *f.* hatred; detestation

°haineusement, (*adv.*) hatefully, spitefully

°haineux(-euse), (*adj.*) full of hatred; malignant; spiteful

°haïr, *v.t.* to hate; to detest

°halage, *m.* hauling; towing (of ship)

°hâle, *m.* sunburn; tan

*haleine, *f.* breath; **hors d'-,** out of breath

°haler, *v.t.* to haul; to tow (a ship)

°haletant, (*adj.*) panting; gasping for breath

°haleter, *v.i.* to pant; to gasp for breath

hall, *m.* (spacious) entrance hall; (hotel) lounge

°halle, *f.* market place (covered in); **les Halles Centrales,** the central market of Paris

°hallebarde, *f.* halberd; **il tombe** (*or* **pleut**) **des hallebardes,** it is raining cats and dogs

°**hallier**, *m.* thicket, copse

°**halte**, *f.* stop, halt; wayside station

haltère, *m.* dumb-bell

°**hamac**, *m.* hammock

°**hameau**, *m.* hamlet

hameçon, *m.* fish-hook

°**hampe**, *f.* staff, pole (flag); shank (of fish-hook)

°**hanche**, *f.* hip; haunch

°**hangar**, *m.* shed; lean-to; hangar (*aviation*)

°**hanneton**, *m.* cockchafer

°**hanter**, *v.t.* to haunt

°**hantise**, *f.* haunting memory; obsession

°**happe**, *f.* cramp-iron; staple

°**happer**, *v.t.* to snap up, snatch; catch (insects, etc.)

°**harangue**, *f.* harangue, speech

°**haranguer**, *v.t.* to harangue

°**haras**, *m.* stud farm; horse breeding establishment, stud

°**harcelant**, (*adj.*) harassing, worrying

°**harcèlement**, *m.* harassing, worrying

°**harceler**, to harass, worry, torment; to harry (enemy, etc.)

hardes, *f.pl.* clothes (already worn)

ᵇ**hardi**, (*adj.*) bold, audacious, daring; rash; impudent; forward (manner)

°**hardiesse**, *f.* boldness; daring, pluck; effrontery, impudence

°**hareng**, *m.* herring, **- fumé**, kipper

°**hargneux(-euse)**, peevish, cross; nagging; snarling (dog)

°**haricot blanc**, *m.* kidney bean; **- de mouton**, haricot mutton; Irish stew

°**haricots verts**, french beans

harmonie, *f.* harmony; agreement

harmonieux(-euse), harmonious

°**harnacher**, *v.t.* to harness

°**harnais**, *m.* harness

°**haro**, *m.* outcry; hue and cry.

°**harpe**, *f.* harp

°**harpon**, *m.* harpoon

°***hasard**, *m.* chance; luck; accident; **jeu de -**, game of chance

°**hasardé**, (*adj.*) risky, foolhardy; indiscreet (remark)

°**hasarder**, *v.t.* to risk, venture

°**hasardeux(-euse**, perilous, risky

°**hâte**, *f.* haste, hurry

°**hâter**, *v.t.* to hasten, to hurry (something on); to expedite; **se -**, *v.r.* to make haste to do something

°**hâtif(-ive)**, (*adj.*) hasty

°**hausse**, *f.* rise, rising; **baromètre en -**, barometer on the rise; **- des prix**, advance (rise) in prices

°**hausser**, *v.t.* to raise, to lift; **- les épaules**, to shrug the shoulders

°**haussier**, *m.* " bull " (Stock Exchange term)

°**haut**, *m.* height, top

°**haut**, (*adj.*) high, tall, lofty; exalted (position); loud (voice)

°**haut**, (*adv.*) above, high (up); **- les mains !** hands up! **en -**, upstairs

°**haute mer**, high sea, open sea

°**haut-fourneau**, *m.* blast furnace

°**hautain(e)**, (*adj.*) haughty

°**hautement**, (*adv.*) highly (thought of)

°**hauteur**, *f.* height

°**haut-parleur**, *m.* loudspeaker

°**havane**, *f.* Havana; havana cigar

°**hâve**, (*adj.*) wan, pale, haggard

°**havir**, *v.t.* to scorch

°**havre**, *m.* harbour, haven

°**havresac**, *m.* knapsack

hebdomadaire, (*adj.*) weekly; once a week; *m.* (weekly) paper

héberger, *v.t.* to harbour; to lodge; to shelter

hébété, (*adj.*) dull, dazed

hébétement, *m.* stupefaction

hébéter, *v.t.* to dull, stupefy (the senses)

hébraïque, (*adj.*) Hebrew

hébreux (**hébraïque**), (*adj.*) Hebrew

hectare, *m.* hectare = 2·50 acres

hectolitre, *m.* hectolitre = 2·75 bushels

hein, (*int.*) what? eh? (indicates surprise or invites agreement) hélas! (*interj.*) alas!

°héler, *v.t.* to hail (a ship); to speak (a ship, etc.)

hélice, *f.* screw, propeller (ship); air-screw (*aviation*)

hélicoptère, *m.* helicopter

hémisphère, *m.* hemisphere

hémorragie, *f.* hæmorrhage

hémorroïdes, *f. pl.* hæmorrhoids, piles

°hennir, *v.i.* to neigh, whinny

°héraut, *m.* herald

herbe, *f.* herb, plant; grass; fines herbes, seasoning herbs

héréditaire, (*adj.*) hereditary

hérédité, *f.* heredity

hérétique, *m.* and *f.* heretic

°hérissé (de), (*adj.*) bristling (with)

°hérisser, *v.t.* to bristle; se -, *v.r.* to stand on end (hair)

°hérisson, *m.* hedgehog

héritage, *m.* inheritance, heritage

hériter, *v.i.* to inherit, succeed to; to come into a fortune

héritier(-ère), *m.* (*f.*) heir (heiress)

hermétique, (*adj.*) tight closed, hermetically sealed

hermine, *f.* ermine

°hernie, *f.* hernia, rupture (*med.*)

héroïne, *f.* heroine; heroin (narcotic drug)

héroïque, (*adj.*) heroic

héroïsme, *m.* heroism

°héros, *m.* hero

°herse, *f.* harrow (*agric.*)

°herser, *v.t.* to harrow

hésitation, *f.* hesitation, hesitancy

hésiter, *v.i.* to hesitate, waver

°hêtre, *m.* beech (tree)

*heure, *f.* hour; o'clock; time of day

heureux(-euse), (*adj.*) happy; lucky; favourable, fortunate

heureusement, (*adv.*) happily; luckily; fortunately

°heurter, *v.t.* and *v.i.* to knock against; run against; run into; se - (à), *v.r.* to run into (somebody, something); to collide

°hibou(x), *m.* owl

°hideux(-euse), (*adj.*) hideous

°hie, *f.* pile-driver

hier, (*adv.*) yesterday

°hiérarchie, *f.* hierarchy

hiéroglyphique, (*adj.*) hieroglyphic(al)

hilarité, *f.* mirth, laughter, hilarity

hippique, (*adj.*) equine; to do with horses

hippodrome, *m.* racecourse; circus, hippodrome

hippopotame, *m.* hippopotamus

hirondelle, *f.* swallow

°hisser, *v.t.* to hoist; to run up (a flag, etc.); to hoist in; se -, *v.r.* to hoist, or pull oneself up

*histoire, *f.* history; a story, tale

historien, *m.* historian

historique, (*adj.*) historic(al)

histrion, *m.* play actor; mountebank (generally *politics*)

hiver, *m.* winter

hivernage, *m.* winter season; winter quarters

hiverner, *v.i.* to winter; to lie up for the winter

°hobereau, *m.* squire, squireen

°hoche, *f.* notch, nick

°hocher, *v.t.* and *v.i.* to shake (one's head); to toss (the head)

°hocher, *v.t.* to notch, to nick

°hochet, *m.* bauble, toy

°hollandais, (*adj.*) Dutch

°homard, *m.* lobster

homicide, *m.* and *f.* homicide; *m.* manslaughter; (*adj.*) homicidal

hommage, *m.* homage; rendre - à, to pay (a) tribute to

hommages, *m. pl.* respects, compliments (to a lady, etc.)

homme, *m.* man; mankind

°hongrois, (*adj.*) Hungarian

honnête, (*adj.*) honest, upright, honourable; straight, decent; respectable (*f.* woman)

honnêteté, *f.* honesty, uprightness; decency; fairness

*honneur, *m.* honour

°honnir, *v.t.* to disgrace; dishonour

honorabilité, *f.* honourable character; respectability; standing (of business, etc.)

honorable, (*adj.*) honourable; respectable

honoraire, (*adj.*) honorary

honoraires, *m. pl.* fees (of lawyer, etc.); honorarium

honorer, *v.t.* to honour (someone); to respect (qualities); to honour (a bill, etc.); to do credit to

°**honte,** *f.* shame (sense of); **avoir - de,** to be ashamed of

°**honteux (-euse),** ashamed, shameful, disgraceful

hôpital(-aux), *m.* hospital, infirmary

°**hoquet,** *m.* hiccough

horaire, *m.* time-table

horizon, *m.* horizon

horizontal(-aux), (*adj.*) horizontal

horloge, *f.* clock (of church, town, etc.)

horloger, *m.* clock and watch maker

horlogerie, *f.* clock and watch making

°**hormis,** (*prep.*) except; but

horreur, *f.* horror; disgust, repugnance; a dreadful thing; shocking thing; a hideous person

horrible, (*adj.*) horrible; awful; horrifying

°***hors,** (*adv.*) out, outside

°**hors,** (*prep.*) out of, outside, without, save, except

°**hors-d'œuvre,** *m.* (invariable), side dishes (at beginning of meal)

horticulteur, *m.* horticulturist

hospice, *m.* hospice, asylum, refuge; monastery

hospitalier(-ère), (*adj.*) hospitable

hospitaliser, *v.t.* to admit to a charitable institution, or to a hospital

hospitalité, *f.* hospitality

hostie, *f.* victim, sacrifice (offering); the Host (*eccles.*)

hostile, (*adj.*) hostile; unfriendly

hostilité, *f.* hostility; ill-will; animosity

hôte, *m.* host (entertainer of guests); landlord (of inn, etc.); guest or visitor

hôtel, *m.* hotel (normal sense); mansion, large house; public building (e.g. post office); **- garni (meublé),** lodging house

hôtel de ville, *m.* town hall

hôtel-Dieu, *m.* hospital

hôtelier(-ère), *m.* (*f.*) innkeeper

hôtellerie, *f.* inn, hostelry

hôtesse, *f.* hostess; guest; landlady

°**hotte,** *f.* basket (on back)

°**hottée,** *f.* basketful

°**houblon,** *m.* hop(s)

°**houblonnière,** *f.* hop-field

°**houe,** *f.* hoe

°**houer,** *v.t.* to hoe

°**houille,** *f.* (pit) coal; **- blanche,** hydro-electric power

°**houillère,** *f.* coal mine

°**houilleur,** *m.* collier, miner

°**houilleux(-euse),** (*adj.*) carboniferous, coal-bearing

°**houle,** *f.* swell, surge (of sea)

°**houleux(-euse),** (*adj.*) swelling, surging (sea)

°**houppe,** *f.* tuft, bunch (of feathers); powder puff

°**houppelande,** *f.* great-coat

°**houpper,** *v.t.* to comb wool

°**hourra,** *m.* and (*interj.*) hurrah

°**houspiller,** *v.t.* to hustle (someone); to handle roughly (someone); to abuse, to rate (someone)

°**houssaie,** *f.* holly plantation

°**housse,** *f.* covering; furniture cover; dust-sheet

°**houx,** *m.* holly

°**hublot,** *m.* port-hole, scuttle-hole

°**huée,** *f.* booing, hooting, jeers

°**huer,** *v.i.* to shout; to hoot

huile, *f.* oil (general use, salad, etc.); **- de ricin,** castor-oil; **- de foie de morue,** cod-liver oil; **- à graisser,** lubricating oil

huiler, *v.t.* to oil; to lubricate, to grease

huileux(-euse), oily, greasy

huilier, *m.* oil and vinegar stand; cruet

huis, *m.* door (rare); **à - clos,** behind closed doors; in camera (*legal*)

huissier, *m.* usher (in court); process server; bailiff (court)

°**huit,** (adj.) and m. eight; **un huit-reflets,** (fam.) top hat
°**huitaine,** f. about eight (days, etc.); **- de jours,** about a week
huître, f. oyster; (slang) a mug
humain(e), (adj.) human
humaniser, v.t. to humanise, to make human; **s'-,** v.r. to become more sociable
humanitaire, (adj.) humanitarian
humanité, f. humanity; human nature; kindness; humaneness
humble, (adj.) humble
humecter, v.t. to moisten, to damp
humeur, f. humour, mood, temper; disposition
humide, (adj.) moist, damp
humidité, f. moisture, dampness, humidity
humiliant, (adj.) humiliating; mortifying
humiliation, f. humiliation, mortification; affront
humilier, v.t. to humiliate, to humble
hunier, m. topsail
°**huppe,** f. tuft, crest (of bird)
°**hure,** f. head (of pig, boar); a kind of pâté made of potted pig's head
°**hurlement,** m. howl, howling (dog, etc.)
°**hurler,** v.i. to howl; to roar (wind, etc.); to howl (person); to bawl
°**hussard,** m. hussar
°**hutte,** f. hut, shed, cabin, hovel
hybride, m. hybrid, cross
hydraulique, (adj.) hydraulic; f. hydraulics
hydrocéphalie, f. water on the brain
hydrogène, m. hydrogen
hydropisie, f. dropsy (med.)
hyène, f. hyena
hygiène, f. hygiene; **- publique,** public health
hygiénique, hygienic, healthy
hymne, m. national, patriotic song; hymn (eccles.)
hypnotiser, v.t. to hypnotise
hypocondre, m. hypochondriac
hypocondriaque, (adj.) hypo-

chondriacal (having morbid anxiety as to one's health)
hypocrisie, f. hypocrisy; cant
hypocrite, (adj.) hypocritical; m. or f. hypocrite
hypothèque, f. mortgage
hypothéquer, v.t. to mortgage (estate, property)
hypothèse, f. hypothesis, assumption
hypothétique, (adj.) hypothetical
hysope, f. hyssop (bot. herb)
hystérie, f. hysteria; hysterics
hystérique, (adj.) hysterical

I

ïambe, m. iambus
ibérique, (adj.) Iberian
ibis, m. ibis (ornith.)
ici, (adv.) here; **- et là,** here and there; **jusqu' -,** hitherto; **par -,** this way; **d' - peu,** before long
iconomètre (-scope), m. viewmeter (finder)
idéal, (adj.) ideal
idéal(s), m. (pl.) ideal
*****idée,** f. idea; notion; conception; purpose; intention; plan; mind
identification, f. identification
identifier, v.t. to identify
identité, f. identity; **plaque (carte) d' -,** identity disk (card)
idéologique, (adj.) ideological
idiomatique, (adj.) idiomatic
idiome, m. idiom; dialect
idiot, (adj.) idiotic, absurd; senseless
idiot(e), m. (f.) idiot, imbecile; fool; (slang) silly ass
idolâtre, (adj.) idolatrous; m. and f. idolater, idolatress
idole, f. idol
idylle, f. idyll
if, m. yew, yew tree
ignare, m. and f. ignoramus, dunce
ignifuge, (adj.) fire-proof
ignoble, (adj.) ignoble, base, filthy, mean
ignominie, f. shame, ignominy, baseness

ignorance, *f.* ignorance

ignorant, (*adj.*) ignorant; illiterate; unacquainted (with)

ignorer, *v.t.* to be ignorant of; to be unaware of; not to know

île, *f.* island; **les îles Normandes,** the Channel Islands

illégal, (*adj.*) illegal; unlawful

illégitime, (*adj.*) illegitimate; unlawful, unjust

illégitimité, *f.* illegitimacy

illettré, (*adj.*) illiterate, ignorant

illicite, (*adj.*) illicit

illico, (*adv.*) (*slang*) at once; forthwith

illimité, (*adj.*) unlimited, boundless

illisible, (*adj.*) illegible

illumination, *f.* illumination; display of lights

illuminé, (*adj.*) illuminated; enlightened; *m.* (*f.*) crank, fanatic

illuminer, *v.t.* to illuminate; to light up; to enlighten

illusion, *f.* illusion (optical); delusion

illusionner, *v.t.* to delude; **s'-,** *v.r.* to delude oneself

illustration, *f.* illustration (*art.*); illustrating; celebrity

illustre, (*adj.*) illustrious

illustrer, *v.t.* to illustrate (book, etc.); to make illustrious

îlot, *m.* small island

image, *f.* image; likeness; picture; effigy; frame (*cin.*)

imaginaire, (*adj.*) imaginary

imagination, *f.* imagination; fancy

imaginer, *v.t.* to imagine; to conceive; to fancy, invent

imbécile, (*adj.*) imbecile, silly; *m.* and *f.* imbecile

imberbe, (*adj.*) beardless

imbiber, *v.t.* to soak; to imbue; to wet

imbroglio, *m.* confused heap; confused situation

imitateur(-trice), *m.* (*f.*) imitator

imiter, *v.t.* to imitate; to copy; to mimic

immaculé, (*adj.*) immaculate, spotless

immangeable, (*adj.*) uneatable

immanquable, (*adj.*) inevitable

immaturité, *f.* immaturity, unripeness

immédiat, (*adj.*) immediate, instantaneous

immense, (*adj.*) immense, huge

immensité, *f.* vastness, immensity, hugeness

immerger, *v.t.* to immerse

immérité, (*adj.*) undeserved, unjust, unmerited

immeuble, *m.* real estate; premises

immigration, *f.* immigration

imminent, (*adj.*) imminent, impending

immiscer, *v.t.* to introduce; mix up; **s'-,** *v.r.* to interfere (with); to meddle (with)

immobile, (*adj.*) motionless, immovable, unmoved

immobilité, *f.* immobility

immobilier(-ère), (*adj.*) real; immovable; **vente -,** sale of property

immobilisation, *f.* immobilisation; tying up

immobiliser, *v.t.* to stop; to tie up (funds, etc.); to fasten

immodéré, (*adj.*) immoderate

immoler, *v.t.* to sacrifice

immonde, (*adj.*) filthy, unclean, disgusting, foul

immondices, *f. pl.* filth, dirt

immoral, (*adj.*) immoral

immoralité, *f.* immorality

immortalité, *f.* immortality

immortel(le), (*adj.*) immortal, everlasting; **les immortels,** the members of the French Academy

immortelle, *f.* everlasting flower

immuable, (*adj.*) unchangeable

impair, (*adj.*) uneven, odd (of numbers); **un gant -,** an " odd " glove

impardonnable, (*adj.*) unpardonable

imparfait, (*adj.*) incomplete, defective, imperfect

imparfait, *m.* imperfect tense

impartial, (*adj.*) impartial

impartialité, *f.* impartiality

impasse, *f.* blind alley; deadlock

impassible, *(adj.)* unmoved, impassive

impatience, *f.* impatience; restlessness

impatient, *(adj.)* impatient, fidgety, restless

impatienter, *v.t.* to provoke, to put out of patience; **s'-,** *v.r.* to lose patience, to fidget, to fret

impayable, *(adj.)* invaluable, priceless; very funny

impeccable, *(adj.)* faultless, perfectly correct; unimpeachable

impénétrable, *(adj.)* impenetrable, impervious, inscrutable

impénitence, *f.* impenitence

impénitent, *(adj.)* impenitent

impératif(-ive), *(adj.)* imperative

impératrice, *f.* empress

impérial, *(adj.)* imperial

impériale, *f.* top deck of bus, etc.

impérieux(-euse), *(adj.)* imperious, domineering, overbearing

impérissable, *(adj.)* imperishable

impéritie, *f.* incapacity, unskilfulness

imperméable, *(adj.)* waterproof, water-tight; *m.* raincoat, mackintosh

impertinence, *f.* impertinence; insolence; rudeness

impertinent, *(adj.)* impertinent, insolent

imperturbable, *(adj.)* unshaken, imperturbable

impétueux(-euse), *(adj.)* impetuous

impétuosité, *f.* impetuosity, violence, vehemence

impie, *(adj.)* impious, godless, ungodly

impiété, *f.* impiety, godlessness

impitoyable, *(adj.)* pitiless, ruthless, relentless

implacabilité, *f.* implacability

implacable, *(adj.)* implacable

implicite, *(adj.)* implicit

impliquer, *v.t.* to implicate; to imply

implorer, *v.t.* to implore; to supplicate; to beg, beseech

impoli, *(adj.)* impolite, uncivil, rude, discourteous

impolitesse, *f.* incivility, rudeness, impoliteness

impopulaire, *(adj.)* unpopular

importance, *f.* importance, worth, consequence; purport

important, *(adj.)* important, momentous, weighty, essential

importation, *f.* importation; imports

importer, *v.t.* to import; *v.i.* to be of consequence; to matter; **n'importe,** it does not matter

importun, *(adj.)* troublesome, tiresome; ill-timed; *m.* intruder, bore

importuner, *v.t.* to annoy, to pester; to dun, to importunate

imposable, *(adj.)* taxable

imposant, *(adj.)* imposing, impressive, grand

imposé, *(adj.)* imposed, taxed

imposer, *v.t.* to impose; to inflict; to force on; to tax

imposition, *f.* infliction; tax; assessment *(not* imposition meaning punishment)

impossible, *(adj.)* impossible

impossibilité, *f.* impossibility

imposteur, *m.* impostor, cheat, swindler

imposture, *f.* imposture, deception, deceit

impôt, *m.* tax, duty

impraticabilité, *f.* impracticability

impraticable, *(adj.)* impracticable; unfeasible; impassable

imprécis, *(adj.)* inaccurate, vague

imprégner, *v.t.* to impregnate

imprenable, *(adj.)* impregnable

impression, *f.* impression; print, issue; edition; stamping

impressionnable, *(adj.)* impressionable; sensitive, nervous

impressionner, *v.* to impress, to make an impression on

imprévoyance, *f.* improvidence; carelessness; want of forethought

imprévu, *(adj.)* unexpected

imprimé, *m.* printed matter

imprimer, *v.t.* to imprint, to impress; to print; to publish

imprimerie, *f.* printing; printing office or house

imprimeur, *m.* printer

improbabilité, *f.* improbability

improbable, (*adj.*) improbable

improbe, (*adj.*) dishonest

improbité, *f.* dishonesty

impropre, (*adj.*) improper, wrong, unfit, inaccurate

improviser, *v.t.* to extemporise, to improvise

improviste, (à l'), without warning

imprudence, *f.* imprudence

imprudent, (*adj.*) imprudent; heedless, foolhardy, unwise

impudence, *f.* impudence; cheek, effrontery

impudent, (*adj.*) impudent, cheeky, shameless

impudeur, *f.* immodesty, indecency

impudique, (*adj.*) immodest, lewd, unchaste

impuissance, *f.* impotence, inability, incapacity

impuissant, (*adj.*) powerless, unable, ineffectual

impulsion, *f.* impulse, impetus

impunément, (*adv.*) with impunity

impuni, (*adj.*) unpunished

impur, (*adj.*) impure, unclean, lewd, unchaste, adulterated

imputer, *v.t.* to impute; to ascribe

inacceptable, (*adj.*) unacceptable

inaccoutumé, (*adj.*) unaccustomed

inachevé, (*adj.*) unfinished, incomplete

inactif(-ive), (*adj.*) inactive, sluggish; unemployed

inaction, *f.* inaction, inertness

inadmissible, (*adj.*) inadmissible

inadvertence, *f.* oversight; par -, inadvertently

inaltérable, (*adj.*) unchangeable

inanimé, (*adj.*) inanimate, lifeless

inanition, *f.* starvation, inanition

inaperçu, unperceived, unheeded

inapplicable, (*adj.*) inapplicable, unfit

inappréciable, (*adj.*) invaluable, inestimable

inassouvi, (*adj.*) unquenched, unsated

inattaquable, (*adj.*) unassailable

inattendu, (*adj.*) unexpected, unforeseen

inattentif(-ive), (*adj.*) inattentive

inauguration, *f.* opening; inauguration

inaugurer, *v.t.* to inaugurate, to open (exhibition, etc.)

incapable, (*adj.*) incapable, unfit, unable

incapacité, *f.* incapacity, inability

incarcérer, *v.t.* to imprison, to incarcerate

incartade, *f.* thoughtless insult; prank

incendiaire, *m.* and *f.* and (*adj.*) incendiary; bombe -, incendiary bomb

incendie, *m.* fire, conflagration

incendier, *v.t.* to set fire to, to burn out; (*fig.*) to inflame

incertain, (*adj.*) uncertain

incertitude, *f.* uncertainty

incessamment, (*adv.*) at once; immediately; unceasingly

incessible, (*adj.*) untransferable; inalienable

inceste, *m.* incest

incidence, *f.* incidence

incident, *m.* incident; (*adj.*) incidental

incidemment, (*adv.*) incidentally

incinération, *f.* incineration

inciser, *v.t.* to make an incision; to gash

incisif(-ive), (*adj.*) incisive, sharp

inciter, *v.t.* to incite, to urge; to stir up

inclémence, *f.* inclemency

inclément, (*adj.*) inclement, rough

inclinaison, *f.* inclination, incline, gradient

inclination, *f.* inclination; bow, stooping

incliner, *v.t.* to incline, to bend, to bow; **s'-,** *v.r.* to bow; to bow down; to incline, to lean

inclus, *(adj.)* enclosed, included; **ci-inclus,** herein enclosed

inclusif(-ive), *(adj.)* inclusive; enclosing

incohérent, *(adj.)* incoherent

incombustible, *(adj.)* incombustible

incommode, *(adj.)* inconvenient; troublesome; tiresome

incommoder, *v.t.* to inconvenience, to incommode; to annoy; to trouble

incommodité, *f.* inconvenience

incomparable, *(adj.)* matchless; unequalled; incomparable

incompatibilité, *f.* incompatibility

incompatible, *(adj.)* inconsistent, incompatible

incomplet, *(adj.)* incomplete; imperfect

incompréhensible, *(adj.)* incomprehensible; unintelligible

incompris, *(adj.)* unappreciated; misunderstood

inconcevable, *(adj.)* inconceivable; incredible

inconduite, *f.* misconduct; immoral behaviour

inconnu(e), *(adj.)* unknown; *m.* *(f.)* a stranger, a nobody

inconséquence, *f.* inconsequence, inconsistency, indiscretion

inconséquent, *(adj.)* inconsequent; inconsistent

inconsidéré, *(adj.)* unconsidered; hasty, incautious (inconsiderate in French would have another rendering, e.g. **qui manque d'égards**)

inconsolable, *(adj.)* inconsolable; disconsolate

inconstant, *(adj.)* inconstant, fickle; unsteady

incontestable, *(adj.)* indisputable; unquestionable

incontinence, *f.* incontinence

incontinent, *(adj.)* incontinent; *(adv.)* at once

inconvenance, *f.* impropriety; unseemliness

inconvenant, *(adj.)* unseemly, unbecoming, shocking

inconvénient, *m.* disadvantage; inconvenience; drawback; objection; harm

incorrect, *(adj.:)* incorrect, inaccurate; unseemly (behaviour)

incorrigible, *(adj.)* incorrigible

incrédule, *(adj.)* incredulous, unbelieving

incrédulité, *f.* incredulity, unbelief

incriminer, *v.t.* to incriminate, to impeach

incroyable, *(adj.)* incredible, past belief; astounding

inculpé(e), *m.* *(f.)* accused; defendant

inculquer, *v.t.* to instil, to inculcate

inculte, *(adj.)* uncultivated (land); unkempt (hair, etc.)

incurable, *(adj.)* incurable

incurie, *f.* carelessness

incursion, *f.* inroad, incursion

indécence, *f.* indecency, immodesty

indécent, *(adj.)* indecent, improper; immodest

indéchiffrable, *(adj.)* undecipherable

indécis, *(adj.)* unsettled; undecided; doubtful, vague

indécision, *f.* indecision; uncertainty

indécrottable, *(adj.)* uncleanable; incorrigible

indéfini, *(adj.)* indefinite; unlimited; undefined

indéfinissable, *(adj.)* undefinable; nondescript

indélicat, *(adj.)* indelicate; coarse; dishonest; unscrupulous

indemniser, *v.t.* to indemnify

indemnité, *f.* indemnity

indépendance, *f.* independence

indépendant, *(adj.)* independent

indescriptible, *(adj.)* indescribable

index, *m.* forefinger; index finger; index (book)

indicateur(-trice), *m.* (*f.*) time-table; guide (railway); (*adj.*) indicating; **poteau -**, signpost

indice, *m.* sign; token, mark

indicible, (*adj.*) unspeakable; inexpressible

indiciblement, unspeakably

indifférence, *f.* indifference, unconcern

indifférent, (*adj.*) indifferent, unconcerned

indigence, *f.* poverty; indigence

indigène, (*adj.*) indigenous; native; *m.* and *f.* native (of foreign country or colony)

indigent, (*adj.*) poor, needy, poverty-stricken

indigeste, (*adj.*) indigestible; undigested

indigestion, *f.* indigestion

indigne, (*adj.*) unworthy

indigné, (*adj.*) shocked, indignant

indigner, *v.t.* to rouse the indignation of; to excite; **s'-**, *v.r.* to be angry; to be exasperated

indiquer, *v.t.* to indicate; to point out, to show; to inform

indirect, (*adj.*) indirect

indiscret(-ète), (*adj.*) indiscreet; inconsiderate; inquisitive

indiscrétion, *f.* indiscretion; imprudence; indiscreetness

indiscutable, (*adj.*) unquestionable; incontestable; indisputable

indispensable, (*adj.*) indispensable

indisponible, (*adj.*) unavailable

indisposé, (*adj.*) unwell, poorly

indisposer, *v.t.* to make somebody unwell; to prejudice; to set against

indisposition, *f.* indisposition, slight illness

individu, *m.* individual, person, fellow (used slightingly)

indivisé, (*adj.*) undivided

indivisible, (*adj.*) inseparable; indivisible

in-dix-huit, (*adj.*) and *m.* decimo-octavo

indocile, (*adj.*) unmanageable, unruly, disobedient

indolent, (*adj.*) lazy, indolent

indomptable, (*adj.*) unconquerable; untamable; indomitable

indubitable, (*adj.*) undoubted

induction, *f.* inference, induction; **bobine d'-**, induction coil

induire, *v.t.* to lead, to induce; to infer

indulgence, *f.* indulgence; leniency; forbearance

indulgent, (*adj.*) indulgent; lenient, forbearing

industrie, *f.* industry; activity; industry (trade, manufacture)

industriel(le), (*adj.*) industrial; *m.* manufacturer; industrialist

industrieux(-euse), industrious; active, busy

inébranlable, (*adj.*) immovable; solid; unshakable; firm (friendship, etc.); steadfast

inédit, (*adj.*) unpublished; new, original

ineffaçable, (*adj.*) ineffaceable (mark); indelible

inefficace, (*adj.*) ineffectual; inefficacious

inégal, (*adj.*) unequal; uneven (ground)

inepte, (*adj.*) inept, foolish, silly

inépuisable, (*adj.*) inexhaustible

inertie, *f.* inertia; sluggishness

inespéré, (*adj.*) unexpected; unhoped for

inévitable, (*adj.*) unavoidable; inevitable

inexact, (*adj.*) inaccurate; incorrect; inexact; unpunctual

inexactitude, *f.* inaccuracy; inexactitude; unpunctuality

inexorable, (*adj.*) inexorable, unrelenting

inexplicable, (*adj.*) inexplicable; unaccountable

inexprimable, (*adj.*) inexpressible

infaillibilité, *f.* infallibility

infaillible, (*adj.*) infallible

infaisable, (*adj.*) impracticable; unfeasible

infamant, (*adj.*) defamatory

infâme, (*adj.*) infamous; foul; unspeakable

infamie, *f.* infamy; dishonour

infanterie, *f.* infantry
infatigable, *(adj.)* indefatigable
infect, *(adj.)* foul
infecter, *v.t.* to infect; pollinate
infectieux(-euse), *(adj.)* infectious
infection, *f.* infection
inférieur, *(adj.)* inferior; lower (in amount); poor (quality); inferior, lower (rank)
infériorité, *f.* inferiority
infernal, *(adj.)* infernal; devilish
infidèle, *(adj.)* unfaithful; false, faithless; dishonest (employee)
s'infiltrer, *v.r.* to infiltrate, seep in
infime, *(adj.)* lowest; minute, tiny
infini, *(adj.)* infinite; boundless (space, etc.); endless
infiniment, *(adv.)* infinitely; exceedingly; ever so much
infirme, *(adj.)* disabled; crippled; infirm; *m.* and *f.* invalid; cripple
infirmerie, *f.* infirmary, hospital; sick-room
infirmier, *m.* hospital attendant; male nurse; medical orderly *(mil.)*
infirmière, *f.* hospital nurse; sick nurse
infirmité, *f.* infirmity; disability
inflammation, *f.* inflammation
infliger, *v.t.* to inflict
influence, *f.* influence; authority; power
influencer, *v.t.* to influence; to put pressure on
influent, *(adj.)* influential
influenza, *f.* influenza
informateur(-trice), *m.* (*f.*) informant
informatif(-ive), informatory, informative
information, *f.* information; enquiry (legal); preliminary investigation (of a case); **bulletin d'informations,** news bulletin
informer, *v.t.* to inform (somebody of something); to acquaint someone with a fact; **s'- (auprès de),** *v.r.* to make enquiries (of someone)
infortune, *f.* misfortune, calamity

infortuné, *(adj.)* unfortunate, unlucky
infraction, *f.* infringement (of rights); breach (of law)
infranchissable, impassable (barrier); insuperable (difficulty)
infructueux(-euse), *(adj.)* unfruitful (land); unavailing (efforts); unprofitable (investment, etc.)
infus, *(adj.)* innate, inborn
ingénieur, *m.* engineer
ingénieux(-euse), *(adj.)* ingenious, clever
ingénu, *(adj.)* artless, simple, ingenuous
ingrat, *(adj.)* ungrateful, barren
ingratitude, *f.* ingratitude; thanklessness (of task)
inhabité, *(adj.)* uninhabited
inhospitalier(-ère), *(adj.)* inhospitable
inhumain, *(adj.)* inhuman
inimaginable, *(adj.)* unimaginable
inimitable, *(adj.)* inimitable; matchless (wit, etc.)
inimitié, *f.* enmity; hostility
inintelligible, *(adj.)* unintelligible
ininterrompu, *(adj.)* uninterrupted; unbroken
iniquité, *f.* iniquity
initial(-aux), *(adj.)* initial (cost, etc.)
initiale, *f.* initial letter
initier, *v.t.* to initiate
injure, *f.* wrong; injury; insult, abuse
injurieux(-euse), insulting; abusive
injuste, *(adj.)* unjust; unfair
injustice, *f.* injustice, unfairness
inné, *(adj.)* innate, inborn
innocence, *f.* innocence; guiltlessness; artlessness; simplicity
innocent, *(adj.)* innocent; guiltless; simple; artless
innombrable, *(adj.)* innumerable; countless
innovation, *f.* innovation
in-octavo, *m.* octavo
inoculation, *f.* inoculation

inodore, (adj.) odourless, scentless (flower)

inondation, f. inundation; flood

inonder, v.t. to inundate; to flood; to overwhelm (with enquiries); to deluge

inopiné, (adj.) sudden, unexpected; unforeseen

inouï, (adj.) unheard of; extraordinary; outrageous

inoxydable, (adj.) rust-proof, stainless

in-quarto, m. quarto

inquiet(-ète), (adj.) anxious, uneasy; fidgety, restless; worried

inquiétant, (adj.) disquieting, disturbing

inquiéter, v.t. to alarm; to make uneasy; to trouble (somebody); **s'-** (de), v.r. to become anxious; to worry (about)

inquiétude, f. anxiety, uneasiness, concern; restlessness

inquisiteur, m. inquisitor

insalubre, (adj.) unhealthy

insalubrité, f. unhealthiness, insanitariness

insatiable, (adj.) insatiable

inscription, f. writing down; registration; inscription

inscrire, v.t. to write down, inscribe; to register (name); to enter (one's name); to enroll (for a course of study)

inscrutable, (adj.) unfathomable, inscrutable

insecte, m. insect

insécurité, f. insecurity

insensé, (adj.) senseless; foolish (action); mad, insane

insensible, (adj.) insensible; unfeeling; indifferent; gradual

inséparable, (adj.) inseparable

insérer, v.t. to insert (an advertisement, clause, etc.)

insigne, (adj.) notorious; arrant

insignifiant, (adj.) insignificant

insinuation, f. insinuation; innuendo; introduction

insinuer, v.t. to insinuate; to hint at; to insert (gently)

insister, v.t. to insist, to lay stress (on)

insobriété, f. intemperance

insolation, f. sunstroke

insolence, f. insolence; impertinence; impudence

insolent, (adj.) insolent; impertinent; impudent

insoluble, (adj.) unsolvable (problem); insoluble

insolvable, (adj.) insolvent

insomnie, f. sleeplessness

insonore, (adj.) sound-proof

insouciant, (adj.) careless; unconcerned

insoucieux(-euse), (adj.) heedless

insoutenable, (adj.) untenable (opinion); indefensible; unbearable

inspecteur(-trice), m. (f.) inspector; inspectress; superintendent; overseer (of works)

inspectorat, m. inspectorate, body of inspectors

inspiration, f. inspiration; suggestion; inhaling

inspirer, v.t. to inspire, to inhale

installation, f. installation (of a bishop, etc.); setting up (of house); arrangements; establishment

installations, f. pl. fittings

installer, v.t. to install; to fit, equip (factory); **s'-**, v.r. to settle down; to install oneself

instamment, (adv.) earnestly; urgently

instance, f. entreaty; solicitation

instant, (adj.) urgent; m. moment, instant

instantané, (adj.) instantaneous; m. un -, a snapshot (phot.)

instar de (à l'), (prep.) after the manner of

instaurer, v.t. to found, to set up

instinct, m. instinct

instinctif(-ive), (adj.) instinctive

instituer, v.t. to institute; to establish, to set up

institut, m. institute, institution

instituteur, m. schoolmaster; schoolteacher (elementary)

institution, f. establishment (educational); boarding school; academy

institutrice, *f.* schoolmistress; governess

instructif(-ive), instructive

instruction, *f.* instruction; education; schooling; training (of troops); preliminary investigation (of a law case); **juge d'-,** examining magistrate

instruire, *v.t.* to teach, educate, instruct; to train (troops), to investigate (a law case)

instrument, *m.* instrument; implement, tool

insu de (à l'), without the knowledge of

insuccès, *m.* failure; miscarriage (of plan)

insuffisant, *(adj.)* insufficient; inadequate

insulaire, *(adj.)* insular; *m.* and *f.* islander

insulte, *f.* insult

insulter, *v.t.* to insult, to affront

insupportable, *(adj.)* insufferable; unbearable; intolerable

insurgé(e), *m.* (*f.*) insurgent

(s')insurger, *v.r.* to rebel; to rise in rebellion

intact, *(adj.)* intact; untouched; undamaged

intaille, *f.* intaglio

intangible, *(adj.)* intangible

intarissable, *(adj.)* inexhaustible; unfailing

intégral(-aux), *(adj.)* whole, entire, integral

intégralement, *(adv.)* wholly, entirely, fully

intègre, *(adj.)* upright, honest

intellect, *m.* intellect, understanding

intellectuel(le), intellectual

intelligence, *f.* understanding; intelligence, intellect

intelligent, *(adj.)* intelligent; sharp; clever

intelligible, *(adj.)* intelligible

intempérance, *f.* intemperance

intempérie, *f.* inclemency (weather)

intenable, *(adj.)* untenable

intendance, *f.* stewardship; managership; commissariat *(mil.)*; direction (managing)

intendant, *m.* steward; manager; bailiff

intense, *(adj.)* intense; severe; intensive

intensif(-ive), *(adj.)* intensive

intensité, *f.* intensity

intenter (un procès contre), *v.t.* to bring (an action against)

*****intention,** *f.* intention; purpose; design

interallié, *(adj.)* inter-allied

intercaler, *v.t.* to insert

interdiction, *f.* prohibition, forbidding

interdire, *v.t.* to forbid

interdit, disconcerted; abashed; speechless; stunned; overwhelmed; **- de séjour,** forbidden to enter a particular area

interdit, *m.* interdict; person interdicted

intéressant, *(adj.)* interesting; deserving help, pity

intéressé, interested, having an interest in, concerned; *m.* and *f.* interested party

intéresser, *v.i.* to interest; to concern; to affect

*****intérêt,** *m.* interest; concern; **avoir un - en jeu,** to have an axe to grind

intérieur, *(adj.)* interior, inner, internal; *m.* inside; home; private life

intermédiaire, *(adj.)* intermediary, intervening; *m.* and *f.* agent; go-between; middleman; intermediary

interminable, *(adj.)* endless

internat, *m.* boarding-school; resident medical student

interne, *m.* and *f.* boarder (at school); **- d'hôpital,** house-surgeon

interplanétaire, *(adj.)* interplanetary (society, rocket, etc.)

interprète, *m.* and *f.* interpreter

interpréter, *v.t.* to interpret

interrogation *f.* **(point d'),** question mark

interrogatoire, *m.* examination (of defendant, witness, etc.)

interroger, *v.t.* to question; to examine, to interrogate (witness)

interrompre, *v.t.* to interrupt; to intercept; to cut short (conversation)

interrupteur, *m.* switch (*elect.*)

intervalle, *m.* interval; distance (between); period (of time)

intervenir, *v.i.* to intervene; to interpose; to interfere

interviewer, *v.t.* to interview; *m.* interviewer

intestat, (*adj.*) intestate

intestins, *m. pl.* intestines; bowels

intime, (*adj.*) intimate; close (friend); interior (home)

intimé(e), *m.* (*f.*) defendant

intimer, *v.t.* to intimate

intimider, *v.t.* to frighten, intimidate

intimité, *f.* intimacy

intitulé, *m.* title (of book, etc.)

intituler, *v.t.* to entitle; give a title to

intolérable, (*adj.*) insufferable; intolerable; unbearable

intolérant, (*adj.*) intolerant

intraitable, (*adj.*) untractable; unmanageable; beyond treatment (*mod.*)

intransigeant, (*adj.*) uncompromising; peremptory; "diehard"

intransigeance, *f.* intolerance; intransigence; uncompromising attitude

intrépide, (*adj.*) bold, dauntless, intrepid

intrépidité, *f.* fearlessness, boldness

intrigue, *f.* intrigue; plot; scheme

intriguer, *v.t.* to puzzle; to intrigue; *v.i.* to plot

introduction, *f.* introduction; preamble; introducing; inserting

introduire, *v.t.* to introduce; put in, to insert; to show in

introuvable, (*adj.*) untraceable; undiscoverable; not to be found; matchless

introverti(e), (*adj.*) and *m.* (*f.*) introvert

intrus(e), (*adj.*) intruding; *m.* (*f.*) intruder; interloper

intuition, *f.* intuition

inusité, (*adj.*) unusual; not in general use

inutile, (*adj.*) useless, unavailing; vain (effort)

invalide, (*adj.*) invalid, infirm; null and void; *m.* and *f.* invalid (person)

invalidité, *f.* infirmity; disability; invalidity

invariable, (*adj.*) invariable, unvarying

invasion, *f.* invasion; inroad

inventaire, *m.* inventory; stock-taking (*commerce*)

inventer, *v.t.* to invent, to discover; to devise; to make up (story)

inventeur, *m.* inventor, discoverer (of process, etc.)

invention, *f.* invention; contrivance; lie

inverse, (*adj.*) inverse, opposite; *m.* opposite, reverse

investir, *v.t.* to invest, to surround (position)

invétéré, (*adj.*) inveterate; confirmed

invincibilité, *f.* invincibility

invincible, (*adj.*) invincible, unconquerable; insurmountable

inviolable, (*adj.*) inviolable

invisible, (*adj.*) invisible

invité(e), *m.* (*f.*) guest

inviter, *v.t.* to invite; (general sense) to request (someone to do something)

involontaire, (*adj.*) involuntary, unintentional

invoquer, *v.t.* to call up; to invoke; call forth

invraisemblable, (*adj.*) improbable, unlikely

invraisemblance, *f.* improbability

iode, *m.* iodine

iris, *m.* iris (flower); rainbow colours

irlandais, (*adj.*) Irish

ironie, *f.* irony

ironique, (*adj.*) ironical

irréconciliable, *(adj.)* irreconcilable

irréfléchi, *(adj.)* thoughtless

irrégularité, *f.* irregularity; unpunctuality

irrégulier(-ère), *(adj.)* irregular; unpunctual

irrémédiable, *(adj.)* irreparable

irrésistible, *(adj.)* irresistible

irrésolu, *(adj.)* irresolute, wavering; unsolved

irrésolution, *f.* indecision

irresponsable, *(adj.)* irresponsible

irrévocable, *(adj.)* irrevocable; binding

irrigateur, *m.* hose (garden, street); syringe *(med.)*

irrigation, *f.* irrigation; washing out (wound, etc.); douche

irritable, *(adj.)* irritable, touchy

irritant, *(adj.)* irritating; *m.* irritant *(med.)*

irriter, *v.t.* to irritate; s'-, *v.r.* to grow angry; to become influenced

Isabelle, *(adj.)* dove-coloured

isolé, *(adj.)* isolated, lonely, remote

isoler, *v.t.* to isolate; to insulate *(elect.);* bouteille isolante, vacuum flask

israélite, *(adj.)* Jewish, Israelitish; *m.* and *f.* Israelite, Jew(ess)

issu, *(adj.)* descended from

issue, *f.* issue, end; conclusion

isthme, *m.* isthmus

italiques, *m. pl.* italics

item, *(adv.)* likewise, also

itinéraire, *m.* itinerary; route; guide-book

ivoire, *m.* ivory

ivre, *(adj.)* drunk; ivre-mort, dead drunk

ivrogne, *m.* drunkard

ivrognerie, *f.* drunkenness

J

jabot, *m.* crop (of bird); frill, ruffle

jaboter, *v.i.* to gabble; to chatter, jabber

jacasser, *v.i.* to chatter

jacasserie, *f.* chatter; idle talk

jachère, *f.* fallow, unploughed land

jacinthe, *f.* hyacinth; - des bois, bluebell

jacobée, *f.* ragwort *(bot.)*

Jacobin, *m.* Jacobin *(eccl., and French history)*

jactance, *f.* bragging; boastfulness

jade, *m.* jade (stone)

jadis, *(adv.)* formerly; once; of old

jaillir, *v.i.* to spring up; to gush (out); to spout (up or out); to spurt (blood)

jais, *m.* jet (mineral)

jalon, *m.* pole, stake; surveying-staff; landmark

jalonner, *v.t.* to set out, stake out; peg out (claim)

jalouser, *v.t.* to envy

jalousie, *f.* jealousy; venetian blind

jaloux(-se), *(adj.)* jealous

*jamais, *(adv.)* ever; (ne) ... -, never

*jambe, *f.* leg

jambon, *m.* ham

jambonneau, *m.* knuckle of ham

jante, *f.* rim (of cycle or car wheel)

janvier, *m.* January

japonais, *(adj.)* Japanese

jappement, *m.* yelping, yapping

japper, *v.i.* to yelp, yap

jaquette, *f.* tail, morning coat; jacket (lady's)

jardin, *m.* garden; - potager, kitchen garden

jardinage, *m.* gardening

jardiner, *v.i.* to garden

jardinet, *m.* small garden

jardinier(ère), *m. (f.)* gardener

jardinière, *f.* flower stand

jargon, *m.* jargon, slang, cant

jargonner, *v.i.* to talk gibberish, jargon

jarnac, *m.* (used with coup de =treacherous blow; stab in the back)

jarre, *f.* earthenware jar

jarret, *m.* bend of the knee; hock (horse); knuckle of veal, etc.; shin of beef

jarretelle, *f.* suspender (stocking, etc.)

jarretière, garter; **ordre de la -,** Order of the Garter

jaser, *v.i.* to chatter; to gossip; to tell tales

jasmin, *m.* jasmine

jasper, *v.t.* to marble, to mottle

jatte, *f.* bowl; platter

jauge, *f.* gauge; tonnage (ship)

jauger, *v.t.* to gauge, measure the capacity (tonnage, etc.)

jaunâtre, *(adj.)* yellowish

jaune, *(adj.)* yellow; *m.* yellow; yolk of egg; **livre-,** Blue Book

jaunir, *v.t.* and *v.i.* to yellow; to turn yellow

jaunisse, *f.* jaundice

javanais, *m.* and *(adj.)* Javanese

Javel (eau de), *f.* bleaching fluid, disinfectant

javelle, *f.* loose sheaf; swath

javelot, *m.* javelin

jésuite, *m.* Jesuit (religious order)

jet, *m.* throw; cast; jet (water, etc.)

jetée, *f.* pier, jetty

***jeter,** *v.t.* to throw, fling; cast

***(se) jeter,** *v.r.* to throw oneself

jeton, *m.* counter, token

***jeu(x),** *m.* game, play, sport; gaming, gambling

jeudi, *m.* Thursday; **- saint,** Maundy Thursday

jeun, (à) *(adv. phrase)* fasting

jeune, *(adj.)* young; youthful; **jeunes gens,** young people

jeûne, *m.* fast, fasting

jeune-premier, *m.* juvenile lead

jeune-première, *f.* leading lady

jeûner, *v.i.* to fast

jeunesse, *f.* youth; boyhood; girlhood

joaillerie, *f.* jewellery, trinkets

joaillier, *m.* jeweller

jobard, *m.(slang)* a mug; easy mark

jobarder, *v.t.* to dupe; to take somebody in

jocrisse, *m.* simpleton

***joie,** *f.* joy; delight; gladness

joindre, *v.t.* to join; to bring together; to add to; **se -,** *v.r.* to join, unite

joint, *(adj.)* joined, united; *m.* join, joint *(not* of meat)

jointure, *f.* join, joint

joli, *(adj.)* pretty, nice; good-looking

joliment, *(adv.)* prettily, finely, nicely; very, awfully

jonc, *m.* rush *(bot.)*

joncher, *v.t.* to strew, spread over

jonction, *f.* junction, joining

jongler, *v.i.* to juggle

jongleur, *m.* mountebank (ancient); juggler (modern)

joue, *f.* cheek

jouer, *v.i.* and *v.t.* to play; to gamble; to trick, make a fool of someone; **se -,** *v.r.* (de quelqu'un) to make game (of someone)

jouet, *m.* toy, plaything

joueur(-euse), *m.* *(f.)* player; gambler

joufflu, *(adj.)* chubby-cheeked

joug, *m.* yoke

jouir (de), *v.i.* to enjoy; to be in the enjoyment (of)

jouissance, *f.* enjoyment; possession; use (of)

joujou(x), *m.* plaything, toy

***jour,** *m.* day; daylight; **faire -,** to dawn; **au - le -,** from hand to mouth; **de nos jours,** nowadays

journal(-aux), *m.* newspaper, journal; day-book *(accountancy)*; **- de navigation,** log-book *(naut.)*; **marchand de journaux,** newsagent

journalier, *(adj.)* daily (task, etc.); everyday (happening)

journalier(-ère), *m.* *(f.)* day-labourer

journaliste, *(adj.)* and *m.* *(f.)* journalist(ic)

journée, *f.* day(time); day's work; **toute la -,** all day long

journellement, *(adv.)* daily; every day

joute, *f.* tilt, joust

jouvence, *f.* youth

jovial, *(adj.)* jolly, merry, breezy

jovialité, *f.* jollity, breeziness

joyau(x), *m.* jewel

joyeux(-euse), *(adj.)* merry; glad

jubilant, (*adj.*) jubilant; in high glee

jubiler, *v.i.* to exult

jucher, *v.i.* to perch; to go to roost

juchoir, *m.* perch; hen-roost

judiciaire, (*adj.*) judicial, judiciary

judicieux(-euse), (*adj.*) judicious

juge, *m.* judge; **- d'instruction,** examining magistrate; **- de paix,** police court magistrate

jugement, *m.* judgment; decision, award; sentence (criminal courts); opinion

juger, *v.t.* to judge; to try (a case); to pass sentence on somebody; to adjudicate

jugulaire, *f.* jugular vein

juif(-ive), *m.* (*f.*) Jew(ess)

juif(-ive), (*adj.*) Jewish

juillet, *m.* July

juin, *m.* June

juiverie, *f.* the Jews; Jewry; sharp practice.

jujube, *m.* lozenge

julienne (potage, *m.*) *f.* vegetable soup

jumeau(-elle), *m.* (*f.*) twin; **lits jumeaux,** twin beds

jumeler, *v.t.* to pair; to arrange in pairs

jumelles, *f. pl.* binoculars; opera-glasses

jument, *f.* mare

jupe, *f.* skirt (woman's)

jupon, *m.* petticoat; underskirt

juré, *m.* juryman

jurer, *v.t.* to swear; promise; to use bad language

juridiction, *f.* jurisdiction

juridique, (*adj.*) juridical, legal

jurisprudence, *f.* statute law

juron, *m.* oath, swear-word

jury, *m.* jury

jus, *m.* juice, gravy

jusque, (*prep.*) till, as far as, up to; **jusqu'ici,** up to now; **jusqu'à ce que,** (*conj.*) till, until

juste, (*adj.*) just, right, exact; **chanter juste (faux),** to sing in (out of) tune; **je ne sais pas au**

juste, I don't exactly know

justesse, *f.* accuracy, correctness

justice, *f.* justice; legal proceedings; **palais de -,** law courts

justificatif(-ive), (*adj.*) justificatory

justification, *f.* justification, proof

justifier, *v.t.* to justify, prove, warrant

jute, *m.* jute

juteux(-euse), juicy

juvénile, (*adj.*) youthful

juxtaposer, *v.t.* to put side by side

juxtaposition, *f.* juxtaposition

K

kakatoès, *m.* cockatoo

kaléidoscope, *m.* kaleidoscope

kangourou, *m.* kangaroo

képi, *m.* soldier's cap (French army).

kermesse, *f.* village fair

k(h)aki, *m.* and (*adj. inv.*) khaki

kilogramme, *m.* measure of weight (kilo = 2·2 lb.)

kilomètre, *m.* measure of distance (1,093 yards)

kiosque, *m.* kiosk, bandstand; newspaper stall; flower stand in Paris

klaxon, *m.* hooter; klaxon (of car)

knout, *m.* knout; Russian scourge

krach, *m.* financial failure, or smash

kyrielle, *f.* litany, string (of words, etc.)

kyste, *m.* cyst; ganglion

kystique, (*adj.*) cystic (tumour)

L

la, (*def. art. f.*) the

là, (*adv.*) there; **là-bas,** (*adv.*) over there, yonder

labeur, *m.* labour; toil, hard work

labial, (*adj.*) labial

laboratoire, *m.* laboratory

laborieux(-euse), (adj.) hard-working, laborious; arduous, hard (work)

labour, m. tilling; ploughing

labourable, (adj.) arable

labourer, v.t. to till, to plough

laboureur, m. ploughman; farm labourer

labyrinthe, m. labyrinth; maze

lac, m. lake

lacer, v.t. to lace up (a shoe)

lacérer, v.t. to lacerate, slash

lacet, m. lace; snare

lâchage, m. dropping (of bomb from aeroplane)

lâche, (adj.) cowardly; dastardly; m. coward

lâcher, v.t. to let loose; to release; to loosen

lâcheté, f. cowardice, cowardliness

laconique, (adj.) laconic

lacrymogène, (adj.) tear-producing; **gaz -**, tear-gas

lacté, (adj.) milky; **la Voie lactée**, the Milky Way

lacune, f. gap (in text); break (in succession); blank (in memory)

là-dedans, (adv.) in there; within

là-dehors, (adv.) without; outside

là-dessous, (adv.) under that; under there

là-dessus, (adv.) on that; thereupon

ladre, (adj.) miserly, stingy; m. skinflint

lagune; f. lagoon

laid, (adj.) ugly; unsightly; plain (of person)

laideur, f. ugliness; plainness (of features)

lainage, m. woollen goods

laine, f. wool

lainerie, f. manufacture of woollen goods

laïque, m. and f. layman, laywoman; (adj.) secular, lay

laisse, f. leash; lead

laisser, v.t. to let, allow; to leave (something in a place)

laisser-aller, m. free-and-easiness

laisser-faire, m. non-interference

laissez-passer, m. pass, permit

lait, m. milk

laitage, m. dairy produce; milk foods, diet

laiterie, f. dairy

laiteux(-euse), milky

laitier(-ère), m. (f.) milkman (dairymaid)

laiton, m. brass

laitue, f. lettuce

lambeau, m. shred; scrap; **en lambeaux**, in tatters

lambin, m. dawdler

lame, f. blade (razor-blade, etc.)

lamentable, (adj.) lamentable; deplorable (accident, etc.); pitiful, pitiable

lamenter, v.t. to lament; to mourn; se -, v.r. to mourn; to whine; to bewail

laminer, v.t. to flatten; to roll (metal)

laminoir, m. rolling mill

lampe, f. lamp (general use)

lampée, f. gulp; draught (of wine, etc.)

lampion, m. light (for illuminations); Chinese lantern

lampisterie, f. lamp-room; lamp trade

lance, f. spear; harpoon; water-hose nozzle

lance-flammes, m. flame-thrower

lance-fusées, m. rocket-gun (anti-aircraft)

lance-torpille, m. torpedo-tube

lancer, v.t. to throw; fling; to hurl; to set going; to launch (a ship); se -, v.r. to rush forward; to dash forward

lancette, f. lancet (surgeon's knife)

lancier, m. lancer (cavalry)

lande, f. heath; moor (sandy)

langage, m. language; speech (of the individual); talk, style of speech

langoureux(-euse), (adj.) languorous, languid

langouste, f. crayfish (very similar to a lobster)

*langue, *f.* tongue; language (of a people); - maternelle, mother tongue

langueur, *f.* languor; listlessness

languir, *v.i.* to pine; to languish

lanière, *f.* thong

lanterne, *f.* lantern

laper, *v.t.* to lap up (milk)

lapider, *v.t.* to throw stones at (someone)

lapin(e), *m.* (*f.*) rabbit (doe)

laps, *m.* a lapse; space of time

laquais, *m.* footman, flunkey

laque, *f.* lac, shellac

laquer, *v.t.* to lacquer; to japan

larcin, *m.* larceny, petty theft

lard, *m.* bacon, pork

larder, *v.t.* to lard

*large, (*adj.*) broad, wide, extensive; generous, liberal (views); abundant; large; le -, the open sea

largement, (*adv.*) extensively, largely, widely, amply; generously, liberally

largesse, *f.* liberality; money bestowed

largeur, *f.* breadth, width

larme, *f.* tear; pleurer à chaudes larmes, to weep bitterly

larmoyer, *v.i.* to weep, to shed tears, to whimper, to snivel

larron, *m.* thief; pilferer

larve, *f.* larva; grub

larynx, *m.* larynx

las(se), (*adj.*) tired, weary

lascif(-ive), (*adj.*) lascivious, lustful

lasser, *v.t.* to tire, to weary, to fatigue; se -, *v.r.* to get tired, to grow weary

latéral, (*adj.*) lateral

*latin, (*adj.*) Latin; le quartier -, the Latin (students') quarter of Paris

latitude, *f.* latitude (*geog.*); room, space; freedom (behaviour, etc.)

latrines, *f. pl.* latrines; privy

latte, *f.* lath

lauréat, *m.* laureate

laurier, *m.* laurel; (*fig.*) honour (generally used in plural)

lavabo, *m.* wash-basin; wash-stand; water-closet

lavage, *m.* washing

lavande, *f.* lavender

lavandière, *f.* washerwoman; laundress

lave, *f.* lava

lavement, *m.* enema (*med.*)

laver, *v.t.* to wash; to wash away; to bathe

laveur(-euse), *m.* (*f.*) washer (washerwoman)

lavis, *m.* colour-wash

lavoir, *m.* washing place

laxatif, *m.* laxative

lazaret, *m.* quarantine hospital

le, (*def. art. m.*) the

lécher, *v.t.* to lick, to lap

leçon, *f.* lesson; - de choses, object lesson

lecteur(-trice), *m.* (*f.*) reader

lecture, *f.* reading

ledit, ladite, the said ...

légal, (*adj.*) legal, lawful

légaliser, *v.t.* to legalise

légat, *m.* legate

légataire, *m.* and *f.* legatee (under will)

légation, *f.* legation (diplomatic)

légendaire, (*adj.*) legendary, fabulous

légende, *f.* legend, myth

léger(-ère), (*adj.*) light; slight; inconsiderate (conduct); flighty; unimportant; soft, gentle

légèrement, (*adv.*) lightly; loosely; slightly; softly; delicately

légèreté, *f.* lightness; inconsiderateness; nimbleness (movement); thoughtlessness

légion, *f.* legion; host; multitude

légionnaire, *m.* legionary; member of the order Legion of Honour; soldier in the Foreign Legion

législateur, *m.* legislator; law-giver

législatif(-ive), (*adj.*) legislative

législation, *f.* legislation; law(s)

légitime, (*adj.*) legitimate; lawful; justifiable

légitimer, *v.t.* to legitimise; to justify; to recognise

legs, *m.* legacy, bequest

léguer, *v.t.* to bequeath; to leave (property, money, etc.)

légume, *m.* vegetable

légumes (grosses), *f. pl. (slang)* the big-wigs; important people

lendemain, *m.* next day, day after

lent, *(adj.)* slow; tardy, backward; dull

lenteur, *f.* slowness; delay; sluggishness

lentille, *f.* lentil; lens

léopard, *m.* leopard

lèpre, *f.* leprosy

lépreux(-euse), *(adj.)* leprous; *m.* (*f.*) leper

lequel, *(pron.)* who(m), which (one)

lèse-majesté, *f.* high treason

lésine, *f.* stinginess

lésiner, *v.i.* to pinch and scrape; to be stingy, mean

lessive, *f.* lye; soiled linen; **faire la -,** to do the washing

lessiver, *v.t.* to wash and boil; to wash in lye

lest, *m.* ballast

leste, *(adj.)* lively, brisk, agile, nimble, light-footed

*lettre, *f.* letter (of alphabet); letter, note; learning; letters; literature; **homme de lettres,** man of letters

lettré, *(adj.)* learned; literate

leur, *(poss. adj.)* their

leur, *(pers. pron. invar.)* to them

leurrer, *v.t.* to lure; to decoy; **se -,** *v.r.* to delude oneself

levage, *m.* raising; lifting

levain, *m.* leaven

levant, *m.* East; Levant; *(adj.)* rising

levée, *f.* levy; rising; collection; **- postale,** collection of letters from post-box

lever, *v.t.* to lift, to lift up; to raise; to elevate; to set up; to levy; to weigh (anchor); to abolish; **se -,** *v.r.* to rise; to get up; to stand up

lever, *m.* rising (of the sun)

levier, *m.* lever

lèvre, *f.* lip

lévrier, *m.* greyhound

levure, *f.* yeast

lexique, *m.* lexicon; dictionary (abridged)

lézard, *m.* lizard

lézarde, *f.* crevice, crack

liaison, *f.* connection; joining; binding together; intimacy; love affair; *(mil.)* liaison

liard, *m.* farthing

liasse, *f.* bundle; file of papers

libelle, *m.* libel; scurrilous satire

libéral, *(adj.)* open-handed; free, generous; Liberal *(polit.)*

libéralité, *f.* liberality, generosity

libérateur, *m.* deliverer, rescuer

libérer, *v.t.* to free, to rid; to discharge, to release; to pay off

liberté, *f.* liberty; freedom; independence; boldness

libertin, *m.* libertine, rake

libraire, *m.* bookseller

libraire-éditeur, *m.* publisher

librairie *f.* book trade; bookshop, publishing house

libre, *(adj.)* free; at liberty; exempt; disengaged; unoccupied; unattached

libre-échange, *m.* free-trade

licence, *f.* licence; leave, permission; **passer sa -,** to sit for one's degree

licencié(e), *m.* licentiate; licence-holder

licencié ès lettres, *m.* Bachelor of Arts

licencier, *v.t.* to discharge, dismiss

licorne, *f.* unicorn

licou, *m.* halter

lie, *f.* dregs

liège, *m.* cork; cork tree

lien, *m.* band; bond; tie

lier, *v.t.* to bind; to tie; to unite

lierre, *m.* ivy

liesse, *f.* mirth

lieu, *m.* place; spot; ground; reason; cause; **au - de,** instead of; **lieux (d'aisance),** water-closet, W.C.

lieue, *f.* league (about 2½ miles, or 4 kilometres)

lieur, *m.* binder, trusser

lieutenant, *m.* lieutenant; subaltern officer; sous-lieutenant, 2nd lieutenant

lièvre, *m.* hare

liftier(-ère), *m.* (*f.*) lift-boy (-girl)

ligne, *f.* line; row, rank; formation

ligoter, *v.t.* to bind, tie up

ligue, *f.* league (association); confederation

liguer, *v.t.* to unite; to band together

lilas, *m.* lilac

limaçon, *m.* snail

limaille, *f.* filings

lime, *f.* file (tool)

limer, *v.t.* to file

limier, *m.* bloodhound; sleuth

limitation, *f.* limitation; restriction

limite, *f.* border; boundary; limit

limiter, *v.t.* to limit; to restrict; to restrain

limon, *m.* mud, slime, ooze

limon, *m.* lime (fruit)

limonade, *f.* lemonade

limonadier, *m.* café owner (seller of lemonade and other drinks)

limousine, *f.* limousine (car); waggoner's cloak

limpide, (*adj.*) limpid; clear; pure

lin, *m.* flax

linceul, *m.* shroud, winding-sheet

linge, *m.* linen; household linen; calico

lingère, *f.* seamstress; wardrobe-keeper; sewing-maid

lingerie, *f.* linen-drapery; underclothing; linen

lingot, *m.* ingot; or en lingots, bullion

linguistique, (*adj.*) and *f.* linguistic(s)

linière, *f.* field of flax

linotte, *f.* linnet (*ornith.*)

linteau, *m.* lintel

lion(ne), *m.* (*f.*) lion(ess)

lippu, (*adj.*) thick-lipped

liqueur, *f.* liquor, drink; liqueur (dessert)

liquidateur, *m.* liquidator

liquidation, *f.* liquidation; winding-up of company

liquide, *m.* liquid (general sense); argent -, ready money

lire, *v.t.* to read; to read out (announcement)

lis, *m.* lily

lisérer, *v.t.* to border; to edge

liseur(-euse), *m.* (*f.*) reader; (*adj.*) fond of reading

liseuse, *f.* reading stand; reading lamp

lisible, (*adj.*) legible

lisière, *f.* edge, border (of field); skirt of forest; leading strings

lisse, *f.* rail; handrail; ribband

lisse, (*adj.*) smooth; glossy

liste, *f.* list; register

*lit, *m.* bed

litanie, *f.* litany

literie, *f.* bedding

lithographe, *m.* lithographer

lithographie, *f.* lithography

litière, *f.* litter; stable litter

litige, *m.* litigation; legal dispute

litre, *m.* litre (a measure = $1\frac{3}{4}$ pints)

littéraire, (*adj.*) literary

littéral, (*adj.*) literal (translation, etc.)

littérateur, *m.* literary man; man of letters

littérature, *f.* literature

littoral, *m.* sea-board; littoral

livide, (*adj.*) livid; ghastly; pale

livraison, *f.* delivery (of goods, etc.); - franco, delivered free; payable à -, payable on delivery; faire - de, to deliver (goods); prendre - de, to take delivery of

livre, *m.* book; - de comptabilité, account book; tenue de livres, book-keeping

livre, *f.* pound (weight); pound (sterling)

livrée, *f.* livery

livrer, *v.t.* to deliver, to give up; to surrender; to deliver (goods); - bataille, to join battle; se - (à), *v.r.* to give oneself up (to)

livret, *m.* small book; booklet;

handbook; - **de banque,** pass-book

livreur(-euse), *m.* (*f.*) delivery man (girl); roundsman; delivery-van

lobe, *m.* lobe of ear

local(-aux), (*adj.*) local

local(-aux), *m.* premises; building

localiser, *v.t.* to localise (confine to one place, or region); to locate; **se -,** *v.r.* to fix one's home in a place

localité, *f.* locality; place; spot

locataire, *m.* and *f.* tenant, occupant (of house, etc.)

location, *f.* hiring; letting out on hire; booking (of seats)

locomotive, *f.* locomotive, engine (used for railways)

locution, *f.* phraseology; expression

loge, *f.* lodge; cabin; hut; box (theatre)

logement, *m.* lodging; housing of people; billeting (troops); accommodation; lodgings

loger, *v.i.* to lodge, to live; to be billeted; *v.t.* to lodge; accommodate; to house (somebody)

logique, (*adj.*) logical; *f.* logic

logis, *m.* home; house (dwelling)

loi, *f.* law (general sense)

loin, (*adv.*) far (general sense)

lointain, (*adj.*) distant, remote, far-off

loir, *m.* dormouse.

loisible, (*adj.*) permissible; optional

loisir, *m.* leisure

lombaire, (*adj.*) lumbar (*anat.*, relating to the loins)

lombes, *m. pl.* lumbar region; the loins

Londres, (generally *m.*) London

long(ue), (*adj.*) long (both space and time); **le - de,** along

longe, *f.* halter, leading rein; loin (of meat, generally veal)

longer, *v.t.* to keep to the side of a road; to skirt (a wood, etc.); to go along

longitude, *f.* longitude (*geog.*)

longtemps, (*adv.*) a long time, long (time)

longueur, *f.* length

longue-vue, *f.* telescope; field glass

lopin, *m.* piece; plot (of ground)

loquace, (*adj.*) loquacious; talkative

loque, *f.* rag; tatter; (in talking of a person means " a wreck ")

loquet, *m.* latch (of door)

lorgner, *v.t.* to cast a side glance; to ogle

lorgnette, *f.* (pair of) opera-glasses

lorgnon, *m.* pince-nez; eyeglasses

lors, (*adv.*) (generally used with **depuis** = from that time, ever since)

lorsque, (*conj.*) when (at the time, or moment)

losange, *m.* lozenge

lot, *m.* lot, share (of estate); portion; prize (lottery)

loterie, *f.* lottery

lotion, *f.* lotion; washing, bathing (of wound)

lotissement, *m.* dividing into lots; development of building land

louable, (*adj.*) praiseworthy

louage, *m.* letting; hiring

louange, *f.* praise; adulation

louche, (*adj.*) cross-eyed; shady (i.e. suspicious); *f.* soup ladle

loucher, *v.i.* to squint

louer, *v.t.* to hire out; to let (house, etc.); to rent (house)

louer, *v.t.* to praise; commend

loufoque, (*adj.*) eccentric; (*slang*) dippy

louis(-d'or), *m.* twenty-franc gold piece

loup, *m.* wolf; **à pas de -,** stealthily; **une faim de -,** ravenous hunger

loupe, *f.* magnifying glass; lens

lourd, (*adj.*) heavy, dull; ponderous; ungainly, close, sultry

lourdaud, *m.* lout, bumpkin

lourdeur, *f.* heaviness, clumsiness, awkwardness; dullness (brain); closeness of weather

loustic, *m.* wag, joker
loutre, *f.* otter
louve, *f.* she-wolf
louveteau, *m.* wolf-cub (also scouting term)
louvoyer, *v.i.* to tack, beat about (yachting)
loyal(-aux), *(adj.)* loyal; straight-forward; fair (dealing)
loyauté, *f.* loyalty; straightfor-wardness; uprightness (in busi-ness)
loyer, *m.* rent
lubrification, *f.* greasing
lubrifier, *v.t.* to grease, lubricate
lucarne, *f.* attic window; skylight
lucide, *(adj.)* lucid, clear
lucidité, *f.* lucidity, clearness
luciole, *f.* fire-fly, glow-worm
lucratif(-ive), *(adj.)* lucrative; profitable
luette, *f.* uvula *(anat.)*
lueur, *f.* gleam, glimmer
luge, *f.* toboggan
lugubre, *(adj.)* mournful, dismal
luire, *v.i.* to shine
luisant, *(adj.)* shining; bright; shiny; glossy (surface, skin, etc.)
lumière, *f.* light (general sense)
lumignon, *m.* snuff (of candle); candle end
luminaire, *m.* luminary; light
lumineux(-euse), *(adj.)* luminous
lunaire, *(adj.)* lunar (month)
lundi, *m.* Monday; **- de Pâques**, Easter Monday
lune, *f.* moon; **- de miel**, honey-moon
lunette, *f.* telescope
lunettes, *f. pl.* spectacles
lupanar, *m.* brothel
luron(ne), *m. (f.)* a good fellow; *f.* a tomboy
lustre, *m.* lustre; polish; gloss; chandelier; lustrum (5 years)
luth, *m.* lute (musical instrument)
luthérien, *(adj.)* Lutheran *(relig.)*
luthier, *m.* stringed instrument maker
lutiner, *v.t.* to tease; plague
lutrin, *m.* lectern
lutte, *f.* wrestling; a struggle, tussle

lutter, *v.i.* to wrestle; to struggle (against); compete with
lutteur, *m.* wrestler
luxe, *m.* luxury, profusion; **train de -**, first class (Pullman) train
luxueux(-euse), *(adj.)* luxurious
luxure, *f.* lewdness
luxurieux(-euse), *(adj.)* lewd, lustful
luzerne, *f.* lucerne, fodder; purple clover
lycée, *m.* lyceum; state-supported college, grammar school
lycéen(ne), *m. (f.)* pupil at a lycée
lyncher, *v.t.* to lynch
lynx, *m.* lynx
lyrique, *(adj.)* lyrical; **théâtre -**, opera house

M

macabre, *(adj.)* gruesome, ghoul-ish; grim; **danse -**, dance of death
macadamiser, *v.t.* to macadam-ise
macaque, *m.* macaque
macaron, *m.* macaroon
mâché, *(adj.)* worn, jagged
mâcher, *v.t.* to chew, to masticate
machin, *m.* what's his name, what d'you call it; gadget
machinal(-aux), *(adj.)* mechan-ical; unconscious (action)
machinalement, *(adv.)* mechan-ically; unconsciously
machine, *f.* machine; engine; locomotive; **- à écrire**, type-writer; **- à coudre**, sewing ma-chine; **- à vapeur**, steam engine; **- outil**, *f.* machine tool
machiner, *v.t.* to scheme, to plot
machinerie, *f.* machine construc-tion; machine shops
machiniste, *m.* sometimes used as engine-man, more often as scene-shifter, stage-hand
mâchoire, *f.* jaw; jawbone
mâchure, *f.* bruise (on fruit); flaw
macis, *m.* mace (cooking)
maçon, *m.* mason; with **franc-**, freemason

maçonnerie, f. masonry

maculature, f. brown paper; waste paper

macule, f. stain, spot; blemish

maculer, v.t. to stain, to spot; to blemish

madame, f. madam, ma'am, wife, Mrs.

mademoiselle, f. Miss, young lady

madère, f. Madeira; m. Madeira wine

madone, f. madonna

madrier, m. thick plank; joist

madrilène, (adj.) of Madrid

magasin, m. shop; store, warehouse; store-room; magazine

magasinage, m. warehousing; storage; warehouse rent

magasinier, m. warehouse-man

mages, m. pl. magi

magicien(ne), m. (f.) magician; necromancer; sorcerer(-ess)

magie, f. magic, charm

magique, (adj.) magic

magistral(-aux), (adj.) masterly authoritative dictatorial; brilliant

magistrat, m. magistrate, judge, justice

magnan, m. silkworm

magnanime, (adj.) magnanimous

magnanimité, f. magnanimity

magnésie (f.) (sulfate m. de), Epsom salts

magnésium, m. magnesium

magnétique, (adj.) magnetic

magnétiser, v.t. to magnetise

magnétisme, m. magnetism, hypnotism, attraction

magnéto, f. magneto

magnificence, f. pomp, magnificence, splendour

magnifique, (adj.) magnificent

magnolier, m. magnolia

magot, m. barbary ape, baboon; hoard; hidden treasure

mahométan(e), (adj.) and m. (f.) Mahometan

mai, m. May

maigre, (adj.) lean; thin, skinny, meagre, scanty

maigreur, f. leanness; thinness; scantiness; poorness

maigrir, v.i. to grow thin; to waste away

maille, f. stitch, knot; mesh

maillet, m. mallet

maillot, m. long clothes; jersey; tights; - de bain, bathing costume

*main, f. hand, fist, handwriting; deal (at cards)

main-d'œuvre, f. work, workmanship; manual labour

main-forte, f. help, assistance

maint(e), (adj.) many a, many

maintenant, (adv.) now, at present

maintenir, v.t. to uphold, to sustain ; to support ; to maintain ; to keep together , to affirm

maintien, m. maintenance

maire, m. mayor; adjoint au -, deputy mayor

mairie, f. mayoralty; town hall (in small town or village)

mais, (conj.) but

maïs, m. Indian corn, maize

maison, f. house; residence, home; household; family; firm (business) ; shop; - de campagne, f. country house; villa; - garnie, meublée, f. furnished house, furnished rooms; - de tolérance, f. licensed brothel

maître, m. master, owner, proprietor, instructor, teacher, chief; a title used by barristers and notaries

maîtresse, f. mistress, owner, proprietress, landlady, teacher; mistress (lady love); - femme, f. a capable or efficient woman

maîtriser, v.t. to master, to control, to subdue

majesté, f. majesty, dignity, stateliness

majestueux(-euse), (adj.) majestic, magnificent, stately

majeur(e), (adj.) major, superior, very important; (legal) of age

major, m. army doctor; surgeon major (mil.); état-major, m. headquarters, headquarters staff

majorer, *v.t.* to increase price

majorité, *f.* majority; coming of age; full age

majuscule, *f.* capital letter

mal, *(adv.)* wrong; ill; badly; on bad terms; in disgrace; uncomfortably; amiss

mal (maux), *m.* evil, ill, wrong, mischief, pain, harm, hurt, sore, misfortune; - aux dents, toothache; - de tête, headache

malade, *(adj.)* sick, ill, unwell, poorly

malade, *m.* and *f.* invalid, patient, sufferer

maladie, *f.* sickness, disease, ailment, mania

maladif(-ive), *(adj.)* sickly

maladresse, *f.* awkwardness, clumsiness

maladroit, *(adj.)* awkward, clumsy, unskilful

malaise, *m.* uneasiness

malaisé, *(adj.)* hard, difficult, awkward

malbâti, ungainly, ill-shaped

malchance, *f.* mishap, ill-luck

malcontent, *(adj.)* discontented, dissatisfied

mâle, *m.* male; man; he (for animals); *(adj.)* masculine, manly, virile

malédiction, *f.* curse, malediction

maléfice, *m.* spell; witchcraft

malencontre, *f.* mischance, mishap

malencontreux(-euse), *(adj.)* unlucky, untoward

malentendu, *m.* misunderstanding, mistake

malfaiteur(-trice), *m.* *(f.)* criminal; evildoer

malfamé, *(adj.)* ill-famed; disreputable

malgré, *(prep.)* in spite of; notwithstanding

malheur, *m.* unhappiness, misfortune, ill-luck, calamity, disaster, accident, misery

malheureux(-euse), *(adj.)* unfortunate, unlucky, disastrous, disagreeable, unpleasant, wretched

malhonnête *(adj.)* dishonest, fraudulent, rude, uncivil

malhonnêteté, *f.* dishonesty; dishonest action; rudeness, incivility

malice, *f.* mischievousness, mischief, spite, maliciousness, harm; malice does not always mean *malice*, which is best translated by *méchanceté* or *rancune*

malicieux(-euse), *(adj.)* mischievous, sly

malin (maligne), *(adj.)* cunning, artful, sharp, shrewd, mischievous, deep

malingre, *(adj.)* sickly, weakly

malitorne, *(adj.)* rude, coarse; *m.* uncouth person

malle, *f:* trunk (luggage); boot (of car)

malléable, *(adj.)* malleable, supple, docile

malmener, *v.t.* to mishandle; to abuse; to insult

malotru, *(adj.)* rough, uncouth, coarse

malpeigné(e), *m.* *(f.)* slovenly person

malpropre, *(adj.)* unclean, dirty, filthy; dishonest; indecent

malpropreté, *f.* dirtiness, nastiness, indecency

malsain, *(adj.)* unhealthy; unwholesome

malséant, *(adj.)* unbecoming, improper, unsuitable

malt, *m.* malt

maltais(e), *(adj.)* Maltese

maltraiter, *v.t.* to ill-treat, to illuse, to handle roughly

malveillance, *f.* ill-will, spite

malveillant, *(adj.)* malevolent; evil-minded; spiteful

malverser, *v.i.* to embezzle

malvoisie, *f.* Malmsey (wine)

maman, *f.* mother, mama

mamelle, *f.* breast; udder

mamelon, *m.* nipple; hillock, hummock, mound

mamelu, *(adj.)* full-breasted

manant, *m.* peasant, clodhopper, bumpkin

manche, *m.* handle, holder; *f.* sleeve; flexible pipe, hose;

heat (sports) ; . - à air, windsock (av.)

manchette, f. cuff, wristband; headline (newspaper)

manchon, m. muff

manchot(e), (adj.) and m. (f.) one-armed, one-handed (person)

mandat, m. mandate, authority, commission; charge, draft, money-order; - d'arrêt, warrant for arrest

mandataire, m. proxy, representative, agent

mander, v.t. to let know; to summon, to call for, to order

mandibule, f. jaw, mandible

manège, m. horsemanship; training of horses; roundabout

manette, f. handle, lever

mangeable, (adj.) eatable

mangeoire, f. manger (stable), crib

manger, v.i. and v.t. to eat, to eat up; to run through a fortune; to squander; to consume

manger, m. eating, food

mangeur(-euse), m. (f.) eater

maniable, (adj.) handy; easy to handle; tractable; pliable

maniaque, (adj.) mad; m. (f.) madman(-woman), crank

manie, f. mania; passion (for); whim, fancy

maniement, m. handling, touching, fingering

manier, v.t. to handle, to touch, to finger

manière, f. manner, way, fashion, style; sort, kind; mannerism; f. pl. manners

maniéré, (adj.) affected

maniérisme, m. mannerism

manifestation, f. demonstration; manifestation

manifeste, (adj.) evident, obvious, plain

manifeste, m. declaration; manifest (shipping paper)

manifester, v.t. to make known, to make clear, to manifest

manipuler, v.t. to operate, to handle

manivelle, f. crank, handle, winch

manne, f. manna; hamper; basket

mannequin, m. lay figure; dummy; girl who shows off dresses

manœuvre, f. action; working (of); proceeding; drilling (of soldiers); manœuvre; trick, stratagem; shunting

manœuvre, m. labourer, navvy

manœuvrer, v.t. to work, operate, manœuvre

manoir, m. manor, manor house

manquant, (adj.) missing, wanting, absent

manque, m. want, lack, deficiency, failure

*manquer, v.t. and v.i. to miss, to fail, to be wanting, to be lacking

mansarde, f. garret, attic

manteau(x), m. cloak, coat, mantle

manucure, m. (f.) manicurist

manuel(le), (adj.) manual: m. handbook, manual

manufacture, f. manufacture, making

manufacturer, v.t. to manufacture, to make

manufacturier(-ère), m. (f.) manufacturer; (adj.) manufacturing

manuscrit, m. manuscript, (print.) copy

manutention, f. administration, management; handling (of goods)

mappemonde, f. map of the world

maquereau, m. mackerel: (vulg.) pimp

maquette, f. model (in clay or wax); rough sketch

maquignon, m. horse dealer; horse-coper

maquillage, m. make-up (the face); making-up

maquiller, v.t. to make up (the face); to fake (picture, cheque)

maquis, m. scrub, bush (especially in Corsica); "underground" army

maraîchage, m. market-gardening

maraîcher, *m*. market-gardener

marais, *m*. marsh; bog

marasme, *m*. depression (mental); stagnation (of business)

marâtre, *f*. stepmother, unnatural mother

maraud(e), *m*. (*f*.) rascal, rogue; bad woman

marauder, *v.i*. to plunder, maraud

marbre, *m*. marble

marbrière, *f*. marble quarry

marbrure, *f*. marbling

marc, *m*. rape (of grapes); dregs; grounds (of coffee)

marchand(e), *m*. (*f*.) merchant; dealer; shopkeeper; tradesman

marchander, *v.t*. to haggle; to bargain for

marchandise, *f*. merchandise, goods

marche, *f*. march; step, stair; march (*mus*.); running (of machine); course of events

*marché, *m*. market; dealing; buying; deal, contract; bon -, cheap, cheapness

marchepied, *m*. footboard, running board (motor); step of carriage

marcher, *v.i*. to tread, to walk, to go; to march; to move (trains, etc.)

marcheur(-euse), *m*. (*f*.) walker (with vieux, old reprobate)

marcotte, *f*. layer (gardening); runner

mardi, *m*. Tuesday; mardi-gras, Shrove Tuesday

mare, *f*. pool, pond

marécage, *m*. bog, swamp

marécageux(-euse), (*adj*.) marshy, swampy

maréchal(-aux), *m*. marshal (field marshal); - ferrant, shoeing smith; - des logis, sergeant (cavalry or artillery)

marée, *f*. tide; - basse (haute), low (high) tide

margarine, *f*. margarine

marge, *f*. border; edge (of road, etc.); margin

margot, *f*. magpie

margotin, *m*. small faggot of wood

marguerite, *f*. daisy; marguerite

mari, *m*. husband

mariable, (*adj*.) marriageable

mariage, *m*. wedding, marriage, matrimony

marié(e), *m*. (*f*.) married person

marier, *v.t*. to marry (i.e. to perform the ceremony); se -, *v.r*. to marry, to get married

marin(e), (*adj*.) marine (engine, etc.)

marin, *m*. sailor, seaman

marine, *f*. seascape; sea service; - de guerre, the Navy; - marchande, merchant service

mariner, *v.t*. to pickle

marionnette, *f*. puppet, marionette

maritime, (*adj*.) maritime (province, etc.)

marmelade, *f*. compote of fruit; orange marmalade; être dans la -, to be in a fine pickle

marmite, *f*. cooking pot, pan; heavy shell (artillery)

marmot, *m*. brat; urchin

marmotte, *f*. marmot

marne, *f*. marl

marocain, (*adj*.) moroccan

maroquin, *m*. moroccan leather

maroquinerie, *f*. fancy leather goods

marotte, *f*. fad, hobby, whim

*marque, *f*. mark; brand (of goods)

marquer, *v.t*. to mark; to put a mark on; to show, to indicate

marqueterie, *f*. inlaid work

marqueur(-euse), *m*. (*f*.) scorer, tally-keeper

marquis, *m*. marquis

marquise, *f*. marchioness; awning; marquee, tent

marraine, *f*. godmother; sponsor (christening)

marrant, (*adj*.) very funny; (*coll*.) boring

(se) marrer, *v.r*. to roar with laughter; (*coll*.) j'en ai marre, I'm fed up with it

marron, *m*. chestnut

marronnier, m. chestnut tree

mars, m. March; Mars; **champ de -**, parade ground

marsouin, m. porpoise; colonial soldier

marteau, m. hammer

marteler, v.t. to hammer; to plague; to knock (engine)

martial(-aux), (adj.) martial, soldier-like, warlike

martre, f. marten

martyr(e), m. (f.) martyr

martyre, m. martyrdom; **souffrir le -**, to be martyred.

marxiste, (adj.) and m. (f.) Marxist

mascarade, f. masquerade

masque, m. mask; - protecteur, - à gaz, gas mask

masquer, v.t. to mask; to hide, screen

massacre, m. massacre

massacrer, v.t. to massacre, to butcher, to slaughter

masse, f. mass, fund, stock; mace

massepain, m. marzipan (cake, etc.)

masser, v.t. to mass (soldiers); to massage

massif(-ive), (adj.) massive, bulky

massif, m. clump (of shrubs, etc.); chain, mountain mass

massue, f. club, bludgeon

mastic, m. mastic, cement, putty.

masure, f. hovel

mat, (adj.) dull (metal); mat (complexion); unpolished

mat, (adj. invar.) (échec et mat) checkmate

mât, m. mast, pole

match, m. match (sport)

matelas, m. mattress

matelot, m. sailor, seaman

mater, v.t. to checkmate (chess); to subdue somebody

matériaux, m. pl. materials, material

matériel(le), (adj.) material; m. material, stores, stock-in-trade

matériellement, (adv.) materially, positively

maternel(le), (adj.) maternal, motherly

maternité, f. maternity, motherhood

mathématicien(ne), m. (f.) mathematician

mathématique, f. (usually pl.) mathematics

mathématique, (adj.) mathematical

matière, f. matter, material, substance; matières premières, raw materials

matin, m. morning, forenoon, dawn

mâtin, m. mastiff; scoundrel, rascal

matinal, (adj.) early, early rising

matinée, f. morning; forenoon; afternoon performance at theatre, etc.; faire la grasse -, to lie abed late

matir, v.t. to deaden

matois, (adj.) cunning, sly, artful

matou(s), m. tom-cat

matraque, f. bludgeon; life-preserver; blackjack

matriculer, v.t. to enter in the register; to register (not to matriculate)

maturité, f. maturity, ripeness, mature age

maudire, v.t. to curse; to execrate

maudit(e), (adj.) cursed; detestable, confounded

maure, (adj.) Moorish; m. a Moor

mauresque, f. Moorish woman

mausolée, m. mausoleum

maussade, (adj.) sulky, sullen

mauvais, (adj.) bad, evil; ill, wicked, naughty, hurtful, unpleasant, injurious

mauviette, f. lark

maxime, f. maxim

maximum, m. maximum

mécanicien, m. mechanician; machinist, mechanic, engine-driver; engine-man

mécanique, (adj.) mechanical, machine-made; f. mechanics

mécanisme, m. mechanism, machinery, contrivance

méchamment, (adv.) wickedly, spitefully, maliciously

méchanceté, *f.* wickedness, spite, malice, spitefulness, naughtiness

méchant, *(adj.)* wicked, evil, bad, spiteful; ill-natured, naughty, bad-tempered; vicious (animal)

mèche, *f.* wick, lock of hair; **sentir la -**, to smell a rat; **vendre la -**, to let the cat out of the bag

mécompte, *m.* miscalculation; mistake, error

méconnaissable, *(adj.)* unrecognisable

méconnaissant, *(adj.)* ungrateful, thankless

méconnaître, *v.t.* to disregard; not to recognise; to disown, to deny (parentage)

méconnu, *(adj.)* unrecognised

mécontent, *(adj.)* displeased, dissatisfied, discontented

mécontentement, *m.* discontent, dissatisfaction

mécontenter, *v.t.* to dissatisfy, to displease

mécréant, *(adj.)* infidel, unbelieving

médaille, *f.* medal, medallion, metal badge

médaillé, *(adj.)* medalled, bemedalled; *m.* medallist, prize-winner

médaillon, *m.* medallion, locket

médecin, *m.* physician; doctor

médecine, *f.* medicine, medical science

médiateur(-trice), *m. (f.)* mediator

médiation, *f.* mediation

médical(-aux), *(adj.)* medical, medicinal

médicament, *m.* medicine, remedy

médicastre, *m.* quack

médiocre, *(adj.)* mediocre, middling, moderate, passable

médire, *v.i.* to slander

médisance, *f.* slander, scandal

méditer, *v.t.* to meditate, to think over, to consider

méditerrané, *(adj.)* inland, midland

médius, *m.* middle finger

méduse, *f.* jelly fish

méfait, *m.* misdeed, misdoing

méfiance, *f.* mistrust, distrust, suspicion

(se) méfier (de), *v.r.* to be suspicious (of), to mistrust, to beware, to mind; **méfiez-vous des pickpockets**, beware of pickpockets

mégarde, *f.* inadvertence; **par -**, inadvertently

mégère, *f.* shrew, vixen

meilleur(e), *(adj.)* better, preferable (comparative of *bon*, good)

mélancolie, *f.* melancholy, sadness, gloom

mélancolique, *(adj.)* melancholy, dismal, gloomy

mélange, *m.* mixture, mixing, blend, medley, jumble

mélanger, *v.t.* to mix, to mingle, to blend, to cross (breeds)

mélasse, *f.* molasses; treacle

mêlée, *f.* scrimmage, tussle, free fight

mêler, *v.t.* to mix (up), to mingle, to entangle; **mêlez-vous de vos affaires**, mind your own business

mélèze, *m.* larch tree

mélodie, *f.* melody

mélodieux(-euse), *(adj.)* melodious, sweet, musical, harmonious

mélodrame, *m.* melodrama

melon, *m.* melon; **chapeau -**, bowler hat

membre, *m.* member, limb

même, *(adj.)* same, self-same, self; (with **lui**, etc. = himself, etc.)

même, *(adv.)* even, also, likewise

mémoire, *f.* memory, recollection, remembrance

mémoire, *m.* memorandum, statement of account; *m. pl.* memoirs

menace, *f.* menace; threat

menacer, *v.t.* to threaten

ménage, *m.* housekeeping; household; family; married couple; **femme de -**, charwoman, housekeeper; **faire bon - ensemble**, to live happily together

ménagement, *m.* consideration, discretion, tact, caution

ménager, *v.t.* to spare, to save, to be sparing of, to economise, to be careful of

ménagère, *f.* housewife, housekeeper

mendiant(e), *m.* (*f.*) beggar

mendicité, *f.* begging; vagrancy

mendier, *v.t.* to beg, to solicit, to beg for

menée, *f.* (usually in plural), underhand dealing, conspiracy

mener, *v.t.* to lead, to guide, to conduct; to manage, to carry on; to drive (car, etc.)

meneur, *m.* (ring)leader

menottes, *f. pl.* handcuffs

mensonge, *m.* lie, falsehood, untruth

mensonger(-ère), (*adj.*) lying, untrue, deceitful

mensualité, *f.* monthly payment, monthly allowance

mensuel(le), (*adj.*) monthly

mental(-aux), (*adj.*) mental

menterie, *f.* falsehood

menteur(-euse), *m.* (*f.*) liar

menthe, *f.* mint, peppermint

mention, *f.* mention

mentionner, *v.t.* to mention, to make mention of

mentir, *v.i.* to lie, to tell a lie, to tell stories

menton, *m.* chin

menu, (*adj.*) slim, slender, spare, thin, small

menu, *m.* minute detail; bill of fare, menu

menuiserie, *f.* carpentry, joinery, woodwork

menuisier, *m.* carpenter, joiner

(se) méprendre, *v.r.* to be mistaken; to make a mistake

mépris, *m.* contempt, scorn, disrespect

méprisable, (*adj.*) contemptible

méprisant, (*adj.*) contemptuous, scornful

mépriser, *v.t.* to scorn, to despise

mer, *f.* sea, deep, ocean; **la grande -,** open sea (high seas); **grosse -,** heavy sea

mercenaire, (*adj.*) mercenary, paid, hired; *m.* hired soldier, mercenary

mercerie, *f.* haberdashery

merci, *f.* mercy, discretion, will

merci, *m.* thanks; (*adv.*) thank you; no, thank you

mercier(-ère), *m.* (*f.*) haberdasher, mercer

mercredi, *m.* Wednesday; **- des Cendres,** Ash Wednesday

mercure, *m.* mercury

mère, *f.* mother; dam (of animals); **belle-mère,** *f.* mother-in-law; step-mother

méridien, *m.* meridian

méridional(-aux), (*adj.*) southern

mérite, *m.* merit, desert, worth

mériter, *v.t.* to merit, to deserve, to earn, to gain

méritoire, (*adj.*) deserving, meritorious

merlan, *m.* whiting

merle, *m.* blackbird

merluche, *f.* haddock, hake, stockfish

merveille, *f.* marvel, wonder, miracle; **à -,** admirably, wonderfully well

merveilleux(-se), (*adj.*) wonderful, marvellous, excellent

mésalliance, *f.* misalliance, bad match (matrimonial)

mésange, *f.* tom-tit

mésaventure, *f.* mischance, misadventure, mishap

mesquin, (*adj.*) petty, shabby, stingy, paltry

message, *m.* message, official communication

messager(-ère), *m.* (*f.*) messenger

messagerie, *f.* goods traffic, goods department (*rail.*)

messe, *f.* mass (R.C. Church)

messieurs, (*pl.* of **monsieur**) gentlemen, Messrs.

mesurable, (*adj.*) measurable

mesure, *f.* measurement, size, bounds, dimension, capacity, limit; **au fur et à -,** in proportion (as), successively

mesuré, (*adj.*) measured, regular, proportioned

mesurer, *v.t.* to measure (out); to proportion; to calculate; to compare

métairie, *f.* small farm; dairy farm

métal(-aux), *m.* metal; **- blanc**, German silver

métallique, *(adj.)* metallic

métallurgiste, *m.* metallurgist

métamorphose, *f.* metamorphosis

métaphore, *f.* metaphor

métayer(-ère), *m.* *(f.)* farmer (who pays rent in kind)

météore, *m.* meteor

météorique, *(adj.)* meteoric

météorologie, *f.* meteorology

méthode, *f.* method, system, way, custom, habit

métier, *m.* trade, profession; loom; **arts et métiers**, arts and crafts

métis(se), *m.* *(f.)* half-breed, half-caste, mongrel

mètre, *m.* metre (3·25 feet)

métrique, *(adj.)* metrical

métropole, *f.* mother country; capital

métropolitain, *(adj.)* metropolitan, home; *m.* Metropolitan *(eccles.)*; **le Métro(politain)**, underground railway in Paris, the " Tube "

mets, *m.* dish; food

metteur en scène, *m.* producer, director

*****mettre**, *v.t.* to put (in), to set, to lay, to place, to introduce, to put on, to wear, to contribute, to devote, to expend; **se - à**, *v.r.* to begin, set to work to; **se - en route**, to start on one's way

meuble, *m.* piece of furniture, suite of furniture

meubler, *v.t.* to furnish; to store; to stock

meule, *f.* millstone, grindstone; rick (hay, etc.)

meunier(-ère), *m.* *(f.)* miller (miller's wife)

meurtre, *m.* murder, manslaughter

meurtrier(-ère), *m.* *(f.)* murderer(-ess); *f.* loophole; *(adj.)* murderous

meurtrir, *v.t.* to bruise; to make black and blue

meute, *f.* pack of hounds; mob

mévente, *f.* sale at a loss

mi, *(prefix invar.)* half-, mid-; **à mi-chemin**, half-way

miauler, *v.i.* to mew

microbe, *m.* microbe

micro(phone), *m.* microphone; *(fam.)* mike

midi, *m.* mid-day, noon; south; **le Midi**, the south of France

mie, *f.* crumb (of bread)

miel, *m.* honey

mielleux(-euse), *(adj.)* honeyed, soft-spoken, fair-spoken, oily

mien(ne), *(poss. adj.* and *poss. pron.)* mine, my own, of mine

miette, *f.* small crumb, particle

mieux, *(adv.)* better; *m.* the best, best thing

mièvre, *(adj.)* dainty, mincing, affected

mignard, *(adj.)* dainty, affected

mignardise, *f.* daintiness, affectation

mignon(ne), *(adj.)* delicately pretty; small and graceful; *m.* and *f.* darling

migraine, *f.* sick headache

migration, *f.* migration

mijoter, *v.i.* and *v.t.* to simmer, to stew gently; to plot, to hatch

mil, *(adj.)* thousand (in dates A.D. only)

milice, *f.* militia

milicien, *m.* militiaman

milieu, *m.* middle, environment, circle, mean; **au -**, in the middle

militaire, *(adj.)* military (profession); *m.* military man; soldier

militarisme, *m.* militarism

militariste, *m.* militarist

mille, *(adj.* and *m. invar.)* (a) thousand; *m.* a mile

mille-pattes, *m.* centipede

millésime, *m.* date on coin

milliard, *m.* thousand million

millier, *m.* about a thousand

millimètre, *m.* millimetre (= 0·039 of an inch)

million, *m.* million

millionnaire, *m.* millionaire (in French money)

mime, *m.* mimic

mimer, *v.t.* to mimic

minable, *(adj.)* shabby, wretched

mince, *(adj.)* thin, slender, slight; *(slang)* **mince alors!** well I'm hanged!

mincer, *v.t.* to mince

mine, *f.* mine (coal, etc.)

mine, *f.* appearance, look, mien; **avoir bonne -,** to look well; **faire - de,** to make as if to, to make a show of

miner, *v.t.* to mine, undermine; **se -,** *v.r.* to waste away

minerai, *m.* ore

minéral(aux), *(adj.)* and *m.* mineral

minet(te), *m.* and *f.* puss

mineur, *m.* miner

mineur(e), *(adj.)* minor; *m.* and *f.* a minor (under 21)

miniature, *f.* miniature

minime, *(adj.)* very small, trifling

ministère, *m.* ministry; government department; **- des Affaires Étrangères,** Foreign Office; **- de l'Intérieur,** Home Office

ministériel(le), *(adj.)* ministerial

ministre, *m.* minister (Government); also minister (clergyman)

minium, *m.* red lead

minorité, *f.* minority

minoterie, *f.* flour mill

minuit, *m.* midnight

minuscule, *(adj.)* tiny minute; *f.* small letter (as opposed to capital)

minute, *f.* minute (of hour, degree)

minuter, *v.t.* to draw up (an agreement, etc.)

minutieux(-euse), *(adj.)* extremely careful (person); thorough, detailed

mioche, *m.* and *f.* small child; mite, urchin

mi-parti, *(adj.)* equally divided

miracle, *m.* miracle

miraculeux(-euse), *(adj.)* miraculous; marvellous

mirage, *m.* mirage

mire, *f.* sight (of rifle)

mirer, *v.t.* to aim at, take aim at

mirobolant, *(adj.)* wonderful, astounding

miroir, *m.* mirror, looking-glass

miroiter, *v.i.* to shine; to flash; to shimmer

misanthrope, *m.* misanthrope; *(adj.)* misanthropic(al)

mise, *f.* placing; stake (bet); attire, dress; **- en marche,** starting (of engine, etc.)

misérable, *(adj.)* miserable, unhappy, unfortunate, wretched

misère, *f.* misery, distress, extreme poverty; trifle

miséricorde, *f.* mercy, mercifulness

missel, *m.* missal (*eccles.*), mass book

mission, *f.* mission

missionnaire, *m.* and *f.* missionary

mistral, *m.* mistral; cold north-east wind

mitaine, *f.* mitten

mite, *f.* mite; clothes moth

mité, *(adj.)* moth-eaten

mitoyen(ne), *(adj.)* intermediate

mitrailler, *v.t.* to rake with machine-gun fire

mitraillette, *f.* light automatic; sub-machine-gun

mitrailleuse, *f.* machine-gun

mitre, *f.* mitre (of bishop)

mitron, *m.* journeyman baker

mixte, *(adj.)* mixed

mobile, *(adj.)* mobile, movable, restless; *m.* motive

mobilier, *m.* furniture, set of furniture

mobiliser, *v.t.* to mobilise (troops); to call up (reservists)

mobilité, *f.* mobility, instability of character

mode, *f.* fashion, fancy; way; *m.* mode; mood (*gram.*)

modelage, *m.* modelling

modèle, *m.* model

modeler, *v.t.* to model, to mould; **se - (sur qn.),** *v.r.* to take someone as a pattern

modérateur(-trice), *(adj.)* restraining, moderating; *m.* regulator

modération, *f.* moderation, restraint

modéré, *(adj.)* moderate, temperate, reasonable (price)

modérer, *v.t.* to moderate, restrain, to slacken (speed)

moderne, *(adj.)* modern

modeste, *(adj.)* modest; unassuming

modicité, *f.* smallness (of means); lowness (of prices)

modifier, *v.t.* to modify; to alter

modique, *(adj.)* moderate, reasonable

modiste, *f.* milliner

module (lunaire), *m.* (lunar) module

moduler, *v.t.* to modulate one's voice

moelle, *f.* marrow (of bone)

moelleux(-euse), *(adj.)* pithy; soft (to the touch)

moellon, *m.* quarry-stone; squared stone (for building)

mœurs, *f. pl.* morals or manners of people; customs of a country

moignon, *m.* stump (of limb)

moindre, *(adj.)* less(er); **le -,** the least

moine, *m.* monk

moineau, *m.* sparrow

*****moins,** *(adv.)* less

moiré, *(adj.)* watered (silk); moiré

mois, *m.* month

moisi, *(adj.)* mouldy, mildewy

moisir, *v.i.* and *v.i.* to mildew

moisissure, *f.* mildew, mould

moisson, *f.* harvest; harvest-time; crop

moissonner, *v.t.* to harvest (crops), to reap

moissonneur(-euse), *m.* *(f.)* reaper, harvester

moite, *(adj.)* moist, clammy

moiteur, *f.* dampness, clamminess

*****moitié,** *f.* half

molaire, *(adj.)* and *f.* molar (tooth)

môle, *m.* mole, breakwater

molester, *v.t.* to molest

mollement, *(adv.)* softly, slackly

mollesse, *f.* softness; flabbiness, slackness; lifelessness

mollet, *m.* calf (of leg)

molleton, *m.* soft flannel; swansdown

mollir, *v.i.* to soften; to become soft

mollusque, *m.* mollusc

môme, *m.* and *f.* brat, kid, youngster

moment, *m.* moment, instant

momentané, *(adj.)* momentary; temporary

momie, *f.* mummy

mon (ma, mes), *poss. adj.* my

monarchie, *f.* monarchy

monarque, *m.* monarch

monastère, *m.* monastery

monceau, *m.* heap, pile

mondain, *(adj.)* worldly

monde, *m.* world; people; society; **tout le -,** everybody

monder, *v.t.* to stone (raisins); to peel

mondial(-aux), *(adj.)* worldwide

monétaire, *(adj.)* monetary

monnaie, *f.* money, coin; change (small change, etc.); **la -,** the Mint

monnayer, *v.t.* to coin, to mint

monnayeur, *m.* coiner; **faux -,** counterfeiter

monologue, *m.* monologue, soliloquy

monomane, *m.* and *f.* monomaniac

monoplace, *(adj.)* and *m.* single-seater (car, plane)

monopole, *m.* monopoly

monotone, *(adj.)* monotonous

monseigneur, *m.* form of address to persons of high rank (Your Royal Highness, My Lord, etc.)

monsieur, *m.* sir; gentleman; Mr.

monstre, *m.* monster

monstrueux(-euse), *(adj.)* monstrous, huge, colossal

mont, *m.* mount, mountain

montagnard(e), *(adj.)* mountain, highland (people); *m. (f.)* mountaineer; highlander

montagne, *f.* mountain

montagneux(-euse), *(adj.)* mountainous, hilly

montant, *m.* amount, total amount; (*adj.*) rising, ascending

mont-de-piété, *m.* pawn office, pawnshop

montée, *f.* rise, ascent

*****monter,** *v.i.* (*être*) to mount, to go up, to climb on to, into (something); to rise, to go up (in price); to amount; to raise; *v.t.* to climb (a hill), to mount; to fit; to erect; to carry up; to set up (a business)

monteur(-euse), *m.* (*f.*) fitter (engineering); setter (jewels); producer (of plays)

montre, *f.* watch; show, display

montre-bracelet, *f.* wrist-watch

montrer, *v.t.* to show, to display; to point out; to teach

montueux(-euse), (*adj.*) hilly

monture, *f.* mount (horse, etc.); setting (of jewel)

monument, *m.* monument, memorial

monumental(-aux), (*adj.*) monumental; huge, colossal

(se) moquer (de), *v.r.* to make fun of, to laugh at, to mock

moquerie, *f.* mockery, ridicule, derision

moqueur(-euse), (*adj.*) mocking, scoffing; *m.* (*f.*) scoffer

moraillon, *m.* clasp of lock

moral(-aux), (*adj.*) moral; *m.* moral nature; morale

morale, *f.* morals, morality; moral (of story, etc.)

moralité, *f.* good moral conduct, morality

morbide, (*adj.*) morbid

morbleu! (*interj.*) hang it!

morceau(x), *m.* piece, morsel (food), bit, fragment

morceler, *v.t.* to cut up into small pieces; to parcel out

mordant, (*adj.*) biting; eating away; corrosive; caustic (criticism)

mordre, *v.t.* to bite, to nip

moresque, (*adj.*) Moorish (see mauresque)

(se) morfondre, *v.r.* to be chilled to the bone; to be bored to death

morgue, *f.* mortuary; pride, conceit

moribond, (*adj.*) at death's door, dying

morne, (*adj.*) gloomy, dreary, dismal

morose, (*adj.*) sulky

morphine, *f.* morphine

mors, *m.* bit (for horse); jaw (of vice)

morsure, *f.* bite

mort, *f.* death

mort(e), (*adj.* and *past part.* of *mourir*) dead, stagnant; *m.* (*f.*) dead person

mortadelle, *f.* Bologna sausage

mortalité, *f.* mortality

mortel(le), (*adj.*) and *m.* (*f.*) mortal

mortellement, (*adv.*) mortally, fatally

mortier, *m.* mortar; (trench) mortar (*mil.*)

mortifiant, (*adj.*) mortifying

mortifier, *v.t.* to mortify; to gangrene

mortuaire, (*adj.*) mortuary; **chambre -,** death chamber

morue, *f.* cod

morve, *f.* glanders (in horses); nasal mucus, (*vulgar*) snot

morveux(-euse), *m.* (*f.*) brat, greenhorn; (*adj.*) snotty

mosaïque, *f.* mosaic

mosquée, *f.* mosque

mot, *m.* word, saying; **bon -,** witty remark

moteur, *m.* motor, engine

moteur(-trice), (*adj.*) motive, driving (power)

motif(-ive), (*adj.*) motive (cause)

motif, *m.* motive, incentive

motion, *f.* motion, proposal

motiver, *v.t.* to state the reason for; to justify, to warrant

motocyclette, *f.* motor-cycle

motorisé, (*adj.*) motorised

motte, *f.* mound; clod of earth; peat

motus! (*interj.*) Mum's the word!

mou (molle), (*adj.*) soft; weak

mou, *m.* lights, lungs (of animals)

mouchard(e), *m.* (*f.*) sneak; (police) informer

mouche, *f.* fly; spot, stain
moucher, *v.t.* to wipe; to snub somebody; **se -,** *v.r.* to blow, to wipe one's nose
moucheron, *m.* gnat
moucheter, *v.t.* to spot; to speckle
mouchoir, *m.* handkerchief
moudre, *v.t.* to grind, to mill
moue, *f.* pout
mouette, *f.* sea-gull, sea-mew
moufle, *m.* and *f.* mittens (usually in plural); tackle
mouflon, *m.* wild sheep
mouillage, *m.* moistening; anchorage, mooring, ground
mouiller, *v.t.* to wet, to moisten; to drop anchor; **se -,** *v.r.* to get wet
mouilleur de mines, *m.* mine-layer (*navy*)
moule, *m.* mould
moule, *f.* mussel
moulé, (*adj.*) moulded; cast (steel)
mouler, *v.t.* to cast; to mould
moulin, *m.* mill; **- à vent (eau),** wind (water) mill
moulinet, *m.* winch; hand mill
moulu (from *moudre*), ground; broken
moulure, *f.* moulding
mourir, *v.i.* to die; **se -,** *v.r.* to be dying
mousquetaire, *m.* musketeer
mousqueton, *m.* blunderbuss
mousse, *f.* moss; foam
mousse, *m.* ship's boy; cabin boy
mousseline, *f.* muslin; **- de soie,** chiffon
mousser, *v.i.* to froth, to foam
mousseux(-euse), (*adj.*) mossy; foaming; sparkling (wine)
moustache, *f.* moustache (frequently plural in French)
moustiquaire, *f.* mosquito-net
moustique, *m.* mosquito
moût, *m.* must (of grapes)
moutarde, *f.* mustard
moutardier, *m.* mustard-pot
mouton, *m.* sheep; mutton
moutonner, *v.i.* to froth, to foam
mouvant, (*adj.*) moving; mobile

mouvement, *m.* movement, motion; traffic (railway)
mouvementé, (*adj.*) animated, lively; full of incident
mouvoir, *v.t.* to move, to start, to drive, to prompt (actuate)
moyen(ne), (*adj.*) middle; average; **le - âge,** Middle Ages
moyen, *m.* means
moyennant, (*prep.*) on condition, for; with **que** = provided
moyenne, *f.* average
muable, (*adj.*) changeable; mutable
mucilage, *m.* gum
mucus, *m.* mucus
mue, *f.* moulting (birds)
muer, *v.t.* to moult, to shed (coat, etc., of animals)
muet(te), (*adj.*) dumb
mufle, *m.* snout, nose; rotter (*slang*)
muflerie, *f.* low-down trick
mugir, *v.i.* to low, to bellow, to roar (sea)
mugissement, *m.* bellowing, roaring, moaning
muguet, *m.* lily of the valley; thrush (*med.*)
mulâtre, (*adj.*) and *m.* and *f.* mulatto, half-caste
mule, *f.* mule (she-mule); slipper (lady's)
mulet, *m.* mule (male)
muletier, *m.* muleteer
mulot, *m.* field mouse
multiple, (*adj.*) multiple, multifarious
multiplier, *v.t.* and *v.i.* to multiply (by); **se -,** *v.r.* to multiply, to increase
multitude, *f.* multitude, crowd
municipal(-aux), (*adj.*) municipal
municipalité, *f.* municipality, town council
munificence, *f.* munificence, bounty
munir (de), *v.t.* to furnish, supply, equip (with)
munition, *f.* munitions (of war); ammunition; stores, supplies
muqueux(-euse), (*adj.*) mucous (membrane)

mur, *m.* wall

mûr, (*adj.*) ripe

muraille, *f.* wall, partition

mural(-aux), (*adj.*) mural

mûre, *f.* mulberry; - sauvage, blackberry

murène, *f.* sea-eel, lamprey

mûrier, *m.* mulberry tree

mûrir, *v.i.* to ripen

murmure, *m.* murmur, whispering, muttering, grumbling

murmurer, *v.i.* and *v.t.* to murmur, to whisper, to grumble

musard(e), *m.* (*f.*) loiterer

musc, *m.* musk-deer; musk

muscade, *f.* nutmeg

muscat, *m.* muscatel (grape); muscatel wine

muscle, *m.* muscle

musclé, (*adj.*) muscular

museau, *m.* snout, muzzle

musée, *m.* museum

museler, *v.t.* to muzzle; to silence (somebody)

muselière, *f.* muzzle; nose-band

muser, *v.i.* to loiter, to moon

musette, *f.* bagpipe; bal -, popular (cheap) dance hall

musical(-aux), (*adj.*) musical (never applied to persons, see musicien)

musicien(ne), (*adj.*) musical (as applied to persons)

musicien(ne), *m.* (*f.*) musician

musique, *f.* music

musqué, (*adj.*) perfumed with musk

mutiler, *v.t.* to maim; *m.* mutilé de guerre, disabled soldier

mutin, (*adj.*) mutinous; *m.* mutineer

mutiner, *v.t.* to mutiny

mutinerie, *f.* mutiny, rebellion, riot

mutisme, *m.* dumbness, mutism

mutuel(le), (*adj.*) mutual, reciprocal

mutuellement, (*adv.*) mutually

myope, (*adj.*) short-sighted

myopie, *f.* short-sightedness

myosotis, *m.* forget-me-not

myrrhe, *f.* myrrh

myrte, *m.* myrtle

myrtille, *f.* bilberry

mystère, *m.* mystery, secret

mystérieux(-euse), (*adj.*) mysterious

mystifier, *v.t.* to hoax; to mystify

mythe, *m.* myth, fiction

mythologie, *f.* mythology

mythologique, (*adj.*) mythological

N

nabab, *m.* nabob

nable, *m.* plug (boat); scuttle-hole

nabot, *m.* dwarf, midget

nacarat, *m.* and (*adj.*) nacarat; orange-red

nacelle, *f.* skiff, dinghy; gondola (of airship); car (balloon); cockpit (aeroplane)

nacre, *f.* mother-of-pearl

nacrer, *v.t.* to give a pearly gloss to

nage, *f.* swimming; paddling; sculling; être en -, to be in a perspiration; passer à la -, to swim across

nageoire, *f.* fin (of fish); float (plane)

nager, *v.i.* to swim; to scull, row

nageur(-euse), *m.* (*f.*) swimmer; rower

naguère, lately; a short time ago

naïf(-ve), (*adj.*) artless; simple

nain(e), *m.* (*f.*) dwarf; pygmy

naissance, *f.* birth; source (of a river); acte de -, birth certificate

naître, *v.i.* to be born; to rise (a river)

naïveté, *f.* artlessness; simplicity

nantissement, *m.* pledge; collateral security

napoléonien(ne), (*adj.*) Napoleonic

nappe, *f.* table-cloth; cloth, cover

narcotique, *m.* and (*adj.*) narcotic; opiate

narguer, *v.t.* to set at defiance; flout

narine, *f.* nostril

narquois(e), *(adj.)* sneering, mocking, jeering

narration, *f.* narration, narrative account

narrer, *v.t.* to narrate, relate

nasal, *(adj.)* nasal

nasalement, *(adj.)* nasally, with a twang

naseau, *m.* nostril (of animal)

nasiller, *v.i.* to speak through the nose

natal, *(adj.)* native (country)

natalité, *f.* birth-rate

natation, *f.* swimming

nation, *f.* nation

national(-aux), *(adj.)* national

nationaliser, *v.t.* to nationalise

nationalité, *f.* nationality

nativité, *f.* nativity; birth

natte, *f.* mat, matting (rush, straw); plait (hair)

natter, *v.t.* to mat; to plait, braid

naturaliser, *v.t.* to naturalise

naturalisation, *f.* naturalisation

naturaliste, *m.* naturalist

nature, *f.* nature ; character; kind ; temperament; **payer en -**, to pay in kind

nature, *(adj. invar.)* plain boiled (potatoes, etc.); **café -,** black coffee

naturel(le), *(adj.)* natural; unaffected; *m.* disposition

naufrage, *m.* shipwreck; **faire -,** to be shipwrecked

naufragé(e), *m.* *(f.)* castaway; *(adj.)* shipwrecked

nauséabond, *(adj.)* nauseating, foul (smell)

nausée, *f.* nausea, disgust

nautique, *(adj.)* nautical

naval(s), *(adj.)* naval

navarin, *m.* mutton stew

navet, *m.* turnip

navette, *f.* shuttle; shuttle service (boat, etc.); colza oil

navigable, *(adj.)* navigable (river); seaworthy

navigateur, *m.* navigator

navigation, *f.* navigation, sailing

naviguer, *v.i. and v.t.* to navigate, to sail

navire, *m.* vessel, ship; **navire-école**, training ship; **navire-citerne**, tanker

navrant, *(adj.)* heart-breaking, heart-rending

navrer, *v.t.* to grieve

navré, *(adj.)* heart-broken; dreadfully sorry

né(e), (from *naître*) born

néanmoins, *(adv.)* nevertheless; for all that; yet

néant, *m.* nought, nothingness

nébuleux, *(adj.)* nebulous; hazy, vague, obscure

nécessaire, *(adj.)* necessary; indispensable

nécessaire, *m.* what is necessary, necessaries; dressing-case

nécessairement, *(adv.)* necessarily; inevitably

nécessité, *f.* necessity; exigency; need, want (poverty)

nécessiter, *v.t.* to necessitate; to make necessary; to entail (something)

nécrologe, *m.* obituary list

nécrologie, *f.* obituary notice

nef, *f.* nave (church) ; ship (*poetical*)

néfaste, *(adj.)* luckless; ill-omened; baneful

nèfle, *f.* medlar (fruit)

négatif(-ive), *(adj.)* negative; *m.* negative (*phot.*)

négation, *f.* negation, denial

négative, *f.* negative, refusal

négligé, *m.* negligée, morning dress; *(adj.)* careless, neglected

négligence, *f.* carelessness, neglect

négligent, *(adj.)* careless, negligent

négliger, *v.t.* to neglect

négociable, *(adj.)* negotiable (securities, etc.)

négociabilité, *f.* negotiability

négociant, *m.* merchant, trader

négociateur(-trice), *m.(f.)* mediator, negotiator

négociation, *f.* negotiation, transaction, mediation, discussion

négocier, *v.t.* to negotiate; discuss

nègre, *m.* negro, black; *(adj.)* negro

négresse, *f.* negress, black woman

négrillon(ne), *m. (f.)* negro boy, negro girl

négroïde, *(adj.)* negroid, black

neige, *f.* snow; **boule de -,** snowball

neiger, *(impers. verb)* to snow

neigeux(-euse), *(adj.)* snowy

nénufar, *m.* water-lily

nerf, *m.* nerve; sinew, tendon; **crise (attaque) de nerfs,** fit of hysterics

nerver, *v.t.* to stiffen

nerveux(-euse), *(adj.)* nervous; wiry; excitable, highly strung

nervosité, *f.* irritability, nervousness

net(te), *(adj.)* clean, spotless; clear; plain (answer); net (weight)

net, *(adv.)* plainly, outright

nettement, *(adv.)* neatly; clearly; frankly; point-blank

netteté, *f.* neatness, clearness

nettoyer, *v.t.* to clean; to scour; cleanse

nettoyeur(-euse), *m. (f.)* cleaner

neuf, *(num. adj.)* and *m.* nine

neuf(-ve), *(adj.)* new; fresh

neurasthénie, *f.* neurasthenia

neurasthénique, *(adj.)* and *m.* neurasthenic

neurotique, *(adj.)* neurotic

neutraliser, *v.t.* neutralise (effort, etc.)

neutralité, *f.* neutrality

neutre, *(adj.)* neuter; neutral

neveu(x), *m.* nephew

névralgie, *f.* neuralgia

névrose, *f.* neurosis

névrosé(e), *(adj.;* and *m. (f.)* neurasthenic subject, patient *(med.)*

*****nez,** *m.* nose

ni, *(conj.)* nor, or; **ni. . . ni. . .,** neither . . . nor . . .

niable, *(adj.)* deniable

niais(e), *(adj.)* simple, inane

niaiserie, *f.* silliness

niche, *f.* nook, recess (wall, etc.); trick, prank; **- à chien,** dog-kennel.

nichée, *f.* nest; brood, litter (of puppies)

nicher, *v.i.* to nest; to nestle

nickel, *m.* nickel

nid, *m.* nest; **- de poule,** pot-hole (road)

nièce, *f.* niece

nier, *v.t.* to deny (general use)

nigaud, *m.* simpleton, booby

nimbe, *m.* halo, nimbus

nippes, *f. pl.* old garments

nitouche (sainte), *f.* little hypocrite

nitrique, *(adj.)* nitric (acid)

niveau, *m.* level; **passage à -,** level crossing; **- de vie,** standard of living

niveler, *v.t.* to survey ground; to level, even up (ground)

nivellement, *m.* surveying; levelling

noble, *(adj.)* noble (descent, birth); stately; *m.* nobleman

noblesse, *f.* nobility; nobleness; **- oblige,** rights imply duties, obligations

noce, *f.* wedding; wedding party; **faire la -,** to lead a fast life

noces, *f. pl.* wedding, nuptials

noceur(-euse), *m. (f.)* dissipated man (woman)

nocher, *m.* pilot, mariner

nocturne, *(adj.)* nightly, nocturnal

nocuité, *f.* noxiousness

Noël, *m.* Christmas; **jour de -,** Christmas Day; **la veillée de -,** Christmas Eve

nœud, *m.* knot; hitch; knot *(naut.)*; **- coulant,** slip-knot

*****noir,** *(adj.)* black

noirâtre, *(adj.)* blackish

noircir, *v.i.* to grow, turn black; to darken; *v.t.* to blacken, cast gloom over

noisetier, *m.* hazel tree

noisette, *f.* hazel nut

noix, *f.* nut, walnut; **- de coco,** coconut

nom, *m.* name; **- de guerre,** penname; **- de théâtre,** stage name; **(pré)nom,** Christian name; **- de famille,** surname

nombre, *m.* number

nombrer, *v.t.* to number

nombreux(-euse), *(adj.)* numerous; **peu -,** few

nombril, *m.* navel

nominal(-aux), *(adj.)* nominal; **appel -,** roll call

nomination, *f.* nomination for appointment; appointment

nommément, *(adv.)* namely

nommer, *v.t.* to name; to give a name to; to mention by name; to appoint (somebody to a post); **se -,** *v.r.* to be called

non, *(adv.)* no, not; used also in compound words, e.g. *non-intervention,* non-interference

nonce, *m.* papal nuncio

nonchalance, *f.* carelessness, listlessness

nonchalant, *(adj.)* careless, unconcerned

nonne, *f.* nun

nonobstant, *(prep.)* notwithstanding

nonpareil(le), *(adj.)* peerless, without equal; *f.* fancy ribbon

nord, *m.* north; **l'Amérique du Nord,** North America; **perdre le -,** to lose one's head, be all at sea

nordique, *(adj.)* Nordic, (also) Scandinavian

normal(-aux), *(adj.)* normal; **école normale,** training college for teachers

normand, *(adj.)* and *m.* Norman

norvégien(ne), *(adj.)* Norwegian

nostalgie, *f.* home-sickness, nostalgia

notable, *(adj.)* notable; considerable

notabilité, *f.* notability; person of distinction

notaire, *m.* notary

notamment, *(adv.)* especially; more particularly; in particular

notation, *f.* notation

note, *f.* note, memorandum; mark (school); notice, account, bill

noter, *v.t.* to note; to take notice of; to put down, make a note of;

un homme bien noté, a man of repute

notice, *f.* notice; review of a book

notification, *f.* notification; intimation

notion, *f.* notion, idea

notoire, *(adj.)* notorious, well known (fact, etc.)

notoriété, *f.* notoriety; repute (of somebody)

notre, *(poss. adj.)* our

Notre-Dame, Our Lady *(eccles.)*

nouer, *v.t.* to knot, to tie; **se -,** *v.r.* to become knotted

noueux(-euse), *(adj.)* knotty; gnarled

nougat, *m.* nougat; almond cake

nouilles, *f. pl.* vermicelli, noodles

nourrain, *m.* young fish; small fry

nourrice, *f.* wet nurse

nourricier(ère), *(adj.)* nutritious; **père -,** foster father

nourrir, *v.t.* to feed, to nourish; to foster (hatred, etc.); to entertain (hope)

nourrissant, *(adj.)* nourishing

nourrisson, *m.* infant at breast; nursling

nourriture, *f.* food, nourishment, sustenance; feed (for cattle)

nouveau (nouvel, nouvelle), *(adj.)* new; fresh, recent; further, additional; **de -,** again

nouveauté, *f.* novelty

nouvelle, *f.* news (piece of)

nouvelles, *f. pl.* news (about something)

novateur(-trice), *m. (f.)* innovator

novembre, *m.* November

novice, *m.* and *f.* novice (in monastery or convent)

noyade, *f.* drowning

noyau, *m.* stone (of fruit); core, kernel

noyer, *m.* walnut (tree, or wood)

noyer, *v.t.* to drown; **se -,** *v.r.* to drown oneself; to be drowned

nu, *(adj.)* naked; unclothed; uncovered, plain

(N.B.—**Nu** before the noun is

invariable and joined to the noun by a hyphen: **nu-pieds,** barefoot; **nu-tête,** bare-headed, but aller la tête nue)

nuage, m. cloud

nuageux(-euse), (adj.) cloudy; overcast; clouded over

nuance, f. shade (of colour or meaning); hue; tint

nucléaire, (adj.) nuclear; **rayonnement -,** nuclear radiation

nudité, f. nakedness

nuée, f. storm-clouds; cloud (of insects, etc.)

nuire, v.t. to hurt, to be hurtful, prejudicial (to somebody or something)

nuisibilité, f. harmfulness

nuisible, (adj.) hurtful, harmful

*****nuit,** f. night; darkness

nuitée, f. night's work

nul(le), (adj.) no, not one; worthless; ineffectual

nullement, (adv.) not at all

nullité, f. nullity; nothingness; incompetent (person)

numéraire, m. specie

numéral(-aux), (adj.) and m. numeral

numérique, (adj.) numerical

numéro, m. number (of house, room, etc.); **- d'appel,** telephone number

numérotage, m. numbering

numéroter, v.t. to number (page, street, etc.)

numismate, m. numismatist

nuptial, (adj.) bridal

nuque, f. nape of the neck

nutritif(-ive), nutritious, nourishing

nutrition, f. nutrition

nylon, m. nylon

nymphe, f. nymph

O

oasis, f. oasis

obéir (à), v.t. to obey; to be obedient (to)

obéissance, f. obedience; dutifulness; allegiance

obéissant, (adj.) obedient; dutiful

obélisque, m. obelisk

obérer, v.t. to involve (in debt); to burden

obèse, (adj.) corpulent, fat, stout

obésité, f. corpulence

obituaire, m. and (adj.) obituary

objecter, v.t. to object; to raise an objection

objectif(-ive), (adj.) objective; m. aim, objective, target; object

objection, f. objection

objet, m. object, thing, article; **- d'art,** work of art

objurgation, f. violent reproof; objurgation

obligation, f. obligation; duty; bond, debenture (finance)

obligatoire, (adj.) compulsory, obligatory

obligeance, f. obligingness; kindness; willingness

obligeant, (adj.) obliging; kind, civil

*****obliger,** v.t. to oblige, to compel; to bind; **s'- (à),** v.r. to undertake (to do something)

obligé, (adj.) obliged, bound, compelled; indispensable

oblique, (adj.) oblique, slanting

oblitération, f. obliteration

oblitérer, v.t. to obliterate, wipe out, destroy; to cancel (stamp)

oblong, (adj.) oblong

obole, f. obolus; farthing, mite, very small gift

obscène, (adj.) obscene, lewd

obscénité, f. obscenity, lewdness, dirty talk

obscur(e), (adj.) dark, dim, obscure, dingy

obscurcir, v.t. to darken, to dim, to obscure; **s'-,** v.r. to grow dark or dim

obscurcissement, m. dimness, darkening, black-out

obscurité, f. darkness, obscurity, gloom

obséder, v.t. to importune; to beset; to haunt

obsèques, f. pl. obsequies; funeral

obséquieux(-euse), (adj.) obsequious

observance, f. observance (of rule, etc.)

observateur(-trice), m. (f.) observer (general sense)

observation, f. observation; remark; mild reproof

observatoire, m. observatory

observer, v.t. to observe; to examine; to watch; to look at; faire -, to point out

obsession, f. obsession

obstacle, m. obstacle, hindrance; obstruction; course d'obstacles, steeplechase; hurdle race

obstétrique, f. obstetrics; midwifery; (adj.) obstetric(al)

obstination, f. obstinacy; stubbornness

obstiné, (adj.) stubborn, obstinate

(s')obstiner (à), v.r. to be stubborn, to persist (in)

obstruction, f. obstruction; stoppage, blocking

obstruer, v.t. to obstruct; to block (the view, etc.)

obtenir, v.t. to obtain, to get; to secure (promise); to procure; to come by

obtention, f. obtainment

obturateur, m. throttle (eng.), shutter (phot.)

obtus(e), (adj.) dulled, blunted; obtuse (angle)

obus, m. shell (artillery); - brisant, high explosive shell; - traceur, tracer shell

obvier, v.t. to obviate

occasion, f. occasion; opportunity; good bargain; motive, reason, cause

occasionnel(le), (adj.) occasional

occasionner, v.t. to cause; to bring about

occident, m. west, occident

occidental, (adj.) western

occupant(e), m. (f.) occupier, occupant; (adj.) occupying

occupation, f. occupation; pursuit; employment; occupancy (legal)

occuper, v.t. to occupy; to take up; to engross; s' - (de), v.r. to busy oneself (with); to apply oneself (to); to see (about)

océan, m. ocean

océanique, (adj.) oceanic

octobre, m. October

octogénaire, (adj.) and m. (f.) octogenarian

octroi, m. town dues; city toll, toll-house; duty

octroyer, v.t. to grant; to concede

oculaire, (adj.) ocular; m. eye-glass

oculiste, m. oculist

odeur, f. odour, smell

odieux(-euse), (adj.) odious; hateful; heinous (crime)

odorat, m. sense of smell

odoriférant, (adj.) fragrant; sweet-smelling

*œil (pl. yeux), m. eye

œil-de-bœuf, bull's eye; circular window

œillade, f. glance, leer, ogle

œillère, f. eye-tooth; blinker

œillet, m. pink, carnation; eyelet (-hole)

œilleton, m. off-shoot, sucker; young bud

œuf, m. egg; - frais, new-laid egg; - à la coque, boiled egg; œufs frits (pochés), fried (poached) eggs; œufs brouillés, scrambled eggs

œuvé, (adj.) hard-roed (fish)

œuvre, f. work, labour; piece of work; finished work

offense, f. offence; transgression

offenser, v.t. to offend (someone); to give offence to; to be offensive to; to shock (the feelings)

offensif(-ive), (adj.) offensive, aggressive, attacking; f. offensive (mil.)

office, m. function; duty; divine service; f. servants' hall

officiel(le), (adj.) official (statement, etc.); formal (call)

officier, v.i. to officiate

officier, m. officer (general sense: army, navy, etc.)

officieux(-euse), (adj.) officious; meddlesome; unofficial

offrande, *f.* offering; present

offre, *f.* offer, proposal; tender (contract)

offrir, *v.t.* to offer; to bid, to tender; s'-, *v.r.* to offer oneself; to present oneself

offusquer, *v.t.* to offend, to shock (somebody)

ogival(e), (*adj.*) Gothic (style)

ogive, *f.* pointed arch; shell-cap (*mil.*)

ogre(sse), *m.* (*f.*) ogre (ogress)

oïdium, *m.* vine blight

oie, *f.* goose

oignon, *m.* onion; petit -, spring onion

oindre, *v.t.* to oil; to anoint

oiseau, *m.* bird; bricklayer's hod

oisif(-ive), (*adj.*) idle

oisiveté, *f.* idleness; leisure

oison, *m.* gosling

olive, *f.* olive

olivier, *m.* olive tree

olographe, *m.* holograph (will written by person in whose name it appears)

ombrage, *m.* shade (of trees); umbrage

ombrager, *v.t.* to shade; to protect against the sun

ombrageux(-euse), (*adj.*) shady

ombre, *f.* shadow; darkness; ghost, shade (of oneself)

ombrelle, *f.* parasol

omelette, *f.* omelet; - aux fines herbes, savoury omelet

omettre, *v.t.* to omit; to leave out

omission, *f.* omission

omnibus, *m.* omnibus (general use); (train) omnibus, slow train

omoplate, *f.* shoulder-blade

on, (*indef. pron.*) one, people, we, they

onagre, *m.* wild ass

oncle, *m.* uncle

onction, *f.* unction; anointing; extrême -, the last sacrament

onctueux, (*adj.*) unctuous

onde, *f.* wave; billow; wave - (wireless)

ondée, *f.* heavy shower

on-dit, *m.* rumour, hearsay

ondoiement, *m.* undulation

ondoyer, to undulate, to wave, to ripple

ondulant, (*adj.*) undulating (country), waving (corn)

ondulation, *f.* undulation; wave; ondulation permanente, permanent wave

onéreux(-euse), (*adj.*) onerous; heavy (expenditure); burdensome

ongle, *m.* nail (of finger, etc.); claw, talon (bird)

onguent, *m.* unguent, salve

onze (*adj. invar.*) eleven

opale, *f.* opal

opéra, *m.* opera; opera house

opération, *f.* operation (*surg. or mil.*); working; performance

opérateur(-trice), *m.* (*f.*) operator

opérer, *v.t.* to operate; to work, to work out, to effect; to bring about

opérette, *f.* light opera, musical comedy

ophtalmie, *f.* ophthalmia

opiner, *v.i.* to be of opinion, to give one's opinion

opiniâtre, (*adj.*) obstinate, stubborn, stiff or stout (resistance)

(s')opiniâtrer, to be obstinate

opiniâtreté, *f.* obstinacy, stubbornness

opinion, *f.* opinion, belief, judgment

opium, *m.* opium

opportun, (*adj.*) opportune, timely, seasonable, favourable, convenient

opportunité, *f.* opportunity; favourable opening; timeliness

opposant(e), (*adj.*) opposing, adverse; *m.* (*f.*) opponent, adversary

opposé, (*adj.*) opposite; contrary in position to; facing

opposer, *v.t.* to oppose; to place opposite to; to stand in the way of; s'- (à), *v.r.* to oppose, to resist, to object (to); to set oneself (against)

opposition, *f.* opposition; antagonism; hindrance; resistance; the opposition (*politics*)

oppresser, *v.t.* to oppress

oppresseur, *m.* oppressor, tyrant

oppression, *f.* oppression, tyranny; difficult breathing

opprimer, *v.t.* to oppress, to crush (by harsh government)

opprobre, *m.* infamy, shame, disgrace, opprobrium

opter, *v.i.* to choose

opticien, *m.* optician

optimisme, *m.* optimism

optimiste, *m.* and *f.* optimist; (*adj.*) optimistic

optique, *f.* optics (science of); (*adj.*) optical

opulence, *f.* wealth, affluence, opulence

opulent, (*adj.*) opulent, wealthy, affluent

or, (*conj.*) now; but; well

or, *m.* gold; gold (currency); gold ornament; gold colour

oracle, *m.* oracle

orage, *m.* tempest, storm, thunderstorm

orageux(-euse), (*adj.*) stormy, tempestuous

oraison, *f.* oration, speech; prayer; - **dominicale**, Lord's Prayer

oral, (*adj.*) oral, verbal

orange, *f.* orange; (*adj.*) orange-coloured

orangeade, *f.* orange juice, orangeade

oranger, *m.* orange tree

orangerie, *f.* orangery

orateur, *m.* orator, speaker

oratoire, (*adj.*) oratorical; *m.* oratory; private chapel

orbe, *m.* orb, orbit, sphere, globe

orbite, *m.* and *f.* orbit (*astron.*); orbit; eye socket

orchestre, *m.* orchestra, band; the musicians (of band)

orchestrer, *v.t.* to orchestrate, arrange musical score

orchidée, *f.* orchid

ordinaire, (*adj.*) ordinary, usual; common; vulgar; *m.* mess (*mil.*)

ordinairement, (*adv.*) usually, generally, ordinarily

ordonnance, *f.* order, disposition;

regulation; statute; prescription (*med.*); - **de police**, police regulation; **officier d'-**, orderly officer; *m.* orderly (batman).

ordonné, (*adj.*) ordered, orderly, methodical

ordonner, *v.t.* to arrange (something); to set in order; to dispose; to order; to direct

****ordre**, *m.* order; command; sequence; writ; regulation

ordure, *f.* filth, dirt; household refuse; filth (talk); obscenity

****oreille**, *f.* ear

oreiller, *m.* pillow

oreillons, *m. pl.* mumps

(d')ores et déjà, (*adv.*) henceforth; from this moment

orfèvre, *m.* goldsmith, silversmith

orfèvrerie, *f.* goldsmith's, silversmith's art (or shop); gold or silver jewellery

orfraie, *f.* osprey

organe, *m.* organ (body); voice

organique, (*adj.*) organic; of the bodily organs

organisation, *f.* organisation; formation; arrangement; system

organisé, (*adj.*) organised; well arranged

organiser, *v.t.* to organise; to get up (meeting, etc.); to form (society); to arrange; to settle

organiste, *m.* and *f.* organist

orge, *f.* barley; **sucre d'-**, barley sugar

orgie, *f.* debauch, drinking-bout; extravagance, excess

orgue, *m.* organ (church, etc.); - **de Barbarie**, barrel-organ

orgueil, *m.* pride, arrogance

orgueilleux(-euse), (*adj.*) proud, haughty, arrogant, boastful

orient, *m.* east, orient

oriental, (*adj.*) eastern, oriental

orienter, *v.t.* to set towards the east; to direct, to set right; **s'-**, *v.r.* to find out one's position, to find one's way

orifice, *m.* opening, aperture

original(-aux), (*adj.*) original; primitive; first, earliest; novel (in character); queer, strange

originalité, *f.* originality; eccentricity; oddness

origine, *f.* origin; source; starting point, beginning; extraction; descent, birth

orme, *m.* elm tree

ormeau, *m.* young elm tree

ornement, *m.* ornament; adornment; knick-knack

orner, *v.t.* to adorn; to decorate, to ornament

ornière, *f.* rut; beaten track

ornithologie, *f.* ornithology

ornithologiste, *m.* and *f.* ornithologist

orpailleur, *m.* gold prospector

orphelin(e), *m.* (*f.*) orphan; (*adj.*) orphaned

orphelinat, *m.* orphanage

orteil, *m.* toe; **gros -,** big toe

orthographe, *f.* orthography, spelling

orthopédique, (*adj.*) orthopædic

orthopédiste, *m.* orthopædist

ortie, *f.* nettle

os, *m.* bone

oscillation, *f.* oscillation; fluctuation, wavering

osciller, *v.i.* to oscillate; to swing; to fluctuate

osé, (*adj.*) bold; daring; venturesome

oseille, *f.* sorrel

oser, *v.t.* to dare, venture; to attempt

oseraie, *f.* osier bed

osier, *m.* water-willow; **d'-,** wicker

ossature, *f.* bony structure; skeleton

osselet, *m.* knuckle-bone

ossements, *m. pl.* bones (of dead persons)

osseux(-euse), (*adj.*) bony

ossuaire, *m.* ossuary; charnel house

ostensible, (*adj.*) ostensible

ostensoir, *m.* monstrance (R.C. Church)

ostentation, *f.* ostentation; vain, stupid display

otage, *m.* hostage

otarie, *f.* sea-lion

ôter, *v.t.* to take away, to remove; to take off (hat, etc.); to pull off (clothes); to take away

ou (*conj.*) or, either, else, otherwise

où, (*adv.*) where, whither, whence; when, from which; to which

ouailles, *f pl.* sheep, flock of sheep; flock (of priest)

ouate, *f.* cotton wool; cotton padding

ouater, *v.t.* to wad, to pad

oubli, *m.* oblivion; forgetfulness

oubliable, (*adj.*) forgettable

oublie, *f.* wafer

oublier, *v.t.* to forget; **s'-,** *v.r.* to forget oneself

oubliette, *f* dungeon

oublieux(-euse), (*adj.*) forgetful

ouest, *m.* west

oui, yes; **je crois que -,** I think so

oui-dire, *m.* (*invar.*) hearsay

ouïe, *f.* sense of hearing

ouïr, *v.t.* to hear

ouistiti, *m.* marmoset

ouragan, *m.* hurricane

ourdir, *v.t.* to warp; to hatch (plot)

ourler, *v.t.* to hem

ourlet, *m.* hem

ours(e), *m.* (*f.*) bear (she-bear)

oursin, *m.* sea-urchin

outil, *m.* tool, implement

outillage, *m.* set of tools; plant, gear

outiller, *v.t.* to equip, to supply, fit out

outrage, *m.* outrage; gross insult (against morals, etc.)

outrageant, (*adj.*) insulting; scurrilous

outrager, *v.t.* to insult; to outrage (nature)

outrance, *f.* excess; **à -,** to the bitter end

outre, (*prep.*) beyond; in addition to; **en -,** besides, moreover

outré, (*adj.*) exaggerated, incensed; exasperated

outrecuidance, *f.* presumptuousness

(d')outremer, (*adv.*) overseas

outrer, *v.t.* to carry to excess; to exaggerate; to overdo; to exasperate

ouvert, *(adj.)* open; exposed; unfortified (town)

ouverture, *f.* opening, aperture; overture *(mus.)*

ouvrable, *(adj.)* working, workable; **jour -,** working day

ouvrage, *m.* work, piece of work; job; workmanship

ouvre-boîtes, *(m. invar.)* tin-opener

ouvreur(-euse), *m.* *(f.)* opener (generally employee of theatre as box-opener)

ouvrier(ère), *m.* *(f.)* workman (-woman); mechanic; operative; *(adj.)* working(-class), labour (relations, etc.)

ouvrir, *v.t.* to open; to unclose; to throw open; to expand; to start (a business); **s'-,** *v.r.* to open one's heart (to somebody); to talk freely

ouvroir, *m.* workroom, workshop

ovaire, *m.* ovary *(med.)*

ovale, *(adj.)* oval; *m.* oval

oxyde, *m.* oxide

oxygène, *m.* oxygen

ozone, *m.* ozone

P

pacage, *m.* pasture, pasturage

pacager, *v.t.* to pasture, to graze (cattle)

pachyderme, *(adj.)* thick-skinned; *m.* pachyderm

pacificateur(-trice), *m.* *(f.)* peace-maker; *(adj.)* peace-making

pacification, *f.* pacification

pacifier, *v.t.* to pacify (a country); to calm

pacifique, *(adj.)* pacific; peaceable

pacifiste, *(adj.)* and *m.* *(f.)* pacifist

pacotille, *f.* shoddy goods

pacte, *m.* pact, agreement

pactiser, *v.i.* to treat with; enter into a compact; to compromise

pagaïe, *f.* disorder, muddle

paganisme, *m.* paganism

page, *f.* page (of book); **ne pas être à la -,** not to be up to date, in the know

page, *m.* page-boy

pagode, *f.* pagoda; temple

paiement, *m.* payment (also spelt **payement**)

païen(ne), *(adj.)* pagan; *m.* *(f.)* pagan, heathen

paillard, *(adj.)* lewd

paillasse, *f.* straw mattress

paillasse, *m.* clown, buffoon

paillasson, *m.* straw mat; door mat

paille, *f.* straw; **homme de -,** dummy; cat's-paw

pailler, *m.* straw stack

pailleter, *v.t.* to spangle

paillette, *f.* spangle

pain, *m.* bread; a loaf of bread; **petit -,** roll; **- de savon,** cake of soap

pair, *(adj.)* equal; even (number); **au-,** board and lodging, but no pay

pair, *m.* peer

paire, *f.* pair (of stockings, etc.)

pairie, *f.* peerage

paisible, *(adj.)* peaceful, peaceable, quiet

paître, *v.t.* to graze cattle; *v.i.* to graze, to feed

paix, *f.* peace

palace, *m.* expensive hotel or cinema

palais, *m.* palace; palate

palan, *m.* pulley-block, tackle

palatine, *f.* fur tippet

pale, *f.* pale, paling

pâle, *(adj.)* pale, pallid

palefrenier, *m.* groom; stud-groom

paleron, *m.* shoulder-bone (of animal)

paletot, *m.* great-coat

pâleur, *f.* paleness, pallor

palier, *m.* landing (of stairs)

pâlir, *v.i.* to turn pale, grow pale; to grow dim (of light, etc.)

palis, *m.* paling; picket fence

palissade, *f.* fence, palisade; hoarding

palissandre, *m.* rosewood
palliatif(-ive), *(adj.)* palliative
palmarès, *m.* honours list
palme, *f.* palm (tree); palm (branch)
palmier, *m.* palm tree
palombe, *f.* wood pigeon; ring dove
pâlot(te), *(adj.)* palish, peaky (child)
palpable, *(adj.)* palpable; obvious
palpe, *f.* feeler (of insect)
palper, *v.t.* to feel; to examine
palpitant, *(adj.)* palpitating; throbbing
palpitation, *f.* palpitation
palpiter, *v.i.* to palpitate; to flutter; to throb (heart)
paludisme, *m.* malaria
(se) pâmer, *v.r.* to faint, to swoon
pamphlet, *m.* pamphlet (often scurrilous)
pamplemousse, *m.* grape-fruit
pan, *m.* panel, flap (of garment); piece, section; patch (of sky)
panacée, *f.* panacea
panache, *m.* plume, tuft
panaché, *(adj.)* plumed; parti-coloured
panacher, *v.t.* to variegate; se -, *v.r.* to deck oneself out, to put on fine feathers
panachure, *f.* variegation
panade, *f.* bread soup
panaris, *m.* whitlow
pancarte, *f.* placard, bill (on hoarding)
pané, *(adj.)* covered with bread-crumbs; fried in breadcrumbs
panier, *m.* basket; - à papier, waste-paper basket
panique, *f.* panic, scare
panne, *f.* plush
panne, *f.* breakdown, hold-up (on railway); rester en -, to have a breakdown (car, etc.)
panneau, *m.* panel; snare (for game); hoarding (*advert., etc.*)
panse, *f.* belly, paunch
pansement, *m.* dressing (for wound)
panser, *v.t.* to dress a wound
pantalon, *m.* pair of trousers

pantelant, *(adj.)* panting; quivering (of body)
panteler, *v.i.* to pant
panthère, *f.* panther
pantin, *m.* nonentity, puppet
pantomime, *f.* dumb show
pantoufle, *f.* slipper
paon(ne), *m.* (*f.*) peacock (peahen)
papal, *(adj.)* papal
papauté, *f.* papacy
pape, *m.* the Pope
paperasse, *f.* official papers; archives; waste paper; "red-tape"
paperasserie, *f.* accumulation of unnecessary documents
papeterie, *f.* paper-making; paper mill; stationer's shop
papetier, *m.* paper-maker; stationer
papier, *m.* paper; document; private papers, business documents
papier-monnaie, *m.* paper currency
papillon, *m.* butterfly
papillonner, *v.i.* to flit, to flutter about
papillote, *f.* curl-paper
Pâque(s), *f.* Easter; Jewish Passover; (Pâques for Easter is usually spelt with " s ")
paquebot, *m.* liner
Pâques-fleuries, Palm Sunday
paquet, *m.* parcel, package; bundle; recevoir son -, (*coll.*) to get the sack
paqueter, *v.t.* to make into a parcel
*par, (*prep.*) by, by means of; through; in
parabole, *f.* parable; parabola
parachute, *m.* parachute
parachutiste, *m.* parachutist; air-borne soldier
parade, *f.* parade (*mil.*); guard-mounting; ostentation, show, parade (of wealth)
paradis, *m.* paradise; upper gallery, the " gods " (*theat.*)
paradoxal, *(adj.)* paradoxical
parafe *or* paraphe, *m.* flourish (flourishing signature)

parage, m. birth, descent

parages, m, pl. parts; regions

paragraphe, m. paragraph

*paraître, v.i. to appear, to seem; to come out (of stars); to come on the stage (actor); to be published (book); to be visible, apparent; faire -, to bring out, to publish

parallèle, (adj.) parallel

paralyser, v.t. to paralyse

paralysie, f. paralysis

paralytique, (adj.) paralytic; m. and f. paralytic

parangon, m. paragon (of virtue); pattern

parapet, m. parapet; breastwork

parapluie, m. umbrella

parasite, m. and f. parasite; pl. interference (W. Tel.); (adj.) parasitic

parasol, m. parasol; sunshade

paratonnerre, m. lightning-conductor

paravent, m. folding screen

parbleu! (interj.) why, of course; rather!

parc, m. park; pleasure grounds; cattle pen; car park

parcage, m. penning of cattle; folding of sheep; parking of cars

parcelle, f. small fragment; plot of land

parce que, (conj.) because

parchemin, m. parchment, vellum

parcimonie, f. parsimony, stinginess

parcimonieux(-euse), (adj.) parsimonious; stingy

parcourir, v.t. to go over; to travel through (a district, country); to wander, ramble (the streets); to skim through (book)

parcours, m. route of omnibus; course (of river); course (of a race); distance covered

pardessous, (prep.) and (adv.) under, underneath

pardessus, m. overcoat

pardessus (prep.) and (adv.) over, over the top of; - le marché, into the bargain

pardi! (interj.) of course!

pardon, m. pardon, forgiveness

pardon! I beg your pardon

pardonnable, (adj.) pardonable, forgiveable

pardonner, v.t. to pardon, to forgive

pare-boue, m. (invar.) mudguard

pare-brise, m. (invar.) windscreen

pare-choc, m. (invar.) bumper, fender (of car)

pareil(le), (adj.) like, alike; similar to; such; like that

parement, m. ornament, adornment; decoration

parent, m. parent; father and mother; relative; connection (family); blood relation

parentage, m. parentage; birth

parenté, f. kinship; relationship

parenthèse, f. parenthesis; brackets (typog.)

parents, m. pl. family, relations

parer, v.t. to adorn; to deck out with; to trim; to parry; to ward off; se -, v.r. to adorn oneself

paresse, f. laziness, idleness

paresseux(-euse), (adj.) lazy, idle; m. (f.) idler, sluggard

parfait, (adj.) perfect; faultless

parfaitement, (adv.) perfectly; certainly; exactly

parfois, (adv.) sometimes; occasionally

parfum, m. perfume; scent (of flowers, etc.)

parfumer, v.t. to scent; to use perfume

parfumerie, f. perfumery

parfumeur(-euse), m. (f.) perfumer

pari, m. bet, wager; - mutuel, totalisator (system)

parier, v.t. to bet, to wager, to lay (a bet)

parieur, m. bettor, backer

parité, f. equality (value, etc.), parity

parjure, m. perjury; se parjurer, v.r. to perjure oneself

parlant, (adj.) speaking; talking; film -, talkie

parlement, m. parliament

parlementaire, *(adj.)* parliamentary; *m.* bearer of a flag of truce

parlementer, *v.i.* to parley (with)

***parler,** *v.i.* to speak; to talk

parloir, *m.* parlour

parmi, *(prep.)* among

parodie, *f.* parody; skit (upon)

parodier, *v.t.* to parody

paroi, *f.* partition; wall

paroisse, *f.* parish

paroissien(ne), *m. (f.)* parishioner

***parole,** *f.* word (spoken); remark; promise, word (of honour); speech

parquer, *v.t.* to pen (cattle); to park (cars, etc.)

parquet, *m.* floor (also inlaid floor); public prosecutor's court, the well of the court (*legal*)

parqueter, *v.t.* to lay a floor

parrain, *m.* godfather

parsemer (de), *v.t.* to strew (with); to sprinkle; to dot (sky, countryside)

part, *f.* share; part; portion; participation; **de ma -,** on my behalf; **quelque (nulle) -,** somewhere (nowhere); **à -,** separately, aside *(theat.)*; **d'une -, d'autre -,** on the one (other) hand

partage, *m.* division; sharing (out); allotment

partager, *v.t.* to divide; to apportion out (property, etc.); to share out

partance, *f.* departure; sailing (time of)

partant, *(adv.)* therefore; *(adj.)* departing; *m. pl.* starters (racing)

partenaire, *m.* and *f.* partner (sport and dancing, *not* business associate)

parterre, *m.* flower-bed; pit (of a theatre)

***parti,** *m.* party; resolve; match (marriageable); **prendre son -,** to make up one's mind

parti pris, *m.* prejudice, bias (of opinion)

partial(-aux), *(adj.)* partial; biased

partialité, *f.* partiality; unfairness

participation, *f.* participation; share, interest (in)

participer, *v.i.* to participate; to have a share

particulariser, *v.t.* to give particulars, details

particularité, *f.* particularity; detail; peculiarity

particulier(-ère), *(adj.)* particular, special; characteristic; private (reasons); *m. (f.)* private individual

partie, *f.* part (of whole); party (pleasure); game (of tennis, etc.); client (of a barrister)

partiel(le), *(adj.)* partial, incomplete

partiellement, *(adv.)* partially; in part

***partir** (with *être*), *v.i.* to depart; to leave, to start; to go off; to walk away; to sail (of ship); to steam off (of train); **à - d'aujourd'hui,** from to-day on (-wards)

partisan(e), *m. (f.)* partisan

partout, *(adv.)* everywhere; on all sides

parure, *f.* ornament; head-dress; set (of jewellery, etc.)

parvenir, *v.i.* to reach; to arrive at; to attain; to manage to do something; to succeed

parvenu(e), *m. (f.)* parvenu, upstart

pas, *m.* pace, step, stride; straits (geog.); step (stair)

pas, *(neg. adv.)* not; **- du tout,** not at all

passable, *(adj.)* passable; tolerable; pretty fair

passage, *m.* passage; crossing (of something); passing over; way through, thoroughfare; fare; "**- interdit,**" "no thoroughfare"; **- clouté,** pedestrian crossing (marked with studs)

passager(ère), *(adj.)* momentary, transient, transitory; migratory (bird); *m. (f.)* passenger

passant(e), *m. (f.)* passer-by

passe, *f.* permit, pass

passé, *(adj.)* past; gone by; *m.* the past

passe-partout, *m.* *(invar.)* master key; mount *(phot.)*

passe-temps, *m.* *(invar.)* pastime

passementer, *v.t.* to trim (with lace, etc.)

passeport, *m.* passport

passer, *v.i.* to pass; to go past; to go (on, along or by); to undergo (trial, suffering); *v.t.* to pass; to cross (bridge, etc.); to exceed; to surpass; **se -,** *v.r.* to happen; to take place; **se - de,** to do without

passereau, *m.* sparrow

passerelle, *f.* footbridge; navigating bridge

passeur(-euse), *m.* *(f.)* ferryman (-woman)

passif(-ive), *(adj.)* passive; *m.* passive; liabilities

passion, *f.* passion

passionnant, *(adj.)* thrilling

passionné, *(adj.)* passionate, ardent

passoire, *f.* strainer (kitchen utensil)

pastèque, *f.* water-melon

pasteur, *m.* pastor, Protestant minister; shepherd

pastille, *f.* lozenge, fruit drop

pat, *m.* stalemate

pataquès, *m.* mistake in pronunciation (showing lack of education)

patauger, *v.i.* to paddle; to splash about; to flounder in mud

pâte, *f.* paste, dough; (with *dentifrice*) toothpaste

pâté, *m.* pie, pasty; blot (of ink)

patelin, *m.* wheedler; smooth-tongued person; *(adj.)* wheedling, glib

patenôtre, *f.* Lord's Prayer

patent, *(adj.)* patent; obvious

patente, *f.* licence (to carry out trade, etc.)

patenter, *v.t.* to licence

patère, *f.* peg (coat or hat); curtain hook

paternel(le), *(adj.)* paternal

paternité, *f.* paternity

pathétique, *(adj.)* pathetic

patience, *f.* patience; long-suffering

patient, *(adj.)* patient; *m.* *(f.)* patient (i.e. in hospital)

patienter, *v.i.* to show patience

patin, *m.* skate; runner

patiner, *v.i.* to skate

patineur(-euse), *m.* *(f.)* skater

patinoire, *f.* skating rink

pâtir, *v.i.* to suffer (in health)

pâtisserie, *f.* pastry; cake shop; tea-rooms

pâtissier(-ère), *m.* *(f.)* pastry-cook

patois, *m.* provincial, country dialect

pâtre, *m.* herdsman

patriarche, *m.* patriarch

patrie, *f.* native land or country

patrimoine, *m.* patrimony, heritage

patriote, *m.* and *f.* patriot; *(adj.)* patriotic (person)

patriotique, *(adj.)* patriotic (speech, song)

patriotisme, *m.* patriotism

patron(ne), *m.* *(f.)* patron; master (mistress) (of house, business); *(slang)* the boss; master (of small ship); *m.* pattern (for dress)

patronage, *m.* patronage; club (especially for young people)

patrouille, *f.* patrol

patrouiller, *v.i.* to patrol

patrouilleur, *m.* member of a patrol; patrol boat

patte, *f.* paw (of dog, cat, etc.); leg (of insect, fly, etc.); claw; **à quatre -s,** on all fours

patte d'oie, *f.* crow's foot (wrinkle)

pâturage, *m.* pasturage

pâture, *f.* feed (of animals); pasture

paume, *f.* palm (of hand); tennis (real, *not* lawn tennis)

paupière, *f.* eyelid

pause, *f.* pause

pauvre, *(adj.)* poor; needy; in want; scanty (vegetation)

pauvre, *m.* and *f.* pauper, poor person

pauvreté, *f.* poverty

(se) pavaner, *v.r.* to strut about

pavé, *m.* pavement; paving-stone; roadway

paver, *v.t.* to pave

paveur, *m.* paver, paviour

pavillon, *m.* pavilion; tent; summer-house (in garden); flag (*navy*)

pavois, *m.* shield (body); bulwark

pavoiser, *v.t.* to deck with flags, to dress (ship)

pavot, *m.* poppy

payable, *(adj.)* payable

payant, *(adj.)* paying (guest, pupil, etc.); *m.* (*f.*) payer, one who pays

paye, *f.* wages (of workmen); pay (of troops)

payement, *m.* payment

payer, *v.t.* to pay; to pay (for something) ; **- d'audace,** to take the risk

payeur(-euse), *m.* (*f.*) payer

pays, *m.* country; land; district; **vin du -,** local wine

paysage, *m.* landscape; countryside

paysagiste, *m.* and *f.* landscape-painter

paysan(ne), *m.* (*f.*) and *(adj.)* peasant; rustic

paysannerie, *f.* peasantry

péage, *m.* toll; turnpike

peau, *f.* skin (of person); hide, pelt, fur (of animal); **peau-rouge,** Redskin (Indian)

peausserie, *f.* skin-dressing

pêche, *f.* fishing; catch (of fish)

pêche, *f.* peach

péché, *m.* sin

pêcher, *m.* peach tree

pécher, *v.i.* to sin

pêcher, *v.t.* to fish

pêcheur(-euse), *m.* (*f.*) fisherman (-woman)

pécheur (pécheresse), *m.* (*f.*) sinner

pécore, *f.* beast; silly, stupid person (generally used of woman)

pécule, *m.* savings; small store of money

pécuniaire, *(adj.)* pecuniary

pédagogue, *m.* (*f.*) pedagogue

pédale, *f.* pedal

pédaler, *v.i.* to pedal; (*slang*) to bike

pédant(e), *(adj.)* pedantic; *m.*(*f.*) pedant

pédestre, *(adj.)* pedestrian

pédicure, *m.* and *f.* chiropodist

peigne, *m.* comb

peigner, *v.t.* to comb (the hair); to comb wool

peignoir, *m.* dressing-gown; morning wrapper (lady's)

peindre, *v.t.* to paint; to coat with paint; portray (in colours); to describe

peine, *f.* sorrow, grief, affliction; pains, trouble; penalty, punishment; **à -,** scarcely

peiner, *v.t.* to pain, to grieve, to distress; to toil

peintre, *m.* a painter (feminine is **femme peintre**)

peinture, *f.* painting (art of); picture, painting

peinturer, *v.t.* to cover with a coat of paint

Pékin, *m.* Pekin (*geog.*); civilian (*mil.*)

pelage, *m.* coat, wool (of animal)

pelé, *(adj.)* bald, hairless

peler, *v.t.* to take the hair off (a hide); to peel, skin (fruit, etc.); **se -,** *v.r.* to lose its hair (of animal)

pèlerin(e), *m.* (*f.*) pilgrim

pèlerinage, *m.* pilgrimage

pèlerine, *f.* woman's cape; tippet

pelisse, *f.* pelisse; fur-lined cloak

pelle, *f.* shovel; **pelle-bêche,** entrenching tool

pelleterie, *f.* fur trade

pelletier(-ère), *m.* (*f.*) furrier

pellicule, *f.* pellicle; film (of ice or of camera, etc.)

pelote, *f.* ball (of wool, string, etc.); **- basque,** *f.* pelota (game of pelota)

peloter, *v.t.* to wind (wool or string) into a ball; to handle

peloton, *m.* platoon, squad (*mil.*)

pelouse, *f.* lawn; plot of grass; enclosure (race-course)

pelu, (adj.) hairy

peluche, f. plush

pelure, f. peel, skin (apple, etc.); rind of cheese

pénal (pl. -als or -aux), (adj.) penal (code)

pénalité, f. penalty

penaud, (adj.) abashed; crest-fallen

penchant, (adj.) sloping, inclined, leaning; m. slope, declivity; a leaning or inclination (for)

pencher, v.i. to lean over; to incline, to lean; se -, v.r. to bend, to stoop

pendable, (adj.) hangable; abominable

pendaison, f. hanging (capital punishment)

pendant, (adj.) hanging, pendent; pending; m. pendant

pendant, (prep.) during; - que (conj.) while

pendard(e), m. (f.) rascal, rogue; forward woman

pendeloque, f. ear-drop

pendentif, m. pendant (worn round neck)

pendiller, v.i. to dangle

pendre, v.t. to hang (up); to hang (a person)

pendule, f. clock, time-piece; m. pendulum

pénétrant, (adj.) penetrating; piercing (wind); keen (glance)

pénétrer, v.i. to enter; v.t. to penetrate

pénible, (adj.) painful; distressing; laborious, hard (work); laboured (breathing)

péniche, f. canal-boat, barge

péninsule, f. peninsula

pénitence, f. penitence; repentance

pénitent, (adj.) and m. (f.) penitent

pénitentiaire, m. penitentiary, prison house

pénombre, f. half light; semi-darkness

pensée, f. thought; pansy (flower)

*penser, v.i. to think; to consider; to imagine

penseur(-euse), m. (f.) thinker

pensif(-ive), (adj.) pensive, thoughtful

pension, f. pension; board and lodging; boarding-house

pensionnaire, m. and f. pensioner; boarder

pensionnat, m. boarding-school

pensum, m. imposition (in school)

pente, f. slope, incline, gradient

Pentecôte, f. Whitsuntide; Pentecost

penture, f. hinge (of door)

pénurie, f. scarcity; shortage; poverty

pépie, f. pip (disease of fowls, birds)

pépier, v.i. to chirp

pépin, m. stone (of grape); pip (of apple)

pépinière, f. nursery (hortic.)

percale, f. cambric

perce-neige, f. (invar.) snowdrop

perce-oreille, m. earwig (pl. perce-oreilles)

percée, f. cutting (in wood), glade; break through (mil.)

percepteur(-trice), (adj.) discerning; m. (f.) tax-collector

perceptible, (adj.) perceptible, discernible

percer, v.t. to pierce, to go through; to lance (an abscess); to penetrate; v.i. to come through

percevoir, v.t. to perceive; to collect taxes; to levy (taxes)

perche, f. perch (fish); perch (for birds); thin pole, perch, rod; pole (measurement)

percher, v.i. to perch, to roost

percheron, m. percheron (horse, heavy draught horse)

perclus, (adj.) stiff-jointed

percussion, f. percussion, impact

perdant(e), (adj.) losing; m. (f.) loser

perdre, v.t. to lose; to ruin; to destroy; se -, v.r. to be lost; to lose one's way

perdreau, m. young partridge

perdrix, f. partridge

perdu, (adj.) lost; ruined
père, m. father
péremptoire, (adj.) peremptory
perfection, f. perfection
perfectionnement, m. perfecting; improving
perfectionner, v.t. to perfect; to improve; se -, v.r. to improve one's knowledge of something
perfide, (adj.) perfidious; treacherous
perforer, v.t. to perforate; to bore through; to puncture
péril, m. peril, danger, risk
périlleux(-euse), (adj.) perilous, dangerous, risky
périmer, v.i. to fall into abeyance; to become out of date
période, f. period of time; age, era
périodique, (adj.) periodical
péripétie, f. vicissitude
périr, v.i. to perish; to be destroyed (périr even in this sense takes avoir)
péritoine, m. peritoneum
péritonite, f. peritonitis
perle, f. pearl; nacre de -, mother-of-pearl
perlé, (adj.), pearly (teeth); pearled; beaded; faire la grève perlée, to work slowly on purpose, ca' canny
perler, v.t. to pearl (barley); to husk rice
permanence, f. permanence; building open day and night
permanent, (adj.) permanent
perméable, (adj.) permeable, porous
*permettre, v.t. to permit; to allow
permis, (adj.) allowed, permitted, permissible
permis, m. permit; - de conduire, driving licence
permission, f. permission; leave; leave of absence (of soldier)
permissionaire, m. soldier (on short leave)
permutation, f. exchange of posts; (maths.) permutations
pernicieux(-euse), (adj.) pernicious; harmful; baneful (influence)
péronnelle, f. silly woman
perpendiculaire, (adj.) perpendicular
perpétuel(le), (adj.) perpetual, everlasting
perpétuer, v.t. to perpetuate
perpétuité, f. perpetuity; à -, in perpetuity, for ever
perplexe, (adj.) perplexed, puzzled
perquisition, f. search (of premises)
perquisitionner, v.t. to make a search
perron, m. flight of steps
perroquet (perruche), m. (f.) parrot
perruque, f. wig
perse, f. chintz (material); (adj.) Persian
persécuter, v.t. to persecute; to pester
persécution, f. persecution
persévérance, f. perseverance
persévérant, (adj.) persevering, dogged
persévérer, v.i. to persevere
persienne, f. Venetian blind
persiflage, m. banter; persiflage
persifler, v.i. to banter (generally ill-natured)
persil, m. parsley
persillé, (adj.) green; streaked (meat)
persister (à), v.i. to persist (in)
personnage, m. personage (of rank); person, individual
personnalité, f. personality; individual characteristic; personage (of note)
personne, f. person; individual; ne ... -, no one, nobody
personnel(le), (adj.) personal; m. personnel, staff
personnifier, v.t. to personify; to impersonate
perspectif(-ive), (adj.) perspective (plan, etc.)
perspective, f. outlook, view, prospect
perspicace, (adj.) shrewd

perspicacité, *f.* perspicacity; shrewdness

persuader, *v.t.* to persuade; to convince

persuasif(-ive), *(adj.)* persuasive

persuasion, *f.* persuasion; conviction; belief

perte, *f.* loss, ruin; à - de vue, as far as the eye can see

pertinent, *(adj.)* pertinent; relevant (to)

pertuis, *m.* narrow pass; sluice

perturbateur(-trice), *m. (f.)* disturber (of the peace, etc.)

perturbation, *f.* perturbation; agitation

pervenche, *f.* periwinkle

pervers, *(adj.)* perverse; depraved

perversion, *f.* perversion

perversité, *f.* perversity

pervertir, *v.t.* to pervert; to corrupt

pesage, *m.* weighing; weighing in; paddock (race-course)

pesant, *(adj.)* heavy, weighty, ponderous

pesanteur, *f.* sluggishness, dullness (of mind), stupidity

pèse-lettre, *m.* letter-weight

peser, *v.t.* to weigh; *v.i.* to be heavy; se -, *v.r.* to weigh oneself

peson, *m.* spring-balance

pessimiste, *m.* and *f.* pessimist; *(adj.)* pessimistic

peste, *f.* plague, pestilence

pestifère, *(adj.)* pestiferous, pestilential

pétard, *m.* petard; detonator (on railway); faire du -, to kick up a row

péter, *v.i.* to break wind; to pop (of cork); to crackle

pétillant, *(adj.)* sparkling; crackling

pétiller, *v.i.* to sparkle; to crackle (wood burning)

petit, *(adj.)* small, little; insignificant, unimportant; en -, in miniature

petit-fils (petite-fille), *m. (f.)* grandson; granddaughter

petitesse, *f.* smallness, pettiness

pétition, *f.* petition; memorial

pétrification, *f.* petrification

pétrifier, *v.t.* to petrify

pétrin, *m.* kneading trough; *(slang)* in the soup

pétrir, *v.t.* to knead (dough)

pétrole, *m.* petroleum

pétrolifère, *(adj.)* oil-bearing

peu, *(adv.)* little; few; sous -, shortly, soon; - à -, bit by bit

peuplade, *f.* small tribe

peuple, *m.* people; nation; the masses

peupler, *v.t.* to people; to populate

peuplier, *m.* poplar tree

peur, *f.* fear; fright; dread

peureux(-euse), *(adj.)* fearful (of); nervous; timid

peut-être, *(adv.)* perhaps, possibly

phare, *m.* lighthouse; headlight (of car)

pharmacie, *f.* chemist's shop; dispensary

pharmacien(ne), *m. (f.)* chemist, pharmacist

phase, *f.* phase; stage, period

phénoménal(-aux), *(adj.)* phenomenal; prodigious

phénomène, *m.* phenomenon; freak

philanthrope, *m.* and *f.* philanthropist

philanthropisme, *m.* philanthropy

philatéliste, *m.* and *f.* stamp collector

philosophe, *m.* and *f.* philosopher; *(adj.)* philosophical

philosophie, *f.* philosophy

phoque, *m.* seal

phosphore, *m.* phosphorus

photographe, *m.* photographer

photographie, *f.* photography

photographique, *(adj.)* photographic

phrase, *f.* sentence

phraséologie, *f.* phraseology

phtisie, *f.* phthisis; consumption

physicien(ne), *m. (f.* natural philosopher *(not* physician); physicist

physiologiste, *m.* physiologist

physionomie, *f.* countenance, face; cast of features

physique, *(adj.)* physical; *f.* physics; *m.* physique

piaffer, *v.i.* to prance; paw the ground (horse); to swagger

piailler, *v.i.* to squall (child); to squeal

pianiste, *m.* and *f.* pianist

piano, *m.* piano, pianoforte

piaulard, *(adj.)* whining, whimpering (child)

piauler, *v.i.* to whine, to whimper

pic, *m.* peak (mountain); pick, pickaxe; à -, perpendicularly

pichenette, *f.* fillip, flip

picoter, *v.t.* to peck (of birds); to prick (holes in something)

pie, *f.* magpie

*****pièce,** *f.* piece (as a whole); piece (part of the whole); room in a house; - d'artillerie, gun

*****pied,** *m.* foot (of man); à -, on foot

piège, *m.* snare, trap

pierraille, *f.* heap of stones

pierre, *f.* stone; Peter (proper name); - à briquet, flint for lighter; - à aiguiser, whetstone

pierreries, *f. pl.* precious stones

pierreux(-euse), *(adj.)* stony

pierrot, *m.* pierrot, clown; (also used as diminutive of *Pierre,* Peter)

piété, *f.* piety; affectionate devotion; **mont de -,** pawnshop

piétiner, *v.t.* to trample; to stamp (on)

piéton, *m.* foot passenger; pedestrian

pieu(x), *m.* stake, post, pile

pieux(-euse), *(adj.)* pious, godly

pigeon(ne), *m.* *(f.)* pigeon; dove; *(slang)* a mug, greenhorn

pigeon-voyageur, carrier pigeon

pigeonnier, *m.* pigeon house; dove-cot

pignon, *m.* gable; pinion; **avoir - sur rue,** to have a house of one's own

pilastre, *m.* pilaster

pile, *f.* pile; battery (torch, etc.);

reverse of coin; - ou face, heads or tails

piler, *v.t.* to pound

pilier, *m.* pillar, post

pillage, *m.* pillage; looting

pillard, *m.* looter

piller, *v.t.* to plunder; to loot

pilonner, *v.t.* to pound, to pulp (paper)

pilori, *m.* pillory

pilote, *m.* pilot; **brevet de pilotage,** pilot's certificate ((aviat.)

piloter, *v.t.* to pilot (ship, aeroplane)

pilotis, *m.* piling, pile-work

pilule, *f.* pill

piment, *m.* pimento; red pepper

pimenter, *v.t.* to season with red pepper

pimpant, *(adj.)* smart, spruce

pin, *m.* pine tree, fir

pinacle, *m.* pinnacle

pince, *f.* hold, handle (of tool); pincers, pliers

pince-feuilles, *m.* (invar.) paper clip

pince-nez, *m.* (invar.) eyeglasses, pince-nez

pinceau, *m.* paint brush (artist's)

pincer, *v.t.* to pinch, to nip; to catch (a thief); **se faire -,** to get pinched, nabbed

pincettes, *f. pl.* tweezers, nippers

pinson, *m.* chaffinch

pintade, *f.* guinea-fowl

pioche, *f.* pickaxe, pick

piocher, *v.t.* to dig with a pick; to study hard, to swat

pion, *m.* pawn (chess); usher; junior master

pionnier, *m.* pioneer

pioupiou, *m.* foot soldier

pipe, *f.* pipe, tube; tobacco pipe

pipelet(te), *m.* *(f.)* porter; concierge (in Paris, of block of flats, etc.)

piper, *v.i.* to peep (small birds); to lure birds (with calls)

piquant, *(adj.)* stinging; sharp (taste); biting (remark); attractive (appearance)

pique, *f.* pike; *m.* spade (cards)

piquer, *v.t.* to prick, to sting; to

offend (someone); to quilt; to stimulate (appetite); - une tête, to dive, take a header

piquet, *m.* peg, post; picket *(mil.)*; piquet (card-game)

piquette, *f.* local wine (of poor quality)

piqûre, *f.* sting, bite (of insect); hypodermic injection

pirate, *m.* pirate

piraterie, *f.* piracy

pire, (comp. of *mauvais*) (*adj.*) worse

pirogue, *f.* canoe

pirouette, *f.* whirligig, pirouette

pis, *m.* udder (of cow)

pis, (*adv.*) (comp. of *mal*) worse; (de) - en -, worse and worse; *m.* - aller, poor substitute, last resort

piscine, *f.* fish-pond; swimming bath

pissenlit, *m.* dandelion

pisser, *v.i.* to make water (vulgar use only)

piste, *f.* running-track, race track; track, scent

pistolet, *m.* pistol

piston, *m.* piston *(mech.)*

pistonner, *v.t.* to back, to recommend; to push, boost (by influence or favour)

pitance, *f.* pittance

piteux(-euse), (*adj.*) piteous, woeful

pitié, *f.* pity, compassion

piton, *m.* eye-bolt; peak of mountain; peg (mountain-climbing)

pitoyable, (*adj.*) pitiable, pitiful; wretched

pittoresque, (*adj.*) picturesque

pivoine, *f.* peony

pivot, *m.* pivot, axis, swivel

pivoter, *v.i.* to pivot; to hinge (upon); to revolve

placard, *m.* poster, placard; wall cupboard

*****place,** *f.* place, position; seat (in train, etc.); locality; **sur -,** on the spot; **- publique,** public square; market place

placement, *m.* placing; investment (money)

placer, *v.t.* to place; to put; to invest; **se -,** *v.r.* to take one's place or seat

plafond, *m.* ceiling; ceiling (of aeroplane)

plage, *f.* beach; shore; seaside resort

plagiaire, *m.* and *f.* plagiarist

plaider, *v.t.* to plead (a cause); to plead (in law court)

plaideur(-euse), *m.* (*f.*) litigant, suitor (legal)

plaidoirie, *f.* counsel's speech; pleading

plaie, *f.* wound, open sore; affliction

plaindre, *v.t.* to pity; **se -,** *v.r.* to complain

plaine, *f.* plain, flat country

plainte, *f.* complaint; groan, moan

plaintif(-ive), (*adj.*) plaintive, querulous

plaire, *v.t.* to please; to be agreeable to; **se -,** *v.r.* to be pleased; to be happy or contented; **s'il vous plaît,** if you (please)

plaisant, (*adj.*) amusing, funny

plaisanter, *v.i.* to joke; to jest

plaisanterie, *f.* joke, jest

plaisir, *m.* pleasure, delight; favour; will; **au - de vous revoir,** hoping to see you again

plan, *m.* plan, drawing, project; **premier -,** foreground

plan, (*adj.*) flat (ground), level

planche, *f.* board, plank; **faire la -,** to float (in bathing)

plancher, *m.* floor (boarded); planking

plançon, *m.* sapling

plane, *m.* plane-tree

planer, *v.i.* to soar; to hover; to smooth

planète, *f.* planet

planeur, *m.* glider (for air-borne troops, etc.)

plant, *m.* plantation; sapling

plante, *f.* plant; sole of the foot

planter, *v.t.* to plant; to fix; set up; **- qn. là,** to leave someone in the lurch

planton, *m.* orderly *(mil.)*

plantureux(-euse), (*adj.*) abundant, copious

plaque, *f.* plate, sheet (of metal); slab of marble; badge (identity)

plaquer, *v.t.* to veneer (wood); to plate (metal); to leave in the lurch *(fam.);* **se -,** *v.r.* to lie flat on ground

plastique, *(adj.)* and *m.* plastic

plastron, *m.* shirt-front

plat, *(adj.)* flat, level; dull

plat, *m.* dish; flat of the hand

platane, *m.* plane tree

plateau, *m.* tray; plateau; table-land

plate-bande, *f.* flower-bed

plate-forme, *f.* platform (of omnibus); footplate (of engine)

platine, *f.* platinum

plâtre, *m.* plaster; plaster-cast

plâtrer, *v.t.* to plaster; to plaster up

plâtrier, *m.* plasterer

plausible, *(adj.)* plausible

plein (de), *(adj.)* full (of); filled (with)

plénipotentiaire, *m.* and *(adj.)* plenipotentiary

pléthore, *f.* superabundance; plethora

pleurer, *v.i.* to shed tears; to cry; *v.t.* to mourn for (someone)

pleurésie, *f.* pleurisy

pleurnicher, *v.i.* to whine; to snivel

pleuvoir, *v. imp.* to rain

pli, *m.* fold, pleat; cover, envelope; **sous ce -,** enclosed herein, herewith

pliant, *(adj.)* flexible; *m.* folding chair

plier, *v.t.* to fold; to fold up

plisser, *v.t.* to pleat; to crease; to crumple

plomb, *m.* lead

plomber, *v.t.* to cover with lead; to weight with lead; to stop, to fill (a tooth); to seal

plomberie, *f.* plumbing; plumber's shop

plombier, *m.* plumber

plonger, *v.i.* to plunge; to dive; *v.t.* to immerse

plongeur(-euse), *m.* *(f.)* diver; washer-up (in restaurant)

pluie, *f.* rain

plumage, *m.* plumage; feathers

plume, *f.* feather; pen

plumeau, *m.* feather duster

plumer, *v.t.* to pluck (poultry); to fleece (somebody)

plumet, *m.* plume

plupart (la), *f.* (the) most; the greatest, or greater part or number

pluriel(le), *m.* and *(adj.)* plural *(gram.)*

***plus,** *(adv.)* more

plusieurs, *(adj.* and *pron.)* several

plutôt, *(adv.)* rather, sooner

pluvier, *m.* plover

pluvieux(-euse), *(adj.)* rainy (season)

pneu, *m.* tyre (of car, bicycle)

pneumatique, *(adj.)* pneumatic

pneumatique, *m.* pneumatic tyre; (in Paris) express letter

pneumonie, *f.* pneumonia

pochard, *m.* drunkard

poche, *f.* pocket; bag; pouch; sack; **- d'air,** air-pocket

pocher, *v.t.* to poach (eggs)

pochette, *f.* pouch, handbag

poêle, *f.* frying-pan

poêle, *m.* stove; cooking-stove or range

poème, *m.* poem

poésie, *f.* poetry; poem

poète (poétesse), *m.* *(f.)* poet (ess)

poétique, *(adj.)* poetic

poids, *m.* weight; importance; **- lourd,** heavyweight (boxing)

poignant, *(adj.)* poignant; agonising, thrilling (sight, spectacle)

poignard, *m.* dagger

poignarder, *v.t.* to stab

poignée, *f.* handful; **- de main,** handshake

poignet, *m.* wrist; cuff, wristband (of shirt)

poil, *m.* hair (of animal); hair (on the body of man); nap (of cloth)

poilu *(adj.)* hairy; *m.* French soldier *(coll.)*

poinçon, *m.* bradawl; bodkin; punch

poinçonner, *v.t.* to bore, to prick; to punch (a hole)

poindre, *v.i.* to dawn

poing, *m.* fist

*****point,** *m.* point; degree; stitch; full-stop; **deux points,** colon; **point et virgule,** semi-colon; **ne... point,** *(adv.)* no, not; **- du tout,** not at all

pointe, *f.* point (of sword, needle, etc.); promontory *(geog.)*

pointe-sèche, *f.* dry-point etching

pointer, *v.t.* to prick, to stab; to aim; to level; to tick off (names, etc., on list)

pointeur, *m.* gun-layer, time-keeper

pointiller, *v.i.* to cavil, bicker, to dot (i's, etc.)

pointu, *(adj.)* pointed

pointure, *f.* size (of shoes, etc.)

poire, *f.* pear; *(slang)* a mug; easy mark (very commonly used)

poiré, *m.* perry (drink made from pears)

poireau, *m.* leek; wart

poirier, *m.* pear-tree

pois, *m.* pea; **petits -,** *m. pl.* green peas; **- de senteur,** sweet peas; **purée de -,** pea soup

poison, *m.* poison

poisson, *m.* fish

poissonnerie, *f.* fish shop or market

poissonnier(-ère), *m.* *(f.)* fish-monger

poitrail, *m.* breast (of horse)

poitrinaire, *m.* and *f.* and *(adj.)* consumptive

poitrine, *f.* chest; breast, bosom (of woman)

poivrade, *f.* sauce seasoned with pepper

poivre, *m.* pepper

poivrer, *v.t.* to season with pepper

poivrière, *f.* pepper-box; pepper-castor; small turret

poix, *f.* pitch; cobbler's wax

polaire, *(adj.)* polar

pôle, *m.* pole (north, south)

polémique, *f.* controversy

poli, *(adj.)* polite, polished; burnished

police, *f.* police, policing; policy (insurance); **agent de -,** police-man

polichinelle, *m.* Punch; buffoon

policier, *m.* policeman; *(adj.)* **roman -,** detective novel

polir, *v.t.* to polish; to burnish

polisson(ne), *m.* *(f.)* rascal, scamp; naughty child

polissonnerie, *f.* mischievousness (of child); depravity, obscenity

politesse, *f.* politeness; good manners

politique, *f.* politics; *(adj.)* political

polluer, *v.t.* to pollute, to defile

polonais, *(adj.)* Polish

poltron(ne), *(adj.)* cowardly, timid; *m. (f.)* coward

pommade, *f.* pomade, pomatum

pomme, *f.* apple; **- de terre,** potato

pommeau, *m.* pommel, butt

pommelé, *(adj.)* dappled, mottled

pommette, *f.* cheek-bone

pommier, *m.* apple-tree

pompe, *f.* pump; pomp, display; **pompes funèbres,** undertaker's establishment; **pompe à incendie,** fire-engine

pomper, *v.t.* to pump

pompeux(-euse), *(adj.)* pompous; high-flown

pompier, *m.* fireman

pompon, *m.* pompon; tuft

(se) pomponner, *v.r.* to smarten oneself up; to titivate

ponce, *f.* pumice-stone

ponceau, *m.* culvert; corn-poppy; *(adj. invar.)* flaming red

ponctualité, *f.* punctuality

ponctuel(le), *(adj.)* punctual

ponctuer, *v.t.* to punctuate; to emphasise

pondaison, *f.* laying of eggs

pondéré, *(adj.)* well-balanced, level-headed

pondre, *v.t.* to lay (eggs)

pont, *m.* bridge; deck (of a ship); **ponts et chaussées,** highways department; **pont suspendu,** *m.* suspension bridge; **pont levis,** *m.* drawbridge; **pont à bascule,** *m.* weighbridge

pontife, *m*. Pontiff (the Pope)

ponton, *m*. pontoon

populace, *f*. the mob, riff-raff

populaire, (*adj*.) popular

populariser, *v.t.* to popularise (an idea)

popularité, *f*. popularity

population, *f*. population

populeux(-euse), (*adj*.) populous

porc, *m*. hog; pig; pork (meat)

porcelaine, *f*. chinaware

porcelet, *m*. young pig

porc-épic, *m*. porcupine

porche, *m*. porch

pore, *m*. pore (of the skin, etc.)

porphyre, *m*. porphyry

port, *m*. port; harbour; carriage, transport of goods; postage (of parcel, etc.)

portable, (*adj*.) portable; wearable (garment)

portage, *m*. conveyance, transport (of goods)

portail(s), *m*. portal

portant, (*adj*.) bearing, carrying; bien (mal) -, in good (bad) health); à bout -, point blank

portatif(-ive), (*adj*.) easily carried; portable

porte, *f*. door, doorway, gateway; - de derrière, back door; - d'entrée, front door

porte-avions, *m*. (*invar*.) aircraft-carrier

porte-bonheur, *m*. (*invar*.) charm; amulet

porte-carte, *m*. map case

porte-cigarettes, *m*. (*invar*.) cigarette case; cigarette holder

porte-clefs, *m*. (*invar*.) key ring

porte-crayon, *m*. (*invar*.) pencil case

portefaix, *m*. street porter; dock hand

portefeuille, *m*. portfolio; note-case; wallet

porte-mine, *m*. (*invar*.) propelling pencil

porte-monnaie, *m*. (*invar*.) purse

porte-parole, *m*. (*invar*.) spokesman

porte-plume, *m*. (*invar*.) pen-holder; - à réservoir, fountain pen

portée, *f*. reach (of arm); range (of gun, etc.); span; litter (of animals)

*porter, *v.t.* to carry, to bear; to support; to wear (clothes); to strike (a blow), e.g. porter un coup à quelqu'un; se -, *v.r.* to repair; proceed to a place; se - bien (mal), to be in good (bad) health

porteur(-euse), *m*. (*f*.) carrier, bearer

portier(-ère), *m*. (*f*.) porter, door-keeper

portière, *f*. door (of railway carriage, car)

portion, *f*. portion, share; part

portionner, *v.t.* to share out

portique, *m*. portico

portrait, *m*. portrait, likeness

pose, *f*. pose, attitude, posture; laying (of cable, etc.)

posé, (*adj*.) steady, sedate

poser, *v.i.* to place, put, set, to lay (down something); to put up; to pose (for one's portrait, etc.); se - sur, to alight, land on

poseur(-euse), *m*. (*f*.) person who poses; who is affected

positif(-ive), (*adj*.) positive, actual

position, *f*. position, situation

posséder, *v.t.* to possess; to be in possession of something

possesseur, *m*. possessor

possession, *f*. possession

possibilité, *f*. possibility

possible, (*adj*.) possible

postal(-aux), (*adj*.) postal (service); carte postale, post card

poste, *f*. post, post office; *m*. post, position, berth, police station; - de T.S.F., radio-set

poster, *v.t.* to post, to station (somebody)

postérieur, (*adj*.) posterior; subsequent to

postérité, *f*. posterity; descendants

posthume, (*adj*.) posthumous

postiche, (*adj*.) false (hair); sham

postuler, *v.t.* to conduct a case; to sue

pot, *m.* pot, jug, jar

pot-au-feu, *m.* boiled beef and vegetables

potable, (*adj.*) drinkable, fit to drink

potage, *m.* soup

potager, *m.* kitchen-garden

potasse, *f.* potash

pot-de-vin, *m.* gratuity; bribe; hush-money; (*pot-de-vin* is often used in connection with political moves and it really means greasing the palm)

poteau, *m.* post, stake

potée, *f.* potful, jugful; swarm (of children)

potelé, (*adj.*) plump; chubby

potence, *f.* gallows, gibbet

poterie, *f.* pottery; stoneware

potiche, *f.* large vase (especially eastern porcelain)

potier, *m.* potter

potin, *m.* pewter; white metal; tittle-tattle; **faire du -,** to kick up a row, to cause a stir

potion, *f.* potion, draught, mixture (*med.*)

potiron, *m.* pumpkin

pou(x), *m.* louse

poubelle, *f.* dustbin

pouce, *m.* thumb; inch

pouding, *m.* pudding; plum-pudding

poudre, *f.* powder (general use)

poudrer, *v.t.* to powder; to sprinkle with powder

poudrerie, *f.* (gun) powder factory

poudreux(-euse), (*adj.*) dusty

poudroyer, *v.i.* to form clouds of dust (on road); *v.t.* to cover with dust

pouffer (de rire), *v.i.* to burst out laughing

pouilleux(-euse), (*adj.*) lousy

poulailler, *m.* hen-house; poulterer; the " gods " (*theat.*)

poulain, *m.* colt, foal

poularde, *f.* fat fowl (ready for table)

poule, *f.* hen; (*fam.*) prostitute, " bird "

poulet, *m.* chicken; love-letter

poulette, *f.* pullet

poulie, *f.* pulley; block

pouls, *m.* pulse

poumon, *m.* lung

poupe, *f.* stern (of ship)

poupée, *f.* doll; puppet

***pour,** (*prep.*) for; on account of; instead of; as to; in order to; for (time); by (time)

pourboire, *m.* tip, gratuity

pourceau, *m.* hog, pig

pourcent, *m.* percentage

pourparlers, *m. pl.* parley; negotiations

pourpre, *m.* crimson, purple

pourquoi? (*adv.* and *conj.*) why? - **faire?** what for?

pourrir, *v.i.* to rot, to decay

pourriture, *f.* rottenness

poursuite, *f.* pursuit; chase; tracking (of criminal)

poursuites, *f. pl.* lawsuit, action; prosecution

poursuivre, *v.t.* to pursue; to go after; to chase; to continue; to sue

pourtant, (*adv.*) nevertheless; however

pourtour, *m.* circumference

pourvoi, *m.* (legal) petition (for mercy, leniency)

pourvoir, *v.t.* to provide; to supply

pourvu que, (*conj.*) provided that

pousse-café, *m.* (*invar.*) liqueur after coffee

poussée, *f.* push, thrust; pushing; growth; sprouting

pousser, *v.t.* to push, to thrust; to utter (a cry); to urge; *v.i.* to sprout; **- qn. un bout (de chemin),** to give someone a lift

poussière, *f.* dust

poussiéreux(-euse), (*adj.*) dusty

poussin, *m.* chick, young chicken

poutre, *f.* beam (of wood)

pouvoir, *m.* power, authority

***pouvoir,** *v.t.* to be able; to be allowed

prairie, *f.* meadow; grassland

praline, *f.* burnt almond; praline (sweet)

praticable, *(adj.)* practicable; feasible

praticien, *m.* practitioner *(med.* or *legal)*

pratique, *(adj.)* practical; useful; *f.* practice; application (of theory); custom

pratiquer, *v.t.* to practise; to employ, use

pré, *m.* meadow

préalable (à), *(adj.)* previous (to)

préambule, *m.* preamble

préau, *m.* courtyard, playground

prébendier, *m.* prebendary (church)

précaire, *(adj.)* precarious; delicate (health, situation)

précaution, *f.* precaution; care

précédemment, *(adv.)* previously

précédence, *f.* precedence; priority

précédent, *(adj.)* preceding, previous; *m.* precedent

précéder, *v.t.* to precede; to go before

précepte, *m.* precept

précepteur, *m.* tutor

prêche, *m.* sermon

prêcher, *v.t.* to preach

précieux(-euse), *(adj.)* precious; valuable; affected

précipice, *m.* precipice

précipitamment, *(adv.)* precipitately, headlong, hurriedly

précipiter, *v.t.* to precipitate; to hurry; to hasten; to hurl

précis, *(adj.)* precise, accurate; *m.* summary

préciser, *v.t.* to specify, to fix (details); to state precisely

précision, *f.* precision, exactness, accuracy

précoce, *(adj.)* precocious, forward (child), early

préconiser, *v.t.* to recommend (somebody); to advocate

prédécesseur, *m.* predecessor

prédiction, *f.* prediction; forecast

prédire, *v.t.* to predict; to foretell

prédominance, *f.* predominance; prevalence

prédominant, *(adj.)* predominant, prevailing

prééminent, *(adj.)* pre-eminent

préface, *f.* preface; foreword

préfectoral(-aux), *(adj.)* prefectoral; of the prefect

préfecture, *f.* prefecture (headquarters of the prefect of a department); **- de police,** headquarters of the Paris police force

préférable, *(adj.)* preferable

préférence, *f.* preference; **action de -,** preference share

préférer, *v.t.* to prefer; to like better

préfet, *m.* prefect (of a department in France); the head of the Paris police

préjudice, *m.* prejudice; detriment

préjugé, *m.* precedent; presumption; prejudice; prepossession

préjuger, *v.t.* to prejudge

prélart, *m.* tarpaulin

(se) prélasser, *v.r.* to lounge about; to put on airs of importance

prélat, *m.* prelate

prélèvement, *m.* deduction (in advance)

prélever, *v.t.* to deduct in advance; to set apart

préliminaire, *(adj.)* preliminary

prélude, *m.* prelude

prématuré, *(adj.)* premature, untimely

préméditation, *f.* premeditation

préméditer, *v.t.* to premeditate

premier(-ère), *(adj.)* first; **premier ministre,** premier, prime minister; **monter en première,** to travel first class

*prendre, *v.t.* to take, to seize; to lay hold of; to capture

prendre, *v.i.* to set (jelly, etc.); to take, get a hold

preneur(-euse), *m. (f.)* taker; lessee

prénom, *m.* first name, Christian name

préoccuper, *v.t.* to preoccupy, to engross; **se - (de),** *v.r.* to give one's attention (to)

préopinant(e), *m.* *(f.)* previous speaker

préparatifs, *m. pl.* preparations

préparation, *f.* preparation, preparing (for)

préparatoire, *(adj.)* preparatory

préparer, *v.t.* to prepare; to get or make ready; **se - (à),** *v.r.* to get ready (for); **il se prépare quelque chose,** something is brewing

prépondérance, *f.* preponderance (over)

préposé, *m.* official in charge; superintendent

près (de), *(adv.)* near; **à peu -,** nearly, about, approximately

présage, *m.* omen

présager, *v.t.* to betoken; to augur

pré-salé, *m.* mutton (fed on salt marshes)

presbyte, *(adj.)* long-sighted

presbytère, *m.* presbytery (Roman Catholic Church); parsonage (Protestant Church)

prescription, *f.* prescription; direction for treatment *(med.)*; regulation

prescrire, *v.t.* to prescribe; lay down

préséance, *f.* precedence; priority

présence, *f.* presence; appearance (at a meeting, etc.)

présent, *(adj.)* present; **à -,** now; *m.* gift

présentation, *f.* presentation (of play, etc.); introduction (to somebody)

présentable, *(adj.)* presentable

présenter, *v.t.* to present; to offer; to introduce; **se -,** *v.r.* to present oneself

préservateur(-trice), *(adj.)* preserving; preservative (from)

préservatif(-ive), *(adj.)* preservative; protective; *m.* preservative

préserver, *v.t.* to preserve; to protect (from)

présidence, *f.* presidency; chairmanship

président(e), *m.* *(f.)* president; chairman (chair-woman)

présider, *v.t.* and *v.i.* to preside; to take the chair

présomptif(-ive), *(adj.)* presumptive

présomption, *f.* presumption

présomptueux(-euse), *(adj.)* presumptuous

presque, *(adv.)* almost, nearly

presqu'île, *f.* peninsula

presse, *f.* press, pressing machine; the press; newspapers; pressure

presse-papiers, *m.* *(invar.)* paperweight

pressé, *(adj.)* crowded, close together; hurried

pressentiment, *m.* presentiment

pressentir, *v.t.* to have a presentiment; to have a foreboding

presser, *v.t.* to press; to hurry; to urge; **se -,** *v.r.* to hasten, make haste; to hurry

pression, *f.* pressure

pressoir, *m.* press (wine, cider, etc.)

pressurer, *v.t.* to press out (the juice)

prestance, *f.* fine bearing; fine appearance

preste, *(adj.)* quick, nimble; sharp

prestidigitateur, *m.* conjurer

prestige, *m.* prestige; high reputation; marvel

prestigieux(-euse), *(adj.)* wonderful, marvellous, amazing (skill)

présumer, *v.t.* to presume, to suppose

présupposer, *v.t.* to take something for granted; to presuppose

prêt, *(adj.)* ready, prepared

prêt, *m.* loan; advance against security

prétendant, *m.* applicant, candidate for; pretender; suitor

prétendre, *v.t.* to claim; to require; to assert; to pretend

prétendu, *(adj.)* alleged; would be; intended (husband)

prétentieux(-euse), *(adj.)* pretentious, assuming

prétention, *f.* pretension; claim

prêter, *v.t.* to lend; **- serment,**

to take the oath; **se -** (**à**), *v.r.* to be a party (to)

prêteur(-euse), *m.* (*f.*) lender; **- sur gages,** pawnbroker

prétexte, *m.* pretext, excuse, plea

prêtre, *m.* priest

preuve, *f.* proof, evidence, token

preux, (*adj.*) gallant

prévaloir, *v.i.* to prevail; to make good one's claim

prévenance, *f.* kindness; kind attention

prévenir, to anticipate, to forestall; to inform; to forewarn; to ward off

prévention, *f.* prepossession; prejudice, bias (against)

prévenu(e), (*adj.*) prejudiced, prepossessed; *m.* (*f.*) the prisoner, accused

prévoir, *v.t.* to foresee, to forecast

prévôt, *m.* provost

prévoyance, *f.* foresight, precaution

prévoyant, (*adj.*) far-sighted; provident

prie-dieu, *m.* praying-stool

prier, *v.t.* to pray; to beg, request

prière, *f.* prayer; entreaty, request

prieur(e), *m.* (*f.*) prior (prioress)

primaire, (*adj.*) primary (education)

primat, *m.* primate (Church)

prime, *f.* premium; bonus; option (Stock Exchange); **de - abord,** to begin with

primer, *v.t.* to excel; to surpass

primeur, *f.* early fruit, vegetables

primevère, *f.* primrose; primula; cowslip

primitif(-ive), (*adj.*) primitive

primo, (*adv.*) in the first place, firstly

primordial(-aux), (*adj.*) prime, first importance

prince, *m.* prince

princesse, *f.* princess

princier(-ère), (*adj.*) princely

principal(-aux), (*adj.*) principal, chief, leading

principal(-aux), *m.* chief, headmaster; great (main) thing

principauté, *f.* principality

printanier(-ère), (*adj.*) spring (season)

printemps, *m.* spring, springtime

priorité, *f.* priority

prise, *f.* hold, grasp; capture; solidification; **- de corps,** arrest; **en -,** in gear; **lâcher -** (**de**), to let go (of); **aux prises** (**avec**), fighting, at grips (with)

priser, *v.t.* to appraise, to value, to prize

prisme, *m.* prism

prison, *f.* prison, gaol

prisonnier(-ère), *m.* (*f.*) prisoner

privation, *f.* privation, hardship; deprivation (of)

privauté, *f.* intimacy, (undue) familiarity

privé, (*adj.*) private [familiarity

priver, *v.t.* to deprive; **se -** (**de**), *v.r.* to do without

privilège, *m.* privilege; licence

privilégier, *v.t.* to privilege; to grant a licence

prix, *m.* value, cost, price, worth; prize; **à tout -,** at any price; **- fixe,** set price; **hors de -,** prohibitive price; **- courant,** market price; price list

probabilité, *f.* probability, likelihood

probable, (*adj.*) probable, likely

probe, (*adj.*) upright, honest

probité, *f.* integrity, honesty

problématique, (*adj.*) problematic

problème, *m.* problem

procédé, *m.* proceeding; dealing; process; method

procéder, *v.i.* to proceed

procédure, *f.* procedure (*legal*)

procès, *m.* proceedings, action at law, lawsuit

processif(-ive), (*adj.*) litigious

procession, *f.* procession

processionnel(le), (*adj.*) processional (hymn, etc.) .

procès-verbal, *m.* official report; minutes of meeting; record of evidence prochain, (adj.) next; nearest; near at hand; m. (f.) neighbour

prochainement, (adv.) soon

proche, (adv.) near, close at hand

proclamer, v.t. to proclaim, to declare

procréateur(-trice), (adj.) procreative; m. (f.) procreator

procréer, v.t. to procreate

procuration, f. procuration; power of attorney; proxy

procurer, v.t. to procure, to obtain; to get

procureur(-atrice), m. (f.) proxy; attorney-at-law; - de la République, public prosecutor

prodigalité, f. prodigality, lavishness

prodige, m. prodigy, wonder

prodigieux(-euse), (adj.) prodigious, stupendous

prodigue, (adj.) prodigal; m. spendthrift

prodiguer, v.t. to lavish

productif(-ive), (adj.) productive

production, f. production

produire, v.t. to produce; to bring forward; to yield; to bear fruit; se -, v.r. to occur, to happen, to arise

produit, m. product, produce

profane, (adj.) profane: m. layman

profaner, v.t. to profane; to desecrate

proférer, v.t. to utter

professer, v.t. to profess (religion); to teach

professeur, m. professor (at university, etc.); teacher (at a lycée)

profession, f. profession; trade; calling

professionnel(le), (adj.) professional

professorat, m. body of teachers; mastership (in college)

profil, m. profile

profit, m. profit; benefit; gain

profitable, (adj.) profitable, advantageous

profiter (de), v.i. to profit (by); to take advantage (of); to make a profit

profond, (adj.) deep

profondeur, f. depth

profusion, f. abundance

progéniture, f. progeny

programme, m. programme

progrès, m. progress; improvement (in work of pupil)

progresser, v.i. to progress; to improve

progressif(-ive), (adj.) progressive

prohiber, v.t. to prohibit; to forbid

prohibitif(-ive), (adj.) prohibitive, exorbitant

proie, f. prey

projecteur, m. searchlight; projector

projectile, m. projectile, missile; - terre-à-avion, ground-to-air missile

projet, m. plan, scheme

projeter, v.t. to plan; to scheme

prolétaire, (adj.) proletarian

prolifique, (adj.) prolific

prologue, m. prologue (to)

prolongation, f. prolongation, extension (of leave, etc.)

prolonger, v.t. to prolong; to extend

*promenade, f. walk(ing); stroll; promenade (public walk)

promener, v.t. to lead about; to take for a walk, etc.; se -, v.r. to walk; to go for a walk, etc.

promeneur(-euse), m. (f.) walker, pedestrian

promenoir, m. promenade (of music hall, etc.); covered walk

promesse, f. promise, assurance

promettre, v.t. to promise; to make a promise

promontoire, m. promontory; cape (geog.)

promoteur(-trice), m. (f.) promoter, originator

promotion, f. promotion; preferment

prompt, (adj.) quick, ready, prompt

promptitude, f. quickness, promptitude

promu, (adj.) promoted, raised (to)

promulguer, v.t. to promulgate (law); to issue (decree)

prône, m. sermon

prôner, v.t. to preach to a congregation; to praise

prononcer, v.t. to pronounce; to deliver sentence; se -, v.r. to express one's opinion

prononciation, f. pronunciation; passing of sentence

pronostic, m. prognostic; prognosis (med.); - du temps, weather forecast

propagande, f. propaganda; publicity

propager, v.t. to spread abroad; to propagate

propédeutique (l'année de -), first year of University study

prophete (prophétesse), m. (f.) prophet(ess)

prophétie, f. prophecy

prophétique, (adj.) prophetic

propice, (adj.) propitious

proportion, f. proportion, ratio

proportionnel(le), (adj.) proportional

proportionner, v.t. to proportion; to adjust

propos, m. purpose; resolution; subject; utterance; à -, by the way; that reminds me

proposer, v.t. to propose (a plan); to propound; se -, v.r. to mean (to do something); to offer oneself (for a position)

proposition, f. proposition, proposal (not of marriage)

*propre, (adj.) proper; suitable; own; clean; neat

propreté, f. cleanness; neatness

propriétaire, m. and f. proprietor, proprietress; owner

propriété, f. property; estate; characteristic; correctness (of language, etc.)

propulseur, m. propeller

propulsion, f. propulsion, propelling; impulsion

propulsif(-ive), (adj.) propulsive, propelling

proroger, v.t. to prorogue; to adjourn

prorogation, f. prorogation (of Parliament); extension of time (legal)

proscrire, v.t. to proscribe; to banish

proscrit(e), m. (f.) outlaw

prose, f. prose

prospère, (adj.) prosperous

prospérer, v.i. to prosper: to thrive

(se) prosterner, v.r. to prostrate oneself; to bow down (to)

prostituée, f. prostitute

prostituer, v.t. to prostitute (person or talent)

prostitution, f. prostitution

protecteur(-trice), m. (f.) protector (protectress); patron(ess)

protection, f. protection; patronage; influence

protectorat, m. protectorate

protéger, v.t. to protect; to shelter; to guard (against)

protégé(e), m. (f.) protégé (protégée); dependant

protestant(e), (adj.) and m. (f.) Protestant

protestantisme, m. Protestantism

protester, v.t. to protest

protêt, m. protest (used both in commercial and legal terms)

protocole, m. protocol; form of procedure

proue, f. bows (of ship); stem, prow

prouesse, f. prowess, valour

prouver, v.t. to prove (a fact)

provenance, f. origin, source

provenir, v.i. to proceed; to result from

proverbe, m. proverb

proverbial(-aux), (adj.) proverbial

providence, f. providence; l'État -, the Welfare State

providentiel(le), (adj.) providential

province, f. province

provincial(-aux), (adj.) provincial; countrified

proviseur, m. headmaster (of a college, lycée)

provision, f. provision; stock; supply; margin (financial)

provisoire, (adj.) provisional

provocant, (adj.) provocative; aggressive; tantalising

provocation, f. provocation

provoquer, v.t. to provoke; to bring about

proximité, f. proximity; nearness

prude, (adj.) prudish; f. prude

prudence, f. prudence; carefulness

prudent, (adj.) prudent; careful

prud'homme, m. expert; experienced man; **conseil des prud'-hommes,** conciliation board (for business disputes)

prune, f. plum

pruneau, m. prune

prunelle, f. pupil (of eye); sloe

prunier, m. plum tree

prussien, (adj.) Prussian

prussique, (adj.) prussic (acid)

psaume, m. psalm

psautier, m. psalm-book

pseudonyme, m. pseudonym; assumed name

psyché, f. dressing-glass

puanteur, f. foul smell; stench

puberté, f. puberty

public(-que), (adj.) public

publication, f. publication; published work

publiciste, m. publicist

publicité, f. publicity

publier, v.t. to publish; to bring out (a book)

puce, f. flea

pucelle, f. maiden, virgin; **la - d'Orléans,** Joan of Arc

pudeur, f. modesty

pudibond, (adj.) prudish

pudique, (adj.) modest, chaste

puer, v.i. to stink

puéril, (adj.) puerile; childish

pugilat, m. boxing; pugilism

pugiliste, m. (professional) boxer

puis, (adv.) then; afterwards; besides; **"et - après,"** "what then," "so what!"

puiser (à), v.t. to draw water (from)

puisque, (conj.) since, as

puissance, f. power (general use)

puissant, (adj.) powerful, mighty

puits, m. well; shaft (of mine)

pulluler, v.i. to swarm

pulmonaire, (adj.) pulmonary

pulpe, f. pulp

pulper, v.t. to pulp

pulsation, f. pulsation; beating of the heart

pulvériser, v.t. to pulverise; to grind to powder

punaise, f. bug; drawing-pin

punir, v.t. to punish

punition, f. punishment

pupille, m. and f. ward (child in care of somebody); pupil

pupitre, m. desk; music stand

pur, (adj.) pure; **pur-sang,** thoroughbred

purée, f. mash (cook.); thick soup

pureté, f. purity; pureness

purgatif, m. purgative

purgatoire, m. purgatory

purger, v.t. to purge, to cleanse, to clear

purification, f. purification; cleansing (of blood); Candlemas

purifier, v.t. to purify; to cleanse; to sweeten (air, etc.)

purpurin, (adj.) purplish

purulent, (adj.) purulent (abscess, etc.)

pus, m. pus, matter

pusillanime, (adj.) pusillanimous; faint-hearted

pusillanimité, f. pusillanimity; faint-heartedness

pustule, f. pustule; pimple

putatif(-ive), (adj.) supposed, presumed

putois, m. polecat; skunk

putréfaction, f. putrefaction

putréfier, v.t. to putrefy

pygmée, m. (f.) dwarf; pygmy

pyjama, m. (pair of) pyjamas

pylône, m. pylon

pyramide, f. pyramid

python, m. python

Q

quadragénaire, (adj.) and m. (f.) quadragenarian

quadrangulaire, (adj.) four-angled

quadrille, m. quadrille

quadrimoteur(-trice), (adj.) and m. four-engined (aircraft)

quadrupède, (adj.) four-footed; m. quadruped

quai, m. quay, wharf, pier; platform (railway station); embankment (along a river)

qualification, f. designation; name; title

qualifié, (adj.) qualified (to do something)

qualifier, v.t. to style, call, term; se -, v.r. to call, style oneself

qualité, f. quality (degree of excellence); qualification; capacity; profession; title; rank

quand, (adv. and conj.) when, whenever; what time? - même, even if, even though

quant à, (prep.) as for, with regard to; concerning

quantité, f. quantity

quarantaine, f. quarantine; (about) forty; toucher à la -, to be getting on for forty

quarante, (adj.and m.invar.) forty

quart, m. quarter, fourth part; watch (naut.); quadrant

quartier, m. quarter, district, neighbourhood; - général, headquarters

quasi, (adv.) quasi, almost

quasimodo, f. Low Sunday

*quatre, m. four; Quatre-Temps, m. pl. Ember Days

quatuor, m. quartet

quatorze, (adj.) and m. inv. fourteen

*que, (rel. pron.) that, whom; *-, (interr. pron.) what? - (conj.) that; ne...-, only

quel(le), (adj. and pron.) what, which

quelconque, any (whatever)

quelque, (adj.) some, any; - chose, something; quelquefois (adv.) sometimes; quelqu'un(e), (indef.pron.) somebody, someone; - part (adv.) somewhere

quenelle, f. fish or forcemeat ball

quenouille, f. distaff

querelle, f. quarrel, dispute

quereller, v.t. to quarrel with somebody; se -, v.r. to wrangle

querelleur(-euse), m. (f.) wrangler; (adj.) quarrelsome

*question, f. question, query

questionnaire, m. list of questions

questionner, v.t. to question (somebody); to ask questions

quête, f. quest, search; collection (church, etc.)

quêter, v.t. to collect (alms, etc.)

queue, f. tail; file of people; cue (billiard); piano à -, grand piano; venir en -, to bring up the rear; faire la -, to queue up

qui (rel. and interr. pron.) who, that; who? whom?; - vive? who goes there?

quiconque, whoever

qui que ce soit, anyone (whatever)

quignon, m. hunk, chunk (of bread, etc.)

quille, f. ninepin, skittle; keel

quincaillerie, f. ironmongery

quincaillier, m. ironmonger

quinconce, (en) m. (trees) planted in alternate rows

quinine, f. quinine

quinquina, m. Peruvian bark; cinchona

quintal, m. (equivalent to) hundredweight

quintuple, (adj.) fivefold

quintupler, v.t. and v.i. to increase fivefold; quintuple

quinzaine, f. fortnight; about fifteen

quinze, (adj.) and m. inv. fifteen

quittance, f. receipt; discharge (commercial term)

quitte, (adj.) free, quit, rid of

quitter, v.t. to leave, quit

*quoi, (rel. pron.) what

quoi, (interr. pron.) what?

quoique, (conj.) though, although

quolibet, m. gibe, jeer

quotidien(ne), (adj.) daily

quotient, m. quotient

quotité, f. quota, amount of share

R

rabâchage, *m.* repetition (of words); drivel

rabâcher, *v.i.* to repeat the same words; to talk drivel

rabais, *m.* reduction in price; rebate; **vendre au -,** to sell at reduced price

rabaisser, *v.t.* to reduce, to lower price

rabat, *m.* turned down piece; flap

rabattre, *v.t.* to turn down, to fold back, to bring down to a lower level

rabbin, *m.* rabbi

rabot, *m.* plane (tool)

raboter, *v.t.* to plane

raboteux(-euse), *(adj.)* uneven

rabougrir, *v.t.* to stunt the growth of

rabrouer, *v.t.* to snub

raccommodage, *m.* mending, repairing, darning

raccommoder, *v.t.* to mend, to repair, to darn

raccorder, *v.t.* to join, to unite, to connect

raccourci, *m.* abridgment

raccourcir, *v.t.* to shorten; to reduce the length of

(se) raccoutumer, *v.r.* to re-accustom oneself to

raccrocher, *v.t.* to hang up again; **se - (à),** *v.r.* to catch on (to)

race, *f.* race (of people), breed

racé, *(adj.)* thoroughbred

rachat, *m.* repurchase; redemption

racheter, *v.t.* to repurchase, buy back; to atone for

rachitique, *(adj.)* rickety

rachitisme, *m.* rickets

racine, *f.* root (of plant, hair or tooth)

raclée, *f.* a thrashing, a licking

racler, *v.t.* to scrape (skin, etc.); to clean

racoler, *v.t.* to recruit, to solicit

racoleur, *m.* tout

raconter, *v.t.* to relate, to tell

radar, *m.* radar (station)

rade, *f.* roadstead, roads (*naut.*)

radeau, *m.* raft

radiateur, *m.* radiator

radical, *(adj.)* and *m.* radical (*politics*)

radier, *v.t.* to erase

radio, *m.* wireless message; wireless operator; *f.* radio, the wireless

radiodiffuser, *v.t.* to broadcast

radiodiffusion, *f.* broadcasting

radiotélégramme, *m.* wireless telegram

radis, *m.* radish; **ne pas avoir un -,** not to have a " bean "

radotage, *m.* drivel, twaddle

radoter, *v.i.* to talk drivel

radouber, *v.t.* to repair hull (of a ship)

radoucir, *v.t.* to soften, to calm; to mollify

rafale, *f.* squall, gust of wind; burst of gunfire

raffermir, *v.t.* to harden; to strengthen; to make firmer

raffiné, *(adj.)* refined, subtle, delicate (taste)

raffiner, *v.t.* to refine

raffinerie, *f.* sugar-refinery

raffoler (de), *v.i.* to dote (on)

rafle, *f.* clean sweep; round-up (by the police)

rafler, *v.t.* to sweep off, carry off; to round up (suspected person)

rafraîchir, *v.t.* to cool, to refresh; **se -,** *v.r.* to turn cooler (weather)

rafraîchissement, *m.* cooling; refreshment; brushing up one's knowledge

rafraîchissant, *(adj.)* refreshing, cooling

ragaillardir, *v.t.* to cheer somebody up

rage, *f.* rabies; rage, fury

rager, *v.i.* to be in a rage, to be furious

rageur(-euse), *(adj.)* passionate, violent (tempered)

ragoût, *m.* stew (of mutton, etc.)

raid, *m.* raid (air-raid, etc.)

raide, *(adj.)* stiff; steep; abrupt (descent)

raideur, *f.* stiffness; steepness; inflexibility

raidir, *v.t.* to stiffen; to tighten;

se -, *v.r.* to grow stiff; to steel oneself

raie, *f.* line (on paper); stripe (on material); skate (fish); parting (hair)

raifort, *m.* horse-radish

rail, *m.* rail

railler, *v.t.* to laugh at, to jeer at

raillerie, *f.* jest, chaff

railleur (-euse), *m.* (*f.*) scoffer; (*adj.*) scoffing, bantering

rainette, *f.* rennet, russet (apple)

rainure, *f.* groove, slot

rais, *m.* spoke (of wheel)

raisin, *m.* grape

*raison, *f.* reason, motive; reasoning; satisfaction; ratio (*maths.*); avoir -, to be right

raisonnable, (*adj.*) reasonable

raisonné, (*adj.*) reasoned; methodical (mind, etc.)

raisonnement, *m.* reasoning

raisonner, *v.i.* to reason, to argue

rajeunir, *v.t.* to rejuvenate; to make young again

rajouter, *v.t.* to add more

rajuster, *v.t.* to readjust; to set to rights; se -, *v.r.* to straighten one's clothes

râle, *m.* rattle (in throat); rail (bird)

ralentir, *v.i.* and *v.t.* to slow down (up); to slacken; se -, *v.r.* to slow up; to relax

ralenti, (*adj.*) slow

râler, *v.i.* to be at one's last gasp; to fume with rage

ralliement, *m.* rallying, assembly

rallier, *v.t.* to rally, to assemble (troops, etc.)

rallonge, *f.* extension piece; leaf (of table)

rallonger, *v.t.* to lengthen; to make longer

rallumer, *v.t.* to relight, to rekindle

ramage, *m.* floral design; warbling of birds

ramas, *m.* heap, pile, collection

ramassé, (*adj.*) thick-set, stocky

ramasser, *v.t.* to gather together; to collect; to pick up; se -, *v.r.* to pick oneself up

rame, *f.* oar, scull; ream of paper

ramé, (*adj.*) trained on sticks (*hort.*)

rameau, *m.* small branch, twig (of tree); dimanche des rameaux, Palm Sunday

ramener, *v.t.* to bring back

ramer, *v.i.* to row; *v.t.* to stick, to stake (in gardening)

ramification, *f.* ramification; branching

(se) ramifier, *v.r.* to branch out

ramollir, *v.t.* to soften; to weaken

ramollissement, *m.* softening (generally of the brain)

ramonage, *m.* chimney sweeping

ramoner, *v.t.* to sweep (chimney); to rake out

ramoneur, *m.* chimney sweep

rampe, *f.* slope; banisters; footlights (theatre)

ramper, *v.i.* to creep; to crawl; to cringe

ramure, *f.* branches, boughs; antlers (of stag)

rance, (*adj.*) rancid, rank

rançon, *f.* ransom

rançonner, *v.t.* to hold to ransom; to fleece (a customer)

rancune, *f.* rancour; grudge, spite

rancunier (-ère), (*adj.*) vindictive, spiteful

randonnée, *f.* outing, excursion (by car, etc.)

rang, *m.* row, line; rank; station in life

rangé, (*adj.*) tidy, orderly; bataille rangée, pitched battle

rangée, *f.* row, line (of persons, etc.)

ranger, *v.t.* to arrange; to tidy; to range (in rows); to put in order; se -, *v.r.* to draw up; line up; to side with (somebody); to get out of the way; to settle down (get married)

ranimer, *v.t.* to revive; to stir up (the fire); to put new life into (something); se -, *v.r.* to come to life again

rapace, (*adj.*) rapacious

rapacité, *f.* rapacity; rapaciousness

râpe, *f.* rasp

râpé, (*adj.*) shabby, worn out; grated (cheese)

râper, *v.t.* to grate; to wear threadbare

rapetisser, *v.t.* to make something smaller; to shrink; to lessen

rapide, *(adj.)* rapid, swift, fast; *m.* express train

rapidité, *f.* rapidity, swiftness

rapiéçage, *m.* patchwork

rapiécer, *v.t.* to patch (garment); to piece

rapin, *m.* art student

rapine (*or* **rapinerie**), *f.* rapine, pillage

rappel, *m.* recall; repeal (of law, etc.)

rappeler, *v.t.* to recall (somebody); to call something to mind; **se -,** *v.r.* to recollect, to remember

rapport, *m.* official report; yield; return (profit); relation; **par - à,** in relation to, regard to

rapporter, *v.t.* to bring back; to bring in; to yield (a profit); to report (a fact); **se -,** *v.r.* to agree (with); to relate to

rapporteur, *m.* reporter, recorder; chairman (of parliamentary committee)

rapprendre, *v.t.* to learn over again

rapprochement, *m.* coming together, reconciliation

(se) rapprocher, *v.r.* to draw near(er) (to something)

rapt, *m.* abduction

raquette, *f.* racquet, racket

rare, *(adj.)* rare; uncommon; exceptional

raréfaction, *f.* rarefaction

raréfier, *v.t.* to rarefy

rareté, *f.* scarceness, scarcity; rare occurrence

ras, *(adj.)* close cropped; smooth

rasant, *(adj.)* *(slang)* boring, tiresome

raser, *v.t.* to raze to the ground; to shave off (to skim over); **se -,** *v.r.* to shave

raseur, *m.* bore

rasoir, *m.* razor; **- de sûreté,** safety-razor

rassasiement, *m.* satisfying (of hunger); surfeit

rassasier, *v.t.* to satisfy (hunger); to satiate

rassemblement, *m.* crowd, assemblage

rassembler, *v.t.* to collect, to gather together

rasseoir, *v.t.* to reseat (somebody); to settle (one's ideas); **se -,** *v.r.* to sit down again

rasséréner, *v.t.* to calm; to restore equanimity; **se -,** *v.r.* to clear up (weather); to recover one's composure

rassis, *(adj.)* settled, staid; stale (bread)

rassurer, *v.t.* to reassure; **se -,** *v.r.* to feel reassured

rastaquouère, *m.* flashy adventurer

rat, *m.* rat

ratatiné, *(adj.)* shrivelled, shrunk

ratatiner, *v.t.* to shrivel up, to shrink

ratatouille, *f.* stew (of doubtful quality)

râteau, *m.* rake

râtelier, *m.* rack (in stable); set of false teeth

rater, *v.i.* and *v.t.* to miss; to fail to go off; **- le coup,** to miss the mark; **- une affaire,** to fail to do business

ratification, *f.* confirmation, ratification

ratifier, *v.t.* to confirm (decision); to ratify (a treaty)

ration, *f.* ration; allowance

rationnel(le), *(adj.)* rational

rationner, *v.t.* to ration

ratisser, *v.t.* to rake; to scrape

rattacher, *v.t.* to refasten, retie

rattraper, *v.t.* to catch again, recapture; to overtake; **se -,** *v.r.* to steady oneself; to save oneself

raturer, *v.t.* to erase, scratch out

rauque, *(adj.)* hoarse

ravage, *m.* ravage, havoc, devastation

ravager, *v.t.* to ravage, devastate

ravaler, *v.t.* to debase; to snub (somebody); to swallow again ravauder, *v.t.* to mend, patch (clothes)

rave, *f.* turnip; rape (seed)

ravin, *m.* ravine, gully

ravir, *v.t.* to ravish; to rob; to enrapture

ravi (de), *(adj.)* enchanted, delighted (to)

(se) raviser, *v.r.* to change one's mind

ravissant, *(adj.)* enchanting, bewitching

ravissement, *m.* carrying off; rapture

ravitaillement, *m.* provisioning

ravitailler, *v.t.* to provision with

ravoir, *v.t.* to recover (something)

rayer, *v.t.* to scratch (glass, etc.); to rule paper; to strike out (off)

rayon, *m.* ray (of sun); beam (of light); radius, spoke (of wheel); shelf (of cupboard); bookshelf; department (of big store)

rayonner, *v.i.* to radiate, to shine

razzia, *f.* raid; police raid

réaction, *f.* reaction; à -, jet propelled

réactionnaire, *(adj.)* and *m.* and *f.* reactionary

réagir (sur), *(v.i.)* to react (upon)

réalisation, *f.* realisation; carrying out (a plan); selling out

réaliser, *v.t.* to realise; to carry out; to sell out (shares, etc.)

réalité, *f.* reality

réapparition, *f.* reappearance

réargenter, *v.t.* to resilver, to replate

rébarbatif(-ive), *(adj.)* grim; forbidding

rebattu, *(adj.)* worn out, hackneyed

rebelle, *(adj.)* rebellious; *m.* (*f.*). rebel

rébellion, *f.* rebellion; revolt

(se) rebiffer, *v.r.* to resist; to kick (over the traces)

reboisement, *m.* replanting, retimbering

rebondi, *(adj.)* plump; chubby

rebondir, *v.i.* to rebound

rebord, *m.* edge; border, rim

rebours, *m.* wrong way; contrary; reverse

rebrousser, *v.t.* to brush up (the hair); - chemin, to retrace one's footsteps

rebuffade, *f.* rebuke; snub

rebut, *m.* waste; scrap

rebutant, *(adj.)* tiresome; tedious

rebuter, *v.t.* to disallow (evidence); to dishearten

récalcitrant, *(adj.)* refractory

récapitulation, *f.* recapitulation; summing-up

récapituler, *v.t.* to recapitulate; to sum up

recéler, *v.t.* to receive stolen goods

receleur(-euse), *m.* (*f.*) receiver of stolen goods, fence

récemment, *(adv.)* recently

recensement, *m.* census (of population)

récent, *(adj.)* recent, late (event)

récépissé, *m.* acknowledgment; receipt

récepteur, *(adj.)* receiving; *m.* receiver

réception, *f.* receipt (of letter); taking delivery (of goods); welcome; reception

recette, *f.* takings (of business, etc.); returns; recipe (for dish, etc.)

recevable, *(adj.)* allowable; admissible (evidence)

receveur(-euse), *m.* (*f.*) receiver; collector, conductor (of bus, etc.)

recevoir, *v.t.* to receive; to get (letter, etc.); to welcome (somebody); to entertain (friends)

rechange, *m.* replacement; spare part

recharger, *v.t.* to recharge (accumulator)

réchaud, *m.* portable stove; chafing-dish; - à gaz, gas-ring

réchauffer, *v.t.* to reheat; to warm up (again)

rêche, *(adj.)* hard, rough

recherche, *f.* search, pursuit; affectation

recherché, *(adj.)* in great demand; select

rechercher, *v.t.* to search for; to enquire into

rechigner, *v.i.* to look sour, sulky; to jib

rechute, *f.* relapse

récidive, *f.* repetition of an offence

récif, *m.* reef

récipient, *m.* container, receptacle

réciprocité, *f.* reciprocity

réciproque, (*adj.*) reciprocal, mutual

récit, *m.* narrative; account (of a happening)

réciter, *v.t.* to recite; to say or repeat a lesson

réclamation, *f.* complaint; protest; claim

réclame, *f.* advertising; publicity; puff advertisement

réclamer, *v.i.* to complain; to clamour for; to protest against

reclus(e), *m.* (*f.*) recluse, hermit

réclusion, *f.* seclusion; confinement; solitary confinement

recoin, *m.* nook, recess

récolte, *f.* crop ; harvest

récolter, *v.t.* to gather in the crop; to harvest

recommandable, (*adj.*) commendable

recommandation, *f.* recommendation; testimonial

recommander, *v.t.* to recommend; to enjoin; to register (letter, parcel)

recommencer, *v.t.* to begin, to start again

récompense, *f.* reward

récompenser, *v.t.* to reward

réconcilier, *v.t.* to reconcile

reconduire, *v.t.* to escort; to see somebody home

réconforter, *v.t.* to comfort, to cheer up; to strengthen

reconnaissance, *f.* recognition; acknowledgment (of debts, etc.); gratitude; reconnaissance (*mil.*)

reconnaissant (de), (*adj.*) grateful (for)

***reconnaître,** *v.t.* to recognise; to know again; to acknowledge; to admit (mistake); to reconnoitre

reconstituer, *v.t.* to reconstitute; to restore (health, etc.)

reconstruire, *v.t.* to rebuild, reconstruct

record, *m.* record (*sport.*); utmost output of production

recourber, *v.t.* to bend; to curve; **se -,** *v.r.* to bend; to curl

recourir (à), *v.i.* to have recourse (to)

recours, *m.* recourse, resort

recouvrer, *v.t.* to recover; to retrieve (one's property)

recouvrir, *v.t.* to recover (roof, etc.); **se -,** *v.r.* to cloud over (the sky)

récréation, *f.* amusement; relaxation; playtime, break (in school)

récréer, *v.t.* to amuse, entertain; to refresh (the mind); to create again

(se) récrier, *v.r.* to exclaim, to cry out, to protest

récrimination, *f.* recrimination

récrire, *v.t.* to rewrite

recroquevillé, (*adj.*) shrivelled, curled up; clenched

recrue, *f.* recruit

recruter, *v.t.* to recruit; to enlist (supporters)

rectangulaire, (*adj.*) rectangular

recteur, *m.* vice-chancellor; rector (of university)

rectifier, *v.t.* to rectify (spirit); to straighten

rectiligne, (*adj.*) rectilinear

recto, *m.* right-hand side (of page)

rectorat, *m.* vice-chancellorship; rectorship

reçu, (*adj.*) received, accepted

reçu, *m.* receipt (for amount paid)

recueil, *m.* selection; anthology (of poems, works)

recueillement, *m.* meditation, contemplation

recueillir, *v.t.* to gather, to collect; to shelter (somebody); **se -,** *v.r.* to collect one's thoughts

recul, *m.* recoil (of gun)

reculade, *f.* falling back, retreat

reculé, (*adj.*) distant; remote (time)

reculer, *v.i.* to move back; to

step back; to retreat; to recoil; to flinch (before something)

récupérer, *v.t.* to recover (debt); **se -,** *v.r.* to recover (from ill-health); to convalesce

récuser, *v.t.* to take exception; to object to

rédacteur, *m.* reporter (newspaper); draftsman (of deed, or bill in Parliament); **- en chef** editor

rédaction, *f.* drafting (of deed or bill); editorial staff; composition (scholastic)

reddition, *f.* surrender (of town)

redevable (à), *(adj.)* indebted (to)

redevance, *f.* rent; dues; royalties (of author)

rédiger, *v.t.* to draw, to draft (agreement, etc.); to write (an article)

redingote, *f.* frock-coat

redire, *v.t.* to repeat, to tell again; **trouver à - à,** to find fault with

redoubler, *v.t.* to redouble, to increase

redoutable, *(adj.)* redoubtable; formidable (enemy)

redoute, *f.* redoubt *(mil.)*

redouter, *v.t.* to dread, to fear

redressement, *m.* setting up again; righting (of wrong, mistake)

redresser, *v.t.* to set upright again; to redress; **se -,** *v.r.* to set up; to right (boat, etc.)

réductible, *(adj.)* reducible

réduction, *f.* reduction; cutting down expenses; conquest (of country)

réduire, *v.t.* to reduce (speed, etc.); to cut down (expenses); to reduce to poverty

réduit, *m.* nook, retreat

réel(le), *(adj.)* real, actual

réélire, *v.t.* to re-elect

refaire, *v.t.* to remake; to do again; **se -,** *v.r.* to recover one's health

réfectoire, *m.* dining-hall (in school)

référer, *v.t.* to refer; to ascribe;

se - (à), *v.r.* to ask the opinion (of)

refermer, *v.t.* to reclose; to shut again

réfléchi, *(adj.)* thoughtful; deliberate (opinion or action)

réfléchir, *v.t.* to reflect; to consider; to ponder

réfléchissement, *m.* reflection

réflecteur, *m.* reflecting mirror; reflector

reflet, *m.* reflection; reflected light

refleurir, *v.i.* to flower again; to flourish again

réflexe, *m.* reflex *(med.)*

réflexion, *f.* thought; reflection (of light or image)

refluer, *v.i.* to flowback; to ebb (tide)

reflux, *m.* ebb-tide; ebbing of tide

réforme, *f.* reform, reformation; discharge (from navy, etc.)

réformé, *m.* man discharged from the services

réformer, *v.t.* to reform (one's conduct); to discharge as unfit

refouler, *v.t.* to drive back; to push back; to repress (desire, etc.)

réfractaire, *(adj.)* refractory, insubordinate; fireproof (brick)

refrain, *m.* refrain, burden (of song)

refréner, *v.t.* to restrain, to curb

réfrigérant, *m.* refrigerator

refroidir, *v.t.* to cool, to chill; to damp (one's enthusiasm)

refroidissement, *m.* cooling (down)

refuge, *m.* refuge

(se) réfugier, *v.r.* to find shelter; to take refuge

réfugié(e), *m.* *(f.)* refugee

refus, *m.* refusal

refuser, *v.t.* to refuse, to decline; to turn down (an offer); to deny (somebody, something); **se -,** *v.r.* to object to

réfuter, *v.t.* to refute

regagner, *v.t.* to regain, to recover; to get back (to a place)

regain, *m.* aftermath; renewal

régal, *m.* feast; succulent dish

régaler, *v.t.* to entertain (one's friends); **se -,** *v.r.* to treat oneself to

regard, *m.* look, glance, gaze

regarder, *v.t.* to regard, to consider; to look at something; to concern; **ça ne vous regarde pas,** that's none of your business

régate, *f.* regatta

régence, *f.* regency

régent, *m.* regent; governor of the Bank of France

régie, *f.* excise office

régime, *m.* form of government; regime; diet

régiment, *m.* regiment

région, *f.* region; territory; area

régional(-aux), *(adj.)* regional, local

régir, *v.t.* to govern; to rule

régisseur, *m.* manager *(theat.)*; agent, steward

registre, *m.* register; minute book; damper (of furnace)

*****règle,** *f.* rule; ruler

règlement, *m.* settlement (of account); regulation

régler, *v.t.* to rule (paper); to order (one's life); to regulate; to settle (account)

réglementaire, *(adj.)* prescribed, regulation

réglisse, *f.* liquorice

règne, *m.* reign

régner, *v.i.* to reign; to rule; to prevail

regommer, *v.t.* to retread (tyre)

regonfler, *v.t.* to pump up a tyre

regorger, *v.i.* to overflow; to abound in

regret, *m.* regret

regretter, *v.t.* to regret, to be sorry for

régularisation, *f.* regularising; putting in order

régulariser, *v.t.* to regularise; to put in order

régularité, *f.* regularity; punctuality

régulier(-ère), *(adj.)* regular; punctual; orderly

réhabiliter, *v.t.* to reinstate, rehabilitate

rehausser, *v.t.* to raise; to enhance

réimpression, *f.* reprint

rein, *m.* kidney; *m. pl.* loins; the back

reine, *f.* queen

reine-claude, *f.* greengage

réintégrer, *v.t.* to reinstate

réitérer, *v.t.* to repeat, reiterate

rejeter, *v.t.* to throw back; to fling back; to cast up; to reject

rejeton, *m.* shoot (of plant); sucker; offspring

rejoindre, *v.t.* to rejoin, reunite; to overtake (somebody); **se -,** *v.r.* to meet again

réjoui, *(adj.)* jolly, merry, cheerful

réjouir, *v.t.* to delight; to rejoice; **se - (de),** *v.r.* to be glad (of); to be delighted (at)

réjouissance, *f.* rejoicing

relâche, *m.* respite, relaxation; no performance (on bills outside theatre, etc.)

relâcher, *v.t.* to loosen; to slacken; to release; **se -,** *v.r.* to become slack (of person)

relais, *m.* relay; stage (relay station)

relater, *v.t.* to relate, to state

relatif(-ive), *(adj.)* relative (value, etc.)

relation, *f.* relation (human intercourse); account, statement, report; **être en - avec,** to be in touch with

relayer, *v.t.* to relieve; to take turns

reléguer, *v.t.* to relegate, to consign

relevant (de), *(adj.)* depending (on)

relève, *f.* relief (of troops); draft, levy (of men)

relevé, *(adj.)* raised, erect; highly seasoned (sauce)

relevé, *m.* summary (of accounts)

relèvement, *m.* raising; revival; statement (of accounts, of business)

relever, *v.t.* to raise again; to make out a statement (com-

mercial); to set off (colour, etc.);
- (de), v.i. to be dependent (on)
relief, m. relief (used in sculpture);
en -, raised
relier, v.t. to bind, tie again; to
bind (book)
relieur, m. bookbinder
religieux(-euse), (adj.) religious,
sacred; m. (f.) monk (nun)
religion, f. religion
reliquat, m. residue, balance (of
account)
relique, f. relic
relire, v.t. to read over again; to
re-read
reliure, f. binding of book
relouer, v.t. to relet, to sublet
reluire, v.i. to shine; to glitter;
to glisten
reluisant, (adj.) shining, glittering, glossy (skin)
remaniement, m. change, alteration
remanier, v.t. to rehandle, to
recast
se remarier, v.r. to re-marry
remarquable, (adj.) remarkable
remarque, f. remark
remarquer, v.t. to remark, to
notice; faire -, to draw one's
attention to; to observe; se
faire -, to attract attention
remballer, v.t. to repack
remblai, m. embankment; earth
(for filling in)
rembourrer, v.t. to stuff, to pad
remboursement, m. reimburse-
ment
rembourser, v.t. to refund; to
repay
rembrunir, v.t. to darken; to
make darker or browner; se -,
v.r. to cloud over, to grow dark
remède, m. remedy, cure
remédier, v.t. to remedy something
remémorer, v.t. to remind (someone of something)
remercier, v.t. to thank; to discharge (employee)
remercîment, m. thanks, acknowledgment
*remettre, v.t. to put back, to

recollect, to postpone, to deliver;
se -, v.r. to recover from an illness
remeubler, v.t. to refurnish
remise, f. delivery (of letter,
etc.); remittance (of money);
rebate; coach-house
remonter, v.i. to go up again;
cela remonte au XV° siècle,
that goes back to the fifteenth
century; v.t. to carry something
up; se -, v.r. to recover one's
strength (after illness)
remontrance, f. remonstrance
remords, m. remorse
remorque, f. towing; trailer
remorquer, v.t. to tow
remorqueur, m. tug-boat, steam
tug
remoudre, v.t. to regrind (corn)
rémoudre, v.t. to regrind (knife);
to resharpen
remous, m. eddy; wash of ship
rempailler, v.t. to rebottom (a
chair)
rempart, m. rampart
remplaçant(e), m. (f.) substitute
remplacement, m. substitution
remplacer, v.t. to take the place
of; to succeed
remplir (de), v.t. to fill up (with);
to refill; to perform (a duty)
remporter, v.t. to carry; to take
away; to carry off (prize, etc.)
remuer, v.t. to move; to shift; se
-, v.r. to bustle about; to stir
oneself
rémunérateur(-trice), (adj.) remunerative
rémunération, f. remuneration
rémunérer, v.t. to remunerate;
to reward (somebody)
renâcler, v.i. to sniff, to snort
renaissance, f. rebirth; revival
renaître, v.i. to be born again; to
revive
rénal(-aux), (adj.) renal
renard, m. fox
renchérir, v.i. to get dearer; to
increase in price; - sur qn., to
outbid someone
rencontre, f. meeting, encounter;
aller à la - de qn., to go to meet
someone

rencontrer, *v.t.* to meet (with)

rendement, *m.* produce; yield (of taxes, etc.); profit (from a business)

rendez-vous, *m. (invar.)* rendez-vous, appointment

(se) rendormir, *v.r.* to go to sleep again

rendre, *v.t.* to give back, return, restore; to repay, render; (with adjective following) to make; **se -,** *v.r.* to proceed to a place; to surrender, give in

rêne, *f.* rein

renégat, *m.* renegade; turncoat

renfermer, *v.t.* to shut up, lock up; to contain

renfermé, *(adj.)* uncommunicative; **sentir le -,** to smell stuffy

renflement, *m.* swelling, bulging

renfler, *v.t.* and *v.i.* to swell, to bulge

renforcer, *v.t.* to reinforce; to strengthen

renfort, *m.* reinforcements

renier, *v.t.* to deny, to disown, to repudiate

renifler, *v.i.* to sniff, to snort, to snuffle

renne, *m.* reindeer

renom, *m.* renown, fame

renommé, *(adj.)* renowned, famed

renommée, *f.* renown, fame

renommer, *v.t.* to reappoint

renoncement, *m.* self-denial; renunciation

renoncer, *v.t.* to renounce; to give up something

renoncule, *f.* ranunculus; buttercup

renouer, *v.t.* to tie, to knot (again); to renew

renouveau, *m.* springtime; renewal

renouveler, *v.t.* to renew, to renovate; **se -,** *v.r.* to happen again

renouvellement, *m.* renewal

rénovation, *f.* renovation, restoration

renseignement, *m.* information; piece of intelligence; indication

renseigner, *v.t.* to inform (somebody); to give information; **se - (sur),** *v.r.* to make enquiries; to find out (about)

rente, *f.* revenue, rent

rentier(-ère), *m. (f.)* person of independent means; annuitant

rentrée, *f.* return; home-coming; reassembly (of Parliament); re-opening (of schools, etc.)

rentrer, *v.i.* to re-enter; to come in again; to go in again; to return home; *v.t.* to take in, bring in; to get in

renverser, *v.t.* to reverse; to overthrow; to knock over; to astound; **se -,** *v.r.* to fall over; to overturn

renvoi, *m.* returning; sending (back); dismissal (of employee)

renvoyer, *v.t.* to send back; to throw back; to postpone (a matter)

réorganiser, *v.t.* to reorganise

réouverture, *f.* reopening

repaire, *m.* den; lair (of wild beasts)

repaître, *v.t.* to feed (animals)

répandre, *v.t.* to spread, to scatter; to strew (flowers, etc.); to pour out; to shed (blood)

répandu, *(adj.)* widespread; widely distributed

reparaître, *v.i.* to reappear

réparation, *f.* reparation; amends; repairing

réparer, *v.t.* to repair; to mend; to make amends

repartie, *f.* retort, rejoinder

répartir, *v.t.* to distribute to share out

repartir, *v.i.* (with *être*) to set out again; (with *avoir*) to retort

répartition, *f.* distribution; sharing out

repas, *m.* meal

repassage, *m.* ironing; grinding (knives, etc.)

repasser, *v.i.* and *v.t.* to pass by again; to cross over (something); to iron clothes; to grind (knife, etc.)

repasseuse, *f.* ironer

repeindre, *v.t.* to repaint

repentir, *m.* repentance; **se -** (de), *v.r.* to repent; to be sorry (for)

repère, *m.* landmark; bench-mark (surveying)

repérer, to locate; to pick out; to mark (an instrument with reference marks)

répertoire, *m.* list, catalogue; repertory (*theat.*)

répéter, *v.t.* to repeat, to say or do again; to rehearse

répétiteur, *m.* assistant master; private tutor

répétition, *f.* duplicate; rehearsal of play

répit, *m.* respite; delay

replet, (*adj.*) stoutish

repli, *m.* fold, crease (in clothes); bend (of river)

replier, *v.t.* to fold up again; to coil up; to turn back

réplique, *f.* rejoinder, retort, cue

répliquer, *v.i.* to rejoin, to retort

répondre, *v.t.* to answer, reply

réponse, *f.* answer

report, *m.* amount carried forward

reportage, *m.* report (newspaper); set of articles (on a subject)

reporter, *v.t.* to carry back; to take something back; *m.* reporter (newspaper)

repos, *m.* rest, repose

reposer, *v.i.* to rest, to lie

reposer, *v.t.* to put back; to re-place; **se -,** *v.r.* to rest, to repose

reposoir, *m.* resting place; temporary altar

repoussant, (*adj.*) repulsive, loathsome

repousser, *v.t.* to repel, to push back, to rebuff

repoussoir, *m.* driving bolt; foil (to beauty, etc.)

répréhensible, reprehensible, blamable

reprendre, *v.t.* to retake; to take back; to reprove; to resume; **se -,** *v.r.* to recover oneself

représailles, *f. pl.* reprisals

représentation, *f.* representa-tion; agency; performance (of play)

représenter, *v.t.* to represent; to act for; to depict; to perform or to act (a play); to reintroduce; **se -,** *v.r.* to offer oneself again (as candidate)

réprimande, *f.* reprimand, re-proof

reprise, *f.* recapture; darning; mending; **à plusieurs reprises,** repeatedly

reproche, *m.* reproach

reprocher, *v.t.* to reproach

reproduire, *v.t.* to reproduce

réprouvé, *m.* reprobate

républicain(e), (*adj.*) republican

république, *f.* republic

répudier, *v.t.* to repudiate; to renounce

répugnance, *f.* repugnance, dis-like for

répugner (à), *v.i.* to feel repug-nance (for); to be repugnant

réputation, *f.* reputation, repute

réputer, *v.t.* to repute, to hold, to deem

requérir, *v.t.* to ask for some-thing; to solicit a favour

requête, *f.* request, petition, suit

requin, *m.* shark

requis, (*adj.* and *past part.*) requisite; due

réquisition, *f.* commandeering, requisitioning

réquisitionner, *v.t.* to requisi-tion; to commandeer (provis-ions, etc.)

réquisitoire, *m.* public prosecu-tor's indictment

rescapé(e), *m.* (*f.*) survivor

réseau, *m.* network, system of roads, railways

réséda, *m.* mignonette

réserve, *f.* reserve, reserving; reserves (*mil.*)

réserver, *v.t.* to reserve, to set aside; to save; **se -,** *v.r.* to reserve oneself; to hold back

réserviste, *m.* reservist

réservoir, *m.* reservoir; fish pond or tank; tank, cistern

résidence, *f.* residence

résider, *v.i.* to reside, to live

résidu, *m.* remainder, residue

résignation, *f.* resignation, submissiveness

résigner, *v.t.* to resign (a possession)

résilier, *v.t.* to cancel, to annul

résine, *f.* resin

résineux(-euse), *(adj.)* resinous

résistance, *f.* resistance; opposition

résister (à), *v.t.* to resist; to oppose; to withstand

résolu, *(adj.)* resolute

résolution, *f.* solution (of problem); termination. (of agreement); resolve; resoluteness

résonner, *v.i.* to resound

résoudre, *v.t.* to resolve; to dissolve; to solve (problem); to cancel; to settle (a question)

respect, *m.* respect

respectable, *(adj.)* respectable

respecter, *v.t.* to respect; to have a regard for

respectueux(-euse), *(adj.)* respectful

respiration, *f.* breathing, respiration

respirer, *v.i.* to breathe

resplendir, *v.i.* to shine brightly; to glitter

resplendissant, *(adj.)* resplendent, shining, dazzling

responsable, *(adj.)* responsible

responsabilité, *f.* responsibility

ressaisir, *v.t.* to seize again; to recapture; **se -,** *v.r.* to regain one's self-control

ressaut, *m.* jutting out, projection ; leap

ressemblance, *f.* resemblance, likeness

ressembler (à), *v.t.* to resemble; **se -,** *v.r.* to be alike

ressentir, *v.t.* to feel (emotion); to resent

resserre, *f.* storage

resserrer, *v.t.* to put away again; to contract

ressort, *m.* elasticity; spring; jurisdiction

ressortir, *v.i.* to come or go out again; *v.t.* to bring out again

ressource, *f.* resource; means; resources

ressusciter, *v.t.* to restore to life; to resuscitate

restant(e), *(adj.)* remaining; *m.* (*f.*) remaining (person); *m.* remainder

restaurant, *m.* restaurant; eating-house

restaurateur, *m.* owner of a restaurant

restaurer, *v.t.* to restore (building, etc.); to re-establish (order, etc.)

reste, *m.* rest, remainder; **du -,** besides

rester (with *être*), *v.i.* to remain, to be left

restituer, *v.t.* to restore, to reinstate

restitution, *f.* restitution

restreindre, *v.t.* to restrict; **se -,** *v.r.* to retrench; to cut down expenses

résultat, *m.* result

résulter, *v.i.* (*imp.*) to result; to follow

résumé, *m.* summary; résumé

résumer, *v.t.* to summarise.

résurrection, *f.* resurrection; revival

rétablir, *v.t.* to re-establish; to restore; to recover

rétablissement, *m.* re-establishment; reinstatement; recovery

retailler, *v.t.* to recut; to resharpen

retaper, *v.t.* to do up; to touch up

*****retard,** *m.* delay; backwardness; **être en -,** to be late

retardataire, *m.* and *f.* latecomer; backward (child, pupil)

retarder, *v.t.* and *v.i.* to delay, to put off; to put back (clock); to be slow (clock)

retenir, *v.t.* to hold back; to detain; to restrain; to keep hold of; to engage (attention); **se -,** *v.r.* to control oneself

retentir, *v.i.* to resound, to echo

retentissant, *(adj.)* resounding

retentissement, *m.* resounding noise; repercussion

retenue, *f.* deduction; discretion; detention

rétif(-ive), *(adj.)* restive; stubborn

rétine, *f.* retina (eye)

retirer, *v.t.* to withdraw (something); to draw back; to draw out; to take away; **se -,** *v.r.* to retire; to withdraw

retors(e), *(adj.)* twisted; crafty

retoucher, *v.t.* to retouch, to touch up

retour, *m.* return, coming back; **être de -,** to be back

retourner, *v.t.* to turn, to return; to give, to send (something back); *v.i.* (with *être*) to go back; **se -,** *v.r.* to turn round

retracer, *v.t.* to retrace

rétracter, *v.t.* to withdraw; to recant

retraite, *f.* retreat, retirement; refuge; **être en -,** to be on the retired list; **mettre à la -,** to pension somebody off

retraiter, *v.t.* to pension off

retranchement, *m.* entrenchment; retrenchment

retrancher, *v.t.* to entrench *(mil.)*; to cut off; to cut out; **se -,** *v.r.* to retrench; to curtail; cut down expenses

rétrécir, *v.t.* to narrow; to straiten; *v.i.* to shrink

rétribuer, *v.t.* to remunerate

rétribution, *f.* remuneration, fee

rétrogradation, *f.* retrogression

rétrograder, *v.i.* to move backwards

retrousser, *v.t.* to roll up; to tuck up; to turn up

retrouver, *v.t.* to find again; **se -,** *v.r.* to meet again; to recover oneself

réunion, *f.* reunion; gathering; meeting

réunir, *v.t.* to reunite; to join together; **se -,** *v.r.* to meet, to assemble, to gather together

réussir (à), *v.t.* to succeed (in); to be successful

réussi, *(adj.)* successful; **mal -,** badly done

réussite, *f.* success; successful result; **faire une -,** to get a game of patience " out "

revanche, *f.* revenge, return match

rêve, *m.* dream

revêche, *(adj.)* harsh; cantankerous

réveil, *m.* waking, awakening

réveille-matin, *m.* alarm clock

réveiller, *v.t.* to awaken; to wake (somebody up); **se -,** *v.r.* to wake up

réveillon, *m.* midnight supper (on Christmas and New Year's Eve)

révélateur(-trice), *(adj.)* revealing; tell-tale; *m. (f.)* revealer; *m.* developer *(phot.)*

révélation, *f.* revelation, disclosure

révéler, *v.t.* to reveal, to disclose

revenant, *m.* ghost

revendeur(-euse), *m. (f.)* retailer; middle-man

revendication, *f.* claim, demand

revendiquer, *v.t.* to claim, to demand

revendre, *v.t.* to resell

revenir (with *être*), *v.i.* to come back, come again; to return; to cost; to recover (consciousness)

revenu, *m.* income

rêver, *v.i.* to dream

réverbère, *m.* street lamp; reflector

réverbérer, *v.i.* to reverberate; *v.t.* to reflect; to throw back

reverdir, *v.i.* to grow green again

révérence, *f.* reverence; bow or curtsey

révérer, *v.t.* to revere; to reverence

rêverie, *f.* dreaming; musing

revers, *m.* reverse; back; wrong side

revêtir, *v.t.* to clothe, to dress; to face (a building with stone, etc.)

rêveur(-euse), *(adj.)* dreamy, dreaming, thoughtful; *m. (f.)* dreamer

revient, *m.* net cost, cost price

revirement. *m.* sudden change; transfer

réviser, *v.t.* to revise; to reconsider

révision, f. revision; overhauling

revivre, v.i. to come to life again; to revive

révocation, f. repeal; revocation; dismissal

revoir, v.t. to see again; to meet somebody again; au -, goodbye for the present

révolte, f. revolt, rebellion, mutiny

révolter, v.t. to revolt, to disgust (somebody); se -, v.r. to revolt, to rebel against; to mutiny

révolutionnaire, (adj.) and m. and f. revolutionary

revolver, m. revolver

revoquer, v.t. to revoke, repeal; to dismiss (from office)

revue, f. revue (mil. and theat.); passer en -, to review (troops)

rez-de-chaussée, m. ground level, ground floor

rhabiller, v.t. to mend, to repair; to dress again; se -, v.r. to buy a set of new clothes

rhabilleur, m. repairer (esp. of clocks)

rhénan, (adj.) Rhenish

rhinocéros, m. rhinoceros

rhubarbe, f. rhubarb

rhum, m. rum

rhumatisme, m. rheumatism

rhume, m. cold, cold in the head

rhythme, m. rhythm

ribambelle, f. long string (of animals); swarm

ribaud, (adj.) ribald

ribote, f. drinking bout

ricanement, m. sneer, sneering laughter

ricaner, v.i. to laugh sneeringly, to sneer, to titter

richard, m. man of means

riche, (adj.) rich; copious

richesse, f. wealth; richness (of soil, etc.)

ricin, m. castor-oil plant; huile de -, castor oil

ricocher, v.i. to rebound, to ricochet

ricochet, m. rebound, ricochet

rictus, m. grin

ride, f. wrinkle (of face)

rideau, m. curtain, screen

rider, v.t. to wrinkle

ridicule, (adj.) ridiculous; m. absurdity

ridiculiser, v.t. to ridicule

*rien, (pron.) anything (when a negative answer is expected); nothing, not anything; m. trifle; rien que, only

rieur(-euse), (adj.) laughing; fond of laughter; m. (f.) laugher

rigide, (adj.) rigid, tense

rigidité, f. rigidity; stiffness

rigole, f. drain, trench, gutter

rigoler, v.i. to laugh; to enjoy oneself

rigolo(te), (adj.) funny, comical

rigoureux(-euse), (adj.) rigorous; hard

rigueur, f. rigour; harshness, severity (of weather); hardship; à la -, strictly; if need be; être de -, to be compulsory, obligatory

rime, f. rhyme

rimer, v.t. to put into rhyme

rimeur, m. rhymester

rincer, v.t. to rinse (clothes), to rinse out

rinçage, rinsing

rince-doigts, m. inv. finger-bowl

ripaille, f. carousal, junketing

ripailler, v.i. to carouse

riposte, f. retort, repartee; counter (stroke)

riposter, v.i. to retort; to counter

*rire, v.i. to laugh

rire, m. laugh, laughter

ris (de veau), sweetbread (cook.)

risée, f. mockery; laughing-stock

risible, (adj.) laughable

risque, m. risk

risquer, v.t. to risk, to chance

rissoler, v.t. to brown (cook.)

ristourne, f. refund; rebate

rite, m. rite

rituel(le), (adj.) and m. ritual

rivage, m. shore; bank (of river)

rival(-aux), (adj.) rival; m. (f.) rival

rive, f. bank (of river); shore (of lake)

river, v.t. to rivet; to clinch

riverain(e), (adj.) riparian; adjoining; m. (f.) riverside dweller rivière, f. river (small); stream

rixe, f. brawl, scuffle

riz, m. rice; poudre de -, face-powder

robe, f. lady's dress, gown; robe, gown (of lawyer, etc.); robe de chambre, dressing-gown; morning-wrapper; - d'intérieur, house-coat

robinet, m. tap; stop-cock

robuste, (adj.) robust, sturdy

roc, m. rock

rocailleux(-euse), (adj.) rocky

roche, f. rock, boulder

rochet, m. ratchet; rochet (eccles.)

rocheux(-euse), (adj.) rocky, stony

rôder, v.i. to prowl, to roam; to stroll (about the streets)

rôdeur(-euse), m. (f.) prowler

rodomontade, f. bluster, swagger

roger-bontemps, a happy-go-lucky fellow

rogner, v.t. to clip, to pare

rognon, m. kidney (of animals, not of persons)

rognures, f. pl. parings, clippings

rogomme, m. spirits, dram

roi, m. king; (jour) (fête) des Rois, Twelfth Night

rôle, m. roll (of parchment), register, list; part, rôle (theat.); à tour de -, in turn, in rotation

romain(e), (adj.) and m. (f.) Roman

roman, m. novel, romance (mediæval literature)

roman(e), (adj.) Romanesque, Norman (archit.)

romancier(-ère), m. (f.) novelist

romanesque, (adj.) romantic (idea)

roman-feuilleton, m. serial story

romantique, (adj.) romantic (literature)

romarin, m. rosemary

rompre, v.t. to break; to break off, up; to train; se -, v.r. to break off

rompu, (adj.) broken, broken-in

ronce, f. briar; bramble; (pl.) thorns

ronceux(-euse), (adj.) brambly

rond, m. round, ring

rond(e), (adj.) round, plump

ronde, f. round, patrol (police)

rondelet(te), (adj.) roundish, plumpish

ronflement, m. snore, snoring; rumbling, whirring

ronfler, v.i. to snore, to roar (wind, fire); to whirr

ronger, v.t. to gnaw, to nibble; to corrode

rongeur(-euse), (adj.) and m. (f.) rodent, gnawing (animal)

ronron, m. purring

ronronner, v.i. to purr

roquefort, m. Roquefort cheese

roquet, m. pug-dog; mongrel

rosace, f. rose-window

rosaire, m. rosary

rosâtre, (adj.) pinkish

rose, f. rose (flower); rose (colour)

rosé, (adj.) rosy; rosé (wine)

roseau, m. reed

rosée, f. dew

rosette, f. rosette

rosier, m. rose tree

rosir, v.i. to blush; to turn pink

rosse, f. an objectionable character; a beast; old horse

rossée, f. thrashing

rosser, v.t. to give somebody a thrashing

rossignol, m. nightingale; unsaleable article

rot, m. belch

roter, v.i. to belch

rôti, m. roast (of meat)

rôtir, v.t. to roast (meat); to scorch, dry up (by sun)

rôtisserie, f. grill-room

rotonde, f. rotunda; circular hall

roturier(-ère), m. (f.) commoner

rouage, m. wheelwork

roublard(e), (adj.) wily, cunning

roucouler, v.i. to coo

roue, f. wheel

rouelle, f. round slice; round (of beef)

rouennerie, f. printed cotton goods

rouer, *v.t.* to thrash somebody; to break on a wheel

roué(e), *m.* (*f.*) profligate, wanton

rouet, *m.* spinning-wheel

rouge, (*adj.*) red, red hot; *m.* red, rouge; **bâton de -,** lipstick

rougeâtre, (*adj.*) reddish

rougeaud(e), *m.* (*f.*) red-faced person

rouge-gorge, *m.* robin redbreast

rougeole, *f.* measles

rougeur, *f.* redness; blush; flush

rougir, *v.t.* to redden; to blush; to flush; to be ashamed of something

rouille, *f.* rust; mildew

rouillé, (*adj.*) rusted, rusty

rouiller, *v.t.* to rust, to mildew

roulage, *m.* carriage, conveyance (of goods)

roulant, (*adj.*) rolling, sliding; **matériel -,** rolling stock

rouleau, *m.* roller; roll of paper; roll, spool

roulement, *m.* rolling, running (of machine); circulation of funds, rumbling

rouler, *v.t.* to roll (general sense); to rumble; **- quelqu'un,** to do somebody; to take somebody in; **se -,** *v.r.* to roll (in the grass, etc.)

roulette, *f.* caster; small wheel; gambling game of roulette

roulier, *m.* carter, carrier

roulis, *m.* rolling of ship

roumain(e), (*adj.*) Roumanian

roupiller, *v.i.* to snooze

rouquin(e), (*adj.*) red-haired

rouspéter, *v.i.* to resist; to protest vigorously

rousseur, *f.* redness (of hair); **tache de -,** freckle

roussir, *v.t.* to redden; to turn brown, russet-coloured

route, *f.* road, path, track; **- nationale,** *or* **grande -,** highway, main road; **en -,** on one's way; let us be off, go on; **se mettre en -,** to start out

routier(-ière), (*adj.*); **carte -,** road map; **gare -,** bus (coach) station

routine, *f.* routine

rouvrir, *v.t.* to reopen

roux(-sse), (*adj.*) reddish-brown; red (haired)

royal(-aux), (*adj.*) royal

royaliste, (*adj.*) and *m.* (*f.*) royalist

royaume, *m.* kingdom

royauté, *f.* royalty

ruban, *m.* ribbon; band

rubis, *m.* ruby

ruche, *f.* beehive; ruche

rude, (*adj.*) arduous; severe; uncouth; harsh (voice); rugged (path); rough (weather); gruff

rudement, (*adv.*) roughly, severely; awfully

rudesse, *f.* severity (of weather); uncouthness, gruffness

rudiments, *m. pl.* rudiments

rudoyer, *v.t.* to treat roughly

rue, *f.* street; thoroughfare

ruée, *f.* rush

ruelle, *f.* lane, narrow street, alley

ruer, *v.i.* to kick out, lash out (animal); **se -,** *v.r.* to hurl oneself on

rugir, *v.i.* to roar; to howl (of wind)

rugissement, *m.* roar, roaring (of animal); howling (of wind)

rugueux(-euse), (*adj.*) rugged, rough; gnarled (tree trunk)

ruine, *f.* ruin; downfall; decay

ruiner, *v.t.* to ruin; to destroy; **se -,** *v.r.* to ruin oneself; to go to ruin

ruineux(-euse), (*adj.*) ruinous

ruisseau, *m.* brook; small stream; street gutter

ruisseler, *v.i.* to stream down; to trickle, to drip

rumeur, *f.* murmur; din; rumour, report

ruminant, (*adj.*) ruminating; chewing the cud

ruminer, *v.t.* to ruminate (over); to chew the cud

rupture, *f.* breaking; rupture; fracture of bone; breaking off; discontinuance (of negotiations)

rural(-aux), (*adj.*) rural

ruse, *f.* ruse, trick, dodge

rusé(e), (*adj.*) artful, sly, cunning

ruser, *v.i.* to use trickery

russe, *(adj.)* and *m.* and *f.* Russian

rustaud, *m.* bumpkin, boor

rustique, *(adj.)* rustic

rustre, *m.* a lout, boor

rutilant, *(adj.)* glowing red; gleaming

rutiler, *v.i.* to glow, to glow red

rythme, *m.* rhythm

rythmique, *(adj.)* rhythmic

S

sabbat, *m.* Sabbath (generally Jewish); sabbath (witchcraft)

sable, *m.* sand; sable (fur)

sableux(-euse), *(adj.)* sandy

sablier, *m.* hour-glass; egg-timer

sablière, *f.* sandpit

sablonneux(-euse), *(adj.)* sandy (shore, etc.)

sabord, *m.* port (-hole)

saborder, *v.t.* to scuttle (a ship)

sabot, *m.* wooden shoe, clog; hoof of horse; drag, skid (of wheel)

sabotage, *m.* malicious destruction; sabotage

saboter, *v.t.* to destroy maliciously (machinery, etc.)

sabotier, *m.* wooden shoe maker

sabre, *m.* sabre, cavalry sword

sabrer, *v.t.* to sabre; to cut down with a sword

sac, *m.* sack, bag; pouch; knapsack; pillage; **l'affaire est dans le -,** *(fam.)* it's "in the bag" (settled)

saccade, *f.* jerk, jolt

saccader, *v.t.* to jerk, to jolt

saccager, *v.t.* to plunder

sachet, *m.* small bag; scent bag

sacoche, *f.* wallet, satchel

sacrement, *m.* sacrament

sacre, *m.* anointing; crowning of king or bishop

sacré, *(adj.)* (after the noun) consecrated, sacred, inviolable; used profanely (before the noun) cursed, damned

sacrer, *v.t.* to anoint, crown (king or bishop); to curse (profane)

sacrifice, *m.* sacrifice

sacrifier, *v.t.* to sacrifice (victim); to offer up in sacrifice

sacrilège, *m.* sacrilege

sacristain, *m.* sacristan; sexton

sacristie, *f.* vestry, sacristy

sadique, *(adj.)* sadistic; *m. (f.)* sadist

safran, *m.* saffron

sagace, *(adj.)* sagacious; shrewd

sagacité, *f.* sagacity; shrewdness

sage, *(adj.)* wise; good; well-behaved; **sois - !** be good!

sage-femme, *f.* midwife

sagesse, *f.* wisdom; discretion

sagou, *m.* sago

saignant, *(adj.)* bleeding; raw (wound); underdone (meat)

saignée, *f.* bleeding; blood-letting (*med.*)

saigner, *v.t.* to bleed (a person); *v.i.* to bleed (from nose, etc.)

saigneux(-euse), *(adj.)* bloody

saillant, *(adj.)* projecting; jutting out; *m.* salient (*mil.*)

saillie, *f.* spring; spurt; sally (*mil.*); flash of wit; **en -,** projecting

saillir, *v.i.* to gush out; to spurt out; to stand out, jut out

sain, *(adj.)* healthy; sound (idea); wholesome; **- et sauf,** safe and sound

saindoux, *m.* lard

saint(e), *(adj.)* holy, saintly, godly; *m. (f.)* saint

Saint-Esprit, *m.* the Holy Ghost

Saint-Père (le), the Pope

sainteté, *f.* holiness, saintliness

saisie, *f.* seizure

saisie-arrêt, *f.* attachment (of goods)

saisir, *v.t.* to seize; to grasp; to perceive; to understand; **se - (de),** *v.r.* to possess oneself of

saisissant, *(adj.)* piercing, nipping (cold); striking

saison, *f.* season (general sense)

salade, *f.* salad; (*slang*) a mix-up

saladier, *m.* salad bowl

salaire, *m.* wages

salaison, *f.* salting; curing; salt meats

salarier, *v.t.* to pay wages

salaud(e), *m.* (*f.*) a dirty fellow (woman); a rotten fellow

sale, (*adj.*) dirty, filthy, unclean

salé (*adj.*) salt(y) (fish, meat, etc.)

saler, *v.t.* to salt, to season with salt

saleté, *f.* dirt, filth, dirtiness; obscenity

salière, *f.* salt-cellar

saligaud(e), *m.* (*f.*) dirty fellow (woman); low type

salin, (*adj.*) saline, briny

saline, *f.* saltworks

salir, *v.t.* to dirty; to soil; to besmirch (somebody); **se -,** *v.r.* to dirty oneself; to get dirty; to dirty one's clothes

salive, *f.* saliva, spittle

salle, *f.* hall (large room); auditorium (of theatre, etc.); **- d'attente,** *f.* waiting room; **- de bain,** *f.* bath-room; **- à manger,** *f.* dining-room

salon, *m.* drawing-room; saloon (ship)

salope, *f.* slattern, slut

saloperie, *f.* filthiness; trash

salopette, *f.* overalls, dungarees

salsifis, *m.* salsify (vegetable)

saltimbanque, *m.* showman; humbug, charlatan

salubre, (*adj.*) salubrious, healthy

saluer, *v.t.* to salute; to bow (to somebody), raise one's hat to

salut, *m.* safety; a bow, greeting; **armée du -,** Salvation Army

salutaire, (*adj.*) salutary, beneficial

salutation, *f.* salutation; greeting; bow

salve, *f.* salvo; volley (of rifle fire, etc.)

samedi, *m.* Saturday

sanatorium, *m.* convalescent home

sanction, *f.* sanction; approval; penalty

sanctionner, *v.t.* to approve; to sanction; to attach a penalty to

sanctuaire, *m.* sanctuary

sandale, *f.* sandal; gym. shoe; (U.S.A.) sneaker

*****sang,** *m.* blood; **pur -,** thorough-bred (horse)

sang-froid, *m.* coolness, composure

sanglade, *f.* lash

sanglant, (*adj.*) bloody; blood-stained; scathing

sangle, *f.* strap; band; girth (of saddle)

sangler, *v.t.* to strap (a parcel, etc.); to thrash; to girth up

sanglier, *m.* wild boar

sanglot, *m.* sob

sangloter, *v.i.* to sob

sangsue, *f.* leech; blood-sucker

sanguin, (*adj.*) full-blooded

sanguinaire, (*adj.*) bloodthirsty; bloody (fight)

sanitaire, (*adj.*) sanitary; **train -,** ambulance train

*****sans,** (*prep.*) without; **- parler,** without speaking; (*conj.*) **- que nous le sachions,** without our knowing

sans-façon, sans-gêne, *m.* home-liness; lack of ceremony

sans-fil, *m.* wireless (telegraphy)

sansonnet, *m.* starling

sans-souci, *m.* and *f.* (*invar.*) carefree person; *m.* unconcern

sans-travail (les), *m. pl.* the unemployed

santé, *f.* health; well-being

saoul, (*adj.*) drunk

saouler, *v.t.* to intoxicate; to make somebody drunk; **se -,** *v.r.* to get drunk. (N.B.—**saoul, saouler,** etc., are sometimes spelt **soûl(er),** etc.)

saper, *v.t.* to sap; to undermine

sapeur, *m.* sapper, pioneer (*mil.*)

sapeur-pompier, *m.* member of fire brigade, fireman

saphir, *m.* sapphire

sapin, *m.* fir tree

sarcasme, *m.* sarcasm

sarcastique, (*adj.*) sarcastic

sarcelle, *f.* teal (bird)

sarcler, *v.t.* to weed a garden; to hoe up (weeds, etc.)

sarcleuse, *f.* weeding machine

sarcloir, *m.* hoe

sarcophage, *m.* sarcophagus

sardine, *f.* sardine; pilchard

sarrasin, *m.* buckwheat; (*adj.*) Saracen

sarrau, *m.* smock

sasse, *f.* bailer; scoop

satané, (*adj.*) devilish; confounded; damned

satanique, (*adj.*) satanic; diabolical; fiendish (cruelty, etc.)

satellite, *m.* and (*adj.*) satellite

satin, *m.* satin

satiné, (*adj.*) glossy (surface)

satire, *f.* satire

satirique, (*adj.*) satirical; *m.* satirist

satisfaction, *f.* satisfaction, gratification

satisfaire, *v.t.* to satisfy, to content; to give satisfaction

satisfait (de), (*adj.*) satisfied, contented (with)

saturer, *v.t.* to saturate; se - (de), *v.r.* to become saturated (with)

satyre, *m.* satyr

sauce, *f.* sauce (*cook.*)

saucière, *f.* sauce-boat

saucisse, *f.* fresh sausage

saucisson, *m.* dry sausage

sauf(-ve), (*adj.*) safe, unhurt

sauf, (*prep.*) except, but

sauf-conduit, *m.* safe-conduct pass

sauge, *f.* sage (herb)

saugrenu, (*adj.*) absurd; ridiculous

saule, *m.* willow tree

saule-pleureur, *m.* weeping willow

saumâtre, (*adj.*) brackish (water)

saumon, *m.* salmon

saunier, *m.* salter, one who makes salt

saupoudrer, *v.t.* to sprinkle; to powder; to dust with powder

saur, *m.* smoked and dried (particularly herring)

saut, *m.* jump, leap

saut-de-lit, *m.* bedside rug

sauté, (*adj.*) sauté potatoes (*cook.*)

saute-mouton, leap-frog

sauter, *v.i.* to jump; to leap; *v.t.* to jump over (obstacle)

sauter, *v.i.* to explode (mine, etc.); to go smash (bank, etc.); (faire) -, to blow up (bridge, etc.)

sauterelle, *f.* grasshopper

sautiller, *v.i.* to skip, to hop

sauvage, (*adj.*) savage; uncivilised; wild; shy; *m.* and *f.* savage

sauvagerie, *f.* savageness

sauvegarde, *f.* safeguard; safekeeping

sauvegarder, *v.t.* to safeguard; to protect

sauver, *v.t.* to save; to rescue; se -, *v.r.* to escape; to run away

sauvetage, *m.* life-saving; bateau de -, life-boat; ceinture de -, life-belt

sauveur, *m.* saviour; the Saviour

savamment, (*adv.*) learnedly; knowingly

savant(e), (*adj.*) learned; *m.* (*f.*) scholar; scientist

savate, *f.* old shoe; French boxing (now rarely seen)

savetier, *m.* cobbler

saveur, *f.* taste, flavour

*savoir, *v.t.* to know; to be aware of something

savoir-faire, *m.* ability, tact

savon, *m.* soap

savonner, *v.t.* to soap; to lather

savonnerie, *f.* soap-works; soap trade

savonnette, *f.* cake of soap (toilet)

savonneux(-euse), (*adj.*) soapy

savourer, *v.t.* to relish (one's food, etc.)

savoureux(-euse), (*adj.*) savoury, tasty

scabreux(-euse), (*adj.*) improper; scabrous; risky

scalper, *v.t.* to scalp

scandale, *m.* scandal

scandaleux(-euse), (*adj.*) scandalous; disgraceful

scaphandrier, *m.* diver

scarifier, *v.t.* to scarify (*surg.*)

scarlatine, *f.* scarlet fever

sceau, *m.* seal (state, and company's seal, etc.); garde des sceaux, keeper of the seals

scélérat(e), *m.* (*f.*) scoundrel, villain; (*adj.*) villainous

scellé, (*adj.*) sealed, under seal

sceller, *v.t.* to seal; to seal up

scène, *f.* scene; scene of action; stage (of theatre, etc.)

sceptique, (*adj.*) sceptical; *m.* and *f.* sceptic

sceptre, *m.* sceptre

sciatique, *f.* sciatica

scie, *f.* saw; a bore, nuisance

sciemment, (*adv.*) knowingly

science, *f.* science; knowledge; skill

scientifique, (*adj.*) scientific

scier, *v.t.* to saw; to bore

scierie, *f.* saw-mill

scintillant, (*adj.*) sparkling, twinkling (star)

scintiller, *v.i.* to sparkle; to twinkle

sciure, *f.* sawdust

sclérose, *f.* sclerosis

scolaire, (*adj.*) scholastic

scooter, *m.* (motor) scooter

scorbut, *m.* scurvy

scorie, *f.* dross (iron); slag

scorpion, *m.* scorpion

scoutisme, *m.* (boy) scouting

scrofules, *f. pl.* scrofula

scrupule, *m.* scruple; doubt (conscientious)

scrupuleux(-euse), (*adj.*) scrupulous

scrutateur(-trice), *m.* (*f.*) scrutiniser; scrutineer; (*adj.*) scrutinising, searching

scruter, *v.t.* to scrutinise; to examine closely

scrutin, *m.* ballot, poll

sculpter, *v.t.* to sculpture; to carve

sculpteur, *m.* sculptor (the feminine is **femme sculpteur**)

sculpture, *f.* sculpture

séance, *f.* sitting, session; meeting; performance (theatre, etc.)

séance tenante, forthwith

séant, (*pres. part.*) sitting (from verb *seoir*, not much used); proper

seau, *m.* bucket; pail

sébile, *f.* wooden bowl

sec (sèche), (*adj.*) dry

sécher, *v.t.* to dry; to dry up (tears)

sécheresse, *f.* dryness; drought; spareness (of figure)

second, (*adj.*) second; second (in command)

seconde, *f.* second (of time)

secondaire, (*adj.*) secondary

seconder, *v.t.* to assist; to back up

secouer, *v.t.* to shake; to shake off; to shake down; **se -,** *v.r.* to shake oneself

secourable, (*adj.*) helpful; willing to help

secourir, *v.t.* to help, to aid

secours, *m.* help, relief, aid; **au - !** help!

secousse, *f.* shock; shaking; jolt; jerk

secret, (*adj.*) secret; hidden; *m.* secret

secrétaire, *m.* and *f.* secretary; *m.* writing-desk

secrétariat, *m.* secretaryship; secretary's office; secretariat

sécréter, *v.t.* to secrete (generally *med.*)

secte, *f.* sect (religious)

secteur, *m.* sector; district

section, *f.* section; cutting; branch (of a department, Civil Service)

séculaire, (*adj.*) secular; century old

secundo, (*adv.*) secondly

sécurité, *f.* security, safety

sédentaire, (*adj.*) sedentary

sédiment, *m.* sediment, deposit

séduction, *f.* seduction; enticement

séduire, *v.t.* to seduce; to lead astray; to captivate

séduisant, (*adj.*) seductive, tempting; fascinating

ségrégation, *f.* segregation; isolation

seigle, *m.* rye

seigneur, *m.* lord (of manor, etc.); nobleman; the Lord

seigneurie, *f.* lordship

sein, *m.* breast; bosom

seine, *f.* draw-net

séjour, *m.* stay, sojourn.

séjourner, *v.i.* to stay (in a place)

sel, *m.* salt (used in general sense); wit

sélecteur(-trice), *m.* (*f.*) selector

sélection, *f.* selection, choice

selle, *f.* saddle; seat; stool (*med.*)

sellier, *m.* saddler

selon, (*prep.*) according to

semailles, *f. pl.* sowing; seed-time

semaine, *f.* week; week's wages

semblable, (*adj.*) alike; similar; like; such

semblant, *m.* semblance; appearance

sembler, *v.i.* to seem; to appear

semelle, *f.* sole (of shoe); sock (in shoe)

semence, *f.* seed

semer, *v.i.* to sow; to spread; to strew

semestre, *m.* half-year

semeur(-euse), *m.* (*f.*) sower; spreader (of news)

sémillant, (*adj.*) bright, sprightly

séminaire, *m.* seminary; training college (usually for clergy)

sémitique, (*adj.*) Semitic

semoir, *m.* drill, sowing machine

semonce, *f.* lecture; (severe) reprimand

semoncer, *v.t.* to lecture; reprimand; to scold

semoule, *f.* semolina

sempiternel(le), (*adj.*) never-ceasing

sénat, *m.* senate, senate house

sénateur, *m.* senator

séneçon, *m.* groundsel

*****sens,** *m.* sense (the five senses); consciousness; judgment; direction (traffic)

sensation, *f.* sensation; excitement

sensationnel(le), (*adj.*) sensational; thrilling

sensé, (*adj.*) sensible, judicious

sensibilité, *f.* sensibility (to pain); sensitiveness; feeling (for)

sensible, (*adj.*) sensitive, susceptible; perceptible

sensiblement, (*adv.*) appreciably, palpably

sensitif(-ive), (*adj.*) having feeling

sensualisme, *m.* sensualism

sensualiste, *m.* sensualist

sensualité, *f.* sensuality

sensuel(le), (*adj.*) sensuous, sensual

senteur, *f.* scent, odour, perfume

sentier, *m.* path; pathway

sentiment, *m.* feeling; sensation (of happiness, etc.); opinion

sentimental, (*adj.*) sentimental

sentinelle, *f.* sentry, sentinel

sentir, *v.t.* to feel; to be conscious of; *v.i.* to smell; to taste

séparation, *f.* separation; severance; parting

séparé, (*adj.*) separate; different

séparément, (*adv.*) separately

séparer, *v.t.* to separate; to part; to keep apart; to divide; **se -,** *v.r.* to part from; to part company

sept, (*num. adj.*) seven; **septième** (*adj.*) seventh

septembre, *m.* September

septentrional, (*adj.*) northern

septique, (*adj.*) septic (poisoning)

septuagénaire, (*adj.*) and *m.* and *f.* septuagenarian

sépulcre, *m.* sepulchre

sépulture, *f.* burial

séquence, *f.* sequence

séquestration, *f.* sequestration (of goods); isolation (of infected beings, etc.)

séquestre, *m.* embargo

séquestrer, *v.t.* to sequester; to lay an embargo on

sérail, *m.* seraglio

serein, (*adj.*) calm, serene; *m.* evening dew

sérénade, *f.* serenade

sérénité, *f.* serenity, calmness

serge, *m.* woollen serge

sergent, *m.* sergeant; **- de ville,** policeman

sergerie, *f.* serge factory

série, *f.* series; succession (of events, etc.); range (of samples, goods); **hors -,** specially made, outsize

sérieux(-euse), *(adj.)* serious; earnest; sober
serin, *m.* canary
seringue, *f.* syringe
serment, *m.* oath (solemn); **prêter -,** to take an oath
sermon, *m.* sermon; preaching
sermonner, *v.t.* to give someone a talking to
serpe, *f.* bill-hook
serpent, *m.* serpent, snake
serpenter, *v.i.* to wind; to meander; to curve
serpette, *f.* pruning knife
serre, *f.* greenhouse; conservatory; claw; grip
serre chaude, *f.* hot-house
serre-frein, *m.* brakesman
serre-papiers, *m.* paper clip
serrer, *v.t.* to squeeze; to press; to close; close up; **se -,** *v.r.* to draw close together; to huddle together
serrure, *f.* lock
serrurerie, *f.* locksmith's shop
serrurier, *m.* locksmith
servante, *f.* maidservant
serveur(-euse), *m.* *(f.)* server, carver; barman (barmaid)
serviable, *(adj.)* obliging; willing to help
*service, *m.* service; course of dishes
serviette, *f.* towel, napkin; brief-case
servile, *(adj.)* servile
*servir, *v.t.* to serve; *v.i.* to be useful to somebody; **se - (de),** *v.r.* to make use (of)
serviteur, *m.* servant
session, *f.* session; sitting
seuil, *m.* threshold; door-step
seul, *(adj.)* (before noun) only, single, sole; (after noun) alone.
seulement, *(adv.)* only
sève, *f.* sap (of plant)
sévère, *(adj.)* severe; hard; harsh
sévérité, *f.* severity; sternness; strictness
sévices, *m. pl.* ill-treatment; brutality
sévir, *v.i.* to rage; to be rampant
sevrer, *v.t.* to wean

sevreuse, *f.* wet-nurse (not often used)
sexagénaire, *(adj.)* and *m. (f.)* sexagenarian
sexe, *m.* sex
sexuel(le), *(adj.)* sexual
si, *(conj.)* if
si, *(adv.)* so, so much; yes (in answer to a negative question)
siècle, *m.* century; age; long period of time
siège, *m.* seat; centre (of learning); seat, chair; siege; **- social,** *m.* registered offices of a company
siéger, *v.i.* to sit; to hold sittings or meetings; to have the head offices (of a company)
sien(ne), *(adj.)* his, hers, its; **le -,** *(pron.)* his, etc.
sieste, *f.* afternoon nap
sifflement, *m.* whistling, hissing
siffler, *v.i.* to whistle, to hiss
sifflet, *m.* whistle
siffleur(-euse), *m. (f.)* whistler; booer (theatre, etc.)
signal(-aux), *m.* signal
signalé, *(adj.)* signal; conspicuous (service)
signalement, *m.* description (of person, etc.); particulars (of car)
signaler, *v.t.* to signalise; to make conspicuous; to draw attention to; **se -,** *v.r.* to distinguish oneself
signataire, *m.* and *f.* signatory
signature, *f.* signature, signing
signe, *m.* sign; indication; symptom of illness; mark (of joy, grief); gesture
signer, *v.t.* to sign; to place one's signature to
signet, *m.* book-marker
significatif(-ive), *(adj.)* significant
signification, *f.* signification; sense (of)
signifier, *v.t.* to signify; to mean
silence, *m.* silence
silencieux(-euse), *(adj.)* silent
silhouette, *f.* silhouette; outline; profile
sillage, *m.* wake, wash (of ship)
sillon, *m.* furrow

sillonner, *v.t.* to furrow; to plough (the seas)

simagrée, *f.* pretence; *pl.* affectation(s)

similaire, *(adj.)* similar to; like

similarité, *f.* similarity; likeness

simple, *(adj.)* simple; single; plain; easy; ingenuous; - **soldat,** private soldier

simplicité, *f.* simplicity; plainness (of manner, dress, etc.); artlessness

simplifier, *v.t.* to simplify

simuler, *v.t.* to simulate; to feign

simultané, *(adj.)* simultaneous

simultanément, *(adv.)* simultaneously

sinapisme, *m.* mustard plaster

sincère, *(adj.)* sincere, candid (opinion)

sincérité, *f.* sincerity, candour.

singe, *m.* monkey, ape

singer, *v.t.* to ape, to mimic

singerie, *f.* grimace; apish trick

singulariser, *v.t.* to make someone conspicuous; **se -,** *v.r.* to make oneself conspicuous

singularité, *f.* singularity; peculiarity; oddness

singulier, *(adj.)* singular; strange; remarkable

sinistre, *(adj.)* sinister; ominous; *m.* disaster; catastrophe

sinon, *(conj.)* otherwise; else; if not

sinueux(-euse), *(adj.)* sinuous; winding; meandering

sinuosité, *f.* sinuosity, winding; bend (of river)

siphon, *m.* siphon; bottle of (soda water, etc.)

sire, *m.* sire (also as form of address)

sirène, *f.* siren; charmer; hooter, buzzer

sirop, *m.* syrup

siroter, *v.t.* to sip

sis, *(adj.)* situate (from *sevir* and used in legal documents)

site, *m.* site; picturesque site (landscape)

sitôt, *(adv.)* as soon

situation, *f.* situation; position; site (of town, etc.); state; condition (in life)

situer, *v.t.* to situate, to place

six, *(num. adj.)* six

sixième, *(adj.)* and *m.* sixth; sixth part

ski, *m.* ski; **faire du -,** to ski, go in for skiing

slovaque, *(adj.)* Slovak

sobre, *(adj.)* sober, temperate, moderate

sobriété, *f.* sobriety; moderation; quietness

sobriquet, *m.* nickname

sociabilité, *f.* sociability

sociable, *(adj.)* sociable; companionable

social, *(adj.)* social; **siège -,** registered office (of company)

socialisme, *m.* socialism

socialiste, *(adj.)* socialistic; *m.* and *f.* socialist

sociétaire, *m.* and *f.* shareholder; stockholder

société, *f.* society; company (business); community; companionship; association; fellowship

socle, *m.* pedestal; base; plinth (of statue)

sœur, *f.* sister; sister of charity; nun

soi, *(pers. pron.)* himself; herself; itself; oneself

soi-disant, *(adj. invar.)* so-called; self-styled

soie, *f.* silk; bristle (of pig)

soierie, *f.* silk trade; silk fabrics

soif, *f.* thirst; **avoir -,** to be thirsty

soigné, *(adj.)* carefully done; well groomed

soigner, *v.t.* to look after; to take care of; to attend to; **se -,** *v.r.* to look after oneself

soigneux(-euse), *(adj.)* careful; painstaking

soin, *m.* care

soir, *m.* evening

soirée, *f.* evening (duration of); evening party

soit! *(interj.)* so be it! agreed!

soixantaine, *f.* about sixty
soixante, (*num. adj.*) sixty
soixante-dix, (*num. adj.*) seventy
sol, *m.* soil, ground
solaire, (*adj.*) solar
soldat, *m.* soldier
soldatesque, *f.* soldiery (depreciatory sense)
solde, *f.* pay (of employees, soldiers, etc.); *m.* balance; surplus stock; remnant (sale)
solder, *v.t.* to pay; to discharge; to pay off; to sell off (surplus stock)
sole, *f.* sole (fish); sole (animal's hoof)
solécisme, *m.* solecism
soleil, *m.* sun; le coucher (lever) du -, sunset (sunrise)
solennel(le), (*adj.*) solemn
solenniser, *v.t.* to solemnize
solennité, *f.* solemnity; gravity; awfulness
solidaire, (*adj.*) jointly responsible (*legal*)
solidairement, (*adv.*) jointly (with conjointement) jointly and severally
solidarité, *f.* joint (and several) liability; solidarity; fellowship
solide, (*adj.*) solid, firm
solidifier, *v.t.* to solidify
solidité, *f.* solidity; strength (of construction, etc.)
soliloque, *m.* soliloquy
solitaire, (*adj.*) solitary; lonely; *m.* hermit; solitaire (game)
solitude, *f.* solitude; loneliness; lonely spot
solive, *f.* joist, beam, rafter
sollicitation, *f.* solicitation; request; entreaty
solliciter, *v.t.* to solicit; to request; to beg (favour, etc.)
solution, *f.* solution (of liquid); answer to problem; settlement (of dispute, etc.)
solutionner, *v.t.* to solve (problem, difficulty)
solvabilité, *f.* solvency
solvable, (*adj.*) solvent
sombre, (*adj.*) dark, gloomy, sombre

sombrer, *v.i.* to founder; to sink
sommaire, (*adj.*) summary; improvised; *m.* summary, abstract
sommation, *f.* summons (*legal*); notice (to fulfil contract)
somme, *f.* sum, amount; *m.* nap; short sleep; bête de -, beast of burden
sommeil, *m.* sleep; slumber
sommeiller, *v.i.* to doze; to sleep lightly
sommelier, *m.* wine butler; wine waiter (in restaurant); cellarman
sommer, *v.t.* to summon; to sum up (*maths.*)
sommet, *m.* summit, top (of hill); crest (of wave)
sommier, *m.* transom; - élastique, spring mattress
sommité, *f.* summit, top (of mountain); apex; prominent person
somnambule, *m.* and *f.* sleepwalker; somnambulist
somnifère, *m.* and (*adj.*) narcotic; soporific
somnolence, *f.* sleepiness; somnolence
somnolent, (*adj.*) sleepy, somnolent
somptueux(-euse), (*adj.*) sumptuous; gorgeous
son, (*m.* of *poss. adj.* son, sa, ses) his, hers, its; one's
son, *m.* sound; *m.* bran
sonate, *f.* sonata
sondage, *m.* sounding (*naut.*)
sonde, *f.* sounding lead; probe (*med.*)
sonder, *v.t.* to take soundings; to sound; to probe; to explore (wood, etc.)
songe, *m.* dream
songer, *v.i.* to dream (of); to think over; to imagine
songerie, *f.* day-dreaming
songeur(-euse), *m.* (*f.*) dreamer
sonner, *v.i.* to sound; to strike (of clock); to ring, to toll (bell); il est six heures sonnées, it's gone six o'clock; elle a cinquante ans (bien) sonnés, she'll never see fifty again
sonnet, *m.* sonnet

sonnette, *f.* small bell; **serpent à sonnettes,** rattlesnake

sonneur, *m.* bell-ringer

sonore, (*adj.*) sonorous; loud-sounding; resonant

soporifique, (*adj.*) inducing sleep; tedious (story)

sorbet, *m.* water-ice; sorbet (*cook.*)

sorcellerie, *f.* sorcery

sorcier, *m.* wizard, sorcerer

sorcière, *f.* sorceress; **vieille -,** old hag

sordide, (*adj.*) sordid, squalid

sornettes, *f. pl.* idle talk

sort, *m.* fate; lot (in life)

sortable, (*adj.*) suitable (employment, match)

sortant, (*adj.*) coming out; winning number (in lottery); retiring (members of committee, etc.)

sorte, *f.* manner; way; kind, sort; **de - que,** so that

sortie, *f.* exit; outlet; way out

sortir, *v.i.* (with *être*) to go out; to come out; to leave

sortir, *v.t.* to take out; bring out; pull out; **faire - qn.,** to take somebody out (for walk, etc.)

sosie, *m.* double (of somebody); counterpart

sot(te), (*adj.*) silly, stupid, foolish; *m.* (*f.*) dolt, blockhead

sottise, *f.* silliness, stupidity; foolish (act or word)

sou, *m.* (formerly) a halfpenny; 5 centimes

soubassement, *m.* base; sub-foundation

soubresaut, *m.* sudden start

soubrette, *f.* soubrette (*theat.*); waiting-maid

souche, *f.* stump; stem; stub; counterfoil

souci, *m.* care, anxiety, worry

(se) soucier (de), *v.r.* to trouble oneself (about); to care for

soucieux(-euse), (*adj.*) anxious; concerned about

soucoupe, *f.* saucer; **- volante,** flying saucer

soudain, (*adj.*) sudden; unexpected; (*adv.*) suddenly

soudainement, (*adv.*) suddenly

soudard, *m.* old soldier; veteran

soude, *f.* soda

souder, *v.t.* to solder; to weld

soudoyer, *v.t.* to hire (usually for evil purpose) ; to bribe

soudure, *f.* soldering; welding

souffle, *m.* breath; puff (of wind); respiration

soufflé, *m.* soufflé (*cook.*)

souffler, *v.i.* to blow; to prompt (*theat.*, etc.); to puff; to utter (a word)

soufflet, *m.* bellows; box (on the ear)

souffleter, *v.t.* to slap

souffleur, *m.* blower; prompter (in theatre)

soufflure, *f.* flaw; blister (on paint)

souffrance, *f.* suffering, pain; suspense

souffrant, (*adj.*) suffering; in pain; unwell

souffrir, *v.t.* to suffer, to endure, to undergo; to permit

soufre, *m.* sulphur

souhait, *m.* wish, desire

souhaitable, (*adj.*) desirable

souhaiter, *v.t.* to wish

souiller, *v.t.* to dirty; to soil

souillon, *m.* and *f.* sloven

souillure, *f.* spot (of dirt); blot; blemish

soûl, (*see* saoul)

soulagement, *m.* relief; comfort

soulager, *v.t.* to relieve; to assist

se soûler (*see* se saouler)

soulèvement, *m.* rising; swell (of waves); uprising; revolt

soulever, *v.t.* to raise; to lift up; to provoke (indignation, etc.)

soulier, *m.* shoe

souligner, *v.t.* to underline; to lay stress on

soumettre, *v.t.* to subdue; to submit, to refer (question)

soumis, (*adj.*) submissive; obedient; subject (to)

soumission, *f.* submission

soupape, *f.* valve

soupçon, *f.* suspicion; slight flavour; dash (of)

soupçonner, *v.t.* to suspect; to conjecture

soupçonneux(-euse), *(adj.)* suspicious; distrustful

soupe, *f.* soup; sop

soupente, *f.* loft, garret

souper, *v.i.* to sup; to have supper; *m.* supper

soupière, *f.* soup tureen

soupir, *m.* sigh

soupirail(-aux), *m.* air-hole; ventilator

soupirer, *v.i.* to sigh   [tilator

souple, *(adj.)* supple; pliant; flexible; lithe

souplesse, *f.* suppleness; flexibility; litheness

source, *f.* source; spring (water); well

sourcier, *m.* water-diviner

sourcil, *m.* eye-brow

sourciller, *v.i.* to frown; wince

sourcilleux(-euse), *(adj.)* supercilious

sourd, *(adj.)* deaf; **sourd-muet,** deaf and dumb

sourdement, *(adv.)* dully; with a dull, hollow sound

sourdine, (à la) secretly, slyly

sourdre, *v.i.* to gush out (used only in 3rd pers. sing.)

souriant, *(adj.)* smiling

souricière, *f.* mouse-trap

sourire, *v.i.* to smile; *m.* smile

souris, *f.* mouse

sournois, *(adj.)* cunning; shifty; underhand

sous, *(prep.)* under, underneath; beneath; below

sous-chef, *m.* assistant manager. (N.B.—Compound nouns in which *sous* forms the first part, vary in the plural)

sous-commission, *f.* sub-committee

souscription, *f.* subscription; signature; contribution

souscrire, *v.t.* to subscribe; sign; to apply for shares

sous-directeur(-trice), *m.* (*f.*) sub-manager(ess)

sous-entendre, *v.t.* to understand; to imply

sous-entendu, *m.* implication

sous-lieutenant, *m.* second-lieutenant, sub-lieutenant

sous-locataire, *m.* and *f.* sub-tenant

sous-location, *f.* sub-letting

sous-louer, *v.t.* to sub-let

sous-marin, *m.* submarine

sous-officier, *m.* non-commissioned officer

sous-préfet, *m.* sub-prefect (of a French department)

sous-sol, *m.* basement; sub-soil

soussigné(e), *m.* (*f.*) undersigned

soussigner, *v.t.* to sign; undersign

soustraction, *f.* removal, withdrawal; subtraction

soustraire, *v.t.* to take away; to withdraw; to subtract

sous-traiter, *v.t.* to sub-contract

soutache, *f.* braid

soutane, *f.* cassock

soutenable, *(adj.)* bearable, supportable

souteneur, *m.* upholder; pimp

soutenir, *v.t.* to sustain, to support; to hold up; to back up (a cause, or a friend); to maintain (an opinion); **se -,** *v.r.* to support oneself; to last, continue

souterrain, *m.* underground (passage); subway; *(adj.)* subterranean

soutien, *m.* support, prop; **soutien-gorge,** *m.* (*invar.*) bust-supporter; bodice; brassiere

souvenir, *m.* remembrance; memory; keepsake; **se - (de),** *v.r.* to remember; to recall

souvent, *(adv.)* often

souverain, *m.* sovereign; *(adj.)* sovereign, supreme

soyeux(-euse), *(adj.)* silky

spacieux(-euse), *(adj.)* spacious,

spadassin, *m.* hired bully

spasme, *m.* spasm

speaker(-ine), *m.* (*f.*) announcer (W. Tel.)

spécial(-aux), *(adj.)* special, especial

spécialiser, *v.t.* to specialise; **se - dans,** *v.r.* to be a specialist (in)

spécialiste, *m.* and *f.* specialist; expert

spécialité, f. speciality

specieux(-euse), (adj.) specious, plausible

spécification, f. specification

spécifier, v.t. to specify; to state quite definitely

spécimen, m. specimen

spectacle, m. spectacle; sight; show (theat.); display (spectacles (pl.) does not mean " spectacles " in the sense of glasses)

spectateur(-trice), m. (f.) spectator; onlooker

spectre, m. spectre, ghost, apparition

spéculateur(-trice), m..(f.) speculator

spéculer, v.i. to speculate; to think over

sphère, f. sphere; globe; orb

sphérique, (adj.) spherical

sphinx, m. sphinx

spiral(-aux), (adj.) spiral; m. spring (of watch, etc.)

spirituel(le), (adj.) spiritual; witty; humorous

spiritueux(-euse)(adj.)spirituous

splendeur, f. splendour; magnificence; brilliance

splendide, (adj.) splendid, magnificent, gorgeous

spoliation, f. plundering; despoiling; robbing

spolier, v.t. to despoil; to rob

spongieux(-euse), (adj.) spongy

spontané, (adj.) spontaneous

spontanéité, f. spontaneity

sporadique, (adj.) sporadic

sport, m. sports; games

sportif(-ive), (adj.) sporting

square, m. public square (with [garden)

squelette, m. skeleton

stabilisation, f. stabilisation, steadying

stabiliser, v.t. to stabilise; to steady (prices, etc.)

stable, (adj.) steady; firm; stable

stade, m. stadium

stage, m. period of probation, of instruction

stagiaire, (adj.) and m. (f.) (person) under instruction

stance, f. stanza; stance

standard, m. switchboard (tel.); - de vie, standard of living

station, f. station, standing; station (on " Tube "); stage (on omnibus route); short stay or stop

stationnaire, (adj.) stationary; standing still

stationnement, m. stopping; parking

stationner, v.i. to stop; to take up a position; to halt; to park (car)

statistique, f. statistics

statuaire, (adj.) statuary; f. statuary (art of)

statue, f. statue

statuer, v.t. to decree

statut, m. statute, ordinance

sténodactylo(graphe), m. and f. shorthand-typist

sténographe, m. and f. stenographer

sténographie, f. shorthand

sténographier, v.t. to write down in shorthand

stéréotype, m. stereotype plate

stérile, (adj.) sterile; barren

stériliser, v.t. to sterilise

stérilité, f. sterility; barrenness

stéthoscope, m. stethoscope

stigmate, m. stigma; brand; stain on character

stigmatiser, v.t. to stigmatise; to put the stamp of shame on

stimulant, (adj.) stimulating; m. stimulant, tonic

stimuler, v.t. to stimulate

stipendier, v.t. to keep in one's 'pay; to hire

stipulation, f. stipulation; provision

stipuler, v.t. to stipulate; to lay down

stock, m. stock (of goods)

stoppage, m. stoppage (of machine); invisible mending

stopper, v.i. to come to a stop; v.t. to repair by invisible mending

store, m. roller blind (inside or out)

strapontin, m. folding seat; flap seat

strass, *m.* paste jewellery
stratégie, *f.* strategy
strict, *(adj.)* strict, severe, exact
strident, *(adj.)* shrill
strié, *(adj.)* scored, striped, streaked (marble, etc.)
stuc, *m.* stucco
studieux(-euse), *(adj.)* studious
studio, *m.* studio (film); one-roomed flat
stupéfait, *(adj.)* stupefied, amazed
stupéfaction, *f.* stupefaction, amazement
stupéfier, *v.t.* to amaze; to astound; to stupefy *(med.)*
stupeur, *f.* stupor
stupide, *(adj.)* stupid; dull-witted
stupidité, *f.* stupidity; foolishness
style, *m.* style (literary, etc.)
styler, *v.t.* to train, to coach (somebody)
stylet, *m.* stiletto; probe *(med.)*
stylo(graphe), *m.* fountain-pen
suaire, *m.* shroud, winding-sheet
suant, *(adj.)* sweating, sweaty
suave, *(adj.)* bland, suave; soft
subalterne, *(adj.)* subordinate, minor (official)
subconscient, *(adj.)* and *m.* subconscious
subdivision, *f.* subdivision
subir, *v.t.* to undergo (operation, etc.); to suffer; to sustain (defeat, etc.); to submit to
subit, *(adj.)* sudden, unexpected
subitement, *(adv.)* suddenly, unexpectedly
subjonctif, *(adj.)* and *m.* subjunctive
subjuguer, *v.t.* to subjugate, to subdue
sublime, *(adj.)* sublime; exalted; lofty (thought)
submerger, *v.t.* to submerge; to put under water
subordonné(e), *(adj.)* subordinate; *m. (f.)* subordinate
suborner, *v.t.* to suborn; to bribe
subséquent, *(adj.)* subsequent; ensuing
subsistance, *f.* subsistence, maintenance

subsister, *v.i.* to subsist; to be in existence
substance, *f.* substance; matter
substantiel(le), *(adj.)* substantial
substituer, *v.t.* to substitute
substitut, *m.* substitute
subtil, *(adj.)* subtle; fine (distinction)
subtiliser, *v.t.* to subtilise; to refine; *(fam.)* to sneak (i.e. steal)
subtilité, *f.* subtlety
suburbain, *(adj.)* suburban
subvenir, *v.t.* to supply, provide for; to assist
subvention, *f.* subsidy; grant of money; subvention
subventionner, *v.t.* to subsidise
subversif(-ive), *(adj.)* subversive
suc, *m.* sap, juice
succéder, *v.t.* to succeed; to follow after
succès, *m.* success; favourable result
successeur, *m.* successor
successif(-ive), *(adj.)* successive
succession, *f.* succession; series, sequence (ideas, etc.)
succin, *m.* yellow amber
succinct, *(adj.)* succinct, concise, short
succomber, *v.i.* to succumb; to die
succulent, *(adj.)* succulent; juicy
succursale, *f.* branch (of establishment)
sucer, *v.t.* to suck
sucre, *m.* sugar
sucrer, *v.t.* to sugar; to sweeten
sucrerie, *f.* sweetmeats; sugar-factory
sucrier, *m.* sugar-basin
sud, *m.* south; *(adj. invar.)* south(erly)
sudation, *f.* sweating *(med.)*
sud-est, *(adj. invar.)* and *m.* south-east
sud-ouest, *(adj. invar.)* and *m.* south-west
suédois, *(adj.)* Swedish
suer, *v.i.* to sweat, to perspire
sueur, *f.* sweat, perspiration
suffire, *v.i.* to suffice; to be sufficient

suffisance, *f.* sufficiency; adequacy; conceit

suffisant, *(adj.)* sufficient, adequate; conceited

suffixe, *m.* suffix

suffocant, *(adj.)* suffocating; choking

suffocation, *f.* suffocation

suffoquer, *v.t.* to suffocate, to stifle; *v.i.* de colère, to choke with anger

suffrage, *m.* suffrage, vote

suggérer, *v.t.* to suggest

suggestif(-ive), *(adj.)* suggestive

suggestion, *f.* suggestion

suicide, *m.* suicide

(se) suicider, *v.r.* to commit suicide

suie, *f.* soot

suif, *m.* tallow; suet

suint, *m.* grease (of wool)

suinter, *v.i.* to ooze, to sweat

suisse, *(adj.)* Swiss; *m.* porter; kind of verger

suite, *f.* continuation; sequel; consequence; retinue; **par -,** consequently; **tout de -,** immediately; **- et fin,** conclusion, concluded (final instalment of a serial story)

suivant, *(adj.)* next, following

suivant, *(prep.)* according to; in accordance with

suivre, *v.t.* to follow; to result (when used impersonally); to pay attention to; **à -,** to be continued; **faire - s'il vous plaît,** please forward

sujet(te), *(adj.)* subject; *m.* *(f.)* subject (i.e. British subject, etc.); *m.* subject, reason, cause; **mauvais -,** bad lot

superbe, *(adj.)* superb; stately; magnificent

supercherie, *f.* deceit; fraud; hoax

superficie, *f.* surface

superficiel(le), *(adj.)* superficial; shallow (character, etc.)

superflu, *(adj.)* superfluous; unnecessary

superfluité, *f.* superfluity

supérieur(e), *(adj.)* superior; higher, upper; *m.* *(f.)* superior (i.e. one's chief)

supériorité, *f.* superiority.

supermarché, *m.* supermarket

superstitieux(-euse), *(adj.)* superstitious

superstition, *f.* superstition

supplanter, *v.t.* to supplant; to supersede

suppléant, *m.* substitute, deputy (for)

suppléer, *v.t.* to supply; make up; to supply a deficiency

supplément, *m.* supplement; excess fare; extra charge

supplémentaire, *(adj.)* supplementary; additional

suppliant, *m.* suppliant

supplice, *m.* torture; severe punishment; torment; **dernier -,** capital punishment

supplier, *v.t.* to implore; to entreat

support, *m.* support, prop

supportable, *(adj.)* bearable, endurable, tolerable

supporter, *v.t.* to support; to hold up; to back somebody up; to tolerate

supposer, *v.t.* to suppose, to assume

supposition, *f.* supposition

supprimer, *v.t.* to suppress; to put down; to abolish

suppuration, *f.* suppuration; running (of wound)

suppurer, *v.i.* to suppurate

suprématie, *f.* supremacy

suprême, *(adj.)* supreme; highest degree

sur, *(prep.)* on, upon; out of (e.g. *un jour sur cinq,* one day out of five)

sûr, *(adj.)* sure, certain; **pour -,** for certain

suranné, *(adj.)* obsolete; out of date

surcharge, *f.* overload, excess weight; overcharge

surchauffer, *v.t.* to overheat

surclasser, *v.t.* to outclass

surcroissance, *f.* overgrowth

surcroît, *m.* addition, increase

surdité, *f.* deafness

sureau, *m.* elder tree

surenchère, *f.* higher bid

surenchérir, *v.i.* to outbid; to bid higher

suret(te), (*adj.*) sourish

sûreté, *f.* safety, security; surety; safekeeping; **la Sûreté,** *f.* the Criminal Investigation Department

surexciter, *v.t.* to over-excite; to excite somebody

surface, *f.* surface; outside

surfaire, *v.t.* to overcharge

surfaix, *m.* surcingle (*harness*)

surfin, (*adj.*) superfine

surgir, *v.i.* to rise, to arise; to loom up

surhumain, (*adj.*) superhuman

surlendemain, *m.* next day but one; day after to-morrow

sur-le-champ, (*adv.*) at once

surmenage, *m.* brain fag; overwork

surmener, *v.t.* to overwork; se -, *v.r.* to work too hard; to over-do it

surmontable, (*adj.*) surmountable

surmonter, *v.t.* to surmount; to get over (difficulty)

surnaturel(le), (*adj.*) supernatural

surnommer, *v.t.* to name; to nickname

surnuméraire, (*adj.*) supernumerary

surpasser, *v.t.* to surpass

surplomb, *m.* overhang (of wall, etc.)

surplomber, *v.i.* to overhang; to jut out

surplus, *m.* surplus, excess; au -, moreover

surprenant, (*adj.*) surprising; astonishing

surprendre, *v.t.* to surprise; to astonish

surprise, *f.* surprise

surproduction, *f.* overproduction

sursaut, *m.* start, jump (with fear or surprise)

surseoir, *v.t.* to suspend; to stay (judgment)

sursis, *m.* delay; stay (of proceedings); reprieve

surtaxe, *f.* supertax; surcharge (on letter, etc.)

surtout, (*adv.*) particularly, especially; *m.* overcoat

surveillance, *f.* supervision, superintendence; watching

surveillant(e), *m.* (*f.*) supervisor; superintendent; (school) master or mistress on duty

survenir, *v.i.* (with *être*) to come unexpectedly; to happen; to occur; to arise (difficulty)

survivant(e), *m.* (*f.*) survivor

survivre, *v.t.* to survive

sus (*adv.*) upon, against; en -, in addition

susceptible, (*adj.*) susceptible; liable to; sensitive

susciter, *v.t.* to raise up; to create (enmity, jealousy, etc.)

susdit(e), (*adj.*) aforesaid

suspect(e), (*adj.*) suspect, suspicious, doubtful; *m.* (*f.*) suspect, suspicious character

suspendre, *v.t.* to suspend; to hang up

(en) suspens, in suspense

suspicion, *f.* suspicion

sustenter, *v.t.* to sustain, to support

s.v.p. (**s'il vous plaît**), if you please

svelte, (*adj.*) slender, slim

syllabe, *f.* syllable

symbole, *m.* symbol; creed

symbolique, (*adj.*) symbolical

symétrique, (*adj.*) symmetrical

sympathique, (*adj.*) sympathetic; attractive; likeable

sympathie, *f.* sympathy; fellow feeling (for somebody)

symptôme, *m.* symptom

syndic, *m.* syndic; - de faillite, official receiver

syndicalisme, *m.* syndicalism

syndicat, *m.* syndicate; trusteeship; association (trade, profession)

synonyme, *m.* synonym; *(adj.)* synonymous

synthétique, *(adj.)* synthetic

systématique, *(adj.)* systematic

système, *m.* system

T

tabac, *m.* tobacco; **débit de -,** tobacconist's shop; **- à priser,** snuff

tabagie, *f.* smoking-room; fuggy room

tabatière, *f.* snuff-box; tobacco-box

***table,** *f.* table

tableau(x), *m.* picture; painting; board; tableau; **- noir,** blackboard; **- de bord,** dashboard

tablette, *f.* shelf (of book-case); flat slab; cake (of chocolate, etc.)

tablier, *m.* apron; footplate (of locomotive); **rendre son -,** to give notice

tabouret, *m.* stool

tac, *m.* click; **répondre du - au -,** to make an instant retort

tache, *f.* spot; stain; blot

tâche, *f.* task; job

tacher, *v.t.* to stain; to spot; to blemish

tâcher, *v.i.* to try; to endeavour

tacheter, *v.t.* to mark with spots; to speckle

tacite, *(adj.)* tacit; implied

taciturne, *(adj.)* taciturn; close-mouthed

tacot, *m.* old motor-car, old train

tact, *m.* sense of touch; tact

tactique, *(adj.)* tactical; *f.* tactics

taffetas *m.* taffeta (material); **- d'Angleterre,** court-plaster

taie d'oreiller, *f.* pillow-slip

taillade, *f.* gash; cut, slash

taillader, *v.t.* to gash, to cut, to slash

taille, *f.* cutting (clothes, etc.); trimming (of hedge); edge; height (of person); figure, waist; **- de cheveux,** hair-cut; **taille-douce,** *f.* copper-plate engraving

tailler, *v.t.* to cut; to trim, clip; to sharpen (pencil); to cut (clothes)

tailleur, *m.* tailor; cutter (of precious stones); a tailor-made suit

taillis, *m.* copse; underwood

tain, *m.* silvering; foil

taire, *v.t.* to say nothing about something; **se -,** *v.t.* to be silent; to hold one's tongue; **faire - to** silence (someone)

talent, *m.* talent, gift; faculty

talisman, *m.* talisman

***talon,** *m.* heel (foot or shoe)

talonner, *v.t.* to follow closely; to urge; to spur on

talus, *m.* slope; embankment

tambour, *m.* drum; drummer

tambouriner, *v.i.* to beat a drum

tambour-major, *m.* drum-major

tamis, *m.* sieve, sifter

tamiser, *v.t.* to sieve, to sift

tampon, *m.* plug, stopper; wad *(surg.);* **état -,** buffer state

tamponnement, *m.* plugging (of wound, etc.); collision

tamponner, *v.t.* to plug (wound, etc.); to run into, collide with

tan, *(adj. invar.)* tan (colour); *m.* tan

tancer, *v.t.* to scold

tandem, *m.* tandem

tandis que, *(conj.)* whilst, whereas

tangage, *m.* pitching (of ship)

tangible, *(adj.)* tangible

tanguer, *v.i.* to pitch (ship movement)

tanière, *f.* den, lair

tanin, *m.* tannin *(chem.)*

tanner, *v.t.* to tan

tanneur, *m.* tanner

tant, *(adv.)* so much, so many; **- mieux,** so much the better; **- pis,** so much the worse; **- que,** so long as

tante, *f.* aunt; **- à la mode de Bretagne,** first cousin once removed

tantinet, *m.* tiny bit; least bit

tantôt, *(adv.)* soon, presently, shortly; a little while ago

tantôt ... tantôt, at one time ... at another time; sometimes ... sometimes taon, *m.* gadfly

tapage, *m.* loud noise, uproar; faire du -, to kick up a row

tapageur(-euse), *(adj.)* noisy, uproarious

tape, *f.* a tap, slap

taper, *v.t.* to tap, to slap; to type (-write)

tapette, *f.* mallet; carpet-beater

tapir, *m.* tapir

(se) tapir, *v.r.* to squat; to cower down; to nestle

tapis, *m.* carpet; cloth, cover (of table)

tapisser, *v.t.* to paper a room; to hang a wall with tapestry

tapisserie, *f.* tapestry making; tapestry, hangings; wall-paper

tapissier, *m.* upholsterer; tapestry-worker

tapissière, *f.* delivery van, furniture van

taquin(e), *(adj.)* teasing; *m. (f.)* tease

taquiner, *v.t.* to tease

tard, *(adv.)* late

tarder, *v.i.* to delay

tardif(-ive), *(adj.)* tardy, backward (fruit, etc.)

tarentule, *f.* tarantula (poisonous spider)

tarière, *f.* auger; drill

tarif, *m.* tariff; price list; scale of charges

tarir, *v.i.* to dry up (spring, etc.); to run dry

tarte, *f.* (open) tart; flan

tartelette, *f.* small tart, tartlet

tartine, *f.* slice of bread and butter, bread and jam

tartufe, *m.* hypocrite, humbug

tas, *m.* heap; à lot of; pile of (stones, etc.); a pack, crew (of persons)

tasse, *f.* cup

tasser, *v.t.* to cram, to squeeze, compress; to heap together; se -, *v.r.* to settle, set (foundations); to crowd together

tâter, *v.t.* to feel, to touch; to finger, to handle (material, etc.); to sound (somebody)

tatillon(ne), *m. (f.)* busybody

tâtonner, *v.i.* to grope, to feel one's way; à tâtons, *(adv. phrase)* groping; feeling one's way

tatouage, *m.* tattooing

tatouer, *v.t.* to tattoo

taudis, *m.* hovel, wretched room

taupe, *f.* mole

taureau, *m.* bull

taux, *m.* rate (discount); scale (of prices, etc.)

taverne, *f.* tavern; public-house; café-restaurant

taxe, *f.* tax, duty; fixed rate

taxer, *v.t.* to tax; to impose a tax on; to regulate the price

taxi, *m.* taxi-cab

taximètre, *m.* taxi-meter

technicien, *m.* technician

technique, *(adj.)* technical; *f.* technique

teck, *m.* teak (wood)

teigne, *f.* ringworm; moth (of clothes)

teindre, *v.t.* to dye; to tinge; se -, *v.r.* to dye one's hair

teint, *m.* dye, colour; complexion

teinte, *f.* tint, shade

teinter, *v.t.* to tint

teinture, *f.* dyeing (general sense); colour, tinge; dye

teinturerie, *f.* dye-works

teinturier(-ère), *m. (f.)* dyer and cleaner

tel(le), *(adj.)* such, like, as; tel père, tel fils, like father, like son; - que, such as

télégramme, *m.* telegram

télégraphie, *f.* telegraphy

télégraphier, *v.t.* to telegraph

télégraphique, *(adj.)* telegraphic; bureau -, telegraph office

téléphone, *m.* telephone; coup de -, telephone call

téléphoner, *v.t.* and *v.i.* to telephone; to ring somebody up

téléphonique, (cabine) *f.* call-box

télescope, *m.* telescope

télescoper, *v.t.* to telescope (railway accidents)

tellement, *(adv.)* to such a degree; to such an extent that

téméraire, *(adj.)* rash, reckless

témérité, *f.* rashness, recklessness

témoignage, *m.* testimony; proof, evidence

témoigner, *v.i.* to testify, to give evidence

témoin, *m.* witness

tempe, *f.* temple (head)

tempérament, *m.* temperament; constitution (physical)

tempérance, *f.* temperance; moderation

tempérant, *(adj.)* temperate; moderate

température, *f.* temperature *(med.)*; degree of heat (climate)

tempérer, *v.t.* to moderate, to temper

tempête, *f.* tempest, storm

temple, *m.* temple (place of worship); (Protestant) church

temporaire, *(adj.)* temporary; provisional

temporel(le), *(adj.)* temporal (opposite of spiritual)

*temps, *m.* time; weather; à -, in time

tenable, *(adj.)* tenable, bearable, defensible (position)

tenace, *(adj.)* tenacious

tenacité, *f.* tenacity

tenailles, *f. pl.* pincers

tenancier, *m.* tenant-farmer

tendance, *f.* tendency, trend

tendelet, *m.* awning

tendon, *m.* tendon, sinew

tendre, *(adj.)* tender; soft; affectionate

tendre, *v.t.* to stretch; to stretch out, hold out (hand); se -, *v.r.* to become strained (relations)

tendresse, *f.* fondness; tenderness

tendu, *(adj.)* tense, tight; strained

ténèbres, *f. pl.* darkness, gloom

ténébreux(-euse), *(adj.)* gloomy, dark

teneur, *f.* purport, tenor; amount

teneur(-euse), *m. (f.)* holder; - de livres, bookkeeper

ténia, *m.* tapeworm

*tenir, *v.i.* to hold; to adhere; to keep; to last; to depend upon; to occupy; - à, to care about; - bon, to hold out; remain firm; (y) -, to prize much; se -, *v.r.* to keep; to remain; to contain oneself

tension, *f.* tension; pressure; - artérielle, blood pressure

tentation, *f.* temptation

tentative, *f.* attempt

tente, *f.* tent; awning

tenter, *v.t.* to tempt; to attempt; to try

tenu, *(adj.)* kept; bien -, well kept, neat

tenue, *f.* bearing; behaviour; dress; en - de golf, in plus-fours

térébenthine, *f.* turpentine

tergiverser, *v.i.* to equivocate; to shuffle

terme, *m.* quarter (day), quarter's rent; term (expression); end; mettre - à qch., to put an end to; marché à terme, time bargain *(commerc.)*

termes, *m. pl.* wording of clause; conditions

terminaison, *f.* ending, termination

terminer, *v.t.* to end, to terminate

terne, *(adj.)* dull, lustreless

ternir, *v.t.* to tarnish, to dull

terrain, *m.* ground; a piece, plot of ground; soil

terrasse, *f.* terrace; bank

terrassement, *m.* banking; earthwork

terrasser, *v.t.* to bank up; to knock down; to dismay, bowl over

terrassier, *m.* navvy

terre, *f.* (the) earth; the world; ground, land

terrestre, *(adj.)* terrestrial; worldly

terreur, *f.* terror; dread

terreux(-euse), *(adj.)* earthy; dull (colour); sickly (complexion)

terrible, *(adj.)* terrible; dreadful; awful; frightful

terrier, *m.* terrier; burrow (of rabbit, etc.)

terrifiant, *(adj.)* terrifying, awe-inspiring

terrifier, *v.t.* to terrify; to scare

terrine, *f.* earthenware dish, or pot; potted meat

territoire, *m.* territory

territorial(-aux), (*adj.*) territorial

terroir, *m.* soil; sentir le terroir, to smack of the soil

terroriser, *v.t.* to terrorise

terrorisme, *m.* terrorism

terroriste, *m.* and *f.* terrorist

tertre, *m.* hillock; mound

testament, *m.* will, testament; Testament (Bible)

testamentaire, (*adj.*) testamentary

testateur(-trice), *m.* (*f.*) testator (-trix)

tester, *v.i.* to make one's will

tétanos, *m.* tetanus; lock-jaw

têtard, *m.* tadpole

*tête, *f.* head; wits

tête-à-tête, *m.* (*invar.*) private interview; face to face

téter, *v.t.* to suck

tétin, *m.* nipple, teat

tétière, *f.* cap (child); cover (of chair); head-stall

têtu, (*adj.*) stubborn; obstinate

texte, *m.* text

textile, (*adj.*) and *m.* (*f.*) textile

textuellement, (*adv.*) textually

thé, *m.* tea

théâtral, (*adj.*) theatrical

théâtre, *m.* theatre; playhouse

théière, *f.* tea-pot

thème, *m.* theme, topic; subject (of speech); exercise (prose)

théologie, *f.* theology

théologien, *m.* theologian

théorème, *m.* theorem

théoricien(ne), *m.* (*f.*) theorist

théorie, *f.* theory

théorique, (*adj.*) theoretical

thermal(-aux), (*adj.*) thermal; eaux thermales, hot springs

thermes, *m. pl.* thermal baths

thermomètre, *m.* thermometer

thésauriser, *v.t.* to hoard, pile up (money)

thèse, *f.* thesis, proposition, argument

thon, *m.* tunny-fish

thym, *m.* thyme

thyroïde, (*adj.*) thyroid; *m.* thyroid gland

tiare, *f.* tiara

tibia, *m.* tibia; shin-bone

tic, *m.* twitching (of face, etc.); tic

ticket, *m.* ticket; check, numbered slip

tiède, (*adj.*) tepid, lukewarm

tiédeur, *f.* tepidness

tiédir, *v.i.* to become tepid; to cool off (friendship)

tien(ne), (*poss. adj.*) yours, thine le tien, la tienne, (*poss. pron.*) yours, thine

tiens! (*interj.*) hullo! well, well!

tiers, *m.* third part, third person

tige, *f.* stem, stalk (flower, etc.); trunk (of tree); shaft (of column); rod (*mech.*)

tigre(sse), *m.* (*f.*) tiger (tigress)

tilleul, *m.* lime tree; infusion made from leaves of lime tree

timbale, *f.* kettle-drum; drinking-cup; pie(-dish)

timbre, *m.* stamp (postage, and on document); bell of clock; timbre (quality in tone)

timbre-quittance, *m.* receipt-stamp

timbrer, *v.t.* to stamp

timide, (*adj.*) timid, shy, bashful

timidité, *f.* shyness, timidity, bashfulness

timon, *m.* pole (of vehicle); tiller

timonerie, *f.* steering of ship

timonier, *m.* helmsman

tintamarre, *m.* din, racket

tinter, *v.t.* to ring. to toll (bell)

tir, *m.* shooting; shooting ground; range; - aux pigeons, pigeon shooting

tirage, *m.* pulling, hauling; number printed; drawing (of lottery)

tiraillement, *m.* tugging, pulling about

tirailler, *v.t.* to pull about

tirailleur, *m.* sharpshooter; colonial soldier

tirant, *m.* string; check-strap; draught (of ship)

tire-botte, *m.* boot-jack

tire-bouchon, *m.* corkscrew

tire-bouton, *m.* buttonhook

tirelire, *f.* money-box

*tirer, *v.t.* to draw; to stretch, to pull (out); to pull; to fire (rifle, etc.)

tiret, *m.* hyphen, dash

tireur(-euse), *m.* (*f.*) drawer; shooter

tiroir, *m.* drawer (of table, etc.)

tisane, *f.* tea made from herbs

tison, *m.* fire-brand; half-burned log

tisonner, *v.t.* to poke the fire

tisonnier, *m.* poker

tissage, *m.* weaving

tisser, *v.t.* to weave

tisserand, *m.* weaver

tissu, *m.* tissue; material (woven); fabric

titanesque, (*adj.*) titanic; gigantic

titre, *m.* title (of nobility, book, etc.); diploma; certificate; bond; claim; à quel -, by what right

tituber, *v.i* to reel, to stagger about

titulaire, (*adj.*) titular; *m.* (*f.*) holder, bearer (office, document)

toast, *m.* toast

toaster, *v.t.* to toast; to drink somebody's health

tocsin, *m.* alarm signal

toge, *f.* gown, robe (of judge, etc.)

toile, *f.* linen, linen cloth; picture (oil painting); curtain (theatre); - d'araignée, cobweb; - cirée, oilcloth

toilette, *f.* toilet cover; wash-stand; dressing-table; woman's dress; lavatory

toise, *f.* fathom

toiser, *v.t.* to measure; to take stock (of somebody)

toison, *f.* fleece

toit, *m.* roof; house-top

toiture, *f.* roofing

tôle, *f.* sheet-iron

tolérable, (*adj.*) tolerable, bearable

tolérance, *f.* tolerance; toleration

tolérant, (*adj.*) tolerant

tolérer, *v.t.* to tolerate

tomate, *f.* tomato

tombe, *f.* tomb, grave

tombeau, *m.* tomb; tombstone; monument over grave

tombée, *f.* fall (of night, rain, etc.)

*tomber, *v.i.* (with *être*) to fall, to fall down, tumble down; to hang down (hair, etc.)

tombereau, *m.* tip-cart; tumbril

tome, *m.* volume (book); tome

ton, *m.* tone, intonation; tone (manners); tint, colour

ton (ta), (*poss. adj.*) thy, your.

tondeuse, *f.* shears, clippers (for hair)

tondre, *v.t.* to shear, to clip

tonique, *m.* tonic; *f.* key-note

tonnage, *m.* tonnage

tonne, *f.* ton (weight); tun

tonneau, *m.* cask, barrel

tonnelle, *f.* arbour; bower

tonner, *v.i.* to thunder

tonnerre, *m.* thunder

tonsure, *f.* tonsure

topographie, *f.* topography, surveying

toque, *f.* cap (worn by a judge, chef); toque (woman's hat)

toqué, (*adj.*) cracked, dotty, off his head; in love with

torche, *f.* torch

torcher, *v.t.* to wipe, to clean (with rag)

torchon, *m.* floor-cloth, dish-cloth

tordant, (*adj.*) very funny, excruciatingly funny

tordre, *v.t.* to twist; to wring (clothes); se ~, *v.r.* to writhe, to twist; to roar with laughter

torpédo, *m.* or *f.* an open touring car

torpeur, *f.* torpor

torpille, *f.* torpedo

torpilleur, *m.* torpedo-boat

torréfier, *v.t.* to roast (coffee, *not* meat)

torrent, *m.* torrent

torrentiel(le), (*adj.*) torrential

torride, (*adj.*) torrid; scorching

torsade, *f.* twisted fringe

torse, *m.* torso (of person)

tort, *m.* wrong, error, fault, harm; **avoir -,** to be wrong; **à - et à travers,** at random

torticolis, *m.* stiff neck

tortiller, *v.t.* to twist, to twirl

tortiller, *v.i.* to wriggle; to prevaricate

tortu, *(adj.)* crooked

tortue, *f.* tortoise

tortueux(-euse), *(adj.)* winding, meandering, crooked

torture, *f.* torture

torturer, *v.t.* to torture

tôt, *(adv.)* soon; **au plus -,** as soon as possible; **- ou tard,** sooner or later

total(-aux), *(adj.)* total, whole

totalisateur, *m.* totalisator; the tote *(racing)*

totalisatrice, *f.* cash register

totaliser, *v.t.* to total up

totalité, *f.* totality; the whole

touage, *m.* towing

touchant, *(adj.)* touching; affecting; moving

touche, *f.* touch, touching; key (of piano); **pierre de -,** touch-stone; **ligne de -,** touch line

toucher, *v.t.* to touch, to move; to affect; to cash (a cheque); to receive (pay); **se -,** *v.r.* to touch (adjoin)

touer, *v.t.* to tow; to warp *(naut.)*

touffe, *f.* tuft; clump (of trees)

touffu, *(adj.)* bushy; thick (wood, etc.)

toujours, *(adv.)* always, ever; nevertheless; all the same

toupet, *m.* tuft of hair; cheek, impudence

toupie, *f.* a top

toupiller, *v.i.* to spin around

toupillon, *m.* small tuft

tour, *f.* tower

*tour, *m.* turn; revolution; trip; turning lathe; circumference; trick; **- de tête,** size in hats

tourbe, *f.* peat, turf; a mob, or rabble

tourbeux(-euse), *(adj.)* peaty, turfy

tourbillon, *m.* whirlwind, eddy

tourbillonner, *v.i.* to whirl round; to eddy

tourelle, *f.* turret; gun-turret

tourillon, *m.* pivot, swivel

tourisme, *m.* touring; **bureau de -,** travel agency

touriste, *m.* and *f.* tourist; tripper

tourment, *m.* torment; torture

tourmente, *f.* gale, tempest

tourmenter, *v.t.* to torment, to torture; **se -,** *v.r.* to be uneasy, to fret

tournailler, *v.i.* to keep turning round and round

tournant, *m.* turning, bend of road; *(adj.)* turning, winding

tournebroche, *m.* roasting spit

tournedos, *m.* fillet steak

tournée, *f.* round; tour (of official or theatrical company)

tourner, *v.t.* to turn; to turn round; to change (direction or colour); to make a film (cinema)

tournesol, *m.* sunflower

tourneur, *m.* turner

tournevis, *m.* screw-driver

tourniquet, *m.* turnstile; tourniquet *(surg.)*

tournoi, *m.* tournament (tennis, etc.)

tournoyer, *v.i.* to turn round and round; to whirl

tournure, *f.* turn, course of events; shape, form

tourte, *f.* covered tart; pie

tourteau, *m.* oil-cake (for cattle)

tourterelle, *f.* turtle-dove

tourtière, *f.* pie-dish

toussaint, *f.* All Saints' Day

tousser, *v.i.* to cough

*tout, toute, *(pl.* **tous, toutes)** all, whole; the whole (treated as an undetermined substantive)

tout, *(pron.)* all, everything; *m.* the whole; *(adv.)* quite, entirely; **- à fait,** quite, altogether, absolutely; **- au plus,** at the very most; **- au moins,** at the very least; **- en parlant,** while speaking; **- à l'heure,** just now; **- de suite,** immediately

toutefois, however, yet, nevertheless

toute-puissance, *f.* omnipotence

tout-puissant, (*adj.*) all powerful

toux, *f.* cough

toxique, (*adj.*) toxic, poisonous

tracasser, *v.t.* to worry; to annoy; to tease; se -, *v.r.* to worry oneself

tracasserie, *f.* annoyance

trace, *f.* trace, track, footprint, trail

tracé, *m.* tracing; outline; diagram

tracer, *v.t.* to trace; to draw (a line); to outline (plan); to map out

traceur(-euse), (*adj.*) tracer; balle traceuse, tracer bullet

trachée, *f.* trachea

trachée-artère, *f.* windpipe

trachéotomie, *f.* tracheotomy (*surg.*)

trachome, *m.* trachoma (eye disease)

traction, *f.* traction; pulling

tradition, *f.* tradition

traditionnel(le), (*adj.*) traditional; standing (custom)

traducteur(-trice), *m.* (*f.*) translator

traduction, *f.* translation

traduire, *v.t.* to translate; to interpret; to summon before a court of justice (*law*)

traduisible, (*adj.*) translatable; liable to be summonsed

trafic, *m.* traffic; trading

trafiquant, *m.* trafficker, trader

trafiquer (en), *v.i.* to traffic in; to trade in

tragédie, *f.* tragedy (general sense)

tragédien(ne), *m.* (*f.*) tragedian

tragique, (*adj.*) tragic

trahir, *v.t.* to betray; to disclose (secret)

trahison, *f.* treason; treachery

*train, *m.* train (railway); line (of vehicles); movement; pace, rate

traînant, (*adj.*) dragging; shambling, drawling

traînard, *m.* laggard, straggler

traîneau, *m.* sledge

traînée, *f.* trail (of smoke); train (of powder)

traîner, *v.t.* to drag, to pull, to haul; to drag on; to trail (behind); to linger (on)

traîneur(-euse), *m.* (*f.*) dragger; straggler

traire, *v.t.* to milk

trait, *m.* pulling; feature; trait (character); stroke, line

traitable, (*adj.*) tractable

traite, *f.* draft; bill (of exchange); trade; - des blanches, white slave traffic

traité, *m.* treaty, agreement, treatise

traitement, *m.* treatment; salary

*traiter, *v.t.* to treat; to negotiate (an affair); to discuss (business); to deal with

traiteur(-euse), *m.* (*f.*) caterer

traître(sse), *m.* (*f.*) traitor (traitress); (*adj.*) treacherous

traîtreusement, (*adv.*) treacherously

trajet, *m.* passage (crossing by sea); journey; path (of bullet, etc.)

tramail, *m.* drag-net

trame, *f.* warp; conspiracy

tramer, *v.t.* to weave (a story); to hatch (a conspiracy)

tramontane, *f.* north wind

tramway, *m.* tram, tramway

tranchant, (*adj.*) sharp, cutting; *m.* edge of knife

tranche, *f.* slice (of bread, etc.)

tranchée, *f.* trench (*mil.*); drain; cutting (railway)

trancher, *v.t.* to cut; to slice (bread, etc.); to settle (a question)

tranquille, (*adj.*) tranquil, quiet, still, placid

tranquilliser, *v.t.* to quieten; to reassure; se -, *v.r.* to set one's mind at rest

tranquillité, *f.* tranquillity; calm; quiet; stillness

transaction, *f.* compromise; transaction, dealing, deal

transatlantique, (*adj.*) transatlantic; *m.* liner; deck-chair

transbordement, *m.* transhipment

transborder, *v.t.* to tranship

transcription, *f.* transcription; transcript, copy

transcrire, *v.t.* to write out; to transcribe; to copy

transe, *f.* (generally plural) fright, fear; trance

transférer, *v.t.* to transfer; to convey; to remove from one place to another

transfiguration, *f.* transfiguration

transformation, *f.* transformation (into)

transformer, *v.t.* to transform; to change into

transfuge, *m.* deserter (*mil.*); turncoat

transfusion, *f.* transfusion (of blood)

transgresser, *v.t.* to break, infringe (the law)

transiger, *v.i.* to compound (with); to compromise

transir, *v.t.* to chill, benumb

transit, *m.* transit; through traffic

transition, *f.* transition

transitoire, (*adj.*) transitory; temporary

transmetteur, *m.* transmitter (telegraphic)

transmettre, *v.t.* to transmit (message, etc.)

transmission, *f.* transmission; conveyance (of estate); assignment (of shares, etc.)

transparence, *f.* transparency

transparent, (*adj.*) transparent

transpiration, *f.* perspiration

transpirer, *v.i.* to perspire; to transpire; to leak out (news)

transplantation, *f.* transplanting

transplanter, *v.t.* to transplant; se -, *v.r.* to go; to settle (in another place)

transport, *m.* transport, carriage (of goods, etc.); outburst (of feeling); transport (troopship)

transportation, *f.* conveyance (of goods); transportation (of convicts)

transporter, *v.t.* to transport; to

convey (goods, etc.); to transfer, to remove; to carry away; se -, *v.r.* to go to a place

transporteur, *m.* forwarding agent; carrier

transvaser, *v.t.* to decant (wine)

tran-tran, (also written **train-train**) *m.* routine

trapèze, *m.* trapezium (*math.*); trapeze

trappe, *f.* trap; pitfall; trap-door

trapu, (*adj.*) thick-set; stocky

traquenard, *m.* trap, snare

traquer, *v.t.* to track down, hunt down; to surround; to beat (for game)

travail(-aux), *m.* work (general sense, intellectual or manual)

travailler, *v.t.* to work, to labour, to toil

travaillé, (*adj.*) worked; wrought (iron, etc.)

travailleur(-euse), *m.* (*f.*) worker, workman (workwoman)

travailliste, *m.* member of Labour Party; (*adj.*) Labour (party)

travers, *m.* breadth; à -, across; (au) - (de), across; de -, askance, askew; defect, failing

traverse, *f.* cross-road; cross-piece; sleeper (railway); set-back

traversée, *f.* passage, crossing by sea

traverser, *v.t.* to traverse; to cross; to go across

traversin, *m.* bolster (of bed); cross-bar

travestir, *v.t.* to disguise (for fancy dress)

trébucher, *v.i.* to stumble; to totter

tréfiler, *v.t.* to wire-draw

trèfle, *m.* trefoil, clover; clubs (cards)

treillage, *m.* lattice-work; trellis-work

treille, *f.* vine-arbour

treillis, *m.* trellis, lattice

treize, *m.* and (*num. adj.*) thirteen

treizième, thirteenth

tréma, *m.* diæresis

tremblaie, *f.* aspen plantation

tremblant, (*adj.*) trembling;

quaking (ground); unsteady (voice)

tremble, *m.* aspen tree

tremblement, *m.* trembling; quivering; shaking; - de terre, earthquake; earth tremor

trembler, *v.i.* to tremble; to quiver; to quake

trémie, *f.* mill-hopper

trémousser, *v.t.* to hustle (somebody); se -, *v.r.* to fidget; to bestir oneself

tremper, *v.t.* to soak; to drench; to steep (in liquid)

tremplin, *m.* spring-board

trentaine, *f.* about thirty

trente, *m.* and (*num. adj.*) thirty

trépaner, *v.t.* to trepan (*surg.*)

trépas, *m.* death

trépasser, *v.i.* to die, depart this life (generally used with *avoir*, but sometimes with *être*)

trépassés(-ées),*m.*(*f.*)*pl.* the dead

trépidation,*f.* trepidation; agitation

trépider, *v.i.* to vibrate, to shake; to be nervous

trépied, *m.* tripod

trépigner, *v.i.* to stamp (with rage); *v.t.* to tread down (earth, etc.)

trépointe, *f.* welt (of shoe)

très, (*adv.*) very; also used as a superlative, most; very much

trésor, *m.* treasure; Treasury

trésorerie, *f.* treasury

trésorier(-ère), *m.* (*f.*) treasurer; paymaster (-mistress)

tressaillement, *m.* start (of surprise); shudder (fear)

tressaillir, *v.i.* to start; to shudder (fear); to thrill

tresse, *f.* plait, tress (of hair); plait (of straw)

tresser, *v.t.* to plait (hair, etc.); to weave (a basket)

tréteau, *m.* trestle; support; stage (on boards)

treuil, *m.* winch; windlass

trève, *f.* truce

triage, *m.* sorting (of letters, etc.); gare de -, marshalling yard (railway)

triangle, *m.* triangle

triangulaire, (*adj.*) triangular

tribord, *m.* starboard (*naut.*)

tribu, *f.* tribe, clan

tribunal(-aux), *m.* tribunal; court of justice; judge's bench

tribune, *f.* tribune; rostrum; speaker's platform; grand stand!

tribut, *m.* tribute (to pay)

tributaire, (*adj.*) tributary; dependent on; *m.* tributary (river)

tricher, *v.i.* and *v.t.* to cheat, to trick

tricheur(-euse), *m.* (*f.*) cheat; trickster

tricolore, (*adj.*) tricoloured

tricorne, *m.* three-cornered hat; (*adj.*) three cornered

tricot, *m.* knitting, knitted wear; jersey, jumper

tricotage, *m.* knitting

tricoter, *v.t.* to knit

trier, *v.t.* to sort (letters, etc.); to marshal (railway trucks); to pick out

trimarder,*v.i.* to be on the tramp

trimardeur, *m.* tramp

trimestre, *m.* quarter; three months; term (scholastic)

trimestriel(le), (*adj.*) quarterly

trimoteur, *m.* three-engined aeroplane

tringle, *f.* rod; bar

tringler, *v.t.* to chalk (a line)

trinité, *f.* the Trinity

trinquer, *v.i.* to clink glasses; to suffer (a loss)

triomphal(-aux),(*adj.*)triumphal

triomphe, *m.* triumph

triompher, *v.i.* to triumph; to exult

tripe, *f.* (*usually pl.*) tripe (*cook.*)

triple, (*adj.*) triple, threefold

triplé(e)s, *m.* (*f.*) triplets

tripler, *v.t.* to treble, to triple

tripot, *m.* gambling den

tripotage, *m.* messing about; underhand work

tripoter, *v.i.* to mess about; to do odd jobs; to handle; to engage in shady transactions

triste, (*adj.*) sad; sorrowful; melancholy (news); unfortunate

tristesse, *f.* sadness; sorrowfulness; melancholy, gloom

trivial(-s or -aux), *(adj.)* trivial, commonplace; trite

trivialité, *f.* trivialities, commonplaces; triteness

troc, *m.* exchange; barter

trochet, *m.* cluster (of fruit)

troène, *m.* privet

trogne, *f.* bloated face

trognon, *m.* core (of apple); stump (of cabbage)

trois, *m.* three

trombe, *f.* water-spout

trompe, *f.* horn; trunk (of elephant)

tromper, *v.t.* to deceive; to cheat; **se -**, *v.r.* to be mistaken; to be wrong

tromperie, *f.* deceit, deception, fraud

trompette, *f.* trumpet; *m.* trumpeter

trompeur(-euse), *m.* (*f.*) deceiver; *(adj.)* deceiving, deceptive

tronc, *m.* trunk (of tree, or body, *not* luggage); stem of tree; collecting box (in church)

tronçon, *m.* piece, stub end

tronçonner, *v.t.* to cut into pieces, sections

trône, *m.* throne

trop, *(adv.)* too; too much; too many; over . . .

trophée, *m.* trophy

tropique, *(adj.)* tropical; *m.* tropic

trop-plein, *m.* overflow

troquer, *v.t.* to exchange; to barter; to have truck with

trot, *m.* trot

trotte, *f.* step, distance, run

trotter, *v.i.* to trot

trottoir, *m.* pavement; footway

trou, *m.* hole; - **d'air**, air pocket

troublant, *(adj.)* disturbing, disquieting

trouble, *(adj.)* murky, cloudy

trouble, *m.* disorder, confusion

troubler, *v.t.* to confuse, to trouble; to disturb (the peace); to agitate; to make (liquid) muddy, cloudy

troubles, *m. pl.* disturbances (riots)

trouée, *f.* gap, opening

trouer, *v.t.* to hole, to make a hole; to pierce

troupe, *f.* troop, band; company (*theat.*); herd (cattle); body of soldiers

troupeau, *m.* herd, drove (of cattle)

troupes, *f. pl.* troops, forces

troupier, *m.* soldier, ranker

trousse, *f.* bundle, package; truss (of hay)

troussé, *(adj.)* tucked up; trussed (chicken, etc.)

trousseau, *m.* bunch (of keys); wedding outfit; school outfit

trousser, *v.t.* to tuck up, to pin up

trouvaille, *f.* lucky find; piece of good luck

trouver, *v.t.* to find; to discover; to invent (process); **se -**, *v.r.* to be; to happen; to feel (better, etc.)

truand, *m.* vagrant

truc, *m.* knack, trick, gadget

trucage, *m.* faking; fake

truchement, *m.* interpreter; go-between

truelle, *f.* trowel

truellée, *f.* trowelful

truffe, *f.* truffle

truie, *f.* sow

truite, *f.* trout

truité, *(adj.)* red-speckled

truquer, *v.t.* to fake; to falsify (accounts)

tuant, *(adj.)* killing; very hard (work)

tube, *m.* tube; pipe

tubercule, *m.* tubercle

tuberculeux(-euse), *(adj.)* tuberculous; consumptive; *m.* (*f.*) consumptive person

tuberculose, *f.* tuberculosis; consumption

tuer, *v.t.* to kill; to slaughter; to slay; **se -**, *v.r.* to kill oneself; to commit suicide

tuerie, *f.* slaughter, massacre, butchery

tue-tête (with *à*), at the top of one's voice

tuf, *m.* tufa; bed-rock

tuile, *f.* tile (of roofing); bad luck

tuilerie, *f.* tile-kiln; **Les Tuileries,** *f. pl.* the Tuileries (gardens in Paris)

tulipe, *f.* tulip

tulle, *m.* net (fabric); tulle

tuméfaction, *f.* swelling

tuméfier, *v.t.* to cause to swell

tumeur, *f.* tumour; growth

tumulaire, *(adj.)* sepulchral

tumulte, *m.* tumult, uproar, hubbub

tumultueux(-euse), *(adj.)* noisy, riotous

tumulus, *m.* mound

tunique, *f.* tunic; coat

tunnel, *m.* tunnel

turbine, *f.* turbine

turbot, *m.* turbot

turbulent, *(adj.)* turbulent; unruly

turlupin, *m.* clown; buffoon

turlupinade, *f.* buffoonery

turne, *f.* *(fam.)* diggings (lodgings)

tutélaire, *(adj.)* guardian; tutelary

tutelle, *f.* guardianship

tuteur(-trice), *m.* *(f.)* guardian

tutoyer, *v.t.* to address somebody as "thou"; to be on familiar terms with somebody

tuyau, *m.* pipe, tube; tip, wrinkle, hint

tympan, *m* tympan; drum of ear

type, *m.* type; pattern; a chap, a fellow; **un drôle de -,** queer fellow

typhoïde, *(adj.)* typhoid; **fièvre -,** typhoid, enteric

typique, *(adj.)* typical; symbolical

typographie, *f.* printing; printing works

typographe, *m.* printer

tyran, *m.* tyrant

tyrannique, *(adj.)* tyrannical

tyranniser, *v.t.* to tyrannise

tzar, *m.* Czar

tzarine, *f.* Czarina

tzigane, *m.* *(f.)* gipsy

U

ubiquité, *f.* ubiquity

udomètre, *m.* rain gauge

ulcère, *m.* ulcer, sore

ulcérer (s'), *v.r.* to ulcerate, fester

ultérieur(e), *(adj.)* ulterior; subsequent

ultra, *m.* extremist, reactionary

ultrasonique, *(adj.)* supersonic

unanime, *(adj.)* unanimous

unanimité, *f.* unanimity

uni, *(adj.)* plain (colour); smooth; united

unifier, *v.t.* to standardise; to amalgamate (industries, etc.)

uniforme, *m.* uniform; · *(adj.)* unvarying, uniform

union, *f.* union; society; association; unity, concord

unique, *(adj.)* only; sole; **rue à sens -,** one way street

unir, *v.t.* to unite, join

unir (s'), *v.r.* to join forces with someone; to become smooth

unité, *f.* unit; unity

univers, *m.* universe

universel(le), *(adj.)* universal

Universitaire, *(adj.)* University; **cité-,** students' hall(s) of residence

université, *f.* university; faculty

urbain, *(adj.)* urban (population)

urgence, *f.* urgency

urgent, *(adj.)* urgent; pressing

uriner, *v.i.* to urinate

urinoir, *m.* public urinal

urne, *f.* urn; ballot box

usage, *m.* usage; custom; practice; **il est d'- de,** it is customary to . . .; **selon l'-,** according to custom, as is the custom

usagé, *(adj.)* that has been used (or worn); second-hand

user, *v.t.* to use something; to use up, consume; to wear out

usine, *f.* factory, works (manufactory)

usité, *(adj.)* in use; current

ustensile, *m.* utensil, implement; household utensils

usuel(le), *(adj.)* usual, customary

usure, *f.* usury; wear and tear

usurier(-ère), *m.* *(f.)* usurer; *(adj.)* usurious

*utile, (*adj.*) useful; serviceable
utilisable, (*adj.*) capable of being turned to account
utiliser, *v.t.* to utilise; to make use of
utilité, *f.* utility; usefulness

V

va! done! agreed!
vacance, *f.* vacancy; vacant post
vacances, *f. pl.* holidays, vacation
vacarme, *m.* uproar, din; racket
vacation, *f.* vacation, recess (of law courts)
vaccin, *m.* vaccine (*med.*); lymph
vaccination, *f.* inoculation; vaccination
vaccine, *f.* cow-pox
vache, *f.* cow; cow-hide (also used abusively of people)
vacherie, *f.* cow-house; (*fam.*) a "dirty trick"
vacillant, (*adj.*) wavering; undecided
vaciller, *v.i.* to waver; to vacillate
vacuité, *f.* emptiness
va-et-vient, *m.* movement to and fro; coming and going
vagabond(e), *m.* (*f.*) vagabond, tramp; (*adj.*) wandering, roving
vagabonder, *v.i.* to rove about the world; to be a vagabond
vagir, *v.i.* to cry; to wail
vague, (*adj.*) vague, indefinite; vacant (stare)
vague, *f.* wave
vaguer, *v.i.* to wander, roam
vaillance, *f.* valour, bravery, courage
vaillant, (*adj.*) valiant, brave; stout hearted; industrious
vain, (*adj.*) vain; fruitless; ineffectual; en -, in vain
vaincre, *v.t.* to defeat, to conquer; to vanquish
vainqueur, *m.* conqueror; victor; winner

vaisseau. *m.* vessel, ship; spatial, space-ship
vaisselle, *f.* plates and dishes; crockery
valable, (*adj.*) valid, good
valet, *m.* footman, man-servant, valet; knave (cards)
valet de ferme, farm-hand
valeur, *f.* worth, value; meaning; valour; *pl.* securities
valeureux(-euse), (*adj.*) gallant, brave, valorous
valide, (*adj.*) valid, good
valise, *f.* suitcase
vallée, *f.* valley
vallon, *m.* little valley; dale
vallonné, (*adj.*) undulating
*valoir, *v.i.* to be worth; to be as good as; to be equal to; to merit; il vaut mieux, it would be better; (en) - (la peine), to be worth while
valse, *f.* valse, waltz
valser, *v.i.* to waltz
value, *f.* value; price
valve, *f.* valve (*not* wireless)
van, *m.* winnowing basket
vandale, *m.* and *f.* vandal
vandalisme, *m.* vandalism
vanille, (*adj.*) vanilla flavoured; *f.* vanilla
vanité, *f.* vanity, conceit; futility
vaniteux(-euse), (*adj.*) vain, conceited
vanne, *f.* water-gate, sluice
vannier, *m.* basket-maker
vantail(-aux), *m.* leaf; hinged flap of a door
vantard(e), *m.* (*f.*) boaster; (*adj.*) boastful, bragging
(se) vanter, *v.r.* to boast; to praise oneself
va-nu-pieds, *m.* (*invar.*) vagabond, ragamuffin
vapeur, *m.* steamer
vapeur, *f.* vapour, steam; bateau à -, steamer
vaporiser, *v.t.* to spray; to sprinkle with; se -, *v.r.* to vaporise; to evaporate
vaquer à, to attend to
varech, *m.* sea-weed; sea-wrack
vareuse, *f.* jersey; tunic

variable, (*adj.*) variable, change-able, fickle

variant, (*adj.*) variant, variable, fickle

varices, *f. pl.* varicose veins

varié, (*adj.*) vari-coloured; varie-gated

varier, *v.t.* to vary; to change

variété, *f.* variety, diversity

variole, *f.* small-pox

varlope, *f.* jointing-plane

vase, *m.* vase; vessel (for flowers, etc.)

vase, *f.* mud, mire, slime

vaseux(-euse), (*adj.*) muddy, slimy; (*fam.*) off colour, seedy

vasque, *f.* basin of fountain

vassal(e), *m.* (*f.*) and (*adj.*) vassal

vaste, (*adj.*) vast, huge, spacious

vau-l'eau (à), down-stream

vaurien, *m.* a good for nothing

vautour, *m.* vulture

vautrer (se), *v.r.* to wallow; to sprawl

veau, *m.* calf; veal; calf's leather

vedette, *f.* picket-boat; star (cin.)

végétal, (*adj.*) vegetable (as apart from mineral)

végétation, *f.* vegetation

végéter, *v.i.* to vegetate

véhémence, *f.* vehemence, impetuosity

véhément, (*adj.*) vehement, ardent, impetuous

véhicule, *m.* vehicle

veille, *f.* watching; waking; vigil; the day before, the " eve "

veillée, *f.* sitting up; evening (in company)

veiller, *v.i.* to sit up, to watch, to keep watch; - à ce que + subjunctive, to see to it that . . .

veilleur, *m.* watchman; guard

veilleuse, *f.* night-light

veinard(e), *m.* and *f.* lucky fellow, lucky devil

veine, *f.* vein; luck

vélin, *m.* vellum

vélo, *m.* bicycle

vélocité, *f.* velocity; speed

vélodrome, *m.* cycling ground, track

velours, *m.* velvet; - à côtes, corduroy

velouté, (*adj.*) velvety; smooth (wine)

velouté, *m.* softness; bloom (of fruit)

velouteux(-euse), (*adj.*) velvety

velu, (*adj.*) hairy, shaggy

venaison, *f.* venison

vénal(-aux), (*adj.*) venal; purchasable

vénalité, *f.* venality

venant(e), *m.* (*f.*) comer (man or woman); à tout venant, to anyone

vendable, (*adj.*) saleable

vendange, *f.* grape harvest; grape-gathering

vendanges (les), *f. pl.* the season for grape-gathering; (the) vintage

vendanger, *v.i.* to harvest the grapes

vendangeur(-euse), *m.* (*f.*) grape-gatherer

vendeur(-euse), *m.* (*f.*) salesman (-woman); shop assistant

vendre, *v.t.* to sell

vendredi, *m.* Friday; - saint, Good Friday

vénéneux(-euse), (*adj.*) venomous, poisonous

vénérable, (*adj.*) venerable

vénérer, *v.t.* to venerate, to reverence

vénérien(ne), (*adj.*) venereal

vengeance, *f.* revenge; vengeance

venger, *v.t.* to avenge; to revenge

vengeur(-eresse), (*adj.*) avenging; revengeful; *m.* (*f.*) avenger

venimeux(-euse), (*adj.*) venomous, spiteful, malignant

venin, *m.* venom, poison

*venir, *v.i.* (with *être*) to come, to arrive, to be coming; - de, to have just

vénitien(ne), (*adj.*) Venetian

vent, *m.* wind, breeze; - de terre (mer), land (sea) breeze; il fait du -, it is windy

vente, *f.* sale; selling; auction; en -, on sale

venter, *v.i.* to blow, to be windy

venteux(-euse), *(adj.)* gusty, squally, windy

ventilateur, *m.* ventilator

ventiler, *v.t.* to ventilate, to air

ventouse, *f.* cupping-glass *(med.)*

ventre, *m.* abdomen; belly; womb; **- à terre**, at full speed

ventrière, *f.* girth; belly band

ventriloque, *m.* *(f.)* ventriloquist; *(adj.)* ventriloquial

venue, *f.* coming, arrival

vêpres, *f. pl.* vespers (Catholic Church service)

ver, *m.* worm; **- luisant**, glow-worm; **- à soie**, silk-worm; **- solitaire**, tape-worm

véranda, *f.* verandah

verbal, *(adj.)* verbal; oral; by word of mouth

verbiage, *m.* idle talk; verbiage

verdâtre, *(adj.)* greenish

verdict, *m.* verdict

verdir, *v.t.* to make green, to grow green

verdoyant, *(adj.)* green, verdant

verdure, *f.* greenness, greenery; green vegetables

véreux(-euse), *(adj.)* wormy, maggoty; shady (character)

verge, *f.* rod, switch

vergé, *(adj.)* laid (paper)

verger, *m.* orchard

verglas, *m.* frost after thaw

vergogne, *f.* shame

véridique, *(adj.)* truthful, veracious

vérification, *f.* verification; examination (of work, etc.)

vérifier, *v.t.* to verify; to examine (statement, etc.)

véritable, *(adj.)* true; genuine; real; veritable

vérité, *f.* truth; **en -,** truly, in truth

verjus, *m.* verjuice

vermeil(-le), *(adj.)* vermilion, bright red; *m.* silver-gilt

vermicelle, *m.* vermicelli

vermifuge, *m.* vermifuge

vermillon, *m.* vermilion, bright red

vermine, *f.* vermin

vermisseau, *m.* small worm

vermoulu, *(adj.)* worm-eaten (wood, etc.)

vermout(h), *m.* vermouth

vernir, *v.t.* to varnish; to polish

vernis, *m.* varnish, polish, glaze

vérole (with *petite*), *f.* small-pox

verrat, *m.* boar

verre, *m.* glass; **- de vin**, glass of wine; **- à vin**, wine-glass

verrerie, *f.* glassworks; glass ware

verrier, *m.* glass-maker, glass-blower

verroterie, *f.* small glass ware; glass beads

verrou, *m.* bolt, bar; **sous les verrous,** in custody, under lock and key

verrouiller, *v.t.* to bolt, to bar

verrue, *f.* wart

vers, *m.* verse, line of poetry

vers, *(prep.)* towards, to

versant, *m.* slope; side (of mountain)

verse, *f.* laying of corn (by wind); **à -,** in torrents (rain)

versé, *(adj.)* skilled, experienced, versed in

versement, *m.* pouring out (liquid); payment (into bank, etc.)

verser, *v.t.* to pour out (liquid); to overturn; to shed (tears); to pay in (to an account)

verseuse, *f.* coffee pot (used in cafés, etc.); bar-maid

versicule, *m.* little verse

version, *f.* version, account (of happening): translation

verso, *m.* back, reverse (of sheet or page)

vert, *(adj.)* green; unripe (fruit); raw (hide); sharp (reprimand)

vert, *m.* green (the colour)

vert-de-gris, *m.* verdigris

vertébral, *(adj.)* vertebral; spinal

vertement, *(adv.)* sharply, briskly

vertical, *(adj.)* vertical, upright

vertige, *m.* giddiness, dizziness

vertigineux(-euse), *(adj.)* dizzy, giddy

vertu, *f.* courage; virtue; chastity; property (of medicine, etc.)

vertueux(-euse), (*adj.*) virtuous; chaste

verve, *f.* animation; zest; spirit

verveine, *f.* verbena

vésicule, *f.* bladder; vesicle

vessie, *f.* bladder

veste, *f.* short jacket

vestiaire, *m.* cloakroom (of hotel, etc.)

vestibule, *m.* entrance hall, lobby

vestige, *m.* mark, trace, vestige

veston, *m.* lounge-coat

vêtement, *m.* garment; *pl.* clothes

vétéran, *m.* veteran

vétérinaire, *m.* veterinary surgeon; (*adj.*) veterinary

vêtir, *v.t.* to clothe, to attire, to dress; **vêtu de**, dressed in

veto, *m.* veto

vétusté, *f.* decay, antiquity, decrepitude

veuf(-ve), *m.* (*f.*) widower (widow); (*adj.*) widowed

veulerie, *f.* flabbiness, listlessness

veuvage, *m.* widowhood

vexant, (*adj.*) provoking, annoying

vexer, *v.t.* to vex, to trouble, to harass

viaduc, *m.* viaduct

viager(-ère), (*adj.*) for life; **rente viagère**, life annuity

viande, *f.* meat

viatique, *m.* viaticum

vibrant, (*adj.*) vibrating; vibrant

vibrer, *v.i.* to vibrate

vicaire, *m.* curate (of parish); - **général**, vicar general

vice, *m.* vice, depravity, flaw

vice-amiral, *m.* vice-admiral

vice-consul, *m.* vice-consul

vice-président, *m.* vice-president

vice-roi, *m.* viceroy

vicié, (*adj.*) vitiated, corrupt

vicieux(-euse), (*adj.*) vicious, depraved

vicinal(-aux), (*adj.*) local; **chemin** -, local road, by-road

vicissitude, *f.* vicissitude; changes of fortune

vicomte(sse), *m.* (*f.*) viscount(ess)

victime, *f.* victim, sufferer

victoire, *f.* victory

victorieux(-euse), (*adj.*) victorious

victuailles, *f. pl.* eatables, victuals

vidange, *f.* night-soil; sediment

vide, (*adj.*) empty; unoccupied; void; *m.* void, gap, blank

vider, *v.t.* to empty; to clear out (room); to drain (a glass)

****vie**, *f.* life; existence; way of living

vieillard, *m.* old man

vieillesse, *f.* old age

vieillir, *v.i.* to grow old; to become obsolete

vielle, *f.* hurdy-gurdy

vierge, *f.* virgin, maiden; (*adj.*) pure, virginal; **la Sainte** -, the Blessed Virgin Mary; **chapelle de la Sainte** -, lady chapel

vieux, vieil (*f.* **vieille**) (*adj.*) old. (N.B.—**vieil** is used before masculine singular nouns beginning with a vowel or " h " mute)

vif(vive), (*adj.*) alive, living; brisk; quick (temper); keen (pleasure); bright; lively; **de vive voix**, by word of mouth

vif-argent, *m.* quicksilver; mercury

vigie, *f.* look-out (man) (*naut.*)

vigilance, *f.* vigilance; watchfulness

vigilant, (*adj.*) vigilant, watchful

vigne, *f.* vine; vineyard

vigneron, *m.* vine-grower

vignoble, *m.* vineyard

vigoureux(-euse), (*adj.*) vigorous, strong, sturdy

vigueur, *f.* vigour, force, strength

vil, (*adj.*) vile, base, mean, foul

vilain, (*adj.*) nasty, unpleasant; ugly

vilebrequin, *m.* brace and bit

vilenie, *f.* meanness; stinginess

vilipender, *v.t.* to vilify, to run down

villa, *f.* villa; suburban house

village, *m.* village

villageois(e), (*adj.*) rustic; *m.* (*f.*) countryman (-woman)

ville, *f.* town; **hôtel de -,** town hall

villégiateur, *m.* visitor at a resort

villégiature, *f.* stay or holiday in the country; **en -,** on holiday

vin, *m.* wine; **- chaud,** mulled wine; **- mousseux,** sparkling wine; **- ordinaire,** table wine

vinaigre, *m.* vinegar

vinaigrer, *v.t.* to season with vinegar

vinaigrette, *f.* vinegar sauce; oil and vinegar dressing

vinaigrier, *m.* oil and vinegar cruet

vindicatif(-ive), *(adj.)* vindictive; spiteful; revengeful

vingt, *(adj.)* and *m.* twenty

vingtaine, *f.* about twenty

vingtième, *f.* twentieth part

vinicole, *(adj.)* wine-growing (generally district)

viol, *m.* rape (crime of)

violacé, *(adj.)* purplish-blue

violation, *f.* violation, infringement

violâtre, *(adj.)* purplish

violence, *f.* violence, force

violent, *(adj.)* violent; high (wind); fierce (battle, etc.)

violer, *v.t.* to violate; to break (the law, etc.)

violet(te), *(adj.)* violet (colour); *f.* violet (flower)

violon, *m.* violin; *(fam.)* the lock-up

violoncelle, *m.* violoncello

vipère, *f.* viper, adder

virage, *m.* turning, sharp turn, corner (of road)

virago, *f.* virago

virement, *m.* transfer (banking term)

virer, *v.i.* to turn; to take a corner (motoring); to bank (aviation)

vireux(-euse), *(adj.)* poisonous

virginal, *(adj.)* virginal, maidenly

virginité, *f.* virginity, maidenhood

virgule, *f.* comma

viril, *(adj.)* virile, manly, male

virilité, *f.* manhood, virility

virole, *f.* ferrule (of stick)

virtuose, *m.* and *f.* virtuoso

virulence, *f.* virulence

virulent, *(adj.)* virulent

virus, *m.* virus

vis, *f.* screw; **serrer la - à qn.,** to put the screw (on somebody)

vis-à-vis, opposite

visage, *m.* face, countenance

visée, *f.* aim; *(mil.)* aiming

viser, *v.i.* to aim (at); to take aim; *v.t.* to countersign, to initial (a paper, etc.)

visibilité, *f.* visibility

visible, *(adj.)* visible; plain; perceptible

visière, *f.* peak of a cap; eye-shade

vision, *f.* vision; eyesight; sight (of something); phantom

visite, *f.* visit; call (social); inspection; **faire (rendre) - à,** to call on, pay a call on

visiter, *v.t.* to visit; to attend a patient; to examine, to inspect; to overhaul (machinery); to search (police)

visiteur, *m.* visitor

vison, *m.* mink (fur)

visqueux(-euse), *(adj.)* sticky, viscous

visser, *v.t.* to screw, to screw on

vital, *(adj.)* vital

vitalité, *f.* vitality

vite, *(adj.)* swift, quick; *(adv.)* quickly. (N.B.—*vitement* as adverb is obsolete)

vitesse, *f.* speed, swiftness, quickness; **passer les vitesses,** to change gear

vitrail(-aux), *m.* stained glass window; church window

vitre, *f.* pane of glass; window-pane

vitré, *(adj.)* glazed; **porte vitrée,** glass door

vitrer, *v.t.* to glaze (window, etc.)

vitrerie, *f.* glass trade

vitrier, *m.* glazier

vitrine, *f.* shop window; glass case; show case

vitriol, *m.* vitriol

vivace, *(adj.)* long-lived; hardy (plant); perennial

vivacité, *f.* vivacity, liveliness; hastiness (temper); heat (discussion)

vivant, *(adj.)* alive, living; lively, animated; **bon -,** man who enjoys life, does himself well

vivat, *m.* and *(interj.)* hurrah, vivat

vive! long live!

vive, *f.* sting-fish

vivement, *(adv.)* briskly, smartly; acutely (feelings)

viveur(-euse), *m.* *(f.)* man (woman) who leads a fast life

vivier, *m.* fish pond

*vivre, *v.i.* to live; to be alive

vivres, *m. pl.* food, provisions, supplies

vocabulaire, *m.* vocabulary

vocation, *f.* vocation, calling (career)

vociférer, *v.i* to shout, to bawl, to yell

vœu(x), *m.* vow; wish

vogue, *f.* fashion, vogue

voguer, *v.i.* to sail *(naut.)*

voici, *(prep.)* here is, here are; **le -,** here he is

voie, *f.* way, road, route, track; **- ferrée,** railway (line)

voies et moyens, ways and means

voilà, *(prep.)* there is, there are; **en - assez,** that will do; that is enough; **- tout,** that is all

voile, *f.* sail *(naut.)*

voile, *m.* veil; cloak; voile (material)

voiler, *v.t.* to veil, to hide one's face; to obscure, dim (light); **se -,** *v.r.* to become overcast

voilier, *m.* sailing ship

*voir, *v.t.* to see (general sense); to set eyes on; to visit (someone, something); to receive (someone); to understand; to discern

voire, *(adv.)* even; in truth

voirie, *f.* the high roads; **service de -,** the highways department

voisin(e), *m.* *(f.)* neighbour; *(adj.)* neighbouring

voisinage, *m.* neighbourhood; proximity; district

voiture, *f.* carriage, conveyance; motor-car; vehicle; **en -!** take your seats!; **- directe,** through carriage, coach; **- restaurant,** dining-car (railway); **- salon,** saloon carriage (railway)

voiturier, *m.* carter, carrier

voix, *f.* voice; **à haute -,** aloud

vol, *m.* flight, flying

vol, *m.* flock, flight; **à - d'oiseau,** as the crow flies

vol, *m.* theft, robbery, stealing

volable, *(adj.)* worth stealing

volage, *(adj.)* fickle

volaille, *f.* poultry, fowls

volailler, *m.* poultry merchant; poultry yard

volant, *(adj.)* flying; fluttering; winged

volant, *m.* steering-wheel (of car); **tenir le -,** to be driving, at the wheel

volcan, *m.* volcano

volcanique, *(adj.)* volcanic

volée, *f.* flight (of bird, etc.); volley

voler, *v.i.* to fly

voler, *v.t.* to steal, to rob

volet, *m.* shutter (inside of window)

voleur(-euse), *m.* *(f.)* thief, robber, burglar

volière, *f.* aviary

volige, *f.* batten; lath

volontaire, *(adj.)* voluntary; spontaneous; *m.* and *f.* volunteer

volonté, *f.* will, will-power

volontiers, *(adv.)* willingly; gladly

volt, *m.* volt

volte-face, *f.* *(invar.)* turning round; face about

voltiger, *v.i.* to fly about; to flutter, to flap

volubilité, *f.* volubility

volume, *m.* volume (book); bulk

volumineux(-euse), *(adj.)* voluminous; bulky; large

volupté, *f.* voluptuousness; sensual pleasure

voluptueux(-euse), *(adj.)* voluptuous, delightful to the senses

vomir, *v.t.* to vomit; to be sick

vomissement, *m.* vomiting

vomitif, *m.* emetic

vorace, *(adj.)* voracious

voracement, (*adv.*) voraciously

votant(e), *m.* (*f.*) voter, person having a vote

vote, *m.* vote; ballot, poll

voter, *v.i.* to vote; to pass, carry a measure

votre (*pl.* **vos**), (*poss. adj.*) your

(le, la) vôtre, (*poss. pro.*) yours

vouer, *v.t.* to vow, to devote, to dedicate

*****vouloir,** *v.t.* to will (something); to be determined; to want; to wish; to require; to be willing; to need (something); **en - à,** to have a grudge against (somebody)

vouloir, *m.* will (of God)

vousseau, *m.* arch-stone

voussure, *f.* curve of arch

voûte, *f.* vault, arch

voûter, *v.t.* to vault, to arch

voyage, *m.* journey, trip, tour

voyager, *v.i.* to travel; to make a journey, trip

voyageur(-euse), *m.* (*f.*) traveller; passenger (in train); **commis -,** commercial traveller

voyant, (*adj.*) seeing; showy, gaudy, loud

voyelle, *f.* vowel

voyou, *m.* loafer, blackguard; street arab

vrai, (*adj.*) true, truthful; **à - dire,** as a matter of fact

vraiment, (*adv.*) really, truly

vraisemblable, (*adj.*) probable, likely

vraisemblance, *f.* probability; likelihood

vrille, *f.* tendril (flower); gimlet

vriller, *v.t.* to bore (with a gimlet)

vrombir, *v.i.* to buzz (fly); to throb (engine)

vu, (*adj.* and *past part.*) seen; considering

vue, *f.* sight; view; prospect; **à -,** at sight (*finance*); **à - (d'œil),** visibly; **perdre de -,** to lose sight of

vulcaniser, *v.t.* to vulcanise

vulcanite, *f.* vulcanite

vulgaire, (*adj.*) vulgar; common; coarse

vulgariser, *v.t.* to vulgarise; to render popular (knowledge)

vulgarité, *f.* vulgarity

vulnérabilité, *f.* vulnerability

vulnérable, (*adj.*) vulnerable

vulnéraire, (*adj.*) healing; *f.* kidney-vetch; cure for wounds

vultueux(-euse), (*adj.*) bloated; puffy; (of face) inflamed

W

wagon, *m.* carriage, coach, car (railway); wagon, truck (goods)

wagon à bestiaux, *m.* cattle-truck

wagon-écurie, *m.* (both vary in plural) horse-box

wagon-frein, *m.* (both vary in plural) brake-van

wagon-lit, *m.* (both vary in plural) sleeping-car; sleeper

wagon-poste, *m.* (*pl.* **wagon-postes**) mail van

wagon-restaurant, *m.* (both vary in plural) dining-car

wagon-salon, *m.* (both vary in plural) saloon-car or carriage

wallace, *f.* drinking-fountain (rarely met with)

wallon(ne), (*adj.*) Walloon

wapiti, *m.* wapiti

watt, *m.* watt, ampere-volt

whisky(s), *m.* whisky

X

xénophobie, *f.* xenophobia, hatred of foreigners

xérès (vin de), *m.* sherry

xylographe, *m.* wood-engraver

xylophone, *m.* xylophone

Y

y, *(adv.* and *pron.)* there, here, thither; to it, at it, etc.
yacht, *m.* yacht
yeuse, *f.* holly oak
yougo-slave, *(adj.)* Yugo-slav
ypérite, *f.* mustard gas
ypréau, *m.* wych elm

Z

zèbre, *m.* zebra
zébré (de), *(adj.)* striped (with)
zébu, *m.* zebu (kind of ox)
zélateur(-trice), *m.* *(f.)* zealot; *(adj.)* zealous
zèle, *m.* zeal, enthusiasm
zélé, *(adj.)* zealous
zénith, *m.* zenith

zéphire, zéphyr(e), *m.* zephyr, breeze
zéro, *m.* nought, cipher, zero
zézaiement, *m.* lisp, lisping
zézayer, *v.i.* and *v.t.* to lisp
zibeline, *f.* sable
zig, *m.* (*fam.*) fellow, chap
zigzag, *m.* zigzag
zigzaguer, *v.i.* to zigzag
zinc, *m.* zinc; zinc counter (in public-house)
zingage, *m.* covering (coating) with zinc
zinguer, *v.t.* to cover with zinc
zingueur, *m.* zinc-worker
zizanie, *f.* tares; dissension
zodiaque, *m.* zodiac .
zona, *m.* shingles *(med.)*
zone, *f.* zone, area; - occupée, occupied zone
zoologie, *f.* zoology
zoologique, *(adj.)* zoological
zouave, *m.* zouave
zut! *(interj.)* bother! drat it!

CHRISTIAN NAMES

Pronoms	*Christian Names*
Achille	Achilles
Adélaïde	Adelaide
Adèle	Adela, Adeline
Adolphe	Adolphus
Adrien	Adrian
Agathe	Agatha
Aimée	Amy
Alphonse	Alphonso
Ambroise	Ambrose
Amélie	Amelia
Anastase (Anastasie)	Anastasius (Anastasia)
André	Andrew
Angélique	Angelica
Anne	Anna, Anne
Antoine	Anthony
Archambaut	Archibald
Arnaud	Arnold
Arthur	Arthur
Auguste	Augustus (Augusta)
Barbe	Barbara
Barthélémy	Bartholomew
Benoît	Benedict
Berthe	Bertha
Bertrand	Bertram
Blanche	Blanche, Bianca
Brigitte	Bridget
Cathérine	Catherine
Cécile	Cecily, Celia
César	Cæsar
Charles	Charles
Chrétien	Christian
Christophe	Christopher
Claire	Clara
Claude	Claude, Claudius
Clément	Clement
Clotilde	Clotilda
Constance	Constance, Constantia
Corneille	Cornelius
Crépin	Crispin
Denis	Dennis, Dionysius
Diane	Diana
Dominique	Dominic
Dorothée	Dorothy
Edmond	Edmund
Édouard	Edward
Élie	Elias
Élisabeth	Elizabeth
Émilie	Emily, Emmy
Emma	Emma
Étienne	Stephen
Eugène	Eugene
Eustache	Eustace
Fabien	Fabian
Fanchon, Fanchette	Fanny
Félicie	Felicity
Flore	Flora
François	Francis, Frank
Frédéric	Frederick
Gaspard	Jasper
Gauthier	Walter
Geneviève	Winifred
Geoffroi	Geoffrey
Gervais	Gervais
Gilles	Giles
Godefroy	Godfrey
Grâce	Grace
Grégoire	Gregory
Guillaume	William
Gustave	Gustavus
Hélène	Helen, Helena
Henri	Henry
Hilaire	Hilary
Horace	Horace, Horatio
Hugues	Hugh
Humfroy	Humphrey
Ignace	Ignatius
Isabelle	Isabel, Isabella
Jacques	James
Jacquot	Jim, Jimmy
Jean	John
Jeanne	Jane
Jeanneton, Jeannette	Janet

Jeannot	Jack, Johnny	Randolphe	Randolph
Jenny	Jenny	Raoul	Ralph
Jérémie	Jeremy	Raymond	Raymund
Jérôme	Jerome	Régine	Regina, Queenie
Jules	Julius		
Julien	Julian	Renaud	Reynold
Justin	Justin, Justinus	Robert	Robert
		Robin	Bob
		Rodolphe	Ralph, Rudolf
Laure	Laura	Roland	Roland, Orlando
Laurent	Lawrence		
Léon	Leo	Rosalinde	Rosalind
Lise	Lizzie	Rosemonde	Rosamund
Louis	Lewis, Louis	Rosette	Rose
Louise	Louisa		
Luc	Luke	Salomon	Solomon
Lucie	Lucy	Samson	Samson
Lucien	Lucien	Sébastien	Sebastian
		Sigismond	Sigismund
Madeleine	Madeline, Magdalen	Silvain	Silvan
		Silvestre	Silvester
Madelon	Maggie, Madge	Sophie	Sophia
Margot	Madge, Marjory, Margot, Meg, Peg, Peggy	Stanislas	Stanislas
		Suzanne	Suzan, Susannah
Marguerite	Margaret	Suzette, Suzon	Susy, Sue
Marie	Maria		
Mariette, Marion	Mary	Théodose	Theodosius, Theo
Marthe	Martha		
Mathilde	Matilda	Thérèse	Theresa
Matthieu	Matthew	Thibaut	Theobald
Maurice	Maurice	Thomas	Thomas
Michel	Michael	Timothée	Timothy
		Tobie	Toby
Nannette, Ninon	Nancy	Toinette	Antonia
Nicolas	Nicholas	Urbain	Urban
		Ursule	Ursula
Olivie	Olive, Olivia		
Olivier	Oliver	Valentin	Valentine
Omfroy	Humphrey	Véronique	Veronica
Othon	Otto, Otho	Vincent	Vincent
Patrice	Patrick	Wilhelmine	Wilhelmina
Paul	Paul		
Philippe	Philip	Zacharie	Zachary
Pierre	Peter		

GEOGRAPHICAL NAMES

L'Abyssinie, *f.* Abyssinia
Achanti, *m.* Ashantee
Les Açores, *f.* the Azores
L'Adriatique, *f.* the Adriatic
L'Afghanistan, *m.* Afghanistan
L'Afrique, *f.* Africa (- du Sud, South Africa)
Aix-la-Chapelle, *f.* Aix-la-Chapelle (*German* Aachen)
Aix-les-Bains, *f.* Aix-les-Bains
Aix-en-Provence, *f.* Aix-en-Provence
L'Alabama, *m.* Alabama
L'Albanie, *f.* Albania
Albe, *f.* Alva
Albion, *f.* Albion
Alep, *m.* Aleppo
Alexandrie, *f.* Alexandria
Alger, *m.* Algiers
L'Algérie, *f.* Algeria
L'Allemagne, *f.* Germany
Les Alpes, *f.* the Alps
L'Alsace, *f.* Alsace
L'Amazone, *m.* the Amazon
Amboine, *m.* Amboyna
L'Amérique, *f.* America
Ancône, *f.* Ancona
L'Andalousie, *f.* Andalusia
Les Andes, *f.* the Andes
Andrinople, *f.* Adrianople
L'Angleterre, *f.* England
Antigue, *f.* Antigua
Les Antilles, *f.* the West Indies
La Mer des Antilles, *f.* the Caribbean Sea
Antioche, *f.* Antioch
Anvers, *m.* Antwerp
Les Apennins, *m.* the Apennines
L'Arabie, *f.* Arabia
Le Golfe Arabique, the Arabian Gulf
L'Aragon, *m.* Aragon
L'Arcadie, *f.* Arcadia
Les Ardennes, *f.* the Ardennes
La (République) Argentine, *f.* the Argentine (Republic)
Arimathée, *f.* Arimathea
L'Arizona, *m.* Arizona
L'Arkansas, *m.* Arkansas
Archangel, *m.* Archangel

L'Arménie, *f.* Armenia
L'Armorique, *f.* Armorica (Brittany)
L'Asie, *f.* Asia (- Mineure, Asia Minor)
L'Assyrie, *f.* Assyria
Athènes, *f.* Athens
L'Atlantique, *m.* the Atlantic Ocean
L'Atlas, *m.* the Atlas
L'Attique, *f.* Attica
Aurigny, *m.* Alderney
L'Australasie, *f.* Australasia
L'Australie, *f.* Australia
L'Autriche, *f.* Austria
Azincourt, *m.* Agincourt
Azof, *m.* Azoff

Bade, *m.* Baden-Baden
Bagdad, *m.* Baghdad
Les Balkans, *m.* the Balkans
La Baltique, *f.* the Baltic
La Barbade, *f.* Barbadoes
La Barbarie, *f.* Barbary
Barcelone, *f.* Barcelona
Batavia, *f.* Batavia
La Bavière, *f.* Bavaria
La Belgique, *f.* Belgium
Bénarès, *f.* Benares
Le Bengale, *m.* Bengal
Berlin, *m.* Berlin
Berne, *f.* Berne
Bersabée, *f.* Beersheba
La Bessarabie, *f.* Bessarabia
Béthanie, *f.* Bethany
La Birmanie, *f.* Burma
La Biscaye, *f.* Biscay
La Bohème, *f.* Bohemia
La Bolivie, *f.* Bolivia
Bologne, *f.* Bologna
La Bosnie, *f.* Bosnia
Le Bosphore, *m.* the Bosphorus
La Bothnie, *f.* Bothnia
La Bourgogne, *f.* Burgundy
Le Brabant, *m.* Brabant
Le Brandebourg, *m.* Brandenburg
Brême, *m.* Bremen
Le Brésil, m. Brazil
La Bretagne, *f.* Brittany

La Grande Bretagne, *f.* Great Britain
Bruxelles, *f.* Brussels
Bucarest, *f.* Bucharest
La Bulgarie, *f.* Bulgaria

Cachemire, *m.* Cashmere
Cadix, *m.* Cadiz
La Cafrerie, *f.* Caffraria
Le Caire, *m.* Cairo
La Calabre, *f.* Calabria
Calais, *m.* Calais
Calais (Le Pas de), the Straits of Dover
La Calédonie, *f.* Caledonia
La Californie, *f.* California
Le Calvaire, *m.* Calvary
La Campanie, *f.* the Campagna
Le Canada, *m.* Canada
Le Cap, *m.* the Cape, Cape Town
Le Cap Vert, *m.* Cape Verde
Capharnaüm, *m.* Capernaum
Le Carmel, *m.* Carmel
La Caroline, *f.* Carolina
Les Carpathes, *m.* the Carpathians (Mountains)
Caspienne, *f.* the Caspian Sea
La Castille, *f.* Castile
La Catalogne, *f.* Catalonia
Le Caucase, *m.* the Caucasus
Cédron, *m.* Kidron
Céphalonie, *f.* Cephalonia
Césarée, *f.* Cæsarea
Le Ceylan, *m.* Ceylon
Chamonix, *m.* Chamonix
Chanaan, *m.* Canaan
Le Chili, *m.* Chili
La Chine, *f.* China
Chypre, *f.* Cyprus
La Circassie, *f.* Circassia
La Colombie, *f.* Colombia
Côme, *m.* Como
Le Congo, *m.* the Congo
Le Connecticut, *m.* Connecticut
Copenhague, *f.* Copenhagen
Les Cordillères, *f.* the Cordilleras
La Corée, *f.* Korea
Corfou, *m.* Corfu
Corinthe, *f.* Corinth
La Corne d'Or, *f.* the Golden Horn
Les Cornouailles, *f.* Cornwall
La Corogne, *f.* Corunna

La Corse, *f.* Corsica
La Côte d'Azur, *f.* the Riviera
La Côte des Esclaves, *f.* the Slave Coast
Cracovie, *f.* Cracow
La Crète, *f.* Crete
La Crimée, *f.* the Crimea
La Croatie, *f.* Croatia
Cuba, *f.* Cuba

La Dalmatie, *f.* Dalmatia
Damas, *m.* Damascus
Damiette, *f.* Damietta
Le Danemark, *m.* Denmark
Le Danube, *m.* the Danube
Les Dardanelles, *f.* the Dardanelles
Le Décan, *m.* the Deccan
Le Delaware, *m.* Delaware
Delphes, *f.* Delphi
La Dominique, *f.* Dominica
Douvres, *f.* Dover
Dresde, *f.* Dresden
Dublin, *m.* Dublin
Dunkerque, *m.* Dunkirk

L'Écosse, *f.* Scotland (La Basse -, the Lowlands; La Haute -, the Highlands)
La Nouvelle Écosse, *f.* Nova Scotia
Eden, *m.* Eden
Édimbourg, *m.* Edinburgh
Égée, *m.* the Ægean
L'Égypte, *f.* Egypt
L'Elbe, *f.* the Elbe
Éphèse, *f.* Ephesus
L'Équateur, *m.* the Equator; Ecuador
L'Érié, *m.* Lake Erie
L'Érythrée, *f.* Eritrea
L'Escaut, *m.* the Scheldt
L'Esclavonie, *f.* Slavonia
L'Espagne, *f.* Spain
L'Esthonie, *f.* Esthonia
L'Estrémadure, *f.* Estramadura
Les États-Unis, *m.* the United States
L'Éthiopie, *f.* Ethiopia
L'Etna, *m.* Mount Etna
L'Étrurie, *f.* Etruria
L'Euphrate, *m.* the Euphrates
L'Europe, *f.* Europe

La Finlande, *f.* Finland
La Flandre, *f.* Flanders
Flessingue, *f.* Flushing
Le Fleuve. Jaune, *m.* the Yellow River
La Floride, *f.* Florida
La Forêt-Noire, *f.* the Black Forest
Formose, *f.* Formosa
La France, *f.* France
Francfort, *m.* Frankfort
'La Frise, *f.* Friesland

Le Gabon, *m.* Gaboon
Gaète, *f.* Gaeta
Galaad, *m.* Gilead
La Galatie, *f.* Galatia
La Galicie, *f.* Galicia
La Galilée, *f.* Galilee
Galles, *f.* (*or* Le Pays de Galles), Wales (- du Sud, South Wales)
La Gambie, *f.* Gambia
Gand, *m.* Ghent
Le Gange, *m.* the Ganges
La Gascogne, *f.* Gascony
La Gaule, *f.* Gaul
Gênes, *f.* Genoa
Genève, *f.* Geneva
La Géorgie, *f.* Georgia
Gessen, *m.* Goshen
Les Ghâtes, *f.* the Ghats
Glasgow, *m.* Glasgow
Le Golfe Persique, *m.* the Persian Gulf
La Gothie, *f.* Gothland
La Grèce, *f.* Greece
La Grenade, *f.* Granada
Le Groenland, *m.* Greenland
La Gueldre, *f.* Guelderland
La Guinée, *f.* Guinea
Guernesey, *m.* Guernsey
La Guyane, *f.* Guyana

Haïti, *m.* Hayti
Hambourg, *m.* Hamburg
Le Hanovre, *m.* Hanover
Harlem *or* Haarlem, *m.* Haarlem
La Havane, *f.* Havana
Le Hâvre, *m.* Havre
Hawaï, *m.* Hawaii
La Haye, *f.* the Hague
Les Hébrides, *f.* the Hebrides

L'Hécla, *m.* Mount Hecla
L'Hellespont, *m.* the Hellespont
Herculanum, *m.* Herculaneum
L'Himalaya, *m.* the Himalayas
L'Hindoustan, *m.* Hindustan
La Hollande, *f.* Holland
La Hongrie, *f.* Hungary

L'Île de Candie, *f.* Candia, Crete
L'Île Maurice, *f.* Mauritius
Les Îles Baléares, *f.* the Balearic Islands
Les Îles Bermudes, *f.* the Bermudas
Les Îles Laquedives, *f.* the Laccadive Islands
Les Îles des Larrons, *m.* the Ladrones
Les Îles Malouines, *f.* the Falkland Islands
Les Îles de la Manche, *f.* (Les Îles Anglo-normandes) the Channel Islands
Les Îles Mariannes, *f.* the Marianas
Les Îles Sorlingues, *f.* the Scilly Islands
L'Illinois, *m.* Illinois
L'Inde, *f.* India
Les Indes, *f.* the Indies
La Mer des Indes, *f.* the Indian Ocean
La Compagnie des Indes, *f.* the East India Company
L'Indiana, *m.* Indiana
L'Indo-Chine, *f.* Indo-China
L'Ionie, *f.* Ionia
L'Iowa, *m.* Iowa
L'Iran, *m.* Iran
L'Irlande, *f.* Ireland
La Mer d'Irlande, *f.* the Irish Sea
L'Islande, *f.* Iceland
L'Italie, *f.* Italy

La Jamaïque, *f.* Jamaica
Le Japon, *m.* Japan
Jéna, *m.* Jena
Jersey, *m.* Jersey
Jérusalem, *f.* Jerusalem
Le Jourdain, *m.* the Jordan
La Judée, *f.* Judea
Le Jura, *m.* the Jura
Le Jutland, *m.* Jutland
Kaboul, *m.* Cabul

La Kamptchatka, *m.* Kamtschatka
Le Kansas, *m.*.Kansas
Les Karpathes, *m.* the Carpathians
Le Kattégat, *m.* the Kattegat
Le Kentucky, *m.* Kentucky

Le Labrador, *m.* Labrador
Le Lac Léman, *m.* Lake Geneva
Le Lac Majeur, *m.* Lake Maggiore
Le Lac Supérieur, *m.* Lake Superior
Le Languedoc, *m.* Languedoc
Laodicée, *f.* Laodicea
La Laponie, *f.* Lapland
Leipzig *or* Liepsick, *m.* Leipzig
La Lettonie, *f.* Latvia
Le Levant, *m.* the Levant
Leyde, *f.* Leyden
Le Liban, *m.* Lebanon
La Libýe, *f.* Libya
Liége, *m.* Liege
Lion, *m.* (Le Golfe du), the Gulf of Lions
Lisbonne, *f.* Lisbon
La Lithuanie, *f.* Lithuania
La Livonie, *f.* Livonia
Livourne, *f.* Leghorn
Lizard, *m.* (Le Cap), the Lizard Point
La Lombardie, *f.* Lombardy
Londres, *f.* London
Le Long Island, *m.* Long Island
La Lorraine, *f.* Lorraine
La Louisiane, *f.* Louisiana
Lucques, *f.* Lucca
Le Luxembourg, *m.* Luxemburg
Lyon, *m.* Lyons

La Macédoine, *f.* Macedonia
Madère, *f.* Madeira
Madrid, *f.* Madrid
Le Maine, *m.* the state (or province) of Maine
Majorque, *f.* Majorca
La Malaisie, *f.* the Malay Archipelago
Malte, *f.* Malta
La Manche, *f.* the English Channel
La Mandchourie, *f.* Manchuria
Manille, *f.* Manilla

Mantoue, *f.* Mantua
Marmara, *f.* Marmora
Le Maroc, *m.* Morocco
Marseille, *m.* Marseilles
La Martinique, *f.* Martinique
Le Maryland, *m.* Maryland
Massachusetts, *m.* Massachusetts
Mayence, *f.* Mainz
La Mecque, *f.* Mecca
Médine, *f.* Medina
La Méditerranée, *f.* the Mediterranean
Menton, *m.* Mentone
La Mer Caspienne, *f.* the Caspian Sea
La Mer Égée, *f.* the Ægean Sea
La Mer du Japon, *f.* the Sea of Japan
La Mer Jaune, *f.* the Yellow Sea
La Mer Morte, *f.* the Dead Sea
La Mer Noire, *f.* the Black Sea
La Mer du Nord, *f.* the North Sea
La Mer Rouge, *f.* the Red Sea
Le Mersey, *m.* the Mersey
La Mésopotamie, *f.* Mesopotamia
Messine, *f.* Messina (Le Détroit de -), the Straits of Messina
Metz, *f.* Metz
Mexico, *m.* (the city of) Mexico
Le Mexique, *m.* (the country of) Mexico (Le Golfe du -, the Gulf of Mexico)
Le Michigan, *m.* Michigan
Le Minnesota, *m.* Minnesota
Minorque, *f.* Minorca
Le Mississippi, *m.* Mississippi
Le Missouri, *m.* Missouri
Moka, *m.* Mocha
La Moldavie, *f.* Moldavia
Le Montana, *m.* Montana
Le Monténégro, *m.* Montenegro
Montréal, *m.* Montreal
La Moravie, *f.* Moravia
La Morée, *f.* the Moree
Moscou, *m.* Moscow

Navarin, *m.* Navarino
La Navarre, *f.* Navarre
Le Nébraska, *m.* Nebraska
Le Népal, *m.* Nepal
La Néva *f.* the Neva
Le Névada, *m.* Nevada
Le New Jersey, *m.* New Jersey

New York, *m.* New York (City) (l'État de -, the state of New York)

Niagara, *m.* Niagara (La Chute de -, the Falls of Niagara)

Le Nil, *m.* the Nile

Ninive, *f.* Nineveh

La Normandie, *f.* Normandy

La Norvège, *f.* Norway

La Nouvelle Calédonie, *f.* New Caledonia

La Nouvelle Écosse, *f.* Nova Scotia

La Nouvelle-Galles du Sud, *f.* New South Wales

La Nouvelle Orléans, *f.* New Orleans

La Nouvelle Zélande, *f.* New Zealand

La Nouvelle Zemble, *f.* Nova Zembla

La Nubie, *f.* Nubia

L'Océanie, *f.* Oceana

L'Ohio, *m.* Ohio

Oliviers (Le Mont des), *m.* the Mount of Olives

L'Olympe, *m.* Olympus

Les Orcades, *f.* the Orkneys (Les Îles -, the Orkney Isles)

L'Orégon, *m.* Oregon

Orléans, *f.* Orleans

Ostende, *f.* Ostend

Ostrante, *f.* Otranto

Ouessant, *f.* Ushant

L'Ouganda, *m.* Uganda

Ourals, *m.* (Les Monts), the Ural Mountains

Oxford, *m.* Oxford

Le Pacifique, *m.* the Pacific

Padoue, *f.* Padua

Le Palatinat, *m.* the Palatinate

Palerme, *f.* Palermo

La Palestine, *f.* Palestine

Palmyre, *f.* Palmyra

Le Paraguay, *m.* Paraguay

Paris, *m.* Paris

Parme, *f.* Parma (the city) (Le Duché de -, the Duchy of Palma)

Le Parnasse, *m.* Parnassus

La Patagonie, *f.* Patagonia

Pavie, *f.* Pavia

Les Pays-Bas, the Netherlands

Pékin, *m.* Pekin

Le Péloponèse, *m.* the Peloponnesus

Le Pendjab, *m.* the Punjab

La Pensylvanie, *f.* Pennsylvania

Pergame, *f.* Pergamos

Pernambouc, *m.* Pernambuco

Le Pérou, *m.* Peru

La Perse, *f.* Persia

Pétrograd, *m.* Petrograd

La Phénicie, *f.* Phœnicia

Philadelphie, *f.* Philadelphia

Philippes, *m.* Philippi

Le Piémont, *m.* Piedmont

Le Pirée, *m.* the Piræus

Pise, *f.* Pisa

La Pologne, *f.* Poland

La Polynésie, *f.* Polynesia

La Poméranie, *f.* Pomerania

Pompée, *m.* Pompeii

Pondichéry, *m.* Pondicherry

Le Pont Euxin, *m.* the Euxine

Port Arthur, *m.* Port Arthur

Porto, *m.* Oporto

Le Portugal, *m.* Portugal

La Provence, *f.* Provence

Les Provinces Unies, *f.* the United Netherlands

La Prusse, *f.* Prussia

Les Pyrénées, *f.* the Pyrenees

Québec, *m.* Quebec

Ratisbonne, *f.* Ratisbon

Ravenne, *f.* Ravenna

Reims, *m.* Rheims

La Rhénanie, *f.* Rhineland

Le Rhin, *m.* the Rhine

Le Rhode Island, *m.* Rhode Island

La Rhodésia, *f.* Rhodesia

Le Rhône, *m.* the Rhone

La Romagne, *f.* the Romagna

Rome, *f.* Rome

La Roumanie, *f.* Rumania

La Russie, *f.* Russia

Le Sahara, *m.* the Sahara

Saint-Ange, *m.* Saint Angelo

Saint-Domingue, *m.* St. Domingo

Sainte-Hélène, *f.* Saint Helena

Sainte-Marie, *f.* Saint Mary's

Le Saint-Gothard, *m.* the Saint Gothard

Saint-Laurent, *m.* the Saint Laurence

Saint-Marin, *m.* San Marino

Salamanque, *f.* Salamanca

Salonique, *f.* Salonika

Samarie, *f.* Samaria

La Saône, *f.* the Saône

Saragosse, *f.* Saragossa

La Sardaigne, *f.* Sardinia

Sarre, *f.* the Saar

La Savoie, *f.* Savoy

La Saxe, *f.* Saxony

La Scandinavie, *f.* Scandinavia

La Seine, *f.* the Seine

Le Sénégal, *m.* Senegal

La Serbie, *f.* Serbia

Le Severn, *m.* the Severn

Le Siam, *m.* Siam

La Sibérie, *f.* Siberia

Sichem, *m.* Shechem

La Sicile, *f.* Sicily

Le Simplon, *m.* the Simplon

Le Sinaï, *m.* Sinai

La Slavonie, *f.* Slavonia

Smyrne, *f.* Smyrna

Sorlingues, *f.* (Les Îles), the Scilly Isles

Le Soudan, *m.* the Soudan

Sparte, *f.* Sparta

Le Spitzberg, *m.* Spitzbergen

Strasbourg, *m.* Strasburg

La Suède, *f.* Sweden

La Suisse, *f.* Switzerland

Supérieur, *m.* (Le Lac), Lake Superior

La Syrie, *f.* Syria

Le Tage, *m.* the Tagus

La Tamise, *f.* the Thames

Tanger, *m.* Tangiers

Tarse, *f.* Tarsus

La Tartarie, *f.* Tartary

La Tasmanie, *f.* Tasmania

Ténériffe, *f.* Teneriffe

Le Tennessée, *m.* Tennessee

La Terre de Feu, *f.* Tierra del Fuego

La Terre-Neuve, *f.* Newfoundland

Le Texas, *m.* Texas

Thèbes, *f.* Thebes

Les Thermopyles, *f.* Thermopylae

La Thessalie, *f.* Thessaly

La Thrace, *f.* Thrace

Le Tibet, *m.* Tibet

Le Tibre, *m.* the Tiber

Le Tigre, *m.* the Tigris

Tolède, *f.* Toledo

Tombouctou, *m.* Timbuctoo

Le Tonkin, *m.* Tonquin

La Toscane, *f.* Tuscany

Le Transvaal, *m.* the Transvaal

La Transylvanie, *f.* Transylvania

Le Trentin, *m.* the Trentino

Trèves, *f.* Trèves, Trier

La Tripolitaine, *f.* Tripoli

Troie, *f.* Troy

La Tunisie, *f.* Tunis

La Turquie, *f.* Turkey

Le Tyne, *m.* the Tyne

Tyr, *f.* Tyre

Le Tyrol, *m.* the Tyrol

Upsal, *m.* Upsala

Utique, *f.* Utica

La Valachie, *f.* Wallachia

Valence, *f.* Valencia

Varsovie, *f.* Warsaw

La Valette, *f.* Valetta

Vaud, *m.* Vaud

Venise, *f.* Venice

Vérone, *f.* Verona

Le Vésuve, *m.* Vesuvius

Vienne, *f.* Vienna

La Virginie, *f.* Virginia

La Vistule, *f.* the Vistula

Le Volga, *m.* the Volga

Les Vosges, *f.* the Vosges

La Westphalie, *f.* Westphalia

Le Wisconsin, *m.* Wisconsin

Xérès, *m.* Jerez

La Yougoslavie, *f.* Jugoslavia

Ypres, *f.* Ypres

La Zambesé, *f.* the Zambesi

La Zélande, *f.* Zealand (La Nouvelle -, New Zealand)

FRENCH WEIGHTS AND MEASURES

(with approximate English equivalents)

un millimètre	= $\frac{1}{25}$ of an inch (approx.)
un centimètre	= slightly less than $\frac{1}{2}$ inch
un décimètre	= about 4 inches
un mètre	= 3 feet 3 inches
un décamètre	= 11 yards (approx.)
un hectomètre	= $\frac{1}{16}$ of a mile (approx.)
un kilomètre	= 5 furlongs (approx.) : $\frac{5}{8}$ of a mile

un centiare (one sq. metre)	= 1·2 sq. yards
un are (100 sq. metres)	= 4 poles
un hectare (10,000 sq. metres)	= 2·47 acres

un centigramme	= 0·154 grain
un décigramme	= 1·54 grain
un gramme	= 15·43 grains
un décagramme	= $\frac{1}{3}$ oz. avoirdupois
un hectogramme	= 3·5 ounces
un kilogramme	= 2·2 lb.

un millilitre	= 17 minims
un centilitre	= 2 drams 50 minims
un décilitre	= 3 fluid ounces
un litre	= 1$\frac{3}{4}$ pints
un décalitre	= 2$\frac{1}{4}$ gallons
un hectolitre	= 22 gallons

REFERENCE TABLE OF PRINCIPAL IRREGULAR VERBS

Infinitive	Participles	Present Indicative	Past Definite	Future	Remarks
acquérir	acquérant acquis	j'acquiers, nous acquérons, ils acquièrent	j'acquis	j'acquerrai	so also: (re)conquérir, s'enquérir
aller	allant allé	je vais, tu vas, il va, nous allons, ils vont	j'allai	j'irai	Pres. Subj. j'aille, n. allions, ils aillent so also: s'en aller
assaillir	assaillant assailli	j'assaille, n. assaillons, ils assaillent	j'assaillis	j'assaillirai	Tressaillir; (re)cueillir and accueillir have future and conditional in -erai (-erais) *not* -irai(s)
s'asseoir	asseyant assis	assieds, assied, asseyons, asseyent	je m'assis	je m'assiéral	Pres. Subj. je m'asseye so also: se rasseoir
avoir	ayant eu	j'ai, tu as, il a, n. avons, ils ont	j'eus	j'aurai	Pres. Subj. j'aie, il ait, n. ayons, ils aient
battre	battant battu	je bats, il bat, n. battons, ils battent	je battis	je battrai	Pres. Subj. je batte so also: abattre, combattre, etc.
boire	buvant bu	je bois, il boit, n. buvons, ils boivent	je bus	je boirai	Pres. Subj. je boive, n. buvions, ils boivent so also: compounds
bouillir	bouillant bouilli	je bous, il bout, n. bouillons, ils bouillent	je bouillis	je bouillirai	Pres. Subj. je bouille
bruire	bruissant none	il bruit ils bruissent	not used	il bruira	bruyant is only used as adjective = noisy
clore	none clos	clos, clôt (no plural)	not used	je clorai	Pres. Subj. je close, n. closions, ils clos- ent

Infinitive	Participles	Present Indicative	Past Definite	Future	Remarks
conclure	concluant conclu	je conclus, il conclut, n. concluons, ils concluent	je conclus	je conclurai	so also: exclure; inclure and reclure have past participle inclus, reclus
conduire	conduisant conduit	je conduis, il conduit, n. conduisons, ils conduisent	je conduisis	je conduirai	so also: construire, séduire, reproduire, introduire. instruire, détruire, cuire, luire and nuire have past participle, lui and nui respectively
confire	confisant confit	je confis, il confit, n. confisons, ils confisent	je confis	je confirai	circoncire has past participle circoncis suffire has past part. suffi.
connaître	connaissant connu	je connais, il connaît, n. connaissons, ils connaissent	je connus	je connaîtrai	always î before t so also reconnaître, etc., and paraître and other verbs in aître, except naître paître lacks past part., past definite and imperf. subj.
coudre	cousant cousu	je couds, il coud, n. cousons, ils cousent	je cousis	je coudrai	Pres. Subj. je couse so also: recoudre, etc.
courir	courant couru	je cours, il court, n. courons, ils courent	je courus	je courrai	Pres. Subj. je coure so also: accourir and other compounds
couvrir	couvrant couvert	je couvre, n. couvrons, ils couvrent	je couvris	je couvrirai	so also ouvrir, découvrir, offrir and souffrir and their compounds
craindre	craignant craint	je crains, il craint, n. craignons	je craignis	je craindrai	Pres. Subj. je craigne so also: all verbs in -aindre, -eindre and -oindre

Infinitive	Participles	Present	Past Def.	Future	Remarks
croire	croyant, cru	je crois, il croit, n. croyons, ils croient	je crus	je croirai	Pres. Subj. je croie
croître	croissant, crû (f. crue)	je croîs, il croît, n. croissons, ils croissent	je crûs	je croîtrai	Pres. Subj. je croisse compounds omit the circumflex in past participle.
cueillir.	See assaillir and remarks none				
déchoir	déchu	je déchois, il déchoit, n. déchoyons, ils déchoient	je déchus	je décherrai	échoir (pres. part. échéant) is used in 3rd person only except in compound tenses choir is rarely used except in infinitive and in compound tenses
devoir	devant, dû (f. due)	je dois, il doit, n. devons, ils doivent	je dus	je devrai	Pres. Subj. je doive. Save for past part. masculine devoir is conjugated like recevoir
dire	disant, dit	je dis, il dit, n. disons, v. dites, ils disent	je dis	je dirai	so also: redire and other compounds (e.g. prédire) have -isez, not -ites, in 2nd person plural of pres. indicative and imperative maudire (past part. maudit) has fut. and cond. maudirai(s); in other tenses, e.g. present imperf. and past def., it resembles the regular verb finir

Infinitive	Participles	Present Indicative	Past Definite	Future	Remarks
dormir	dormant, dormi	je dors, il dort, n. dormons, ils dorment	je dormis	je dormirai	Pres. Subj. je dorme so also: compounds and partir, sentir, servir, sortir, mentir, etc., but ressortir and répartir follow the model of finir
écrire	écrivant, écrit	j'écris, il écrit, n. écrivons, ils écrivent	j'écrivis	j'écrirai	so also: décrire, inscrire, souscrire, etc.
envoyer	envoyant, envoyé	j'envoie, n. envoyons, ils envoient	j'envoyai	j'enverrai	verbs ending in -oyer and -uyer change y into i before a mute syllable; with verbs in -ayer this change is optional; verbs in -eyer make no such change
être	étant, été	je suis, tu es, il est, n. sommes, vous êtes, ils sont	je fus	je serai	Pres. Subj. je sois, il soit, n. soyons, ils soient Imperative sois, soyons, soyez
faillir	faillant, failli	je faux, il faut, n. faillons, ils faillent	je faillis	je faudrai or je faillirai	seldom used except in infinitive, past def. and compound tenses
faire	faisant, fait	je fais, il fait, n. faisons, v. faites, ils font	je fis	je ferai	Pres. Subj. je fasse so also: compounds, e.g. refaire, satisfaire
falloir (impersonal)	none, fallu	il faut	il fallut	il faudra	Pres. Subj. il faille Imp. ind. il fallait
fuir	fuyant, fui	je fuis, n. fuyons, ils fuient	je fuis	je fuirai	Pres. Subj. je fuie so also: s'enfuir

gésir	gisant none	il gît, n. gisons, ils gisent	none	none	Imperf. ind. je gisais only used in the forms shown. N.B.—ci-gît (" here lies "), epitaph
haïr	haïssant haï	je hais, il hait, n. haïssons, ils haïssent	je haïs	je haïrai	Pres. Subj. je haïsse. haïr has no diaeresis in singular of present and imperative; nor does it take a circumflex accent in past def. and imperf. subj. In other respects it is like finir
lire	lisant lu	je lis, n. lisons, ils lisent	je lus	je lirai	so also: élire, relire
luire. See conduire and remarks					
mettre	mettant mis	je mets, il met, n. mettons, ils mettent	je mis	je mettrai	Pres. Subj. je mette so also: admettre, etc.
moudre	moulant moulu	je mouds, il moud, n. moulons, ils moulent	je moulus	je moudrai	so also: émoudre, etc.
mourir	mourant mort	je meurs, n. mourons, ils meurent	je mourus	je mourrai	Pres. Subj. je meure, n. mourions, ils meurent
mouvoir	mouvant mû (f. mue)	je meus, il meut, n. mouvons, ils meuvent	je mus	je mouvrai	so also: émouvoir (but no circumflex in past participle)
naître	naissant né	je nais, il naît, n. naissons, ils naissent	je naquis	je naîtrai	circumflex over i before t

Infinitive	Participles	Present Indicative	Past Definite	Future	Remarks
paraître.	See connaître				
plaire	plaisant plu	je plais, il plaît, n. plaisons, ils plaisent	je plus	je plairai	so also: compounds taire is similarly conju- gated, but has no cir- cumflex in 3rd person sing. pres. ind.
pourvoir	pourvoyant pourvu	je pourvois, n. pourvoyons, ils pourvoient	je pourvus	je pourvoirai	Pres. Subj. je pourvoie
pouvoir	pouvant pu	je peux (je puis), il peut, n. pouvons, ils peuvent	je pus	je pourrai	Pres. Subj. je puisse
prendre	prenant pris	je prends, n. prenons, ils prennent	je pris	je prendrai	Pres. Subj. je prenne, n. prenions, ils prennent so also: apprendre, com- prendre and other com- pounds
résoudre	résolvant résous and résolu	je résous, il résout, n. résolvons, ils résolvent	je résolus	je résoudrai	Pres. Subj. je résolve absoudre and dissoudre have past part. absous (f. absoute) and dissous (dissoute) respectively. These two verbs are not used in past def. and imperf. subjunctive
rire	riant ri	je ris, il rit, n. rions, ils rient	je ris	je rirai	Pres. Subj. je rie, n. riions, ils rient so also: sourire

savoir	sachant, su	je sais, il sait, n. savons, ils savent	je sus	je saurai	Imperative sache, sachons, sachez, Pres. Subj. je sache, etc.
soufrir.	See couvrir				
suivre	suivant, suivi	je suis, il suit, n. suivons, ils suivent	je suivis	je suivrai	so also: poursuivre, s'ensuivre (impers.)
tenir	tenant, tenu	je tiens, il tient, n. tenons, ils tiennent	je tins, il tint, n. tînmes, v. tîntes, ils tinrent	je tiendrai	Pres. Subj. je tienne, n. tenions, ils tiennent. so also: appartenir, contenir and other compounds
traire	trayant, trait	je trais, il trait, n. trayons, ils traient	none	je trairai	Pres. Subj. je traie. so also: abstraire, distraire, extraire and soustraire
vaincre	vainquant, vaincu	je vaincs, il vainc, n. vainquons, ils vainquent	je vainquis	je vaincrai	Pres. Subj. je vainque. so also: convaincre
valoir	valant, valu	je vaux, il vaut, n. valons, ils valent	je valus	je vaudrai	Pres. Subj. je vaille, n. valions, ils vaillent. so also: équivaloir. prévaloir has pres. subj. je prévale, etc.
venir	venant, venu	je viens, il vient, n. venons, ils viennent	je vins, il vint, n. vînmes, v. vîntes, ils vinrent	je viendrai	so also: convenir, devenir and other compounds
vêtir	vêtant, vêtu	je vêts, il vêt, n. vêtons, ils vêtent	je vêtis	je vêtirai	so also: dévêtir and revêtir

Infinitive	Participles	Present Indicative	Past Definite	Future	Remarks
vivre	vivant, vécu	je vis, il vit, n. vivons, ils vivent	je vécus	je vivrai	so also: revivre and survivre
voir	voyant, vu	je vois, il voit, n voyons, ils voient	je vis	je verrai	so also: entrevoir and revoir; prévoir has future and conditional prévoirai(s), etc.; so has pourvoir, which also has past def. pourvus
vouloir	voulant, voulu	je veux, il veut, n. voulons, ils veulent	je voulus	je voudrai	Pres. Subj. je veuille, n. voulions, ils veuillent Imperative veuille, veuillez

SOME IDIOMS AND PHRASES

à • • •   *au mois de mai,* in (the month of) May
une machine à écrire, a typewriter
j'ai beaucoup de choses à faire, I have a great deal to do
c'est à vous de jouer, its your turn to play
ce livre est à moi, this book is mine
sa tante à elle, her aunt (i.e. not someone else's)
à la française, in the French style, or fashion
au secours! help!
ces choses se vendent à la douzaine, these things are sold by the dozen
je suis à vous, I am at your disposal
c'est gentil à vous, it's nice of you

abonner • •   *je suis abonné depuis longtemps au "Temps,"* I have taken *The Times* for a long while

s'accommoder   *je vous conseille de vous accommoder avec lui au plus tôt,* I advise you to come to terms (to an agreement) with him as soon as possible
on devrait apprendre à s'accommoder de tout, one ought to learn to put up with everything (i.e. to adapt oneself)

acheter •   *je le lui ai acheté,* I bought it from him
je vais lui acheter un cadeau, I am going to buy him a present

action • •   *cette belle action lui a valu une citation (à l'ordre du jour),* this brave action earned him a mention in despatches
action ordinaire (privilégiée), ordinary (preference) share
il est capable de vous intenter une action, he is quite capable of bringing an action against you

affaire • •   *la belle affaire!* is that all? (stuff and nonsense)
l'affaire est dans le sac, the matter is as good as settled (it's "in the bag")
mêlez-vous de vos affaires! mind your own business!
vous allez vous attirer une mauvaise affaire, you'll get into a mess (a lot of trouble)
cela fera mon affaire, that will suit me
ne vous inquiétez pas, j'en ferai mon affaire, don't worry, I'll look after that (I'll take on the job myself)
cela ne fait rien à l'affaire, that has nothing to do with it
vous avez affaire à un ennemi redoutable, you're up against (dealing with) a formidable opponent

âge. • •   *quel âge lui donnez-vous?* what age do you put him at?
le moyen âge, the Middle Ages
un homme d'âge mûr } a middle-aged man
un homme entre deux âges

air • • *il a un faux air de...*, he has a faint resemblance to...
il y a un courant d'air, there's a draught
il a l'air distingué, he looks distinguished

aise • • *à cette nouvelle l'enfant ne se sentit pas d'aise*, the child was overjoyed at this news
je suis bien aise de faire votre connaissance, I am so pleased to make your acquaintance
à votre aise, just as you like

aller • • *comment ça va?* how goes it? how are you?
comment allez-vous? how are you? (less familiar than *comment ça va?*)
ce chapeau lui va bien, that hat suits her
cela va de soi, that goes without saying, that stands to reason
allons-y! come on! here goes!
vous n'y allez pas par quatre chemins, you don't beat about the bush, you don't mince your words
il y va de sa vie, his life is at stake
allons donc! nonsense! (i.e. expressing incredulity or impatience)
il est allé jusqu'à, he went so far as to..., to the length of...

appeler • *je l'ai appelé à m'aider*, I called on him (invited him) to help me
j'en appelle à vous, I appeal to you

apprendre • *je lui apprendrai à...*, I will teach him (show him how) to...
je viens d'apprendre que..., I have just heard that...

après • • *après avoir écouté ce discours, il partit*, after listening to this speech, he went away
d'après ce qu'il m'a dit, according to what he told me
bientôt après, soon after(wards)
après qu'il fut parti, after he had left
après son arrivée, after his arrival

argent • *mais, je vous assure qu'il est tout cousu d'argent*, but, I give you my word, he's rolling in money
argent comptant, ready money

arracher • *on se l'arrache*, they're all after him, he's in great demand
il faut que je me fasse arracher cette dent de sagesse, I must have this wisdom tooth (pulled) out

arranger • *il m'a arrangé de la belle façon*, he gave me a proper dressing down
cela s'arrangera, that will settle itself, that can be managed somehow

arriver • • *en arriver à...*, (1) to get to the stage of..., (2) to be reduced to...
il n'arrivera jamais à rien, he'll never get anywhere (i.e. achieve anything of importance)
je ne faisais que d'arriver, I had only just arrived
qu'est-ce qui est arrivé? what's happened?

assez • • *vous êtes assez riche pour...,* you're rich enough to...
avez-vous assez d'argent? have you sufficient money?
j'en ai assez, (1) I have sufficient, (2) I've had
enough of it!

assiette • • *elle ne se sentait pas dans son assiette,* she was not
feeling up to the mark

attendre • *je ne m'y attendais pas,* I wasn't expecting it
je m'attendais à ce qu'il vînt, I was expecting him to
come
je suis fâché de vous avoir fait attendre, I'm sorry to
have kept you waiting
j'attendrai (jusqu'à ce) qu'il vienne, I shall wait till
he comes

auprès • • *auprès de vous,* compared with you
il a fait une démarche auprès du gouvernement, he
approached the government (i.e. made repre-
sentations)

autant • • *autant dire que...,* you might as well say that...
c'est autant de gagné, that's so much to the good
*je suis d'autant plus étonné de son retour que je le
croyais parti pour de bon,* I am the more amazed
at his return as I thought he had gone for good

autre • • *comme dit l'autre,* as the saying is
à d'autres! rubbish! (tell that to the marines!)
ni l'un ni l'autre, neither of them
nous autres marins, we sailors
nous en avons vu bien d'autres, we've been through
worse things than this (this isn't the first time
things like this have happened to us)
c'est (tout) autre chose, that's a different matter

avancer • • *votre montre avance de cinq minutes,* your watch is
five minutes fast
les troupes alliées avancent rapidement vers..., the
allied troops are advancing rapidly towards...
j'ai une idée à avancer, I have an idea to put forward

avant • • *avant de partir,* before leaving
avant que vous (ne) partiez, before you leave
avant demain, before to-morrow
bien avant dans la nuit, far into the night
en avant, in front; forward!

avis • • *avis au public!* notice to the public!
à mon avis, in my opinion
m'est avis que..., it strikes me that..., it's my
opinion that...
changer d'avis, to change one's mind

avoir • • *qu'avez-vous?* what's the matter with you?
il en a contre (à) sa cousine, he's angry with (has a
grudge against) his cousin
elle eut un mouvement de colère, she made an angry
movement
il y a du monde! there are a lot of people!
il a dix ans, he's ten years old

son cachot avait dix pieds de long sur huit de large, his cell was ten feet long and (by) eight wide

elle avait les cheveux blonds, she had fair hair

bas. ● ● *il parlait (tout) bas,* he was whispering

il est mort en bas âge, he died young (i.e. before he was grown up)

ils ont fait main basse sur la ville, they looted the town

en bas de l'échelle, at the foot of the ladder

malheureusement j'ai la vue basse, unfortunately I am shortsighted

à bas les tyrans! down with the tyrans!

la garnison mit bas les armes, the garrison laid down their arms

beau ● ● *bel et bien battu,* fairly and squarely beaten

vous l'avez échappé belle, you've had a narrow escape

le temps se met au beau, it's clearing up, going to be fine

il fait beau (temps), it's fine

le beau monde, the rank and fashion, " society "

tout cela est bel et bon, that's all very fine

vous avez beau parler, vous ne me convaincrez pas de votre sincérité, it's useless (in vain) for you to talk, you will not convince me of your sincerity

vous voilà dans de beaux draps! you're in a fine mess! (i.e. a predicament)

bien ● ● *eh bien, que voulez-vous que je fasse?* well, what do you want me (expect me) to do?

êtes-vous bien là? are you comfortable there?

il est très bien, ce jeune homme, that young man is very attractive (*or* good looking *or* presentable)

est-ce bien lui? is it really he?

bien que je ne le connaisse que de vue, although I only know him by sight

tant bien que mal, somehow or other, after a fashion

bien entendu, of course, naturally

il est du dernier bien avec le capitaine, he is on very good terms (extremely intimate) with the captain

il va très bien (se porte très bien), he is very well (i.e. in health)

j'ai eu bien du mal à..., I had great difficulty in...

bois ● ● *je ne sais (plus) de quel bois faire flèche,* I don't know which way to turn, I'm at my wits' end

je vais vous faire voir de quel bois je me chauffe, I'll show you the stuff I'm made of (what manner of man I am)

bon ● ● *cela est bon à dire,* that's easy enough to say (i.e. but to do it is another matter)

il fait bon ici, it's nice (snug) here

à quoi bon? what's the good (of it)?

le bon de l'affaire, c'est..., the best part of the business is...

elle est bonne (mauvaise), (at tennis) it's in the court, (out of court, a fault)

est-ce pour de bon? you mean it? seriously?

bouche
c'est une fine bouche, he's an epicure
une bouche d'incendie, (fire) hydrant
cela m'a fait venir l'eau à la bouche, it made my mouth water

bout
sa patience est encore une fois à bout, his patience is again exhausted
je suis à bout de forces, I'm exhausted
il n'a mangé que du bout des lèvres, he merely pecked at his food, made a show of eating
nous sommes à bout d'essence, we're out of petrol (gas)
au bout de la rue (semaine), at the end of the street (week)
puis-je vous pousser un bout de chemin? can I give you a lift?

ça (cela)
c'est ça, that's it, that's right
comme ci comme ça, so-so (in health)
comme ça, like that ; and so
il n'y a que cela, there's nothing like it
qu'est-ce que c'est que ça (cela)? what is that?

carte
je vous donne carte blanche, I give you a free hand (i.e. to take what steps seem best)
il connaît le dessous des cartes, he is in the know
il tirait (faisait) les cartes à son oncle, he was telling his uncle's fortune
la carte des vins, the wine list

cas
je fais grand cas de lui, I have a high opinion of him
au cas où..., in the event of...
le cas échéant..., should it so happen...
en ce cas, in that case

casser
se casser la tête, to rack one's brains
à tout casser, terrific, rare old (row, dinner, spree, etc., according to context)

charger
je me charge de cela, I'll look after that, I'll see to that
une lettre chargée, a registered letter

chemin
chemin faisant, on the way
je n'y vais pas par quatre chemins, I don't beat about the bush, I'll come straight to the point
il fera son chemin, celui-là, he'll get on in the world, he will.
voulez-vous m'indiquer le chemin de la gare? will you direct me to the station?
permettez-moi de faire un bout de chemin avec vous, let me go with you for a bit of the way

cœur
il n'a pas de cœur, he is hard-hearted, has no feelings
au fond du cœur, in one's heart of hearts
de bon (grand) cœur, gladly, willingly
je me sentais le cœur gros, I was heavy-hearted

je veux en avoir le cœur net, (1) I want to make a clean breast of it, (2) I must get to the bottom of it

avoir (prendre) à cœur de..., to set one's heart on, be bent on...

de gaieté de cœur, wantonly, thoughtlessly

à cœur joie, to one's heart's content

comme • • *qu'est-ce que vous avez comme fruits?* what have you in the way of fruit?

comme il est content! how pleased he is!

c'est tout comme, it comes to the same thing

comme ci comme ça, so-so

comme dans un rêve, as though in a dream

comme vous voudrez, as you like

un homme comme il faut, a perfect gentleman

compte • • *en fin de compte (tout compte fait)*, all things considered, taking everything into account

je tiens le plus grand compte de cet événement, I attach the greatest importance to this event

je vais régler son compte, I'll settle his hash

tenir les comptes, to keep the accounts

je me rends compte de cela, I realise, understand that

compter • • *sans compter...*, not to mention...

à compter du huit mai, reckoning as from May 8th

je compte sur vous, I count (rely) on you

je compte le faire bientôt, I intend (expect) to do it soon

connaissance • *une dame de ma connaissance*, a lady of my acquaintance

il a perdu (repris) connaissance, he lost (regained) consciousness

sans connaissance, unconscious

j'ai fait connaissance avec lui il y a quelques ans, I got to know him (made his acquaintance) some years ago

en connaissance de cause, (1) in full knowledge of the matter, (2) on good grounds

connaître • *on ne lui connaît pas d'amis*, he is not known to have any friends

je le connais de vue (de réputation), I know him by sight (by repute)

connu! that's an old story!

je crois me connaître en peinture, I (like to) think I'm a good judge of painting

il est bien connu, he is well known

corps • • *un corps-à-corps*, a hand-to-hand struggle

à son corps défendant, reluctantly, against one's will (or judgment)

vous avez pris du corps, you've put on flesh

côté • • *à côté de*, beside, next to

le côté cour (jardin), right (left) side of the stage

il a un petit appartement de l'autre côté de la rue, he has a small flat on the other side of (across) the street

de mon côté, for my part
voilà son côté faible, that's his weak spot
de quel côté est la cathédrale? whereabouts is the cathedral?

coup • • *il m'a fait un sale coup,* he played a dirty trick on me
ils en sont venus aux coups, they came to blows
à coup sûr, for certain, assuredly
du coup, at once
il faut donner un coup de collier, we must make a supreme effort
un coup de tête, an ill-considered (desperate) action
il a fait d'une pierre deux coups, he killed two birds with one stone

couper • • *je vais me faire couper les cheveux,* I'm going to get my hair cut
il m'a coupé la parole, he interrupted me, cut me short
ne me coupez pas, mademoiselle! don't cut me off, operator!
couper au plus court, to take a short cut

coûter • • *ces bas de soie (lui) ont coûté les yeux de la tête,* these silk stockings cost her a mint of money
coûte que coûte, at all costs
il lui en coûta de renoncer à son projet, it was with reluctance that he gave up his scheme

croire • • *à ce que je crois,* to the best of my belief
c'est à ne pas y croire! it passes belief!
je vous croyais plus intelligent, I thought you had more sense
je crois le voir venir, I think I see him coming
je crois que vous avez tort, I believe you're wrong
je le crois bien! I should just think so!

dans • • *il est dans l'enseignement,* he is in the teaching profession
il prit un mouchoir dans sa poche, he took a handkerchief out of his pocket
boire dans un verre, to drink out of a glass
nous partirons dans deux heures, we shall start in two hours (from now)
en deux heures, in (i.e. within) two hours
en Amérique, in America
dans l'Amérique du Nord, in North America

date • • *vous vous trompez de date,* you're making a mistake about the date

dater • • *à dater du vingt courant,* on and after the 20th inst.

de • • *âgé de vingt ans,* twenty years old
si j'étais de lui, if I were in his place
cela ne présage rien de bon, that bodes nothing good
long de six pouces, six inches long

déclarer • *déclarer pique,* to call spades
c'est un athée déclaré, he is an avowed atheist

dedans • • *on lui a dressé un piège et il a donné dedans*, they set a trap for him and he fell into it
au dedans et au dehors, inside and out

défaut • • *sans défaut*, faultless, flawless
au défaut de, for lack of, failing
c'est un défaut grave, it's a grave defect

défendre. • *il est défendu aux messieurs les voyageurs de...*, travellers are forbidden to...
l'ennemi se tenait sur la défensive, the enemy was on the defensive
défense (absolue) d'entrer, no admittance

dehors • • *sous les dehors de*, under the cloak (mask) of
malgré ses vingt ans de service(s) on le mit dehors, despite his 20 years of service he was dismissed

demander • *on demande petit commissionnaire*, errand-boy wanted
je vous demande un peu! I ask you! did you ever!
il ne demandait pas mieux, he asked nothing better (i.e. it was just what he wanted)

démarche • *l'ambassadeur a fait une démarche auprès du Ministre des Affaires étrangères*, the Ambassador has approached the Foreign Secretary on the matter

demi • • *une demi-heure*, half an hour
une heure et demie, an hour and a half
il n'est pas bête, il entend à demi-mot, he's no fool, he can take a hint
un demi-litre, half a litre; in asking for beer, *un demi* is sufficient by itself

démordre • *elle n'en démordra pas*, she won't change her opinion, go back on her decision

dent • • *il n'a pas desserré les dents de toute la journée*, he has not opened his mouth (said a word) all day
je vais passer chez X pour me faire arracher une dent, I'm going to see X to have a tooth out
manger à belles dents, to eat hungrily, heartily

dépasser • *on lui a dressé une contravention parce qu'il a dépassé la limite de vitesse*, he had to appear in court for exceeding the speed-limit
cela me dépasse, that beats me (I can't understand it)

dernier • • *ce dernier*, the latter
le dernier des hommes, the most contemptible of men
dernières nouvelles, latest news; stop press
en dernier ressort, in the last resort

descendre • *je suis descendu au " Cheval Blanc,"* I am staying at, have put up at, the " White Horse "
faites descendre les bagages de monsieur, bring this gentleman's luggage down
il a descendu l'escalier, he came down the stairs

dessous • • *bras dessus bras dessous*, arm in arm
il voit bien le dessous des cartes, he's in the know

dessus • • *un dessus de lit*, a bedspread
le dessus du panier, the pick of the basket

destination • un paquebot à destination de..., a liner bound for...
cette lettre est à sa destination, this letter is addressed to him

dette • • il est criblé de dettes, he is heavily in debt

devant • • il commence à bâtir sur le devant, he's beginning to put on flesh

devenir • que deviendrons-nous? what will become of us?

devoir • • j'ai cru devoir me lever, I thought it advisable to get up
je voudrais rendre mes devoirs à, I should like to pay my respects to
vous devez être fatigué, you must be tired
dût-il revenir je ne le reverrais plus, even were he to return, I should not see him again

diable • • du diable si je le fais! I'm hanged if I'll do it!
que le diable vous emporte! confound you!
un bruit de tous les diables se fit entendre, a deuce of a noise broke out

dire • • cela ne me dit rien, that doesn't appeal (mean a thing) to me
dites donc! look here! I say!
et dire que...! and to think that...!
il n'y a pas à dire, there's no denying
je ne croyais pas si bien dire, I had no idea I (what I said) was so near the mark
je vous le disais bien! I told you so!

doigt • • mon petit doigt me l'a dit, a little bird told me
vous avez mis le doigt dessus, you've put your finger on it (you've hit it)
nous étions à deux doigts de la mort, we were within an ace (an inch) of death

donc • • (often used for emphasis) venez donc! do come!

donner • • étant donné que..., inasmuch as...
quel âge lui donnez-vous? how old would you say he is?
ma chambre donne sur la cour, my room looks on to the courtyard
c'est donné, it's dirt cheap (given away)

dormir • • un conte à dormir debout, (1) a tedious story, (2) a cock-and-bull story
je n'ai pas dormi de toute la nuit, I didn't get a wink of sleep

dos. • • je n'ai rien à me mettre sur le dos, I haven't a rag to wear
j'en ai plein le dos, I'm fed up with it

eau. • • porter de l'eau à la mer, to carry coals to Newcastle
nager entre deux eaux, to swim under water, also to run with the hare and hunt with the hounds
le temps est à l'eau, it's rainy weather
prendre les eaux, to take the waters (at a spa)

échapper • vous l'avez échappé belle, you've had a narrow shave
échapper à la mort, to escape death
s'échapper d'une prison, to escape from a prison

école • • *faire l'école buissonnière,* to play truant
école normale, training college for teachers
faire école, to found a school, be leader of a movement in art or literature

égal • • *cela m'est égal,* it's all one to me, doesn't matter to me

égard • • *à l'égard de,* with regard (respect) to
il l'a fait par égard pour vous, he did it out of consideration for you

empêcher • • *que cela ne vous empêche pas d'agir à votre guise,* don't let that prevent you from doing as you like
c'est un empêcheur de danser en rond, he's a kill-joy

en • • *en été,* in summer
en forgeant on devient forgeron, practice makes perfect
il arriva en courant, he came running up
où en étions-nous? where had we got to? (in the story, etc.)

ensemble • *dans l'ensemble,* on the whole
le tout ensemble, the general effect, the whole

entre • • *entre deux âges,* middle-aged
l'un d'entre vous est menteur, one of you is a liar
entre autres choses, je vous prie de prendre bonne note de..., among other things, I beg you to take due note of...

entrer • • *défense d'entrer!* no admittance!
entrer en matière, to broach the subject, embark on a discourse
faites entrer le monsieur, show the gentleman in

envie • • *j'ai eu envie de rire,* I wanted to laugh

épreuve • *c'est un ami à toute épreuve,* he is a friend one can rely on
cette épreuve est en bon à tirer, this proof is ready for the press
pour m'assurer de sa loyauté je vais mettre son amitié à l'épreuve, to make certain of his loyalty, I am going to put his friendship to the test
un abri à l'épreuve des bombes, a bomb-proof shelter

espèce • • *allez-vous-en, espèce de gredin!* clear out, you scoundrel!
la Chambre a approuvé le payement en espèces de cette somme, the House approved the payment in cash (*not* in kind) of this sum
l'espèce humaine, the human species, mankind

estomac • *je crois qu'il a de l'estomac,* I think he has courage ("guts")
après avoir marché pendant deux heures, il se sentit l'estomac dans les talons, after walking for two hours, he felt ravenously hungry

état • • *cet état de choses ne peut durer longtemps,* this state of things cannot go on for long
ce cheval n'est plus en état de travailler, this horse is no longer fit to work

le général fit grand état de ses subordonnés, the general had a high opinion of his subordinates
un homme d'état, a statesman
le tiers état, the third estate, i.e. the common people

façon   •   •   *pas de façons, je vous en prie,* do not stand on ceremony, I beg
c'est une façon de parler, it's a manner of speaking
de cette façon, in this way, thus
je l'ai arrangé de la belle façon, I gave him a proper talking to (dressing down)
il parlait de telle façon que je ne l'ai pas compris, he was talking in such an (odd) way that I could not understand him

faire   •   •   *c'est à vous de faire (les cartes),* it's your turn to deal
je me suis fait faire un nouvel habit, I have had a new coat made for me
le long de la route nationale il faisait toujours du cent à l'heure, along the main road he always travelled at a hundred (kms.) per hour
il ne faisait que d'arriver chez lui, he had only just got home
ça ne fait rien, it doesn't matter
il fait dans les textiles, he's in the textile trade
qu'est-ce que cela me fait (à moi)? what does that matter to me?
réflexion faite, all things considered, on second thoughts
faites donc! go ahead! carry on!
je n'aime pas les vêtements tout faits, I don't care for ready-made clothes
cela fera mon affaire, that will suit me, that's just what I want
combien cela fait-il? how much does that come to?
c'en est fait d'elle, it's all up with her
rien n'y fit, nothing was any good, it was all to no purpose
il ne se le fit pas dire deux fois, he needed no second bidding
on peut se faire à tout, one can get used to anything

falloir   •   •   *il s'en faut de beaucoup,* far from it
peu s'en fallut qu'il ne le tuât, he all but killed him
il m'a fallu beaucoup de temps pour..., it took me a long time to...
c'est un monsieur très comme il faut, he's a very gentlemanly person
il fallait l'entendre! you ought to have heard it!
il faut $\left\{ \begin{array}{l} \textit{nous dépêcher} \\ \textit{que nous nous dépêchions} \end{array} \right\}$ we must hurry

faux   •   •   *chanter faux,* to sing out of tune
il a un petit air de faux bonhomme, there's a slightly shifty look about him
je m'inscris en faux contre cette accusation, I emphatically deny this accusation

nous avons fait fausse route, we've taken the wrong road

fenêtre • • *en regardant par la fenêtre, j'ai vu passer la plupart d'une division blindée,* while looking out of the window I saw the better part of an armoured division go by

il vaut mieux faire des économies que de jeter son argent par la fenêtre, it is better to save one's money than play ducks and drakes with it

feu • • • *avez-vous du feu, monsieur?* can you give me a light?

il a mis (le) feu à la maison, he has set fire to the house

la maison a pris feu, the house has caught fire

faire feu, to fire

faire feu sur, to shoot at

feu de joie (d'artifice), bonfire (fireworks)

fil • • • *vous me faites perdre le fil de mes idées,* you're making me lose the thread of my ideas

monsieur X est au bout du fil, Mr. X is on the phone (i.e. wanting to speak to you)

il m'a donné bien du fil à retordre, he caused me no end of trouble

fil de fer (barbelé), (barbed) wire

fin • • • *à la fin du compte,* to cut a long story short

il ferait n'importe quoi pour (en) arriver à ses fins, he would do anything to gain his ends

il espère avant longtemps mener l'affaire à bonne fin, he hopes before long to bring the matter to a successful conclusion

force • • *de toutes ses forces,* with all one's might

à force de, by dint of

je l'ai forcé à tomber d'accord, I compelled him to agree

il fut forcé d'y consentir, he was forced to consent to it

il a fait un atterrissage forcé, he made a forced landing

un tour de force, a feat of exceptional strength (*or* skill)

frais • • *moi, j'ai fait tous les frais de la conversation,* I bore the whole burden of the conversation (I kept the conversation going)

eh bien, vous en êtes pour vos frais, well, you've had your trouble for nothing (have lost your money for nothing)

c'est à peine si je couvrirai mes frais, I shall barely cover expenses

frapper • • *il fut frappé de stupeur,* he was dumbfounded

du champagne frappé, iced champagne

on frappe, someone's knocking

froid • • *il n'a pas froid aux yeux, celui-là,* he's got plenty of nerve (*or* cheek)

il sembla à X qu'on lui battait froid, X had the impression that he was being cold-shouldered

garde(r) • • *garde à vous!* attention!
prenez garde de ne pas être en retard, take care not to be late
je vous assure que je l'ai fait sans y prendre garde, I assure you I did it unintentionally
il n'est pas précisément malade, mais il garde sa chambre, he's not exactly ill, but he's keeping to his room
je me garderai bien de l'offenser, I shall take good care not to offend him

goutte • • *la nuit était tellement obscure que je n'y voyais goutte,* it was so dark that I couldn't see a thing
goutte à goutte, drop by drop

grâce • • *de grâce!* for pity's sake!
je vous ferai grâce du reste, I will let you off the rest

guise • • *il fait (agit) toujours à sa guise,* he always goes his own way (behaves as he likes)

habitude • • *comme d'habitude,* as usual
il a pris récemment l'habitude de..., he has got into the habit lately of...

haleine • • *retenir son haleine,* to hold one's breath
perdre haleine, to get out of breath
un ouvrage (travail) de longue haleine, a long job, voluminous or exacting piece of work

hasard • • *par hasard,* by chance
au hasard, at random
un coup de hasard, a stroke of luck, fluke

heure • • *à la bonne heure!* well and good! capital! well done!
de bonne heure, early
à mes heures perdues, in my leisure moments, at odd times
tout à l'heure, just now, presently
à tout à l'heure! see you later!

histoire • • *histoire de rire,* for a joke, for the fun of the thing
c'est toujours la même histoire, it's the old story
en voilà des histoires (pour si peu de chose)! what a fuss (about nothing)!

honneur • • *faire les honneurs,* to do the honours
je me ferai honneur de..., I shall be proud to...
j'ai l'honneur de vous faire part de..., I beg to inform you of...
faire honneur à ses obligations, to meet one's obligations

hors • • *hors de combat,* out of action
hors concours, unrivalled, beyond competition
être hors de soi, to be beside oneself (with rage)
hors lui, il n'y avait personne qui..., except for him there was no one who...

idée • • *vous vous faites des idées,* you're imagining things
il n'est plus jeune, mais il a encore ses idées, there's life in the old dog yet
en voilà une idée! did you ever!
une idée fixe, an obsession

intention • *j'ai l'intention de...*, I intend to...

intérêt • *méfiez-vous des hommes politiques, ils ont toujours un intérêt en jeu*, beware of politicians, they always have an axe to grind

intérêt simple (composé), simple (compound) interest

il est de votre intérêt de..., it is in your own interest to...

jamais • • *au grand jamais!* never! (emphatic)

mieux vaut tard que jamais! better late than never!

jambe • • *ils s'enfuirent à toutes jambes*, they took to their heels (ran off at full speed)

il prit ses jambes à son cou, he showed a clean pair of heels

jeter • • *il jeta un regard scrutateur sur...*, he looked searchingly at...

jeter un cri, to utter a cry

ce petit ruisseau se jette dans la Tamise, this little stream flows into the Thames

le malheureux se jeta par la fenêtre, the poor wretch threw himself out of the window

jeu • • *à beau jeu, beau retour*, one good turn deserves another

faites vos jeux, put down your stakes

c'est vieux jeu, that's out of date, old-fashioned

un jeu de cartes, a pack (*not* a game) of cards

je crois voir clair dans son jeu, I think I can see through his little game

joie • • *feu de joie*, bonfire

c'est un monsieur très serviable qui se fera une joie de vous aider, he is an obliging man who will delight in helping you

jour • • *il y a beau jour qu'il ne vient plus ici*, he stopped coming here a good while ago

du jour au lendemain, at a moment's notice

je viens de donner ses huit jours à la bonne, I've just given the maid a week's notice

langue • • *elle a la langue bien pendue*, she has the gift of the gab

c'est une mauvaise langue, he's a scandalmonger

donner sa langue aux chiens, to give up guessing

la langue verte, slang

large • • *le sentier n'a que deux mètres de large* ⎫
le sentier n'est large que de deux mètres ⎬ the path is only two yards wide ⎭

il y a gros à parier qu'il n'en menait pas large à ce moment-là, it's long odds that he felt very small (cut a sorry figure) at that moment

il se promenait fiévreusement de long en large, he was walking feverishly up and down

latin • • *j'y perds mon latin*, it beats me, I can't make head or tail of it

lettre • • *au pied de la lettre*, literally

il a des lettres, he is well read

lit . . . *il est un peu souffrant et garde le lit depuis trois jours,* he is seedy and has been in bed three days

chambre à un (deux) lit(s), single (double) room

un lit d'ami, a spare bed

un enfant du second lit, a child of the second marriage

main . . *les Allemands ont fait main basse sur la ville,* the Germans looted the town

un ami de longue main, a friend of long standing

nous étions sur le point d'en venir aux mains, we were about to come to blows

je vous donnerai volontiers un coup de main, I'll gladly lend you a hand

j'en mettrais la main au feu, I could swear to it

vous n'y allez pas de main morte, you don't do things by halves (you put your back into it)

serrer la main à ⎫ to shake hands
donner une poignée de main à ⎬ with

manquer . *il ne manquait plus que cela!* it only needed that! (it's the last straw!)

je veillerai à ce que vous ne manquiez de rien, I shall see to it that you want for nothing

manquer à sa parole (son devoir), to break one's word (fail in one's duty)

vous avez manqué une belle occasion, you've missed a fine opportunity

marché . . *le marché noir,* the black market

par-dessus le marché, into the bargain

vous en êtes quitte à bon marché, you got off lightly

à meilleur marché, cheaper

marque . *marque de commerce,* trade mark

une des meilleures marques, one of the best makes (brands)

mèche . *il est de mèche avec les conspirateurs,* he is hand in glove with (in league with) the plotters

mémoire . *si j'ai bonne mémoire,* if I remember aright

mettre . *combien de temps mettez-vous pour aller à...?* how long do you reckon it takes to go to...?

on m'a mis dedans, I've been fooled (taken in)

mettre le couvert, to lay the table

mettons que vous n'avez rien dit, let's consider that unsaid

elle est toujours bien mise, she is always well dressed

le temps de mettre mon chapeau et je suis à vous, just a minute while I put on my hat and I'll be ready (at your disposal)

moins . . *moins que vous,* less than you

moins de dix francs, less than ten francs

en moins de rien, in less than no time

au moins, at least (i.e. not less than)

du moins, at least (i.e. at all events)

à moins que vous ne lui obéissiez, unless you obey him

moitié • • *je suis de moitié avec vous dans l'affaire,* I'll go halves with you in the deal
acheter à moitié prix, to buy at half-price

monter • • *c'est un coup monté,* it's a put up job
voulez-vous faire monter (descendre) les bagages, will you bring up (down) the luggage
c'est un monte en l'air, joli métier! he's a cat burglar, a fine profession!
elle est très collet monté, she's very prim (straitlaced)
monter sur un arbre, to climb a tree
monter à cheval (à bicyclette), to ride a horse (a bicycle)

nez • • *il m'a dans le nez,* he can't stand me (I get under his skin)
elle mène son mari par le bout du nez, she leads her husband by the nose
il faut qu'il fourre son nez (or son doigt) partout, he must poke his nose into everything (have a finger in every pie)
piquer du nez, to nose-dive

noir • • *il voit tout en noir,* he always looks on the dark side
être dans une misère noire, to be in abject poverty
il fait noir (comme dans un four), it's (pitch) dark

nuit • • *elle n'a pas dormi de toute la nuit,* she did not close her eyes all night
passer une nuit blanche, to spend a sleepless night

obliger • • *je l'ai obligé à s'exécuter,* I compelled him to pay up
il fut obligé de partir aussitôt, he was compelled to leave at once

œil • • *en entendant cette nouvelle elle a ouvert de grands yeux,* on hearing this news, she opened her eyes wide
mon tailleur m'a coûté les yeux de la tête, my tailor made cost me a fortune
à vue d'œil, visibly
ils se consultèrent de l'œil, they exchanged glances
il fit de l'œil à la petite, he made eyes at the girl
cela saute aux yeux, that's obvious

ordre • • *jusqu'à nouvel ordre,* until further notice
ordre du jour, order of the day (military); agenda (committee, etc.)
étant un homme prudent il commença de mettre ordre à ses affaires, being a prudent man he began to put his affairs in order
l'Ordre de la Jarretière, the Order of the Garter
un hôtel de tout premier ordre, a really first-class hotel

oreille • • *je vous conseille de faire la sourde oreille à ses plaintes,* I advise you to turn a deaf ear to his complaints
je crois qu'elle a l'oreille dure, I think she's hard of hearing
dresser (tendre) l'oreille, to prick up one's ears

il va revenir l'oreille basse, he'll come back crestfallen (with his tail between his legs)

par. • • *deux fois par mois*, twice a month
par ici, monsieur, this way, sir
par le temps qu'il fait, in this weather
elle regardait par la fenêtre, she was looking out of the window
il le fait par amitié, he does it out of friendship

paraître. • • *un roman qui vient de paraître chez Flammarion*, a novel just published by Flammarion
à ce qu'il paraît, apparently, as it appears
il paraît que..., it seems that

parler • • *moi qui vous parle*, I, myself (emphatic)
n'en parlons plus, let's say no more about it
parler boutique, to talk shop
j'en ai entendu parler, I've heard (tell) of it
un film parlant, "talkie"

parole • • *manquer de parole* (or *à sa parole*), to break faith (one's word)
demander la parole, to ask leave to speak
le parole est à vous, it is your turn to speak (you have the floor)

parti • • *il a pris le parti de...*, he made up his mind to...
c'est un bon parti, he (she) is a good match (i.e. eligible party in marriage)
agir de parti pris, to act deliberately (or with bias)
il sait tirer parti de tout, he can turn anything to good account

partir • • *j'ai maille à partir avec lui*, I have a bone to pick with him
à partir de demain, (starting) from to-morrow
la voilà partie, now she's off
le train est parti, the train has started (gone)

penser • • *je pense à lui*, I am thinking of him
que pensez-vous de lui? what is your opinion of him?
je pense (crois) que oui, I think (believe) so

permettre • • *je lui ai permis de s'en aller*, I allowed him (gave him permission) to go
permettez! excuse me! allow me!
si le temps le permet, weather permitting
elle se croit tout permis, she thinks she can do whatever she likes

piece • • *deux francs (la) pièce*, two francs each
une petite maison de cinq pièces, a little five-roomed house
une pièce de théâtre, a play
la pièce a fait four, the play was a "flop" (i.e. failed)
une pièce de dix francs, a ten-franc piece

pied • • *j'ai le pied marin, dieu merci!* I'm a good sailor, thank goodness!
le pied lui manqua, he lost his footing
je devrai faire le pied de grue, I shall have to hang about (i.e. waiting for someone)

il a un pied-à-terre tout près d'ici, he has a little place close by

un coup de pied, a kick

place(r) • • *au Casino on est bien placé pour vingt francs*, you can get a good seat for 20 francs at the Casino

faites place, s'il vous plaît, make way, please

une voiture de place, a hackney carriage

une voiture à quatre places, a four-seater

elle ne pouvait pas tenir en place, she couldn't keep still

à votre place, j'accepterais, if I were you, I should accept

j'ai trouvé une place chez..., I've got a job with...

plus • • *de plus en plus*, more and more

plus ou moins, more or less

une vue des plus magnifiques, a splendid view (sight)

ni moi non plus, neither do (am, have) I

de plus, moreover

une semaine de plus, a week longer, a week extra

nous ne le reverrons plus, we shall never see him again

(tout) au plus, at the (very) most

point • • *mettre au point*, to adjust, perfect, tune (engine)

vous arrivez à point nommé, you've come in the nick of time

le rôti est cuit à point, the meat is done to a turn

au point où en est l'affaire, as matters stand

porter • • *tirer à bout portant*, to fire point blank

tout le portait à croire que..., everything led him to think that...

un de nos avions a été porté manquant, one of our aircraft failed to return (is reported missing)

pour • • *pour ce qui est de vous*, as far as you are concerned

pour ainsi dire, so to speak

c'est pour de bon? you really mean it?

il est pour beaucoup dans cette affaire, he counts for a good deal in this business

il fait trop froid pour qu'il vienne nous faire visite, it's too cold for him to come and see us

pouvoir • • *cela se peut (bien)*, it's possible

cela ne peut (pas) se faire, it can't be done

vous pouvez nager, you can swim (i.e. are fit to swim)

vous savez nager, you can (know how to) swim

prendre • • *à bien prendre les choses*, if we consider things in their true light

à tout prendre, on the whole (all things considered)

c'est à prendre ou à laisser, you can take it or leave it

ne vous en prenez pas à moi, don't blame me for it

je ne sais pas comment m'y prendre, I don't know how to set about it

il s'est laissé prendre, he let himself be caught
il est pris de boisson, he is the worse for drink
je vous conseille de prendre le train pour..., I advise you to take the train for...

promenade .
allons faire une promenade, let's go for a walk
je vais faire une promenade en voiture, I'm going for a drive
je l'ai envoyé promener! I sent him about his business!

propre . .
il faut que vous alliez en propre personne, you must go in person
un propre à rien, a good for nothing
son propre mouchoir, his own handkerchief
son mouchoir propre, his clean handkerchief
c'est du propre! that's a fine thing, I don't think!

quatre . .
travailler comme quatre, to work like mad
un marchand des quatre saisons, a hawker, costermonger
entre quatre yeux, between you and me (confidentially)
le quatre septembre, the fourth of September
Henri quatre, Henry IV

que . .
c'est que..., the fact is that...
que s'est-il passé? what's happened?
qu'il le veuille ou non, whether he likes it or not
qu'elle est vilaine! how ugly she is!
qu'en pensez-vous? what do you think of it?

question .
il m'a posé beaucoup de questions, he asked me a number of questions
c'est là la question, that's the question

quoi . .
quoi qu'il en soit, be that as it may
il n'y a pas de quoi, don't mention it
c'est en quoi vous vous abusez, that's where you're wrong
il a de quoi vivre à son aise, he has ample means, he's comfortably off

raison . .
raison de plus pour..., all the more reason to...
vous perdez la raison? have you taken leave of your senses?
je le ferai entendre raison, I'll make him see reason
elle a eu raison de mes scrupules, she got the better of my scruples

reconnaître .
je le reconnais bien là, that's just like him
je ne m'y reconnais pas, I don't know where I am (I'm all at sea)
je l'ai reconnu à l'attitude qui lui est particulière, I recognised him by the attitude peculiar to him

règle . .
il faut faire les choses en règle, one must do things correctly
les règles du jeu, the rules (laws) of the game
il se faisait une règle d'arriver à l'heure exacte, he made it a rule to turn up punctually

remettre .
je préfère remettre à demain la décision, I prefer to postpone decision until to-morrow

nous devons nous remettre en route, we must be on our way again

vous ne me remettez pas? don't you remember me?

retard • • *le train a cinq minutes de retard*, the train is five minutes late

vous allez me mettre en retard, you'll make me late

rien • • *de rien, madame*, don't mention it (i.e. in disclaiming thanks)

en moins de rien, in less than no time

pour un rien je vous flanquerais à la porte, I've half a mind to throw you out

cela ne fait rien, it doesn't matter

il n'en est rien, (it's) nothing of the sort

rire • • *rire tout bas*, to chuckle

il n'y a pas de quoi rire, it's no laughing matter

vous voulez rire! you're joking!

rire du bout des dents, to force a laugh

sang • • *bon sang ne ment pas*, blood will tell

ne vous faites pas de mauvais sang, don't worry

sans • • *sans faute*, without fail

sans cela, but for that

cela va sans dire, that goes without saying, as a matter of course

savoir • • *reste à savoir*, (it) remains to be seen

pas que je sache, not that I know of

je ne saurais le dire, I couldn't say

sens • • *rue à sens unique*, one-way street

sens interdit, no entry

cela n'a pas le sens commun, there's no sense in that

service • • *être de service*, to be on duty

qu'y a-t-il pour votre service? what can I do for you?

les services de ravitaillement, the supply services

il y a des autobus qui font le service entre Paris et Versailles, there's a bus service between Paris and Versailles

servir • • *cet objet-là, à quoi sert-il?* what is that (used) for?

en temps de guerre on se sert de n'importe quoi, in wartime one makes use of anything

jadis ce bâtiment servait de caserne, formerly this building served as a barracks

table • • *mettre la table* (or *le couvert*), to lay the table

il tient table ouverte, he keeps open house

nous étions sur le point de nous mettre à table, we were about to sit down to table (to dinner)

talon • • *nous avons joué des talons*, we showed a clean pair of heels

marcher sur les talons de..., to follow hard on the heels of...

temps • • *de temps en temps*, from time to time

il est grand temps de..., it's high time to...

nous avons tout le temps (voulu), we have heaps of time

par le temps qui court, nowadays

il y a beau temps que..., it's a long time since...

il faut être de son temps, one must move with the times

de mon temps, in my day

il fait beau temps, it's fine (of weather)

il fait un temps de chien, it's wretched weather

tenir *je tiens (beaucoup) à le faire,* I am longing (am very keen) to do it

qu'à cela ne tienne, don't let that stand in your way

s'il ne tient qu'à cela, if that's the only difficulty

il ne put se tenir de rire, he couldn't help laughing

tenez la gauche, keep to the left

tenez bon, hold firm, stand fast

il ne tient qu'à vous de..., it rests with you to...

je ne sais pas à quoi m'en tenir, I don't know what to believe

tête *j'en ai par-dessus la tête,* I've had more than enough of it

étant égoïste il en fera à sa tête, being selfish, he will do as he pleases

je ne sais pas où donner de la tête, I don't know which way to turn

se mettre en tête de..., to take it into one's head to...

tirer *il se tirera d'affaire je ne sais comment,* he'll get out of the difficulty (he'll manage) somehow

ce ruban tire sur le gris, this ribbon has a greyish tinge

tirons à la courte paille, let us draw lots

bon à tirer, passed for the press (i.e. ready to print)

il a été tiré de cet ouvrage mille exemplaires, a thousand copies of this work have been printed

tomber *ça tombe mal,* that comes at a bad moment

vous avez laissé tomber quelque chose, you've dropped something

ne laissez pas tomber le feu, don't let the fire go out

tour *il m'a fait un mauvais tour,* he played me a nasty trick

allons faire un tour du jardin, let's stroll round the garden

ce fut fait en un tour de main, it was the work of a moment

à qui le tour? whose turn is it?

tout *à toute vitesse,* at full speed

une fois pour toutes, once and for all

elle fut tout oreilles, she was all ears

tout en longeant la rue, while going along the street

c'est tout ce qu'il y a de plus malheureux, nothing could be more unfortunate

tous les deux, both

tous les deux jours, every other day

pas du tout, not at all

train *aller bon train,* to go at a good pace

aller son petit train, to jog along (in one's usual way)

il menait son train de vie ordinaire, he was leading his normal life

être en train de, to be in the act of (busy doing)
être mal en train, to be dispirited, out of sorts
train de voyageurs (de marchandises), passenger (goods) train

traiter • • *il m'a traité de maladroit*, he called me clumsy
ce roman traite des aventures..., this novel deals with (is about) the adventures...
le docteur X le traite depuis longtemps, mais sa condition empire, Dr. X has been treating him for a long while, but he's getting worse

utile • • *puis-je vous être utile à quelque chose?* can I help you in any way?

valoir • • *il ne vaut pas grand'chose*, he's not much good, not up to much
il vaut mieux mourir que de vivre sans honneur, it is better to die than to live without honour
il vaudrait mieux ne pas le faire, it would be better not to do so
vaille que vaille, at all costs

venir • • *je vous vois venir*, I see what you're after
il venait de partir, he had just left
soyez le bienvenu! (be) welcome!
le nouveau venu, the new-comer
cela vient de ce que..., this is due to the fact that...

vie • • *jamais de la vie!* never!
il gagne bien sa vie, he earns quite a good living
il y va de la vie, it's a matter of life and death
mener (faire) la vie, to lead a fast life

vivre • • *il vit au jour le jour*, he lives from hand to mouth
il fait cher vivre à Paris, living in Paris is expensive
un roman vécu, a novel true to life

voir • • *cela se voit*, that's obvious
à le voir on aurait l'idée que..., to see him one would get the idea that...
nous nous voyons tous les lundis, we meet every Monday
faites voir! show (it) to me!
vous n'avez rien à voir à cette affaire, this affair is no concern of yours
il est mal vu, he is out of favour, in bad odour

vouloir • • *je crois qu'il m'en veut*, I fancy he has a grudge against me
il voulut m'assassiner, he tried (intended) to kill me
je voudrais bien être mort, I wish I were dead
je voudrais bien le voir, I should very much like to see it
si vous voulez, if you like
que veut-il que je fasse? what does he want me to do?

TEACH YOURSELF BOOKS
CONCISE
ENGLISH AND FRENCH
DICTIONARY

AN ENGLISH-FRENCH DICTIONARY

A

a, an, un, une

A1, de première qualité *f.*

aback, (*adv.*) déconcerté; à l'arrière

abaft, (*adv.*) en arrière

abandon, *v.t.* abandonner, délaisser, quitter, renoncer à

to abandon oneself to, se livrer à

abandoned, abandonné; dépravé

abandoned wretch, misérable *m.* and *f.*

abandonment, abandonnement *m.*, délaissement *m.*; abandon *m.*

abase, *v.t.* abaisser, avilir

abasement, abaissement *m.*, avilissement *m.*

abash, *v.t.* déconcerter, confondre

abashed, (*adj.*) confus (de)

to abate, *v.t.* diminuer, amoindrir, rabattre, abaisser

abate, *v.i.* s'affaiblir, se calmer, s'apaiser (weather); tomber, baisser, perdre de sa force (wind); *v.t.* diminuer

abatement, diminution *f.*, réduction *f.*, remise *f.*, rabais *m.*, affaiblissement *m.*

abbacy, dignité d'abbé *f.*

abbess, abbesse *f.*

abbey, abbaye *f.*

abbot, abbé *m.*

abbreviate, *v.t.* abréger, raccourcir

abbreviation, abréviation *f.*

abdicate, *v.t.* abdiquer; renoncer à

abdication, abdication *f.*

abdomen, abdomen *m.*, bas ventre *m.*

abduction, enlèvement de mineur *m.*

abductor, abducteur *m.*, ravisseur *m.*

abeam, (*adv.*) (*naut.*) par le travers

abed, (*adv.*) couché, au lit; alité (ill)

abet, *v.t.* soutenir, encourager, appuyer

abeyance, vacance *f.*, suspension *f.*

in abeyance, en suspens

into abeyance (to fall into -), cesser d'être en vigueur

abhor, *v.t.* abhorrer, avoir en horreur, détester

abhorrence, aversion extrême *f.*, horreur *f.*

abhorrent, (*adj.*) répugnant(e)

abide, *v.i.* demeurer, séjourner, habiter

abide, *v.t.* attendre; supporter, subir, souffrir

abiding, constant, durable, immuable

ability, faculté *f.*, pouvoir *m.*, capacité *f.*, talents *m. pl.*

to the best of my ability, de mon mieux

abject, (*adj.*) abject; vil; bas (basse)

abjection, abjection *f.*

abjuration, abjuration *f.*

to abjure, *v.t.* abjurer, renoncer à

ablaze, (*adj.*) en feu, en flammes

able, (*adj.*) capable, habile

able-bodied, robuste, vigoureux (-euse); **A.B.,** matelot

ablution, ablution *f.*

ably, (*adv.*) habilement

abnegation, abnégation *f.*, renonciation *f.*

abnormal, (*adj.*) anormal(-aux), irrégulier(-ère)

aboard, (*adv.*) à bord de

(to go) aboard, s'embarquer, aller à bord

abode, demeure *f.,* habitation *f.;* séjour *m.*

abolish, *v.t.* abolir, annuler

abolition, abolition *f.*

abominable, *(adj.)* détestable, infâme, abominable

abominate (to), *v.t.* détester

abomination, horreur *f.*

aboriginal, *(adj.)* primitif(-ive)

aborigines, *pl.* aborigènes *m. pl.*

abortion, avortement *m.*

abortive, *(adj.)* manqué, avorté

abound (in), *v.i.* abonder (en), regorger (de)

about, *(prep.)* autour de; environ; auprès de; au sujet de, à l'égard de; en train de (faire, etc.)

about that, à ce sujet

about (two) o'clock, vers (deux) heures

to talk about, parler de

to set about something, se mettre à quelquechose

round about, tout autour de

to be about to, être sur le point de

above, *(prep.)* au-dessus de, pardessus, plus de; au delà de

above all, surtout

above board, ouvertement, franchement

above, *(adv.)* en haut, là-haut, au-dessus

over and above, en outre, en sus

abrade, *v.t.* user par le frottement

abrasion, écorchure *f.;* abrasion

abreast, *(adv.)* de front, à côté l'un de l'autre, vis-à-vis

abridge, *v.t.* abréger, raccourcir, réduire

abridgment, abrégé *m.,* précis *m.,* diminution *f.,* réduction *f.*

abroad, *(adv.)* dehors, à l'étranger (in a foreign country)

to get abroad (rumour), courir, se répandre

abrogate, *v.t.* abroger

abrupt, *(adj.)* brusque; abrupt

abruptly, *(adv.)* brusquement, tout à coup, subitement

abruptness, brusquerie *f.,* rudesse *f.*

abscess, abcès *m.*

abscond, *v.i.* disparaître, fuir la justice

absence, absence *f.,* éloignement *m.*

absence (of mind), distraction *f.*

absent, *(adj.)* absent

to absent oneself, s'absenter

absent-minded, distrait

absentee, absent(e) de son poste (de son pays) *m. and f.*

absently, *(adv.)* d'un air distrait

absinth, absinthe *f.*

absolute, *(adj.)* absolu, illimité; pur et simple

absolutely, *(adv.)* absolument

absolve, *v.t.* absoudre de; délier, dégager

absorb, *v.t.* absorber; engloutir

absorbent, *(adj. and subst.)* absorbant *m.*

absorption, absorption *f.*

abstain, *v.i.* s'abstenir (de)

abstainer, quelqu'un qui s'abstient

abstemious, *(adj.)* sobre, tempérant, abstème

abstention, abstinence *f.;* abstention *f.*

abstract, *(subst.)* sommaire *m.,* résumé *m.,* précis *m.*

abstract, *v.t.* abstraire; soustraire (de)

in the abstract, dans l'abstrait

abstracted, abstrait

absurd, *(adj.)* absurde

absurdity, absurdness, absurdité *f.*

absurdly, *(adv.)* absurdement

abundance, abondance *f.;* grande quantité *f.*

abundant, *(adj.)* abondant, riche

abuse, *(subst.)* abus *m.,* insultes *f. pl.,* injures *f. pl.*

abuse, *v.t.* abuser; dire du mal de; injurier, insulter

abusive, *(adj.)* abusif(-ive), injurieux(-euse)

abut, *v.i.* aboutir (à)

abutment, culée *f.* (of bridge), arc-boutant *m.*

abyss, abîme *m.,* gouffre *m.*

acacia, acacia *m.*

academic(al), (*adj.*) académique

academy, académie (learned society of France); université *f.*, pensionnat *m.*, institution *f.*

acanthus, acanthe *f.*

accede, *v.i.* accéder, consentir à, monter (sur le trône)

accelerate, *v.t.* accélérer, activer, précipiter, hâter

accelerator, accélérateur *m.*

accent, (*subst.*) accent *m.*

(acute) accent, accent aigu

(circumflex) accent, accent circonflexe

(grave) accent, accent grave

accentuate, *v.t.* accentuer, appuyer sur

accentuation, accentuation *f.*

accept, *v.t.* accepter, agréer

to accept the consequences, subir les conséquences

acceptability, acceptabilité *f.*

acceptable, acceptable; agréable

acceptance, acceptation, acceptation *f.*; réception *f.*; approbation *f.*; accueil *m.*

acceptor (business term), accepteur *m.*

access, accès *m.*; entrée *f.*, admission *f.*

accessible, (*adj.*) accessible, abordable

accession, accession *f.*, acquisition *f.*, addition *f.*

accessory, (*adj.*) accessoire; complice *m.* (of a person)

accident, accident *m.*, malheur *m.*; sinistre *m.*

(by) accident, par hasard

accidental, (*adj.*) accidentel; fortuit

accidentally, accidentellement; fortuitement; par hasard

acclaim, *v.t.* acclamer, approuver

acclimatisation, acclimatation *f.*

acclimatise, *v.t.* acclimater

accommodate, *v.t.* accommoder; loger; recevoir; contenir; fournir; donner

accommodating, (*adj.*) accommodant, obligeant

accommodation, logement *m.*; adaptation *f.*, convenance *f.*;

bien-être *m.*; commodité *f.*; complaisance *f.*

accompaniment, accompagnement *m.*

accompany, *v.t.* accompagner (de)

accomplice, complice *m.* and *f.*

accomplish, *v.t.* accomplir, achever; effectuer; remplir

accomplishment, accomplissement *m.*; talent *m.*; qualité *f.*

accord, *v.t.* accorder

accord, *v.i.* s'accorder *v.r.*, être d'accord

accord, accord *m.*, consentement *m.*

in accord, d'accord (avec), conformément (à)

according, conforme (à)

according as, selon que, suivant que

according to, selon, suivant

accordingly, donc, en conséquence

accordion, accordéon, *m.*

accost, *v.t.* accoster, aborder

account, compte *m.*, mémoire *m.*, rapport *m.*, compte rendu *m.*; récit *m.* (narrative)

accountant, comptable *m.* and *f.*

accountable, responsable

account-book, livre (*m.*) de comptes

(to keep) accounts, tenir les livres

to account for, rendre compte de, expliquer

on account of, à cause de

on no account, sous aucun prétexte

accoutre, *v.t.* équiper

accoutrement, parure *f.*; équipement *m.*

accredit, *v.t.* accréditer

accrue, *v.i.* s'accroître, résulter

accumulate, *v.t.* accumuler, entasser

accumulate, *v.i.* s'accumuler *v.r.*

accumulator, accumulateur (-trice) *m.* (*f.*); (electric) accumulateur *m.*

accuracy, exactitude *f.*; précision *f.*; justesse *f.*

accurate, (*adj.*) exact, juste, correct, précis

accursed, (*adj.*) maudit, exécrable

accusation, accusation *f.*

accuse *v.t.* accuser

accuser, accusateur(-trice) *m.* (*f.*)

accustom, *v.t.* accoutumer, habituer; **to get accustomed (to),** s'habituer (à)

ace, as *m.*

acetic, (*adj.*) acétique

ache, mal *m.*, douleur *f.*

headache, mal de tête *m.*

toothache, mal de dents *m.*

to ache, *v.i.* faire mal

achieve, *v.t.* exécuter, accomplir, achever

achievement, exploit *m.*, accomplissement *m.*

aching, endolori

achromatic, (*adj.*) achromatique

acid, acide *m.* and (*adj.*)

acidulate, *v.t.* aciduler

acknowledge, *v.t.* reconnaître; avouer; accuser réception de (acknowledge a letter)

acknowledgment, reconnaissance *f.*; accusé de réception *m.*; remercîments *m. pl.*

acme, comble *m.*, sommet *m.*

acorn, gland *m.*

acoustics, acoustique *f.*

acquaint, *v.t.* informer (de); faire savoir (à)

to be acquainted with (person), connaître

to get acquainted with (person), faire la connaissance (de)

acquaintance, connaissance *f.*

acquiesce, *v.i.* accéder (à), acquiescer (à)

acquire, *v.t.* acquérir; obtenir, gagner

acquirement, acquis *m.*, acquisition *f.*, talent *m.*

acquit, *v.t.* acquitter, absoudre (de)

acquittal, acquittement *m.*

acre, arpent *m.*

acrid, (*adj.*) âcre

acrimonious, (*adj.*) acrimonieux (-euse)

acrimoniously, avec aigreur

acrimony, acrimonie *f.*, aigreur *f.*

acrobat, acrobate *m.* and *f.*

across, (*prep.*) à travers, sur

across, (*adv.*) à travers, en travers; de l'autre côté

across (to come), rencontrer; tomber sur

act, action *f.*; fait *m.*; acte *m.*

act, *v.i.* agir; se conduire (behave); se comporter; opérer

act, *v.t.* jouer; représenter

(in the) act of, en train de

action, action *f.*, fait *m.*, procès *m.* (*legal*); bataille *f.*, combat *m.*

active, (*adj.*) actif(-ive); agile, alerte

actively, (*adv.*) activement

activity, activité *f.*

actor, acteur *m.*; comédien *m.*

actress, actrice *f.*, comédienne *f.*

actual, réel(le), véritable, effectif (-ive)

actually, en effet

actuary, actuaire *m.*

actuate, *v.t.* animer (à), pousser, mettre en action

acumen, finesse *f.*, pénétration *f.*

acute, (*adj.*) aigu; violent; fin; perçant

acutely, vivement; (to suffer) d'une manière poignante

acuteness, finesse *f.*

adage, adage *m.*, proverbe *m.*

adapt, *v.t.* adapter, ajuster (to one's use); approprier

adapted (to), propre (à); approprié

add, *v.t.* ajouter; joindre

add up, *v.t.* additionner

adder, vipère *f.*

addict, *v.r.* s'adonner à, se livrer à

addition, addition *f.*, surcroît *m.*, supplément *m.*

additional, supplémentaire, de plus

address, adresse *f.*, discours *m.* (speech)

address, *v.t.* adresser; s'adresser à; mettre l'adresse (on letters)

addressee, destinataire *m.* or *f.*

addressor, celui (celle) qui adresse

adduce, *v.t.* produire; alléguer

adept, *(adj.)* and *m.* and *f.* adepte; versé *(adj.)*

adequacy, suffisance *f.*

adequate, suffisant, proportionné

adhere, *v.i.* adhérer, s'attacher, s'en tenir (à)

adherence, adhérence *f.*, attachement *m.*

adherent, partisan *m.*, adhérent *m.*

adhesive, *(adj.)* collant; tenace; *m.* adhésif

adieu, adieu *m.*

adit, *(mining)* galerie *(f.)* d'écoulement

adjacency, voisinage *m.*, contiguïté *f.*

adjacent, *(adj.)* adjacent, contigu *(fem.* -guë)

adjoin, *v.i.* être contigu (à); adjoindre

adjoin, *v.t.* joindre; toucher, se joindre à

adjoining, avoisinant, contigu (à)

adjourn, *v.t.* ajourner, remettre

adjournment, ajournement *m.*, délai *m.*

adjudge, adjudicate, *v.t.* adjuger; juger; condamner

adjudication, adjudication *f.*; jugement *m.*; décision *f.*

adjure, *v.t.* adjurer

adjust, *v.t.* ajuster, régler; arranger

adjustable, réglable

adjustment, accord *m.*, arrangement *m.*; raccommodement *m.*, ajustement *m.*

adjutant, capitaine adjudant major *m.* (the English word "adjutant" must not be confused with the French "adjudant" who is not an officer)

administer, *v.t.* administrer; gérer; fournir; rendre

administration, administration *f.*; gouvernement *m.*; gestion (estate) *f.*

administrator, administrateur *m.*

admirable, admirable

admiral, amiral(-aux) *m.*

rear-admiral, contre-amiral *m.*

vice-admiral, vice-amiral *m.*

admiralty, amirauté *f.*

First Lord of the Admiralty, ministre *(m.)* de la marine

admiration, admiration *f.*

admire, *v.t.* admirer

admirer, admirateur(-trice) *m.* *(f.)*

admissible, *(adj.)* admissible

admission, admission *f.*; entrée *f.*

admit, *v.t.* admettre; laisser entrer; avouer; reconnaître

admittance, accès *m.*; entrée *f.*, admission *f.*

no admittance, défense d'entrer

admonish, *v.t.* avertir, exhorter; réprimander

admonition, avertissement *m.*, réprimande *f.*

adolescence, adolescence *f.*

adolescent, adolescent *(adj.* and *subst.)*

adopt, *v.t.* adopter; (career, etc.) embrasser, choisir

adorable, *(adj.)* adorable

adorably, *(adv.)* adorablement

adoration, adoration *f.*

adore, *v.t.* adorer

adorn, *v.t.* orner; parer; embellir

adornment, parure *f.*; ornement *m.*

adrift, à la dérive

adroit, *(adj.)* adroit, habile

adroitness, dextérité *f.*

adulate, *v.t.* aduler

adulation, adulation *f.*

adulterate, *v.t.* falsifier, adultérer

adulteration, falsification *f.*

adulterer, adultère *m.* and *f.*; femme adultère

adultery, adultère *m.*

advance, avance *f.*, avancement *m.*, progrès *m.*

advance, *v.t.* avancer, faire avancer, élever, augmenter (prices, etc.); hausser (stocks, etc.)

in advance, d'avance

advance-guard, avant-garde *f.*

advantage, avantage *m.*; profit *m.*; intérêt *m.*

to have the advantage, avoir le dessus

to one's advantage, à son avantage

to take advantage (of), profiter (de)

to turn to advantage, mettre à profit

advantageous, avantageux (-euse)

advantageously, avantageusement

advent, venue f.; Avent m. (relig.)

adventure, aventure f., hasard m.

adventurer(-ess), aventurier (-ère) m. (f.)

adventurous, aventureux(-euse), hardi

adversary, adversaire m.

adverse, (adj.) adverse, contraire, défavorable

adversity, adversité f.

advert, v.i. faire allusion (à)

advertise, v.t. annoncer, faire annoncer; afficher

advertisement, annonce f. (in newspaper); avis m. (public notice)

advertising, publicité f.

advertising-agent, agent (m.) de publicité

advice, avis m., conseil m.

to take advice, prendre conseil

advisable, (adj.) judicieux(-euse), convenable (pour or de); prudent

advise (to), v.t. conseiller; donner avis (de)

advisedly, (adv.) de propos délibéré, avec réflexion

advocate, avocat m., défenseur m.

advocate, v.t. défendre; plaider; soutenir

adze, (h)erminette f.

aerated, (adj.) gazeux(-euse)

aerated waters, eaux minérales f.

aerial, (adj.) aérien(ne); antenne f. (wireless)

aerolite, aérolithe m.; bolide m.

aeroplane, avion m.

aerostat, aérostat m.

aerodynamics, aérodynamique f.

æsthetic, (adj.) esthétique

afar, (adv.) de loin, au loin

affability, affabilité f.

affable, (adj.) affable

affably, (adv.) avec affabilité

affair, affaire f.

affect, v.t. affecter; intéresser, toucher, émouvoir

affectation, affectation f.

affected, (adj.) affecté, précieux (-euse), maniéré, prétentieux (-euse) (style); disposé pour (inclined to)

affection, affection f.; tendresse f.

affectionate, (adj.) affectueux (-euse)

affiance, v.t. fiancer

affianced, (adj.) fiancé(e)

affidavit, déposition f.

affinity, affinité f.

affirm, v.t. affirmer, confirmer

(in the) affirmative, (adv.) affirmativement

affix, v.t. attacher (à); apposer (à)

afflict, v.t. affliger

afflicting, (adj.) chagrinant, affligeant

affliction, affliction f., douleur f.; calamité f., malheur m.

affluence, opulence f.; affluence f.

affluent, (adj.) abondant, riche; affluent m.

afford, v.t. donner; fournir; accorder; avoir les moyens de, pouvoir

I cannot afford (it), mes moyens ne me le permettent pas

affray, rixe f.; échauffourée f.

affright, effroi m., épouvante f.

affright, v.t. effrayer

affront, affront m.

affront, v.t. offenser, insulter

afire (aflame), (adv.) en feu, en flammes

afloat, (adv.) à flot

afoot, (adv.) à pied

afore, (adv.) auparavant

aforementioned,(adj.) mentionné plus haut, précité

aforesaid, susdit m., and (adj.) le dit m.

afraid, (adj.) effrayé

to be afraid, avoir peur

afresh, (adv.) de nouveau
African, (adj. and subst.) africain(e)
aft, (adv.) à l'arrière
after, (prep.) après, à la suite de, selon, (conj.) après que
after all, après tout, aussi bien
after, (adv.) après, d'après .
aftermath, regain m.
afternoon, après-midi m. and f.
afterthought, réflexion (f.) après coup
afterwards, (adv.) ensuite, après, plus tard
again, (adv.) encore, encore une fois, de nouveau
again and again, maintes fois, à plusieurs reprises
never again, jamais plus
against, (prep.) contre; vis-à-vis, vers
over against, vis-à-vis
agate, agate f.
age, âge m., siècle m.; génération f.
middle ages, moyen âge m.
of age, majeur m.
under age, mineur m.
aged, vieux (vieil, vieille), âgé
age, v.i. vieillir
agency, agence (commer.) f., action f.
servants' agency, bureau (m.) de placement
agenda, ordre du jour m.
agent, représentant m., agent m., mandataire m., homme d'affaires m.
aggrandise, v.t. agrandir
aggrandisement, agrandissement m.
aggravate, v.t. aggraver, exagérer; taquiner (tease); agacer; provoquer
aggravation, exagération f.; provocation f., agacement m.; aggravation f.
aggregate, masse f., total m.
in the aggregate, en somme
aggregate, v.t. rassembler
aggression, agression f.
aggressive, (adj.) agressif(-ive), offensif(-ive)
aggressiveness, caractère agressif m.

aggressor, agresseur m.
aggrieve, v.t. chagriner
aghast, (adj.) ébahi, consterné, frappé d'effroi
agile, (adj.) agile
agility, agilité f.
agitate, v.t. agiter, exciter, remuer
agitation, agitation f.
agitator, agitateur m., meneur m.
ago, (adj. and adv.) passé, il y a
a year ago, il y a un an
agog, (adv.) empressé; en émoi
agonise, v.i. souffrir l'agonie
agonising, déchirant
agony, agonie f.
agree, v.i. s'accorder (à or avec), être d'accord, consentir (à), convenir (de)
agreeable, agréable; conforme à
I am agreeable, je veux bien
agreeably, agréablement
agreed, d'accord
agreement, accord m., rapport m.; contrat m., convention f.
agricultural, (adj.) agricole
agriculture, agriculture f.
agriculturer, agriculteur m.
aground, (adv.) échoué
(to run) aground, échouer, faire échouer
ague, fièvre intermittente f.
ahead, (adv.) en avant; en tête
aid, aide f. assistance f.; secours m.; hearing -, aide-ouïe, m. inv.
aid, v.t. aider, assister, secourir
ail, v.i. être souffrant
ailing, (adj.) souffrant, maladif (-ive)
ailment, mal (maux) m.
aim, v.t. (to take) viser; aspirer (à); avoir pour but
aim, point de mire m.; but m.
air, air m., brise f.; vent m.; mine (appearance) f.; expression f.
breath of air, souffle de vent m.
airborne, aéroporté
aircraft, appareil m. (d'aviation)
aircraft carrier, un porte-avions
airfield, aéroport m.
airgun, fusil à vent m.

air-hole, aspirail *m.*; (of furnace) évent *m.*

airman, aviateur *m.*

air-pump, machine pneumatique *f.*

air-shaft, puits d'aérage *m.*

airship, dirigeable *m.*

airtight, (*adj.*) imperméable à l'air

air, *v.t.* aérer, donner de l'air à

in the open air, en plein air ·

airing, aérage *m.*; prendre l'air (a short walk)

aisle (of a church), nef latérale *f.*

ajar, (*adj.*) entr'ouvert

akimbo, (*adv.*) appuyé sur la hanche

akin, allié (à), parent (de)

alabaster, albâtre *m.*

alacrity, empressement *m.*, vivacité *f.*

alarm, alarme *f.*; (warning) alerte *f.*

alarm-bell, tocsin *m.*

alarm-clock, réveille-matin *m.* or réveil *m.*

false alarm, fausse alerte

alarm, *v.t.* alarmer; effrayer

alarming, alarmant; inquiétant

alas! (*interj.*) hélas!

album, album, *m.* ·

albumen, albumine *f.*

alcohol, alcool *m.*

alcoholic, (*adj.*) and *m.* (*f.*) alcoolique

alcoholism, alcoolisme *m.*

alcove, niche *f.*

alder (tree), aune *m.*

alderman, conseiller (*m.*) municipal(-aux)

ale, bière *f.*

ale-house, cabaret *m.*

alert, (*adj.*) alerte, vigilant

alert, alerte *f.*

on the alert, sur le qui-vive

algebra, algèbre *f.*

Algerian, (*adj.* and *subst.*) algérien(ne)

Algiers, Alger

alien, (*adj.*) étranger(-ère)·

alien, étranger(-ère) *m.* (*f.*)

alienate, *v.t.* aliéner, détacher

alienation of mind, égarement (*m.*) d'esprit

alienist, aliéniste *m.*

alight, *v.i.* descendre; mettre pied à terre

alike, (*adj.*) semblable; pareil(le)

alike, (*adv.*) également; de même

aliment, aliment *m.*

alimentary, (*adj.*) alimentaire

alimony, pension (*f.*) alimentaire

alive, (*adj.*) en vie, vivant; vif (vive) (alert); éveillé; sensible à (alive to)

alkali, alcali *m.*

all, (*adj.*) tout *m.* (*pl.* tous), toute *f.* (*pl.* toutes)

All Saints' Day, le jour de la Toussaint

All Souls' Day, jour des morts

all but, presque

all the way, tout le long du chemin

all, (*adv.*) tout, entièrement

all at once, tout d'un coup

all the better, tant mieux

not at all, point du tout

nothing at all, rien du tout

it is all right, c'est bien entendu

allay, *v.t.* apaiser, adoucir, calmer

allegation, allégation *f.*

allege, *v.t.* prétendre (que); déclarer, alléguer

alleviate, *v.t.* alléger, soulager

alleviation, soulagement *m.*, allègement *m.*

alley, ruelle *f.*, allée *f.*

(blind) alley, cul-de-sac *m.*, impasse *f.*

alliance, alliance *f.*

allied, (*adj.*) allié

alligator, alligator *m.*, caïman *m.*

allocate, *v.t.* assigner, allouer

allot, *v.t.* assigner; répartir

allotment, partage *m.*, lot *m.*, distribution *f.*

allotment (land), lopin de terre *m.*

allow, *v.t.* permettre, autoriser, accorder, admettre, reconnaître

allowable, (*adj.*) permissible

allowance, pension *f.*; allocation *f.*; indemnité *f.*, indulgence *f.*, ration *f.*

to make allowance for, tenir compte (de)

alloy, alliage *m.*
alloy, *v.i.* allier
allude, *v.t.* faire allusion (à)
allure, *v.t.* attirer, séduire, inviter à
allurement, amorce *f.*; charme *m.*; attrait *m.*
allusion, allusion *f.*
alluvial, (*adj.*) alluvial, d'alluvion
ally, allié *m.*, confédéré *m.*
ally, *v.t.* allier; *v.r.* s'allier (avec)
almanac, almanack, almanach *m.*, calendrier *m.*
all-mightiness, toute-puissance *f.*
almighty, (*adj.*) tout puissant
almond, amande *f.*
burnt almond, praline *f.*
almond tree, amandier *m.*
almost, presque
alms, aumône *f.*
almshouse, hospice *m.*
alone, (*adj.*) seul; solitaire; unique
along, (*adv.*) le long de
all along, tout le temps
aloof, (*adj.*) éloigné; à l'écart
aloud, (*adv.*) à haute voix; haut
alpine, (*adj.*) alpestre, alpin
alpine climber, alpiniste *m.* and *f.*
already, (*adv.*) déjà
also, (*adv.*) aussi; également
altar, autel *m.*
high altar, maître-autel
alter, *v.t.* changer, modifier
alter, *v.i.* changer; se changer
alterable, (*adj.*) variable
alteration, changement *m.*, modification *f.*
altercation, altercation *f.*; querelle *f.*
alternate, alternative, (*adj.*) alternatif(-ive)
alternation, alternance *f.*
alternative, alternative *f.*
although, (*conj.*) quoique; bien que; quand même
altitude, altitude *f.*, élévation *f.*, hauteur *f.*
altogether, (*adv.*) tout à fait; entièrement
aluminium, aluminium *m.*
always, toujours

amass, *v.t.* amasser
amateur, amateur, *m.*
amaze, *v.t.* étonner; éblouir; émerveiller
amazement, étonnement *m.*; stupeur *f.*
amazing, étonnant, épatant
ambassador(-dress), ambassadeur(-drice) *m.* (*f.*)
amber, ambre, *m.*
ambergris, ambre-gris *m.*
ambiguity, ambiguïté *f.*, équivoque *f.*
ambiguous, douteux(-euse), ambigu; équivoque
ambition, ambition *f.*
ambitious, ambitieux(-euse)
ambulance, ambulance *f.*
ambush, embuscade *f.*; guet-apens *m.*
ambush, *v.t.* embusquer; mettre en embuscade
ameliorate, *v.t.* améliorer
amelioration, amélioration *f.*
amenable, responsable; soumis, sujet à
amend, *v.t.* réformer, corriger, amender
amend, *v.i.* se corriger, s'amender
amendment, amélioration *f.*; amendement *m.*
amends, compensation *f.*
make amends for, dédommager (de)
American, (*adj.*) and *m.* and *f.* américain(e)
amiability, amabilité *f.*
amiable, (*adj.*) aimable
amicable, (*adj.*) amical(-aux)
amid(st), (*prep.*) au milieu de
amiss, (*adj.* and *adv.*) mal, en mal, de travers
to take amiss, prendre en mauvaise part
amity, amitié *f.*
ammonia, ammoniaque *f.*
amnesty, amnistie *f.*
among, (*prep.*) parmi, entre (for two persons or things only); au milieu de, chez, avec
amorous, (*adj.*) amoureux(-euse)
amount, *v.i.* s'élever, se monter, revenir à

amount, montant *m.*, total(-aux) *m.*; somme *f.*; chiffre *m.*

amour, amourette *f.*

amphibious, (*adj.*) amphibie

amphitheatre, amphithéâtre *m.*

ample, (*adj.*) ample, large, spacieux, abondant, copieux, très suffisant

amplify, *v.t.* amplifier, étendre

amplitude, largeur *f.*, étendue *f.*

amply, (*adv.*) amplement

amputate, *v.t.* amputer

amuck (to run), devenir fou, furieux, s'emballer

amuse, *v.t.* amuser, divertir

amusement, amusement *m.*, divertissement *m.*

amusing, amusant, divertissant

anæmia, anémie *f.*

anaesthetic, anesthésique *m.*

analogous, analogue

analyse, *v.t.* analyser

anarchist, anarchiste *m.* and *f.*

anarchy, anarchie *f.*

anatomy, anatomie *f.*

ancestor(-tress), aïeul(e) *m.* (*f.*), ancêtre *m.* (*f.*)

ancestral, héréditaire

anchor, ancre *f.*

cast anchor, jeter l'ancre

weigh anchor, lever l'ancre

anchorage, mouillage *m.*

anchovy, anchois *m.*

ancient, (*adj.*) ancien(ne), antique, vieux, vieil(le)

and, (*conj.*) et

andiron, chenet *m.*

anecdote, anecdote *f.*

anew, de nouveau

angel, ange *m.*

guardian angel, ange (*m.*) gardien

anger, colère *f.*, courroux *m.*

anger, *v.t.* fâcher, irriter, mettre en colère

angina (pectoris), angine (*f.*) de poitrine

angle, angle *m.*, coin *m.*

angle, *v.i.* pêcher à la ligne

angler, pêcheur (*m.*) à la ligne

angling, pêche (*f.*) à la ligne

angry, (*adj.*) en colère, fâché, irrité; **to get ~,** se fâcher, se mettre en colère

angrily, en colère, avec colère

anguish, angoisse *f.*, douleur *f.*

angular, (*adj.*) angulaire

aniline, aniline *f.*

animal, animal(-aux) *m.*; also (*adj.*)

animate, *v.t.* animer, encourager

animated, (*adj.*) animé

animation, animation *f.*; vivacité *f.*

animosity, animosité *f.*

anise, anis, *m.*

ankle, cheville *f.* (du pied)

annex, *v.t.* annexer, joindre à

annex, annexe *f.*

annexation, annexation *f.*

annihilate, *v.t.* anéantir, détruire

annihilation, anéantissement *m.*

anniversary, anniversaire *m.*

annotate, *v.t.* annoter

annotation, annotation *f.*

announce, *v.t.* annoncer; proclamer

announcement, annonce *f.*, avis *m.*; (of marriage, birth, etc.) lettre (*f.*) de faire part

announcer, (*T.V.*) speaker(-ine) *m.* (*f.*) annonceur *m.*

annoy, *v.t.* ennuyer; agacer, tourmenter

annoyance, ennui *m.*, tourment *m.*, chagrin *m.*

annual, (*adj.*) annuel(le)

annual, annuaire *m.*

annul, *v.t.* annuler

annular, (*adj.*) annulaire

Annunciation, Annonciation *f.*

anoint, *v.t.* oindre

anon, tout à l'heure, bientôt

anonymous, anonyme

another, (*adj.* and *pron.*) autre, un autre, encore un (une)

one after another, l'un après l'autre

one another, l'un l'autre

answer, *v.t.* répondre; répondre à; remplir (with meaning of answering a purpose)

answer, *v.i.* répondre (de), answer (for); réussir (meaning of succeed)

answer, réponse *f.*; raisonnement *m.*

answerable, susceptible de ré-

ponse; responsable (de); conforme (à)
ant, fourmi *f.*
ant-eater, fourmilier *m.*
ant-hill, fourmilière *f.*
antagonise, *v.t.* rendre hostile
antagonism, opposition *f.*
antagonist, antagoniste *m.*; adversaire *m.*
Antarctic, Antarctique, *m.*
antecedent, antécédent *m.*
antechamber, antichambre *f.*
antediluvian, (*adj.*) antédiluvien(ne)
antelope, antilope *f.*
anterior, (*adj.*) antérieur(e)
anthem, motet *m.*; hymne *m.*
anthracite, anthracite *m.*
anthrax, anthrax *m.*
anthropoid, anthropoïde *m.*
anthropology, anthropologie *f.*
anthropophagous, (*adj.*) anthropophage
anti, (*prefix*) contre, anti
anti-aircraft, contre-avion
antic, tour *m.*, farce *f.*, bouffonnerie *f.*
anticipate, *v.t.* anticiper, prévenir, devancer, s'attendre (à), prévoir
anticipation, anticipation *f.*, avant-goût *m.*
antipathy, antipathie *f.*
antiquary, antiquaire *m.* and *f.*
antiquated, (*adj.*) suranné, démodé, antique
antique, (*adj.*) ancien(ne), antique
antiquity, antiquité *f.*
antiseptic, (*adj.* and *m.*) antiseptique *m.*
antithesis, antithèse *f.*
antler, andouiller *m.*
antonym, antonyme *m.*, contraire *m.*
anvil, enclume *f.*
anxiety, anxiété *f.*, inquiétude *f.*, sollicitude *f.*
anxious, inquiet(-ète), soucieux (-euse), désireux(-euse) (de)
any, (*adj.*) quelque, tout, en, aucūn; n'importe lequel
at any rate, en tout cas
anybody, anyone, quelqu'un

I have not any, je n'en ai pas
not any more, pas davantage
scarcely any, presque pas
anyhow, de toute façon, en tout cas, quand même
anything, quelque chose; quoi que ce soit; n'importe quoi
anywhere, quelque part
apace, (*adv.*) vite, à grands pas
apart, (*adv.*) à part, séparément
apartment, chambre *f.*, pièce *f.* (d'un appartement), logement *m.*
ape, singe *m.*; guenon *f.*; singer *v.t.*
aperient, (*adj.*) laxatif(-ive); laxatif *m.*
aperture, ouverture *f.*
apex, sommet *m.*
apiary, rucher *m.*
apiece, (*adv.*) la pièce; par tête, par personne
apologise, *v.i.* faire des excuses; s'excuser
apologue, apologue, *m.*
apology, excuses *f. pl.*; apologie *f.*
apoplectic, (*adj.*) apoplectique
apoplexy, apoplexie *f.*
fit of apoplexy, coup (*m.*) de sang
apostle, apôtre *m.*
apothecary, apothicaire *m.*, pharmacien *m.*
appal, *v.t.* épouvanter, effrayer, consterner
appalling, épouvantable, effrayant
apparatus, appareil *m.*
apparel, habillement *m.*, vêtement *m.*
apparent, visible, évident, manifeste
apparition, apparition *f.*, spectre *m.*
appeal, *v.i.* appeler, faire appel à
appeal (legal), se pourvoir en cassation
appear, *v.i.* paraître; apparaître; se montrer (à), se présenter (à)
appearance, apparition *f.*; apparence *f.*; figure *f.*
appease, *v.t.* apaiser; pacifier; calmer
appellant, appelant *m.*
appellation, dénomination *f.*

append, *v.t.* apposer (à), annexer (à)

appendage, apanage *m.*; accessoire *m.*

appendicitis, appendicite *f.*

appendix, appendice *m.*

appertain, *v.i.* appartenir (à)

appetite, appétit *m.*

appetiser, apéritif *m.*

appetising, appétissant

applaud, *v.t.* applaudir

applause, applaudissement *m.* (generally in plural)

apple, pomme *f.*

apple-pie, tourte (*f.*) aux pommes

apple-tree, pommier *m.*

appliance, moyen *m.*; instrument *m.*

application, application *f.*, demande *f.*, sollicitation *f.*

apply, *v.t.* appliquer (à), s'adresser (à)

apply (oneself), *v.r.* s'appliquer (à), se mettre (à)

appoint, *v.t.* nommer; désigner

appointment, nomination *f.*; emploi *m.*; rendez-vous *m.*

apportion, *v.t.* répartir, partager

appraise, apprécier, évaluer, estimer

appraiser, commissaire-priseur *m.*, expert *m.*

appreciable, appréciable

appreciate, *v.t.* apprécier, estimer

apprehend, *v.t.* appréhender, arrêter; craindre; comprendre

apprehension, crainte *f.*; compréhension *f.*

apprehensive, craintif(-ive)

apprentice, apprenti *m.*

apprentice, *v.t.* mettre en apprentissage

apprenticeship, apprentissage *m.*

apprise, *v.t.* prévenir

approach, *v.i.* approcher *v.t.*; s'approcher (de)

approach, approche *f.*; rapprochement *m.*; abord *m.*

approachable, abordable, accessible

approbation, approbation *f.*

appropriate, approprié; convenable; propre

approval, approbation *f.*

approve, *v.t.* approuver; trouver bon que (with subjunctive)

approvingly, avec approbation

approximate, (*adj.*) approximatif(-ive)

apricot, abricot *m.*

apricot tree, abricotier *m.*

april, avril *m.*; **make an April fool of,** faire un poisson d'avril à

apron, tablier *m.*

apse, abside *f.*

apt, (*adj.*) apte; propre

aqua fortis, eau-forte *f.*

aquatic, (*adj.*) aquatique

aqueduct, aqueduc *m.*

aquiline, (*adj.*) aquilin; d'aigle (of nose)

Arab, (*adj.* and *subst.*) arabe

arable, (*adj.*) labourable

arbiter, arbitre *m.*

arbitrary, arbitraire

arbitration, arbitrage *m.*

arbitrator, arbitre *m.*

arbour, berceau *m.*; tonnelle *f.*

arc, arc *m.*

arcade, arcade *f.*; passage *m.*

arch, arche *f.*, voûte *f.*

arch, *v.t.* voûter, courber (meaning bend)

archangel, archange *m.*

archbishop, archevêque *m.*

archbishopric, archevêché *m.*

archdeacon, archidiacre *m.*

archduke (-duchess), archiduc *m.*, archiduchesse *f.*

arched, voûté; courbé

archer, archer *m.*

archery, tir à l'arc *m.*

archipelago, archipel *m.*

architect, architecte *m.*

architecture, architecture *f.*

archive, archives *f. pl.*

archway, portail (*pl.* -s) *m.*

arctic, (*adj.*) arctique

ardent, ardent

ardour, ardeur *f.*; zèle *m.*

arduous, (*adj.*) ardu, rude, pénible, difficile

area, étendue *f.*; surface *f.*; sous-sol *m.*

arena, arène *f.*

argil, argile *f.*

argue, *v.i.* discuter (avec); raisonner(sur); argumenter(contre); plaider (*legal*)

argument, argument *m.*, raisonnement *m.*; discussion *f.*

arid, (*adj.*) aride

aridness, aridité *f.*

aright, (*adv.*) juste; bien

arise, *v.i.* se lever; s'élever; provenir; résulter; survenir

aristocracy, aristocratie *f.*

aristocrat, aristocrate *m.* and *f.*

aristocratic, (*adj.*) aristocratique

arithmetic, arithmétique *f.*

ark, arche *f.*

arm, bras *m.*, arme *f.* (weapon)

arm, *v.i.* s'armer (de); prendre des armes

arm, *v.t.* armer; donner des armes

arm-chair, fauteuil *m.*

armpit, aisselle *f.*

arm-in-arm, bras-dessus bras-dessous

under arms, sous les armes

armature, armature *f.*; induit *m.*

armistice, armistice *m.*

armour, armure *f.*; (of modern weapons) blindage *m.*

armour-bearer, écuyer *f.*

armoured car, char blindé *m.*

armourer, armurier *m.*

army, armée *f.*

army corps, corps d'armée

aroma, arome *m.*; bouquet *m.* (of wine)

around, (*prep.*) autour, à l'entour

around, (*adv.*) autour, aux alentours; à l'entour

arouse, *v.t.* éveiller, exciter

arpeggio, (*mus.*) arpège *m.*

arrack, eau (*f.*) de vie de riz

arraign, *v.t.* accuser, poursuivre en justice

arrange, *v.t.* arranger; régler; organiser; disposer

arrangement, arrangement *m.*; disposition *f.*

arrant, (*adj.*) (meaning downright); fieffé(e), franc (franche)

array, *v.t.* ranger; déployer; parer (meaning to clothe); revêtir

array, ordre *m.*, étalage *m.*

arrear(s), arriéré *m.*; (*m. pl.*) arrérages

in arrears, en retard

arrest, *v.t.* arrêter; saisir; suspendre

arrest, arrestation *f.*; prise de corps *f.*; arrêt *m.*; suspension *f.*

arrival, arrivée *f.*, arrivage *m.* (of goods)

arrival platform, quai d'arrivée *m.*

arrive, *v.t.* arriver (à) (with être)

arrogance, arrogance *f.*

arrogant, arrogant; hautain

arrogate, *v.t.* s'arroger

arrow, flèche *f.*

arsenal, arsenal *m.*

arsenic, arsenic *m.*

arson, crime d'incendie *m.*

art, art *m.*; habileté *f.*

fine arts, beaux-arts *m. pl.*

arterial, (*adj.*) artériel(le)

artesian, (*adj.*) artésien(ne)

artful, rusé; fin

artichoke, artichaut *m.*

article, article *m.*; objet *m.*

articulate, *v.i.* and *v.t.* articuler

artifice, artifice *m.*; ruse *f.*; finesse *f.*

artificer, artisan *m.*, ouvrier *m.*

artificial, artificiel(le)

artilleryman, artilleur *m.*

artillery, artillerie *f.*

artisan, artisan *m.*, ouvrier *m.*

artist, artiste *m.* and *f.*

artistic, (*adj.*) artistique

artless, ingénu, naïf (naïve); sans art

as, (*conj.*) comme, tel que, aussi . . . que, puisque

as for, quant à

as it were, pour ainsi dire

asbestos, asbeste *m.*

ascend, *v.i.* monter (à, or sur)

ascend, *v.t.* monter, gravir; faire l'ascension de

ascendency, supériorité *f.*, influence *f.*

ascension, ascension *f.*

Ascension Day, jour de l'Ascension

ascent, montée *f.*; pente *f.*

ascertain, *v.t.* s'assurer; s'informer; constater

ascribe, *v.t.* attribuer; imputer à

ash tree, frêne *m.*, sorbier *m.* (mountain ash)

ash, cendres *f. pl.*; Ash Wednesday, mercredi des Cendres

ash-coloured, (*adj.*) cendré

ashpit, ash-tray, cendrier *m.*

ashamed, honteux(-euse)

ashlar (squared or hewed stone), moellon *m.*

ashore, (*adv.*) à terre

ashore (of ship), (*adj.*) échoué

ashy, (*adj.*) cendré

asiatic, (*adj.* and *subst.*) asiatique

aside, (*adv.*) de côté; à part

ask, *v.t.* demander, prier (de); inviter (à); interroger (ask questions); poser (question)

askance, (*adv.*) de travers

asleep, (*adj.*) endormi

fall asleep, *v.r.* s'endormir

asparagus, asperge *f.*; aspergière *f.* (asparagus bed)

aspect, aspect *m.*

aspen (tree), tremble *m.*

asperity, âpreté *f.*; rudesse *f.*; sévérité *f.*

aspersion, calomnie *f.*

asphalt, asphalte *m.*

asphyxiate, *v.t.* asphyxier

aspirant, candidat *m.*

aspire, aspirer (à), souhaiter ardemment

aspirin, aspirine *f.*; an aspirin tablet, un comprimé d'-

ass, âne *m.*, ânesse *f.*

assail, *v.t.* assaillir, attaquer

assassin, assassin *m.*

assassinate, *v.t.* assassiner

assassination, assassinat *m.*

assault, *v.t.* attaquer; assaut *m.*

assay (of metals, etc.), essai *m.*

assemble, *v.i.* s'assembler; se réunir

assemble, *v.t.* assembler, réunir

assembly, assemblée *f.*, réunion *f.*

assembly room, salle de réunion *f.*

assent, consentement *m.*, sanction *f.*

assent, *v.i.* assentir (à)

assert, *v.t.* affirmer; prétendre; revendiquer

assertion, assertion *f.*, revendication *f.*

assess, *v.t.* imposer, taxer

assets, actif *m.*

assiduity, assiduité *f.*

assiduous, (*adj.*) assidu, appliqué

assign, *v.t.* assigner; transférer à

assignation, transfert *m.*; assignation *f.*; rendez-vous *m.*

assignee, cessionnaire *m.*, syndic *m.* (*law*)

assignment, transfert *m.*, cession (*f.*) de biens; attribution *f.*

assimilate, *v.t.* assimiler

assimilate, *v.i.* s'assimiler

assist, *v.t.* assister; aider

assistance, assistance *f.*; aide *f.*; secours *m.*

assistant, aide *m.* and *f.*; commis *m.* (male shop assistant); demoiselle (*f.*) de magasin (shopgirl); assesseur (*law*)

assistant, (*adj.*) auxiliaire

assizes, assises *f. pl.*

associate, *v.i.* s'associer

associate, *v.t.* associer (avec)

associate, associé *m.*, complice *m.*

association, association *f.*; société *f.*

assort, *v.t.* assortir

assorted, (*adj.*) assorti

assortment, assortiment *m.*

assuage, *v.t.* apaiser, calmer

assume, *v.t.* prendre (sur soi); s'attribuer; s'arroger

assumption, présomption *f.*

Assumption (religious festival), l'Assomption *f.*

assurance, assurance *f.*

assure, *v.t.* assurer

aster, aster *m.*

asterisk, astérisque *m.*

astern, (*adv.*) à l'arrière, de l'arrière

asthma, l'asthme *m.*

asthmatic(al), (*adj.*) asthmatique

astir, (*adj.*) en émoi, debout (up in morning)

astonish, *v.t.* étonner

astonishing, (*adj.*) étonnant

astonishment, étonnement *m.*

astound, *v.t.* étonner, ébahir

astounding, (*adj.*) foudroyant

astray, égaré, hors du bon chemin

astride, (*adv.*) à califourchon

astringent, (*adj. and subst.*) astringent *m.*

astronaut, astronaute *m.*

astronomer, astronome *m.*

astronomy, astronomie *f.*

asylum, asile *m.*, refuge *m.*

asylum (lunatic), maison *f.*, hospice d'aliénés *m.*; maison de santé *f.*

at, (*prep.*) à, en, dans; contre

at first, d'abord

at hand, sous la main

at home, chez soi

at last, enfin

at least, au moins

at once, tout de suite, à la fois

at the same time, en même temps

atheism, athéisme *m.*

atheist, athée *m. and f.*

athlete, athlète *m.*

atlas, atlas *m.*

atmosphere, atmosphère *f.*

atmospheric, (*adj.*) atmosphérique

atom, atome, *m.*

atomic, (*adj.*) atomique

atone, *v.i.* expier; racheter

atonement, expiation *f.*

atrocious, (*adj.*) atroce

atrocity, atrocité *f.*

attach, *v.t.* attacher; lier; saisir (goods, etc.)

attachment, attachement *m.*; saisie-arrêt *f.*

attack, attaque *f.*, agression *f.*

attack, *v.t.* attaquer; frapper (de)

attain, *v.t.* atteindre; parvenir (à)

attainment, acquisition *f.*, réalisation *f.*

attempt, essai *m.*, effort *m.*, tentative *f.*

attempt, *v.t.* essayer (de); tenter; tâcher (de)

attend, *v.t.* faire attention (à), écouter; servir; soigner (the sick); accompagner; assister à

attendance, service *m.*; assistance (at a concert, meeting, etc.) *f.*; soins (for a sick person) *m.pl.*

attendant, (*adj.*) qui dépend de; qui accompagne

attendant, domestique *m. and f.*; gardien(ne); ouvreuse *f.* (in theatre)

attention, attention *f.*, soins *m. pl.*; (English = attentions) prévenances *f. pl.*

attention! (look out!), prenez garde! attention!

to call one's attention, faire remarquer à

attentive, (*adj.*) attentif(-ive), assidu; prévenant

attenuate, *v.t.* atténuer; diminuer; amoindrir

attenuation, atténuation *f.*; amoindrissement *m.*

attest, *v.t.* attester

attestation, attestation *f.*

attic, mansarde *f.*; grenier *m.*

attire, vêtement *m.*, costume *m.*, parure *f.*

attire, *v.t.* vêtir, parer

attitude, attitude *f.*, pose *f.*

attorney, avoué *m.*, procureur *m.*

attorney-general, procureur-général *m.*

(power of) attorney, procuration *f.*, pouvoirs *m. pl.*

attract, *v.t.* attirer

attraction, attraction *f.*, attraits *m. pl.*

attractive, (*adj.*) attrayant, séduisant

attractiveness, charme *m.*

attribute, attribut *m.*, qualité *f.*

attribute, *v.t.* attribuer; imputer (à)

attune, *v.t.* accorder

auburn, (*adj.*) châtain clair

auction, vente (*f.*) aux enchères

auctioneer, commissaire-priseur *m.*

audacious, audacieux(-euse)

audaciousness, audacity, audace *f.*

audible, (*adj.*) distinct, intelligible; audible

audience, spectateurs *m. pl.*;

assistants m. pl.; assistance f.; audience f. (of the Pope, etc.)

auditor, vérificateur des comptes (financial); auditeur m.

auger, tarière f.

aught, quelque chose

augment, v.t. augmenter; accroître

augur, v.i. and v.t. présager, augurer

augury, augure m.

August (month), août m.

august, (adj.) auguste, majestueux(-euse)

aunt, tante f.

aurora borealis, aurore boréale f.

auspicious, (adj.) favorable, propice

austere, austère, âpre

austerity, austérité f.

Australian, (adj. and subst.) australien(ne)

Austrian, (adj. and subst.) autrichien(ne)

authentic, (adj.) authentique

authenticity, authenticité f.

author, auteur m., femme auteur f.

authorise, v.t. autoriser

authoritative, impérieux(-euse), autoritaire

authority, autorité f.

autograph, (subst.) autographe m.

autograph, v.t. autographier

automatic, (adj.) automatique

automatically, automatiquement

automaton, automate m.

automobile, automobile f.; voiture f.; (coll.) auto f.

autumn, automne m.

avail, v.i. profiter; servir

avail oneself of, se servir de

(to be of no) avail, ne servir à rien

available, disponible; valable

avalanche, avalanche f.

avarice, avarice f.

avaricious, avare

avenge, v.t. venger

to avenge oneself, se venger (de)

avenue, avenue f., boulevard m.

aver, v.t. affirmer

average, moyenne f.; avarie f. (naut. term); (adj.) moyen(ne)

averse, opposé à

aversion, répugnance f.; aversion f.

aviary, volière f.

aviation, aviation f.

aviator, aviateur m., pilote m.

avoid, v.t. éviter; esquiver (i.e. to dodge a blow)

avoidable, (adj.) qu'on peut éviter

avoirdupois, poids (m.) du commerce (16 onces à la livre)

avow, v.t. avouer, confesser, déclarer

avowal, aveu m.

await, v.t. attendre

awake, v.t. éveiller, réveiller

awake, v.i. s'éveiller

awake (wide), éveillé

award, v.t. adjuger, décerner

be aware, savoir, se rendre compte

away, (adv.) absent; loin, au loin

go away, v.i. s'en aller

send away, v.t. renvoyer

take away, v.t. enlever

awe, crainte f.; terreur f.

awe, v.t. inspirer du respect; effrayer

awful, terrible, redoutable; solennel(le)

awhile, (adv.) pendant quelque temps; un instant

awkward, gauche; maladroit

awl, alène f.; poinçon m.

awning, tente f.; bâche f.; tendelet m. (naut.)

awry, (adj. and adv.) de travers

axe, hache f., cognée f.

axis, axe m.

axle, essieu m.

azalea, azalée f.

azote, azote m.

azure, azur m.; (adj.) azuré

B

baa, v.i. bêler

baaing, bêlement m.

babble, babil m., murmure m.

babble, *v.i.* babiller, murmurer (stream)

babbler, babillard(e) *m.* (*f.*) bavard(e) *m.* (*f.*)

babbling, (*adj.*) babillard

babe, bambin *m.*; petit enfant *m.*

baboon, babouin *m.*

baby, bébé *m.*

baby linen, layette *f.*

babyhood, première enfance *f.*

babyish, (*adj.*) enfantin

bacchanalian, (*adj.*) bacchique

bachelor, célibataire *m.* bachelier *m.* (scholastic); B.A., licencié(e) ès lettres

bacillus, bacille *m.*

back, dos *m.*; derrière *m.*; revers *m.* (of hill); reins *m.* *pl.*; fond *m.*

back, (*adv.*) en arrière, de retour

back, *v.i.* reculer

back, *v.t.* appuyer; soutenir (uphold); endosser (a bill); faire reculer, renverser, jouer (a horse)

back out of, se tirer de

backbite, *v.t.* calomnier

backbone, épine dorsale *f.*

backer, partisan *m.*, parieur *m.*

background, arrière-plan *m.*, fond *m.*

backing, recul *m.* (recoil); remplage *m.* (stiffening)

backroom, chambre de derrière *f.*

backside, derrière *m.*

backsight (of arms), hausse *f.*

backslider, apostat *m.*

backstairs, escalier de service *m.*

backward, backwards, (*adv.*) en arrière, en retard; (*adj.*) tardif (-ive)

back-yard, arrière-cour *f.*

bacon, lard *m.*, bacon *m.*

bacteriology, bactériologie *f.*

bacterium, bactérie *f.*

bad, (*adj.*) mauvais, méchant, triste (weather)

badge, marque *f.*; signe *m.*

badger, blaireau *m.*

badger, *v.t.* harceler

badly, (*adv.*) mal

badness, méchanceté *f.*, mauvais état *m.*

baffle, *v.t.* déjouer, dérouter

bag, sac *m.*; bourse *f.*; poche *f.*

bag, *v.t.* empocher; abattre (shooting)

bagful, sac plein *m.*

baggage, bagage *m.*

baggage-wagon, fourgon *m.*

bagging, toile à sac *f.*

bagpipe, cornemuse *f.*

bail, caution *f.*, liberté sous caution *f.*

bail, *v.t.* donner caution pour (go bail for); écoper l'eau (of a boat)

bailiff, huissier *f.*

bairn, enfant *m.*

bait, appât *m.*

bait, *v.t.* amorcer (a hook); (*fig.*) tourmenter

bake, *v.t.* cuire au four; faire cuire

baker, boulanger *m.*

bakery, boulangerie *f.*

baking, cuisson *f.*

balance, balance *f.*; équilibre *m.*; solde de compte *m.* (of account)

balance, *v.i.* se balancer, s'équilibrer

balance, *v.t.* balancer, peser

balance-sheet, bilan *m.*

balcony, balcon *m.*

bald, (*adj.*) chauve

balderdash, galimatias *m.*

baldness, calvitie *f.*

bale, balle *f.*; ballot *m.*

bale, *v.t.* emballer

ball, balle *f.*; boule *f.*; pelote *f.* (of wool); ballon *m.* (football); bille *f.* (billiard); prunelle *f.* (eyeball)

ball (dance), bal *m.*

ball-room, salle de bal *f.*

ballad, ballade *f.*

ballast, lest *m.*, ballast *m.* (railway line)

in ballast, sur lest

ballast, *v.t.* lester, ensabler (railway line)

ballet, ballet *m.*

ballet-dancer, danseur(-euse) d'opéra *m.* (*f.*); ballerine *f.*

ballistics, balistique *f.*

balloon, ballon *m.*

ballot, scrutin *m.*

balk (*or* **baulk**), poutre *f.*

balk, *v.t.* frustrer

balm, baume *m.*

balsam, baume *m.*

balmy, (*adj.*) embaumé, parfumé

Baltic (sea), mer Baltique *f.*

balustrade, balustrade *f.*

bamboo, bambou *m.*

bamboozle, *v.t.* tromper, enjôler

ban, ban *m.*, interdiction *f.*

ban, *v.t.* interdire

banal, (*adj.*) banal

banana, banane *f.*

band, bande *f.* (i.e. gang); lien *m.* (i.e. bond); ruban *m.*

band, musique *f.*, orchestre *m.*

band, *v.i.* se liguer

band, *v.t.* réunir en troupe

bandage, bandage *m.*; pansement *m.*

bandbox, carton *m.*

bandit, bandit *m.*

bandsman, musicien *m.*

bandy (words), *v.i.* se disputer

bandy-legged, (*adj.*) bancal

bang, coup *m.*; grand bruit *m.*; détonation *f.*

bang, *v.t.* rosser (to beat); fermer avec fracas

bangle, bracelet *m.*

banish, *v.t.* bannir, exiler

bank, rivage *m.*, bord *m.* (river, etc.); berge *f.* (of river); remblai *m.* (mound, etc.); banc *m.* (of sand)

bank (financial), banque *f.*

bank, *v.t.* déposer en banque

bank up, *v.t.* terrasser

bank-book, livret de banque *m.*

bank-clerk, commis de banque *m.*

banker, banquier *m.*

banking, la banque *f.*

bank-note, billet de banque *m.*

bankrupt, (*adj.*) failli, en faillite *f.*

bankrupt, banqueroutier *m.*, failli *m.*

bankruptcy, banqueroute *f.*, faillite *f.*

banns, bans de mariage *m. pl.*

banter, badinage *m.*, raillerie *f.*

banter, *v.t.* badiner, railler

baptise, *v.t.* baptiser

baptism, baptême *m.*

bar, barre *f.*; barreau *m.* (law), parquet *m.* (law); comptoir *m.*

(public-house); buvette *f.* (drinking); banc des accusés *m.*; (*fig.*) obstacle *m.*

bar, *v.t.* barrer, empêcher

barbarian, barbare *m.* and *f.*

barbaric, (*adj.*) barbare

barbarous, (*adj.*) barbare

barbed (wire), fil de fer barbelé *m.*

barbel, barbeau *m.* (fish)

barber, coiffeur *m.*

bare, (*adj.*) nu, découvert; (*fig.*) simple, strict (necessities)

bare, *v.t.* mettre à nu, découvrir

bare-faced, (*adj.*) effronté

bare-foot, (*adj.*) nu-pieds, les pieds nus

bare-headed, (*adj.*) nu-tête, la tête nue

bare-legged, (*adj.*) nu-jambes, les jambes nues

(N.B.—nu, preceding, remains unchanged, but changes when placed after the word with which it is connected)

barely, (*adv.*) à peine, tout juste

bareness, nudité *f.*, pauvreté *f.*

bargain, accord *m.*; contrat *m.*; occasion *f.* (shopping, etc.)

bargain, *v.i.* marchander

into the bargain, par-dessus le marché

barge, barque *f.*; chaland *m.*.

bargee, batelier *m.*, chalandier *m.*

bark, écorce *f.* (of tree)

bark, *v.t.* écorcer

bark (of dog), aboiement *m.*

bark (dog), *v.i.* aboyer

barley, orge *f.*, orge perlé *m.* (pearl barley)

barmaid, fille de comptoir *f.*

barman, garçon de comptoir *m.*

barn, grange *f.*

barnacle, bernache *f.*

barometer, baromètre *m.*

baron(-ess), baron(ne) *m.* (*f.*)

baronet, barronet *m.*

barrack, *v.t.* huer (i.e. to hoot)

barracks (*mil.*), caserne *f.*; (cavalry) quartier *m.*

barrel, baril *m.*, fût *m.* (wine, etc.); canon *m.* (of rifle); cylindre *m.* (machine)

double-barrelled gun, fusil à deux coups *m.*

barren, (*adj.***)** stérile

barricade, barricade *f.*

barricade, *v.t.* barricader

barrier, barrière *f.*

barrister, avocat *m.*

barrow, brouette *f.*

barter, échange *m.*, troc *m.*

barter, *v.t.* échanger, faire échange, troquer

basalt, basalte *m.*

base, (*adj.***)** bas(se); vil

base, base *f.*; fondement *m.*

base-line, ligne (*f.*) de fond (tennis)

basement, sous-sol *m.*

baseness, bassesse *f.*, lâcheté *f.*

bashful, (*adj.***)** timide; modeste

basilisk, basilic *m.*

basin, bassin *m.*; cuvette *f.*; lavabo *m.* (lavatory basin)

basis, base *f.*; fondement *m.*

bask, *v.i.* se chauffer (in the sun, etc.)

basket, panier *m.*, corbeille *f.*

bass, basse *f.* (*mus.*)

bass (fish), bar *m.*, perche *f.*

bassinet, voiture (*f.*) d'enfant, bercelonnette *f.*

bassoon, basson *m.*

bastard, bâtard *m.*

bastinado, bastonnade *f.*

bat, chauve-souris *f.*; batte *f.* (cricket)

batch, fournée *f.*; tas *m.* (heap of)

bath, bain *m.* -tub, baignoire, *f.*

bathe, *v.i.* se baigner

bather, baigneur(-euse) *m.* (*f.*)

bathing, bain *m.*

bathing-dress, costume de bain *m.*; maillot *m.*

bathing-gown, peignoir *m.*; robe-de-chambre *f.*

bathing resort, station balnéaire *f.*

battalion, bataillon *m.*

batten, *v.t.* voliger (carpentry)

batten, *v.i.* s'engraisser (i.e. to grow fat)

batter, pâte (*f.*) lisse

batter, *v.t.* battre; battre en brèche; ébranler

battery, batterie *f.*

battle, bataille *f.*; combat *m.*

battle, *v.i.* combattre; lutter; batailler

give battle, livrer bataille

pitched battle, bataille rangée *f.*

battle-cruiser, croiseur cuirassé *m.*

battlefield, champ de bataille *m.*

battlement, créneau *m.*

battleship, cuirassé *m.*

bauble, babiole *f.*

Bavarian, bavarois(e)

bawdy, (*adj.***)** obscène

bawl, brailler; (*coll.*) gueuler

bawling, cris *m. pl.*; braillements *m. pl.*

bay (tree), laurier *m.*

bay, baie *f.*; golfe *m.*

bay, *v.i.* aboyer (of hounds)

bay-window, fenêtre en saillie *f.*

at bay, aux abois

bayonet, baïonnette *f.*

bayonet, *v.t.* tuer à coups de baïonnette

bazaar, bazar *m.*

be, (*v. aux.*) être

beach, plage *f.*; rivage *m.*

beach, *v.t.* échouer (a ship)

beacon(-light), phare *m.*; fanal *m.*

beadle, suisse *m.* (in Roman Catholic church); bedeau *m.*

beagle, (chien**)** bigle *m.*

beak, bec *m.*; maître *m.* (in school); magistrat *m.*

beaker, gobelet *m.*

beam, poutre *f.* (*arch.*); balancier *m.* (engine); rayon *m.* (light); largeur *f.* (ship)

beam, *v.i.* rayonner

bean, fève *f.*; haricot vert (french bean); haricot blanc *m.* (kidney bean)

bear, ours(e) *m.* (*f.*): baissier *m.* (Stock Exchange)

bear, *v.t.* porter, soutenir, endurer, souffrir, subir; donner naissance à (give birth to)

beard, barbe *f.*

bearded, (*adj.***)** barbu

beardless, (*adj.***)** imberbe

bearer, porteur *m.*, porteuse *f.*
stretcher-bearer, brancardier *m.*
beast, bête *f.*; animal(-aux) *m.* (*pl.*)
beast of burden, bête de somme *f.*
beastly, (*adj.*) bestial (*pl.* -aux)
beastliness, bestialité *f.*
beat, *v.t.* battre; frapper; l'emporter sur (outdo); fouetter (whip); vaincre (conquer)
beaten, (*adj.*) battu
beating, rossée *f.*, correction *f.*; battement *m.* (of heart, etc.)
beau, prétendant *m.*, galant *m.*
beautiful, (*adj.*) beau, bel *m.*, belle *f.*; magnifique
beautifully, (*adv.*) admirablement; parfaitement
beautify, *v.t.* embellir
beauty, beauté *f.*
beauty spot, grain de beauté *m.*
beaver, castor *m.*
because, (*conj.*) parce que; (*prep. phrase*) à cause de
beck, signe (*m.*) de doigt (de tête)
beckon, *v.t.* faire signe
become, *v.i.* devenir; commencer à être
become, *v.t.* aller bien; convenir
becoming, (*adj.*) attrayant; qui va bien
bed, lit *m.*; couche *f.*; assise *f.* (*geol.*); flower-bed, plate-bande *f.*; river bed, lit de rivière *m.*
bed-clothes, draps *m. pl.*, couvertures *f. pl.*
bedding, literie *f.*
bed-ridden, (*adj.*) alité
bedroom, chambre à coucher *f.*
bedstead, lit *m.*
bed-time, l'heure du coucher
bedaub, *v.t.* barbouiller
bedeck, *v.t.* parer
bedew, *v.t.* humecter de rosée
bee, abeille *f.*
bee-hive, ruche *f.*
beech (tree), hêtre *m.*
beech (nut), faîne *f.*
beef, bœuf (meat)
boiled beef, bouilli *m.*
beef-steak, bifteck *m.*
beef-tea, bouillon de bœuf *m.*
beer, bière *f.*; bock *m.* (glass of beer)

beet (beetroot), betterave *f.*
beetle, scarabée *m.*; escarbot *m.*; (hammer) mailloche *f.*
beetle, *v.i.* surplomber; faire saillie
befall, *v.i.* arriver
befit, *v.t.* convenir à
before, (*adv.*) avant (time, order); auparavant; préalablement
before, (*prep.*) devant (place); avant (time)
beforehand, à l'avance, d'avance
befriend, *v.t.* aider, protéger
beg, *v.t.* demander (à); prier (de); mendier (alms)
beget, *v.t.* engendrer
beggar, mendiant(e) *m.* (*f.*); poor beggar! pauvre diable!
beggar, *v.t.* appauvrir; ruiner
begin, *v.t.* commencer; débuter; entamer; se mettre à
begin, *v.i.* commencer par
beginner, commençant *m.*, débutant(e) *m.* (*f.*)
beginning, commencement *m.*
begrime, *v.t.* barbouiller, souiller
begrudge, *v.t.* envier à, refuser
beguile, *v.t.* séduire; charmer
in behalf of, en faveur de
on behalf of, au nom de
behave, *v.i.* se conduire, se comporter
behaviour, conduite *f.*, tenue *f.*
behead, *v.t.* décapiter
behind, (*prep.*) derrière, en arrière de, en retard de
behind, (*adv.*) derrière, par derrière
behindhand, en retard
behold! (*interj.*) voici! voilà!
behold, *v.t.* regarder, voir
being, être *m.*, existence *f.*
belabour, *v.t.* rosser
belated, (*adj.*) attardé
belch, *v.i.* roter
beleaguer, *v.t.* assiéger
belfry, beffroi *m.*, clocher *m.*
Belgian, (*adj.* and *subst.*) belge
belie, *v.t.* démentir
belief, croyance *f.*, foi *f.*
believable, (*adj.*) croyable
believe, *v.i.* and *v.t.* croire
believer, croyant(e) *m.* (*f.*), fidèle *m.* and *f.*

bell, cloche *f.*, clochette *f.*, sonnette *f.* (of house); timbre *m.* (on cycles, etc.); grelot *m.* (small round bell)

bell-push (pull), bouton (*m.*) (cordon) de sonnerie

bell-ringer, sonneur *m.*

bell-shaped, (*adj.*) en forme de cloche

bellicose, belliqueux(-euse)

belligerent, (*adj.* and *subst.*). belligérant(e)

bellow, *v.i.* beugler, mugir

bellow, beuglement *m.*, mugissement *m.*

bellows, soufflet *m.*

belly, ventre *m.*

belly, *v.i.* se gonfler

belly-ache, mal (*m.*) au ventre

belong, *v.i.* appartenir, être à

belongings, effets *m. pl.*

beloved, (*adj.*) bien-aimé, chéri

below, (*prep.*) sous; au-dessous de; en aval de

below, (*adv.*) au-dessous; dessous; en bas

belt, ceinturon *m.*; ceinture *f.*; courroie *f.* (for motors)

bench, banc *m.*, banquette *f.*, parquet *m.* (law); magistrature *f.*

bend, *v.t.* plier; courber; faire plier

bend, *v.i.* se courber, se plier

bend, courbe *f.* (of road, river, etc.), coude *m.*; virage *m.*

beneath, (*prep.*) sous, au-dessous de

beneath, (*adv.*) au-dessous; en bas

benefactor, bienfaiteur *m.*

benefactress, bienfaitrice *f.*

benefice, bénéfice *m.*

beneficence, bienfaisance *f.*

beneficent, bienfaisant

beneficial, (*adj.*) salutaire

benefit, bienfait *m.*, profit *m.*, avantage *m.*, bénéfice *m.*

benevolent, (*adj.*) bienveillant

benign, (*adj.*) bénin (*f.* bénigne); doux (*f.* douce); affable

bent, (*adj.*) courbé, plié

bent on, résolu à

benumb, *v t.* engourdir

benzine, benzine *f.*

bequeath, *v.t.* léguer

bequest, legs *m.*

bereave, *v.t.* priver de

bereavement, perte *f.*, deuil *m.*

berry, baie *f.*

berth, couchette *f.* (on ship, étc.); place *f.* (situation)

berth, *v.i.* mouiller, aborder à quai (of ship)

beseech, *v.t.* supplier

beset, *v.t.* obséder, assaillir

besetting, habituel(le)

beside, (*prep.*) a côté de, auprès de; hormis, excepté

besides, (*adv.*) d'ailleurs; en outre; de plus

besiege, *v.t.* assiéger

besmear, *v.t.* souiller

besmirch, *v.t.* tacher, salir

bespeak, *v.t.* retenir (i.e. to order, book)

best, (*adj.*) and *noun,* le (la) meilleur(e); (*adv.*) and *noun,* le mieux

bestial, bestial (*pl.* bestiaux)

bestir, *v.i.* se remuer

bestow, *v.t.* accorder, donner

bestride, *v.t.* être à cheval sur; enjamber (a ditch, gutter, etc.)

bet, pari *m.*

bet, *v.i.* and *v.t.* parier

betake oneself, se rendre à

betimes, (*adv.*) de bonne heure

betray, *v.t.* trahir

betroth, *v.t.* fiancer

betrothal, fiançailles *f. pl.*

better, (*adj.*) meilleur

better, (*adv.*) mieux

to better oneself, améliorer sa situation

get the better of, prendre le dessus sur, l'emporter sur

between, (*prep.*) entre

bevel, biais *m.*, biseau *m.*

bevel, *v.t.* tailler en biseau, biseauter

beverage, boisson *f.*

bevy, volée *f.*; troupe *f.* compagnie *f.* (of young people, etc.)

bewail, *v.t.* déplorer, pleurer

beware, *v.i.* se garder de; se méfier de

bewilder, *v.t.* ahurir; confondre

bewildered, (adj.) effaré, égaré, ahuri

bewilderment, égarement m.; trouble m.

bewitch, v.t. ensorceler, enchanter

beyond, (prep.) au delà de; outre

beyond, (adv.) là-bas; au delà

bias, parti pris m.; penchant m.

bias, v.t. prédisposer en faveur de (or contre)

bib, bavette f.

Bible, Bible f.

bicarbonate, bicarbonate m.

bicker, v.i. se quereller

bicycle, bicyclette f., vélo m.

bicyclist, cycliste m. (f.)

bid, offre f.; enchère f.

bid, v.t. commander (de); inviter (à); offrir; enchérir

bidder, enchérisseur m.; highest bidder, le plus offrant

bide, v.t. attendre, souffrir

bier, civière f.

big, (adj.) gros (f. grosse); grand, vaste

bigamy, bigamie f.

bigness, grosseur f.; grandeur f.

bigot, sectaire, m. (f.)

bigotry, fanatisme m.

bigwig, gros bonnet m.

bile, bile f.

bilious, bilieux(-euse)

bill, compte m., facture f. (invoice); note f. (hotels); addition f. (restaurant); billet m., effet m. (commerce)

Bill (Parliament), projet de loi m.

bill of exchange, lettre de change f.

bill of fare, menu m., carte f.

bill of lading, connaissement m.

bill of sale, lettre de vente f.

bill at sight, billet à vue m.

bill payable, billet à payer m.

bill receivable, billet à recevoir m.

bill-broker, courtier de change m.

hand-bill, affiche f.

billet, billet (m.) de logement (mil.); bûche f. (of wood)

billet, v.t. loger

billiards, billard m.

billiard-ball, bille f.

billiard-cue, queue f.

billow, flot m., vague f.

billow, v.i. ondoyer

bimetalism, bimétallisme m.

bind, lier; relier (books); obliger (to force)

binder, relieur m.

binding, reliure f.

binnacle, habitacle m.

biographer, biographe m.

biography, biographie f.

biologist, biologiste m.; biologue m.

biology, biologie f.

birch, bouleau m. (tree); verges f. pl. (rods)

birch, v.t. fouetter (à coups de verges)

bird, oiseau m.

bird-cage, cage d'oiseau f.

bird-fancier, amateur d'oiseaux m.

bird's-eye view, vue à vol d'oiseau f.

birth, naissance f.; (fig.) origine f.

birthday, anniversaire m.; jour de naissance m.

birth-place, lieu de naissance m.

birthright, droit d'aînesse m.; droit de naissance

biscuit, biscuit m.

bishop, évêque m.

bishopric, évêché m.

bishop's palace, évêché m.

bit, morceau m.; pièce; mèche f. (tool); mors m. (of bridle)

bitch, chienne f.

bite, morsure f., bouchée f. (of food, etc.)

bite, v.t. mordre

bitter, (adj.) amer(-ère), acharné (struggle)

bitterly, (adv.) amèrement

bitterness, amertume f.; aigreur f.; rancune f.

bitumen, bitume m.

bivouac, bivouac m.

bivouac, v.i. bivouaquer

blab, v.i. bavarder, jaser

blabber, bavard m.

black, (adj.) noir (fig.); obscur, sombre

black, *v.t.* noircir, cirer (shoes)

black-ball, *v.t.* rejeter au scrutin

blackberry, mûre *f.*

blackbird, merle *m.*

blackboard, tableau noir *m.*

black-currant, cassis *m.*

blackguard, goujat *m.*, gredin *m.*

blacking, cirage *m.*,

blackish, *(adj.)* noirâtre

blackleg, renard *m.* (in strikes, etc.), jaune

blackmail, chantage *m.*

blackmail, *v.t.* faire chanter

blackmailer, maître-chanteur *m.*

black-pudding, boudin *m.*

blacksmith, forgeron *m.*

blacksmith's shop, forge *f.*

bladder, vessie *f.* (anatomy); vésicule *f.* (gall-bladder)

blade, lame *f.* (cutting instrument); brin *m.* (of grass)

blamable, *(adj.)* blâmable

blame, blâme *m.*; faute *f.*

blame, *v.t.* blâmer; censurer

blameless, *(adj.)* irréprochable

blameworthy, *(adj.)* digne de blâme

bland, *(adj.)* doux (douce), aimable

blandish, *v.t.* cajoler, flatter

blandishments, cajoleries *f. pl.*

blank, *(adj.)* blanc (blanche); en blanc

blank, blanc *m.*, lacune *f.*

blanket, couverture *f.*

blaspheme, *v.i.* and *v.t.* blasphémer

blasphemer, blasphémateur (-trice) *m. (f.)*

blasphemy, blasphème *m.*

blast, coup de vent *m.*; explosion *f.*

blast, *v.t.* faire sauter

blast-furnace, haut fourneau *m.*

blasting, sautage *m.*, explosion *f.*, mine *f.*

blasting-powder, poudre *(f.)* de démolition

blaze, flamme *f.*; *(fig.)* feu *m.*

blaze, *v.i.* être en flammes; flamber

bleach, *v.t.* blanchir

bleak, *(adj.)* morne, triste

bleat, bleating, bêlement *m.*

bleat, *v.i.* bêler

bleed, *v.t.* and *v.i.* saigner

bleeding, saignement *m.*, saignée *f.* (*surg.*)

blemish, tache *f.*, défaut *m.*

blemish, *v.t.* ternir, gâter

blench, *v.t.* broncher

blend, *v.t.* mêler, mélanger

blend, mélange *m.*

bless, *v.t.* bénir

blessing, bénédiction *f.*; bonheur *m.*

blind, *(adj.)* aveugle

blind, *v.t.* aveugler

blind alley, cul-de-sac *m.*; imblind in one eye, borgne [passe *f.*

blind (of window), store *m.* (of window); jalousie *f.* (venetian)

blind man's buff, colin-maillard *m.*

blindfold, *v.t.* bander les yeux

blindly, *(adv.)* aveuglément

blindness, cécité *f.*, aveuglement *m.*

blink, *v.i.* cligner, clignoter

blink, clignotement *m.*

bliss, félicité *f.*; béatitude *f.*

blissful, *(adj.)* bienheureux(-euse)

blister, ampoule *f.*, vésicatoire *m.*

blister, *v.i.* s'élever en ampoules; (of paint) se cloquer

blithe, *(adj.)* gai, joyeux(-euse)

bloat, *v.t.* bouffir, gonfler

bloater, hareng saur *m.*

block, bloc *m.*; billot *m.*; cliché *m.* (stereotype); gravure sur bois *f.*; poulie *f.* (block and tackle); obstacle *m.*; embouteillage *m.* (traffic)

block, *v.t.* bloquer, boucher

blockade, blocus *m.*

blockhead, sot *m.*, lourdaud *m.*

blood, sang *m.*

blood-horse, cheval pur-sang *m.*

bloodhound, limier *m.*

blood-letting, saignée, *f.*

blood-poisoning, empoisonnement du sang *m.*

blood-red, *(adj.)* rouge comme le sang

bloodshed, effusion *(f.)* de sang

bloodthirsty, (*adj.*) sanguinaire
bloody, ensanglanté; (*coll.*) sacré
bloom, blossom, fleur *f.*; duvet *m.* (bloom on a peach, etc.)
bloom, blossom, *v.i.* fleurir
blooming, florissant, fleurissant
blot, tache *f.*
blot, *v.t.* tacher, sécher (i.e. to dry)
blot out, *v.t.* effacer
blotting paper, papier buvard *m.*
blouse, blouse *f.*; chemisette *f.*
blow, coup (with a stick or fist); soufflet *m.*
blow, *v.i.* souffler (wind)
blow, *v.t.* sonner (horn, etc.)
blow away, *v.t.* chasser
blow one's nose, se moucher
blow up (bridge, etc.), faire sauter
blowpipe, chalumeau *m.*
bludgeon, gourdin *m.*, trique *f.*
blue, (*adj.*) bleu
blue, *v.t.* teindre en bleu
bluebottle, mouche bleue *f.*; bleuet *m.*
blue-eyed, (*adj.*) aux yeux bleus
bluejacket, matelot *m.*
bluestocking, bas-bleu *m.*, femme savante *f.*
bluff, (*adj.*) brusque
bluff, escarpement *m.*, falaise *f.*
bluff, *v.t.* bluffer
bluish, (*adj.*) bleuâtre
blunder, étourderie *f.*; bévue *f.*; faux pas *m.*; gaffe *f.*
blunder, *v.i.* s'embrouiller; faire une gaffe
blunt, (*adj.*) émoussé, brusque
blush, rougeur *f.*
blush, *v.i.* rougir; avoir honte
bluster, tapage *m.*, fureur (storm) *f.*
bluster, *v.i.* tempêter
blusterer, tapageur *m.*; bravache *m.*
blustering, (*adj.*) bruyant, orageux(-euse) (stormy)
boar, sanglier *m.*
board, planche *f.*; table *f.*; pension *f.* (full board); conseil d'administration *m.* (of company); carton *m.* (i.e. cardboard)

board, *v.i.* être en pension
board, *v.t.* nourrir; (a ship) aborder
boarder, pensionnaire *m.* and *f.*
boarding-house, pension *f.*
boarding-school, pensionnat *m.*
boast, vanterie *f.*
boast, *v.i.* se vanter
boat, bateau *m.*, canot *m.*, barque *f.*, embarcation *f.*; navire *m.*
boatman, batelier *m.*
boatswain, maître d'équipage *m.*
boating, promenade en bateau *f.*, canotage *m.*
bob, *v.t.* écourter (tail)
bob-tailed, (*adj.*) à queue écourtée
bobbin, bobine *f.*
bobby, gardien de la paix *m.* (*coll.*)
bode, *v.t.* and *v.i.* présager
bodice, corsage *m.*
bodily, (*adj.*) corporel(le)
boding, pressentiment *m.*
body, corps *m.*
dead body, cadavre *m.*
main body (of army), gros *m.*
public body, corporation *f.*
body-guard, garde du corps *m.*
bog, marais *m.*
boggy, marécageux(-euse)
bogus, (*adj.*) faux (fausse)
Bohemian, (*adj.* and *subst.*) bohémien(ne)
boil, *v.i.* bouillir; cuire à l'eau
boil, *v.t.* faire bouillir, faire cuire à l'eau
boil, furoncle *m.*
boiled, (*adj.*) bouilli, cuit à l'eau
boiler, chaudière *f.*
boiler-maker, chaudronnier *m.*
boiler manufactory, chaudronnerie *f.*
boiling, (*adj.*) bouillant
boiling point, point (*m.*) d'ébullition
boisterous, (*adj.*) turbulent, orageux (weather)
bold, (*adj.*) hardi; audacieux (-euse), effronté (impudent)
boldly, (*adv.*) hardiment; impudemment

boldness, hardiesse *f.*, audace *f.*, impudence *f.*
bolster, traversin *m.*
bolster (up), *v.t.* rembourrer; soutenir; étayer
bolt, verrou *m.*, boulon *m.* (pin)
bolt, *v.t.* gober (food); verrouiller (door); *v.i.* décamper (of person)
bomb, bombe *f.*
bombard, *v.t.* bombarder
bombardment, bombardement *m.*
bomber, bombardier *m.*; avion de bombardement *m.*
bomb-proof, à l'épreuve des bombes
bond, lien *m.*; liaison *f.*; obligation *f.*; bon *m.* (*finan.*)
in bond, à l'entrepôt
bondage, esclavage *m.*
bonded goods, marchandises entreposées
bone, os *m.*, arête *f.* (of fish)
bones, ossements *m. pl.*
bonfire, feu de joie *m.*
bonnet, bonnet *m.*, chapeau *m.*, capot *m.* (of car, etc.)
bony, osseux(-euse)
booby, nigaud *m.*
book, livre *m.*; livret *m.*
book, *v.t.* enregistrer; porter au compte; inscrire; retenir (a place)
book through, prendre un billet direct pour
bookbinder, relieur *m.*
bookbinding, reliure *f.*
bookcase, bibliothèque *f.*
book-keeper, comptable *m.*
book-keeping, comptabilité *f.*
bookseller, libraire *m.*
bookshelf, rayon *m.*
bookshop, librairie *f.*
booking, enregistrement *m.*
booking-office, bureau (*m.*) de distribution des billets *m.*; guichet *m.* (railway station)
boom, grondement *m.* (noise); grande hausse (business and financial); barrage *m.*
boon, bienfait *m.*, avantage *m.*
boor, rustre *m.*
boot, bottine *f.*, botte *f.*, chaus-

sure *f.*, brodequin *m.* (ankle-boot)
boot-lace, lacet *m.*
bootless, (*adj.*) vain; sans chaussures
boot-maker, cordonnier *m.*
boot-tree, embauchoir *m.*
booted, botté
booth, baraque *f.*
booty, butin *m.*
booze, *v.i.* se griser
border, bord *m.*, bordure *f.* (edging); frontière *f.* (country); parterre *m.* (garden)
border, *v.i.* toucher à
bore, trou *m.*, calibre *m.*; raseur *m.* (tiring companion); ennui *m.*
bore, *v.t.* percer; sonder; creuser; forer; ennuyer (to tire, annoy)
boredom, ennui *m.*
boring, (*adj.*) ennuyeux(-euse); assommant
boring, sondage *m.*
born, (*adj.*) né
borough, bourg *m.*; ville *f.*
borrow (from), *v.t.* emprunter (à)
borrower, emprunteur *m.*
bosh, bêtise *f.*, galimatias *m.*
bosom, sein *m.*; (*fig.*) cœur *m.*
Bosphorus, Bosphore *m.*
boss, bosse *f.* (*arch.*); patron *m.*, chef *m.* (employer, etc.)
botanical, (*adj.*) botanique
botany, botanique *f.*
botch, travail (*m.*) mal fait
botch, *v.t.* ravauder; saboter (a piece of work)
both, (*adj.*) tous les deux, tous deux, l'un et l'autre
both . . . and, et . . . et
bother, ennui *m.*, tracas *m.*
bother, *v.t.* tracasser; gêner
bottle, bouteille *f.*
bottle, *v.t.* mettre en bouteille
bottom, fond *m.*, bas *m.*, pied *m.*, derrière *m.*
bottomless, sans fond
bough, rameau *m.*, branche *f.*
boulder, grosse pierre *f.*, bloc *m.*
bounce, *v.i.* rebondir
bound, borne *f.*, limite *f.*; saut *m.*
bound, *v.i.* bondir, sauter; *v.t.* limiter

bound for, en partance pour; à destination de

boundary, limite f., borne f., frontière f.

boundless, (adj.) illimité; sans bornes

bounty, munificence f.; prime f.

bow, révérence f.

bow, v.i. s'incliner; saluer

bow, archet m. (violin); nœud m. (knot); arc m. (archery)

bow (of ship), avant m.

bow-legged, bancal(-als)

bowels, entrailles f. pl.

bower, berceau de verdure m., tonnelle f.

bowie-knife, couteau-poignard m.

bowl, bol m., vase m.; coupe f.; fourneau m. (of pipe)

bowls (sport), boules f. pl.

bowsprit, beaupré m.

box, boîte f.; caisse f.; malle f. (trunk); loge f. (theatre); buis m. (hedge, etc.)

box, v.i. boxer (pugilism)

box on the ear, soufflet m.

Christmas box, étrennes f. pl.

boxer, boxeur m., pugiliste m.

boxing, la boxe f.

Boxing Day, lendemain de Noël m.; jour des étrennes m.

boy, garçon m., garçonnet m., enfant m.

boycott, v.t. boycotter

boyhood, enfance f.

boyish, (adj.) puéril

brace, couple f.; paire f.; attache f.; écharpe f.

brace, v.t. lier, serrer

brace up, v.t. fortifier

bracelet, bracelet m.

braces, bretelles f. pl.

bracing, (adj.) fortifiant

bracket, support m.; console f.; crochet m., parenthèse f. (print.)

bracket, v.t. encadrer (target); mettre entre crochets

brackish, (adj.) saumâtre

Bradshaw, indicateur des chemins de fer m.

brag, v.i. se vanter

braggart, vantard m.

braid, tresse f. (of hair); galon m. (on uniform); ganse f.

brain, cerveau m. (organ); cervelle f. (substance)

brain fever, fièvre cérébrale f.

brainless, sans cervelle

brake, frein m.

brake, v.t. appliquer le frein; freiner

brake-van, wagon-frein m.

bramble, ronce f.

bran, son m.

branch, branche f.; rameau m.; succursale f. (of bank, firm); embranchement m. (railway line)

branch off, v.i. s'embrancher, se bifurquer

brand, marque f. (of goods); brandon m. (fire); (fig.) stigmate m.

brand, v.t. marquer, stigmatiser

brand-new, (adj.) tout neuf(-ve)

brandish, v.t. brandir

brandy, eau-de-vie f., cognac m.; (liqueur brandy) fine champagne f.

brass, cuivre jaune m.; laiton m.; airain m.

brass-foundry, fonderie de cuivre jaune f.

brassière, soutien-gorge m. (invar.)

brave, (adj.) courageux(-euse) vaillant

bravely, (adv.) courageusement

bravery, bravoure f., vaillance f.

brawl, dispute f., querelle f., rixe f.

brawl, v.i. brailler, disputer

brawn, pâté de cochon m.; (fig.) muscles m. pl.

brawny, (adj.) musculeux(-euse); charnu

bray, v.i. braire

brazen, (adj.) d'airain; (fig.) effronté

Brazilian, brésilien(ne)

breach, brèche f., rupture f., infraction f.

bread, pain m.

brown bread, pain bis m.

fresh bread, pain frais m.

stale bread, pain rassis m.

breadth, largeur *f.*

break, *v.t.* rompre, briser (heart, courage, etc.); casser (a limb, etc.); violer (the law, etc.)

break (in) *or* **open,** *v.t.* enfoncer

break in, *v.t.* dresser (animals)

break off, *v.t.* rompre, inter-rompre

break, *v.i.* se briser, se casser, se rompre

break down, *v.i.* s'abattre; s'effondrer

break loose, *v.i.* s'échapper (de)

break out, *v.i.* éclater

break up, *v.i.* se séparer, changer (of weather)

break up, *v.i.* se disperser (crowd, etc.)

break with, *v.i.* rompre avec

break, rupture *f.*, ouverture *f.*, interruption *f.*, changement *m.* (weather)

break-down, accident *m.* (railway); panne *f.* (motor); débâcle *f.*

breakage, rupture *f.*; casse *f.* (commercial)

breakfast, petit déjeuner *m.*

break-neck (speed), *(adj.)* vertigineux(-euse)

breakwater, digue *f.*

breast, sein *m.* (of woman); poitrine *f.*

breath, haleine *f.*; souffle *m.*; existence *f.* (breath of life)

out of breath, hors d'haleine

to take one's breath away, couper la respiration

breathe, *v.i.* respirer; souffler

breathing, respiration *f.*

breathless, *(adj.)* essoufflé

bred, *(adj.)* élevé; (ill-bred) mal élevé

breech, culasse *f.* (of arms)

breeches, culottes *f. pl.*

breed, race *f.*; lignée *f.*

breed, *v.t.* élever; faire naître; engendrer

breed, *v.i.* multiplier

breeding, élevage *m.* (cattle, etc.); éducation *f.* (manners)

breeze, brise *f.*

breezy, *(adj.)* venteux(-euse) (weather); jovial (person)

brethren, frères *m. pl.*; confrères *m. pl.*

Breton, *(adj.* and *subst.)* breton(ne)

brevity, brièveté *f.*; concision *f.*

brew, *v.i.* faire (brasser) de la bière; *(fig.)* se préparer

brewer, brasseur *m.*

brewery, brasserie *f.*

bribe, pot-de-vin *m.*

bribe, *v.t.* acheter, corrompre

brick, brique *f.*

brick, *(adj.)* en briques

brick-kiln, four *(m.)* à briques

bricklayer, maçon *(m.)* en briques

brickwork, briquetage *m.*

bridal, *(adj.)* nuptial, de noces

bride, nouvelle mariée *f.*; fiancée *f.*

bridegroom, nouveau marié *m.*; fiancé *m.*

bridesmaid, demoiselle d'honneur *f.*

bridge (cards), bridge *m.*

bridge, pont *m.*, passerelle *f.* (of a ship)

bridge-head, tête *(f.)* de pont

bridle, bride *f.*; *(fig.)* frein *m.*

brief, *(adj.)* bref (brève)

brier, ronce *f.*; bruyère *f.*

brig, brick *m.*

brigade, brigade *f.*

bright, *(adj.)* brillant; clair; lumineux(-euse); *(fig.)* intelligent

brighten, *v.i.* s'éclaircir (weather)

brighten, *v.t.* faire briller; égayer

brilliance, éclat *m.*, lustre *m.*

brilliant, brillant, éclatant

brilliantly, avec éclat, brillamment

brim, bord *m.*

brimstone, soufre *m.*

brine, saumure *f.*

bring, *v.t.* apporter; amener; conduire

bring about, *v.t.* occasionner, provoquer

bring down, *v.t.* descendre (luggage); abattre (game); abaisser (price)

bring forth, *v.t.* produire

bring forward, *v.t.* avancer, reporter (book-keeping)

bring in, *v.t.* faire entrer

bring nearer, v.t. rapprocher
bring together, v.t. réconcilier; réunir
bring up, v.t. élever
brink, bord m.
brisk, (adj.) vif(-ve); animé; frais (fraîche) (weather)
bristle, poil raide m.; soie f. (of hog)
bristle, v.i. se hérisser
British, (adj.) britannique, anglais
brittle, (adj.) fragile, cassant
broach, v.t. percer; entamer (a subject)
broad, (adj.) large, vaste, gros
broadcast, radiodiffusion f. (wireless); émission f:
broadcast, v.t. radiodiffuser
broaden, v.i. s'élargir
broadly, (adv.) largement
broadside (of guns), salve f.; bordée f.
broil, v.t. griller
broken, (adj.) cassé, brisé, rompu
broker, courtier m. (bill-broker); agent (m.) de change (stock-broker)
brokerage, courtage m.
bronze, bronze m.
bronze, v.t. bronzer
brooch, broche f.
brood, couvée f.
brood, v.i. couver
brook, ruisseau m.
brook, v.t. souffrir (no interference, etc.)
broom, balai m., genêt m. (plant)
broomstick, manche (m.) à balai
broth, bouillon m.
brother, frère m.
brother-in-law, beau-frère m.
brotherhood, fraternité f., confraternité f.
brow, sourcil m. (eyebrow); front 'm. (forehead); sommet m. (of hill)
brown, (adj.) brun; châtain (of hair)
brown, v.i. se brunir
brown, v.t. brunir, rissoler (cook.)
browse, v.t. brouter (on grass, etc.)
bruise, contusion f., bleu m.
bruise, v.t. meurtrir, contusionner

brush, brosse f.; pinceau m. (paint.); balai m.; escarmouche f. (skirmish)
brush, v.t. brosser, balayer
brushwood, broussailles f. pl.
Brussels sprouts, choux (m. pl.) de Bruxelles
brutal, (adj.) brutal, cruel(le)
brutalise, v.t. abrutir
brutality, brutalité f.
brutally, (adv.) brutalement
brute, brute f., animal m.
brutish, (adj.) abruti
bubble, bulle f.; chimère f. (foolish fancy)
bubble, v.i. bouillonner
buccaneer, boucanier m.; flibustier m.
buck, daim m., chevreuil m.
buck-rabbit, mâle (m.) du lapin; vieux marcheur m. (old "buck")
buck-shot, chevrotine f.
bucket, seau m.
buckle, boucle f.
buckle, v.t. boucler; buckle (to) (fig.) s'appliquer (à); gauchir (of metal, etc.)
buckram, bougran m.
buckwheat, sarrasin m.
bud, bourgeon m., bouton m.
bud, v.i. bourgeonner
budge, bouger; se remuer
budget, budget m.
buff, (adj.) de couleur chamois
buffalo, buffle m.
buffer, tampon m.; amortisseur m.
buffet, buffet m. (sideboard); coup de poing m. (blow)
buffet, v.t. frapper à coups de poing
buffoon, bouffon m.
bug, punaise f.
bugbear, épouvantail m.
bugle, clairon m. (mil.)
bugler, clairon m.
build, v.t. bâtir, faire bâtir, construire
build, forme f.; taille f.
builder, entrepreneur (m.) en bâtiments
building, édifice m.; bâtiment m.; construction f.

bulb, bulbe *m.*; oignon *m.*; ampoule *f.* (electric light)

bulbous, bulbeux(-euse)

Bulgarian, (*adj.*) bulgare

bulk, volume *m.*; grosseur *f.*; masse *f.*; **in bulk,** en vrac, en gros

bulky, (*adj.*) gros (grosse)

bull, taureau *m.*; haussier *m.* (Stock Exchange); bulle *f.* (Papal)

bull-dog, bouledogue *m.*

bull-fight, course (*f.*) de taureaux

bullfinch, bouvreuil *m.*

bull's-eye, noir *m.* (of a target)

bullet, balle *f.*

bullet-proof, (*adj.*) à l'épreuve des balles

bullion, or (argent) en lingots *m.*

bullock, bœuf *m.*

bully, bravache *m.*; souteneur *m.* (pimp)

bully, *v.t.* intimider, malmener

bully-beef, conserve (*f.*) de bœuf salé; singe *m.* (*mil. slang*)

bulrush, jonc *m.*

bulwark, rempart *m.*

bump, coup *m.*; choc *m.*; bosse *f.* (on body, etc.)

bump, *v.i.* se heurter, se cogner

bumper, rasade *f.*; pare-chocs *m.* (of car)

bumpkin, rustre *m.*

bumptious, (*adj.*) présomptueux (-euse)

bumpy, cahoteux(-euse) (road, etc.)

bunch, botte *f.*; bouquet *m.* (of flowers); grappe *f.* (of grapes)

bundle, faisceau *m.*; fagot *m.*; paquet *m.*

bundle, *v.t.* empaqueter

bundle out, mettre à la porte

bung, bondon *m.*

bung-hole, bonde *f.*

bungle, *v.t.* bousiller, gâcher

bungler, maladroit(e) *m.* (*f.*); gâcheur(-euse) *m.* (*f.*)

bunion, oignon *m.*

bunker, soute *f.*

bunting, drapeaux *m. pl.*

buoy, bouée *f.*

buoy up, *v.t.* soutenir

buoyant, flottant; léger

burden, fardeau *m.*

burden, *v.t.* surcharger

burdensome, onéreux(-euse)

bureau, bureau *m.* (office); secrétaire *m.* (desk)

bureaucrat, bureaucrate *m.*; rond-de-cuir *m.*

burgess, bourgeois *m.*; citoyen *m.*

burglar, cambrioleur, *m.*

burglary, cambriolage *m.*

burgle, *v.t.* cambrioler

burgomaster, bourgmestre *m.*

Burgundy, Bourgogne *f.* (province); (vin de) Bourgogne *m.* (wine)

burial, enterrement *m.*, inhumation *f.*

burial-ground, cimetière *m.*

burlesque, (*adj.*) burlesque

burly, solide; (*coll.*) costaud

burn, brûlure *f.*

burn, *v.t.* brûler, incendier; *v.i.* brûler

burn to the ground, brûler de fond en comble

burner, bec *m.* (of gas, etc.)

burnish, *v.t.* polir

burrow, terrier *m.*

burrow, *v.i.* se terrer

bursar, économe *m.*

bursary, bourse (*f.*) d'études

burst, éclat *m.*; explosion *f.*

burst, *v.i.* crever, faire irruption

burst open, *v.t.* enfoncer (a door)

burst into tears, fondre en larmes

burst out laughing, éclater de rire

bury, *v.t.* enterrer, ensevelir

bus, omnibus *m.*; (motor-bus) autobus *m.*

bush, buisson *m.*

bushel, boisseau *m.*

bushy, (*adj.*) touffu

business, affaire *f.*; métier *m.*; commerce *m.*; clientèle *f.* (connexion); affaires *f. pl.* (trade, etc.); **to go into business,** entrer dans les affaires

businesslike, (*adj.*) pratique; sérieux(-euse)

bustle, mouvement *m.*, agitation *f.*

bustle, *v.i.* se remuer, s'empresser
busy, *(adj.)* affairé, occupé
but, *(conj.)* mais
but, *(adv.)* seulement, excepté
butcher, boucher(-ère) *m.* (*f.*)
butcher, *v.t.* massacrer
butchery, boucherie *f.*; massacre *m.*
butler, maître d'hôtel *m.*
butt, coup *m.* de tête (by animal); crosse *f.* (of rifle); cible *f.* (target); pipe *f.* (of wine, etc.)
butt, *v.i.* donner un coup de corne (as goat, etc.)
butter, beurre *m.*
butter, *v.t.* beurrer
buttercup, bouton d'or *m.*
butterfly, papillon *m.*
buttermilk, petit lait *m.*
button, bouton *m.*; "**buttons**" (page-boy), chasseur *m.*
button, *v.t.* boutonner
buttonhole, boutonnière *f.*
buttonhook, tire-bouton *m.*
buttress, arc-boutant *m.* (*arch.*)
buxom, *(adj.)* gaillard (of woman); rondelette
buy (from), *v.t.* acheter (à); corrompre (to bribe)
buyer, acheteur *m.*; acheteuse *f.*
buying, achat *m.*
buy up, *v.t.* accaparer
buzz, *v.i.* bourdonner
buzzing, bourdonnement *m.*
by, *(prep.)* par; de; sur; près de; auprès de (near); en (with participles)
by all means, par tous les moyens possibles; faites donc!, je vous en prie
by and by, bientôt
by day, de jour, le jour
by far, de beaucoup
by night, de nuit, la nuit
by no means, nullement
by oneself, tout seul
by the by, à propos
by turns, tour à tour
by-election, élection (*m.*) de remplacement
by-law, arrêté (*m.*) municipal
by-pass, route (*f.*) d'évitement
by-pass, *v.t.* contourner

by-path, sentier (*m.*) détourné
by-product, sous-produit *m.*
bystander, spectateur(-trice) *m.* (*f.*)
by-street, rue de traverse *f.*; rue latérale *f.*
by-word, dicton *m.*; proverbe *m.*; risée *f.* (laughing-stock)
bye, balle passée *f.* (cricket)

C

cab, fiacre *m.*; voiture de place *f.*; taxi *m.*
cab-stand, station (*f.*) de voitures
cabal, cabale *f.*
cabbage, chou *m.*
cabin, cabine *f.* (ship's); cabane *f.* (hut)
cabin-boy, mousse *m.*
cabinet, cabinet *m.*
cabinet (government), conseil de ministres *m.*
cabinet-maker, ébéniste *m.*
cabinet minister, ministre d'état *m.*
cable, câble *m.*; dépêche *f.*
cable, *v.t.* câbler; télégraphier
cackle, caquet *m.*
cackle, *v.i.* caqueter
cactus, cactus *m.*
cad, goujat *m.*; cuistre *m.*
cadaverous, cadavéreux(-euse)
caddy, boîte (*f.*) à thé; caddy *m.* (golf)
cadence, cadence *f.*
cadet, cadet *m.*; officier-élève *m.*
café, café *m.*
cafeteria (café), libre-service *m.*
cage, cage *f.*
cage, *v.t.* mettre en cage
cajole, *v.t.* cajoler
cake, gâteau *m.*; pâtisserie *f.*; tablette *f.* (chocolate, etc.); pain *m.* (of soap)
calamitous, *(adj.)* désastreux
calamity, calamité *f.*; désastre *m.*; sinistre *m.* (accident, fire, etc.)
calcareous, *(adj.)* calcaire
calcine, *v.t.* calciner
calculable, *(adj.)* calculable

calculation, calcul *m.*, compte *m.*
calculate, *v.t.* calculer
calculus, calcul *m.*
calendar, calendrier *m.*
calendar month, mois solaire *m.*
calf, veau *m.* (animal); mollet *m.* (of persons)
calibrate, *v.t.* (artillery) calibrer
calibre, calibre.*m.*
calico, calicot *m.*; indienne *f.* (printed calico)
call, appel *m.*; voix *f.*; demande *f.*; visite *f.*
call, *v.t.* appeler; nommer; convoquer
at anybody's call, aux ordres de tout le monde
call at, toucher (*naut.*)
call-box, cabine téléphonique *f.*
call in, (a doctor, etc.) faire venir
call names, injurier
call on, passer chez . . .
call to mind, se rappeler
call to order, rappeler à l'ordre
call up, appeler
calligraphy, calligraphie *f.*
calling, (trade, etc.) métier *m.*; état *m.*
callosity, callosité *f.*
callous, (*adj.*) endurci; insensible
callously, avec insensibilité *f.*
callousness, insensibilité *f.*
callow, (*adj.*) jeune, novice
calm, (*adj.*) calme, tranquille
calm, calme *m.*; tranquillité *f.*
calm, *v.t.* calmer; apaiser
calmly, tranquillement
calomel, calomel *m.*
calorie, calorie *f.*
calumniate, *v.t.* calomnier
calumny, calomnie *f.*
Calvary, le Calvaire *m.*
calve, *v.i.* vêler
cam, came *f.*
camber, cambrure *f.*; bombement *m.*
cambric, batiste *f.*
camel, chameau *m.*
cameo, camée *m.*
camera, appareil photographique *m.*; caméra *f.* (for cinema work)
in camera, à huis clos
camisole, cache-corset *m.* (*invar.*)

camomile, camomille *f.*
camp, camp *m.*
camp, *v.i.* camper
camp-bed, lit de sangle *m.*
camp-stool, pliant *m.*
campaign, campagne *f.*
camphor, camphre *m.*
camphorated, (*adj.*) camphré
can, pot *m.*; broc *m.*; bidon *m.*; boîte (*f.*) en fer blanc (tin)
can, *v.t.* mettre en boîte (for preserving)
can, (*v. aux.*) pouvoir (to be able); savoir (to know how to)
he can write (etc.), il sait écrire
I can do it, je sais le faire
canal, canal *m.*
canary (bird), serin *m.*
Canadian, canadien(ne)
cancel, *v.t.* effacer; annuler; rayer; résilier (contract)
cancer, cancer *m.*
cancerous, (*adj.*) cancéreux (-euse)
candelabrum, candélabre *m.*
candid, (*adj.*) candide; franc (*f.* franche)
candidate, candidat *m.*; aspirant *m.*
candied, (*adj.*) confit; glacé
candle, chandelle *f.*; bougie *f.*; cierge *m.* (church candle)
Candlemas, la Chandeleur *f.*
candlestick, bougeoir *m.*, chandelier *m.*
candour, candeur *f.*; franchise *f.*; sincérité *f.*
cane, canne *f.*; jonc *m.*
cane, *v.t.* donner des coups de canne; corriger
cane-sugar, sucre de canne *m.*
canicular, (*adj.*) caniculaire
canister, boîte (*f.*) en fer blanc
canker, chancre *m.*; ver rongeur *m.*
canker, *v.t.* ronger
cankerous, (*adj.*) chancreux (-euse)
cannibal, cannibale *m.* and *f.*; anthropophage *m.* and *f.*
cannon, canon *m.* (gun)
cannon-ball, boulet *m.*
canoe, canot *m.*; périssoire *f.*

canon, chanoine *m.* (church dignitary); canon *m.* (rule)

canopy, baldaquin *m.* (*arch.*); voûte *f.* (of the heavens)

cant, hypocrisie *f.*; inclinaison *f.* (slope)

canteen, cantine *f.*

canter, petit galop *m.*

canticle, cantique *m.*

canting, (*adj.*) hypocrite

canto, chant *m.*

canvas, canevas *m.*; toile *f.*; peinture *f.*

canvass, sollicitation *f.* (of votes)

canvass, *v.t.* solliciter

cap, bonnet *m.*; toque *f.* (university); casquette *f.*; chapeau *m.* (in machinery)

cap, *v.t.* coiffer, couvrir

capability, capacité *f.*

capable, (*adj.*) capable

capacious, (*adj.*) spacieux(-euse); vaste; ample

capaciousness, capacité *f.*; étendue *f.*

capacitate, *v.t.* rendre capable de

capacity, capacité *f.*

in the capacity of, en qualité de

cape, cap *m.*; promontoire *m.*; pèlerine *f.* (clothing)

caper, cabriole *f.*; câpre *f.* (plant)

caper, *v.i.* cabrioler

capital, capital *m.* (finance); capitale *f.* (city); fonds sociaux *m. pl.* (finance)

capital, majuscule *f.* (letter); (*adj.*) capital; principal; essentiel(le); excellent

capitulate, *v.i.* capituler

caprice, caprice *m.*

capricious, (*adj.*) capricieux

capsize, *v.i.* chavirer; *v.t.* faire chavirer

capstan, cabestan *m.*

captain, capitaine *m.*; chef *m.*

caption, en-tête *m.* (in book); rubrique *f.* (*journ.*)

captivate, *v.t.* captiver; charmer

captivating, (*adj.*) séduisant

captive, (*adj.*) captif(-ive)

captive, captif(-ive) *m.*(*f.*); prisonnier(-ère) *m.* (*f.*)

captivity, captivité *f.*

capture, capture *f.*; prise *f.*

capture, *v.t.* capturer

car, char *m.*; nacelle *f.* (balloon); wagon *m.* (railway); auto *f.*; automobile *f.* (motor-car)

caravan, caravane *f.*; roulotte *f.*

carbine, carabine *f.*

carbineer, carabinier *m.*

carbolic acid, acide phénique *m.*

carbon, carbone *m.*

carbonic, (*adj.*) carbonique

carbonise, *v.t.* carboniser

carbuncle, escarboucle *f.*; clou *m.*, furoncle *m.* (*med.*)

carburetter, carburateur *m.*

carcass, cadavre *m.*

card, carte *f.*; billet de faire part *m.* (invitation)

cardboard, carton *m.*

card-index, fichier *m.*

card-table, table (*f.*) de jeu

cardinal, (*adj.*) cardinal; principal

cardinal, cardinal *m.*

care, souci *m.* (worry); soin *m.* (attention); sollicitude *f.*; attention *f.*

care for, soigner (i.e. to tend the sick)

I don't care, cela m'est égal; je m'en moque

to care, *v.i.* se soucier de; s'inquiéter de

take care of, avoir soin de; s'occuper de

with care, avec soin

career, carrière *f.*; course *f.*

careful, (*adj.*) soigneux(-euse); prudent; économe

carefully, (*adv.*) soigneusement; attentivement

carefulness, soin *m.*

careless, (*adj.*) insouciant; négligent

carelessness, insouciance *f.*; négligence *f.*

caress, caresse *f.*

caress, *v.t.* caresser

caretaker, concierge *m.* (*f.*); gardien *m.* (museum, etc.)

cargo, cargaison *f.* chargement *m.*

caricature, caricature *f.*

caricature, *v.t.* caricaturer

caries, carie *f.*

carnage, carnage *m.*; tuerie *f.*
carnal, *(adj.)* charnel(le); sensuel(le)
carnation, œillet *m.*
carnival, carnaval *m.*
carnivorous, *(adj.)* carnivore; carnassier (of animals)
carol, chant de Noël *m.*; chanson *f.* (de Noël)
carol, *v.i.* and *v.t.* fredonner, chanter
carousal, orgie *f.*
carouse, *v.i.* riboter; faire la fête
carp, carpe *f.*
carp, *v.i.* critiquer, chicaner sur
carpenter, menuisier *m.*; charpentier *m.*
carpentry, charpenterie *f.*
carpet, tapis *m.*
carpet, *v.t.* garnir de tapis
carriage, voiture *f.*; wagon *m.* (railway); transport *m.*; factage *m.* (of parcels); port *m.*; affût *m.* (gun-carriage); frais de transport *m.* (commercial); tenue *f.* (deportment)
carriage forward, en port dû
carriage free, franc de port
carriage paid, port payé *m.*
carrier, porteur *m.*; voiturier *m.*
carrion, charogne *f.*
carrot, carotte *f.*
carry, *v.r.* porter, transporter, conduire
carry away, *v.t.* emporter; entraîner; enlever
carry off, *v.t.* enlever; emporter
carry on, *v.i.* continuer, exercer
carry out, *v.t.* exécuter
carry over, *v.t.* transporter, reporter (book-keeping)
carry through, *v.t.* accomplir
carry up, *v.t.* faire monter; monter
carried forward, à reporter
cart, charrette *f.*
cart, *v.t.* charrier; transporter
cartel, cartel *m.*
carter, charretier *m.*
cart-horse, cheval *(m.)* de trait
cartilage, cartilage *m.*
cartridge, cartouche *f.*
cartridge-pouch, cartouchière *f.*

carve, *v.t.* graver; tailler; sculpter; découper (meat, etc.)
carving, boiserie *f.* (wood); sculpture *f.*; découpage *m.* (meat)
carving-knife, couteau *(m.)* à découper
case, étui *m.* (cigarette, etc.); caisse *f.* (packing)
case, cas *m.*; cause *f.* (law); vitrine *f.* (show case)
as the case may be, selon les circonstances
in any case, en tout cas
casement, croisée *f.*; fenêtre *f.*
cash, argent *m.*; argent comptant *m.*; caisse *f.*; encaisse *f.* (cash balance)
cash, *v.t.* toucher (cheque)
cash book, livre *(m.)* de caisse
cash on account, accompte *m.*
cashier, caissier(-ère) *m.* *(f.)*
cashier, *v.t.* dégrader (mil.); casser
cashmere, cachemire *m.*
casing, enveloppe *f.*; couverture *f.*
cask, baril *m.*; fût *m.*; barrique *f.*; tonneau *m.*
casket, écrin *m.* (jewels); coffret *m.*
cast, coup *m.*; (throw) jet *m.*; moule *m.* (mould); fonte *f.* (metal); distribution des rôles *f.* (theat.)
cast, *v.t.* jeter (throw off, away); rejeter (cast forth); jeter par terre; fondre (of metal)
cast down, *v.t.* baisser (the eyes)
cast up, *v.t.* additionner, calculer
cast-iron, fonte *f.*
cast-iron, *(adj.)* en fonte
caste, caste *f.*
casting-vote, voix prépondérante *f.*
castle, château *m.*
castor, roulette *f.*
castor-oil, huile *(f.)* de ricin
castor-sugar, sucre *(m.)* en poudre
castrate, *v.t.* châtrer
casual, *(adj.)* accidentel(le), de passage
casually, en passant; par hasard
casualty, perte *f.* (naval, mil., etc.); accident *m.*

cat, chat(te) *m.* (*f.*)
catalogue, catalogue *m.*; liste *f.*
catalogue, (*v.t.*) cataloguer
catapult, lance-pierre *m.*; catapulte *f.* (for aircraft, etc.)
cataract, cataracte *f.*
catarrh, catarrhe *m.*
catastrophe, catastrophe *f.*
catch, prise *f.*; attrape *f.*; aubaine *f.* (good fortune); crampon *m.* (of door); jeu de mot *m.*; cliquet *m.* (of wheel)
catch, *v.t.* attraper; prendre; saisir; surprendre (surprise in the act); ne pas manquer (train); frapper (catch the eye)
catch cold, *v.i.* s'enrhumer
catchword, réplique *f.* (*theat.*); rengaine *f.* (slogan)
catchy, (*adj.*) populaire
catechism, catéchisme *m.*
categorical, (*adj.*) catégorique
category, catégorie *f.*
caterpillar, chenille *f.*
catgut, corde (*f.*) à boyau
cathedral, cathédrale *f.*
catholic, (*adj.*) catholique
catkin, chaton *m.*
cattle, bétail *m.*; *pl.* bestiaux
cauldron, chaudron *m.*
cauliflower, chou-fleur *m.*; *pl.* choux-fleurs
cause, cause *f.*; raison *f.*; motif *m.*
cause, *v.t.* causer; être cause de; occasionner
causeway, chaussée *f.*; digue *f.*
caustic, (*adj.*) caustique
caution, avis *m.* (warning); précaution *f.*; circonspection *f.*; garantie *f.*
caution, *v.t.* avertir; mettre en garde (contre)
cautious, (*adj.*) prudent
cavalry, cavalerie *f.*
cave, caverne *f.*; souterrain *m.*
caviare, caviar *m.*
caw, *v.i.* croasser
cawing (of rooks), croassement *m.*
cease, *v.i.* cesser, discontinuer
ceaseless, continuel(le), incessant
ceaselessly, sans cesse
cedar, cèdre *m.*

ceiling, plafond *m.*
celebrate, *v.t.* célébrer, glorifier
celebrated, (*adj.*) célèbre
celebration, célébration *f.*
celebrity, célébrité *f.*; renommée *f.*
celerity, vitesse *f.*
celery, céleri *m.*
celestial, (*adj.*) céleste
celibacy, célibat *m.*
celibate, (*adj.*) célibataire *m.* and *f.*
cell, cellule *f.*; cachot *m.*
cellar, cave *f.*; caveau *m.*
celluloid, celluloïd(e) *m.*
cement, ciment *m.*; -mixer, bétonnière *f.*
cement, *v.t.* cimenter: fortifier
cemetery, cimetière *m.*
censor, censeur *m.*; to censor, passer par la censure
censorious, (*adj.*) sévère
censure, censure *f.*; blâme *m.*
censure, *v.t.* censurer; blâmer
census, recensement *m.*
cent, sou *m.*
not a red cent, pas un sou (un liard)
per cent, pour cent
centenary, centenaire *m.*
centipede, mille-pattes *m.*
central, (*adj.*) central
centralise, *v.t.* centraliser
centre, centre *m.*; milieu *m.*; foyer *m.*
centre, *v.i.* se concentrer
centrifugal, (*adj.*) centrifuge
century, siècle *m.*
ceremonial, de cérémonie
ceremony, cérémonie *f.*; étiquette *f.*
certain, (*adj.*) certain; sûr
certainly, (*adv.*) certainement
certainty, certitude *f.*
certificate, certificat *m.*; diplôme *m.*; brevet *m.*; acte *m.* (birth, death)
certify, *v.t.* certifier
cessation, cessation *f.*
cesspit, cesspool, fosse *f.*; cloaque *m.*
chafe, *v.i.* s'user, s'irriter; *v.t.* frictionner

chafer (cock-), hanneton *m.*

chaff, paille hachée *f.*; plaisanterie *f.* (making fun of)

chaff, *v.t.* railler; taquiner

chaffinch, pinson *m.*

chain, chaîne *f.*

chain, *v.t.* enchaîner; attacher avec une chaîne

chain-bridge, pont (*m.*) suspendu

chain-store, magasin (*m.*) à succursales multiples

chains, fers *m. pl.*

chair, chaise *f.*; siège *m.*; chaire *f.* (of professor); fauteuil *m.* (of president or chairman)

arm-chair, fauteuil *m.*

chairman, président *m.*

chalk, craie *f.*; crayon *m.* (for drawing)

chalk, *v.t.* marquer *or* écrire à la craie

chalky, crayeux(-euse)

challenge, défi *m.*; provocation *f.*; qui vive *m.*

challenge, *v.t.* défier; provoquer; récuser (jury)

chamber, chambre *f.*; salle *f.*; pièce *f.*

chambers (of lawyer), étude *f.*; bureaux *m. pl.*

chamberlain, chambellan *m.*

chambermaid, femme de chambre *f.*

chamber-pot, pot (*m.*) de chambre

chameleon, caméléon *m.*

chamois, chamois *m.*

chamois leather, peau (*f.*) de chamois

champagne, (vin de) champagne *m.*

champion, champion(ne) *m.* (*f.*)

championship, championnat *m*

chance, chance *f.*; hasard *m.*

chance, *v.i.* arriver par hasard

chance, (*adj.*) accidentel(le)

chancel, sanctuaire *m.*

chancellery, chancellerie *f.*

chancellor, chancelier *m.*

chancellor of the exchequer, ministre (*m.*) des finances

lord chancellor, grand chancelier *m.*

chandelier, lustre *m.*

change, changement *m.*; phase *f.* (of moon); (petite) monnaie *f.* (money)

change, *v.t.* changer, transformer;

"all change," tout le monde descend

change places, changer de place

changeable, (*adj.*) variable; inconstant

channel, canal *m.*; lit *m.* (of river); passe *f.* (of harbour); détroit *m.* (*naut.*)

Channel Islands, les Îles Anglo-normandes

English Channel, la Manche

chap, *v.i.* and *v.t.* gercer; se gercer

chap, garçon *m.*; (coll.) type *m.*

chapped (hands, etc), plein de gerçures

old chap, mon vieux

chapel, chapelle *f.*; temple *m.*

chapfallen, déconcerté

chaplain, aumônier *m.*

chapter, chapitre *m.*

char, *v.t.* carboniser

character, caractère *m.*; réputation *f.*; rôle *m.* (*theat.*); qualité *f.*; certificat (*m.*) de moralité

characteristic, (*adj.*) caractéristique

charcoal, charbon de bois *m.*

charcoal-burner, charbonnier *m.*

charge, charge *f.*; prix *m.*; soin *m.* (care of); accusation *f.* (*law*); fardeau *m.* (burden)

charge, *v.t.* charger; accuser; faire payer

chargeable, (*adj.*) à charge, imposable

charges, frais *m. pl.*; dépens *m. pl*

chariot, chariot *m.*

charitable, (*adj.*) charitable

charity, charité *f.*; aumône *f.*; œuvre de bienfaisance *f.*

charm, charme *m.*; breloque *f.* (trinket, etc.); attraits *m. pl.*

charm, *v.t.* charmer; enchanter

charming, (*adj.*) charmant; délicieux(-euse); ravissant

charnel house, charnier *m.*

chart, carte marine *f.*; carte *f.*

charter, acte *m.*; charte *f.*; privilège *m.*

charter, *v.t.* fréter (*commer.*)

charwoman, femme (*f.*) de ménage

chase, chasse *f.*; poursuite *f.*

chase, *v.t.* chasser; poursuivre; ciseler (metal)

chasm, abîme *m.*; ouverture *f.*; vide *m.*

chaste, (*adj.*) chaste

chastise, *v.t.* châtier

chastisement, châtiment *m.*

chastity, chasteté *f.*; pureté *f.*

chat, causerie *f.*

chat, *v.i.* bavarder, causer

chattels, biens *m. pl.*

chatter, babil *m.*

chatter, *v.i.* jaser; claquer (teeth)

chatterbox, moulin (*m.*) à paroles

cheap, (*adj.*) à bon marché

cheapen, *v.t.* diminuer la valeur de

cheapness, bas prix *m.*

cheat, fourbe *m.* and *f.*; tricheur (-euse) *m.* (*f.*) (cards)

cheat, *v.t.* duper; tricher; tromper

cheating, tromperie *f.*; friponnerie *f.*; tricherie *f.* (cards, etc.)

check, échec *m.*; obstacle *m.*; toile (*f.*) à carreaux (cloth)

check, *v.t.* réprimer (repress); arrêter; vérifier; contrôler; enrégistrer (luggage)

checkmate, échec et mat *m.*

cheek, joue *f.*; impudence *f.*

cheeky, (*adj.*) insolent

cheer, chère *f.* (food, etc.); gaieté *f.*

cheer, *v.i.* se réjouir; applaudir

cheerful, (*adj.*) gai; joyeux(-euse)

cheerless, (*adj.*) triste; morne

cheers, applaudissements *m. pl.*; bravos *m. pl.*; à la vôtre!

cheese, fromage *m.*

chemical, (*adj.*) chimique

chemicals, produits chimiques *m.*

chemist, chimiste *m.* (scientist); pharmacien *m.* (druggist)

chemist's shop, pharmacie *f.*

chemistry, chimie *f.*

cheque, chèque *m.*

crossed cheque, chèque barré

cheque-book, carnet (*m.*) de chèques

chequered, (*adj.*) varié

chequered career, une vie pleine de vicissitudes *f.*

cherish, *v.t.* chérir; entretenir (hopes)

cherry, cerise *f.*

cherry (tree), cerisier *m.*

chess, échecs *m. pl.*

chess-board, échiquier *m.*

chess-man, pièce *f.*

chest, coffre *m.*; caisse *f.*; poitrine *f.* (of body)

chest of drawers, commode *f.*

chestnut, marron *m.*; châtaigne *f.*

chestnut coloured, châtain

chestnut (tree), châtaignier *m.*

chew, *v.t.* mâcher; ruminer (the cud)

chewing, mastication *f.*

chewing-gum, gomme (*f.*) à mâcher

chicken, poulet *m.*; poussin *m.* (chick)

chicken-hearted, (*adj.*) poltron

chicken-pox, varicelle *f.*

chicory, chicorée *f.*

chief, (*adj.*) principal; premier (-ère)

chief, chef *m.*

chilblain, engelure *f.*

child, enfant *m.* (in the singular may also be feminine)

with child, enceinte

childbirth, enfantement *m.*

childhood, enfance *f.*

childish, childlike, (*adj.*) enfantin

childishness, enfantillage *m.*

chill, froid *m.*; refroidissement *m.*; frisson *m.*

chill, *v.t.* refroidir, glacer

chilly, (*adj.*) un peu froid (things); frileux(-euse) (persons)

chime, carillon *m.*

chime, *v.t.* carillonner

chimney, cheminée *f.*

chimney corner, coin (*m.*) du feu

chimney-sweep, ramoneur *m.*

chin, menton *m.*

china, porcelaine *f.*

chine, échine *f.*

Chinese, chinois
chink, fente *f.*; crevasse ·*f.*; tintement *m.* (sound)
chink, *v.t.* faire sonner
chintz, cretonne *f.*
chip, copeau *m.*; éclat *m.*
chip, *v.t.* tailler, hacher
chips, chipped potatoes, pommes de terre frites *f. pl.*
chirp, *v.i.* gazouiller
chirping, gazouillement *m.*
chisel, ciseau *m.*
chisel, *v.t.* ciseler
chitchat, babillage *m.*
chivalrous, (*adj.*) chevaleresque
chivalry, chevalerie *f.*
chlorate, chlorate *m.*
chloride, chlorure *m.*; chlorure de chaux (of lime)
chlorine, chlore *m.*
chloroform, chloroforme *m.*
chloroform, *v.t.* chloroformer
chocolate, chocolat *m.*
choice, (*adj.*) choisi; de choix
choice, choix *m.*
choir, chœur *m.*
choke, *v.i.* étouffer, suffoquer; engorger (of things)
choking, étouffement *m.*; engorgement *m.*
cholera, choléra *m.*
choose, *v.t.* choisir; faire choix de
chop, côtelette *f.*
chop, *v.t.* couper en morceaux; hacher
chop down, *v.t.* abattre
choppy, clapoteux(-euse) (sea)
chord, accord *m.* (mus.)
chorus, chœur *m.*
Christ, le Christ *m.*
Christendom, chrétienté *f.*
christening, baptême *m.*
Christian, chrétien(ne)
Christianity, christianisme *m.*
Christmas, Noël *m.*; la fête de Noël *f.*
Christmas carol, chant de Noël *m.*
Christmas box, étrennes *f. pl.*
Christmas Eve, la veille de Noël
chronic, (*adj.*) chronique
chronicle, chronique *f.*
chronometer, chronomètre *m.*

chrysanthemum, chrysanthème *m.*
chuck, *v.i.* glousser (of fowls); jeter, lancer (of stones, etc.)
chuckle, *v.i.* rire tout bas
chuckle, ricanement *m.*
chum, copain *m.*
chunk, gros morceau (of wood); miche *f.* (of bread)
church, église *f.*
churchyard, cimetière *m.*
churl, rustre *m.*
churn, baratte *f.*
churn, *v.t.* baratter
cider, cidre *m.*
cigar, cigare *m.*
cigarette, cigarette *f.*
cigarette-case, étui (*m.*) à cigarette
cinder, cendre *f.*
Cinderella, Cendrillon *f.*
cinema, cinéma *m.*; ciné *m.*
cinema-star, vedette *f.* (de l'écran)
cinnamon, cannelle *f.*
cipher, chiffre *m.*; zéro *m.*; nullité *f.*
circle, cercle *m.*
circle, *v.i.* se mouvoir autour de
circle, *v.t.* entourer
circuit, révolution *f.*; circuit *m.*; tour *m.*
circuitous, (*adj.*) détourné
circular, circulaire *f.*; bulletin *m.*
circular, (*adj.*) circulaire
circulate, *v.t.* faire circuler, mettre en circulation; *v.i.* circuler
circulation, circulation *f.*; tirage *m.* (of newspaper)
circumcision, circoncision *f.*
circumference, circonférence *f.*
circumflex, (*adj.*) circonflexe
circumscribe, *v.t.* circonscrire
circumstance, circonstance *f.*
circumstantial, (*adj.*) détaillé; indirect (evidence)
circus, cirque *m.*; rond-point *m.* (streets)
cistern, citerne *f.*; réservoir *m.*
citation, citation *f.*
cite, *v.t.* citer
citizen(-ess), citoyen(ne) *m.* (*f.*); bourgeois(e) *m.* (*f.*); habitant(e) *m.* (*f.*)

citizenship, droit (m.) de bourgeoisie

citrate, citrate m.

citric, (adj.) citrique

citron, cédrat m.

city, ville f.; cité f.

civil, (adj.) civil; municipal

civilian, civil m.; bourgeois m.;
pékin m. (used by military con-
temptuously)

civilisation, civilisation f.

civilise, v.t. civiliser

civility, civilité f.; politesse f.

claim, demande f.; prétention f.;
titre m.; droit m.; concession f.
(mining)

claim, v.t. demander; prétendre;
revendiquer; réclamer

claimant, prétendant m.

clamber, v.i. grimper

clammy, (adj.) visqueux(-euse);
gluant

clamorous, (adj.) bruyant

clamour, clameur f.; bruit m.

clamour, v.i. vociférer

clamp, crampon m.

clamp, v.t. agrafer, brider

clang, cliquetis m.; son (m.)
métallique

clang, clank, v.t. faire résonner

clanging, clanking, cliquetis m.;
bruit (m.) métallique

clap, coup m. (thunder); battement (m.) de mains

clap, v.t. battre des mains; applaudir

claret, vin de Bordeaux m.

clarinet, clarinette f.

clash, choc m.; conflit m.

clash, v.i. s'entrechoquer; résonner

clasp, agrafe f.; fermoir m.

clasp, v.t. agrafer; presser; serrer
(of hands)

class, classe f.; cours m.; catégorie f.

class, v.t. classer

classic, classique m.

classical, classic, (adj.) classique

classification, classification f.

classify, v.t. classifier

classing, classement m.

classroom, salle de classe f.

clatter, bruit m.; tapage m.;
tintamarre m.

clause, clause f.

clavicle, clavicule f.

claw, griffe f.

claw, v.t. griffer; déchirer avec
les griffes

clay, argile f.; terre glaise f.

clay soil, sol argileux m.

clayey, argileux(-euse)

clean, (adj.) propre; pur

clean, v.t. nettoyer; laver; purifier; cirer (shoes); éplucher
(vegetables); dégraisser (clothes)

cleaning, nettoyage m.; dégrais-
sage m.

cleanliness, cleanness, propreté
f.; pureté f.; innocence f.

cleanse, v.t. nettoyer; purifier
(system, blood, etc.)

clear, (adj.) clair, net; évident;
sans tache

clear, v.i. s'éclaircir (air, atmosphere, weather); se libérer (to
free from); se débarrasser (de)

clear, v.t. éclaircir; faire évacuer
(room, etc.); déblayer (rubbish);
gagner (a profit); disculper (one's
character); balayer (mil.); to
clear a way for oneself, se
frayer un chemin

clear-headed, à l'esprit clair

clearance, dégagement m.

clearance sale, vente (f.) de
soldes

clearing, éclaircissement m.;
levée f. (letter boxes)

clearly, (adv.) clairement, nettement, évidemment

clearness, clarté f.

cleave, v.t. fendre, diviser; v.i. se
fendre

cleft, fente f.; crevasse f.

clemency, clémence f.; douceur f.
(of weather)

clement, clément

clench, v.t. serrer (the fist)

clergy, clergé m.

clergyman, ecclésiastique m.;
prêtre m.; abbé m.; curé (Roman
Catholic) m.; pasteur m.; ministre m. (Protestant)

clerical, (adj.) clérical

clerk, clerc *m.* (law); commis *m.* (commerce); employé *m.* (civil service); greffier *m.* (law)

clever, (*adj.*) habile; adroit

cleverly, (*adv.*) habilement

cleverness, habileté *f.*; adresse *f.*

click, cliquet *m.*; tic-tac *m.*

click, *v.i.* cliqueter; faire tic-tac

cliff, falaise *f.*

climate, climat *m.*

climax, (*fig.*) comble *m.*

climb, *v.t.* and *v.i.* grimper; gravir; faire l'ascension; prendre de l'altitude (*aviation*)

climber, grimpeur *m.*; alpiniste *m.* and *f.*

climber, plante grimpante *f.* (plant)

cling, *v.i.* se cramponner

clip, *v.t.* couper; tondre (horses, dogs, etc.); contrôler (tickets)

clippings, rognures *f. pl.*

cloak, manteau *m.*; (*fig.*) prétexte *m.*

cloak, *v.t.* couvrir d'un manteau; (*fig.*) masquer; cacher

cloakroom, consigne *f.* (railway); vestiaire *m.* (hotel, etc.)

clock, horloge *f.*; pendule *f.*

clockmaker, horloger *m.*

clock-making, horlogerie *f.*

clod, motte (*f.*) de terre

clog, sabot *m.* (wooden shoe); socque *f.*

close, (*adj.*) fermé, serré, de près (close to); lourd (weather)

close, enclos *m.*

close, *v.t.* fermer (shut); clore; conclure (to terminate); serrer; lever (a sitting)

close in, *v.t.* enfermer

close up, *v.t.* boucher

closely, (*adv.*) de près, étroitement, strictement

closeness, lourdeur *f.* (weather); proximité *f.* (nearness)

closet, cabinet *m.*; garde-robe *f.*; placard *m.*

closure, clôture *f.*

clot, caillot *m.*

cloth, drap *m.* (woollen); toile *f.* (linen); nappe *f.* (table)

cloth trade, draperie *f.*

clothe, *v.t.* habiller, vêtir, couvrir (de)

clothes, habits *m. pl.*; vêtements *m. pl.*

clothing, habillement *m.*

cloud, nuage *m.*

cloudy, (*adj.*) nuageux(-euse); trouble (water, etc.)

clout, torchon *m.*; taloche *f.* (blow)

clove, clou (*m.*) de girofle

cloven, (*adj.*) fendu; fourchu (of hoof)

clover, trèfle *m.*

clown, rustre *m.*; bouffon *m.*; clown *m.*

club, *v.t.* massue *f.*; cercle *m.*; club *m.*; trèfle *m.* (cards)

club, *v.i.* frapper avec une massue; se cotiser (to club together)

cluck, *v.i.* glousser (of hens)

clump, masse *f.*; massif *m.* (of trees)

clumsily, (*adv.*) maladroitement

clumsy, (*adj.*) gauche, maladroit

cluster, grappe *f.* (fruit); bouquet *m.* (flowers); groupe *m.*

cluster, *v.i.* se grouper; se rassembler

clutch, prise *f.*; étreinte *f.*; embrayage *m.* (motor)

clutch, *v.t.* saisir, empoigner; embrayer (motor)

coach, voiture *f.*; carrosse *m.*; instructeur *m.* (tuition); entraîneur *m.* (sport)

coach, *v.t.* préparer aux examens

coach-house, remise *f.*

coachman, cocher *m.*

coagulate, *v.t.* coaguler

coal, charbon *m.* (de terre); houille *f.*

coal-mine, mine (*f.*) de charbon; houillère *f.*

coal scuttle, seau à charbon *m.*

coal seam, couche (*f.*) de charbon

coal tar, goudron (*m.*) de houille

coarse, (*adj.*) grossier; brut (sugar)

coarse-grained, à gros grains

coarsely, (*adv.*) grossièrement

coarseness, grossièreté *f.*

coast, côte *f.*; rivage *m.*; littoral *m.*

coast, v.t. côtoyer, longer la côte
coast-guard, garde-côtes m.
coast-line, littoral m.
coasting-vessel, caboteur m.
coastwise, le long de la côte
coat, habit m.; jaquette f.; couche f. (of paint); pardessus m. (overcoat)
coat, v.t. revêtir
coat and skirt, tailleur m.
coat of arms, écusson m.
coax, v.t. cajoler
cobbler, savetier m.
cobweb, toile d'araignée f.
cock, coq m.; robinet m. (tap); chien m. (rifle)
cock, v.t. relever (hat, etc.); armer le chien (rifle)
cockade, cocarde f.
cockchafer, hanneton m.
cockroach, cafard m.; blatte f.
cockscomb, crête (f.) de coq; (fig.) fat m.
cocksure, très sûr
cocoa, cacao m.
coconut, noix (f.) de coco; coco-tier m. (palm)
cod, morue f.
cod-liver oil, huile (f.) de foie de morue
code, code m.
coerce, v.t. contraindre; forcer
coercion, contrainte f.
coffee, café m.
coffee-cup, tasse (f.) à café
coffee-house, café m. (café has a much wider meaning in France than coffee-house)
coffee-pot, cafetière f.
coffin, bière f.; cercueil m.
cog, dent f.
cog-wheel, roue (f.) d'engrenage
cogitate, v.i. méditer
cognate, (adj.) analogue
cognomen, surnom m.; sobriquet m.
coherent, (adj.) cohérent; suivi
cohesion, cohésion f.
coif, cornette f.; béguin m.
coil, rouleau m. (hair); repli m. (serpents); bobine f. (electricity)
coil, v.t. replier
coil, v.i. se replier

coin, monnaie f.; pièce de monnaie f.
coin, v.t. monnayer; frapper (to mint)
coinage, monnayage m.; monnaie f.
coincide, v.i. s'accorder, coïncider
coincidence, coïncidence f.
coiner, faux monnayeur m.
coke, coke m.
colander, passoire f.
cold, (adj.) froid
cold, froid m.; rhume m. (in the head); refroidissement m.; froi-deur f. (coldness)
catch cold, v.i. s'enrhumer
coldly, froidement
colic, colique f.
collaborate, v.i. collaborer
collaboration, collaboration f.
collaborator, collaborateur m.; collaboratrice f.
collapse, affaissement m.; écroule-ment m.; débâcle f.
collapse, v.i. s'affaisser, s'écrouler
collar, collier m.; col m. (of shirt); collet m. (of coat); faux-col. m. (detachable collar)
collar, v.t. saisir (prendre) au collet
collateral, (adj.) collatéral
collation, collation f.
colleague, collègue m. and f.
collect, v.t. recueillir; ramasser; percevoir (taxes); faire la quête (for charity); faire la levée (letters)
collection, collection f.; ras-semblement m.; amas m.
collector, collectionneur m. (art, etc.); percepteur m. (taxes)
college, collège m.; lycée m.
collide, v.i. se heurter; entrer en collision
collie dog, chien de berger m.
collier, charbonnier m. (ship); houilleur m. (i.e. miner)
colliery, mine (f.) de charbon; houillère f.
collision, collision f.; choc m.
collodion, collodion m.
colloquial, (adj.) familier
colon, colon m. (anat.); deux points m. pl. (gram.)

colonel, colonel *m.*

colonial, (*adj.*) colonial

colonise, *v.t.* coloniser

colonist, colon *m.*

colony, colonie *f.*

colossal, (*adj.*) colossal

colosseum, colisée *m.*

colour, couleur *f.*; drapeau *m.* (*mil.*); pavillon *m.* (*navy*)

colour, *v.t.* colorer

colour-blind, atteint de daltonisme

colouring, coloris *m.*; couleur *f.*

colourless, (*adj.*) incolore

colt, poulain *m.*

column, colonne *f.*

colza, colza *m.*

comb, peigne *m.*; crête *f.* (of cock); rayon *m.* (honey)

comb, *v.t.* peigner

combat, combat *m.*; lutte *f.*

combat, *v.i.* and *v.t.* combattre

combatant, combattant *m.*

combination, combinaison *f.*; coalition *f.*; ligue *f.*

combine, *v.t.* combiner; réunir; allier

combine, *v.i.* se syndiquer

combustible, (*adj.*) combustible

combustion, combustion *f.*; embrasement *m.*

come, *v.i.* venir; arriver; parvenir; se présenter

come in! entrez!

come on! allons!

just come out, vient de paraître (books)

come about, *v.i.* arriver

come against, *v.t.* heurter

come apart, *v.i.* se détacher

come back, *v.i.* revenir

come between, *v.i.* intervenir

come by, *v.i.* passer par; *v.t.* acquérir, obtenir

come down, *v.i.* descendre; baisser (prices)

come forward, *v.i.* avancer; se présenter

come home, *v.i.* rentrer

come in, *v.i.* entrer

come off, *v.i.* se détacher; (*fig.*) réussir

come out, *v.i.* sortir; tomber (of the hair); paraître

come out with, *v.t.* laisser échapper (secret, etc.)

come to, *v.i.* venir à; reprendre connaissance (regain consciousness)

come together, *v.i.* se réunir

come to terms, *v.i.* tomber d'accord

come up with, *v.t.* atteindre

comedian, comédien(ne) *m.* (*f.*)

comedy, comédie *f.*

comely, (*adj.*) beau (belle); avenant

comer, venant *m.*; venu(e) *m.* (*f.*)

comet, comète *f.*

comfort, confort *m.*; aisance (*f.*); agrément *m.*; soulagement *m.*; consolation *f.*

comfort, *v.t.* conforter; soulager; consoler

comfortable, (*adj.*) confortable; bien; à son aise; dans l'aisance

comfortably, (*adv.*) confortablement; bien

comforter, consolateur *m.*; consolatrice *f.*; cache-nez *m.* (scarf)

comfortless, (*adj.*) désolé, triste

comic, comical (*adj.*) comique, drôle

comma, virgule *f.*

command, ordre *m.*; commandement *m.*; autorité *f.*

command, *v.t.* commander; dominer; inspirer (respect); donner sur (a view of)

command (of sea, etc.), maîtrise *f.*

commandant, commandant *m.*

commandeer, *v.t.* réquisitionner

commander, commandant *m.*; commandeur *m.* (of order of knighthood); capitaine *m.* (de frégate, etc.)

commanding, (*adj.*) commandant; imposant

commandment, commandement *m.*

commemorate, *v.t.* célébrer, solenniser, commémorer

commemoration, célébration *f.*; commémoration *f.*

commence, *v.t.* commencer

commencement, commencement *m.*

commend, *v.t.* louer (praise); recommander

commendable, (*adj.*) louable; recommandable

comment, commentaire *m.*; appréciation *f.*

comment, *v.i.* commenter

commentator, commentateur (-trice) *m.* (*f.*); radio-reporter *m.*

commerce, commerce *m.*

commercial, (*adj.*) commercial; industriel(le)

commercial traveller, commis voyageur *m.*

commiserate, *v.t.* and *v.i.* avoir compassion de

commiseration, commisération *f.*; compassion *f.*

commissariat, intendance (*f.*) militaire

commissary, commissaire *m.*

commission, commission *f.*; brevet *m.* (*mil.*); mandat *m.* (*law*)

commission agent, commissionnaire *m.*

commission, *v.t.* charger, autoriser

commissioner, commissaire *m.* (police); préfet (*m.*) de police (chief commissioner)

commit, *v.t.* commettre; confier; livrer; consigner (to prison)

committee, comité *m.*

commode, commode *f.*

commodious, (*adj.*) spacieux (-euse)

commodity, commodité *f.*; marchandise *f.*

common, (*adj.*) commun; ordinaire; vulgaire

common, pré communal *m.*

common council, conseil municipal *m.*

commoner, bourgeois *m.*

commonplace, (*adj.*) banal

House of Commons, Chambre (*f.*) des Communes

commonwealth, république *f.*; état *m.*

commotion, agitation *f.*; commotion *f.*

communicate, *v.t.* communiquer; faire connaître

communication, communication *f.*; communiqué *m.*

communicative, (*adj.*) communicatif(-ive); expansif(-ive)

communion, la communion *f.*

community, communauté *f.*

commute, *v.t.* changer; commuer (*legal*)

compact, (*adj.*) serré; bien lié; concis

compact, contrat *m.*; pacte *m.*

companion, compagnon *m.*; compagne *f.*; camarade *m.* and *f.*

companion-way, escalier (*m.*) des cabines

companionable, (*adj.*) sociable

companionship, camaraderie *f.*

company, compagnie *f.*; société *f.*; troupe *f.* (*theat.*)

comparable, (*adj.*) comparable

comparative, (*adj.*) comparatif (-ive)

compare, *v.t.* comparer

comparison, comparaison *f.*

compartment, compartiment *m.*

compass, boussole *f.* (of ship, etc.); portée *f.* (range); étendue *f.* (voice)

compass, *v.t.* entourer, faire le tour de

compassion, compassion *f.*; pitié *f.*

compassionate, (*adj.*) compatissant

compatibility, compatibilité *f.*

compatible, (*adj.*) compatible (avec)

compatriot, compatriote *m.* and *f.*

compel, *v.t.* forcer, obliger (used in active, *à* before following infinitive; in passive, *de*)

compensate (for), *v.t.* dédommager (de)

compensation, compensation *f.*

compete, *v.i.* faire concurrence à

competence, capacité *f.*; compétence *f.* (*legal*)

competent, (*adj.*) compétent (pour); capable (de)

competition, concurrence *f.*; concours *m.* (for a prize)
competitor, concurrent *m.*
complacence, complaisance *f.*
complacent, (*adj.*) complaisant
complain, *v.i.* se plaindre
complainant, plaignant *m.*
complaint, plainte *f.*; maladie *f.*
complement, complément *m.*
complete, *v.t.* compléter; achever
complete, (*adj.*) total, achevé, complet(-ète)
completion, achèvement *m.*; accomplissement *m.*
complex, (*adj.*) compliqué
complexion, teint *m.*; caractère *m.*
compliance, consentement *m.*
in compliance with, conformément à
compliant, (*adj.*) flexible
complicate, *v.t.* compliquer
complicated, (*adj.*) compliqué
complication, complication *f.*
compliment, compliment *m.*; salutations *f. pl.*; souhaits *m. pl.*
compliment, *v.t.* féliciter
complimentary, (*adj.*) flatteur (-euse)
comply, *v.i.* se soumettre; se conformer
component, (*adj.*) constituant; (*noun*) partie (*f.*) composante
compos mentis, sain d'esprit
compose, *v.t.* composer; écrire; rédiger; calmer
composed, (*adj.*) calme; tranquille
composer, compositeur(-trice) *m.* (*f.*) (*mus.*)
composition, composition *f.*; nature *f.*
composure, calme *m.*; tranquillité *f.*
compound, (*adj.*) composé
compound, composition *f.*; composé *m.*
comprehend, *v.t.* comprendre
comprehensible, (*adj.*) compréhensible; intelligible
comprehension, compréhension *f.*
comprehensive, (*adj.*) compréhensif(-ive); étendu

compress, compresse *f.*
compress, *v.t.* comprimer; condenser
comprise, *v.t.* contenir; comprendre
compromise, compromis *m.*; arrangement *m.*
compulsion, contrainte *f.*
compulsory, (*adj.*) obligatoire
compunction, remords *m.*
compute, *v.t.* calculer
computer, calculateur (électronique) *m.*
comrade, camarade *m.* and *f.*
concave, (*adj.*) concave; creux (-euse)
conceal, *v.t.* cacher; dissimuler; celer (à)
concealment, dissimulation *f.*; recèlement *m.*
concede, *v.t.* concéder
conceit, suffisance *f.*; vanité *f.*
conceited, suffisant; vain
conceivable, (*adj.*) concevable
conceive, *v.t.* concevoir
concentrate, *v.t.* concentrer
conception, conception *f.*; idée *f.*; projet *m.*
concern, soin *m.*; souci *m.*; anxiété *f.*; entreprise *f.* (commercial undertaking); (*fig.*) affaire *f.*
concern, *v.t.* concerner, regarder
concerning, touchant, à l'égard de
concert, concert *m.*
concert, *v.i.* se concerter
concession, concession *f.*
concessionary, concessionnaire *m.*
conciliate, *v.t.* concilier
concise, (*adj.*) concis
conciseness, concision *f.*
conclude, *v.t.* conclure; terminer; estimer
concluding, (*adj.*) final; dernier
conclusion, conclusion *f.*; décision *f.*
conclusive, (*adj.*) concluant, final
concord, accord *m.* (*mus.*); concorde *f.*
concourse, affluence *f.*; foule *f.*
concrete, (*adj.*) concret(-ète)

concrete, béton m.; béton armé (reinforced concrete)

concrete, v.t. bétonner

concubinage, concubinage m.

concubine, concubine f.

concupiscence, concupiscence f.

concur, v.i. être d'accord avec

concurrence, concours m.

concussion, choc m.; commotion (f.) cérébrale

condemn, v.t. condamner (à); blâmer

condemnation, condamnation f.

condense, v.t. condenser

condensed (milk, etc.), conservé

condenser, condensateur m.

condescend, v.i. s'abaisser; daigner

condescension, condescendance f.

condition, condition f.; état m.

conditional, (adj.) conditionnel(le)

condole, v.i. s'affliger avec

condolence, condoléance f.

conduct, conduite f.; direction f.

conduct, v.t. conduire (à); diriger, mener

conductor, conducteur(-trice) m. (f.); guide m. and f.; paratonnerre m. (lightning); chef d'orchestre m.; receveur m. (on tram, etc.)

conduit, conduit m.; tuyau m.

cone, cône m.

cone-shaped, (adj.) conique

confection, confit m.; confection f.

confectioner, confiseur m.

confectionery, confiserie f.

confederacy, confédération f. (of states); ligue f.

confederate, (adj.) confédéré (avec); allié (à)

confederation, fédération f.

confer, v.t. conférer

conference, conférence f.; entretien m.

confess, v.t. confesser; avouer; reconnaître

confess, v.i. se confesser

confession, confession f.; aveu m.

confessor (father-), directeur (relig.) m.; confesseur m.

confide, v.t. confier (à)

confide, v.i. se confier, se fier (à)

confidence, confiance f.; assurance f.

confident, (adj.) confiant, certain, assuré

confidential, (adj.) confidentiel(le)

confine, v.t. enfermer; emprisonner, retenir, borner

confinement, emprisonnement m., détention f.; couches f. pl. (of women)

confirm, v.t. confirmer

confirmation, confirmation f.

confirmed, (adj.) invétéré; incorrigible

confiscate, v.t. confisquer

confiscation, confiscation f.

conflagration, incendie m.

conflict, conflit m.; lutte f.

conflict, v.i. être en contradiction avec

conflicting, contradictoire

confluence, confluent m.

conform, v.i. se conformer (à)

in conformity with, conformément à

confound, v.t. confondre; bouleverser

confused, (adj.) confus

confusion, confusion f.

congeal, v.i. congeler

congestion, congestion f.

congratulate, v.t. féliciter

congratulation, félicitation f.

congress, congrès m.

congruous, conforme (à); convenable

conic, conique

conjecture, conjecture f.

conjecture, v.i. and v.t. conjecturer

conjugate, v.t. conjuguer

conjunction, union f.; conjonction f.

conjure, v.t. conjurer, adjurer; v.i. faire des tours de passe-passe

conjure up, v.t. évoquer

conjurer, prestidigitateur m.

conjuring, prestidigitation f.

connect, v.t. joindre; unir; lier

connected, joint; uni; lié; bien apparenté (well connected)

connection, connection *f.*; liaison *f.*; rapport *m.*

connivance, connivence *f.*

connive at, *v.i.* fermer les yeux sur

connoisseur, connaisseur *m.*; amateur *m.*

conquer, *v.t.* conquérir, vaincre

conqueror, conquérant *m.*

conquest, conquête *f.*

conscience, conscience *f.*

conscientious, *(adj.)* consciencieux(-euse)

conscious, conscient; qui a sa connaissance

consciously, en parfaite connaissance

consciousness, conscience *f.*; connaissance *f.*

conscript, *(adj.)* conscrit *m.*

consecrate, *v.t.* consacrer

consecutive, *(adj.)* consécutif (-ive); de suite

consent, consentement *m.*; accord *m.*

consent, *v.i.* consentir (à)

consequence, conséquence *f.*; effet *m.*; suite *f.*

consequently, par conséquent

conservative, *(adj.)* conservateur (-trice) *m.* (*f.*)

conservative, conservateur *m.* (*politic.*)

conservatory, serre *f.*

consider, *v.t.* considérer; réfléchir; avoir égard à; estimer

considerable, *(adj.)* considérable; important

considerate, *(adj.)* attentif(-ive); indulgent; prévenant

consideration, considération *f.*; examen *m.*; récompense *f.*

consign, *v.t.* consigner; envoyer (*commer.*); confier à

consignment, consignation *f.*; envoi *m.* (of goods)

consist (of), *v.i.* consister (en); se composer (de)

consistence, suite *f.*

consistent, compatible (avec); toujours égal

console, *v.t.* consoler

consolidate, *v.t.* consolider

consoling, consolateur(-trice)

consols (finance, Government funds), consolidés *m. pl.*

consonant, consonne *f.*

consort, époux *m.*; épouse *f.*

consort (with), *v.i.* s'associer (à)

conspicuous, *(adj.)* éminent; visible; remarquable; en évidence

conspiracy, conspiration *f.*; complot *m.*

conspirator, conspirateur(-trice) *m.* (*f.*)

conspire, *v.i.* comploter (contre)

constable, agent de police *m.*

constancy, constance *f.*; stabilité *f.*

constant, *(adj.)* constant; stable, fidèle

consternation, consternation *f.*

constipate, *v.t.* constiper

constipation, constipation *f.*

constituency, circonscription électorale *f.*

constitutional, *(adj.)* constitutionnel(le)

constrain, *v.t.* contraindre

construct, *v.t.* construire; bâtir

construction, construction *f.*; (*fig.*) interprétation *f.*

constructive, *(adj.)* constructif (-ive)

construe, *v.t.* traduire; interpréter

consul, consul *m.*

consulate, consulat *m.*

consult, *v.t.* consulter

consume, *v.t.* consommer (use); dissiper

consumer, consommateur *m.*

consuming, *(adj.)* dévorant

consummate, *v.t.* achever, accomplir

consumption, consomption *f.*; phtisie *f.*

consumptive, *(adj.)* phtisique, poitrinaire

contact, to make (break) -,, établir (rompre) le contact

contagious, contagieux(-euse)

contain, *v.t.* contenir; retenir; renfermer

contaminate, *v.t.* souiller

contemplate, *v.t.* contempler; envisager (course of action, etc.)

contemporary, (adj.) contemporain

contempt, mépris m.; dédain m.

contemptible, (adj.) méprisable

contemptuous, dédaigneux (-euse)

contend, v.i. lutter; combattre (contre)

content, contentement m.; contenu m. (contents of)

content, (adj.) content, satisfait

content, v.t. contenter, satisfaire

contents, contenu m.

contest, lutte f.; combat m.: concours m. (competition)

contest, v.t. contester; disputer

contiguous, (adj.) contigu(-guë)

continence, continence f.; chasteté f.

continent, continent m.

continent, (adj.) continent

contingency, éventualité f.; hasard m.

continual, (adj.) continuel(le)

continuation, continuation f.; suite f. (of serial story)

continue, v.t. continuer, prolonger

continuity, uniformité f.; - girl (cin.) script-girl f.

continuous, continu

continuously, (adv.) sans interruption

contraband, (adj.) de contrebande; contrebande f.

contract, contrat m.; convention f.; entreprise (f.) à forfait (building contract, etc.)

contract, v.t. rétrécir (shrink); contracter, prendre (a habit); froncer (eyebrows); v.i. traiter pour (contract for)

contraction, rétrécissement m.; contraction f.

contractor, entrepreneur m.; fournisseur m.

contradict, v.t. contredire; démentir

contradiction, contradiction f.; démenti m.

contradictory, (adj.) contradictoire

contrariety, opposition f.; contrariété f.

contrary, contraire

on the contrary, au contraire

contrast, contraste m.

contrast, v.t. mettre en contraste

contributary, (adj.) tributaire

contribute, v.t. and v.i. contribuer; payer; collaborer (à)

contribution, contribution f.

contributor, contribuant, collaborateur(-trice) m. (f.)

contributory, (adj.) tributaire

contrivance, invention f.; truc m. (gadget)

contrive, v.t. inventer, trouver

contrive, v.i. trouver moyen (de)

control, contrôle m.; autorité f.

control, v.t. contrôler; diriger

controversy, polémique f.; dispute f.

contumacious, (adj.) obstiné, contumace (legal)

contumacy, obstination f.; contumace f.

contumely, injure f.; insulte f.

conundrum, énigme f.

convalescence, convalescence f.

convalescent, (adj.) convalescent

convenience, commodité f.; convenance f.; cabinet (m.) d'aisances (public convenience)

convenient, (adj.) commode; convenable

convent, couvent m.

convention, convention f.; pacte m.; assemblée f.

conventional, (adj.) conventionnel(le)

conversation, conversation f.; entretien m.

converse, v.i. causer, s'entretenir

conversion, conversion f.; changement m.

convert, v.t. convertir; transformer

convex, (adj.) convexe

convey, v.t. transporter (goods); porter; transmettre; donner (ideas); présenter (thanks)

conveyance, transport m.; transfert m.; voiture f. (vehicle)

convict, condamné(e) *m.* (*f.*); forçat *m.*
convict, *v.t.* condamner
conviction, conviction *f.*
convince, *v.t.* convaincre
convoke, *v.t.* convoquer
convoy, convoi *m.*; escorte *f.*
convoy, *v.t.* convoyer; escorter
convulse, *v.t.* convulser; (*fig.*) ébranler (shake badly)
convulsion, convulsion *f.*; commotion *f.*
cook, cuisinier(-ère) *m.* (*f.*)
cook, *v.i.* cuire; faire la cuisine; *v.t.* faire cuire
cookery, cooking, cuisine *f.*
cool, (*adj.*) frais (fraîche), froid
cool, fraîcheur *f.*
cool, *v.t.* rafraîchir, refroidir
cool, *v.i.* se refroidir
coolness, fraîcheur *f.*; (*fig.*) indifférence *f.*; sang-froid *m.*
cooper, tonnelier *m.*
co-operation, coopération *f.*; concours *m.*
co-operate, *v.i.* coopérer, concourir (à)
cope (with), *v.i.* venir à bout (de), se débrouiller
copious, (*adj.*) copieux(-euse), abondant
copper, cuivre *m.*; chaudière *f.*; chaudron *m.* (small boiler)
copper, (*adj.*) de cuivre
copper-smith, chaudronnier *m.*
copper-wire, fil de cuivre *m.*
copper-works, fonderie (*f.*) de cuivre
coppers, petite monnaie *f.*
coppice, copse, taillis *m.*
copy, copie *f.*; exemplaire *m.*; numéro *m.* (newspaper)
copy, *v.t.* copier, imiter
fair copy, copie (*f.*) au net
rough copy, brouillon *m.*
copy-book, cahier *m.*
copyright, droits (*m. pl.*) d'auteur
coquet, *v.i.* faire la coquette avec
coquettish, (*adj.*) coquet(te)
coral, corail *m.*
cord, corde (*f.*); cordon *m.*
cord, *v.t.* corder, lier, fagoter
cordial, (*adj.*) cordial

cordiality, cordialité *f.*
cordially, (*adv.*) cordialement
corduroy, velours côtelé *m.*
core, cœur *m.*; trognon *m.* (of apple, etc.)
cork, liège *m.*; bouchon *m.* (of bottle)
cork, *v.t.* boucher
cork (tree), chêne-liège *m.*
corkscrew, tire-bouchon *m.*
corn, grain *m.*; froment *m.*; blé *m.* (wheat); maïs *m.* (Indian corn); cor *m.* (on foot, etc.)
corn, *v.t.* saler (beef, etc.)
ear of corn, épi (*m.*) de blé
cornfield, champ (*m.*) de blé
cornflour, farine (*f.*) de maïs
cornflower, bluet *m.*
corned beef, bœuf (*m.*) salé
corner, coin *m.*; angle *m.*
corner, *v.t.* (*fig.*) pousser dans un coin; accaparer (*commerce*)
cornice, corniche *f.*
coronation, couronnement *m.*
coronet, petite couronne *f.* (of nobility)
corporal, (*adj.*) corporel(le)
corporal, caporal *m.*; brigadier *m.* (artillery)
corps, corps *m.*; corps d'armée *m.* (army corps)
corpse, cadavre *m.*
corpulence, corpulence *f.*; embonpoint *m.*
corpulent, (*adj.*) corpulent
Corpus Christi, la fête-Dieu *f.*
correct, (*adj.*) correct, exact, juste, convenable
correct, *v.t.* corriger; rectifier
correction, correction *f.*
correctly, (*adv.*) correctement; exactement
correspond, *v.i.* correspondre (avec); répondre (à); s'accorder (avec) (agree with)
correspondence, correspondance *f.*; rapport *m.*
corridor, corridor *m.*; passage *m.*
corridor carriage, wagon à couloir *m.*
corridor train, train à couloir *m.*
corroborate, *v.t.* corroborer; confirmer

corrode, *v.t.* corroder; ronger
corrosive, (*adj.*) corrosif(-ive);
  rongeur(-euse)
corrugate, *v.t.* rider; plisser; onduler
corrugated iron, tôle (*f.*) ondulée
corrupt, *v.t.* corrompre
corrupt, (*adj.*) corrompu
corruption, corruption *f.*
corset, corset *m.*
Corsican, Corse
cost. prix *m.*; frais *m. pl.*; coût *m.*
  (*commercial*); dépens *m. pl.* (*legal*)
cost, *v.i.* coûter
cost price, prix coûtant *m.*
at any cost, à tout prix; coûte que
  coûte
net cost, prix de revient *m.*
coster, costermonger, marchand
  (*m.*) des quatre saisons
costive, (*adj.*) constipé
costly, (*adj.*) coûteux(-euse); de
  luxe
costume, costume *m.*
cosy, (*adj.*) à l'aise, confortable
cot, lit d'enfant *m.*
cottage, chaumière *f.*; cabane *f.*;
  petite maison *f.*
cotton, coton *m.*; percale *f.*
  (cotton cambric); cotonnade *f.*
  (cotton goods)
cotton-mill, filature (*f.*) de coton
cotton-wool, ouate *f.*
couch, canapé *m.*; couche *f.*
couch, *v.i.* se coucher; (*fig.*)
  rédiger (par écrit)
cough, toux *f.*
cough, *v.i.* tousser
council, conseil *m.*
counsel, conseil *m.*; avis *m.*;
  avocat *m.* (barrister)
counsel, *v.t.* conseiller
count, calcul *m.*; compte *m.*;
  charge *f.* (*legal*); comte *m.*; comtesse *f.* (title)
count, *v.t.* compter
countenance, figure *f.*; mine *f.*;
  (*fig.*) contenance *f.*
countenance, *v.t.* appuyer, encourager
counter, comptoir *m.* (in shop);
  jeton *m.* (cards, etc.); calculateur
  m.

counter, (*adv.*) contre, contraire-
  ment à
counter-attack, contre-attaque *f.*
counteract, *v.t.* neutraliser
counteraction, résistance *f.*; opposition *f.*
counter-balance, *v.t.* contre-
  balancer
counterfeit, (*adj.*) contrefait;
  faux (fausse); imité
counterfeit, *v.t.* contrefaire; imiter
countermand, *v.t.* contremander
counterpane, couvre-pied *m.*
counterpart, contre-partie *f.*;
  double *m.* (*legal*)
countersign, mot (*m.*) d'ordre
countersign, *v.t.* contresigner
counting, compte *m.*; dépouille-
  ment *m.* (of votes, etc.)
counting-house, bureau(x) *m.*
  (*pl.*); caisse *f.*
countrified, (*adj.*) campagnard,
  provincial
country, pays *m.*; campagne *f.*
  (as opposed to town); patrie *f.*
  (fatherland)
country house, maison de campagne *f.*
country seat, château *m.*
countryman, paysan *m.*; compatriote *m.*
countrywoman, paysanne *f.*;
  compatriote *f.*
county, comté *m.*
couple, couple *f.*; couple *m.* (male
  and female)
couple, *v.i.* s'accoupler
couple, *v.t.* coupler, accoupler
courage, courage *m.*
courageous, (*adj.*) courageux
  (-euse)
courier, courrier *m.*
course, cours *m.* (stream, etc.);
  cours *m.* (studies); service *m.* (of
  a meal); courant *m.* (duration);
  terrain (*m.*) de course (race-course)
course, *v.t.* faire courir
course, *v.i.* circuler (of blood)
in course of time, avec le temps
in due course, en temps voulu
of course, (*adv.*) bien entendu;
  naturellement

courser, coursier *m.*
court, cour *f.*; tribunal *m.* (*law*); impasse *f.* (small poor street, etc.)
court of appeal, cour (*f.*) de cassation
criminal court, cour (*f.*) de justice criminelle
to court, pay court, *v.i.* faire la cour à
court-martial, conseil (*m.*) de guerre
court-plaster, taffetas (*m.*) d'Angleterre
courteous, (*adj.*) courtois, poli
courtesy, courtoisie *f.*; politesse *f.*
courtier, courtisan *m.*
courtship, cour *f.*; recherche (*f.*) en mariage
courtyard, cour *f.*
cousin, cousin(e) *m.* (*f.*)
first cousin, cousin(e) germain(e) *m.* (*f.*)
covenant, convention *f.*; pacte *m.*
cover, couvert *m.*; couverture *f.*; couvercle *m.* (saucepans, etc.)
cover, *v.t.* couvrir; voiler; cacher
coverlet, couverture (*f.*) de lit
covert, (*adj.*) caché, secret (-ète)
covert, couvert *m.*; gîte *m.*
covet, *v.t.* convoiter
covetous, (*adj.*) avide; cupide
covetousness, convoitise *f.*; cupidité *f.*
cow, vache *f.*
cow, *v.t.* intimider, dompter
coward, lâche *m.*; poltron(ne) *m.* (*f.*)
cowardice, lâcheté *f.*
cowardly, (*adj.*) lâche, poltron(ne)
cower, *v.i.* se blottir, s'accroupir
cowhide, peau (*f.*) de vache
cowl, capuchon *m.*
coxcomb, fat *m.*
coy, (*adj.*) timide, réservé
crab, crabe *m.*; pomme sauvage *f.*
crabbed, (*adj.*) acariâtre
crack, fente *f.*; crevasse *f.*; fissure *f.*; craquement *m.* (noise); détonation *f.*; as *m.* (expert player, etc.)
crack, *v.i.* se fendre, se gercer (skin)

crack, *v.t.* fendre, gercer
cracked, (*adj.*) fendu; timbré (insane)
cracker, pétard *m.*
crackle, *v.i.* pétiller, crépiter
cradle, berceau *m.*
craft, métier *m.* (trade); bâtiment *m.* (*naut.*); ruse *f.* (trickery)
crafty, (*adj.*) rusé
crag, rocher escarpé *m.*
cram, *v.t.* fourrer; bourrer; chauffer (students)
crammer, préparateur *m.*; chauffeur *m.*
cramp, crampe *f.*; crampon *m.* (clamp)
cranberry, canneberge *f.*
crane, grue *f.* (both for bird and mechanical crane)
travelling crane, grue roulante *f.*
crank, manivelle *f.*; loufoque *m.* (eccentric person)
cranky, fantasque
cranny, fente *f.*; crevasse *f.*
crape, crêpe *m.*
crash, fracas *m.*; grand bruit *m.*; faillite *f.* (financial ruin)
crash, *v.i.* faire un grand fracas; retentir; s'abattre
crate, caisse *f.*
crater, cratère *m.*; entonnoir *m.* (shell or bomb)
cravat, cravate *f.*
crave, *v.t.* implorer; (*fig.*) désirer ardemment
craving, désir (*m.*) ardent
crawfish, crayfish, écrevisse *f.*; langouste *f.* (commercial term)
crawl, *v.i.* ramper; (of taxi seeking fare) marauder
crayon, crayon *m.*; pastel *m.*
craze, folle idée *f.*; passion folle *f.*
crazy, (*adj.*) fou (folle); toqué
creak, *v.i.* craquer; grincer
creaking, grincement *m.*
cream, crème *f.*
creamy, crémeux(-euse)
crease, pli *m.*
crease, *v.t.* plisser (of trousers); chiffonner (to rumple)
create, *v.t.* créer; produire; faire naître; engendrer; occasionner

creation, création *f.*; univers *m.*
creator, créateur *m.*
creature, créature *f.*
credence, croyance *f.*; foi *f.*
credentials, lettres de créance *f. pl.*
credible, (*adj.*) croyable; digne de foi
credit, crédit *m.* (*commercial*); influence *f.*
credit, *v.t.* croire (à); faire crédit (*commercial*); porter au crédit (book-keeping)
creditable, honorable; digne d'éloge
creditor, créancier(-ère), *m.* (*f.*)
credulous, (*adj.*) crédule
creed, credo *m.* (prayer); symbole *m.* (Apostles' Creed); profession de foi (*f.*); croyance *f.*
creek, crique *f.*
creeper, plante grimpante *f.*
creeping, (*adj.*) rampant, grimpant
cremation, crémation *f.*
crematory, crématoire *m.*
crescent, (*adj.*) croissant *m.*
cress, cresson *m.*
crest, crête *f.* (of ridge or cock); écusson *m.* (*heraldry*); cimier *m.* (helmet)
crestfallen, (*adj.*) abattu; penaud
crevice, crevasse *f.*
crew, équipage *m.* (*naut.*)
crib, crèche *f.*; mangeoire *f.*
cricket, grillon *m.* (insect); cricket *m.* (game)
crier, crieur *m.*
crime, crime *m.*
criminal, (*adj.*) criminel(le)
criminal, criminel(le) *m.* (*f.*)
crimp, *v.t.* friser (hair)
crimson, (*adj.*) cramoisi
cringe (to), *v.i.* faire le chien couchant auprès de
cripple, estropié *m.*; boiteux (-euse) *m.* (*f.*)
cripple, *v.t.* estropier; paralyser; avarier (*naut.*)
crippled, estropié
crisis, crise *f.*
crisp, (*adj.*) croquant

critic, critique *m.*
critical, (*adj.*) critique; délicat
criticise, *v.t.* critiquer; censurer (to reprove)
croak, croassement *m.*
croak, *v.i.* croasser
crock (old), vieux clou *m.*
crockery, faïence *f.*; vaisselle *f.*
crocodile, crocodile *m.*
crofter, petit fermier *m.*
crook, escroc *m.* (swindler); courbure *f.* (curve); crosse *f.* (of bishop)
crooked, (*adj.*) courbé; malhonnête (dishonest); pervers
crop, récolte *f.*; moisson *f.*; jabot *m.* (of bird)
crop, *v.t.* tondre, couper
cross, croix *f.*; carrefour *m.* (roads)
cross, (*adj.*) en travers; de travers; de mauvaise humeur (ill temper)
cross, *v.t.* croiser; marquer d'une croix; barrer (cheque); franchir (get over); contrarier
cross-examination, contre-interrogatoire *m.*
cross off, *v.t.* biffer
cross-section, section (*f.*) transversale
crossing, croisement *m.*; passage *m.*; level crossing, passage (*m.*) à niveau
crotchet, noire *f.* (*mus.*)
crotchety, (*adj.*) capricieux(-cuse)
crouch, *v.i.* se blottir
croup, croupion *m.* (birds); croup *m.* (sickness)
crow, corbeau *m.*; corneille *f.*
crow, *v.i.* chanter
crowd, foule *f.*; rassemblement *m.*
crowd, *v.i.* se serrer; se presser en foule
crowd, *v.t.* serrer, encombrer
crowded, (*adj.*) serré, encombré
crown, couronne *f.*; sommet *m.* (of hill, etc.)
crown, *v.t.* couronner
crowning, (*adj.*) final, suprême
crowning, couronnement *m.*
crucible, creuset *m.*
crucifix, crucifix *m.*

crucifixion, crucifixion *f.*

crude, *(adj.)* cru; grossiér(-ère) (coarse)

cruel, *(adj.)* cruel(le)

cruelty, cruauté *f.*

cruet, huilier *m.*

cruise, croisière *f.*

cruise, *v.i.* croiser

cruiser, croiseur *m.*; croiseur cuirassé *m.* (battle-cruiser)

crumb, mie *f.*; miette *f.*

crumble, *v.t.* émietter (bread); broyer (crush); réduire en poussière; *v.i.* s'écrouler (fall in ruins)

crumbling, écroulement *m.*

crumple, *v.t.* chiffonner; froisser

crusade, croisade *f.*

crusader, croisé *m.*

crush, cohue *f.* (crowd)

crush, *v.t.* écraser; broyer

crushing, *(adj.)* écrasant

crust, croûte *f.*; croûton *m.* (of bread)

crusty, couvert d'une croûte; *(fig.)* bourru

crutch, béquille *f.*

crux, point difficile *m.*

cry, cri *m.*

cry, *v.i.* crier; pleurer (weep)

cry, *v.t.* crier

crying, *(adj.)* criant

crying, larmes *f. pl.*; cris *m. pl.*

crying shame, une vraie honte *f.*

crypt, crypte *f.*

cub, petit *m.* (d'un animal); ourson *m.* (bear); lionceau *m.* (of lion)

cube, cube *m.*

cubic, *(adj.)* cubique

cubicle, cellule *f.* (of dormitory)

cuckold, cocu *m.*; cornard *m.* (husband of an unfaithful wife)

cuckoo, coucou *m.*

cucumber, concombre *m.*

cuddle, *v.t.* embrasser étroitement

cudgel, bâton *m.*; trique *f.*

cudgel, *v.t.* rosser

cue, queue de billard *f.*; réplique *f.* (*theat.*); indice *m.* (hint)

cuff, manchette *f.* (of sleeve); coup (*m.*) de poing

cuff, *v.t.* donner des coups de poing

cuirass, cuirasse *f.*

cuirassier, cuirassier *m.*

culinary, *(adj.)* culinaire

cull, *v.t.* cueillir

culminate, *v.i.* culminer, se terminer

culpability, coupabilité *f.*

culprit, coupable *m.* and *f.*; accusé *m.*; accusée *f.*

cultivate, *v.t.* cultiver

cultivation, culture *f.*

cultivator, cultivateur *m.*

culture, culture *f.*

culvert, petit aqueduc *m.*

cumber, *v.t.* embarrasser, encombrer

cumbersome, gênant; difficile à manier

cunning, *(adj.)* rusé

cunning, finesse *f.*; ruse *f.*

cup, tasse *f.*; coupe *f.*; ventouse *f.* (*med.*)

cupboard, armoire *f.*; placard *m.* (in wall)

cupidity, cupidité *f.*

cupola, coupole *f.*

cur, roquet *m.*; (*fig.*) cuistre *m.*

curable, *(adj.)* guérissable

curate, vicaire *m.*

curator, conservateur *m.*

curb, *v.t.* réprimer; brider; mettre un frein (put a brake on)

curd, lait caillé *m.*

curdle, *v.i.* se cailler

cure, guérison *f.*; remède *m.*; cure *f.* (of souls)

cure, *v.t.* guérir; saler (meat)

curfew, couvre-feu *m.*

curio, curiosité *f.*

curiosity, curiosité *f.*

curious, *(adj.)* curieux(-euse)

curl, boucle *f.*

curl, *v.t.* boucler; friser

curly, *(adj.)* frisé

curmudgeon, pingre *m.*; ladre *m.*

currant, groseille *f.*

currency, monnaie *f.*

current, *(adj.)* courant; courant *m.* (electric)

curriculum, cours (*m.*) d'études

currish, *(adj.)* brutal, hargneux (-euse)

curry, *v.t.* étriller (horse)
curry-comb, étrille *f.*
curry-powder, cari *m.*; curry *m.*
curse, malédiction *f.*; imprécation *f.*; fléau *m.* (scourge)
curse, *v.t.* maudire
cursed, (*adj.*) maudit
cursory, (*adj.*) précipité, rapide
curt, (*adj.*) brusque, sec (sèche)
curtail, *v.t.* retrancher; raccourcir
curtain, rideau *m.*
curtly, (*adv.*) brusquement, sèchement
curtsey, révérence *f.*
curtsey, *v.i.* faire la révérence
curvature, courbure *f.*
curve, courbe *f.*
curve, *v.i.* se courber; décrire une courbe
curvet, courbette *f.*
curvet, *v.i.* faire des courbettes
cushion, coussin *m.*
custard, flan *m.*; une crème *f.*
custodian, gardien(ne) *m.* (*f.*)
custody, garde *f.*; arrestation *f.*; détention *f.*
custom, coutume *f.*; habitude *f.*; usage *m.*
custom-house, douane *f.*
customs, douane *f.*
customs duty, droit (*m.*) de douane
customs officer, douanier *m.*
customary, (*adj.*) ordinaire, d'usage
customer, client(e) *m.* (*f.*)
cut, coup *m.* (of sword, etc.); coupe *f.* (of clothes); taille *f.* (shape); tranche *f.* (slice); gravure *f.* (engraving); coupure *f.* (incision)
cut, *v.t.* couper; tailler; trancher; découper (carve); faire (les dents)
cut an acquaintance, *v.t.* passer sans saluer
cut down, *v.t.* abattre; réduire (expenses)
cut out, *v.t.* tailler; (*fig.*) éclipser
cut short, *v.t.* couper la parole (à)
cut to pieces, *v.t.* tailler en morceaux
cut up, *v.t.* découper, dépecer
cutaneous, (*adj.*) cutané

cute, (*adj.*) fin; rusé
cuticle, épiderme *m.*
cutlass, coutelas *m.*
cutler, coutelier *m.*
cutlery, coutellerie *f.*
cutlet, côtelette *f.*
cutter, coupeur *m.*; coupoir *m.* (tools)
cuttle-fish, seiche *f.*
cycle, bicyclette *f.*; vélo *m.*; cycle *m.* (of time)
cycle, *v.i.* faire de la bicyclette
cyclist, cycliste *m.* and *f.*
cyclone, ouragan *m.*; cyclone *m.*
cyclopædia, encyclopédie *f.*
cygnet, jeune cygne *m.*
cylinder, cylindre *m.*
cymbal, cymbale *f.*
cynic, cynique *m.*
cynical, (*adj.*) cynique
cypress, cyprès *m.*
Cyprus, la Chypre *f.*
cyste, kyste *m.*
cystitis, cystite *f.*
Czar, Czar *m.*
Czarina, Czarine *f.*
Czech, Tchèque

D

dab, coup léger *m.*; tache *f.*; limande *f.* (fish)
dab, *v.t.* éponger à petits coups
dab (to be a - at), être calé en ...
dabble, *v.t.* barbouiller
dabble (in), *v.r.* se mêler (de)
dabbler, barboteur *m.*; amateur *m.*
dad *or* daddy, papa *m.*
daffodil, narcisse (*m.*) des prés
daft, (*adj.*) idiot
dagger, poignard *m.*
dahlia, dahlia *m.*
daily, (*adj.*) quotidien(ne)
daily, (*adv.*) journellement; tous les jours
daintiness, délicatesse; goût (*m.*) difficile
dainty, (*adj.*) friand, délicat; difficile

dainty, friandise *f.*

dairy, laiterie *f.*

dais, dais *m.*

daisy, marguerite *f.*

dale, vallée *f.*

dalliance, badinage *m.*

dally, *v.i.* perdre son temps; badiner avec; flirter (avec)

dam, mère *f.* (of animals)

dam, digue *f.*; barrage *m.*

dam, *v.t.* endiguer

damage, dommage *m.*; dégât *m.*; (*fig.*) préjudice *m.*; avarie *f.* (*commercial*)

damage, *v.t.* endommager; avarier (in transport); faire tort à (reputation)

damages, dommages-intérêts *m. pl.* (*legal*)

damaging, (*adj.*) nuisible, préjudiciable

damask, damas *m.*

dame, dame *f.*

damn, *v.t.* damner; (*fig.*) condamner

damnable, odieux(-euse); damnable

damnation, damnation *f.*

damp, (*adj.*) humide, moite

damp (fire damp), grisou *m.*; mofette *f.* (choke damp)

damp, *v.t.* mouiller; rendre humide; (*fig.*) abattre

dampness, humidité *f.*

damsel, jeune fille *f.*; demoiselle *f.*

damson, prune (*f.*) de Damas

dance, danse *f.*; bal *m.*

dance, *v.t.* and *v.i.* danser

dance-hall, bal public *m.*; dancing *m.*

dancer, danseur *m.*; danseuse *f.*

dancing, danse *f.*

dandelion, pissenlit *m.*

dandle, *v.t.* bercer

dandruff, pellicules *f. pl.*

dandy, élégant *m.*; gandin *m.*

Dane, Danish, (*adj.* and *subst.*) danois(e)

danger, danger *m.*; péril *m.*

dangerous, dangereux(-euse)

dangerously, (*adv.*) dangereusement

dangle, *v.i.* pendiller; être suspendu

dangle, *v.t.* balancer, laisser pendre

dank, (*adj.*) humide

dapper, (*adj.*) pimpant (spruce)

dapple, (*adj.*) pommelé

dare, *v.i.* oser

dare, *v.t.* risquer

daring, (*adj.*) hardi, intrépide

dark, (*adj.*) obscur; sombre; noir

dark, ténèbres *f. pl.*; obscurité *f.*

darken, *v.i.* s'obscurcir, se rembrunir (complexion)

darken, *v.t.* obscurcir

darling, chéri *m.*; chérie *f.*; favori *m.*; favorite *f.*; mignon *m.*; mignonne *f.*

darn, *v.t.* raccommoder, repriser

darn(ing), reprise *f.*

dart, dard *m.*; darts (game), fléchette *f.*

dart, *v.i.* s'élancer sur

dash, coup *m.*; impétuosité *f.*; entrain *m.*; élan *m.*; trait *m.* (of pen); soupçon *m.* (a small quantity of)

dash, *v.t.* jeter, précipiter; briser (break); éclabousser (spatter); *v.i.* se précipiter

dashing, (*adj.*) brillant; fougueux (-euse)

dastard, lâche *m.*

data, données *f. pl.*

date, date *f.*; datte *f.* (fruit)

date, *v.t.* dater

daub, *v.t.* barbouiller

daughter, fille *f.*

daughter-in-law, belle-fille *f.*; bru *f.*

dauntless, intrépide

dawdle, *v.i.* flâner

dawn, aube *f.*; point (*m.*) du jour

dawn, *v.i.* poindre

day, jour *m.*; journée *f.* (of work, etc.)

all day, toute la journée

any day, n'importe quel jour

by day, au jour, le jour

nowadays, de nos jours

day after to-morrow, après-demain

day before yesterday, avant-hier

in former days, autrefois, jadis

day-boarder, demi-pensionnaire *m.* and *f.*

day-book, journal *m.* (book-keeping)

day-work, travail à la journée *m.*

day's work, journée *f.*

daze, *v.t.* étourdir, hébéter

dazzle, *v.t.* éblouir

dazzling, (*adj.*) éblouissant

deacon, diacre *m.*

dead, (*adj.*) mort; inanimé; sourd (sound); mat (of colours)

dead beat, éreinté

dead body, cadavre *m.*

dead heat, épreuve (*f.*) nulle

dead-letter office, bureau (*m.*) des rebuts

dead loss, perte (*f.*) sèche

dead march, marche (*f.*) funèbre

deaden, *v.t.* amortir, assourdir (sound)

deadlock, impasse *f.*

deadly, (*adj.*) mortel(le)

deaf, (*adj.*) sourd, insensible

deaf and dumb, (*adj.*) sourd-muet

deafen, *v.t.* assourdir

deafness, surdité *f.*

deal, quantité *f.*; donne *f.* (cards)

deal (wood), bois (*m.*) de sapin

deal (business), affaire *f.*

deal, *v.t.* distribuer, donner (cards)

deal, *v.i.* traiter avec (deal with); se servir chez (at a shop)

a great deal, beaucoup de

to have to deal with, avoir affaire à

dealer, marchand *m.*; donneur *m.* (cards)

dealings, affaires *f. pl.*

dean, doyen *m.*

dear, (*adj.*) cher (chère); coûteux (-euse) (expensive)

oh dear! *interj.* oh là là!; mon Dieu!

dearly, (*adv.*) chèrement

death, mort *f.*; décès *m.* (*legal*)

death-blow, coup (*m.*) mortel

death-throes, agonie *f.*

death-wound, blessure (*f.*) mortelle

debase, *v.t.* abaisser, falsifier

debatable, contestable

debate, débat *m.*; discussion *f.*

debate, *v.t.* débattre, discuter

debater, orateur *m.*

debauch, debauchery, débauche *f.*

debauch, *v.t.* débaucher; pervertir

debenture, obligation *f.*

debit, débit *m.*; doit *m.*

debit, *v.t.* passer au débit; débiter

debt, dette *f.*; créance *f.*

debtor, débiteur *m.*; débitrice *f.*

début, début *m.*

decadence, décadence *f.*

decamp, *v.i.* décamper, filer

decant, *v.t.* décanter

decanter, carafe *f.*

decapitate, *v.t.* décapiter

decay, décadence *f.*; délabrement *m.*; carie *f.* (of teeth)

decay, *v.i.* se tomber en ruines; se délabrer; se carier (of teeth)

decease, décès *m.*; mort *f.*

decease, *v.i.* décéder, mourir

deceit, tromperie *f.*

deceitful, (*adj.*) trompeur(-euse)

deceive, *v.t.* tromper, abuser

December, décembre *m.*

decency, bienséance *f.*; convenances *f. pl.* (of life, etc.)

decent, (*adj.*) décent, honnête

deception, tromperie *f.*; duperie *f.*

decibel, décibel *m.*

decide, *v.t.* décider (de); se décider (à); trancher (a question)

decided, (*adj.*) décidé; positif(-ive)

decision, décision *f.*

decisive, (*adj.*) décisif(-ive)

deck, pont *m.* (of ship)

deck-chair, transatlantique *m.*

declaim, *v.i.* and *v.t.* déclámer

declaration, déclaration *f.*; proclamation *f.*

declare, *v.i.* se déclarer

declare, *v.t.* déclarer

decline, déclin *m.*; baisse *f.*

decline, *v.t.* refuser

decline, *v.i.* décliner; baisser (of prices); être en pente (of ground)

declivity, déclivité *f.*; pente *f.*
declutch, *v.i.* débrayer
decompose, *v.i.* se décomposer
decorate, *v.r.* décorer, embellir
decoration, décoration *f.* (medals, etc.); embellissement *m.*
decorative, décoratif(-ive)
decorous, (*adj.*) convenable
decorum, bienséance *f.*
decoy, appât *m.*; piège *m.*
decrease, décroissance *f.*; diminution *f.*
decrease, *v.i.* décroître, diminuer
decree, décret *m.*; arrêt *m.* (*legal*)
decree, *v.t.* décréter, arrêter
decrepit, (*adj.*) caduc (caduque)
decry, *v.t.* décrier
dedicate, *v.t.* dédier, dévouer
dedication, dédicace *f.*
deduce, *v.t.* déduire
deduction, retenue *f.* (*commercial*); déduction *f.*
deed, action *f.*; fait *m.*; titre *m.* (*law*)
deem, *v.t.* juger, croire
deep, (*adj.*) profond; foncé (colour); grave (sound)
deepen, *v.t.* approfondir; rendre plus foncé
deeply, profondément.
deep-seated, (*adj.*) enraciné
deer, cerf *m.*; daim *m.*
defamatory, (*adj.*) diffamatoire
defame, *v.t.* diffamer
default, défaut *m.*, manque *m.*
default, *v.i.* faire défaut; manquer (à)
defaulter, réfractaire *m.* (*mil.*, etc.)
defeat, défaite *f.*
defeat, *v.t.* battre; vaincre
defect, défaut *m.*
defective, (*adj.*) défectueux(-euse)
defence, défense *f.*
defend, *v.t.* défendre (de), protéger (contre)
defendant, défenseur *m.*; défenderesse *f.*; accusé(e), (criminal case)
defender, défenseur *m.*
defensive, (*adj.*) défensif(-ive)
on the defensive, sur la défensive
defer, *v.t.* différer, ajourner; *v.i.* déférer (à)

deference, déférence *f.*
defiance, défi *m.*
deficiency, défaut *m.*; insuffisance *f.*
deficient, défectueux(-euse)
deficit, déficit *m.*
defile, *v.t.* souiller; violer; défiler (of troops)
definable, définissable
define, *v.t.* déterminer; définir
definite, (*adj.*) déterminé; défini (*gram.*)
definition, définition *f.*
definitive, définitif(-ive)
deflate, *v.t.* dégonfler (of tyre)
deform, *v.t.* défigurer, déformer
deformity, difformité *f.*; laideur *f.*
defraud, *v.t.* frauder
defray, *v.t.* couvrir les frais
deft, (*adj.*) adroit, habile
defy, *v.t.* défier
degeneracy, dégénération *f.*
degenerate, (*adj.*) dégénéré
degenerate, *v.i.* dégénérer
degeneration, dégénération *f.*
degradation, dégradation *f.*
degrade, dégrader; casser
degree, degré *m.*; rang *m.*; ordre *m.*
by degrees, peu à peu
deign, *v.t.* daigner
deity, divinité *f.*
deject, *v.t.* décourager
delay, délai *m.*; retardement *m.*
delay, *v.t.* différer; retarder; *v.i.* s'attarder (à)
delegate, délégué *m.*
delegate, *v.t.* déléguer
delegation, délégation *f.*
delf(t), faïence (*f.*) de Delft
deliberate, délibéré, réfléchi
deliberate, *v.t.* and *v.i.* délibérer
deliberation, délibération *f.*
delicacy, délicatesse *f.*; friandise *f.* (food, dainty)
delicate, délicat
delicious, (*adj.*) délicieux(-euse), exquis
delight, délices *f. pl.*; joie *f.*
delight, *v.t.* plaire à; enchanter
delight (in), *v.i.* se plaire (à)
delightful, délicieux(-euse), ravissant

delinquency, délit *m.*; juvenile -, criminalité juvénile *f.*

delinquent, coupable *m.* and *f.*

delirium, délire *m*

deliver, *v.t.* délivrer, sauver; distribuer (letters); livrer (goods or a place); accoucher (childbirth)

delivery, délivrance *f.*; livraison *f.* (of goods, etc.), distribution *f.* (of letters); accouchement *m.* (of a mother); payment on delivery, livraison contre rémboursement

delude, *v.t.* tromper

deluge, déluge *m.*

deluge (with), *v.t.* inonder (de)

delusion, illusion *f.*; erreur *f.*

delusive, (*adj.*) illusoire

demagogue, démagogue *m.*

demand, demande *f.*; réclamation *f.*

demand, *v.t.* réclamer, exiger

in great demand, très recherché

demarcation, démarcation *f.*

demean oneself, *v.i.* s'abaisser

demeanour, conduite *f.*

dementia, démence *f.*

demilitarise, *v.t.* démilitariser

demobilise, *v.t.* démobiliser

democracy, démocratie *f.*

democratic, (*adj.*) démocratique

demolish, *v.t.* démolir

demolition, démolition *f.*

demon, démon *m.*; diable *m.*

demoniac, demoniacal, (*adj.*) démoniaque

demonstrate, *v.t.* démontrer; *v.i.* manifester (*political*)

demonstration, démonstration *f.*; manifestation *f.*

demur, *v.i.* hésiter; faire des difficultés

demure, (*adj.*) réservé, posé

den, antre *m.*; repaire *m.* (of thieves, beasts, etc.); fumoir *m.* (a man's " den ")

deniable, (*adj.*) niable

denial, dénégation *f.*; démenti *m.*

denominate, *v.t.* dénommer

denomination, dénomination *f.*

denominator, dénominateur *m.*

denote, *v.t.* dénoter, indiquer

denounce, *v.t.* dénoncer

dense, (*adj.*) dense, épais(se); stupide

densely, (*adv.*) en foule compacte; en masse

density, densité *f.*

dent, brèche *f.*; renfoncement *m.*

dental, (*adj.*) dentaire

dentifrice, dentifrice *m.*

dentist, dentiste *m.*

dentition, dentition *f.*

denture, denture *f.*; (*coll.*) râtelier *m.*

deny, *v.t.* nier, démentir, refuser

depart, *v.i.* partir, s'en aller; (*fig.*) mourir

departed, (*adj.*) défunt

department, département *m.*; service *m.*; comptoir *m.* (shop); rayon *m.* (shop)

departure, départ *m.*; (*fig.*) trépas *m.*

depend (on), *v.i.* dépendre (de); compter (sur)

dependable, sur lequel on peut compter (of persons)

dependant, personne (*f.*) dépendante; protégé(e) *m.* (*f.*)

dependency, dépendance *f.*

depict, *v.t.* peindre

deplorable, (*adj.*) déplorable

deplore, *v.t.* déplorer

depopulate, *v.t.* dépeupler

deport, *v.t.* déporter

deportation, déportation, expulsion *f.*

deportment, tenue *f.*

depose, *v.t.* déposer

deposit, dépôt *m.*; versement (*financial*, etc.)

deposit, *v.t.* déposer, verser

deposit (in advance), arrhes *f. pl.*

deposit account, compte en dépôt *m.*

deposition, déposition *f.*

depot, dépôt *m.*

deprave, *v.t.* corrompre, dépraver

depravity, dépravation *f.*

deprecate, *v.i.* désapprouver

depreciate, *v.t.* déprécier

depreciate, *v.i.* perdre de sa valeur

depreciation, dépréciation *f.*

depress, *v.t.* abaisser; baisser; déprimer

depressed, (*adj.*) abattu

depression, dépression *f.*; creux *m.* (in ground); (*fig.*) abattement *m.*; marasme *m.* (in business)

deprive, *v.t.* priver (de)

depth, profondeur *f.*; **depths of winter,** le plus fort de l'hiver

deputation, délégation *f.*

depute, *v.t.* députer, déléguer

deputy, député *m.*; adjoint *m.*; délégué *m.*

deputy-chairman, vice-président *m.*

deputy-governor, sous-gouverneur *m.*

deputy-mayor, adjoint au maire *m.*

derail, *v.t.* faire dérailler; *v.i.* dérailler (to come off the rails)

derailment, déraillement *m.*

derange, *v.t.* déranger; troubler l'esprit

derelict, (*adj.*) abandonné

deride, *v.t.* se moquer de

derision, dérision *f.*; objet (*m.*) de dérision

derisive, dérisoire

derive, *v.t.* and *v.i.* tirer (de), provenir (de)

derogate, *v.i.* déroger (à)

derogatory, (*adj.*) dérogatoire

derrick, grue *f.*

descend, *v.i.* descendre (with *être*); tomber (with *être*); *v.t.* descendre (with *avoir*)

descendant, descendant *m.*; descendante *f.*

descent, chute *f.*; pente *f.*; descendance *f.* (lineage)

describe, *v.t.* décrire; dépeindre

describable, (*adj.*) descriptible

description, description *f.*; désignation *f.* (of person)

descriptive, (*adj.*) descriptif(-ive)

descry, *v.t.* apercevoir

desecrate, *v.t.* profaner

desert, mérite *m.*

desert, désert *m.*

desert, *v.t.* déserter .

deserter, déserteur *m.*

deserve, *v.t.* mériter; être digne de

deservedly, à juste titre

design, dessein *m.*; projet *m.*

design (drawing), dessin *m.*

design, *v.t.* dessiner; faire le plan de; projeter; destiner (à)

designate, *v.t.* désigner, nommer

designing, (*adj.*) intrigant

desirable, (*adj.*) désirable, à désirer

desire, désir *m.*; envie *f.*

desire, *v.t.* désirer, souhaiter, prier (de)

desirous, désireux(-euse)

desist, *v.i.* se désister (de); cesser (de)

desk, pupitre *m.*; chaire *f.* (in college); bureau *m.* (in office)

desolate, (*adj.*) désolé, solitaire

despair, désespoir *m.*

despair, *v.i.* désespérer (de)

desperate, désespéré, acharné

desperation, désespoir *m.*; acharnement *m.*

despicable, (*adj.*) méprisable

despise, *v.t.* mépriser

despite, (*prep.*) en dépit de, malgré

despondency, découragement *m.*

despondent, (*adj.*) découragé, abattu

despot, despote *m.*

despotic, (*adj.*) despotique

despotism, despotisme *m.*

dessert, dessert *m.*

destination, destination *f.*

destine, *v.t.* destiner

destiny, destin *m.*

destitute, (*adj.*) dépourvu; sans le sou

destroy, *v.t.* détruire, exterminer

destroyer, contre-torpilleur *m.* (*naval*)

destroying, (*adj.*) destructeur (-trice); destructif(-ive)

destruction, destruction *f.*; massacre *m.*

destructive, (*adj.*) destructeur (-trice)

desultory, sans suite; décousu

detach, *v.t.* détacher, séparer

detached, (*adj.*) isolé, détaché

detachment, détachement *m.*

detail, détail *m.* (*pl.* détails)

detail, *v.t.* détailler; affecter (*mil.*)

in detail, minutieusement

detain, v.t. détenir, retenir

detect, v.t. découvrir

detection, découverte f.

detective, agent (m.) de la Sûreté; - story, roman (m.) policier

deter, v.t. dissuader de

deteriorate, v.i. se détériorer

deterioration, détérioration f.

determinate, établi, définitif (-ive)

determination, détermination f.; décision f.; résolution f.

determine, v.t. and v.i. déterminer, décider

determined, (adj.) résolu

detest, v.t. détester

detestable, détestable

dethrone, v.t. détrôner

detonate, v.t. faire détoner

detour, détour m.

detract, v.i. déroger à

detriment, détriment m.; préjudice m.

detrimental, préjudiciable

deuce, diantre; deux m. (of cards); égalité f. (tennis)

devastate, v.t. dévaster, ravager

devastating, (adj.) dévastateur (-trice)

devastation, dévastation f.

develop, v.t. développer; v.i. se développer

developer, révélateur m. (phot.)

development, développement m.

deviate, v.i. dévier; s'écarter de

deviation, déviation f.

device, expédient m.; moyen m.; emblème m.; truc m. (gadget)

devil, démon m.; diable m.

devilish, diabolique

devilry, diablerie f.

devious, (adj.) tortueux(-euse)

devise, v.t. imaginer, trouver, inventer

devoid, (adj.) dénué (de); dépourvu (de)

devolve, v.i. incomber (à); v.t. transmettre

devote, v.t. dévouer; s'adonner (à)

devoted, (adj.) dévoué

devotion, dévotion f. (piety); empressement m.; dévouement m.

devour, v.t. dévorer

devouring, (adj.) dévorant

devout, (adj.) pieux(-euse); dévot

dew, rosée f.

dexterity, adresse f.; dextérité f.

dexterous, adroit

diabetes, diabète m.

diabetic, (adj.) diabétique

diabolic(al), diabolique

diadem, diadème m.

diaeresis, tréma m.

diagnose, v.t. diagnostiquer

diagnosis, diagnostic m.

diagonal, diagonale f.; (adj.) diagonal

diagram, diagramme m.; graphique m.

dial, cadran m.; sundial, cadran solaire

dialect, dialecte m.; patois m.

dialogue, dialogue m.

diameter, diamètre m.

diamond, diamant m.; carreau m. (cards)

diaphragm, diaphragme m.

diarrhœa, diarrhée f.

diary, journal m.; agenda m.

diatribe, diatribe f.

dice, dés m. pl.

dictate, précepte m.

dictate, v.t. dicter

dictate, v.i. commander à

dictation, dictée f.

dictator, dictateur m.

dictatorial, impérieux(-euse); dictatorial

dictionary, dictionnaire m.

die, dé m. (singular of dice)

die (for stamping), coin m.; étampe f.

die, v.i. mourir (with être); s'éteindre (of sound); crever (of animals)

diet, régime m. (food in sickness)

diet (parliamentary assembly), diète f.

diet, v.t. mettre au régime

differ, v.i. différer (de); n'être pas d'accord

difference, différence f.; dispute f.;

divergence *f.* (opinion); différend *m.* (discrepancy)
different, (*adj.*) différent, divers
differential, différentiel *m.* (of motor-car)
difficult, (*adj.*) difficile
difficulty, difficulté *f.*; peine *f.*
diffidence, modestie *f.*; timidité *f.*
diffident, (*adj.*) modeste; timide
diffuse, *v.t.* diffuser
dig, *v.t.* creuser, bêcher; **dig up,** déraciner
digest, *v.t.* digérer
digest, abrégé *m.*; sommaire *m.*
digestible, (*adj.*) digestible
digestion, digestion *f.*
digger, terrassier *m.*; bêcheur *m.*
digit, doigt *m.*; chiffre
dignified, (*adj.*) plein de dignité
dignity, dignité *f.*
digress, *v.i.* s'écarter de
digression, digression *f.*
dike, digue *f.*, levée *f.*
dilapidated, délabré
dilate, *v.i.* se dilater
dilatory, (*adj.*) négligent, tardif (-ive)
dilemma, dilemme *m.*
dilettante, amateur des beaux arts *m.*; dilettante *m.*
diligence, assiduité *f.*; diligence *f.*
diligent, (*adj.*) assidu, appliqué
dilute, *v.t.* diluer; couper (wine, etc.)
dim, (*adj.*) terne, pâle, faible
dim, *v.t.* obscurcir
dimension, dimension *f.*; proportion *f.*
diminish, *v.t.* diminuer, amoindrir; *v.i.* diminuer
diminution, diminution *f.*
diminutive, petit; (*gram.*) diminutif *m.*
dimness, obscurité *f.*; faiblesse *f.* (of sight)
dimple, fossette *f.*
din, vacarme *m.*; tapage *m.*
dine, *v.i.* dîner
dingy, (*adj.*)terne; crasseux(-euse)
dining-car, wagon-restaurant *m.*
dining-hall, réfectoire *m.*

dining-room, salle à manger *f.*
dinner, dîner *m.*
by dint of, à force de
diocese, diocèse *m.*
dip, *v.t.* plonger dans; mouiller; *v.i.* plonger
diphtheria, diphtérie *f.*
diploma, diplôme *m.*
diplomacy, diplomatie *f.*
diplomat(ist), diplomate *m.*
direct, (*adj.*) direct, droit
direct, *v.t.* diriger; ordonner; adresser (letters); gérer (manage a business)
direction, direction *f.*; instruction *f.*; sens *m.*
director, directeur *m.*; gérant *m.*
directory, livre (*m.*) d'adresses; annuaire *m.*
directress, directrice *f.*
dirigible, (*adj.*) dirigeable
dirt, saleté *f.*; boue *f.*; crasse *f.*
dirty, (*adj.*) sale; crasseux(-euse); immonde
dirty, *v.t.* salir, crotter; (*fig.*) souiller
disability, incapacité *f.*
disable, *v.t.* rendre incapable; désemparer (naval)
disabled, (*adj.*) hors d'état; estropié (*mil.*); désemparé (naval)
disabuse, *v.t.* détromper, désabuser
disadvantage, désavantage *m.*; inconvénient *m.*
disadvantageous, (*adj.*) désavantageux(-euse)
disaffect, *v.t.* aliéner
disaffected, (*adj.*) mal disposé pour; mécontent
disaffection, désaffection *f.*
disagree, *v.i.* ne pas s'accorder; se brouiller (quarrel)
disagreeable, (*adj.*) désagréable
disagreement, désaccord *m.*; mésentente *f.*
disappear, *v.i.* disparaître
disappearance, disparition *f.*
disappoint, *v.t.* désappointer, décevoir
disappointment, désappointement *m.*,; déception *f.*
disapproval, désapprobation *f.*

disapprove, *v.t.* and *v.i.* désapprouver

disarm, *v.t.* and *v.i.* désarmer

disarmament, désarmement *m.*

disaster, désastre *m.*; malheur *m.*; sinistre *m.* (especially of train accidents, etc.)

disastrous, *(adj.)* désastreux (-euse)

disavow, *v.t.* désavouer

disavowal, désaveu *m.*

disbelief, incrédulité *f.*

disbelieve, *v.t.* ne pas croire

disburse, *v.t.* débourser

disbursements, débours *m. pl.*

disc (disk), disque *m.*; **identity-disk,** plaque (*f.*) d'identité

discard, *v.t.* mettre de côté, écarter

discern, *v.t.* discerner, distinguer

discernible, perceptible

discerning, judicieux(-euse); pénétrant

discernment, pénétration *f.*

discharge, déchargement *m.*; décharge *f.* (of firearms); mise en liberté *f.* (from prison)

discharge, *v.t.* décharger; congédier (an employee)

discharge, *v.t.* acquitter (a debt or a prisoner on trial); remplir (duty)

disciple, disciple *m.* and *f.*

discipline, discipline *f.*

disclaim, *v.t.* désavouer; nier

disclose, *v.t.* révéler

disclosure, révélation *f.*

discoloration, décoloration *f.*

discolour, *v.t.* décolorer

discomfiture, déroute *f.*

discomfort, incommodité *f.*; malaise *m.*

discommode, *v.t.* incommoder, gêner

discompose, *v.t.* agiter, troubler

disconnect, *v.t.* désembrayer (machinery)

disconnected, *(adj.)* décousu; sans suite (of ideas or speech); débrayé (of machinery)

disconsolate, *(adj.)* inconsolable

discontent, mécontentement *m.*

discontented, *(adj.)* mécontent

discontinue, *v.t.* discontinuer; cesser

discord, discorde *f.*; dissonance *f.* (*mus.*)

discount, escompte *m.*; rabais *m.*

discount, *v.t.* escompter

discourage, *v.t.* décourager

discouragement, découragement *m.*

discouraging, *(adj.)* décourageant

discourse, discours *m.*

discourse, *v.i.* traiter (de), causer (de)

discover, *v.t.* découvrir, trouver

discovery, découverte *f.*

discredit, déshonneur *m.*; doute *m.*

discredit, *v.t.* discréditer

discreditable, *(adj.)* déshonorant, indigne

discreet, discret (discrète)

discretion, discrétion *f.*

discriminate, *v.t.* distinguer; *v.i.* faire des distinctions (entre)

discuss, *v.t.* discuter

discussion, discussion *f.*; **to start a discussion,** entamer une discussion

disdain, dédain *m.*

disdain, *v.t.* dédaigner

disdainful, dédaigneux(-euse)

disease, maladie *f.*

diseased, *(adj.)* malade; dérangé (mind)

disembark, *v.t.* and *v.i.* débarquer

disembarkment, débarquement *m.*

disengage, *v.t.* dégager; *v.i.* se dégager

disengaged, libre; pas occupé

disfigure, *v.t.* défigurer

disfigurement, enlaidissement *m.*; défaut *m.*

disgrace, disgrâce *f.*; honte *f.*; déshonneur *m.*

disgrace, *v.t.* disgracier, déshonorer

disgraceful, honteux(-euse)

disguise, déguisement *m.*

disguise, *v.t.* déguiser

disgust, dégoût *m.*

disgust, *v.t.* dégoûter

dish, plat *m.*; mets *m. pl.* (food); vaisselle *f.* (dishes, etc.)

dish up, *v.t.* servir

dishearten, *v.t.* décourager

dishonest, (*adj.*) malhonnête

dishonesty, improbité *f.*; malhonnêteté *f.*

dishonour, déshonneur *m.*

dishonour, *v.t.* déshonorer

disillusion, *v.t.* désillusionner

disinclination, aversion *f.*

disinfect, *v.t.* désinfecter

disinfectant, désinfectant *m.*

disinherit, *v.t.* déshériter

disinterested, (*adj.*) désintéressé

disk, disque *m.*

dislike, aversion *f.*; dégoût *m.*

dislike, *v.t.* ne pas aimer

dislodge, *v.t.* déplacer

disloyal, (*adj.*) infidèle, déloyal

dismal, (*adj.*) triste, lugubre

dismantle, *v.t.* démonter

dismay, effroi *m.*; épouvante *f.*

dismay, *v.t.* épouvanter

dismiss, *v.t.* congédier, renvoyer (servant); mettre à la porte; rejeter (an appeal)

dismissal, renvoi *m.*; congé *m.*; destitution *f.*

dismount, *v.i.* mettre pied à terre

dismount, *v.t.* démonter (a gun, etc.)

disobedience, désobéissance *f.*

disobedient, (*adj.*) désobéissant

disobey, *v.t.* désobéir

disoblige, *v.t.* désobliger

disobliging, (*adj.*) désobligeant

disorder, désordre *m.*; indisposition *f.*

disorderly, (*adj.*) en désordre, désordonné; turbulent

dispatch, *v.t.* expédier; dépêcher

dispensary, pharmacie *f.*

dispensation, dispensation *f.*

dispense, *v.t.* distribuer, dispenser

dispense (with), *v.i.* se passer (de)

dispersal, dispersion *f.*

disperse, *v.t.* disperser, disseminer

display, manifestation *f.*; étalage *m.* (window display)

display, *v.t.* montrer, exposer, étaler

displease, *v.t.* déplaire (à), mécontenter

displeasing, (*adj.*) déplaisant; désagréable

displeasure, mécontentement *m.*; courroux *m.*

displeased, (*adj.*) mécontent

disposable, (*adj.*) disponible

disposal, disposition *f.*, vente *f.*

dispose, *v.t.* and *v.i.* disposer; se défaire de (get rid of)

disposition, disposition *f.*; caractère *m.*

dispossess, *v.t.* déposséder

dispute, dispute *f.*; querelle *f.*

dispute, *v.t.* disputer, contester

disquiet, inquiétude *f.*

disregard, insouciance *f.*; indifférence *f.*

disregard, *v.t.* négliger

disreputable, (*adj.*) de mauvaise réputation; mal famé

dissatisfaction, mécontentement *m.*

dissatisfied (with), (*adj.*) mécontent (de)

dissatisfy, *v.t.* mécontenter

dissect, *v.t.* disséquer

dissemble, *v.i.* dissimuler

dissension, dissension *f.*

dissent, *v.i.* différer (de)

dissenter, dissident *m.*

dissimilar, (*adj.*) dissemblable

dissipate, *v.t.* dissiper

dissipated, (*adj.*) dissipé

dissipation, dissipation *f.*

dissolute, (*adj.*) dissolu

dissolve, *v.t.* dissoudre; *v.i.* se dissoudre

dissuade, *v.t.* dissuader

distaff, quenouille *f.*

distance, distance *f.*; éloignement *m.*; lointain *m.*; perspective *f.*; trajet *m.* (journey)

distant, (*adj.*) éloigné; lointain

distantly, de loin

distaste, aversion *f.*

distemper, maladie des chiens *f*; détrempe *f.* (of walls)

distemper, *v.t.* détremper

distil, *v.t.* distiller

distillery, distillerie f.
distinct, (adj.) distinct, net(te)
distinction, distinction f.
distinctive, distinctif(-ive)
distinguish, v.t. distinguer; v.i. faire une distinction
distinguished, (adj.) distingué
distort, v.t. tordre, contourner
distract, v.t. distraire; détourner (de); bouleverser (upset)
distracted, (adj.) bouleversé, fou (folle)
distraction, distraction f.; folie f.
distress, misère f. (poverty); détresse f.; affliction f.
distress, v.t. affliger, inquiéter
distribute, v.t. distribuer, répartir
distribution, distribution f.; répartition f.
district, contrée f.; région f.; arrondissement m. (of town); quarticr m. (of town)
distrust, méfiance f.; soupçon m.
distrust, v.i. se méfier de
disturb, v.t. déranger, troubler
disturbance, trouble m.; émeute f. (riot); tapage m.
disunion, désunion f.
disunite, v.i. se désunir; v.t. désunir
disuse, désuétude f.
disused, inusité
ditch, fossé m.
ditto, (adv.) idem; dito m. (invar.)
ditty, chanson f.
divan, divan m.
dive, v.i. plonger,. faire un plongeon; piquer (of plane)
diver, plongeur m.; scaphandrier m.
diverge, v.i. diverger
divers, (adj.) divers
diversion, divertissement m.; détournement m. (of traffic, etc.)
divert, v.t. détourner; divertir
divide, v.t. diviser; séparer; v.i. se partager, se séparer
divine, (adj.) divin
divine, ecclésiastique m.
divinity, divinité f.; théologie f.
divisible, (adj.) divisible

division, division f.; partage m.
divisor, diviseur m.
divorce, divorce m.; séparation f.
divorce, v.t. divorcer, séparer de
divulge, v.t. divulguer
dizziness, étourdissement m.; vertige m.
dizzy, (adj.) étourdi, vertigineux (-euse)
do, v.t. faire, finir (finish)
do again, refaire
do away with, supprimer, détruire (destroy)
do good, faire du bien
how do you do, comment allez-vous, comment vous portez-vous
that will do, cela suffit; assez!
to do without, se passer de
dock, bassin m.; banc des accusés (in court)
dry-dock, cale sèche f.
graving-dock, bassin de radoub m.
dockyard, chantier m.
doctor, docteur m.; médecin m.
doctor of law, docteur en droit m.
doctor of science, docteur ès sciences
doctor, v.t. soigner; frelater (wine, etc.)
doctorate, doctorat m.
document, document m.
dodge, tour m.; ruse f.; truc m.
dodge, v.i. se jeter de côté; (fig.) éviter
dodger, roublard m.
doe, daine f.
dog, chien m.; (coll.) coquin m. (rascal)
dog, v.t. suivre à la piste; harceler (harass)
dog-days, jours caniculaires m.pl.
dog-kennel, chenil m.
lead a dog's life, mener une vie de chien
watch-dog, chien de garde m.
dogged, (adj.) obstiné
doggedly, (adv.) résolument
doggerel, vers burlesques m. pl.
dogma, dogme m.
dole, aumône f.; secours m. (de chômage)

doleful, (*adj.*) triste, lugubre

doll, poupée *f.*

dollar, dollar *m.*

dolphin, dauphin *m.*

dome, dôme *m.*; coupole *f.*

domestic, (*adj.*) casanier (i.e. home-loving); domestique (of animals)

domestic, domestique *m.* (*f.*)

domesticated, (*adj.*) apprivoisé (animals)

domicile, domicile *m.*

domiciliary, (*adj.*) domiciliaire

to become domiciled, se domicilier

dominate, *v.t.* and *v.i.*, dominer

domination, domination *f.*

domineering, impérieux(-euse), autoritaire

dominion, autorité *f.*; dominion *m.* (e.g. Canada)

domino, domino *m.*

don, *v.t.* mettre

donation, donation *f.*; don *m.*

donkey, baudet *m.*; âne *m.*; ânesse *f.*; bourrique *m.*

donkey-engine, petit cheval *m.*

donor, donateur(-trice) *m.* (*f.*)

doom, jugement *m.*; sort *m.*

doom, *v.t.* condamner

doomsday, jour du jugement dernier

door, porte *f.*; portière *f.* (of car, etc.)

door-keeper, portier *m.*

door-mat, paillasson *m.*

doorway, portail *m.*

dormitory, dortoir *m.*

dormouse, loir *m.*

dose, dose *f.*

dose, *v.t.* doser; médicamenter

dot, point *m.*

dot, *v.t.* pointiller

dotage, radotage *m.*

dotard, radoteur *m.*

dote, *v.i.* raffoler, radoter

double, (*adj.*) double; en deux

double, *v.t.* doubler; plier en deux

double, (*adv.*) au double

double back, revenir sur ses pas

double-bedded, (chambre) à deux lits

double-dealing, duplicité *f.*

double-faced, (*adj.*) fourbe, hypocrite

doubt, doute *m.*; hésitation *f.*; appréhension *f.*

doubt, *v.i.* douter; craindre (fear)

beyond a doubt, sans aucun doute

beyond all doubt, indubitable

without doubt, sans doute

doubtful, (*adj.*) douteux(-euse)

doubtless, sans doute

dough, pâte *f.*

dove, colombe *f.*; pigeon *m.*

dove-coloured, couleur (*f.*) gorge-de-pigeon

dove-cot, colombier *m.*

dowager, douairière *f.*

down, duvet *m.*

downs, les dunes *f. pl.*

down, (*adv.*) en bas, à terre, en aval (stream); à bas

down, (*prep.*) en bas de

downcast, (*adj.*) abattu

downfall, chute *f.*

down-hearted, (*adj.*) découragé

down-hill, en pente

downpour, averse *f.*; pluie torrentielle *f.*

downright, (*adj.*) direct, véritable

downstairs, (*adv.*) en bas de l'escalier

downwards, (*adv.*) en bas, en descendant

downy, (*adj.*) duveteux(-euse); (*coll.*) rusé

dowry, dot *f.*

doze, somme *m.*

doze, *v.i.* s'assoupir, sommeiller

dozen, douzaine *f.*

drab, (*adj.*) gris brun

draft, brouillon *m.* (draft copy); dessin *m.* (sketch)

draft, *v.t.* rédiger; dessiner

drag, drague *f.*; sabot *m.* (on wheel, etc.)

drag, *v.t.* tirer, traîner

drag away, *v.t.* arracher, entraîner

drag-net, seine *f.*

dragon, dragon *m.*

dragoon, dragon *m.*

drain, tranchée *f.*; égout *m.*

drain, *v.t.* faire écouler; assécher

drainage, écoulement *m.*

drake, canard *m.*

dram, drachme *f.* (chemist); petit verre *m.* (of spirits)

drama, drame *m.*

dramatic, (*adj.*) dramatique

dramatist, auteur dramatique *m.*; dramaturge *m.*

draper, drapier *m.*; marchand (*m.*) d'étoffes

drapery, draperie *f.*

drastic, (*adj.*) énergique

draught, tirage *m.*; trait *m.*; dessin *m.* (sketch)

draught, courant d'air *m.*; coup *m.* (drink)

draughts, jeu (*m.*) de dames

draught-board, damier *m.*

draught-horse, cheval (*m.*) de trait

draughtsman, dessinateur *m.*

draw, *v.t.* tirer, dessiner (picture); toucher (salary); arracher (tooth); puiser (water)

draw back, *v.i.* se retirer

drawback, désavantage *m.*, inconvénient *m.*

draw-bridge, pont-levis *m.*

draw lots, tirer au sort

draw near, *v.i.* s'approcher

draw up, *v.t.* rédiger (contract, etc.); aligner (troops, etc.)

drawer (of a table, etc.), tiroir *m.*

chest of drawers, commode *f.*

drawers, caleçon *m.* (for men); pantalon (*m.*) de dames

drawing, dessin *m.*

drawing-pin, punaise *f.*

drawing-room, salon *m.*

drawl, *v.i.* traîner les paroles

drawl, voix (*f.*) traînante

dray, camion *m.*

drayman, camionneur *m.*

dread, terreur *f.*; crainte *f.*

dread, *v.t.* craindre, redouter

dreadful, (*adj.*) affreux(-euse); épouvantable

dreadfully, (*adv.*) affreusement, horriblement

dream, rêve *m.*; rêverie *f.*

dream, *v.t.* and *v.i.* rêver; (*fig.*) s'imaginer

dreamer, rêveur(-euse) *m.* (*f.*)

dreamland, pays (*m.*) des rêves

dreamy, (*adj.*) rêveur(-euse); songeur(-euse)

dreary, (*adj.*) morne, triste

dredge, drague *f.*

dredge, *v.t.* and *v.i.* draguer

dredger, drague *f.*

dregs, lie *f.*

drench, *v.t.* mouiller; tremper

dress, habillement *m.*; robe *f.* (woman's dress); costume *m.*; toilette *f.*; tenue *f.* (*mil.*)

dress, *v.t.* habiller, vêtir, panser (wound)

dress oneself, s'habiller; faire sa toilette

dress-coat, habit (*m.*) de soirée

dressmaker, couturière *f.*

dressmaking, confections pour dames *f. pl.*

dresser, dressoir *m.* (furniture); externe *m.* (hospital)

dressing, pansement *m.* (of wound)

dressing-case, nécessaire *m.*

dressing-gown, robe de chambre *f.*

dressing-room, cabinet (*m.*) de toilette

dressing-table, table (*f.*) de toilette

drift, monceau *m.* (snow); glace (*f.*) flottante (drift-ice); cours *m.* (of events)

drift, *v.i.* flotter; s'amasser (of snow); dériver (*naut.*)

drifter, chalutier *m.* (ship)

drill, semoir *m.* (*agric.*); manœuvre *f.* (*mil.*); foret (tool)

drill, *v.t.* faire l'exercice; forer

drill-ground, terrain (*m.*) de manœuvre

drink, boisson *f.*; ivresse *f.* (drunkenness)

drink, *v.t.* boire

drinkable, (*adj.*) potable

drinker, buveur *m.*; buveuse *f.*

drinking, la boisson *f.*

drinking-booth, buvette *f.*

drinking-fountain, fontaine (*f.*) publique

drinking-trough, abreuvoir *m*

drip, *v.i.* tomber goutte à goutte

dripping, graisse (*f.*) de rôti

drive, promenade (*f.*) en voiture; avenue *f.* (of house); battue *f.* (*sport*); transmission *f.* (*machine*)

drive, *v.t.* chasser (drive away); conduire (a car); pousser

drive, *v.i.* se diriger, aller à

drivel, bave *f.*; radotage *m.* (nonsense)

drivel, *v.i.* radoter, bavarder

driveller, radoteur(-euse) *m.* (*f.*)

driver, chauffeur (of car); voiturier *m.*; mécanicien (of engine); conducteur *m.* (of bus)

driving-belt, courroie *f.*

driving-shaft, arbre moteur *m.*

driving-wheel, roue motrice *f.*

drizzle, bruine *f.*

drizzle, *v.i.* bruiner

droll, (*adj.*) drôle

drollery, plaisanterie *f.*

dromedary, dromadaire *m.*

drone, bourdon *m.*; bourdonnement *m.* (sound)

drone, *v.i.* bourdonner

droop, *v.i.* languir; pencher

drooping, (*adj.*) languissant; penché

drop, goutte *f.*; chute *f.* (fall); pendant *m.* (for ear); pastille *f.* (sweet)

drop, *v.t.* laisser tomber; tomber par gouttes; abandonner (desist); lâcher (let go)

drop down, *v.i.* tomber par terre

drop in, *v.i.* entrer en passant

drop from fatigue, tomber de fatigue

dropsy, hydropisie *f.*

drought, sécheresse *f.*

drove, troupeau *m.*

drown, *v.t.* noyer; étouffer (noise); inonder; *v.i.* se noyer

drowsy, (*adj.*) somnolent

drudge, *v.i.* peiner

drudgery, travail pénible *m.*; corvée *f.*

drug, drogue *f.*

drug, *v.t.* donner un narcotique

drug-store, pharmacie *f.*

druggist, pharmacien *m.*

drum, tambour *m.*

drummer, tambour *m.*

drunkard, ivrogne *m.*

drunkenness, ivresse *f.*; ivrognerie *f.*

dry, *v.t.* sécher, faire sécher; *v.i.* sécher

dry, (*adj.*) sec (sèche); aride

dry-goods, mercerie *f.*

drying, (*adj.*) qui sèche, desséchant

dryness, sécheresse *f.*; aridité *f.*

dry up, *v.i.* se dessécher; (*coll.*) se taire

dual, (*adj.*) duel (*gram.*); double

dub, *v.t.* (*coll.*) qualifier

dubious, douteux(-euse); louche (i.e. shady)

dubiously, douteusement

dubiousness, douté *m.*; incertitude *f.*

ducal, (*adj.*) ducal

ducat, ducat *m.*

duchess, duchesse *f.*

duchy, duché *m.*

duck, canard *m.*; cane *f.*; coutil *m.* (material)

duckling, caneton *m.*

duct, conduit *m.*; canal *m.* (*anat.*)

ductile, (*adj.*) ductile

dudgeon, mauvaise humeur *f.*

due, (*adj.*) dû (*f.* due); juste, propre, convenable

duel, duel *m.*

fight a duel, se battre en duel

duellist, duelliste *m.*

duet, duo *m.*

duffer, imbécile *m.*

dug, trayon *m.* (of animals); pis *m.* (of cow)

dug-out, abri *m.*

duke, duc *m.*

dull, (*adj.*) stupide, lourd, ennuyeux (boring); sombre (weather); émoussé (blunt); terne (of colours)

dullard, lourdaud *m.*

dullness, stupidité *f.*; ennui *m.* (boredom)

duly, (*adv.*) dûment

dumb, (*adj.*) muet(te)

dumbfound, *v.t.* confondre

dumbness, mutisme *m.*

dump, dépôt *m.*

dump, *v.t.* déposer

dumping on market, inondation (f.) du marché par des produits étrangers
dumpling, boulette f.
dumpy, (adj.) trapu
dun, (adj.) brun foncé
dun, créancier importun m.
dun, v.t. importuner
dunce, ignorant(e) m. (f.)
dung, fumier m.
dungeon, cachot m.
dupe, dupe f.
dupe, v.t. duper, tromper
duplicate, (adj.) double
duplicate, double m.
duplicity, duplicité f.; mauvaise foi f.
durability, durabilité f.
durable, (adj.) durable
durance, captivité f.
duration, durée f.
duress, contrainte f.
during, (prep.) durant, pendant
dusk, brune f.; crépuscule m.; obscurité f.; nuit tombante f.
duskiness, teint (m.) sombre
dusky, (adj.) brunâtre, noirâtre
dust, poussière f.; balayures f. pl. (sweepings)
dust, v.t. épousseter
dust-bin, poubelle f.; boîte aux ordures f.
duster, torchon m.
dusty, (adj.) poussiéreux(-euse)
Dutch, (adj.) hollandais
dutiable, (adj.) taxable (articles for customs); déclarable
dutiful, obéissant, respectueux (-euse)
duty, devoir m.; droit m. (of customs); service (mil., etc.)
on duty, de service
dwarf, nain(e) m. (f.)
dwarfish, (adj.) nain
dwell, v.i. demeurer, habiter
dweller, habitant m.; habitante f.
dwelling, demeure f.; habitation f.
dwelling-place, résidence f.; domicile m.
dwindle, v.i. diminuer, s'amoindrir
dye, teinture f.

dye, v.t. teindre
dyeing, teinture f.
dyer, teinturier m.
dying, (adj.) mourant
dyke, digue f.
dynamic, dynamique
dynamics, dynamique f.
dynamite, dynamite f.
dynamo, dynamo f.
dynasty, dynastie f.
dysentery, dysenterie f.
dyspepsia, dyspepsie f.
dyspeptic, (adj.) dyspeptique
dyspnœa, dyspnée f.

E

each, (adj.) chaque
each, (pron.) chacun m.; chacune f.
each other, l'un l'autre, les uns les autres
eager, avide, empressé
eagerness, avidité f.; empressement m.
eagle, aigle m.
eaglet, aiglon m.
ear, oreille f.; épi m. (of corn)
ear-ache, mal (m.) à l'oreille
ear-drum, tympan m.
ear-mark, v.t. assigner
ear-ring, boucle (f.) d'oreille
ear-trumpet, cornet (m.) acoustique
ear-wax, cérumen m.
earl, comte m.
earldom, comté m.
early, (adj.) matinal; prématuré; (adv.) de bonne heure
earn, v.t. gagner; (fig.) mériter
earnest, (adj.) sérieux(-euse); sincère
earnest, gage m.
earnings, salaire m.; gages m. pl.
earth, terre f.; monde m.; terrier m. (of fox, etc.)
earth, v.t. terrer; relier à la terre (elect.)
earthen, (adj.) de terre
earthenware, poterie f.; faïence f.

earthly, (*adj.*) terrestre; mondain
earthquake, tremblement (*m.*) de terre
earth-work, terrassement *m.*; travaux (*m. pl.*) en terre
earthy, (*adj.*) terreux(-euse)
earwig, perce-oreille *m.*
ease, aise *f.*; aisance *f.*; facilité *f.*
ease, *v.t.* soulager
easel, chevalet *m.*
easiness, aisance *f.*; facilité *f.*
east, est *m.*; l'orient *m.*
Far East, l'extrême Orient
Easter, Pâques *m.*
eastern, (*adj.*) oriental
East Indies, Indes orientales *f. pl.*
easy, (*adj.*) facile; aisé; confortable; naturel(le) (style, etc.)
easy-going, peu exigeant
eat, *v.t.* manger; ronger (corrode)
eatable, (*adj.*) mangeable
eatables, comestibles *m. pl.*
eating-house, restaurant *m.*
eaves, avant-toit *m.*
eavesdrop, *v.i.* écouter aux portes
eavesdropper, écouteur (*m.*) aux portes
ebb, reflux *m.*; déclin *m.*
ebb, *v.i.* refluer; décliner
ebony, ébène *f.*
ebullition, ébullition *f.*
eccentric, (*adj.*) excentrique
eccentricity, excentricité *f.*
ecclesiastic, (*adj.*) ecclésiastique
ecclesiastic, ecclésiastique *m.*
echo, écho *m.*
echo, *v.t.* répéter en écho; (*fig.*) répéter
eclectic, (*adj.*) éclectique
eclipse, éclipse *f.*
eclipse, *v.t.* éclipser
economic(al), (*adj.*) économique
economics, économie *f.* (politique)
economy, économie *f.*
ecstasy, extase *f.*; ravissement *m.*
eddy, tourbillon *m.*
edge, tranchant *m.* (of knife); bord *m.* (rim); lisière *f.* (of wood)
edge, *v.t.* affiler, aiguiser, border (to border)

edging, bordure *f.*
edible, (*adj.*) mangeable
edict, édit *m.*
edifice, édifice *m.*
edify, *v.t.* édifier
edifying, (*adj.*) édifiant
edit, *v.t.* éditer, diriger;
edition, édition *f.*
editor, éditeur *m.* (of text); rédacteur (*m.*) en chef (of newspaper)
editorial, article (*m.*) de fond; (*adj.*) éditorial
educate, *v.t.* instruire
educated, (*adj.*) instruit, lettré
education, enseignement *m.*; éducation *f.*; instruction *f.*
educator, éducateur *m.*; éducatrice *f.*
eel, anguille *f.*
efface, *v.t.* effacer
effect, effet *m.*
effect, *v.t.* effectuer, accomplir
effective, (*adj.*) effectif(-ive)
effects, effets *m. pl.*; biens *m. pl.*
effectual, (*adj.*) efficace
effectuate, *v.t.* effectuer
effeminate, efféminé
effervescent, (*adj.*) effervescent
effete, (*adj.*) caduc (caduque)
efficacious, (*adj.*) efficace
efficacy, efficacité *f.*
efficiency, efficacité *f.*; capacité *f.*
efficient, (*adj.*) efficace, capable (of persons)
effigy, image *f.*
efflorescence, fleuraison *f.*; efflorescence *f.*
effluvium, exhalaison *f.*
effort, effort *m.*
effrontery, effronterie *f.*; impudence *f.*
effulgent, (*adj.*) resplendissant, éclatant
effusion, effusion *f.*; harangue *f.*
effusive, (*adj.*) expansif(-ive); extravagant
eft, salamandre *f.*
egg, œuf *m.*
egg-cup, coquetier *m.*
egg-plant, aubergine *f.*
egg-shaped, en forme d'œuf

egg-shell, coquille d'œuf *f.*
boiled egg, œuf à la coque *m.*
fried egg, œuf sur le plat
hard-boiled egg, œuf dur *m.*
poached egg, œuf poché
scrambled eggs, œufs brouillés
eglantine, églantier *m.*; églantine *f.*
egoism, égoïsme *m.*
egoist, égoïste *m.* (*f.*)
egotism, égotisme *m.*
egotist, égotiste *m.* and *f.*
egregious, fameux(-euse); fieffé
egress, sortie *f.*
Egyptian, (*adj.*) égyptien(ne)
eider, eider *m.*
eiderdown, édredon *m.*
eight, (*adj.*) huit
eighteen, (*adj.*) dix-huit
eighteenth, (*adj.*) dix-huitième
eightfold, (*adj.*) octuple
eighth, (*adj.*) huitième
eightieth, (*adj.*) quatre-vingtième
eighty, (*adj.*) quatre-vingts
either, (*pron.* and *adj.*) l'un ou l'autre; l'une ou l'autre; l'un d'eux; l'une d'elles; ni l'un ni l'autre (negatively); (*prep.* and *conj.*) ou ... ou ...; soit ... soit ...
ejaculate, *v.i.* s'écrier
ejaculation, exclamation *f.*
eject, *v.t.* rejeter; chasser
eke, *v.t.* augmenter; allonger (time)
elaborate, (*adj.*) élaboré; soigné
elaborate, *v.t.* élaborer
elapse, *v.i.* s'écouler
elastic, (*adj.*) élastique; *m.* élastique
elasticity, élasticité *f.*
elate, *v.t.* élever, exalter, transporter
elated, (*adj.*) exalté, gonflé
elbow, coude *m.*
elder, (*adj.*) aîné, plus âgé; ancien *m.* (*eccles.*)
elder (tree), sureau *m.*
elderly, (*adj.*) d'un certain âge
eldest, l'aîné(e), le (la) plus âgé(e)
elect, *v.t.* élire, nommer; choisir
elect, (*adj.*) élu
election, élection *f.*

elector, électeur(-trice) *m.* (*f.*); votant(e) *m.* (*f.*)
electoral, (*adj.*) électoral
electric, electrical, (*adj.*) électrique
electrician, électricien *m.*
electricity, électricité *f.*
electrify, *v.t.* électriser
electron, électron *m.*
elegance, élégance *f.*
elegant, élégant, chic
elegy, élégie *f.*
element, élément *m.*
elementary, (*adj.*) élémentaire; (of school) primaire
elephant, éléphant *m.*
elevate, *v.t.* élever, exalter
elevation, élévation *f.*
elevator (lift), ascenseur *m.*
eleven, onze
elf, lutin *m.*; fée *f.*
eligible, (*adj.*) éligible
elk, élan *m.*
ell, aune *f.*
elm, orme *m.*
elope, *v.i.* se faire enlever (par)
elopement, enlèvement *m.*
eloquence, éloquence *f.*
eloquent, (*adj.*) éloquent
else, (*adv.*) autrement; ou bien
elsewhere, (*adv.*) ailleurs
elude, *v.t.* esquiver; éviter
emaciate, *v.i.* amaigrir
emaciation, amaigrissement *m.*
emanate, *v.i.* émaner
emancipate, *v.t.* émanciper, affranchir
embalm, *v.t.* embaumer
embalming, embaumement *m.*
embank, *v.t.* endiguer; remblayer
embankment, quai *m.* (by river, etc.); talus
embark, *v.i.* s'embarquer
embarkation, embarquement *m.*
embarrass, *v.t.* embarrasser; gêner
embarrassment, embarras *m.*; gêne *f.*
embassy, ambassade *f.*
embedded, (*adj.*) enfoncé
embellish, *v.t.* embellir
embellishment, embellissement *m.*

embers, braise *f.*

Ember days, les Quatre-Temps *f.*

embezzle, *v.t.* détourner; s'approprier

embezzlement, détournement (*m.*) de fonds

embitter, *v.t.* rendre amer; (*fig.*) aigrir

emblem, emblème *m.*

emblematic(al), emblématique

embody, *v.t.* incorporer (dans); réunir

embrace, embrassement *m.*

embrace, *v.t.* embrasser

embroider, *v.t.* broder

embroidery, broderie *f.*

embroil, *v.t.* brouiller

emerald, émeraude *f.*

emerge, *v.i.* surgir; sortir

emergency, circonstance imprévue *f.*; crise *f.*

in an emergency, en cas d'urgence

emery, émeri *m.*

emetic, émétique *m.*

emigrant, émigrant(e) *m.* (*f.*)

emigrate, *v.i.* émigrer

emigration, émigration *f.*

eminence, éminence *f.*; monticule *m.* (small hill)

eminent, (*adj.*) éminent

emission, émission *f.*

emit, *v.t.* émettre (*finan.*); exhaler, dégager

emolument, émoluments *m. pl.*; traitement *m.*

emotion, émotion *f.*

emperor, empereur *m.*

emphasise, *v.t.* souligner; appuyer sur

emphatic, énergique

empire, empire *m.*

employ, *v.t.* employer

employee, employé(e) *m.* (*f.*)

employer, maître *m.*; maîtresse *f.*; patron *m.*; patronne *f.*; employeur *m.*

employment, emploi *m.*; situation *f.*

emporium, entrepôt *m.*

empower, *v.t.* autoriser; donner plein pouvoir à

empress, impératrice *f.*

empty, (*adj.*) vide; désert (streets, etc.)

empty, *v.t.* vider, décharger

emulate, *v.t.* rivaliser avec; imiter

enable, *v.t.* mettre en état (de)

enact, *v.t.* ordonner, arrêter, jouer (a play)

enactment, ordonnance *f.*; acte législatif *m.*

enamel, émail *m.* (*pl.* émaux)

enamel, *v.t.* émailler

enamoured, (*adj.*) amoureux (-euse); épris

encamp, *v.t.* and *v.i.* camper

encase, *v.t.* encaisser

enchant, *v.t.* enchanter, charmer

enchanter(-tress), enchanteur (-eresse) *m.* (*f.*)

enclose, *v.t.* renfermer; entourer; contenir

enclosed, (*adj.*) entouré; sous ce pli (letter, etc.); ci-inclus

enclosure, pièce (*f.*) annexée (in letter, etc.); enclos *m.*; enceinte *f.* (space enclosed)

encore! (*interj.*) bis!

encounter, rencontre *f.*

encounter, *v.t.* rencontrer; (*fig.*) éprouver

encourage, *v.t.* encourager

encouragement, encouragement *m.*

encroach, *v.i.* empiéter (sur)

encumber, *v.t.* embarrasser; encombrer

encumbrance, embarras *m.*; charge *f.*

encyclopædia, encyclopédie *f.*

end, fin *f.*; bout *m.*; extrémité; but *m.* (object in view); **in the end,** à la fin

end, *v.t.* finir, terminer, achever

endanger, *v.t.* mettre en danger

endear, *v.t.* rendre cher à

endeavour, effort *m.*; tentative *f.*

endeavour, *v.i.* tâcher (de); essayer (de); s'efforcer (de)

endless, (*adj.*) infini, sans fin

endorse, *v.t.* endosser; viser (passport)

endorsement, endossement *m.*; endos *m.*; visa *m.*

endow, *v.t.* doter (de), douer

endowment, dotation *f.*; don *m.*

endurable, (*adj.*) supportable

endure, *v.t.* supporter, souffrir; durer (to last)

enemy, ennemi *m.*; ennemie *f.*

energetic, énergique

energy, énergie *f.*

enervate, *v.t.* énerver

enervation, énervement *m.*

enfeeble, *v.t.* affaiblir

enforce, *v.t.* donner de la force à; faire respecter; faire exécuter

enfranchise, *v.t.* admettre au suffrage

enfranchisement, admission (*f.*) au suffrage

engage, *v.t.* engager, retenir (a place, seat); louer (to hire); occuper (attention)

engage, *v.i.* s'engager

engaged, (*adj.*) fiancé; occupé (busy)

engagement, engagement *m.*; occupation *f.*; fiançailles *f. pl.*

engender, *v.t.* faire naître, engendrer

engine, machine *f.*; moteur *m.*; locomotive *f.* (railway)

engine-driver, mécanicien *m.*

engine-shed, dépôt (*m.*) des machines

engine trouble, panne (*f.*) de moteur

twin-engined, bimoteur; à deux machines

engineer, ingénieur *m.*

engineer, (*mil.*) soldat (*m.*) du génie

civil engineer, ingénieur civil *m.*

engineers, génie *m.*

English, (*adj.*) anglais

engrave, *v.t.* graver

engraver, graveur *m.*

engraving, gravure *f.*

engross, *v.t.* absorber, occuper; écrire en grosse

enigma, énigme *f.*

enigmatic(al), (*adj.*) énigmatique

enjoin, *v.t.* prescrire (à)

enjoy, *v.t.* jouir de; posséder (possess); trouver bon; aimer

enjoyable, (*adj.*) agréable

enjoyment, jouissance (de) *f.*; plaisir *m.*

enlarge, *v.t.* élargir, augmenter, agrandir

enlargement, agrandissement (*phot.*, etc.) *m.*; augmentation *f.*

enlighten, *v.t.* éclairer, illuminer

enlist, *v.t.* engager; *v.i.* s'engager

enliven, *v.t.* animer, égayer

enmity, inimitié *f.*; animosité *f.*

ennoble, *v.t.* ennoblir

enormity, énormité *f.*

enormous, (*adj.*) énorme

enormously, (*adv.*) énormément

enough, (*adj.* and *adv.*) assez

to be enough, suffire

enquire, *v.i.* s'informer

enrage, *v.t.* exaspérer, irriter

enrapture, *v.t.* ravir, transporter

enrich, *v.t.* enrichir

ensign, enseigne *f.*; drapeau *m.*; pavillon *m.* (*naval*)

ensign (bearer), porte-drapeau *m.*

enslave, *v.t.* asservir

ensue, *v.i.* s'ensuivre

entail, *v.t.* imposer; substituer à; entraîner

entail (estate), bien (*m.*) substitué

entangle, *v.t.* emmêler, embrouiller

enter, *v.t.* entrer (dans); pénétrer; inscrire (names, etc.); enregistrer (parcels); porter (bookkeeping)

enterprise, entreprise *f.*

enterprising, (*adj.*) entreprenant

entertain, *v.t.* divertir, amuser; recevoir (guests); concevoir (an idea)

entertaining, (*adj.*) divertissant, amusant

entertainment, amusement *m.*; hospitalité *f.*; divertissement *m.*

enthusiasm, enthousiasme *m.*

enthusiast, enthousiaste *m.* and *f.*

enthusiastic, (*adj.*) enthousiaste

entice, *v.t.* attirer; entraîner; allécher

entire, (*adj.*) entier(-ère)

entitle, *v.t.* intituler; donner droit (à) (give the right to)

entrails, entrailles *f. pl.*

entrance, entrée *f.*; début *m.* (beginning)

entrance fee, prix (*m.*) d'entrée
entreat, *v.t.* supplier
entreaty, supplication *f.*
entrust, *v.t.* charger (de); confier (à)
enumerate, *v.t.* énumérer
enumeration, énumération *f.*
envelop, *v.t.* envelopper (de *or* dans)
envelope, enveloppe *f.*
enviable, (*adj.*) digne d'envie, enviable
envious, (*adj.*) envieux(-euse)
to be envious, porter envie à
environment, environnement *m.*
envy, envie *f.*
envy, *v.t.* envier
ephemeral, (*adj.*) éphémère
epic, (*cdj.*) épique; poème épique *m.*; épopée *f.*
epicure, gourmet *m.*
epidemic, (*adj.*) épidemique
epidemic, épidémie *f.*
epigram, épigramme *f.*
epigrammatic, (*adj.*) épigram· matique
epilepsy, épilepsie *f.*
episcopal, (*adj.*) épiscopal
episode, épisode *m.*
epistle, épître *f.*
epitaph, épitaphe *f.*
epoch, époque *f.*
Epsom salts, sulfate (*m.*) de magnésie
equal, (*adj.*) égal (*pl.* égaux)
equalisation, égalisation *f.*
equality, égalité *f.*
equanimity, égalité (*f.*) d'âme
equation, équation *f.*
equator, équateur *m.*
equilibrium, équilibre *m.*
equinox, équinoxe *m.*
equip, *v.t.* équiper; ·outiller (a factory)
equity, équité *f.*; justice *f.*
equivalent, équivalent *m.*
equivocal, (*adj.*) équivoque
era, ère *f.*
erase, *v.t.* raturer, effacer
erasure, rature *f.*
ere, (*prep.*) avant
erect, *v.t.* ériger, dresser, établir
erect, (*adj.*) debout, droit

erection, érection *f.*; construction *f.*
ermine, hermine *f.*
err, *v.i.* errer, se tromper
errand, course *f.*; commission *f.*
errand boy, petit commissionaire *m.*
erratic, (*adj.*) erratique; excentrique
erratum, faute (*f.*) d'impression; erratum *m.*
erroneous, (*adj.*) faux (fausse)
error, erreur *f.*
eruption, éruption *f.*
escape, évasion *f.*; échappement *m.*; fuite *f.*
escape, *v.t.* échapper à, éviter
escape, *v.i.* s'échapper, s'évader
escort, escorte *f.*
escort, *v.t.* escorter
escutcheon, écusson *m.*
especial, (*adv.*) spécial, particulier(-ère)
espouse, *v.t.*·épouser
esquire, écuyer *m.* (There is *no* equivalent to *Esq.* in French as used now)
essay, essai *m.*; composition *f.*
essayist, essayiste *m.*
essence, essence *f.*; fond *m.*
essential, (*adj.*) essentiel(le)
establish, *v.t.* établir; fonder; constituer
established, (*adj.*) établi, fondé (founded)
establishment, établissement *m.*; institution *f.*
estate, état *m.*; rang *m.* (condition of person); propriété *f.*; domaine *m.*; fortune *f.*
estate agent, agent (*m.*) de location
personal estate, biens (*m. pl.*) mobiliers
real estate, biens (*m. pl.*) immobiliers
esteem, estime *f.*; considération *f.*
esteem, *v.t.* estimer
estimable, (*adj.*) estimable
estimate, évaluation *f.*; calcul *m.*
estimate, *v.t.* évaluer, calculer, apprécier

estimation, estimation *f.* ; opinion *f.*
estrange, *v.t.* éloigner, aliéner
estrangement, éloignement *m.*; aliénation *f.*
etch, *v.t.* graver à l'eau forte
etching, gravure (*f.*) à l'eau forte
eternal, (*adj.*) éternel(le)
èternity, éternité *f.*
ether, éther *m.*
ethereäl, (*adj.*) éthéré
eulogy, éloge *m.*
European, (*adj.*) européen(ne)
evacuate, *v.t.* évacuer
evacuation, évacuation *f.*
evade, *v.t.* éviter
evaporate, *v.i.* s'évaporer
evaporation, évaporation *f.*
evasion, détour *m.*
evasive, (*adj.*) évasif(-ive)
eve, veille *f.*
even, (*adj.*) égal (*pl.* égaux); uni (smooth); pair (number); (*prep.*) au niveau de (even with); à fleur de (level with)
even, (*adv.*) même; aussi bien
even, *v.t.* rendre égal. égaliser
even if, quand même
even as, comme
even now, à l'instant même
evening, soir *m.*; soirée *f.*
evening dress, toilette (tenue) (*f.*) de soirée
event, événement *m.*
eventful, plein d'événements; mouvementé
eventual, (*adj.*) éventuel(le)
eventually, (*adv.*) en fin de compte
ever, (*adv.*) toujours; jamais
ever since, depuis
evergreen, (*adj.*) toujours vert
everlasting, (*adj.*) éternel(le); perpétuel(le)
evermore, (*adv.*) toujours; éternellement
every, (*adj.*) chaque, tout, tous les
everybody, tout le monde *m.*
everything, tout *m*
everywhere, (*adv.*) partout
evidence, évidence *f.*, témoignage *m.*

evideut, évident
evidently, évidemment
evil, (*adj.*) mauvais; méchant; malin (maligne)
evil, mal *m.*; malheur *m.*; calamité *f.*
evil-doer, malfaiteur(-trice) *m.* (*f.*)
ewe, brebis *f.*
exact, (*adj.*) exact, précis
exact, *v.t.* exiger
exacting, (*adj.*) exigeant
exactness, exactitude *f.*
exaggerate, *v.t.* exagérer
exaggeration, exagération *f.*
exalt, *v.t.* exalter, élever; (*fig.*) louer (praise)
examination, examen *m.*; inspection *f.*
examine, *v.t.* examiner; interroger
examiner, examinateur *m.*
example, exemple *m.*
for example, par exemple
exasperate, *v.t.* exaspérer
excavate, *v.t.* creuser
excavation, fouilles *f. pl.*
exceed, *v.t.* dépasser
exceedingly, (*adv.*) fort, très; extrêmement
excel, *v.t.* surpasser; *v.i.* exceller (à)
excellence, perfection *f.*; excellence *f.*
excellency (title), excellence *f.*
excellent, (*adj.*) excellent
except, *v.t.* excépter, exclure
except, (*prep.*) excepté, sauf; à l'exception de
exception, exception *f.*; objection *f.*
exceptional, (*adj.*) exceptionnel(le)
take exception to, s'offenser de; s'opposer à
excerpt, extrait *m.*
excess, excès *m.*
excessive, (*adj.*) excessif(-ive)
exchange, échange *m.*; change *m.* (*commer.*); bourse *f.* (stock, corn, building)
exchange, *v.t.* échanger, changer (pour)

bill of exchange, lettre (*f.*) de change

exchange office, bureau (*m.*) de change

exchequer, trésor (*m.*) public

Chancellor of the Exchequer, Ministre (*m.*) des Finances

excise, contributions indirectes *f. pl.*

excise office, régie *f.*

excitability, excitabilité *f.*

excitable, (*adj.*) excitable, irritable

excite, *v.t.* exciter, irriter

excitedly, (*adv.*) d'une manière agitée

excitement, émotion *f.*; agitation *f.*; excitation *f.*

exciting, émouvant, passionnant; excitant (especially sexually)

exclaim, *v.i.* s'écrier, s'exclamer

exclamation, exclamation *f.*; cri *m.*

exclude, *v.t.* exclure

excluding, (*prep.*) sans compter; à l'exclusion de

exclusive, exclusif(-ive)

excrescence, excroissance *f.*

excursion, excursion *f.*; promenade *f.*

excursion ticket, billet (*m.*) d'excursion

excursionist, touriste *m.* and *f.*

excuse, excuse *f.*

excuse, *v.t.* excuser; pardonner; dispenser de

execrable, (*adj.*) exécrable

execrate, *v.t.* exécrer

execute, *v.t.* exécuter; accomplir

execution, exécution *f.*; accomplissement *m.*; saisie *f.* (*legal*)

executioner, bourreau *m.*

executive, pouvoir (*m.*) exécutif

executive, (*adj.*) exécutif(-ive)

executor, exécuteur (*m.*) testamentaire

executrix, exécutrice (*f.*) testamentaire

exemplary, (*adj.*) exemplaire

exempt, *v.t.* exempter (de)

exempt, (*adj.*) exempt

exemption, exemption *f.*

exercise, exercice *m.*; thème *m.*; devoir *m.* (lesson)

exercise, *v.t.* exercer; faire l'exercice

exercise-book, cahier *m.*

exert, *v.t.* exercer, employer

exert oneself, *v.i.* faire des efforts; s'efforcer de

exertion, effort *m.*

exhalation, exhalaison *f.*

exhale, *v.t.* exhaler, émettre

exhaust, *v.t.* épuiser

exhaust, échappement *m.*

exhaust pipe, tuyau d'échappement *m.*

exhaustion, épuisement *m.*

exhaustive, à fond; approfondi

exhaustless, (*adj.*) inépuisable

exhibit, *v.t.* exhiber; montrer; faire voir

exhibition, exposition *f.*; bourse *f.* (at college)

exhibitor, exposant *m.*

exhilarate, *v.t.* réjouir, égayer

exhilarating, divertissant, réjouissant

exhilaration, réjouissance *f.*; joie (*f.*) de vivre

exhort, *v.t.* exhorter (à)

exhumation, exhumation *f.*

exhume, *v.t.* exhumer; déterrer

exigence, exigence *f.*; nécessité *f.*

exigency, besoin *m.*

exigent, (*adj.*) exigeant

exile, exil *m.*; exilé(e) *m.* (*f.*)

exile, *v.t.* exiler, bannir

exist, *v.i.* exister, régner (conditions, etc.)

existence, existence *f.*

exit, sortie *f.*

exonerate, *v.t.* décharger, exonérer

exoneration, décharge *f.*; exonération *f.*

exorbitant, (*adj.*) excessif(-ive)

exotic, (*adj.*) exotique

expand, *v.t.* étendre; dilater; *v.i.* se dilater

expanse, étendue *f.*

expansion, expansion *f.*; dilatation *f.*

expansive, expansif(-ive)

ex parte, d'une seule partie

expatiate, *v.i.* s'étendre sur

expatriate, *v.t.* expatrier
expatriation, expatriation *f.*
expect, *v.t.* attendre, s'attendre à, compter sur; espérer; croire
expectancy, attente *f.*; espérance *f.*
expectation, attente *f.*; espérance *f.*
expectorate, *v.t.* cracher
expediency, convenance *f.*; utilité *f.*
expedient, (*adj.*) convenable, expédient; expédient *m.*
expedite, *v.t.* expédier, accélérer
expedition, expédition *f.*; promptitude *f.*
expeditious, (*adj.*) prompt
expel, *v.t.* expulser, chasser, faire sortir
expend, *v.t.* dépenser
expenditure, dépense *f.*; dépenses *f. pl.*
expense, dépense *f.*; dépens *m.*; frais *m. pl.*
expensive, coûteux(-euse), cher (-ère)
expensiveness, prix (*m.*) élevé
experience, expérience *f.*; pratique *f.*
experience, *v.t.* éprouver
experienced, (*adj.*) expérimenté
experiment, expérience *f.*
expert, (*adj.*) expert, habile
expert, expert *m.*
expertness, habileté *f.*
expiate, *v.t.* expier
expiation, expiation *f.*
expiatory, (*adj.*) expiatoire
expiration, expiration *f.*; fin *f.*
expire, *v.i.* expirer, mourir
explain, *v.t.* expliquer
explainable, (*adj.*) explicable
explanation, explication *f.*; éclaircissement *m.*
explanatory, explicatif(-ive)
expletive, explétif *m.*
explicit, (*adj.*) explicite, formel(le)
explicitly, explicitement, formellement
explode, *v.t.* faire éclater, faire sauter (a mine); discréditer (a theory); *v.i.* éclater, faire explosion

exploit, exploit *m.*
exploit, *v.t.* exploiter
exploitation, exploitation *f.*
exploration, exploration *f.*; (*fig.*) recherche *f.*
explore, *v.t.* explorer
explorer, explorateur *m.*
explosion, explosion *f.*
explosive, (*adj.*) explosif(-ive), explosible; explosif *m.*
export, exportation *f.*
export, *v.t.* exporter
exporter, exportateur *m.*
expose, *v.t.* exposer; (*fig.*) découvrir, démasquer; étaler (goods)
exposition, exposition *f.*
expostulate, *v.i.* faire des remontrances (à)
expostulation, remontrance *f.*
exposure, exposition *f.*; pose *f.* (*photo.*); dévoilement *m.* (crime)
expound, *v.t.* expliquer, exposer
express, (*adj.*) exprès, formel(le)
express, express *m.*; train (*m.*) express; rapide *m.* (railway)
express, *v.t.* exprimer
expressible, (*adj.*) exprimable
expression, expression *f.*
expressive, (*adj.*) expressif(-ive)
expropriate, *v.t.* exproprier
expulsion, expulsion *f.*
expunge, *v.t.* effacer
exquisite, (*adj.*) exquis
exquisite, élégant *m.*
extant, (*adj.*) actuel(le), existant
extemporary, (*adj.*) improvisé
extemporise, *v.t.* and *v.i.* improviser
extend, *v.t.* étendre, prolonger; *v.i.* s'étendre; se prolonger
extension, étendue *f.*; prolongation *f.*
extensive, (*adj.*) vaste, ample, spacieux (-euse)
extent, étendue *f.*; point *m.*
extenuate, *v.t.* exténuer
extenuating, (*adj.*) atténuant (circumstances)
exterior, (*adj.*) extérieur, en dehors
exterior, extérieur *m.*
exterminate, *v.t.* exterminer

external, (adj.) extérieur

externals, dehors m. pl.

extinct, (adj.) éteint, disparu

extinguish, v.t. éteindre

extinguisher, éteignoir m.; extincteur m.

extirpate, v.t. extirper

extol, v.t. exalter, louer

extort, v.t. extorquer, arracher

extortion, extorsion f.

extra, (adj.) en sus; supplémentaire

extra charge, supplément m. (de prix)

extract, extrait m.

extract, v.t. extraire, tirer de, arracher (tooth)

extraction, extraction f.

extradite, v.t. extrader

extradition, extradition f.

extraordinary, (adj.) extraordinaire, remarquable

extravagance, extravagance f.; prodigalité f.

extravagant, (adj.) extravagant, dépensier(-ère)

extreme, (adj.) extrême

extremity, extrémité f.

extricate, v.t. débarrasser; dégager

exuberance, exubérance f.

exuberant, exubérant.

exude, v.i. exsuder

exult, v.i. se réjouir, exulter.

eye, œil m. (pl. yeux); trou (m.) d'aiguille (of needle)

eye, v.t. regarder, observer

eyeball, prunelle f.

eyebrow, sourcil m.

eyeglass, lorgnoh m.; monocle m.

eyelash, cil m.

eyelet-hole, œillet m.

eyelid, paupière f.

eyesight, vue f.

eyewash, (fam.) boniment m.

eyewitness, témoin oculaire m.

eyrie, aire f.

F

fable, fable f.; apologue m.

fabric, construction f.; édifice m.; ouvrage m.; étoffe f.; tissu m.

fabricate, v.t. fabriquer

fabrication, fabrication f.; invention f.

fabulous, (adj.) fabuleux(-euse)

face, figure f.; visage m.; face f. (of things); (fig.) apparence f.; mine f.; physionomie f.; façade f. (front)

face, v.t. faire face à

facer, coup (m.) de poing au visage; obstacle m.

facetious, (adj.) facétieux(-euse)

facilitate, v.t. faciliter

facility, facilité f.

facing, revers m. (of coat, etc.); revêtement m. (of building)

fact, fait m.

in fact, en effet

faction, faction f.; cabale f.

factor, agent m.; facteur m.

factory, usine f.; fabrique f.

faculty, faculté f.

fad, caprice m.; marotte f.

faddy, capricieux(-euse)

fade, v.i. se faner, se déteindre

fag, v.i. piocher (à); travailler dur

fagged out, (adj.) éreinté

faggot, fagot m.

fail, v.i. faillir; · manquer à; échouer (not to succeed in exam., etc.)

failing, défaut m.; faute f.; faillite f. (commer.)

failing, (adj.) défaillant

failure, manque m.; défaut m.; affaiblissement m. (of health, etc.); faillite f. (bankruptcy); insuccès m.

fain, (adv.) volontiers

faint, v.i. s'évanouir

faint(ing), évanouissement m.

faint, (adj.) faible

faint-hearted, (adj.) découragé, timide

faint-heartedness, pusillanimité f.

faintness, faiblesse f.

fair, (adj.) beau (belle); blond (of persons); clair; favorable (wind, etc.); juste (just); permis (allowed); (fig.) assez bon

fair, foire f.

fair-dealing, bonne foi f.

fair-haired, aux cheveux blonds; blond

fairly, (*adv.*) franchement, loyalement

fairness, couleur blonde (of hair); (*fig.*) beauté *f.*; probité *f.* (in deals, etc.)

fairy, fée *f.*

fairy (*adj.*) féerique

faith, foi *f.*; croyance *f.*; fidélité *f.*

faithful, (*adj.*) fidèle

faithfulness, fidélité *f.*; loyauté *f*

faithless, infidèle; perfide

falcon, faucon *m.*

fall, chute *f.*; baisse *f.* (in price); tombée *f.* (of night); éboulement *m.* (of earth); diminution *f.*

fall (water), cascade *f.*

fall, *v.i.* tomber, s'abaisser, descendre, diminuer

fall asleep, *v.i.* s'endormir

fall back, *v.i.* se replier

fall down, *v.i.* tomber par terre

fall due, *v.i.* échoir

fall in, s'écrouler; (*mil.*) former les rangs

fall off, *v.i.* diminuer

fall out, *v.i.* se brouiller (avec); (*mil.*) rompre les rangs

fallacy, fausseté *f.*; illusion *f.*

fallibility, faillibilité *f.*

falling, chute *f.*

falling away, décadence *f.*; défection *f.*

fallow, (*adj.*) en jachère

false, (*adj.*) faux (fausse); perfide, déloyal

falsehood, mensonge *m.*

falsification, falsification *f.*

falsify, *v.t.* falsifier

falter, hésiter, bégayer (in one's speech)

faltering, hésitation *f.*

falteringly, avec hésitation, en tremblant

fame, renom *m.*; renommée *f.*; gloire *f.*

famed, (*adj.*) renommé

familiar, (*adj.*) familier(-ère), intime

familiarise, *v.t.* familiariser

familiarity, familiarité *f.*

family, famille *f.*

family, (*adj.*) de famille

in the family way, enceinte

famine, famine *f.*; disette *f.*

famish, *v.t.* affamer, faire mourir de faim

famish, *v.i.* être affamé

famished, (*adj.*) affamé

famous, fameux(-euse), célèbre

fan, éventail *m.* (*pl.* -s)

fan, *v.t.* éventer

fanatic(al), (*adj.*) fanatique; *m.* fanatique

fanaticism, fanatisme *m*

fancied, (*adj.*) imaginé, supposé

fancier, amateur *m.*

fanciful, fantasque, capricieux (-euse)

fancy, fantaisie *f.*; imagination *f.*; idée *f.*; goût *m.* (fancy for); caprice *m.*

fancy, *v.i.* s'imaginer; se figurer; *v.t.* aimer (like)

fancy dress, travesti *m.*

fancy goods, nouveautés *f. pl.*; objets (*m. pl.*) de fantaisie

fancy work, broderie *f.*

fang, croc *m.* (of dog, etc.); défense *f.* (of boar)

fantastic(al), (*adj.*) fantastique

fantasy, fantaisie *f.*; imagination *f.*

far, (*adj.*) lointain, éloigné

far, (*adv.*) loin, au loin; beaucoup (sense of " much ")

by far, de beaucoup

how far is it? combien y a-t-il? *or* quelle distance y a-t-il?

far-famed, (*adj.*) célèbre

far-fetched, (*adj.*) forcé, outré

far-seeing, (*adj.*) clairvoyant

farce, farce *f.*

farcical, (*adj.*) drôle, burlesque

fare, prix de la course *m.*; chère *f.*; nourriture *f.*; prix du passage *m.*

fare, *v.i.* se porter, se trouver

farewell, adieu *m.*

farinaceous, farineux(-euse), farinacé

farm, ferme *f.*; métairie *f.*

farm, *v.t.* cultiver

farmer, fermier *m.*; cultivateur *m.*

farming, agriculture *f.*
farm-yard, basse-cour *f.*
farther, (*adj.*) plus loin
farthest, (*adj.*) le plus éloigné
farthing, liard *m.*
fascinate, *v.t.* fasciner
fascinating, (*adj.*) enchanteur (-eresse)
fascination, fascination *f.*; séduction *f.*; charme *m.*
fashion, façon *f.*; manière *f.*; la mode *f.*
fashion, *v.t.* façonner
fashionable, (*adj.*) à la mode
fashionably, élégamment
fast, jeûne *m.*
fast, *v.i.* jeûner; faire maigre
fast, (*adj.*) ferme (firm); solide; rapide (quick); dissipé (rakish)
fast, (*adv.*) fidèle (staunch); vite, rapidement (quickly); profondément (asleep)
fasten, *v.t.* attacher; fixer; fermer (shut)
fastening, attache *f.*
fat, (*adj.*) gras (grasse)
fat, graisse *f.*
fatal, (*adj.*) fatal, funeste
fatality, fatalité *f.*
fate, destin *m.*; sort *m.*
fateful, (*adj.*) fatal
father, père *m.*; **godfather,** parrain *m.*; **grandfather,** grand-père *m.*
father-in-law, beau-père *m.*
fatherhood, paternité *f.*
fatherland, pays natal *m.*; patrie *f.*
fatherless, (*adj.*) orphelin; sans père
fathom, brasse *f.* (*naut.*)
fathom, *v.t.* sonder
fatigue, fatigue *f.*; (*mil.*) corvée *f.*
fatigue, *v.t.* fatiguer, lasser
fatiguing, (*adj.*) fatigant *or* fatiguant (*pres. part.*)
fatten, *v.t.* engraisser; (*fig.*) enrichir
fatten, *v.i.* engraisser
fault, faute *f.*; défaut *m.*; vice *m.*
faultless, (*adj.*) sans défaut, parfait, irréprochable
faulty, défectueux(-euse)

favour, faveur *f.*; grâce *f.*; bonnes grâces *f. pl.* (in somebody's favour); service *m.* (good turn)
favour, *v.t.* favoriser
favourable, (*adj.*) favorable
favourite, (*adj.*) favori(te) *m.* (*f.*)
fawn, faon *m.*
fawn upon, *v.t.* flatter, caresser
fear, peur *f.*; crainte *f.*; terreur *f.*
fear, *v.t.* craindre, redouter, avoir peur de
fearful, (*adj.*) peureux(-euse) (timid); terrible; affreux(-euse); effrayant (alarming)
fearfully, (*adv.*) terriblement
fearless, (*adj.*) intrépide
feasible, (*adj.*) praticable
feast, festin *m.*; fête *f.*; régal *m.*
feast, *v.t.* fêter; *v.i.* se régaler
feat, exploit *m.*; tour (*m.*) de force
feather, plume *f.*
feather-bed, lit (*m.*) de plume
feature, trait *m.*; physionomie *f.*; visage *m.*
febrifuge, fébrifuge *m*
February, février *m.*
federal, (*adj.*) fédéral
federate, *v.t.* fédérer
federation, fédération *f.*; ligue *f.*; alliance *f.*
fee, honoraires *m. pl.*
feeble, (*adj.*) faible
feebleness, faiblesse *f.*
feed, *v.t.* donner à manger; nourrir; alimenter
feed, *v.i.* se nourrir, manger; paître (of cattle)
feel, *v.t.* sentir, tâter, toucher; *v.i.* se sentir
feeler, ballon d'essai *m.* (putting out a feeler); antenne *f.* (of insect)
feeling, sentiment *m.*; toucher *m.*
feelingly, (*adv.*) avec émotion
feign, *v.t.* feindre, simuler
feint, feinte *f.*
felicitate, *v.t.* féliciter
felicitous, (*adj.*) heureux(-euse)
felicity, félicité *f.*
fell, *v.t.* abattre (a tree)
fellow, compagnon *m.*; camarade *m.*; membre *m.* (university); individu *m.* (uncomplimentary)

felt, feutre *m.*

female, femelle *f.* (animals only); femme *f.*

female, (*adj.*) féminin; de femme; femelle (animals)

feminine, féminin *m.* (*gram.*)

fen, marais *m.*

fence, clôture *f.*

fence, *v.t.* clôturer (enclose); *v.i.* faire de l'escrime (with foils)

fencing, clôture *f.*; escrime *f.*

fender, garde-feu *m.*; pare-chocs *m.* (of car)

ferment, ferment *m.*; fermentation *f.*

ferment, *v.i.* fermenter

fern, fougère *f.*

ferocious, féroce

ferocity, férocité *f.*

ferro-concrete, béton armé *m.*

ferruginous, ferrugineux(-euse)

ferry, bac *m.*

ferry, *v.t.* and *v.i.* passer en bac

ferryman, passeur *m.*

fertile, (*adj.*) fertile, fécond

fertility, fertilité *f.*; fécondité *f.*

fervent, (*adj.*) fervent, ardent

fester, *v.i.* suppurer

festival, fête *f.*

festivity, fête *f.*; réjouissance *f.*

fetch, *v.t.* aller chercher; rapporter (at sale); amener (person)

fetter, *v.t.* enchaîner

fetters, fers *m. pl.*

feudal, (*adj.*) féodal

fever, fièvre *f.*

feverish, fiévreux(-euse)

feverishness, état (*m.*) de fièvre

few, (*adj.*) peu (de); quelques; quelques-uns *m. pl.*; quelques-unes *f. pl.*

fewer (comparative), moins de

fewest (superlative), le moins de

fewness, petit nombre *m.*

fib, mensonge *m.*

fibre, fibre *f.*

fickle, (*adj.*) inconstant

fiction, fiction *f.*

works of fiction, romans *m. pl.*

fiddle, violon *m.*

fiddle, *v.i.* jouer du violon

fidelity, fidélité *f.*

fidget, *v.i.* se remuer

fidgety, (*adj.*) remuant; nerveux (-euse)

field, champ *m.*; pré *m.* (meadow)

field artillery, artillerie de campagne *f.*

field battery, batterie de campagne *f.*

field-glass, jumelle *f.*

field-gun, pièce (*f.*) de campagne

field-hospital, ambulance *f.*

field-marshal, maréchal *m.*

field-officer, officier *m.* supérieur

in the field, en campagne

fiend, démon *m.*; diable *m.*

fierce, (*adj.*) féroce; farouche; furieux(-euse)

fierceness, férocité *f.*; fureur *f.*; violence *f.*

fieriness, fougue *f.*

fiery, (*adj.*) enflammé; fougueux (-euse)

fife, fifre *m.*

fifteen, quinze

fifty, cinquante

fig, figue *f.*

fig (tree), figuier *m.*

fight, combat *m.*; action *f.*; bataille *f.*; lutte *f.*

fight, *v.i.* and *v.t.* se battre avec; combattre, livrer (a battle)

fighter, avion (*m.*) de combat; chasseur *m.*

figurative, (*adj.*) figuré; métaphorique

figure, taille *f.* (of person); chiffre *m.* (*math.*); personnage *m.*

figure, *v.i.* figurer; chiffrer; *v.t.* se figurer, se représenter

figure of speech, façon (*f.*) de parler

filbert, aveline *f.*

filch, *v.t.* escamoter

file, lime *f.* (tool); dossier *m.* (or papers); file *f.* (*mil.*)

file, *v.t.* limer; classer (documents)

filial, (*adj.*) filial

filigree, filigrane *m.*

filing, classement *m.*

filings, limaille *f.*

fill, *v.t.* remplir, occuper (a situation); bourrer (a pipe)

fillet, filet *m.* (of meat)

filling, remplissage *m.*; plombage *m.* (of teeth)

fillip, to give a, *v.t.* encourager

film, pellicule *f.* (*photo.*); film *m.* (*cin.*); *v.t.* tourner un film (une scène)

silent film, film muet

talking film, film parlant

filter, filtre *m.*

filter, *v.t.* filtrer

filth, ordure *f.*; immondice *f.*

filthy, (*adj.*) sale; immonde

fin, nageoire *f.*

final, (*adj.*) final

finance, finance *f.*; finances *f. pl.*

financial, (*adj.*) financier(-ère)

financier, financier *m.*

finch, pinson *m.*

find, *v.t.* trouver; découvrir; s'apercevoir; déclarer (*legal*)

find, trouvaille *f.*

finding, déclaration *f.* (*legal*)

fine, amende *f.* (penalty)

fine, *v.t.* frapper d'une amende

fine, (*adj.*) fin; délicat; beau (of weather)

all very fine, but..., bel et bon, mais ...

fine arts, beaux arts *m. pl.*

finery, parure *f.*

finesse, finesse *f.*; impasse *f.* (cards)

finger, doigt *m.*

first finger, index *m.*

little finger, auriculaire *m.*

finger, *v.t.* manier, toucher

fingering, maniement *m.*; doigté *m.* (*mus.*)

finish, fin *f.*; fini *m.*

finish, *v.t.* finir; achever; terminer

finished, accompli

finishing, (*adj.*) qui complète; dernier(-ère)

fir (tree), sapin *m.*

fire, feu *m.*; incendie *m.*; (*fig.*) ardeur *f.*

fire, *v.t.* mettre le feu; incendier; tirer, faire feu (gun)

fire, *v.i.* s'enflammer

fire-brick, brique (*f.*) réfractaire

fire-brigade, corps de sapeurs-pompiers *m.*

fire-damp, grisou *m.*

fire-engine, pompe (*f.*) à incendie

fire-escape, échelle (*f.*) de sauvetage

fire-insurance, assurance (*f.*) contre l'incendie

fireman, pompier *m.*; (of locomotive) chauffeur *m.*

fireplace, cheminée *f.*

fireproof, (*adj.*) à l'épreuve du feu, ignifuge, réfractaire

fireside, foyer *m.*; coin du feu *m.*

fireworks, feu (*m.*) d'artifice

firing, chauffage *m.* (heating); combustible *m.* (fuel)

firm, maison (*f.*) de commerce; raison sociale *f.*; firme *f.*

firm, (*adj.*) ferme; solide

firmament, firmament *m.*

first, (*adj.*) premier(-ère)

first-born, premier-né

first-class, first-rate, (*adj.*) de premier ordre; de premier choix

firstly, (*adv.*) premièrement, d'abord

fish, poisson *m.*

fish, *v.t.* and *v.i.* pêcher

fisherman, pêcheur *m.*

fisherwoman, pêcheuse *f.*

fishing, pêche *f.*

fishing-rod, canne (*f.*) à pêcher

fissure, fente *f.*

fist, poing *m.*

fit, accès *m.*; attaque *f.* (illness, etc.); coupe *f.* (clothes)

fit, (*adj.*) bon, convenable, propre

fit, *v.t.* adapter; ajuster; convenir à

fit, *v.i.* s'adapter à, s'ajuster à

five, (*adj.* and *subst.*) cinq

fix, *v.t.* fixer, attacher, établir

fix, embarras *m.*; difficulté *f.*

fixture, engagement *m.*; match *m.*; meuble (*m.*) à demeure

flabby, (*adj.*) flasque

flag, drapeau *m.*; pavillon *m.* (*naut.*); dalle *f.* (stone)

flag, *v.i.* languir

flagrant, (*adj.*) flagrant

flail, fléau *m.*

flake, flocon *m.*; écaille *f.*

flame, flamme *f.*; feu *m.*

flame, *v.i.* flamber, flamboyer

flame-coloured, (*adj.*) couleur de feu

flame-thrower, lance-flammes m.

flange, rebord m.

flank, flanc m.; côté m.

flank, v.t. flanquer

flannel, flanelle f.

flap, battant m. (of table); pan m. (of coat); tape f. (with hand, etc.)

flare, v.i. étinceler; flamber

flare, fusée éclairante f.; feux (m. pl.) d'atterrissage (flare path for planes); godet (dress)

flaring, (adj.) étincelant

flash, éclair m.

flash, v.i. briller; étinceler

flashy, voyant (of clothes, etc.)

flat, (adj.) plat, uni, étendu (on the ground); bémol (mus.); faux (out of tune)

flat, appartement m.

flatness, égalité f.; aplatissement m.

flatten, v t. aplatir, aplanir; v.i. s'aplatir

flatter, v.t. flatter

flatterer, flatteur(-euse) m. (f.)

flattering, (adj.) flatteur(-euse)

flattery, flatterie f.

flavour, saveur f.; bouquet m.

flaw, défaut m.; fente f.

flax, lin m.

flaxen, (adj.) de lin; très blond (of hair)

flay, v.t. écorcher

flea, puce f.

flee, v.i. s'enfuir, fuir

fleece, toison f.

fleece, v.t. dépouiller (to rob); tondre (shear)

fleet, flotte f.

fleet, (adj.) rapide, léger(-ère)

fleeting, (adj.) passager, fugitif (-ive)

Flemish, (adj.) flamand

flesh, chair f.; viande f. (meat)

flesh-coloured, (adj.) couleur de chair

fleshiness, état (m.) charnu

fleshy, (adj.) charnu

flex, flexible m. (electric)

flexible, (adj.) souple

flexibility, flexibilité f.

flicker, v.i. vaciller (of light)

flickering, (adj.) vacillant

flickering, vacillement m.

flight, fuite f.; vol m. (of birds, etc.); cours m. (of time)

flighty, (adj.) volage

fling, v.t. lancer, jeter

fling away, v.t. rejeter, gaspiller (waste)

fling down, v.t. jeter à terre

flint, pierre (f.) à briquet; silex m.

flippancy, légèreté f.

flippant, (adj.) léger

flirt, v.i. coqueter, flirter

flirt, coquette f.

flirtation, coquetterie f.; flirt m.

float, v.i. flotter; faire la planche (swimming); v.t. flotter

float (a company), v.t. fonder (une société)

flock, troupeau m.; bande f.

flock, v.i. s'attrouper

floe, glaçon m.

flog, v.t. fouetter

flood, déluge m.; inondation f.; crue f.

flood, v.t. inonder

floor, plancher m; parquet m.; étage m. (of house)

floor, v.t. parqueter; (fig.) terrasser

florid, (adj.) fleuri, vermeil(le)

florin, florin m.

florist, fleuriste m. and f.

flotilla, flotille f.

flounder, carrelet m.

flounder, v.i. se débattre

flour, farine f.

flourish, éclat m.; parafe m. (after a signature, etc.); fanfare f.

flourish, v.i. fleurir; v.t. brandir

flow, écoulement m.; flux m.

flow, v.i. s'écouler, couler

flower, fleur f.; élite f.

flower, fleurir; être en fleur

flower-bed, plate-bande f.; parterre m.

flowery, (adj.) fleuri

fluctuate, v.i. flotter; osciller

fluctuating, (adj.) flottant

fluctuation, fluctuation f.

flue, tuyau (m.) de cheminée

fluency, facilité f.

fluent, (*adj.*) coulant, facile

fluently, couramment (of language)

fluid, fluide *m.*

fluke, coup (*m.*) de veine (luck); queue *f.* (of whale)

flurry, bouffée (*f.*) de vent; rafale *f.*; agitation *f.*

flurry, *v.t.* troubler, agiter

flush, rougeur *f.*; (*adj.*) (*level*) de niveau, ras

flush, *v.i.* rougir

fluster, *v.t.* ahurir; agiter

flute, flûte *f.*

flutter, émoi *m.*; battement *m.* (of wings)

flutter, *v.t.* agiter; battre des ailes

flutter, *v.i.* s'agiter; battre irrégulièrement

fly, mouche *f.*

fly, *v.i.* voler, s'envoler; prendre la fuite; *v.t.* survoler; piloter (plane)

flying, (*adj.*) volant

flying-ground, aérodrome *m.*; terrain (*m.*) d'aviation

fly-wheel, volant *m.*

foal, poulain *m.*; pouliche *f.*

foal, *v.t.* mettre bas

foam, écume *f.*

foam, *v.i.* écumer

focus, foyer *m.*

in focus, au point

foe, ennemi *m.*

fog, brouillard *m.*, brume *f.*

foggy, (*adj.*) brumeux(-euse)

fog-horn, corne (*f.*) de brun

foil, feuille (*f.*) de métal

foil, *v.t.* frustrer

fold, pli *m.*, repli *m.*

fold, *v.t.* plier

folding-bed, lit pliant *m.*

folding-chair, pliant *m.*

folding-door, porte brisée *f.*

foliage, feuillage *m.*

folio, in-folio *m.*; folio *m.*

folk, gens *m.* and *f. pl.*; personnes *f. pl.*

follow, *v.t.* suivre; poursuivre; s'attacher (à)

follow, *v.i.* s'ensuivre, résulter

follower, partisan (*m.*), disciple *m.*

following, (*adj.*) suivant

folly, folie *f.*; sottise *f.*; bêtise *f.*

foment, *v.t.* fomenter

fomentation, fomentation *f.*

fond, (*adj.*) affectueux(-euse); tendre, indulgent; cher (of hopes)

to be fond of, aimer, tenir à

fondle, *v.t.* caresser

food, nourriture *f.*; aliment *m.*; vivres *m. pl.*

fool, sot(te) *m.* (*f.*); imbécile *m.* and *f.*

fool, *v.t.* duper; se moquer (de)

fooling, bouffonnerie *f.*

foolish, sot(te); bête; imbécile; ridicule

foot, pied *m.*

on foot, à pied

football, ballon *m.*; football *m.* (game)

foot-board, marche-pied *m.*

footbridge, passerelle *f.*

foothold, point d'appui *m.*

footlights, rampe *f.* (theatre)

footman, valet *m.*

foot-passenger, piéton *m.*

footpath, sentier *m.*

footprint, empreinte *f.*

footsore, (*adj.*) pieds meurtris

foot-stool, tabouret *m.*

foot-way, trottoir *m.*

fop, fat *m.*

foppish, (*adj.*) affecté

for (*prep.*) pour; de, à, pendant (during); depuis (since); en faveur de; à cause de

for, (*conj.*) car; parce que

for all that, malgré tout cela

forage, *v.i.* and *v.t.* fourrager

forbear, *v.t.* and *v.i.* s'abstenir

forbear, ancêtre *m.*

forbearance, patience *f.*

forbid, *v.t.* défendre; empêcher

force, force *f.*; violence *f.*

in force, en vigueur (law, etc.); en force (*mil.*)

forces, forces (armées) *f. pl.*

force, *v.t.* forcer; obliger; violer (violate)

forcible, (*adj.*) puissant; énergique

ford, gué *m.*

fore, antérieur, de devant

fore-arm, avant-bras *m.*

forebode, *v.t.* présager

foreboding, pressentiment *m.*

forecast, prévoyance *f.*; pronostic *m.*

forefathers, aïeux *m. pl.*

forefinger, index *m.*

foreground, premier plan *m.*

forehead, front *m.*

foreland, promontoire *m.*

foreman, contremaître *m.*

foremost, le plus avancé

forenoon, matinée *f.*

forerunner, précurseur *m.*

foresee, *v.t.* prévoir

foretaste, avant-goût *m.*

foretell, *v.t.* prédire

forethought, prévoyance *f.*

forewarn, *v.t.* prévenir

forewoman, première ouvrière *f.*

foreign, (*adj.*) étranger(-ère)

foreign office, ministère (*m.*) des affaires étrangères

foreigner, étranger(-ère) *m.* (*f.*)

forest, forêt *f.*

forfeit, amende *f.*; confiscation *f.*

forfeit, *v.t.* confisquer; perdre par confiscation

forge, forge *f.*

forge, *v.t.* forger; contrefaire (money); commettre un faux

forger, faussaire *m.*; faux monnayeur *m.*

forgery, crime de faux *m.*; falsification *f.*

forget, *v.t.* oublier

forgetful, oublieux(-euse)

forgetfulness, oubli *m.*; négligence *f.*

forgive, *v.t.* pardonner à; faire grâce à (or de)

forgiveness, pardon *m.*; grâce *f.*

fork, fourchette *f.* (table); fourche *f.*; bifurcation *f.* (of roads)

fork, *v.t.* enlever avec une fourche

fork, *v.i.* (se) bifurquer (of road); faire fourche

forked, (*adj.*) bifurqué; fourchu (branch)

forlorn, (*adj.*) abandonné, solitaire

form, forme *f.*; modèle *m.*;

classe *f.* (school); tournure *f.* (of phrase); banc *m.* (bench); imprimé *m.* (printed)

form, *v.t.* façonner; former

formality, formalité *f.*

formally, (*adv.*) formellement

formation, formation *f.*; ordre *m.*

former, (*adj.*) précédent, ancien (-ne); (*pron.*) celui-là

formerly, (*adv.*) autrefois, jadis

formidable, (*adj.*) formidable, redoutable

formula, formule *f.*

forsake, *v.t.* abandonner

forswear, *v.t.* répudier

fort, forteresse *f.*; fort *m.*

forth, (*adv.*) en avant; hors; dehors; au dehors

and so forth, et ainsi de suite

forthcoming, (*adj.*) prêt à paraître, prochain

forthwith, (*adv.*) sur-le-champ

fortification, fortification *f.*

fortify, *v.t.* fortifier

fortifying, (*adj.*) fortifiant

fortnight, quinze jours *m. pl.*; quinzaine *f.*

fortnightly, tous les quinze jours

fortress, place forte *f.*; forteresse *f.*

fortuitous, (*adj.*) imprévu, fortuit

fortuitously, par hasard

fortunate, heureux(-euse)

fortunately, (*adv.*) heureusement, par bonheur

fortune, fortune *f.*; sort *m.* (lot)

fortune-teller, diseur(-euse) *m.* (*f.*) de bonne aventure

forty, (*adj.*) quarante

about forty, une quarantaine *f.*

forward, (*adj.*) avancé; en avant; précoce

forward, *v.t.* avancer; activer; envoyer; expédier; faire suivre (letters)

forwarding, expédition *f.*

forwarding agent, commissaire (*m.*) expéditeur

forwardness, avancement *m.*; précocité *f.*; effronterie *f.*

foster, *v.t.* élever; nourrir; encourager

foster-brother, frère (*m.*) de lait
foster-mother, mère nourricière *f.*
foster-sister, sœur (*f.*) de lait
foul, (*adj.*) sale; immonde; infect (air); obscène; (*sport*) faute *f.*
found, *v.t.* fonder, établir; fondre (to cast)
foundation, fondation *f.*; établissement *m.*
foundations, fondements *m. pl.*
founder(-ress), fondateur(-trice) *m.* (*f.*)
founder, *v.i.* sombrer
foundry, fonderie *f.*
fountain, fontaine *f.*; source *f.*
fountain-pen, plume (*f.*) à réservoir; stylo *m.*
four, (*adj.*) quatre
four-cornered, (*adj.*) à quatre coins
four score, quatre-vingts
fourteen, (*adj.*) quatorze
fourteenth, (*adj.*) quatorzième
fowl, oiseau *m.*; poule *f.* (hen); volaille *f.* (for cooking)
fowl-house, poulailler *m.*
fox, renard *m.*
foxglove, digitale *f.*
fox-hunting, chasse (*f.*) au renard
fraction, fraction *f.*
fractional, (*adj.*) fractionnaire
fracture, fracture *f.*
fragile, (*adj.*) fragile
fragment, fragment *m.*
fragrance, parfum *m.*
fragrant, (*adj.*) odoriférant; parfumé
frail, (*adj.*) frêle, fragile
frailty, fragilité *f.*
frame, charpente *f.*; châssis *m.* (car, etc.); fuselage *m.* (of aeroplane); cadre *m.* (picture); construction *f.*; système *m.*
frame, *v.t.* encadrer
franchise, droit (*m.*) électoral, franchise *f.*
frank, (*adj.*) franc(-che), sincère
frantic, (*adj.*) frénétique, furieux (-euse)
fraternal, (*adj.*) fraternel(le)
fraternity, fraternité *f.*
fraud, fraude *f.*; supercherie *f.*

fraudulent, (*adj.*) frauduleux (-euse); trompeur(-euse)
fraudulently, en fraude
fraught (with), plein (de), chargé (de)
fray, mêlée *f.*; bagarre *f.*
freak, caprice *m.*; phénomène *m.*; bizarrerie *f.*
freakish, (*adj.*) bizarre; capricieux(-euse)
freckle, (tache de) rousseur *f.*
free, (*adj.*) libre; exempt; gratuit; libéral (generous); ouvert (manner)
freehold, propriété (*f.*) foncière libre
freeholder, propriétaire (*m.*) foncier
freemason, franc-maçon *m.*
freemasonry, franc-maçonnerie *f.*
free-thinker, libre penseur *m.*
free-trade, libre échange *m.*
freedom, liberté *f.*; indépendance *f.*; droit (*m.*) de cité (of city)
freely, (*adv.*) librement, gratuitement
freeze, *v.t.* geler; *v.i.* (se) geler
freezing, (*adj.*) glacial
freezing, congélation *f.*
freight, cargaison *f.*; chargement *m.*
freight, *v.t.* affréter
freighter, cargo *m.*
French, (*adj.*) français
frenzied, (*adj.*) forcené, frénétique
frenzy, frénésie *f.*; délire *m.*
frequent, (*adj.*) fréquent
frequent, *v.t.* fréquenter
frequently, (*adv.*) fréquemment, souvent
fresco, fresque *f.*
fresh, (*adj.*) frais (fraîche); récent; nouveau (nouvelle); (eau) douce (water)
freshen, *v.t.* rafraîchir
freshness, fraîcheur *f.*
fret, *v.i.* se chagriner; se tourmenter; *v.t.* ronger
fretful, (*adj.*) irritable
fretfulness, mauvaise humeur *f.*
friar, moine *m.*; religieux *m.*
friction, frottement *m.*; friction *f*

Friday, vendredi *m.*
friend, ami(e) *m.* (*f.*)
friendless, sans ami, délaissé
friendliness, bienveillance *f.*
friendly, (*adj.*) amical
friendship, amitié *f.*
fright, effroi *m.*; frayeur *f.*; épouvante *f.*
frighten, *v.t.* épouvanter, effrayer
frightful, épouvantable, effroyable; affreux(-euse)
frigid, froid
frill, jabot *m.*
fringe, frange *f.*; bord *m.*
fringe, *v.t.* franger
frippery, friperie *f.*
frisk, *v.i.* sautiller, gambader
friskiness, vivacité *f.*
frisky, (*adj.*) vif; fringant (of horse)
fritter, beignet *m.* (*cook.*)
fritter away, *v.t.* gaspiller
frivolity, frivolité *f.*
frivolous, (*adj.*) frivole
frock, robe *f.*; redingote *f.* (frock-coat)
frog, grenouille *f.*
frolic, escapade *f.*; gambade *f.*
frolic, *v.i.* folâtrer
from, de, depuis, à, à partir de
frond, fronde *f.*
front, front *m.*; façade *f.* (of building); devant *m.*
front, *v.t.* faire face à; donner sur
front door, porte (*f.*) d'entrée
front room, chambre sur le devant *f.*
front view, vue de face *f.*
frontage, façade *f.*; devanture *f.* (of a shop)
frontal, (*adj.*) frontal
frontier, frontière *f.*
fronting, vis-à-vis
frontispiece, frontispice *m.*
frost, gelée *f.*
frost-bitten, (*adj.*) gelé
frosty, (*adj.*) glacé, froid
froth, écume *f.*
froth, *v.i.* écumer
frown, *v.i.* froncer les sourcils
frowzy, (*adj.*) malpropre
frozen, (*adj.*) gelé

fructify, *v.i.* fructifier
frugal, (*adj.*) frugal, économe
fruit, fruit *m.*
fruit tree, arbre fruitier *m.*
fruitful, (*adj.*) fertile; fécond
fruitfully, abondamment
fruition, jouissance *f.*
fruitlessly, (*adv.*) inutilement
frump, une (femme) mal attifée
frustrate, *v.t.* frustrer
frustration, frustration *f.*
fry, friture *f.*
fry, *v.t.* frire
frying-pan, poêle (*f.*) à frire
fuchsia, fuchsia *m.*
fuddle, *v.i.* griser
fuel, chauffage *m.*; combustible *m.*
fugitive, fugitif *m.*
fugue, fugue *f.*
fulfil, *v.t.* remplir, accomplir, réaliser
fulfilment, accomplissement *m.*
full, (*adj.*) plein; rempli; entier (-ère); ample; complet (of bus, etc.)
full-dress, grande (*f.*) tenue
full-faced, (*adj.*) au visage plein
full-length, en pied (of portrait)
full-steam, à toute vapeur
full-stop, point *m.*
fuller's earth, terre (*f.*) à foulon
fulminate, *v.i.* fulminer
ful(l)ness, plénitude *f.*; plein *m.*
fulsome, (*adj.*) gonflé; servile
fumble, *v.i.* tâtonner
fumbling, à tâtons
fume, vapeur *f.*; fumée *f.*
fume, *v.i.* fumer; s'exhaler
fret and fume, se faire du mauvais sang
fumigate, *v.t.* fumiger; désinfecter
fumigation, fumigation *f.*
fun, gaieté *f.*; amusement *m.*
function, fonction *f.*
function, *v.i.* fonctionner, marcher
functional, fonctionnel(le)
functionary, fonctionnaire *m.*
fund, fonds *m. pl.*; caisse *f.*
fundamental, (*adj.*) fondamental
funded, (*adj.*) consolidé
funeral, funérailles *f. pl.*; obsèques *f. pl.*

funereal, (*adj.*) funèbre

fungous, (*adj.*) fongueux

fungus, mycète *m.*

funk, venette-*f.*; peur (*f.*) bleue

funnel, entonnoir *m.*; cheminée *f.* (steamers)

funny, (*adj.*) drôle

fur, fourrure *f.*;

fur coat, manteau (*m.*) de fourrure

furbish, *v.t.* fourbir

furious, (*adj.*) furieux(-euse)

furl, *v.t.* ferler, serrer

furlough, congé *m.*; permission *f.*

furnace, fourneau *m.*

furnish, *v.t.* fournir; meubler (a house)

furnisher, fournisseur *m.* (of goods)

furniture, meubles *m. pl.*; mobilier *m.*; ameublement *m.*

furrier, fourreur *m.*; pelletier *m.*

furrow, sillon *m.*

furrow, *v.t.* rider (the face); sillonner

further, (*adj.*) plus éloigné, ultérieur

further, *v.t.* avancer; faciliter

furthermore, (*adv.*) de plus, en outre

furthermost, (*adj.*) le plus éloigné

furtive, (*adj.*) furtif(-ive), dérobé

fury, furie *f.*; fureur *f.*

furze, ajonc *m.*

fuse, *v.t.* and *v.i.* fondre; sauter (of electric lights)

fuse, fusée *f.*

delayed action fuse, fusée (*f.*) en retard

percussion fuse, fusée (*f.*) percutante

fusion, fusion *f.*; fonte *f.*

fuss, fracas *m.*; embarras *m.*

fussy, tracassier(-ère)

fustian, futaine *f.*

fusty, (*adj.*) moisi

futile, (*adj.*) futile, vain

futility, futilité *f.*

future, avenir *m.*

future, (*adj.*) futur

futurity, avenir *m.*

fuzzy, (*adj.*) flou, crêpelu

G

gab, faconde *f.*

to have gift of the gab, avoir la langue bien pendue

gabble, *v.i.* babiller; bavarder

gabbler, bavard *m.*

gable, pignon *m.*

gable-end, pignon *m.*

gaby, nigaud *m.*

gad (about), *v.i.* courir ça et là; battre le pavé

gadfly, taon *m.*

gadget, machin *m.*; truc *m.*

gaff, gaffe *f.*

gag, bâillon *m.*

gag, *v.t.* bâillonner

gage, gage *m.*

gaiety, gaieté *f.*

gaily, (*adv.*) gaiement

gain, gain *m.*; profit *m.*; avantage *m.*

gain, *v.t.* gagner; acquérir; obtenir

gainer, gagnant *m.*

gainings, profits *m. pl.*

gainsay, *v.t.* contredire

gait, démarche *f.*; allure *f.*

gaiters, guêtres *f. pl.*

gala, gala *m.*

galaxy, galaxie *f.*; voie (*f.*) lactée

gale, tempête *f.*; vent frais *m.*; brise *f.*

gall, fiel *m.*; écorchure *f.* (soreness); (*fig.*) rancune *f.*

gall-bladder, vésicule (*f.*) biliaire

gall-stone, calcul (*m.*) biliaire

gallant, (*adj.*) brave, noble, vaillant, intrépide, galant

gallant, galant *m.*; amoureux *m.*

gallantry, valeur *f.*; bravoure *f.*; galanterie *f.*

galleon, galion *m.*

gallery, galerie *f.*

galley, galère *f.*; cuisine *f.* (ship's galley)

Gallic, (*adj.*) gaulois

galling, (*adj.*) irritant, vexant

gallivant, *v.i.* vagabonder

gallon, quatre litres et demi

gallop, galop *m.*

gallop, *v.i.* galoper; aller au galop

gallows, potence *f.*

galosh, galoche *f.*; caoutchouc *m.*

galvanic, *(adj.)* galvanique

galvanise, *v.t.* galvaniser

gamble, *v.i.* jouer

gambler, joueur(-euse) *m. (f.)*

gambling, jeu *m.*

gambling-house, maison *(f.)* de jeu, tripot *m.*

gamboge, gomme-gutte *f.*

gambol, *v.i.* gambader

game, jeu *m.*; partie *f.*; gibier *m.* (wild game, etc.); **-'s up,** il n'y a rien à faire

game-bag, gibecière *f.*; carnassière *f.*

gamekeeper, garde-chasse *m.*

game-leg, jambe boiteuse *f.*

gamester, joueur *m.*

gammon, quartier de lard *m.*

gammon *(slang),* blague *f.*; *v.i.* blaguer

gamut, *(mus.)* gamme *f.*

gander, jars *m.*

gang, bande *f.*; troupe *f.*; équipe *f.* (of workmen)

ganger, chef *(m.)* d'équipe

gangrene, gangrène *f.*

gangway, passage *m.*; passavant *m.* (of ship); coupée *f.*; passerelle *f.*

gaol, prison *f.*

gap, brèche *f.*; ouverture *f.*; passage *m.*; lacune *f.* (book, etc.); trouée *f.* (in forest)

to fill a gap, remplir une lacune

to stop a gap, boucher un trou

gape, *v.i.* bâiller; avoir la bouche béante

garage, garage *m.*

garb, habit *m.*; vêtement *m.*

garbage, détritus *m. pl.*; entrailles *f. pl.*

garble, *v.t.* tronquer (a version or quotation)

garden, *m.* jardin

kitchen garden, jardin potager

garden, *v.i.* jardiner

gardener, jardinier *m.*

gardening, jardinage *m.*

garden-plot, parterre *m.*

gargle, *v.i.* se gargariser

gargoyle, gargouille *f.*

garish, *(adj.)* voyant, criard

garland, guirlande *f.*

garlic, ail *m.*

garment, vêtement *m.*; habillement *m.*

garner, *v.t.* amasser, entasser

garnet, grenat *m.*

garnish, *v.t.* garnir; parer

garret, mansarde *f.*; grenier *m.*

garrotte, *v.t.* garrotter; étrangler

garrison, garnison *f.*

garrulity, loquacité *f.*

garrulous, *(adj.)* babillard, loquace

garter, jarretière *f.*

gas, gaz *m.*

gas-bomb, bombe *(f.)* asphyxiante

gas-burner, bec *(m.)* de gaz

gas-holder, gazomètre *m.*

gas-lamp, réverbère *m.*

gas-lighting, éclairage *(m.)* au gaz

gas-mask, masque *(m.)* à gaz

gas-meter, compteur *(m.)* à gaz

gas-pipe, tuyau *(m.)* de gaz

gasworks, usine *(f.)* à gaz

poison gas, gaz asphyxiant

tear-gas, gaz lachrymogène

gaseous, *(adj.)* gazeux(-euse)

gash, balafre *f.*; entaille *f.*

gash, *v.t.* balafrer, taillader

gasp, *v.i.* haleter; respirer avec difficulté

gastric, *(adj.)* gastrique

gastritis, gastrite *f.*

gate, porte *f.*; grande porte *f.*; porte cochère *f.*; grille *f.* (iron gate)

gate-keeper, portier *m.*

gateway, porte *(f.)* cochère; portail *m.*

gather, *v.t.* ramasser; rassembler, assembler, cueillir (fruit)

gather, *v.i.* se rassembler, se réunir; former un abcès *(med.)*

gatherer, percepteur *m.* (of taxes, etc.)

gathering, rassemblement *m.*; réunion *f.*; récolte *f.* (harvest); abcès *(med.)*

gaudiness, éclat *m.*; faste *m.*

gaudy, (*adj.*) voyant, fastueux (-euse)

gauge, jauge *f.*; mesure *f.*

gauge, *v.t.* jauger, mesurer; (*fig.*) juger (judge)

gaunt, (*adj.*) maigre, décharné

gauze, gaze *f.*

gawky, (*adj.*) gauche, dégingandé

gay, (*adj.*) gai

gaze, *v.i.* regarder fixement

gaze, regard (*m.*) fixe

gazelle, gazelle *f.*

gazette, journal (*m.*) officiel

gazetteer, dictionnaire (*m.*) géographique

gear, appareil (*m.*); accoutrement (*m.*); engrenage *m.* (machinery); vitesse *f.* (of car)

gear, *v.t.* embrayer; *v.i.* s'embrayer

gelatine, gélatine *f.*

gelatinous, (*adj.*) gélatineux (-euse)

geld, *v.t.* châtrer

gelding, cheval (*m.*) hongre

gem, pierre précieuse *f.*; joyau *m.*

gender, genre *m.*

genealogical, (*adj.*) généalogique

genealogy, généalogie *f.*

general, (*adj.*) général; commun; ordinaire; d'ensemble; universel (-le)

general servant, bonne (*f.*) à tout faire

general use, à l'usage de tout le monde

general (officer), général *m.*

generality, généralité *f.*; la plupart

generally, en général, généralement

generate, *v.t.* engendrer, générer

generation, génération *f.*

generosity, générosité *f.*

generous, généreux(-euse)

genial, (*adj.*) sympathique; génial, affable

geniality, bonne humeur *f.*; bienveillance *f.*

genius, génie *m.*

gentile, (*adj.*) and *m.* and *f.* gentil(e)

gentle, (*adj.*) doux (douce); paisible; aimable

gentleman, monsieur *m.*; homme (*m.*) comme il faut

gentlemanly, bien élevé, distingué

gentleness, douceur *f.*

gently, (*adv.*) doucement

gentry, haute bourgeoisie *f.*; petite noblesse *f.*

genuine, (*adj.*) véritable; pur

geographer, géographe *m.*

geography, géographie *f.*

germ, germe *m.*

German, allemand

germinate, *v.i.* germer

gesticulate, *v.i.* gesticuler

gesture, geste *m.*

get, *v.t.* obtenir, acquérir, se procurer; recevoir (receive); gagner (earn); apprendre (to learn); arriver à, atteindre (reach); aller chercher (fetch); trouver (find); attraper (catch)

get, *v.i.* devenir (become); se faire (become)

get about, se répandre (rumour)

get abroad, se répandre

get across, traverser

get a footing, s'établir

get along, s'avancer, faire des progrès

get away, s'en aller, s'échapper à

get behind, rester en arrière; être en retard (to be late)

get done, faire faire

get down, descendre

get drunk, s'enivrer

get friends, se faire des amis

get hold of, s'emparer (de); saisir

get home, arriver chez soi

get in, monter; entrer dans

get in debt, se faire des dettes

get killed, se faire tuer

get near, s'approcher de, approcher

get off, descendre de

get old, vieillir

get on, réussir, faire des progrès

get out (of trouble, etc.), se tirer de

get the better of, l'emporter sur

get up, se lever, arranger

get wet, se mouiller

ghastly, pâle comme la mort; horrible

gherkin, cornichon *m.*

ghost, âme *f.*; esprit *m.*; fantôme *m.*; revenant *m.*

giant, géant *m.*

gibberish, jargon *m.*

gibbet, potence *f.*; gibet *m.*

giddy, (*adj.*) étourdi; vertigineux (-euse)

gift, don *m.*; présent *m.*; cadeau *m.*; talent *m.*

gifted, (*adj.*) doué

gigantic, (*adj.*) gigantesque

giggle, *v.i.* pousser des rires nerveux

gild, *v.t.* dorer

gilding, dorure *f.*

gilliflower, giroflée *f.*

gimlet, vrille *f.*

gin, genièvre *m.* (alcohol); égreneuse de coton; trébuchet *m.* (a snare)

ginger, gingembre *m.*

gingerbread, pain (*m.*) d'épices

gipsy, bohémien(ne) *m.* (*f.*); tzigane *m.* and *f.*

girder, poutre *f.*; solive *f.*; traverse *f.*

girdle, ceinture *f.*

girl, fille *f.*; jeune fille

girlhood, jeunesse *f.*

give, *v.t.* donner; rendre (give back); accorder; faire (credit or answer); porter (a blow); prononcer (verdict, etc.)

give in, give way, *v.i.* céder, s'abandonner à (give way to)

give up, *v.t.* abandonner

glacier, glacier *m.*

glad, joyeux(-euse), content, heureux(-euse)

gladden, *v.t.* réjouir; *v.i.* se réjouir

glade, clairière *f.*

gladly, volontiers, avec plaisir

glance, *v.i.* jeter un coup d'œil

glance, regard *m.*; coup d'œil *m.*

gland, glande *f.*

glare, éclat *m.*; lumière (*f.*) éblouissante; lueur *f.*; regard (*m.*) farouche

glare, *v.i.* regarder d'un air farouche; éblouir; luire

glaring, (*adj.*) voyant, criant, éclatant, éblouissant; flagrant

glass, verre *m.*; vitre *f.* (glass window); (train, car), glace *f.*

glasses (spectacles), lunettes *f. pl.*

glasses (field), jumelles *f. pl.*

glass (looking-), miroir *m.*

plate-glass, glace *f.*

stained glass, vitrail (*m.*) peint

glass works, verrerie *f.*

glaze, *v.t.* vitrer

glazier, vitrier *m.*

glazing, vitrage *m.* (windows); vernissage *m.*

gleam, *v.i.* briller, luire

gleam, rayon *m.*; lueur *f.*

glean, *v.t.* glaner

glee, joie *f.*

glen, vallon *m.*

glide, *v.i.* glisser; se glisser dans; couler

glider, (*aviat.*) planeur *m.*

glimmer, lueur *f.*; faible rayon *m.*

glimmer, *v.i.* jeter une faible lueur

glimpse, lueur *f.*; coup d'œil *m.*; vue (*f.*) rapide

to catch a glimpse of, entrevoir

glisten, glitter, étinceler; briller

globe, globe *m.*

gloom, obscurité *f.*; ténèbres *f. pl.*; tristesse *f.*

gloomy, (*adj.*) sombre; obscur; mélancolique; morne

glorify, *v.t.* glorifier

glorious, (*adj.*) glorieux(-euse); splendide; magnifique

glory, gloire *f.*

gloss, lustre *m.*

gloss, *v.i.* lustrer

glossary, glossaire *m.*

glove, gant *m.*

glover, gantier *m.*

glove-shop, ganterie *f.*

glow, chaleur *f.*; ardeur *f.*; incandescence *f.*

glow, *v.i.* rougir; briller

glue, colle (*f.*) forte

glut, surabondance *f.*

glutton, glouton(ne) *m.* (*f.*)
gluttonous, (*adj.*) glouton(ne), goulu
glycerine, glycérine *f.*
gnarled, (*adj.*) noueux(-euse)
gnash, *v.t.* grincer (des dents)
gnat, moucheron *m.*
gnaw, *v.t.* ronger
gnawing, (*adj.*) rongeant, rongeur
go, *v.t.* aller; marcher; passer
go abroad, aller à l'étranger
go against, aller contre, s'opposer à
go ahead, marcher; poursuivre son chemin
go away, s'en aller
go back, revenir; remonter (in time)
go-between, intermédiaire *m.* and *f.*
go for, aller chercher
go in for, se présenter à, concourir pour
go on, continuer, marcher
go out, sortir
go slow, faire la grève perlée
go to sleep, s'endormir
go up, monter
go without, se passer de
goal, but *m.*
goat, chèvre *f.*; (he-goat) bouc *m.*
goblet, gobelet *m.*
God, Dieu *m.*
godchild, filleul(e) *m.* (*f.*)
godfather, parrain *m.*
godmother, marraine *f.*
godsend, bonne aubaine *f.*; trouvaille *f.*
goddess, déesse *f.*
godly, pieux(-euse)
gold, or *m.*
gold, (*adj.*) d'or, en or
goldsmith, orfèvre *m.*
gondola, gondole *f.*
gonorrhœa, gonorrhée *f.*
good, (*adj.*) bon(ne); honnête; convenable; sage (child)
good-bye, adieu *m.*
good-for-nothing, vaurien *m.*
Good Friday, vendredi saint
good-humoured, de bonne humeur; gai
goodly, (*adj.*) considérable; beau

good-natured, bienveillant
goodness, bonté *f.*
thank goodness, Dieu merci
goodness knows, Dieu sait
goodwill, bonne volonté; (*commer.*) clientèle *f.*
goods, marchandise *f.*
goose, oie *f.*; (*fig.*) nigaud(e) *m.* (*f.*)
gooseberry, groseille (*f.*) (à maquereau)
gooseberry bush, groseillier *m.*
gore, sang *m.*
gorge, gorge *f.*; gosier *m.* (throat)
gorge, *v.i.* avaler, gorger
gorgeous, (*adj.*) splendide; magnifique; fastueux(-euse)
gorse, ajonc *m.*
gospel, évangile *m.*
gossamer, fil (*m.*) de la vierge
gossip, *v.i.* bavarder
gossip, (a) commère *f.*; causeur *m.*; causeuse *f.*
gossip(ing), commérage *m.*
Gothic, (*adj.*) gothique
gourd, gourde *f.*; calebasse *f.*
gout, goutte *f.*
gouty, (*adj.*) goutteux(-euse)
govern, *v.t.* gouverner, régir, diriger
governess, gouvernante *f.*
government, gouvernement *m.*
governor, gouverneur; directeur *m.* (of institution)
gown, robe *f.*
dressing-gown, peignoir *m.*; robe (*f.*) de chambre
grab, *v.t.* empoigner; saisir
grace, grâce *f.*; faveur *f.*; bénédicité *m.* (before meals); grâces *f. pl.* (after meals)
grace, *v.t.* orner, embellir
graceful, (*adj.*) gracieux(-euse)
gracious, (*adj.*) gracieux(-euse); favorable, clément
grade, grade *m.*; degré *m.*; rang *m.*
gradient, pente *f.*; rampe *f.*
gradual, (*adj.*) graduel(le); par degrés
graduate, *v.t.* graduer; *v.i.* passer sa licence
grain, grain *m.*; céréales *f. pl.*; gramme *m.* (weight)

grammar, grammaire *f.*
granary, grenier *m.*
grand, *(adj.)* magnifique, sublime, grandiose
grandeur, grandeur *f.*; éclat *m.*
granddaughter, petite-fille *f.*
grandfather, grand-père *m.*
grandmother, grand'mère *f.*
grandson, petit-fils *m.*
grange, ferme *f.*
granite, granit *m.*
grant, concession *f.*
grant, *v.t.* accorder, concéder; convenir, avouer
grape, raisin *m.*; grain (*m.*) de raisin; raisins *m. pl.*
grapple, *v.i.* venir aux prises (avec)
grasp, *v.t.* empoigner; saisir
grass, l'herbe *f.*; gazon *m.*
grass-blade, brin (*m.*) d'herbe
grasshopper, sauterelle *f.*
grassland, prairie *f.*
grass-plot, pelouse *f.*
grassy, *(adj.)* herbeux(-euse)
grate, grille *f.*; foyer *m.* (hearth)
grate, *v.t.* râper; frotter
grate the teeth, grincer des dents
grate upon, écorcher; (*fig.*) choquer
grateful, *(adj.)* reconnaissant
gratification, satisfaction *f.*; contentement *m.*
gratify, *v.t.* satisfaire; contenter
grating, grille *f.*; grillage *m.*; grincement *m.* (sound)
gratis, *(adv.)* gratuitement
gratitude, reconnaissance *f.*; gratitude *f.*
gratuitous, *(adj.)* gratuit
grave, tombe *f.*; fosse *f.*; (*fig.*) tombeau *m.*
grave, *(adj.)* grave; sérieux(-euse)
grave-digger, fossoyeur *m.*
grave-digging, fossoyage *m.*
graveyard, cimetière *m.*
gravel, gravier *m.*
graving, gravure *f.*
graving-dock, bassin (*m.*) de radoub
gravity, pesanteur *f.*; air (*m.*) sérieux
gravy, jus *m.*

gray(ish), *(adj.)* gris(âtre)
graze, *v.i.* faire paître; paître; brouter
graze, *v.t.* frôler
grease, graisse *f.*
grease, *v.t.* graisser
greasiness, graisse *f.*
greasy, *(adj.)* gras(se); graisseux (-euse)
great, *(adj.)* grand; considérable
great-coat, paletot *m.*
great-grandfather, bisaïeul *m.*
great-grandson, arrière-petit-fils *m.*
greatness, grandeur *f.*
greed, greediness, voracité *f.*; cupidité *f.*
greedy, *(adj.)* vorace, glouton(ne), avide
Greek, *(adj.)* grec (grecque)
green, *(adj.)* vert; jeune; frais (fraîche); novice
greenfinch, verdier *m.*
greengage, reine-claude *f*
greengrocer, fruitier *m.*
greenhorn, blanc-bec *m.*
greenhouse, serre *f.*
greenish, verdâtre
greensward, pelouse *f.*
greet, *v.t.* saluer
greeting, salut *m.*
gregarious, *(adj.)* grégaire
grenade, grenade *f.*
grey, *(adj.)* gris
greyhound, lévrier *m.*
greyish, *(adj.)* grisâtre
grid, grille *f.*
gridiron, gril *m.*
grief, chagrin *m.*; douleur *f.*
grieve, *v.i.* se chagriner; *v.t.* chagriner, affliger
grieving, doléance *f.*
grievous, grave; douloureux (-euse); affligeant
grill, *v.t.* faire griller
grim, *(adj.)* sévère, sinistre
grin, *v.i.* sourire (à belles dents)
grind, *v.t.* moudre; aiguiser (sharpen); *v.i.* grincer
grinder, rémouleur *m.*; dent (*f.*) molaire
grindstone, meule *f.* (à aiguiser)
grip, *v.t.* empoigner; serrer; saisir

gripe, *v.t.* donner la colique

gripes, colique *f.*

grist, blé (*m.*) à moudre

grit, grès *m.*; cran *m.* (courage)

groan, *v.i.* gémir; grogner

groan, gémissement *m.*; grognement *m.*

groats, gruau (*m.*) d'avoine

grocer, épicier(-ère) *m.* (*f.*)

grocery, épicerie *f.*

groin, aine *f.* (*anat.*); arête *f.* (*arch.*)

groom, palefrenier *m.*

groove, rainure *f.*; coulisse *f.*

groove, *v.t.* canneler; creuser

grope, *v.i.* tâtonner

grope about, aller à tâtons

gross, grosse *f.*

gross, (*adj.*) gros(se); grossier (-ère); grivois (coarse)

grotto, grotte *f.*

ground, terre *f.*; fond *m.*; raison *f.* (reason)

ground, *v.t.* fonder, baser

ground, *v.i.* échouer

ground-floor, rez-de-chaussée *m.*

ground-plan, plan (*m.*) horizontal

ground-rent, rente foncière *f.*

group, groupe *m.*

grouper, *v.t.* grouper

grouse (game), coq (*m.*) de bruyère

grouse, *v.i.* grogner; rouspéter (*slang*)

grow, *v.i.* croître, pousser, devenir; *v.t.* cultiver

growl, grognement *m.*; grondement *m.*

growl, *v.i.* grogner; gronder

growth, croissance *f.*; accroissement *m.*

grub, larve *f.*; (*slang for food*) mangeaille *f.*, boulot *m.*

grudge, rancune *f.*; malice *f.*

to have or bear a grudge, en vouloir à quelqu'un

gruel, gruau *m.*

gruff, (*adj.*) brusque; renfrogné

grumble, **grunt**, *v.i.* grogner; grommeler (grumble)

grunt, grognement *m.*

guarantee, garant *m.*; garantie *f.*; caution *f.*

guarantee, *v.t.* garantir

guard, garde *f.*; défense *f.*; protection *f.*

guard (railway), chef de train *m.*

guard, *v.i.* se garder, se tenir sur les gardes

guard, *v.t.* garder; défendre; protéger; veiller sur

guardedly, (*adv.*) avec réserve

guardian, gardien(ne) *m.* (*f.*); tuteur *m.* (for minors)

guardianship, tutelle *f.*

guess, *v.i.* and *v.t.* deviner

guess, **guesswork**, conjecture *f.*

guest, hôte *m.*; invité(e) *m.* (*f.*); client(e) *m.* (*f.*)

guidance, conduite *f.*; direction *f.*

guide, guide *m.*; conducteur (-trice) *m.* (*f.*)

guide, *v.t.* conduire; diriger

guide-book, guide *m.*

guide-post, poteau (*m.*) indicateur

guild, corporation *f.*

guildhall, hôtel (*m.*) de ville

guile, artifice *m.*; astuce *f.*

guileful, (*adj.*) astucieux(-euse)

guileless, (*adj.*) sincère

guillotine, guillotine *f.*

guillotine, *v.t.* guillotiner

guilt, culpabilité *f.*; faute *f.*

guiltless, (*adj.*) innocent

guilty, (*adj.*) coupable

guinea, guinée *f.*

guinea-fowl, pintade *f.*

guise, manière *f.*

guitar, guitare *f.*

gulf, golfe *m.*; baie *f.*; (*fig.*) gouffre *m.*; abîme *m.*

gull, mouette *f.*; (*fig.*) dupe *f.*

gullet, gosier *m.*

gullibility, crédulité *f.*

gullible, (*adj.*) crédule

gully, ravin *m.*

gulp, gorgée *f.*

gulp, *v.t.* avaler

gum, gomme *f.*; gencive *f.* (of teeth)

chewing-gum, gomme (*f.*) à mâcher

gum, *v.t.* gommer

gummy, (*adj.*) gommeux(-euse)

gumption, savoir *m.*; esprit *m.*

gun, fusil *m.*; pièce d'artillerie *f.*; canon *m.*

field gun, pièce (*f.*) de campagne

heavy gun, artillerie (*f.*) lourde

gun-barrel, canon (*m.*) de fusil

gun-boat, canonnière *f.*

gun-carriage, affût *m.*

gun-cotton, coton-poudre *m.*

gunmetal, métal (*m.*) à fonte

gunner, canonnier *m.*

gunpowder, poudre (*f.*) à canon

gunsmith, armurier *m.*

gunwale, plat bord *m.*

gurgle, *v.i.* murmurer; faire glouglou

gurgling, glouglou *m.*; murmure *m.*

gurnet, rouget *m.*; grondin *m.*

gush, écoulement *m.*; jaillissement *m.*

gush, *v.i.* jaillir; ruisseler

gushing, (*adj.*) effusif(-ive); empressé (manner); torrentiel(le)

gusset, gousset *m.*

gust, coup de vent *m.*; rafale *f.*; bouffée *f.* (de vent)

gusto, goût *m.*; plaisir *m.*

gusty, (*adj.*) orageux(-euse)

gut, boyau *m.*; intestin *m.*

gut, *v.t.* éventrer

guts, intestins *m. pl.*; cran *m.* (*slang*)

gutta-percha, gutta percha *f.*

gutter, gouttière *f.* (of house); ruisseau *m.* (street); caniveau *m.* (road)

gutter, *v.t.* canneler; *v.i.* couler (of candle)

guttural, (*adj.*) guttural

guy, épouvantail(-aux); (*slang*) type *m.*

guzzle, *v.t.* and *v.i.* bouffer, s'empiffrer

gymnasium, gymnase *m.*

gymnastics, gymnastique *f.*

gypsum, gypse *m.*

gyrate, *v.t.* tourner en rond; tournoyer

gyration, mouvement (*m.*) giratoire

gyves, fers *m. pl.*

H

haberdasher, mercier *m.*; chemisier *m.*

haberdashery, mercerie*f.*; chemiserie *f.*

habit, habitude *f.*

habitable, (*adj.*) habitable

habitation, habitation *f.*

habitual, (*adj.*) habituel(le)

habituate, *v.t.* habituer, accoutumer

habitude, habitude *f.*; coutume *f.*

hack, *v.t.* hacher; couper, tailler en pièces

hack, cheval de louage *m.*; entaille *f.*; écrivain (*m.*) à la tâche

hackney-carriage, voiture (*f.*) de place

haddock, aiglefin *m.*

haft, manche *m.*; poignée *f.*

hag, vieille sorcière *f.*; furie *f.*

haggard, (*adj.*) hagard, égaré

haggle, *v.i.* marchander

hail, grêle *f.*; -**stone,** grêlon *m.*

hail, *v.i.* grêler; *v.t.* saluer, acclamer

hailstone, grêlon *m.*

hair, cheveu *m.*; cheveux *m. pl.*; poil *m.* (of animals); chevelure *f.* (head of hair)

hair-brush, brosse (*f.*) à cheveux

hair-cut, coupe (*f.*) de cheveux

hairdresser, coiffeur *m.*

hairless, (*adj.*) chauve

hair-net, filet (*m.*) à cheveux

hairpin, épingle (*f.*) à cheveux

hairy, (*adj.*) poilu, velu, chevelu

hake, merluche *f.*

halcyon, (*adj.*) serein

hale, robuste, sain, vigoureux (-euse)

half, (*adj.*) demi

half, moitié *f.*; demi(e) *m.* (*f.*)

half, (*adv.*) à demi, à moitié

half-pay, demi-solde *f.*

half-price, moitié prix *m.*

half-way, à mi-chemin

half-witted, sot(te); idiot

half-year, semestre *m.*

half-yearly, (*adv.*) tous les six mois, semestriel(le)

halfpenny, sou *m.*

hall, salle *f.*; vestibule *m.* (entrance-hall)

halloo, *v.i.* crier

hallow, *v.t.* sanctifier, consacrer

halo, halo *m.*; auréole *f.*; nimbe *m.*

halt, halte *f.*

halt, (*adj.*) estropié (lame)

halt, *v.i.* faire halte

halter, corde *f.* (for hanging); licou *m.*

halting-place, halte *f.*

halve, *v.t.* partager en deux

ham, jambon *m.*

hamlet, hameau *m.*

hammer, marteau *m.*

hammer, *v.t.* marteler

hammock, hamac *m.*

hamper, panier *m.*; banne *f.*

hamper, *v.t.* gêner

hamstring, tendon (*m.*) du jarret

hamstring, *v.t.* couper le jarret

hand, main *f.*; écriture *f.* (writing); jeu *m.* (of cards); aiguille *f.* (of watch); ouvrier(-ère) *m.* (*f.*) (factory hand)

hand, *v.t.* donner; passer

hand down, *v.t.* transmettre

hand over, *v.t.* remettre

hand-bag, sac (*m.*) à main; pochette *f.*

hand-book, manuel *m.*

hand-cart, voiture (*f.*) à bras

handcuff, menotte *f.*

handcuff, *v.t.* mettre les menottes

hand gallop, petit galop *m.*

hand-grenade, grenade *f.* (à main)

handicap, handicap *m.*

handicap, *v.t.* handicaper

handicraft, métier (*m.*) manuel

handily, (*adv.*) adroitement

handiness, adresse *f.*; dextérité *f.*

handiwork, ouvrage *m.*; travail *m.*

handkerchief, mouchoir *m.*

handle, manche *m.*; bouton *m.* (of door)

starting-handle, manivelle (*f.*) de mise en marche

handle, *v.t.* manier; traiter (a deal, case, etc.)

handling, maniement *m.*

handmaid, servante *f.*; soubrette *f.*

handrail, rampe *f.*

handsome, (*adj.*) beau (belle); joli

handy, (*adj.*) adroit, commode

hang, *v.t.* pendre; suspendre; s'accrocher (à); baisser (the head)

hang, *v.i.* être suspendu; pendre

hang-dog look, mine patibulaire *f.*

hanger-on, parasite *m.* or *f.*

hanging, suspension *f.*; pendaison *f.* (execution)

hangings, tenture *f.*

hangman, bourreau *m.*

hanker, *v.i.* soupirer après

happen, *v.i.* arriver, advenir, se passer

happily, (*adv.*) heureusement, par bonheur

happiness, bonheur *m.*

happy, (*adj.*) heureux(-euse), content

harangue, harangue *f.*

harangue, *v.t.* haranguer

harass, *v.i.* harceler

harassing fire, feu (*m.*) harcelant

harbour, port; (*fig.*) asile *m.*

harbour, *v.t.* héberger; donner asile à

harbour-dues, droits de mouillage *m. pl.*

harbour-master, capitaine du port *m.*

hard, (*adj.*) dur; ferme; rude (weather)

hard-earned, (*adj.*) péniblement gagné

hard-featured, (*adj.*) aux traits durs

hard-hearted, (*adj.*) inhumain, insensible

hard-working, laborieux(-euse)

harden, *v.t.* durcir; rendre dur; tremper (steel)

harden, *v.i.* devenir dur; s'endurcir

hardihood, audace *f.*

hardiness, tempérament (*m.*) robuste

hardly, (adv.) à peine; ne...
guère (scarcely); difficilement
hardness, dureté f.; rigueur f.
hardship, peine f.; privation f.;
souffrance f.
hardware, quincaillerie f.
hardy, (adj.) fort, robuste
hare, lièvre m.
hare-brained, (adj.) étourdi
jugged hare, civet (m.) de lièvre
hark! écoutez!
harlot, prostituée f.
harm, tort m.; dommage m.;
mal m.
harm, v.t. faire du mal
harmless, (adj.) innocent, in-
offensif(-ive)
harmonious, harmonieux(-euse)
harmonise, v.i. s'accorder; v.t.
harmoniser
harmony, harmonie f.; accord m.
harness, harnais m.
harness, v.t. harnacher, atteler
(to something)
harp, harpe f.
harrow, herse f.
harrow, v.t. herser
harrowing, navrant (i.e. to the
feelings)
harry, v.t. harceler
harsh, (adj.) âpre; rude; sévère
hart, cerf m.
harvest, moisson f.; récolte f.
harvest, v.t. récolter; moissonner
hash, hachis m.
hash, v.t. hacher
make a hash of, gâcher (i.e.
spoil)
haste, hâte f.; précipitation f.
haste, v.t. hâter; dépêcher; avancer
hasten, v.i. se hâter, se dépêcher
(make haste)
hastily, (adv.) brusquement; à la
hâte
hastiness, précipitation f.; em-
portement m.; vivacité f.
hasty, (adj.) précipité, rapide;
vif (temper)
hat, chapeau m.
bowler-hat, chapeau melon
soft-hat, chapeau mou
top-hat, chapeau haut de forme

hat-maker, hatter, chapelier m.
hat-stand, porte-chapeaux m.
hatch, couvée f. (of chickens);
éclosion f. (of eggs)
hatch, couver; faire éclore
hatches, écoutilles f. pl. (naut.)
hate, haine f.
hate, v.t. haïr; détester
hateful, (adj.) odieux(-euse);
détestable
hatred, haine f.
haughtiness, hauteur f.; arrogance f.
haughty, (adj.) hautain, arrogant
haulage, camionnage m.
haulier, camionneur m.
haunt, v.t. hanter, fréquenter
have (v. aux.), avoir; v.t. avoir,
posséder
haversack, havresac m.
havoc, ravage m.
hawk, faucon m.
hawker, colporteur m.; camelot
m.
hawser, amarre f.
hawthorn, aubépine f.
hay, foin m.
haymaking, fenaison f.
hay-rick, hay-stack, meule (f.)
de foin
hazard, hasard m.
hazard, v.t. risquer
hazardous, hasardeux(-euse)
haze, brume f. (mist)
hazel-nut, noisette f.
hazy, brumeux(-euse); vague
he, (pron.) il; lui
head, tête f.; chef m.
head, v.t. se mettre à la tête de;
diriger
head, (adj.) principal, en chef
head-ache, mal (m.) de tête
head-dress, coiffure f.
headland, promontoire m.
head-light, phare m.
headline, manchette f.
headlong, (adj.) précipité
head-master, principal m.
headquarters, quartier-général
m.
headstrong, (adj.) opiniâtre,
entêté
headway, progrès m.

heal, *v.t.* guérir; *v.i.* se guérir

healing, (*adj.*) curatif(-ive)

healing, guérison *f.*

health, santé *f.*; salubrité *f.* (of place)

healthily, (*adv.*) sainement, en santé

healthiness, salubrité *f.*

healthy, (*adj.*) sain, salubre

heap, tas *m.*; amas *m.*; monceau *m.*

heap, *v.t.* entasser

hear, *v.t.* entendre, entendre dire; apprendre (learn)

hearer, auditeur *m.*

hearing, ouïe *f.*; audition *f.* (of witnesses)

hearsay, ouï-dire *m.*

hearse, corbillard *m.*

heart, cœur *m.*; courage *m.*

at heart, au fond

by heart, par cœur

heart-ache, chagrin *m.*

heart-break, crève-cœur *m.*

heart-breaking, (*adj.*) navrant

hearten, *v.t.* encourager

heartily, (*adv.*) cordialement

heartiness, cordialité *f.*; vigueur *f.* (appetite)

heartless, (*adj.*) sans pitié, cruel (-le)

heartlessness, cruauté *f.*

hearty, (*adj.*) cordial, sincère; bon (of meals)

heat, chaleur *f.*; ardeur *f.*; épreuve *f.* (race)

heat, *v.t.* chauffer, échauffer

heater, appareil (*m.*) de chauffage; réchaud *m.*

heath, bruyère *f.*; lande *f.*

heathen, (*adj.*) païen(ne)

heather, brande *f.*; bruyère *f.*

heaven, ciel *m.* (*pl.* cieux)

heavenly, (*adj.*) céleste

heaviness, lourdeur *f.*

heavy, (*adj.*) lourd, pesant

Hebrew, Hébreu *m.*; hébraïque

hectic, (*adj.*) hectique

hedge, haie *f.*

hedge, *v.i.* parier pour et contre

hedge in, *v.t.* enfermer

hedgehog, hérisson *m.*

heed, soin *m*

heed, *v.t.* prendre garde à

heedless, (*adj.*) étourdi

heel, talon *m.*

to show a clean pair of heels, montrer les talons

height, hauteur *f.*; élévation *f.*; taille *f.* (of person)

heighten, *v.t.* surélever, augmenter

heir, héritier *m.*

heiress, héritière *f.*

helicopter, hélicoptère *m.*

hell, enfer *m.*

gambling hell, tripot *m.*

hellish, (*adj.*) infernal

hello, allô (telephone)

helm, gouvernail *m.*

helmet, casque *m.*

help, secours *m.*; aide *f.*; assistance *f.*

help, *v.t.* aider; assister; secourir; venir en aide à

helper, aide *m.* and *f.*

helpful, (*adj.*) utile, serviable

helpless, (*adj.*) faible, impuissant

helpmate, aide *m.* and *f.*

hem, ourlet *m.*

hem, *v.t.* ourler

hemisphere, hémisphère *m.*

hemorrhage, hémorrhagie *f.*

hemorrhoids, hémorrhoïdes *f. pl.*

hemp, chanvre *m.*

hen, poule *f.*

hen-house, poulailler *m.*

hen-roost, juchoir *m.*

hence, (*adv.*) d'ici; de là

henceforth, **henceforward**, (*adv.*) désormais

her, (*pron.*) elle, la; (*adj.*) son, sa, ses

herb, herbe *f.*

sweet herbs, fines herbes *f. pl.*

herbalist, herboriste *m.* and *f.*

herd, troupeau *m.*; troupe *f.*

here, ici, voici

hereabout(s), (*adv.*) près d'ici

hereafter, (*adv.*) ci-après, désormais

hereby, (*adv.*) par ces présentes (*legal*); par ce moyen

hereditary, (*adj.*) héréditaire

hereupon, (*adv.*) là-dessus; sur ce

herewith, (*adv.*) ci-joint
heritage, héritage *m.*
hermetic, (*adj.*) hermétiqu
hermit, ermite *m.*
hermitage, ermitage *m.*
hernia, hernie *f.*
hero, (le) héros *m.*
heroic, héroïque
heroine, (l')héroïne *f.*
heroism, héroïsme *m.*
heron, héron *m.*
herring, hareng *m.*
hers, (*pron.*) le sien *m.*; la sienne *f.*; les siens *m. pl.*; les siennes *f. pl.*
herself, (*pron.*) elle-même, elle; soi-même
by herself, (*pron.*) toute seule
hesitancy, hésitation *f.*
hesitate, *v.i.* hésiter
hesitating, (*adj.*) hésitant
hew, *v.t.* couper, tailler
hibernate, *v.i.* hiverner
hiccough, hoquet *m.*
hickory, noyer américain *m.*
hidden, (*adj.*) caché, secret(-ète)
hide, peau *f.*; cuir *m.* (leather)
hide-bound, (*adj.*) à l'esprit étroit; bigot
hide, *v.t.* cacher; *v.i.* se cacher
hide-and-seek, cache-cache *m.*
hideous, (*adj.*) hideux(-euse); affreux(-euse)
hiding, raclée *f.* (a thrashing)
hiding-place, cachette *f.*
high, (*adj.*) haut, élevé
high-born, de haute naissance
highland, pays montagneux
highlander, montagnard écossais *m.*
highness, hauteur *f.*
highness (title), Altesse *f.*
highway, grande route *or* grand'-route *f.*; chemin (*m.*) de grande communication
highwayman, voleur (*m.*) de grand chemin
hilarity, gaieté *f.*, hilarité *f.*
hill, colline *f.*; coteau *m.*; côte *f*
hillock, monticule *m.*
hilly, (*adj.*) montagneux(-euse)
hilt, poignée *f.*
hind, (*adj.*) de derrière, arrière

hind, biche *f.* (deer)
hinder, *v.t.* empêcher, gêner, retarder
hinge, charnière *f.*; pivot *m.*
hint, suggestion *f.*; insinuation *f.*; allusion *f.*
hint, *v.i.* insinuer; faire allusion à; suggérer
hip, hanche *f.*; églantine *f.* (fruit)
hippopotamus, hippopotame *m.*
hire, louage *m.*; gages *m. pl.*
hire, *v.t.* louer; engager; employer
his, (*poss. adj.*) son, sa, ses
hiss, *v.i.* and *v.t.* siffler
hiss, sifflement *m.*
hissing, sifflement *m.*
historian, historien *m.*
historic(al), historique
history, histoire *f.*
hit, coup *m.* (blow); succès *m.* (theatre piece, etc.)
hit, *v.t.* frapper, heurter; atteindre (the mark)
hitch, *v.t.* accrocher; attacher
hitch, obstacle *m.*, anicroche *f.*
hitch-hike, *v.i.* faire de l'autostop
hither, (*adv.*) ici, y
hitherto, (*adv.*) jusqu'ici
hive, ruche *f.*
hoar-frost, gelée blanche *f.*
hoard, *v.t.* amasser; accumuler
hoard, magot *m.*; monceau *m.*
hoarse, (*adj.*) rauque, enroué
hoarseness, enrouement *m.*
hoary, (*adj.*) blanchi; aux cheveux gris
hoax, mauvaise plaisanterie *f.*; mystification *f.*
hobble, *v.i.* clopiner
hobby, marotte *f.*
hobby-horse, dada *m.*
hock, vin du Rhin *m.*; jarret *m.* (of a horse)
hoe, *v.t.* houer, sarcler
hoe, houe *f.*
hog, cochon *m.*; porc *m.*
hoggishness, gloutonnerie *f.*; grossièreté *f.*
hoist, *v.t.* hisser
hold, prise *f.*; appui *m.*; soutien *m.*
hold, *v.t.* tenir, retenir; détenir;

contenir (contain); occuper (to have or occupy)

hold, *v.i.* se maintenir; durer

hold back, *v.t.* retenir; *v.i.* rester en arrière

hold fast, tenir bon

hold forth, *v.i.* pérorer

hold good, *v.i.* être valable

hold on, *v.i.* tenir ferme, tenir bon

hold out, *v.i.* tenir bon; *v.t.* tendre (hand, etc.)

hold up, *v.t.* soutenir; arrêter

take hold of, *v.t.* saisir

hole, trou *m.*; ouverture *f.*

hole, *v.t.* trouer

holiday, fête *f.*; jour de fête *m.*; congé *m.*

holidays, vacances *f. pl.*

holiness, sainteté *f.*

hollow, (*adj.*) creux (*f.* creuse)

hollow, creux *m.* (of hand); cavité *f.*

hollow, *v.t.* creuser

holly, houx *m.*

holy, (*adj.*) saint

Holy Land, Terre sainte *f.*

homage, hommage *m.*

home, maison *f.*; foyer domestique *m.*; logis *m.*; (*fig.*) demeure *f.*

at home, chez soi

home-bred, (*adj.*) du pays

home-grown, (*adj.*) indigène

home rule, autonomie *f.*

homeliness, simplicité *f.*

homely, simple

homesick, (*adj.*) qui a le mal du pays

homesickness, nostalgie *f.*

homeward(s), (*adv.*) de retour, vers la maison

homework, devoirs (*m. pl.*) du soir

homicidal, (*adj.*) meurtrier(-ère)

homicide, homicide *m.*

honest, (*adj.*) honnête, loyal, sincère

honesty, honnêteté *f.*; loyauté *f.*; sincérité *f.*

honey, miel *m.*

honeycomb, rayon (*m.*) de miel

honeymoon, lune (*f.*) de miel

honeysuckle, chèvrefeuille *m.*

honorary, (*adj.*) honoraire

honour, honneur *m.*

honour, *v.t.* honorer

honourable, (*adj.*) honorable

hood, coiffe *f.*; capuchon *m.*; capote *f.* (of car)

hoof, sabot *m.*

hook, crochet *m.*; hameçon *m.* (fish-hook)

hook, *v.t.* agrafer

hook-nose, nez (*m.*) crochu

hooked, (*adj.*) crochu, recourbé

hooligan, voyou *m.*

hoop, cercle *m.*; cerceau *m.*

hoot, *v.t.* huer; *v.i.* corner (to sound motor-horn)

hoot, hooting, huée *f.*

hop, saut *m.*

hop, *v.i.* sauter, sautiller

hope, espérance *f.*; espoir *m.*; attente *f.*

hope, *v.i.* espérer

hopeful, (*adj.*) plein d'espérance

hopefully, avec espoir

hopeless, sans espoir; inutile

hopelessness, désespoir *m.*

hops, houblon *m.*

horizon, horizon *m.*

horn, corne *f.*; cor *m.*

hornet, frelon *m.*

horrible, horrible, affreux(-euse)

horrid, affreux(-euse), horrible

horror, horreur *f.*

horse, cheval *m.*

horse-artillery, artillerie (*f.*) à cheval

horseback, à cheval

horse-box, wagon (*m.*) à chevaux

horse-coper, maquignon *m.*

horse-doctor, vétérinaire *m.*

horseman, cavalier *m.*

horsemanship, équitation *f.*

horse-power, cheval-vapeur *m.* (*abbrev.* c.v.)

horse-race, course (*f.*) de chevaux

horse-radish, raifort *m.*

horse-shoe, fer (*m.*) à cheval

horse-whip, *v.t.* cravacher

horticulture, horticulture *f.*

hose, hose-pipe, manche (*f.*) à eau, tuyau *m.*

hosier, bonnetier et chemisier *m.*

hosiery, bonneterie et lingerie *f.*

hospitable, hospitalier(-ère)
hospital, hôpital; infirmerie *f.*
hospital nurse, infirmière *f.*
hospitality, hospitalité *f.*
host, hôte *m.*; aubergiste *m.*; hostie *f.* (Roman Catholic)
hostile, (*adj.*) hostile
hot, (*adj.*) chaud; ardent; brûlant; violent (temper)
hot-bed, couche *f.*
hot-blooded, (*adj.*) passionné
hot-house, serre chaude *f.*
hotly, (*adv.*) chaudement; avec chaleur
hotness, chaleur *f.*; passion *f.*
hot-water bottle, bouillotte *f.*
hotel, hôtel *m.*
private hotel, hôtel de famille
hotel-keeper, hôtelier(-ère) *m.* (*f.*)
hound, chien (*m.*) de meute
hound, *v.t.* traquer, poursuivre
hour, heure *f.*
an hour ago, il y a une heure
hourly, (*adj.* and *adv.*) d'heure en heure; à chaque heure
hour-glass, sablier *m.*
house, maison *f.*; logis *m.*; habitation *f.*; ménage *m.* (household); famille *f.* (family)
house, *v.t.* loger, héberger
house-agent, agent (*m.*) de location; agent immobilier *m.*
household, ménage *m.*
housekeeper, femme (*f.*) de charge; ménagère *f* (housewife)
housekeeping, ménage *m.*
housemaid, femme (*f.*) de chambre, bonne
house-porter, concierge *m.*
house-rent, loyer *m.*
hovel, taudis *m.*
hovercraft, aéroglisseur *m.*
how, (*adv.*) comment, comme
how much, combien
however, (*conj.*) cependant, pourtant
however, (*adv.*) de quelque manière que; quelque... que
however that may be, quoi qu'il en soit
howl, *v.i.* hurler, crier
howl, hurlement *m.*; cri *m.*

howling, hurlement *m.*; mugissement *m.*; grondement *m.* (of the sea)
hubbub, vacarme *m.*
huddle, *v.i.* se coudoyer, se tasser
hue, couleur *f.*
hug, *v.t.* embrasser, serrer
huge, (*adj.*) énorme
hull, coque *f.* (of a ship)
hulk, carcasse *f.* (of a ship)
hum, *v.i.* and *v.t.* fredonner, bourdonner (of bees, etc.)
hum, humming, bourdonnement *m.*
human, (*adj.*) humain
humane, humain, compatissant
humanity, humanité *f.*
humble, (*adj.*) humble
humble, *v.t.* humilier
humbug, blague *f.*; farce *f.*
humdrum, (*adj.*) ennuyeux (-euse); banal
humid, (*adj.*) humide
humidity, humidité *f.*
humiliate, *v.t.* humilier
humming-bird, colibri *m.*
humorist, humoriste *m.*
humorous, (*adj.*) plaisant
humour, humeur *f.*; disposition *f.*; plaisanterie *f.*
hump, bosse *f.*
humpback, bossu(e) *m.* (*f.*)
hunch, miche *f.* (of bread); bosse *f.* (on back)
hunchback, bossu(e) *m.* (*f*)
hundred, (*adj.* and *m.*) cent
about a hundred, une centaine
hundredfold, centuple
hundredweight, quintal *m.*
Hungarian, (*adj.*) and *m.* (*f*) hongrois(e)
hunger, faim *f.*
hunger, *v.i.* avoir faim
hungrily, (*adv.*) avidement
hungry, (*adj.*) affamé
hunt, *v.t.* chasser; poursuivre; chercher
hunt, *v.i.* chasser; aller à la chasse
hunter, chasseur; cheval (*m.*) de chasse
hunting, chasse *f.*

huntsman, chasseur *m.*; veneur *m.*

hurdle, claie *f.*

hurdle-race, course de haies *f.*

hurdy-gurdy, vielle *f.*

hurl, *v.t.* lancer, jeter

hurricane, ouragan *m.*

hurried, (*adj.*) précipité, pressé

hurriedly, précipitamment

hurry, hâte *f.*; précipitation *f.*

hurry, *v.i.* se hâter; se dépêcher; se presser; *v.t.* hâter, presser

hurt, mal *m.*; blessure *f.*; tort *m.*

hurt, *v.t.* faire mal à; nuire à; blesser

hurt, *v.i.* faire du mal

hurtful, (*adj.*) nuisible

husband, mari *m.*; époux *m.*

husbandry, agriculture *f.*

hush, *v.t.* faire taire

hush! (*interj.*) taisez-vous! silence! chut!

husk, cosse *f.*; gousse *f.*

husk, *v.t.* écorcer, écosser

huskiness, enrouement *m.*

husky, (*adj.*) rauque

hussy, coquine *f.*; friponne *f.*

hustle, *v.t.* bousculer, presser

hut, hutte *f.*; baraque *f.*

huts, (*mil.*) baraquements *m. pl.*

hutch, huche *f.*

hyacinth, jacinthe *f.*

hybrid, hybride *m.*

hydrant, prise (*f.*) d'eau

fire hydrant, bouche (*f.*) d'incendie

hydraulic, (*adj.*) hydraulique

hydraulics, hydraulique *f.*

hydrogen, hydrogène *m.*

hydroplane, hydravion *m.*

hyena, hyène *f.*

hygiene, hygiène *f.*

hymn, hymne *m.*

hyperbole, hyperbole *f.*

hyphen, trait (*m.*) d'union

hypnotic, (*adj.*) hypnotique

hypnotism, hypnotisme *m.*

hypocrisy, hypocrisie *f.*

hypocrite, hypocrite *m.* and *f.*

hypocritical, (*adj.*) hypocrite

hypothesis, hypothèse *f.*

hysterical, (*adj.*) hystérique

I

I, (*pron.*) je, moi

iambic, (*adj.*) ïambique

iberian, ibérien(ne)

ibex, bouquetin *m.*; ibex *m.*

ice, glace *f.*

ice, *v.t.* glacer; frapper (wine, etc.)

iceberg, montagne de glace *f.*; iceberg *m.*

icebound, cerné par les glaces

ice-box (*or* **safe**), glacière *f.*

Icelandic, (*adj.*) islandais

icicle, glaçon *m.*

iciness, froid glacial *m.*

icing, glacé *m.*; frappage *m.*

icy, (*adj.*) glacé, glacial

idea, idée *f.*

ideal, (*adj.*) idéal; idéal *m.*

idealism, idéalisme *m.*

identical, (*adj.*) identique

identify, *v.t.* identifier, reconnaître

identity, identité *f.*

identity papers, pièces (*f.*) d'identité

identity disk, plaque (*f.*) d'identité

idiocy, idiotie *f.*

idiom, idiome *m.*; idiotisme *m.*

idiot, idiot(e) *m.* (*f.*); imbécile *m.* and *f.*

idiotic, (*adj.*) idiot(e)

idle, (*adj.*) paresseux(-euse), oisif(-ive); en chomâge (out of work)

idle, *v.i.* faire le paresseux; fainéanter

idleness, paresse *f.*; oisiveté *f.*

idler, fainéant(e) *m.* (*f.*); paresseux(-euse) *m.* (*f.*)

idol, idole *f.*

idolatrous, (*adj.*) idolâtre

idolatry, idolâtrie *f.*

idolise, *v.t.* idolâtrer

idyll, idylle *f.*

i.e., c'est-à-dire

if, (*conj.*) si; quand, quand même

if necessary, s'il (le) faut; au besoin

if not, sinon

ignoble, (*adj.*) ignoble, vil

ignominious, (*adj.*) ignominieux (-euse)

ignominy, ignominie *f.*

ignoramus, ignorant(e) *m.* (*f.*)

ignorance, ignorance *f.*

ignorant, (*adj.*) ignorant

ignore, *v.t.* ne tenir aucun compte de; ne pas vouloir connaître (person)

ill, (*adj.*) mauvais, malade, souffrant

ill, (*adv.*) mal

ill, mal *m.*

ill-bred, (*adj.*) mal élevé

ill-doing, mauvaise action *f.*

ill-favoured, (*adj.*) laid

ill-mannered, (*adj.*) mal élevé

ill-nature, méchanceté *f.*

ill-starred, (*adj.*) de mauvais augure; néfaste

ill-treat, *v.t.* maltraiter

ill-will, rancune *f.*

illegal, (*adj.*) illégal, illicite

illegality, illégalité *f.*

illegible, (*adj.*) illisible

illegitimacy, illégitimité *f.*

illegitimate, (*adj.*) illégitime

illicit, (*adj.*) illicite; défendu

illiterate, (*adj.*) illettré; ignorant

illness, maladie *f.*; indisposition *f.*

illogical, (*adj.*) illogique

illuminate, *v.t.* illuminer; éclairer

illumination, illumination *f.*

illusion, illusion *f.*

illusive, (*adj.*) illusoire

illustrate, *v.t.* illustrer; (*fig.*) expliquer, éclaircir

illustration, illustration *f.*; explication *f.*; éclaircissement *m.*; gravure *f.*

illustrious, (*adj.*) illustre; célèbre

image, image *f.*; (*fig.*) portrait *m.*

imagery, images *f. pl.*

imaginable, (*adj.*) imaginable

imagination, imagination *f.*

imaginative, imaginatif(-ive)

imagine, *v.t.* se figurer; imaginer; concevoir

imbecile, (*adj.*) idiot, imbécile

imbecile, imbécile *m.* and *f.*

imbecility, imbécilité *f.*

imbibe, *v.t.* absorber

imbue, *v.t.* imprégner

imitate, *v.t.* imiter

imitation, imitation *f.*; contrefaçon *f.* (*commer.*)

imitative, (*adj.*) imitatif(-ive)

imitator, imitateur(-trice) *m.* (*f.*)

immaculate, (*adj.*) immaculé, impeccable

immaterial, (*adj.*) immatériel(le)

immature, (*adj.*) pas mûr; prématuré

immaturely, (*adv.*) prématurément; avant la maturité

immeasurable, (*adj.*) immense; incommensurable

immediate, (*adj.*) immédiat, urgent

immemorial, (*adj.*) immémorial

immense, (*adj.*) immense

immensely, (*adv.*) immensément; énormément

immensity, immensité *f.*

immerse, *v.t.* plonger, immerger

immigrant, immigrant(e) *m.* (*f.*); immigré(e) *m.* (*f.*)

immigrate, *v.i.* immigrer

imminence, imminence *f.*

imminent, (*adj.*) imminent

immobilise, *v.t.* immobiliser

immobility, immobilité *f.*

immoderate, (*adj.*) excessif(-ive); immodéré

immodest, (*adj.*) immodeste, impudique

immolate, *v.t.* immoler

immoral, (*adj.*) immoral

immorality, immoralité *f.*

immortal, (*adj.*) immortel(le)

immortality, immortalité *f.*

immovable, (*adj.*) fixe; inébranlable

immunity, exemption *f.*, immunité *f.*

imp, petit drôle *m.*; diablotin *m.*

impact, choc *m.*

impair, *v.t.* détériorer, abîmer (of health)

impart, *v.t.* communiquer; faire connaître

impartial, (*adj.*) impartial, désintéressé

impartiality, impartialité *f.*

impassable, (*adj.*) impraticable, infranchissable

impassioned, (*adj.*) passionné

impassive, (*adj.*) impassible

impatience, impatience *f.*

impatient, (*adj.*) impatient

to grow impatient, *v.i.* s'impatienter

impeach, *v.t.* mettre en accusation

impeachment, accusation *f.*

impeccable, (*adj.*) impeccable

impecuniosity, manque (*m.*) d'argent

impecunious, besogneux(-euse)

impede, *v.t.* empêcher; gêner

impediment, empêchement *m.*; obstacle *m.*

impel, *v.t.* pousser, forcer

impend, *v.i.* être imminent

impending, (*adj.*) imminent

impenetrable, (*adj.*) impénétrable

impenitence, impénitence *f.*

imperceptible, (*adj.*) imperceptible

imperfect, (*adj.*) imparfait, incomplet(-ète)

imperfection, imperfection *f.*

imperial, (*adj.*) impérial; (*fig.*) majestueux

imperialism, impérialisme *m.*

imperious, (*adj.*) impérieux (-euse)

impermeable, (*adj.*) imperméable

impersonal, (*adj.*) impersonnel(le)

impersonate, *v.t.* personnifier; se faire passer pour

impertinence, impertinence *f.*; insolence *f.*

impertinent, (*adj.*) impertinent, insolent

impetuous, (*adj.*) impétueux (-euse)

impetuousness, impétuosité *f.*

impetus, impulsion *f.*; élan *m.*

impious, (*adj.*) impie

impish, (*adj.*) de diablotin

implacable, (*adj.*) implacable

implement, outil *m.*; ustensile *m.*

implement, *v.t.* exécuter

implication, insinuation *f*

implicit, (*adj.*) implicite

implore, *v.t.* implorer, supplier

imply, *v.t.* impliquer; vouloir dire

impolite, (*adj.*) impoli

import, portée *f.*; signification *f.*; sens *m.*; importation *f.* (*commer.*)

import, *v.t.* importer

import duty, droit (*m.*) d'entrée

importance, importance *f.*

important, (*adj.*) important

importer, importateur *m.*

importunate, (*adj.*) importun

importune, *v.t.* importuner

impose, *v.t.* imposer; *v.i.* en imposer à (to impose on someone)

imposition, impôt *m.* (taxes); pensum *m.* (school task); imposition *f.*

impossibility, impossibilité *f.*; chose (*f.*) impossible

impossible, (*adj.*) impossible

impostor, imposteur *m.*

impotence, impuissance *f.*

impotent, (*adj.*) impuissant

impoverish, *v.t.* appauvrir

impracticable, (*adj.*) impraticable

impregnable, (*adj.*) imprenable

impregnate, *v.t.* imprégner

impress, empreinte *f.*

impress, *v.t.* imprimer; impressionner (someone)

impression, impression *f.*; tirage *m.* (of book, etc.)

impressionable, (*adj.*) impressionnable

impressive, (*adj.*) impressionnant; frappant

imprint, *v.t.* imprimer; empreindre

imprison, *v.t.* emprisonner

imprisonment, emprisonnement *m.*

improbable, (*adj.*) improbable; invraisemblable

improbability, improbabilité *f.*

improper, (*adj.*) inconvenant, peu convenable

improve, *v.i.* se perfectionner, s'améliorer; faire des progrès

improve, *v.t.* améliorer

improvement, amélioration *f.*; progrès *m.*

improvidence, imprévoyance *f.*

improvise, *v.t.* improviser

imprudence, imprudence *f.*

imprudent, (*adj.*) imprudent

impudence, impudence *f.*; effronterie *f.*

impudent, (*adj.*) impudent, effronté

impulse, impulsion *f.*

impulsive, (*adj.*) impulsif(-ive)

impunity, impunité *f.*

impure, (*adj.*) impur

impute, *v.t.* imputer

in, (*prep.*) en; dans; à, chez (at someone's house); parmi (among)

in, (*adv.*) dedans, au dedans; chez soi, à la maison, y

inability, impuissance *f.*; incapacité *f.*

inaccessible, (*adj.*) inabordable

inaccuracy, inexactitude *f.*

inaccurate, (*adj.*) inexact

inaction, inaction *f.*; repos *m.*

inactive, (*adj.*) inactif(-ive)

inadequacy, insuffisance *f.*

inadequate, (*adj.*) insuffisant

inadmissible, (*adj.*) inadmissible

inanimate, inanimé, mort

inasmuch, (*adv.*) vu que

inattentive, (*adj.*) inattentif(-ive)

inaudible, (*adj.*) qu'on ne peut entendre, imperceptible

inaugurate, *v.t.* inaugurer

inauguration, inauguration *f.*

inborn, (*adj.*) inné

incalculable, (*adj.*) incalculable

incapable, (*adj.*) incapable

incapability, incapacité *f.*

incarcerate, *v.t.* incarcérer

incarnate, (*adj.*) incarné

incautious, (*adj.*) imprudent

incendiary, (*adj.*) incendiaire; incendiaire *m.*

incense, encens *m.*

incense, *v.t.* irriter, exaspérer

incentive, stimulant *m.*

incessant, continuel(le); incessant

inch, pouce *m.* (about 2½ centimetres)

incident, incident *m.*; événement *m.*

incipient, naissant

incise, *v.t.* inciser

incision, incision *f.*

incite, *v.t.* exciter, encourager

inclemency, inclémence *f.*; rigueur *f.* (weather)

inclement, inclément, rigoureux (-euse)

inclination, pente *f.*, inclinaison *f.* (slope); inclination *f.* (of head); penchant *m.* (liking for)

incline, *v.t.* and *v.i.* incliner; *v.i.* être porté (à)

incline, pente *f.*

include, *v.t.* comprendre, renfermer

included, (*adj.*) y compris

including, inclusive, comprenant, y compris

inclusion, inclusion *f.*

incoherent, (*adj.*) incohérent

incombustible, (*adj.*) incombustible

income tax, impôt (*m.*) sur le revenu

incommode, *v.t.* incommoder

incomparable, (*adj.*) incomparable

incompatibility, incompatibilité *f.*

incompatible, (*adj.*) incompatible

incomplete, (*adj.*) imparfait, inachevé, incomplet(-ète)

inconceivable, (*adj.*) inconcevable

inconclusive, (*adj.*) inconcluant

incongruous, (*adj.*) incongru

inconsiderable, (*adj.*) peu considérable

inconsiderate, (*adj.*) inconsidéré

inconsistent, (*adj.*) incompatible (avec); contradictoire

inconsolable, (*adj.*) inconsolable

inconstant, (*adj.*) inconstant; peu conforme

incontestable, (*adj.*) incontestable

inconvenience, inconvénient *m.*; dérangement *m.*; embarras *m.*; incommodité *f.*

inconvenience, *v.t.* déranger; incommoder; gêner

inconvenient, *(adj.)* incommode, gênant

incorporate, *v.t.* incorporer

incorrect, *(adj.)* incorrect, inexact

incorrectly, *(adv.)* incorrectement, inexactement

incorrigible, *(adj.)* incorrigible

incorruptible, *(adj.)* incorruptible

increase, accroissement *m.*; augmentation *f.*

increase, *v.i.* augmenter; croître; s'accroître; *v.t.* augmenter

increasing, *(adj.)* croissant

incredible, *(adj.)* incroyable

incredulous, *(adj.)* incrédule

incriminate, *v.t.* inculper, incriminer

incriminating documents, pièces *(f. pl.)* à conviction

incumbent, *(adj.)* imposé, obligatoire

incumbent, bénéficiaire *m.*

incur, *v.t.* encourir; contracter (debts)

incurable, *(adj.)* inguérissable

indebted, *(adj.)* redevable (à)

indecency, indécence *f.*

indecent, *(adj.)* indécent

indecisive, *(adj.)* indécis (of person); peu concluant

indeed, *(adv.)* en effet; en vérité; vraiment

indefatigable, infatigable

indefinite, indéfini

indelible, ineffaçable, indélébile

indemnify, *v.t.* indemniser, dédommager

indemnity, indemnité *f.*; dédommagement *m.*

indent, *v.t.* denteler (to notch or jag); réquisitionner

indentation, dentelure *f.*

indenture, contrat *(m.)* d'apprentissage

independence, indépendance *f.*

independent, *(adj.)* indépendant; libre

indescribable, *(adj.)* indescriptible

indestructible, *(adj.)* indestructible

indeterminate, *(adj.)* indéterminé

index, table *(f.)* des matières (books); index *(m.)* (finger); aiguille *f.* (hand of watch)

india paper, papier *(m.)* de Chine

indiarubber, gomme *(f.)* à effacer; caoutchouc *m.*

Indian, *(adj.)* indien(ne)

Indian corn, maïs *m.*

indicate, *v.t.* indiquer

indication, indication *f.*; signe *m.*

indicator, indicateur *m.*

indict, *v.t.* accuser, inculper

indifference, indifférence *f.*

indifferent, *(adj.)* indifférent; médiocre

indigestible, *(adj.)* difficile à digérer; indigeste

indigestion, indigestion *f.*

indignant, *(adj.)* indigné; plein d'indignation

indignation, indignation *f.*

indigo, indigo *m.*

indirect, *(adj.)* indirect

indiscreet, *(adj.)* indiscret(-ète)

indispensable, *(adj.)* indispensable

indispose, *v.t.* indisposer (contre); déranger

indisposed, indisposé, souffrant

indisposition, indisposition *f.*

indistinct, indistinct; vague

individual, *(adj.)* individuel; particulier(-ère)

individual, individu *m.*; particulier(-ère) *m.* *(f.)*

indolence, indolence *f.*; paresse *f.*

indolent, *(adj.)* indolent; paresseux(-euse)

indomitable, *(adj.)* indomptable

indoors, à (dans) la maison

indubitable, *(adj.)* incontestable

induce, *v.t.* décider, persuader; induire *(electric.)*

indulge, *v.i.* se livrer (à), s'abandonner (à); *v.t.* gâter

indulgence, indulgence *f.*

indulgent, *(adj.)* complaisant; indulgent

industrial, (*adj.*) industriel(le)
industrialist, industriel *m.*
industrious, (*adj.*) diligent, laborieux(-euse)
industry, industrie *f.* (manufacture); diligence *f.*; travail *m.*
inebriate, *v.t.* enivrer
inebriating, (*adj.*) enivrant
ineffective, (*adj.*) sans effet, inefficace
ineffectual, (*adj.*) inutile, inefficace
inefficiency, incapacité *f.*
inefficient, (*adj.*) incapable, inefficace
inequality, inégalité *f*
inert, (*adj.*) inerte
inertia, force (*f.*) d'inertie
inestimable, (*adj.*) incalculable; inestimable
inevitable, (*adj.*) inévitable
inexcusable, (*adj.*) inexcusable
inexhaustible, (*adj.*) inépuisable
inexorable, (*adj.*) inexorable
inexpensive, (*adj.*) pas cher (chère); (à) bon marché
inexperienced, (*adj.*) sans expérience, inexpérimenté
inexplicable, (*adj.*) inexplicable
inexpressible, (*adj.*) inexprimable
infallibility, infaillibilité *f.*
infallible, (*adj.*) infaillible
infamous, infâme, honteux(-euse)
infamy, infamie *f.*
infancy, (première) enfance *f.*; minorité *f.* (*legal*)
infant, petit(e) enfant *m.* (*f.*)
infantile, (*adj.*) enfantin
infantry, infanterie *f.*
infantryman, fantassin *m.*
infect, *v.t.* infecter
infection, contagion *f.*; infection *f.*
infectious, (*adj.*) contagieux (-euse); infectieux(-euse)
infer, *v.t.* déduire (de); supposer; conclure
inference, inférence *f.*; déduction *f.*
inferior, (*adj.*) inférieur
inferiority, infériorité *f.*
infernal, (*adj.*) infernal

infidel, infidèle *m.* and *f.*
infiltrate, *v.t.* infiltrer; *v.i.* s'infiltrer
infinite, (*adj.*) infini
infinitive, infinitif *m.*
infirm, (*adj.*) infirme, maladif (-ive)
infirmary, hôpital *m.*; infirmerie *f.*
infirmity, infirmité *f.*; faiblesse *f.*
inflame, *v.t.* enflammer; exciter
inflammable, (*adj.*) inflammable
inflammation, inflammation *f.*
inflexible, (*adj.*) inflexible
inflict, *v.t.* infliger
infliction, peine *f.*; châtiment *m.*; infliction *f.*
influence, influence *f.*
influence, *v.t.* influencer
influential, (*adj.*) qui a de l'influence; influent
influenza, grippe *f.*
inform, *v.t.* informer, aviser, faire savoir
inform against, *v.t.* dénoncer
information, renseignement *m.*; renseignements *m. pl.*; nouvelle *f.*; avis *m.*
informer, mouchard *m.* (*coll.*); dénonciateur(-trice) *m.* (*f.*)
infrequency, rareté *f.*
infrequent, (*adj.*) rare, infréquent
infringe, *v.t.* enfreindre, violer
infringement, violation *f.*
infuriate, *v.t.* rendre furieux (-euse)
infuriated, (*adj.*) furieux(-euse)
ingenious, (*adj.*) ingénieux(-euse)
ingenuous, (*adj.*) ingénu; naïf (naïve)
ingot, lingot *m.*
ingratiate, *v.t.* s'insinuer
ingratitude, ingratitude *f.*
ingredient, ingrédient *m.*; élément *m.*
inhabit, *v.t.* habiter
inhabitant, habitant(e) *m.* (*f.*)
inhabited, (*adj.*) habité
inherit, *v.t.* hériter
inheritance, héritage *m.*; patrimoine *m.*
inhuman, (*adj.*) inhumain, cruel (-le)

inimitable, (*adj.*) inimitable
iniquitous, (*adj.*) inique
iniquity, iniquité *f.* .
initial, (*adj.*) premier; initial
initial, initiale *f.*
initial, *v.t.* mettre ses initiales à
initiate, *v.t.* initier, commencer
initiation, initiation *f.*
initiative, initiative *f.*
inject, *v.t.* injecter
injection, injection *f.*; piqûre *f.*
injudicious, (*adj.*) injudicieux (-euse)
injunction, injonction *f.*
injure, *v.t.* nuire (à); faire tort (à); blesser; avarier (*commer.*, damage to goods)
injurious, (*adj.*) nuisible
injury, tort *m.*; mal *m.*; préjudice *m.*; dégât, dommage *m.* (goods); lésion *f.* (*med.*)
injustice, injustice *f.*
ink, encre *f.*
inkstand, encrier *m.*
inlaid, (*adj.*) incrusté; marqueté
inland, (*adj.*) intérieur; intérieur *m.*
inland revenue, fisc *m.*
inlet, entrée *f.*; passage *m.*; petit bras (*m.*) de mer
inn, auberge *f.*
innate, (*adj.*) inné
innings, tour *m.*
innkeeper, aubergiste *m.*; hôtelier(-ère) *m.* (*f.*)
innocence, innocence *f.*
innocent, (*adj.*) innocent
innocuous, (*adj.*) inoffensif(-ive)
innovation, innovation *f.*
innuendo, insinuation *f.*
innumerable, (*adj.*) innombrable
inoffensive, (*adj.*) inoffensif (-ive), innocent
inordinate, (*adj.*) démesuré
inquest, enquête *f.*
inquire, *v.i.* and *v.t.* s'informer; demander
inquiring, (*adj.*) curieux(-euse)
inquiry, demande *f.*; recherche *f.*
inquiry office, bureau (*m.*) de renseignements
inquisitive, (*adj.*) curieux(-euse)
insane, (*adj.*) fou (folle); aliéné

insanitary, (*adj.*) malsain
insanity, folie *f.*; démence *f.*
insatiable, (*adj.*) insatiable
inscribe, *v.t.* inscrire
inscription, inscription *f.*
insect, insecte *m.*
insecure, (*adj.*) en danger; hasardeux(-euse); peu solide
insecurity, manque (*m.*) de sûreté; péril *m.*
insensible, (*adj.*) insensible (unfeeling); évanoui; sans connaissance
insensibility, insensibilité *f.*; évanouissement *m.*; perte (*f.*) de connaissance
inseparable, (*adj.*) inséparable
insert, *v.t.* insérer; faire insérer dans
inside, dedans *m.*; intérieur *m.*; estomac *m.*
insides, entrailles *f. pl.*
insight, pénétration *f.*; aperçu *m.*
insignificant, (*adj.*) insignifiant
insincere, (*adj.*) peu sincère; faux (fausse)
insinuate, *v.t.* insinuer
insipid, (*adj.*) fade
insist, *v.i.* insister (sur)
insolence, insolence *f.*
insolent, (*adj.*) insolent
insoluble, (*adj.*) insoluble
insolvency, faillite *f.*
insolvent, (*adj.*) en faillite
insomnia, insomnie *f.*
insomuch, à un tel point que
inspect, *v.t.* inspecter, examiner
inspection, inspection *f.*; revue *f.* (troops); examen *m.*; surveillance *f.*
inspector, inspecteur *m.*
inspiration, inspiration *f.*
inspire, *v.t.* inspirer, animer (de)
instal, *v.t.* installer
installation, installation *f.*
instalment, paiement (*m.*) à terme; acompte *m.*
instance, demande *f.*; exemple *m.*
instant, (*adj.*) pressant, immédiat, courant (of month)
instant, instant *m.*; moment *m.*
instantly, (*adv.*) à l'instant; sur-le-champ; tout de suite

instantaneous, (adj.) instantané
instead of, (adv.) au lieu de
instep, cou-de-pied m.
instigate, v.t. provoquer, instiguer
instil, v.t. instiller ; inculquer
instinct, instinct m.
instinctive, (adj.) instinctif(-ive)
institute, institut m.
institute, v.t. instituer; établir
instruct, v.t. instruire
instruction, instruction f.; enseignement m. (teaching)
instructive, (adj.) instructif(-ive)
instrument, instrument m.
insufferable, (adj.) intolérable
insufficiency, insuffisance f.
insufficient, (adj.) insuffisant
insular, (adj.) insulaire
insularity, insularité f.
insulate, v.t. isoler
insulation, isolement m
insulator, isolateur m.
insult, insulte f.
insult, v.t. insulter
insulting, (adj.) injurieux(-euse)
insuperable, (adj.) insurmon-
table
insupportable, (adj.) insupportable, intolérable
insurance, assurance f.
fire insurance, assurance. (f.)
contre l'incendie
insurance company, compagnie
(f.) d'assurances
life insurance, assurance (f.) sur
la vie
insure, v.t. assurer; (fig.) garantir
insured person, assuré(e) m. (f.)
insurgent, insurgé(e) m. (f.)
intact, (adj.) intact
intake, prise f. (d'eau, etc.)
integral, (adj.) intégral
intellect, intelligence f.; esprit m.
intellectual, (adj.) intellectuel(le)
intelligence, intelligence f.; esprit m.; renseignements m. pl.;
nouvelle f. (information)
intelligence department, bureau (m.) de renseignements;
deuxième bureau (military intelligence)
intelligent, (adj.) intelligent
intelligible, (adj.) intelligible

intemperate, (adj.) immodéré,
excessif(-ive)
intend, v.t. avoir l'intention de
intense, (adj.) intense; vif (vive)
intensify, v.t. rendre plus vif
intensity, violence f.; intensité f.
intensive, (adj.) intensif(-ive)
intention, intention f.; dessein
m.
intentional, (adj.) intentionnel(le)
inter, v.t. enterrer
intercept, v.t. intercepter
intercession, intercession f.;
médiation f.
intercourse, relations f. pl.;
rapports m. pl.; commerce m.
interest, intérêt m.; profit m.
interest, v.t. intéresser; s'intéresser à (take an interest in)
interested, (adj.) intéressé
interesting, (adj.) intéressant
interfere, v.i. intervenir; se mêler
interim, (adv.) entre-temps; in-
térim m.
interior, (adj.) intérieur; intérieur
m.
interject, v.t. lancer, émettre
interlude, intermède m.
intermediary, intermédiaire m.
intermediate, (adj.) intermédiaire
interminable, (adj.) interminable
intermingle, v.t. entremêler; v.i.
s'entremêler
intermission, interruption f.
intern, v.t. interner
internal, (adj.) interne, internal
international, (adj.) international
interpose, v.t. interposer
interpret, v.t. interpréter
interpreter, interprète m. and
f.
interrogate, v.t. interroger
interrupt, v.t. interrompre
intersect, v.i. se croiser (roads,
etc.), couper
interval, intervalle m.; entr'acte
m. (theat.)
intervene, v.i. intervenir; s'interposer
intervention, intervention f.
interview, entrevue f.; interview
m. (journalism)

interview, *v.t.* avoir une entrevue avec

interweave, *v.t.* entrelacer

intestinal, (*adj.*) intestinal

intestine, intestin *m.*

intimacy, intimité *f.*

intimate, (*adj.*) intime

intimate, *v.t.* donner à entendre

intimidate, *v.t.* intimider

intolerable, (*adj.*) intolérable

intolerant, (*adj.*) intolérant

intone, *v.i.* entonner

intoxicate, *v.t.* enivrer

intoxication, ivresse *f.*

intractable, (*adj.*) intraitable

intrepid, (*adj.*) intrépide

intricacy, embrouillement *m.*; complication *f.*

intricate, (*adj.*) embrouillé, compliqué

intrigue, intrigue *f.*

intrigue, *v.i.* intriguer

intriguing, (*adj.*) intrigant, intrigant

introduce, *v.t. and v.i.* introduire; faire entrer; présenter (persons to each other)

introduction, introduction *f.*; présentation *f.*

introductory, (*adj.*) préliminaire

intrude, *v.i.* se fourrer; s'introduire; déranger

intruder, importun *m.*; intrus(e) *m.* (*f.*)

intuition, intuition *f.*

inundate, *v.t.* inonder

inundation, inondation *f.*; débordement *m.*

inutility, inutilité *f.*

invade, *v.t.* envahir

invader, envahisseur *m.*

invalid, (*adj.*) non valable, de nul effet; infirme

invalid, malade *m. and f.*

invalidate, *v.t.* annuler; casser

invaluable, (*adj.*) inestimable, sans prix

invariable, (*adj.*) invariable

invasion, invasion *f.*; envahissement *m.*

invective, invective *f.*

inveigh, *v.i.* invectiver contre

inveigle, *v.t.* séduire

invent, *v.t.* inventer

invention, invention *f.*

inventive, inventif(-ive)

inventor, inventeur(-trice) *m.* (*f.*)

inventory, inventaire *m.*

inverse, (*adj.*) inverse

inversely, (*adv.*) en sens inverse

invert, *v.t.* renverser

inverted commas, guillemets *m. pl.*

invest, *v.t.* investir (*mil.*); placer (money)

investigate, *v.t.* examiner; faire une enquête (sur)

investigation, recherche *f.*

investiture, investiture *f.*

investment, placement *m.* (money)

investor, actionnaire *m.* (*f.*)

inveterate, (*adj.*) invétéré

invidious, odieux(-euse); désagréable

invincible, (*adj.*) invincible

invigorate, *v.t.* fortifier

inviolable, (*adj.*) inviolable

inviolability, inviolabilité *f.*

invisibility, invisibilité *f.*

invisible, (*adj.*) invisible

invitation, invitation *f.*

invite, *v.t.* inviter; (*fig.*) appeler

inviting, (*adj.*) appétissant, tentant

invoice, facture *f.*

invoice, *v.t.* facturer

involuntary, (*adj.*) involontaire

involve, *v.t.* entraîner; compliquer; entraîner (entail)

invulnerable, (*adj.*) invulnérable

inward, (*adj.*) intérieur

inwards, (*adv.*) en dedans

iodine, teinture (*f.*) d'iode; iode *m.*

iota, iota *m.*; rien *m.*

i.o.u., billet à ordre *m.*

irascible, (*adj.*) irascible

ire, courroux *m.*

iris, iris *m.*

Irish, (*adj.*) irlandais

irk, ennuyer

irksome, (*adj.*) ennuyeux(-euse)

iron, (*adj.*) de fer

iron, fer *m.* (metal)

iron, *v.t.* repasser (linen); mettre en fers

cast-iron, fonte *f.*

corrugated-iron, tôle (*f.*) ondulée

flat-iron, fer (*m.*) à repasser

old-iron, ferraille *f.*

pig-iron, gueuse *f.*

sheet-iron, tôle *f.*

iron-foundry, fonderie *f.*

ironmonger, quincaillier *m.*

ironmongery, quincaillerie *f.*

iron ore, minerai (*m.*) de fer

iron-work, ouvrage (*m.*) en fer; ferronnerie *f.*

iron-works, forges *f. pl.*

ironer, repasseuse *f.* (of linen, etc.)

ironic(al), (*adj.*) ironique

ironing, repassage *m.*

irony, ironie *f.*

irradiate, *v.i.* rayonner, éclairer

irrational, (*adj.*) déraisonnable

irreclaimable, (*adj.*) incorrigible

irreconcilable, (*adj.*) irréconciliable

irredeemable, (*adj.*) non amortissable; incorrigible

irrefutable, (*adj.*) incontestable

irregular, (*adj.*) irrégulier(-ère)

irregularity, irrégularité *f.*

irrelevant, (*adj.*) hors de propos; inapplicable (à)

irremediable, (*adj.*) irrémédiable

irreproachable, (*adj.*) irréprochable

irresistible, (*adj.*) irrésistible

irresolute, (*adj.*) irrésolu

irrespective, (*adj.*) sans égard (à)

irresponsible, (*adj.*) étourdi

irretrievable, (*adj.*) irréparable

irreverence, irrévérence *f.*

irreverent, (*adj.*) irrévérent

irrevocable, (*adj.*) irrévocable; irréparable

irrigate, *v.t.* arroser, irriguer

irrigation, arrosage *m.*; irrigation *f.*

irritable, (*adj.*) irritable

irritate, *v.t.* irriter

irruption, irruption *f.*; invasion *f.*

isinglass, colle (*f.*) de poisson

island, isle, île *f.*

islander, insulaire *m.* and *f.*

islet, îlot *m.*

isolate, *v.t.* isoler

isolation, isolement *m.*

isosceles, (*adj.*) isocèle

issue, issue *f.*; sortie *f.*; émission *f.* (of banknotes, etc.); résultat *m.*; distribution *f.* (rations, etc.); postérité *f.* (children); question *f.* (*legal*); publication *f.* (books)

issue, *v.i.* sortir, jaillir de

issue, *v.t.* publier, distribuer, mettre en circulation; émettre; faire délivrer (tickets, etc.); lancer un mandat (a writ)

isthmus, isthme *m.*

it, (*pron.*) il *m.*; elle *f.*; le *m.*; la *f.* (accusative); lui (dative); ce, cela (impersonal); y (at it, in it, to it); en, y, pour cela (for it); en (from it)

Italian, (*adj.*) italien(ne)

italics, italiques *m. pl.*

itch, gale *f.* (disease); démangeaison *f.*

itch, *v.i.* démanger

item, article *m.*; item *m.*

item, (*adv.*) item

itinerant, (*adj.*) ambulant; - salesman (hawker), marchand forain *m.*

itinerary, itinéraire *m.*

itself, (*pron.*) lui, elle, soi, lui-même, elle-même

itself, (*reflexive*) se

ivory, ivoire *m.*

ivy, lierre *m.*

J

jab, (*verb*), piquer; (*noun*) piqûre *f.*

jabber, *v.i.* bredouiller, bavarder

jabber, bavardage *m.*

jack, brochet *m.* (fish, pike); cric *m.* (car); valet *m.* (cards)

jackal, chacal *m.* (*pl.* -s)

jackass, âne *m.*; baudet *m.*; (*coll.*) idiot *m.*

jackdaw, choucas *m.*

jacket, jaquette *f.* (woman's); veste *f.*; veston *m.* (man's); smoking *m.* (dinner jacket) jack-pot, (le) gros lot

jade, rosse *f.*; coquine *f.*

jade (mineral), jade *m.*

jaded, (*adj.*) éreinté

jag, brèche *f.*; saillie *f.*

jagged, déchiqueté, ébréché

jail, prison *f.*

jailer, geôlier *m.*

jam, confitures *f. pl.*; embouteillage *m.* (of traffic)

jam, *v.t.* serrer; *v.i.* se coincer

jamb, montant *m.* (of door)

jangle, *v.i.* cliqueter

janitor, concierge *m.* and *f.*

January, janvier *m.*

japan, *v.t.* vernir, laquer

Japanese, (*adj.*) japonais(e)

jar, cruche *f.*; pot *m.*; choc *m.*

jar, *v.i.* être discordant; choquer, vibrer

jar, *v.t.* ébranler, faire trembler; agacer

jarring, bruit discordant *m.*

jaundice, jaunisse *f.*

jaunty, (*adj.*) insouciant

jaw, mâchoire *f.*

jay, geai *m.*

jealous, (*adj.*) jaloux(-ouse)

jealousy, jalousie *f.*

jeer, raillerie *f.*; moquerie *f.*

jeer, *v.i.* railler (de); se moquer (de)

jelly, gelée *f.*

jeopardise, *v.t.* risquer, mettre en péril

jerk, saccade *f.*; secousse *f.*

jerk, *v.t.* secouer; donner une secousse à

jessamine (jasmin), jasmin *m.*

jest, plaisanterie *f.*

jest, *v.i.* plaisanter

Jesuit, jésuite *m.*

jet, jet *m.*; jet d'eau; jais *m.* (mineral); (of engine), à réaction

jetty, jetée *f.*

Jew(ish), (*adj.*) juif *m.*, juive *f.*; israélite

jewel, bijou *m.*; joyau *m.*; pierre (*f.*) précieuse

jewel-case, écrin *m.*

jeweller, bijoutier *m.*

jewellery, joaillerie *f.*

jig (dance), gigue *f.*

jingle, tintement *m.* (of bells); cliquetis *m.* (of glasses and metals)

jingle, *v.i.* tinter; *v.t.* cliqueter; faire cliqueter

jingo, chauvin(e) *m.* (*f.*)

jingoism, chauvinisme *m.*

job, travail *m.*; ouvrage *m.*; besogne *f.*; affaire *f.*

job, *v.i.* travailler à la tâche

jobber (stocks, etc.), agioteur *m.*

jockey, jockey *m.*

jocose, (*adj.*) plaisant; jovial

jog, *v.t.* secouer du coude (elbow); marcher lentement (jog along)

join, *v.t.* joindre, unir; rejoindre (overtake)

join, *v.i.* se joindre, s'unir

joiner, menuisier *m.*

joinery, menuiserie *f.*

joint, jointure *f.*; joint *m.*; articulation *f.* (of limbs); morceau *m.* (meat)

joint-stock company, société (*f.*) anonyme

joint-stock bank, banque (*f.*) par actions

joke, plaisanterie *f.*

joke, *v.i.* plaisanter

jollification, noce *f.*

jolly, (*adj.*) gai; joyeux(-euse); réjoui

jolt, cahot *m.*

jolt, *v.t.* cahoter

jorum, bol *m.*

jostle, *v.t.* pousser; heurter; bousculer

jot, iota *m.*; brin *m.*

jottings, notes *f. pl.*

journal, journal *m.*

journalism, journalisme *m.*

journalist, journaliste *m.* and *f.*

journey, voyage *m.*; trajet *m.*

journey, *v.i.* voyager

journeyman, garçon *m.*; ouvrier *m.*

jovial, (*adj.*) jovial

joy, joie *f.*

to wish joy, féliciter

joyful, (*adj.*) joyeux(-euse)

joyfully, (*adv.*) joyeusement

joyless, (*adj.*) sans joie; triste

joyous, (*adj.*) joyeux(-euse)

joy-stick, levier (m.) de commande
jubilant, (adj.) réjoui; triomphant
jubilation, jubilation f.; joie f.
jubilee, jubilé m.
Judaic, (adj.) judaïque
Judaism, judaïsme m.
judge, juge m.; arbitre m.; connaisseur m. (of art, etc.)
judge, v.t. juger; estimer; décider
judgment, jugement m.; arrêt
m.; sentence f.
judgment-day, jugement (m.)
dernier
judicature, judicature f.; justice
f.
judicial, (adj.) judiciaire; juridique
judicious, (adj.) prudent, sage
jug, cruche f.; broc m.; pot (m.)
d'eau (of water)
jugged-hare, civet (m.) de lièvre
juggle, v.i. faire des tours de
passe-passe; (fig.) escamoter
juggle, jonglerie f.; tour (m.) de
passe-passe
juggler, jongleur m.
juice, jus m.; sève f. (sap); (coll.)
essence f. (petrol)
juiciness, succulence f.
juicy, (adj.) juteux(-euse); plein
de jus; succulent
jujube, jujube m.; boule (f.) de
gomme
July, juillet m.
jumble, mélange m.; confusion f.
jumble, v.t. mêler ensemble;
confondre
jump, saut m.; sursaut m. (of
surprise, etc.)
jump, v.i. sauter, bondir
jumping-off place, (mil.) base
(f.) avancée
junction, jonction f.; gare (f.)
d'embranchement (railway)
juncture, conjoncture f.
June, juin m.
jungle, jungle f.; fourré m.
junior, (adj.) (plus) jeune;
cadet(te); cadet(te) m. (f.)
juniper, genièvre m.
junk, jonque f. (vessel)
junket, lait (m.) caillé

junta, junte f.
juridical, (adj.) juridique
jurisdiction, juridiction f.
jurisprudence, jurisprudence f.
jurist, juriste m.
juror, juré m.
jury, jury m.
just, (adj.) juste, équitable
just, (adv.) juste, justement,
précisément; tout juste; un peu
just now, tout à l'heure
just tell me, dites-moi donc
not just yet, pas encore
justice, justice f.; juge m. (magistrate)
justice of the peace, juge de
paix
justifiable, (adj.) justifiable,
légitime
justifiably, (adv.) légitimement;
d'une manière justifiable
justly, (adv.) exactement; à bon
droit
justness, justice f.; justesse f.;
exactitude f.
jut out, v.i. avancer; faire saillie
jute, jute m.
jutting, (adj.) en saillie, saillant
juvenile, (adj.) juvénile; de
jeunesse
juxtapose, v.t. juxtaposer
juxtaposition, juxtaposition f.

K

Kaffir, Cafre m.
kale, chou m. (pl. -x)
sea-kale, chou (m.) marin
kaleidoscope, kaléidoscope m.
kangaroo, kangourou m.
kedge, ancre (f.) à jet
keel, quille f.; carène f.
keen, (adj.) aigu; aiguisé; tranchant (edge); vif (f. vive); ardent;
mordant; perçant (sight); pénétrant (wind)
keen-eyed, aux yeux perçants
keen-sighted, à la vue perçante
keen-witted, à l'esprit perçant
keenness, finesse f. (of edge); zèle
m.

keep, *v.t.* tenir, retenir, garder; maintenir; conserver (preserve); entretenir (support); nourrir (to keep in board); célébrer; protéger

keep on, *v.i.* continuer; *v.t.* garder

keep waiting, *v.t.* faire attendre

keep, donjon *m.*

keeper, garde *m.*; gardien *m.*; surveillant *m.*

gamekeeper, garde-chasse *m.*

keeping, surveillance *f.*

keepsake, souvenir *m.*

keg, baril *m.*

kennel, chenil *m.*; niche *f.*

kerbstone, bordure (*f.*) de trottoir

kerchief, fichu *m.*

kernel, amande *f.*

kestrel, émouchet *m.*

ketch, quaiche *f.*; ketch *m.*

kettle, bouilloire *f.*

kettle-drum, timbale *f.*

key, clé *f.*; clef *f.*; ton *m.* (*mus.*); touche *f.* (piano)

master key, passe-partout *m.*

keyhole, trou (*m.*) de (la) serrure

key-position, (*mil.*) position-clef *f.*

keyless watch, montre (*f.*) à remontoir

kick, coup de pied *m.*; ruade *f.* (of animals); recul *m.* (of gun, etc.)

kick, *v.t.* donner un coup de pied; *v.i.* reculer (of gun)

kick up a row, faire du tapage

kickshaw, colifichet *m.*

kid, chevreau *m.*; gosse *m.* and *f.* (small child)

kid gloves, gants (*m. pl.*) de chevreau

kidnap, *v.t.* enlever

kidney, rein *m.* (human); rognon *m.* (animal)

kill, *v.t.* tuer; faire mourir; abattre (slaughter)

killer, tueur *m.*

killing, tuerie *f.*; boucherie *f.*; massacre *m.*

kiln, four *m.*

brick-kiln, four (*m.*) à briques

kilt, jupon (*m.*) écossais

kin, parent *m.*; parenté *f.*

kind, espèce *f.*; sorte *f.*; genre *m.*

kind, (*adj.*) bienveillant; bon; bienfaisant

kind-hearted, bienveillant; bienfaisant

kindle, *v.t.* allumer; enflammer; *v.i.* s'enflammer

kindliness, bienveillance *f.*

kindness, bonté *f.*

kindred, parenté *f.*; parents *m. pl.*

kine, vaches *f. pl.*

king, roi *m.*

kingdom, royaume *m.*

kingfisher, martin pêcheur *m.*

kink, coque *f.*; nœud *m.*; lubie *f.*

kinsman, parent *m.*

kiosk, kiosque *m.*

kipper, hareng (*m.*) salé et fumé

kiss, baiser *m.*

kiss, *v.t.* embrasser

kit (soldier's), fourniment *m.*

kitchen, cuisine *f.*

kitchen-garden, jardin potager *m.*

kitchen-maid, fille (*f.*) de cuisine

kitchen-range, fourneau (*m.*) de cuisine

kitchen-utensils, batterie (*f.*) de cuisine

kite, milan *m.* (bird); cerf-volant *m.*

kith and kin, parents et amis *m. pl.*

kitten, chaton *m.*; petit(e) chat(te) *m.* (*f.*)

kleptomania, kleptomanie *f.*

knack, tour (*m.*) de main; talent *m.*

knacker, équarisseur *m.*; abatteur (*m.*) de chevaux

knapsack, havresac *m.*

knave, coquin *m.*; fripon *m.*; valet *m.* (cards)

knavery, friponnerie *f.*; coquinerie *f.*

knavish, (*adv.*) fripon(ne); fourbe

knead, *v.t.* pétrir

kneading-trough, pétrin *m.*

knee, genou *m.* (*pl.* -x)

knee-cap, rotule *f.*

knee-deep, jusqu'aux genoux
knee-joint, articulation (f.) du genou
knock-kneed, (adj.) cagneux (-euse)
kneel, v.i. s'agenouiller; se mettre à genoux
knickerbocker, culotte f.
knick-knack, bibelot m.
knife, couteau m.; bistouri (surg.); canif m. (penknife)
knife-blade, lame (f.) de couteau
knife-grinder, repasseur (m.) de couteau
knife-rest, porte-couteau m.
knight, chevalier m.
knight, v.t. faire chevalier
knighthood, chevalerie f.
knit, v.t. tricoter
knitting, tricot m., tricotage m.
knitting-needle, aiguille (f.) à tricoter
knob, bouton m. (door); bosse f.
knock, coup m. (de marteau)
knock, v.t. frapper, heurter, cogner
knock down, v.t. renverser; abattre; adjuger (at auction)
knocker (door), marteau m.
knoll, monticule m.; tertre m.
knot, nœud m.; groupe m. (of persons)
knot, v.t. nouer; lier
knotty, (adj.) noueux(-euse)
knout, knout m.
know, savoir; apprendre; connaître (to be acquainted)
know someone, connaître quelqu'un
know something, savoir quelque chose
knowing, intelligent; instruit; rusé
knowledge, connaissance f.; science f.; savoir m.
knuckle, jointure (f.) du doigt jarret m. (meat)
knuckle-bone, osselet m.
knuckle-duster, coup de poing (m.) américain
knuckle under, v.i. se soumettre

L

laager, campement m.
label, étiquette f.
label, v.t. étiqueter; (fig.) désigner sous le nom de...
labial, (adj.) labial; labiale f.
laboratory, laboratoire m.
laborious, (adj.) laborieux(-euse)
labour, travail m.; labeur f.; peine f.; couches f. pl. (childbirth)
labour, main (f.) d'œuvre (hands)
Labour Party, Parti Travailliste (Socialiste)
labour, v.t. travailler
labour, v.i. peiner, travailler
labour exchange, bureau (m.) de placement
labourer, ouvrier m.; journalier m. (daily labourer)
labouring class, classe (f.) ouvrière
lac, laque f.
lace, dentelle f.; point m.; lacet m. (boot-lace)
lace, v.t. lacer
lace manufacture, fabrication (f.) de dentelle
lace-work, dentelles f. pl.
lacerate, v.t. lacérer, déchirer
laceration, déchirure f.
lack, manque m.; besoin m.; défaut m.
lack, v.t. and v.i. manquer (de)
lackadaisical, (adj.) languissant
lackey, laquais m.
laconic, (adj.) laconique
lacquer, laque m.
lad, garçon m.; jeune homme m.
ladder, échelle f.
lade, v.t. charger (de)
lading, chargement m.
bill of lading, connaissement m.
ladies, mesdames f pl. (e.g. in a speech)
ladle, cuiller (f.) à pot, louche f.
lady, dame f.
young lady, demoiselle f.; jeune fille f.
lady-bird, bête (f.) à bon Dieu
Lady Day, fête (f.) de l'Annonciation

lady-like, (*adj.*) comme il faut; distinguée

lady's maid, femme (*f.*) de chambre

ladyship, madame, la (baronne, comtesse, etc.)

lag, *v.i.* se traîner en arrière

lag, retard *m.*

lager, bière blonde *f.*

laggard, traînard *m.*; (*adj.*) lent

lagoon, lagune *f.*

laic, (*adj.*) laïque, séculier(-ère)

lair, repaire *m.*

laird, seigneur (*m.*) écossais

laity, laïques *m. pl.*

lake, lac *m.*

lamb, agneau *m.*

lamb, *v.i.* agneler

lambkin, agnelet *m.*

lamb-like, comme un agneau

lame, (*adj.*) boiteux(-euse)

lame, *v.t.* estropier

lameness, boitement *m.*

lament, lamentation *f.*; complainte *f.*

lament, *v.t.* and *v.i.* lamenter; pleurer

lamentable, (*adj.*) déplorable

lamented, (*adj.*) regretté

lamp, lampe *f.*; lanterne *f.*

headlamp, phare *m.*

lamp-post, lampadaire *m.*; réverbère *m.*

lamp-shade, abat-jour *m*

street lamp, réverbère *m.*

lampoon, pasquinade *f.*; satire *f.*; libelle *m.*

lamprey, lamproie *f.*

lance, lance *f.*

lance, *v.t.* percer (an abscess, etc.)

lancer, lancier *m.*

lancet, lancette *f.*

land, terre *f.*; pays *m.* (country); terrain *m.*; sol *m.* (soil)

land, *v.t.* débarquer; mettre à terre; atterrir (aeroplane)

land-owner, propriétaire (*m.*) foncier

landscape, paysage *m.*; vue *f.*

landslide, éboulement (*m*) de terre

land-tax, impôt (*m.*) foncier

landworker, travailleur (*m.*) agricole

landed property, propriété (*f.*) foncière

landing, palier *m.* (on staircase); débarquement *m.* (from ship)

landing gear (of plane), train (*m.*) d'atterrissage

landing-ground, terrain (*m.*)d'atterrissage

landing-stage, débarcadère *m.*

landlady, hôtesse *f.*; propriétaire *f.*

landless, (*adj.*) sans terre

landlocked, (*adj.*) enfermé entre les terres

landlord, hôtelier *m.*; hôte *m.*; propriétaire *m.*

landmark, borne *f.*; point (*m.*) de repère

lane, ruelle *f.*; passage *m.*

language, langage *m.*; langue *f.*

bad language, grossièretés *f. pl.*

languid, (*adj.*) languissant, mou (molle)

languish, *v.i.* languir

languishing, (*adj.*) languissant

languor, langueur *f.*

lankness, maigreur *f.*

lanky, (*adj.*) maigre, décharné

lantern, lanterne *f.*

lap, giron *m.*; genoux *m. pl.*; tour (*m.*) de piste (of race)

lap, *v.t.* laper (lap up, lick)

lapel, revers *m.*

lapidary, lapidaire *m.*

lappet, pan *m.* (of coat)

lapse, laps *m.* (of time); erreur *f.* (fault)

larceny, larcin *m.*; vol *m.*

larch, mélèze *m.*

lard, saindoux *m.*

lard, *v.t.* larder

larder, garde-manger *m.*

large, (*adj.*) gros(se); grand; étendu; considérable

largeness, grandeur *f.*; étendue *f.*; ampleur *f.*

largess, largesse *f.*; libéralité *f.*

lark, alouette *f.*; (*fig.*) escapade *f.*

larva, larve *f.*

larynx, larynx *m.*

lash, coup de fouet *m.*; cil *m.* (eye)

lash, *v.t.* and *v.i.* cingler, fouetter; *v.t.* lier (to secure)

lass, jeune fille *f.*
last, (*adj.*) dernier(-ère)
at last, enfin
last, *v.i.* durer
last, forme *f.* (for shoes)
lasting, (*adj.*) durable, permanent
lastly, en dernier lieu
latch, loquet *m.*
latchkey, passe-partout *m.*
late, tard, tardif(-ive); feu (deceased)
lately, (*adv.*) dernièrement
lateness, retard *m.*; heure avancée *f.*
lathe, tour *m.*
lather, mousse (*f.*) de savon
lather, *v.t.* savonner
Latin, Latin *m.*; (*adj.*) latin(e)
latitude, latitude *f.*
latter, dernier, celui-ci, ceux-ci, celle-ci, celles-ci
latterly, (*adv.*) dernièrement
lattice, treillis *m.*
laud, *v.t.* louer
laudable, (*adj.*) louable
laugh, rire *m.*; risée *f.* (of derision, sneer)
laugh, *v.i.* rire
laughable, (*adj.*) risible
laugher, rieur *m.*; rieuse *f.*
laughter, rire *m.*
launch, chaloupe *f.*; vedette *f.*
launch, *v.i.* se jeter, se lancer; *v.t.* lancer
launching, mise à l'eau *f.*; lancement *m.*
laundress, blanchisseuse *f.*
laundry, blanchisserie *f.*; buanderie *f.*
laureate, lauréat *m.*
laurel, laurier *m.*
lava, lave *f.*
lavatory, cabinet (*m.*) de toilette
lavender, lavande *f.*
lavish, (*adj.*) prodigue
lavish, *v.t.* prodiguer
law, loi *f.*; droit *m.*
civil law, droit civil
commercial law, droit commercial
criminal law, droit criminel
lawful, (*adj.*) légitime, légal

lawn, pelouse *f.* (turf); batiste *f.* (material)
lawsuit, procès *m.*
lawyer, avocat *m.* (barrister); avoué *m.* (solicitor)
lax, (*adj.*) dissolu (morals, etc.); mou (molle)
laxative, laxatif *m.*; laxatif(-ive) (*adj.*)
lay, *v.t.* mettre; placer; poser; pondre (an egg); pointer une pièce (a gun)
lay, (*adj.*) laïque
layer, couche *f.*; bonne pondeuse *f.* (hen)
laying, mise *f.*; pose *f.*; ponte *f.* (of eggs)
layman, laïque *m.*
laziness, paresse *f.*
lazy, paresseux(-euse); fainéant, indolent
lead, plomb *m.* (metal); sonde *f.* (naut.)
leads, mines *f. pl.* (for pencils)
leaden, de plomb
lead-works, plomberie *f.*
lead, conduite *f.*; direction *f.*; main *f.* (cards)
lead, *v.t.* and *v.i.* mener; guider; conduire; aboutir à (result in)
leader, chef *m.*; meneur *m.*; premier(-ère) *m.* (*f.*); article (*m.*) de fond (leading article in paper)
leadership, direction *f.*; commandement *m.*
leading, premier; principal
leading-strings, lisière *f.*
leaf, feuille *f.*; feuillet *m.* (book); pliant *m.* (table)
turn over a new leaf, changer de conduite
leafage, feuillage *m.*
leafy, couvert de feuilles
league, ligue *f.*; lieue *f.* (3 miles)
league, *v.i.* se liguer
leak, fuite (*f.*) d'eau
leak, *v.i.* faire eau; fuir
leakage, coulage *m.*; fuite *f.*
lean, (*adj.*) maigre
lean, *v.i.* s'appuyer; se pencher; *v.t.* appuyer, pencher
lean on, *m.* s'appuyer sur
leanness, maigreur *f.*

leap, saut *m.*; bond *m.*

leap, *v.i.* sauter, bondir; *v.t.* sauter; franchir

leap-year, année (*f.*) bissextile

learn, *v.t.* apprendre

learned, (*adj.*) savant, instruit

learning, érudition *f.*; instruction *f.*

lease, bail *m.* (*pl.* baux)

long lease, bail (*m.*) à long terme

lease, *v.t.* donner à bail; louer

leaseholder, locataire *m.* (*f.*)

least, (*adj.*) le moindre, le plus petit

least, (*adv.*) le moins

at least, au moins, du moins

leather, cuir *m.*

patent leather, cuir verni

leathern, (*adj.*) de cuir, en cuir

leave, permission *f.*; congé *m.*

leave, *v.t.* laisser, quitter; partir de

leave off, *v.t.* cesser (de)

leave-taking, adieux *m. pl.*

leavings, restes *m. pl.*

lecture, conférence *f.*; leçon *f.*

lecture, *v.i.* faire une conférence; faire un cours (à); *v.t.* sermonner (reprimand)

lecturer, conférencier(-ère) *m.* (*f.*)

ledge, rebord *m.*

ledger, grand livre *m.* (book-keeping)

leech, sangsue *f.*

leek, poireau *m.*

left, (*adj.*) gauche

left-handed, gaucher(-ère)

leg, jambe *f.*; cuisse *f.* (of chicken); gigot *m.* (of mutton)

legacy, legs *m.*

legal, (*adj.*) légal

legalisation, légalisation *f.*

legalise, *v.t.* légaliser

legality, légalité *f.*

legatee, légataire *m.* and *f.*

legation, légation *f.*

legend, légende *f.*

legendary, (*adj.*) légendaire; fabuleux(-euse)

legged, (*adj.*) à jambes, à pieds

leggings, jambières *f. pl.*

legibility, lisibilité *f.*

legible, (*adj.*) lisible

legislate, *v.i.* faire des lois

legislative, (*adj.*) législatif(-ive)

legislator, législateur *m.*

legislature, législature *f.*

legitimacy, légitimité *f.*

legitimate, (*adj.*) légitime, juste

leisure, loisir *m.*

leisured, désœuvré

lemon, citron *m.*; limon *m.*

lemonade, limonade *f.*

lemon-peel, écorce (*f.*) de citron

lemon-squash, citronnade *f.*

lend, *v.t.* prêter

lender, prêteur *m.*; prêteuse *f.*

lending, prêt *m.*

lending-library, bibliothèque (*f.*) de prêt

length, longueur *f.*; étendue *f.*; pièce *f.* (of cloth, etc.); durée *f.* (of time)

lengthen, *v.t.* allonger, étendre; prolonger (time)

leniency, indulgence (pour) *f.*

lenient, (*adj.*) indulgent

lens, lentille *f.* (optical)

Lent, Carême *m.*; mi-Carême *f.* (mid-Lent) (carnival)

lentil, lentille *f.*

leopard, léopard *m.*

leper, lépreux(-euse) *m.* (*f.*)

leprosy, lèpre *f.*

leprous, (*adj.*) lépreux(-euse)

less, (*adj.*) moindre, plus petit, inférieur

less, (*adv.*) moins

grow less, *v.i.* diminuer, s'amoindrir

lessen, *v.t.* amoindrir, diminuer, rapetisser

lesson, leçon *f.*

lest, de peur que (*always takes subjunctive*)

let, *v.t.* laisser, permettre, louer (a house); faire (to cause)

let in, *v.t.* laisser (faire) entrer; admettre

let out, *v.t.* laisser sortir; laisser échapper

letter, lettre *f.*

letter-box, boîte (*f.*) aux lettres

letter-paper, papier (*m.*) à lettres

letter-writer, épistolier(-ère) *m.* (*f.*)

letting, louage *m.*

lettuce, laitue *f.*

levee, réception officielle *f.*

level, (*adj.*) de niveau (avec); au niveau (de); égal (égaux)

level, *v.t.* aplanir, niveler

level-crossing, passage (*m.*) à niveau

lever, levier *m.*

lever up, *v.t.* soulever au moyen d'un levier

leveret, levraut *m.*

leviathan, léviathan *m.*

levity, légèreté *f.*

levy, levée *f.*

levy, *v.t.* lever (troops); percevoir (taxes)

lewd, (*adj.*) dissolu, impudique

liabilities, (*pl.*) passif *m.*; engagements *m. pl.*

liability, responsabilité *f.*; passif *m.* (*commer.*)

liable, (*adj.*) responsable (de); exposé (à)

liar, menteur(-euse) *m.* (*f.*)

libel, diffamation *f.*

libel, *v.t.* diffamer, calomnier

libellous, (*adj.*) diffamatoire

liberal, (*adj.*) libéral; généreux (-euse)

liberalism, libéralisme *m.*

liberality, libéralité *f.*

librarian, bibliothécaire *m.*

library, bibliothèque *f*

licence, licence *f.*; permis *m.*; patente *f.* (*commer.*)

licence, *v.t.* autoriser; accorder un permis

licensed, (*adj.*) autorisé; patenté (*commer.*)

licensee, détenteur (*m.*) de patente

licentious, (*adj.*) licencieux(-euse), libertin

lick, *v.t.* lécher; laper; (*slang*) rosser (hit)

licking, raclée *f.*

lid, couvercle *m.*; paupière *f.* (of eye)

lie, mensonge *m.*; disposition (*f.*) du terrain (lie of the land)

lie, *v.i.* mentir (i.e. to tell lies)

lie, *v.i.* être couché; se coucher; être situé; reposer; rester

lieutenant, lieutenant *m.*

life, vie *f.*; vivacité *f.*; entrain *m.* (spirits)

for life, à vie

life annuity, rente (*f.*) viagère

lifebelt, ceinture (*f.*) de sauvetage

lifeboat, canot (*m.*) de sauvetage

lifeguards, garde (*f.*) du corps

life insurance, assurance (*f.*) sur la vie

lifeless, (*adj.*) sans vie, inanimé

lifelike, très ressemblant

lifelong, de toute la vie

life-size, de grandeur naturelle

lifetime, vivant *m.*

lift, action (*f.*) de lever; action (*f.*) de soulever; ascenseur *m.*, lift *m.* (in hotel, etc.)

lift, *v.t.* lever, soulever, hausser

ligature, ligature *f.*

ligature, *v.t.* ligaturer

light, lumière *f.*; jour *m.* (daylight); clair *m.* (of the moon); feu *m.* (army and navy); feux de circulation (traffic lights)

light, *v.t.* allumer, éclairer

light, (*adj.*) léger(-ère)

light blue, bleu clair

lighten, *v.i.* faire des éclairs (storm); *v.t.* alléger (a burden, etc.)

lighter, chaland *m.* (craft); briquet *m.* (for cigarettes)

lighthouse, phare *m.*

lightning, les éclairs *m. pl.*; foudre *f.*

a lightning war, une guerre éclair (*blitzkrieg*)

lightning-conductor, paratonnerre *m.*

like, *v.t.* aimer, trouver bien, trouver bon, vouloir, désirer

like, (*adj.*) ressemblant, semblable, tel(le), pareil(le), même

likelihood, probabilité *f.*; vraisemblance *f.*

likely, (*adj.*) probable, vraisemblable

liken, *v.t.* comparer (à or avec)

likeness, ressemblance *f.*; portrait *m.*

likewise, (*adv.*) également, de même, aussi

lilac, lilas *m.*

lily, lis *m.*

lily of the valley, muguet *m.*

limb, membre *m.*

lime, chaux *f.*

lime (tree), tilleul *m.*

limit, limite *f.*; borne *f.*

limit, *v.t.* limiter; borner; restreindre

limitation, limitation *f.*; restriction *f.*

limited, *(adj.)* limité

limp, boitement *m.*

limp, *v.i.* boiter

limp, *(adj.)* flasque

line, *v.t.* doubler (clothes); aligner, mettre en ligne; *v.i.* s'aligner

line, ligne *f.*; corde *f.*; alignement *m.* (row); voie *f.* (railway); rangée *f.* (row)

linen, toile *(f.)* de lin; linge *m.* (clothes)

linen, *(adj.)* de toile

linen-draper, marchand *(m.)* de toiles; marchand de nouveautés

linen-drapery, nouveautés *f. pl.*

linen-room, lingerie *f.*

liner, paquebot *m.*; transatlantique *m.*

linger, *v.i.* tarder; languir

lining, doublure *f.*

link, *v.t.* relier (avec); enchaîner (dans)

link, chaînon *m.*; anneau *m.*

cuff-links, boutons *(m.)* de manchettes

golf-links, terrain *(m.)* de golf

linnet, linotte *f.*

linseed, graine *(f.)* de lin

linseed-meal, farine *(f.)* de lin

linseed-oil, huile *(f.)* de lin

lint, charpie *f.*; pansement *m.* (dressing for wound)

lion, lion *m.*

lioness, lionne *f.*

lip, lèvre *f.*

lipstick, bâton *(m.)* de rouge

thick-lipped, *(adj.)* lippu

liquid, *(adj.)* liquide; liquide *m.*

liquidate, *v.t.* liquider

liquidation, liquidation *f.*; acquittement *m.*

liquidator, liquidateur *m.*

liquor, liqueur *f.*; boisson *(f.)* alcoolique

liquorice, réglisse *f.*

lisp, *v.i.* zézayer

lissom, *(adj.)* souple

list, liste *f.*; (textile) lisière *f.*

army list, annuaire *(m.)* de l'armée

civil list, liste *(f.)* civile

wine list, carte *(f.)* des vins

list, *v.t.* enregistrer, cataloguer

list, *v.i.* donner de la bande *(naut.)*

listen (to), *v.t.* écouter

to listen in, être à l'écoute

listener, auditeur *m.*; écouteur *m.*

listless, *(adj.)* apathique

listlessness, nonchalance *f.*; apathie *f.*

literal, *(adj.)* littéral

literally, *(adv.)* littéralement

literary, littéraire, lettré

literature, littérature *f.*

lithograph, lithographie *f.*

lithograph, *v.t.* lithographier

litter, litière *f.*; (rubbish) fumier *m.*; désordre *m.*

little, *(adj.)* petit; minime

little, peu *m.*

little, *(adv.)* peu; pas beaucoup

littleness, petitesse *f.*

live, *v.i.* vivre; demeurer (reside); habiter (reside)

live, *(adj.)* vivant, ardent

live-stock, bestiaux *m. pl.*

livelihood, gagne-pain *m.*; vie *f.*

lively, *(adj.)* vif (vive), gai

liver, foie *m.*

livery, livrée *f.*

livery company, corps *(m.)* de métier

lizard, lézard *m.*

Lloyd's list, journal *(m.)* des mouvements maritimes

load, fardeau *m.*; charge *f.*; poids *m.* (weight); chargement *m.*

load, *v.t.* charger; *(fig.)* accabler

loading, chargement *m.*

loaf, pain *m.*

loafer, fainéant *m.*; badaud *m.*

loam, terre *(f.)* glaise; terre grasse

loan, prêt *m.*; emprunt *m.*

loan, *v.t.* prêter

loathe, v.t. détester, abominer

loathing, dégoût m.; répugnance f.

loathsome, (adj.) dégoûtant, odieux(-euse)

lobby, vestibule m.

lobby, v.t. and v.i. faire les coulisses (de la chambre, etc.)

lobster, homard m.

local, (adj.) local

locality, localité f.

lock, serrure f.; écluse f.; (on river, canal, etc.); mèche f. (of hair); boucle f. (of hair)

lock, v.t. fermer à clef; v.i. s'enrayer (of wheels)

locksmith, serrurier m.

locomotive, locomotive f.; machine f.

locust, sauterelle f.

lodge, loge f.

lodge, v.t. loger; abriter; mettre

lodger, locataire m. and f.

lodging, logement m.

lodging-house, hôtel (m.) garni

loft, grenier m.

loftiness, élévation f.; hauteur f.; sublimité f.

lofty, (adj.) haut, élevé; pompeux (-euse)

log, bûche f.; tronc (m.) d'arbre

logic, logique f.

loin, filet m. (of veal, etc.); reins m. pl.

loiter, v.i. flâner, traîner

loiterer, flâneur(-euse) m. (f.)

loitering, flânerie f.

Londoner, Londonien(ne) m. (f.)

lone, (adj.) isolé, solitaire

loneliness, solitude f.

lonely, (adj.) isolé, délaissé

lonesome, solitaire

lonesomeness, solitude f.

long, (adj.) long; étendu, prolongé, allongé

long-sighted, presbyte

long-suffering, (adj.) endurant, patient

long-winded, (adj.) interminable (speech), verbeux(-euse) (person)

longevity, longévité f.

longish, (adj.) un peu long

longitude, longitude f.

look, regard m.; air m.

look, v.i. regarder; avoir l'air; sembler

look after, v.t. soigner

look for, v.t. chercher

look ill, v.i. avoir mauvaise mine

look out, v.i. prendre garde

look well, v.i. avoir bonne mine

looker-on, spectateur m.; spectatrice f.

looking-glass, miroir m.

loom, métier m.

loop, boucle f.

loophole, créneau m.; trou m.

loose, (adj.) détaché; large (clothes); (fig.) relâché, licencieux (-euse) (in conduct)

loose, v.t. lâcher; (fig.) déchaîner

loosely, (adj.) librement, négligemment, vaguement

loosen, v.t. délier; détacher; défaire; ébranler (shake)

loosen, v.i. se relâcher

looseness, relâchement m.; ampleur f.; caractère (m.) lâche

loot, butin m.

loot, v.t. piller

lop, v.t. ébrancher

lop-eared, (adj.) oreillard (horse)

loquacious, (adj.) loquace; babillard

loquacity, loquacité f.

lord, seigneur m.; maître m.; lord m. (title)

lordliness, hauteur f.; orgueil m.

lordship, seigneurie f.

lore, science f.

lorry, camion m.

lorry-driver, camionneur m.

lose, v.t. perdre, faire perdre; manquer (a train); v.i. retarder (of a watch)

lose one's way, s'égarei

loser, perdant m.

loss, perte f.; perte sèche (dead loss)

lot, lot m.; sort m. (fate); beaucoup (de) (quantity)

lotion, lotion f.

lottery, loterie f.

loud, (adj.) haut; bruyant; retentissant; tapageur(-euse) (noisy); criard (colours) loud-speaker, haut-parleur *m.* (*wireless*)

loudly, (*adv.*) à haute voix, bruyamment

loudness, grand bruit *m.*

lounge, *v.i.* flâner

lounge, promenoir *m.*; salon *m.*

lounge-chair, chaise (*f.*) longue

lounger, flâneur *m.*

louse, pou *m.* (*pl.* -x)

lousy, (*adj.*) pouilleux(-euse)

lout, rustre *m.*; lourdaud *m.*

lovable, (*adj.*) aimable

love, amour *m.*; affection *f.*

fall in love (with), s'éprendre (de)

love, *v.t.* aimer

loveless, (*adj.*) sans amour

loveliness, beauté *f.*

lovely, (*adj.*) beau (belle); charmant; ravissant

lover, amant (*m.*); amoureux *m.*

loving, (*adj.*) aimant; affectueux (-euse); tendre

low, (*adj.*) bas (basse); abattu; vulgaire

low-bred, (*adj.*) mal élevé

low-priced, (*adj.*) à bas prix; bon marché

low-spirited, (*adj.*) triste; découragé

low, *v.i.* beugler

Low Countries, Pays Bas *m. pl.*

lower, (*comparative*) inférieur; plus bas

lower, *v.t.* baisser; amener (sails)

lowering, menaçant

lowlands, terres basses *f. pl.*

lowness, bassesse *f.*

loyal, (*adj.*) loyal; fidèle

lozenge, pastille *f.*

lozenge shaped, en losange

lubricant, lubrifiant *m.*

lubricate, *v.t.* lubrifier, graisser

lubrication, lubrication *f.*

lucid, (*adj.*) lucide; transparent

lucidity, lucidité *f.*

luck, fortune *f.*; chance *f.*; bonheur *m.*

luckily, (*adv.*) heureusement

luckless, (*adj.*) malheureux(-euse)

lucky, (*adj.*) heureux(-euse)

lucrative, (*adj.*) lucratif(-ive)

ludicrous, (*adj.*) risible, comique

lug, *v.t.* tirer; traîner

luggage, bagages *m. pl.*

left luggage-office, consigne *f.*

luggage-ticket, bulletin (*m.*) de bagages

luggage-van, fourgon *m.*

lugubrious, (*adj.*) lugubre

lukewarm, (*adj.*) tiède

lullaby, berceuse *f.*

lumbago, lumbago *m.*

lumber, bois (*m.*) de charpente (wood); fatras *m.* (rubbish in a room)

luminary, luminaire *m.*

luminous, (*adj.*) lumineux(-euse)

lump, masse *f.*; morceau *m.* (of sugar); bloc *m.*

lunacy, folie *f.*; démence *f.*

lunar, (*adj.*) lunaire

lunatic, fou *m.*; folle *f.*; aliéné(e) *m,* (*f.*)

lunch(eon), déjeuner *m.*

lunch, *v.i.* déjeuner

lung, poumon *m.*

lurch, embarras *m.* (i.e. left in the lurch); coup (*m.*) de roulis (of ship, etc.)

lurcher, chien de braconnier *m.*

lure, leurre *m.*

lure, *v.t.* leurrer, allécher

lurk, *v.i.* se cacher; être aux aguets

lurking, (*adj.*) caché

luscious, (*adj.*) succulent

lust, convoitise *f.*; luxure *f.*

lust, *v.i.* désirer immodérément

lustful, (*adj.*) lascif(-ive)

lustily, (*adv.*) vigoureusement

lustre, éclat *m.*; lustre *m.* (of chandelier, etc.)

lusty, (*adj.*) robuste

luxuriance, exubérance *f.*; luxuriance *f.*

luxuriant, exubérant, surabondant; fort riche

luxurious, (*adj.*) luxueux(-euse); somptueux(-euse)

luxury, luxe *m.*; somptuosité *f.*

lye, lessive *f.*

lying, (*adj.*) menteur(-euse) (untruthful)

lying, mensonge *m.*

lying, lying in, couches *f. pl.*
lying-in hospital, hôpital (*m.*) pour les femmes en couches
lymph, lymphe *f.* ; vaccin *m.*
lynch, *v.t.* lyncher
lynx, lynx *m.*
lyre, lyre *f.*
lyrical, (*adj.*) lyrique

M

M.A., licencié(e) ès lettres
macadam, macadam *m.*
macadamise, *v.t.* macadamiser
macaroni, macaroni *m.*
macaroon, macaron *m.*
mace, masse *f.* (staff) ; macis *m.* (of nutmeg)
mace-bearer, massier *m.*
macerate, *v.t.* and *v.i.* macérer
machination, machination *f.* ; complot *m.*
machine, machine *f.* ; appareil *m.* (aeroplane)
machine-gun, mitrailleuse *f.*
machine-gunner, mitrailleur *m.*
machined, (*adj.*) usiné
machine-made, fait à la machine
machine-tool, machine-outil *f.*
machinery, mécanisme *m.*
machinist, machiniste *m.* ; mécanicien(ne) *m.* (*f.*)
mackerel, maquereau *m.*
mackintosh, imperméable *m.*
mad, fou, fol (folle) ; furieux (-euse) ; enragé (of dogs)
madam, madame *f.*
madden, *v.t.* rendre fou ; faire enrager
maddening, (*adj.*) enrageant ; à rendre fou
madness, folie *f.* ; fureur *f.* ; rage *f.* (of dogs, etc.)
madonna, madone *f.*
magazine, magasin *m.* (of rifle, etc.) ; magazine *m.* (periodical) ; soute (*f.*) aux poudres (powder magazine)
maggot, ver *m.* ; larve *f.*
magic, (*adj.*) magique
magic, magic *f.*
magician, magicien(ne) *m.* (*f.*)

magisterial, (*adj.*) de maître ; de magistrat ; magistral
magistrate, magistrat *m.* ; juge *m.*
magistracy, magistrature *f.*
magnanimity, magnanimité *f.*
magnanimous, (*adj.*) magnanime
magnet, aimant *m.*
magnetic, (*adj.*) magnétique ; d'aimant
magnetism, magnétisme *m.*
magnificence, magnificence *f.*
magnificent, (*adj.*) magnifique ; superbe
magnify, *v.t.* grossir, agrandir
magnified, (*adj.*) grossi
magnifying glass, loupe *f.*
magnitude, grandeur *f.* ; importance *f.*
magnolia, magnolia *m.*
magpie, pie *f.*
mahogany, acajou *m.*
maid, fille *f.* ; jeune fille *f.* ; bonne *f.* (servant)
maid of all work, bonne (*f.*) à tout faire
maiden, (*adj.*) virginal ; de jeune fille ; de début (speech, etc.)
maidenly, (*adj.*) chaste, modeste
mail, mailles *f. pl.* (armour)
mail, courrier *m.* (post) ; dépêches *f. pl.*
mail-bag, sac (*m.*) de dépêches
mail-train, train-poste *m.*
mail-boat, paquebot-poste *m.*
maim, *v.t.* estropier
main, (*adj.*) principal ; premier (-ère) ; important
main, grand conduit *m.* (water. etc.)
mainly, (*adv.*) principalement ; surtout
main body (of troops), gros *m.* (de la troupe, etc.)
mainland, continent *m.* ; terre (*f.*) ferme
main line, voie (*f.*) principale
mainmast, grand mât *m.*
main road, grande route *f.*
mainspring, grand ressort *m.*
maintain, *v.t.* maintenir, soutenir

maintenance, maintien *m.*; entretien *m.*

maize, maïs *m.*

majestic, (*adj.*) majestueux(-euse)

majesty, majesté *f.*

majolica, majolique *f.*

major, (*adj.*) majeur, plus grand

major, commandant *m.*; chef (*m.*) de bataillon; personne majeure *f.* (*legal*)

major-general, général (*m.*) de brigade

majority, majorité *f.*

make, *v.t.* faire, créer, façonner, fabriquer, rendre, forcer; amasser, gagner (money)

make for, se diriger vers

make over to, céder à

make sure of, s'assurer de

make up, arranger (a quarrel); confectionner (clothes); se maquiller (one's face); préparer (prescription)

make-believe, feinte *f.*

make-up, maquillage *m.* (of face, etc.)

make-weight, supplément *m.*

maker, créateur *m.*; fabricant *m.*

making-up, façon *f.*; confection *f.*

makeshift, pis-aller *m.*

maladministration, mauvaise administration *f.*

malady, maladie *f.*

malaria, malaria *f.*; paludisme *m.*

malcontent(e), (*adj.*) and *m.* (*f.*) mécontent

male, (*adj.*) mâle, masculin

male, mâle *m.*

malediction, malédiction *f.*

malefactor, malfaiteur(-trice) *m.* (*f.*)

malevolence, malveillance *f.*

malevolent, (*adj.*) malveillant

malice, méchanceté *f.*; rancune *f.*

to bear malice, en vouloir à (quelqu'un)

malicious, (*adj.*) malicieux (-euse), méchant

malignant, (*adj.*) malin (maligne); méchant

malignity, malignité *f.*

malinger, *v.i.* faire le malade

malingerer, faux malade *m.*

malleable, (*adj.*) malléable

mallet, maillet.*m.*

malt, malt *m.*

Maltese, (*adj.*) maltais

maltreat, *v.t.* maltraiter

mamma, maman *f.*

mammal, mammifère *m.*

man, *v.t.* garnir (a fort, etc.); armer (a ship)

man, homme *m.*; valet *m.* (valet)

man-of-war, vaisseau (*m.*) de guerre

man-power, effectifs *m. pl.*; main (*f.*) d'œuvre

manacles, *pl.* menottes *f. pl.*

manage, *v.t.* diriger, administrer, gérer; ménager (to scheme); manier

manage, *v.i.* s'arranger

manageable, (*adj.*) traitable, maniable

management, direction *f.*; administration *f.*; gestion *f.*

manager, directeur *m.*; gérant *m.* (*commer.*); **good manager** (i.e. housewife), bonne ménagère (*f.*)

manageress, directrice *f.*; gérante *f.*

mane, crinière *f.*

man-eater, anthropophage *m.*

manful, (*adj.*) viril, vaillant

manger, mangeoire *f.*

mangle, *v.t.* mutiler, déchirer; calandrer (linen)

mangle, calandre *f.* (for linen)

manhandle, *v.t.* manutentionner (goods, etc.)

manhole, trou (*m.*) d'homme

manhood, virilité *f.*

mania, manie *f.*; folie *f.*

manicurist, manucure *m.* (*f.*)

manifest, *v.t.* manifester, témoigner; montrer

manifest, (*adj.*) évident

manifest, manifeste *m.* (shipping paper)

manifestation, manifestation *f.*

manifold, (*adj.*) multiple, divers

mankind, genre humain *m.*

manliness, caractère (*m.*) viril

manly, (*adj.*) d'homme; viril; mâle

mannequin, mannequin *m.*

manner, manière *f.*; air *m.*; genre *m.*; sorte *f.*; espèce *f.*; habitude *f.*

mannerly, (*adj.*) poli

manners, mœurs *f. pl.*; politesse *f.* (good manners)

manœuvre, *v.t.* and *v.i.* manœuvrer

manœuvre, manœuvre *f.*

manor, manoir *m.*; château *m.*

manservant, domestique *m.*

mansion, château *m.*; hôtel *m.* (town house)

manslaughter, homicide *m.*

mantelpiece, manteau (*m.*) de cheminée

mantle, manteau *m.*; mante *f.*; manchon *m.* (gas)

manual,(*adj.*) manuel(le); de main

manual labour, travail manuel

manual, manuel *m.* (book)

manufactory, fabrique *f.*; usine *f.*

manufacture, *v.t.* fabriquer, manufacturer

manufacture, manufacture *f.*; industrie *f.*

manufacturer, manufacturier *m.*; industriel *m.*; fabricant *m.*

manufactures, industrie *f.*; produits (*m. pl.*) manufacturés

manure, engrais *m.*; fumier *m.*

manure, *v.t.* engraisser, fumer

manuscript, manuscrit *m.*

many, (*adj.*) beaucoup (de); bien (des) nombreux(-euse); **how many,** combien (de); **too many,** trop (de); **so many,** tant (de)

map, carte (*f.*) géographique; plan *m.* (of town)

maple (tree), érable *m.*

mar, *v.t.* gâter; défigurer

marble, marbre *m.*

marble-cutting, marbrerie *f.*

marble-quarry, carrière (*f.*) de marbre

marbled, (*adj.*) marbré

March, mars *m.* (month)

march, marche *f.*; étape *f.* (day's march)

march, *v.i.* se mettre en marche, marcher

march, *v.t.* faire marcher

quick march ! en avant, marche!

march past, défilé *m.*

marching, marche *f.*

marchioness, marquise *f.*

mare, jument *f.*

margarine, margarine *f.*

margin, bord *m.*; marge *f.*

marine, (*adj.*) marin; de mer; naval

marine, infanterie (*f.*) de marine

mariner, matelot *m.*; marin *m.*

maritime, (*adj.*) maritime

mark, marque *f.*; signe *m.*; empreinte *f.*; but *m.* (target); témoignage *m.* (of esteem)

mark, *v.t.* marquer; faire attention à; coter (an exercise)

market, marché *m.*; halle *f.* (covered market); **black market,** marché noir

market, cours *m.* (current price)

market, *v.t.* acheter *or* vendre au marché

market-day, jour de marché *m.*

market-garden, jardin (*m.*) maraîcher

market-gardener, maraîcher *m.*

market-price, cours (*m.*) du marché

market-town, ville (*f.*) où se tient un marché

marketing, marché *m.*

to go marketing, aller faire le marché

marking, marquage *m.*

marking-ink, encre (*f.*) à marquer

marl, marne *f.*

marmalade, marmelade (*f.*) d'oranges

marmot, marmotte *f.*

marquess, marquis, marquis *m.*

marriage, mariage *m.*; noces *f. pl.* (wedding)

marriage portion, dot *f.*

marriage settlement, contrat (*m.*) de mariage

marrow, moelle *f.*; courge *f.* (vegetable)

marry, *v.t.* se marier avec; épouser; marier (i.e. to perform ceremony or give in marriage)

marry, *v.i.* se marier

marsh, marais *m.*

marsh-land, pays (*m.*) marécageux

marshal, maréchal *m.*

field marshal, maréchal *m.*

marshy, marécageux(-euse)

mart, marché *m.*; entrepôt *m.*

marten, martre *f.*

martial, (*adj.*) martial; de guerre; guerrier(-ère)

martyr, martyr(e) *m.* (*f.*)

martyr, *v.t.* martyriser

martyrdom, martyre *m.*

marvel, merveille *f.*; chose merveilleuse *f.*

marvel (at), *v.i.* s'émerveiller (de); s'étonner (de)

marvellous, merveilleux(-euse), étonnant

marvellously, à merveille, merveilleusement

masculine, (*adj.*) mâle; d'homme; masculin (*gram.*)

mash, mâche *f.*, purée *f.*

mash, *v.t.* écraser, broyer

mask, masque *m.*; mascarade *f.*

gas mask, masque à gaz

mask, *v.t.* déguiser, masquer; se masquer (one's face)

mason, maçon *m.*

masonry, maçonnerie *f.*

mass, masse *f.*; gros *m.*; foule *f.*

mass, 'messe *f.* (Roman Catholic service)

mass, *v.t.* masser; *v.i.* se masser

massacre, massacre *m.*

massacre, *v.t.* massacrer

massive, (*adj.*) massif(-ive)

mast, mât *m.*

master, maître *m.*; patron *m.*; professeur *m.*

master, *v.t.* maîtriser

masterly, de maître; magistral

masterpiece, chef (*m.*) d'œuvre

mastery, empire *m.*; pouvoir *m.*; supériorité *f.*

mastiff, mâtin *m.*

mat, natte *f.*; paillasson *m.*

mat, *v.t.* natter, tresser; s'emmêler (of hair)

match, allumette *f.*; égal *m.* (equal); parti *m.* (marriage); lutte *f.* (contest); match *m.* (*sport*); **to strike a match,** frotter une allumette

match, *v.t.* égaler; *v.i.* s'assortir (of colours); être pareil

match-box, boîte (*f.*) à allumettes

mate, camarade *m.*; compagnon *m.*; officier (of ship)

mate, *v.t.* accoupler; faire échec et mat (chess)

material, (*adj.*) matériel(le); essentiel(le)

material, matière *f.*; étoffe *f.*; tissu *m.*; matériel *m.* (de guerre), war material

raw materials, matières premières

materialise, *v.t.* matérialiser

materialism, matérialisme *m.*

materialist, matérialiste *m.*

maternal, (*adj.*) maternel(le)

maternity, maternité *f.*

mathematician, mathématicien (-ne) *m.* (*f.*)

mathematics, mathématiques *f. pl.*

matrimony, mariage *m.*

matter, matière *f.*; chose *f.*; affaire *f.*; sujet *m.*; pus *m.* (*med.*)

matter of course, (*adj.*) tout naturel

matter of fact, (*adj.*) pratique, positif(-ive)

no matter, n'importe

matter, *v.i.* importer; **it does not matter,** cela ne fait rien

mattress, matelas *m.*

mature, *v.t.* mûrir

mature, (*adj.*) mûr

maturity, maturité *f.*

maudlin, (*adj.*) gris (drunk); larmoyant (tearful)

maul, *v.t.* rouer de coups, meurtrir

mausoleum, mausolée *m.*

mauve, (*adj.*) mauve; mauve *m.*

maximum, maximum *m.*; maximum (*adj.*)

may, (v. aux.) pouvoir

may, mai m.

maybe, (adv.) peut-être

may-blossom, aubépine f.

may-bug, hanneton m.

may-day, premier mai

mayor, maire m.

mayoress, femme (f.) du maire

maze, labyrinthe m.

meadow, prairie f.; pré m.

meadow-land, prairie f.

meagre, (adj.) maigre; pauvre

meagreness, maigreur f.

meal, repas m.; farine f. (flour)

mean, v.t. signifier, vouloir dire, entendre, se proposer de

mean, (adj.) bas (basse), méprisable, vil, moyen(ne), médiocre, mesquin (stingy)

mean, milieu m.; moyenne f. (math.)

meander, v.i. serpenter

meaning, signification f.

meanness, bassesse f.; avarice f.

means, moyens m. pl.; fortune f.

by means of, au moyen de

by no means, nullement

in the meantime, en attendant

measles, rougeole f.

measure, mesure f.; capacité f.; projet (m.) de loi

measure, v.t. mesurer; arpenter (land); prendre mesure (for clothes)

measured, (adj.) mesuré

measurement, mesure f.; dimension f.

meat, viande f.

meatless day, jour (m.) maigre

mechanic, ouvrier m.; artisan m.; mécanicien m.

mechanical, (adj.) mécanique; machinal

mechanician, mécanicien m.

mechanics, mécanique f.

mechanism, mécanisme m.

medal, médaille f.

meddle, v.i. se mêler (de); toucher à; intervenir

mediæval, (adj.) du moyen âge

mediate, v.i. intervenir; s'interposer (dans)

mediator, médiateur(-trice) m. (f.)

medical, (adj.) médical

medical student, étudiant(e) m. (f.) en médecine

medicament, médicament m.

medicine, médecine f.; médicament m., remède m.

mediocrity, médiocrité f.

meditate, v.t. méditer

Mediterranean, Méditerranée f.

medium, milieu m.; moyen m.; voie f.; médium m. (spiritualism)

through the medium of, par l'intermédiaire de

medley, mélange m.

meek, (adj.) doux (douce); paisible

meerschaum, écume (f.) de mer

meet, v.t. rencontrer; faire la rencontre de; faire honneur à (a bill, etc.)

meet, v.i. se rencontrer; s'assembler

meeting, rencontre f.; réunion f.

melancholy, mélancolie f.

melancholy, (adj.) mélancolique

mellow, (adj.) mûr; doux (douce)

melody, mélodie f.

melon, melon m.

melt, v.t. fondre; faire fondre

melt, v.i. se fondre; s'attendrir

melting-pot, creuset m.

member, membre m.

memoir, mémoire m.

memorable, (adj.) mémorable

memorandum, mémorandum m.; carnet m. (note-book)

memorial, monument (m.) commémoratif m.

memory, souvenir m.; mémoire f. (faculty of remembering)

menace, menace f.

menace, v.t. menacer

menagerie, ménagerie f.

mend, v.t. raccommoder; réparer; stopper (" invisible " mending)

mend, v.i. s'améliorer; se corriger

mendicant, mendiant m.

menial, domestique m. and f.

mensuration, mesurage m.

mental, (adj.) mental; - home, maison (f.) de santé

mention, mention *f.*; indication *f.*

mention, *v.t.* mentionner; faire mention de; citer (in dispatches)

don't mention it! il n'y a pas de quoi!

mercantile, (*adj.*) marchand, de commerce, mercantile

mercenary, (*adj.*) mercenaire; vénal

mercenary, mercenaire *m.*

mercer, mercier *m.*; marchand (*m.*) de soieries

merchandise, marchandise *f.*

merchant, négociant *m.* (wholesale); commerçant *m.*; marchand *m.* (retail)

merchant ship, navire (*m.*) marchand

merchant-service, marine (*f.*) marchande

merciful, (*adj.*) miséricordieux (-euse)

merciless, (*adj.*) impitoyable

mercury, mercure *m.*

mercy, miséricorde *f.*; compassion *f.*; indulgence *f.*; merci *f.*

mere, (*adj.*) seul, unique

mere, étang *m.*

merge, *v.t.* fusionner

merger, fusion *f.*

meridian, méridien *m.*

meridional, méridional

merit, mérite *m.*

merit, *v.t.* mériter

meritorious, (*adj.*) méritant (persons); méritoire (things)

mermaid, sirène *f.*

merry, (*adj.*) gai, joyeux(-euse)

merry-go-round, chevaux (*m. pl.*) de bois; carrousel *m.*

mesh, maille *f.* (net); prise *f.* (machinery)

mess, gâchis *m.*; saleté *f.* (dirt); mets *m.* (dish); popote *f.* (officers'); embarras *m.* (difficulty)

mess up, *v.t.* salir; (*fig.*) gâcher

message, message *m.*

messenger, messager(-ère) *m.(f.)*; chasseur *m.* (hotel, etc.)

metal, métal *m.*

metal, *v.t.* empierrer (a road)

metallic, (*adj.*) métallique

metallurgic, (*adj.*) métallurgique

metamorphosis, métamorphose *f.*

metaphor, métaphore *f.*

meteor, météore *m.*

meter, compteur *m.*

method, méthode *f.*

methylated spirit, alcool (*m.*) à brûler

metre, mètre *m.*

metrical, (*adj.*) métrique

metropolis, métropole *f.*

metropolitan, métropolitain

mettle, courage *m.*; fougue *f.*

mettlesome, fougueux(-euse)

mew, *v.i.* miauler (of cat)

mewing, miaulement *m.*

mews, écuries *f. pl.*

mica, mica *m.*

Michaelmas, la Saint-Michel *f.*

microphone, microphone *m.*; (*coll.*) micro *m.* (" mike ")

microscope, microscope *m.*

microscopic, (*adj.*) microscopique

mid, (*adj.*) mi; du milieu

mid-day, midi *m.*

middle, (*adj.*) du milieu, central

middle, milieu *m.*; centre *m.*

middle (in the - of), au milieu de

middle-aged, entre deux âges

Middle Ages (the), le Moyen Age *m.*

middling, médiocre

midnight, minuit *m.*

midshipman, aspirant (*m.*) de la marine de guerre

midsummer day, la Saint-Jean *f.*

midwife, sage-femme *f.*

might, puissance *f.*; pouvoir *m.*; force *f.*

mighty, (*adj.*) puissant, fort

migrate, *v.i.* émigrer

migratory, (*adj.*) migratoire

mild, (*adj.*) doux (douce); léger (-ère)

mile, mille *m.*

milestone, borne (*f.*) routière; borne kilométrique

militant, (*adj.*) militant

militarism, militarisme *m.*

military, (*adj.*) militaire

militia, milice *f.*

milk, lait *m.*

milk, *v.t.* traire

milk diet, régime (*m.*) lacté

milkman (-maid), laitier(-ère) *m.* (*f.*)

milk-white, (*adj.*) blanc comme le lait

milky, laiteux(-euse)

milky way, voie (*f.*) lactée

mill, moulin *m.*; filature *f.* (spinning)

mill, *v.t.* moudre (grain); fouler (cloth)

mill-stone, meule (*f.*) de moulin

miller, meunier *m.*

milliner, modiste *f.*

million, million *m.*

millionaire, millionnaire, *m.* (*f.*)

mimic, *v.t.* imiter

mimic, imitateur(-trice) *m.* (*f.*); (*adj.*) mimique

mince, hachis *m.*

mince, *v.t.* hacher menu

mind, esprit *m.*; intelligence *f.*; opinion *f.*; envie *f.*

mind, *v.t.* faire attention à, songer à; s'occuper de; soigner (nurse)

make up one's mind, se décider; prendre son parti

I don't mind, cela m'est égal

never mind, n'importe

mindful, attentif(-ive)

mine, mine *f.*

mine, *v.t.* miner, creuser

mine-field, champ (*m.*) de mines

mine-layer, mouilleur (*m.*) de mines

miner, mineur *m.*

mine-sweeper, dragueur (*m.*) de mines

mineral, (*adj.*) minéral; minéral *m.*; minerai *m.*

mineralogist, minéralogiste *m.*

mineralogy, minéralogie *f.*

mingle, *v.i.* se mêler

miniature, miniature *f.*

miniature, (*adj.*) en miniature

mining, exploitation (*f.*) des mines; travail (*m.*) dans les mines

minister, ministre *m.*; pasteur *m.* (*eccles.*)

minister of state, ministre (*m.*) d'état

minister of war, ministre (*m.*) de la guerre

prime minister, premier ministre

ministry, ministère *m.*

minor, (*adj.*) moindre, secondaire

minor, mineur(e) *m.* (*f.*)

minority, minorité *f.*

minster, cathédrale *f.*

minstrel, ménestrel *m.*

mint, menthe *f.*

mint, monnaie *f.* (*finan.*): hôtel de la monnaie *m.* (the Mint)

mint, *v.t.* monnayer; frapper de la monnaie

minute, (*adj.*) menu, très petit

minute, minute *f.*; instant *m.*; moment *m.*; -s (of a meeting), procès-verbal *m.*

minutely, (*adv.*) minutieusement; en détail

miracle, miracle *m.*

miraculous, (*adj.*) miraculeux (-euse)

mirage, mirage *m.*

mire, boue *f.*; vase *f.*; bourbe *f.*

mirth, gaieté *f.*; joie *f.*; hilarité *f.*

mirthful, gai, joyeux(-euse)

mirth-provoking, désopilant

miry, (*adj.*) bourbeux(-euse)

misadventure, mésaventure *f.*, contretemps *m.*

misalliance, mésalliance *f.*

misapplication, mauvaise application *f.*

misappropriation, détournement *m.* (of funds)

misbehave, *v.i.* se comporter mal

miscalculate, *v.i.* and *v.t.* calculer mal

miscarriage, erreur (*f.*) judiciaire (of justice); fausse couche *f.* (in childbirth)

miscarry, *v.i.* échouer

mischance, malchance *f.*; malheur *m.*

mischief, mal *m.*; dommage *m.*; tort *m.*

mischief (to make -), *v.t.* semer la discorde; brouiller

mischief-maker, brouillon *m.*; mauvaise langue *f.*

mischievous, (*adj.*) méchant, malicieux(-euse)

misconduct, mauvaise conduite *f.*; adultère *m.* (in divorce proceedings)

miscreant, vaurien *m.*; scélérat *m.*

misdeed, méfait *m.*

misdemeanour, délit *m.*

miser, avare *m.* (*f.*)

miserable, (*adj.*) misérable, pitoyable, malheureux(-euse)

miserly, (*adj.*) avare, sordide

misery, misère *f.*; supplice *m.*

misfire, *v.i.* rater

misfortune, malheur *m.*

misgiving, appréhension *f.*, doute *m.*

misgovern, *v.t.* gouverner mal

mishandle, *v.t.* maltraiter

misjudge, *v.t.* juger mal

mislay, *v.t.* égarer

mislead, *v.t.* égarer, tromper

misprint, faute (*f.*) d'impression

misrule, désordre *m.*

miss, *v.t.* manquer, regretter vivement

miss, manque *m.*; coup manqué *m.*; mademoiselle *f.*

missile, projectile *m.*

mission, mission *f.*

missionary, missionnaire *m.*

mist, brume *f.*; bruine *f.*

mistake, erreur *f.*; faute *f.*

mistake, *v.t.* comprendre mal; faire erreur

mistakenly, par méprise

be mistaken, se tromper

mistletoe, gui *m.*

mistress, maîtresse *f.*; madame *f.*

mistrust, méfiance *f.*; défiance *f.*

mistrust, *v.t.* se méfier

misty, brumeux(-euse)

misunderstand, *v.t.* mal comprendre, méconnaître

misunderstanding, malentendu *m.*

misuse, abus *m.*

misuse, *v.t.* maltraiter; faire mauvais emploi (de)

mitigate, *v.t.* adoucir, atténuer

mitten, mitaine *f.*

mix, *v.t.* mêler, mélanger

mix, *v.i.* se mêler

mixed, (*adj.*) mixte

mixture, mélange *m.*

moan, gémissement *m.*; plainte *f.*

moan, *v.i.* gémir, déplorer

moat, fossé *m.*

mob, populace *f.*; foule *f.* (crowd)

mobile, (*adj.*) mobile

mobilise, *v.t.* mobiliser

mobilisation, mobilisation *f.*

mock, *v.t.* se moquer de

mockery, moquerie *f.*; raillerie *f.*

mocking, (*adj.*) moqueur(-euse)

mode, mode *f.*; façon *f.*; manière *f.*

model, modèle (*adj.*) and person *m.* (*f.*), thing *m.*

model, *v.t.* modeler

modelling, modelage *m.*

moderate, (*adj.*) modéré; ordinaire; médiocre

moderate, *v.t.* modérer, tempérer

moderation, modération *f.*

modern, (*adj.*) moderne

modernise, *v.t.* moderniser

modest, modeste

modesty, modestie *f.*

modify, *v.t.* modifier

modulate, *v.t.* moduler

moist, (*adj.*) moite, humide

moisten, *v.t.* humecter, mouiller

moisture, humidité *f.*

molar, (*adj.*) molaire

mole, taupe *f.*; grain (*m.*) de beauté (on skin); môle *m.* (pier)

mole-hill, taupinière *f.*

molest, *v.t.* molester

mollify, *v.t.* adoucir

moment, moment *m.*; instant *m.*

momentary, (*adj.*) momentané, passager(-ère)

momentous, important

monarch, monarque *m.*

monarchy, monarchie *f.*

monastery, monastère *m.*

Monday, lundi *m.*

monetary, monétaire

money, argent *m.*; monnaie *f.*

ready money, argent comptant

money-box, tirelire *f.*; caisse *f.*

money-lender, usurier *m.*; prêteur (*m.*) d'argent
money-market, bourse *f.*;
marché (*m.*) financier
money-order, mandat *m.*
monk, moine *m.*
monkey, singe *m.*
monogram, monogramme *m.*
monopoly, monopole *m.*
monotonous, (*adj.*) monotone
monster, monstre *m.*
monstrous, monstrueux(-euse)
month, mois *m.*
monthly, (*adj.*) mensuel(le)
monument, monument *m.*
mood, humeur *f.*; disposition *f.*;
mode *m.* (*gram.*)
moody, (*adj.*) de mauvaise
humeur; maussade
moon, lune *f.*
moonbeam, rayon (*m.*) de lune
moonlight, clair (*m.*) de lune
moonlit, éclairé par la lune
moor, lande *f.*; bruyère *f.*
moor, *v.t.* amarrer; *v.i.* s'amarrer
mooring, amarrage *m.*
moorish, (*adj.*) mauresque
moorland, lande *f.*
mop, balai (*m.*) à laver
mop, *v.t.* éponger
to mop up (after attack), nettoyer
moral, (*adj.*) moral
moral, morale *f.*
morale, moral *m.* (of troops, etc.)
morals, mœurs *f. pl.*; moralité *f.*
morbid, (*adj.*) malsain, morbide
more, (*adj.*) (*comp.*) plus, plus
(de); plus nombreux; encore;
(*adv.*) plus, davantage
no more, ne... plus
moreover, (*adv.*) d'ailleurs
morning, matin *m.*; matinée *f.*
(forenoon)
moroccan leather, maroquin *m.*
moroccan, (*adj.*) marocain
morose, (*adj.*) maussade
morphine, morphine *f.*
morrow, lendemain *m.*
morsel, morceau *m.*
mortal, (*adj.*) mortel(le)
mortality, mortalité *f.*
mortar, mortier *m.*
mortgage, hypothèque *f.*

mortgage, *v.t.* hypothéquer
mortgagee, créancier (*m.*) hypo-
thécaire
mortification, mortification *f.*
mortify, *v.i.* humilier, mortifier
mosaic, (*adj.* and *subst.*) mosaïque
f.
mosque, mosquée *f.*
mosquito, moustique *m.*
mosquito net, moustiquaire *f.*
moss, mousse *f.*
mossy, moussu
most, (*adj.*) le plus; le plus
grand; la plupart de; (*adv.*) le
plus; très; fort
mostly, pour la plupart; principalement
moth, papillon (*m.*) de nuit; mite
f. (in clothes)
mother, mère *f.*
mother-in-law, belle-mère *f.*
mother-of-pearl, nacre *f.*
motherhood, maternité *f.*
motherly, (*adj.*) maternel(le)
motion, mouvement *m.*; signe *m.*;
proposition *f.* (at meeting)
motion, *v.t.* faire signe (à)
motionless, (*adj.*) immobile
motive, motif *m.*
motor, *v.i.* aller (voyager) en auto
motor, moteur *m.*
motor-bicycle, motocycle(tte) *f.*
motor-boat, canot (*m.*) automobile
motor-bus, autobus *m.*
motor-car, automobile *f.*; auto *f.*
motor-coach, autocar *m.*; car *m.*
motorised, (*adj.*) motorisé
motorist, automobiliste *m.* (*f.*)
motto, devise *f.*
mould, moisi *m.* (mouldiness);
moule *m.*; (*fig.*) modèle *m.*
mould, *v.t.* mouler
moulder, *v.i.* s'effriter
mouldiness, moisissure *f.*
mouldy, (*adj.*) moisi
moult, *v.i.* muer.
mound, tertre *m.*; butte *f.*
mount, mont *m.*; armement *m.*
(of machine)
mount, *v.t.* and *v.i.* monter,
monter (sur)
to mount guard, monter la garde

mountain, montagne *f.*
mountaineer, montagnard *m.*
mountainous, montagneux (-euse)
mounted, (*adj.*) monté, à cheval
mourn, *v.t.* and *v.i.* déplorer, pleurer
mournful, (*adj.*) triste, lugubre
mourning, le deuil *m.*
mouse, souris *f.*
mouse-trap, souricière *f.*
moustache, moustache *f.* (often plural)
mouth, bouche *f.* (of persons); gueule *f.* (of animals); embouchure *f.* (of rivers)
mouthful, bouchée *f.*
mouth-piece, embouchure *f.*; porte-parole *m.* (spokesman)
movable, (*adj.*) mobile
movables, biens meubles *m.*; effets mobiliers *m. pl.*
move, *v.t.* remuer; mettre en marche; faire aller; attendrir (qn.)
move, *v.i.* bouger, se remuer, se mouvoir, s'avancer, déménager
move forward, *v.t.* avancer; *v.i.* (s')avancer
movement, mouvement *m.*
mover, moteur *m.*; (of proposal, etc.).auteur *m.*
moving, mobile; (*fig.*) émouvant
moving, mouvement *m.*; déménagement *m.* (of furniture, etc.); déplacement *m.*
moving staircase, escalier roulant *m.*
mow, *v.t.* faucher, tondre
mowing machine, faucheuse *f.*
much, (*adj.*) beaucoup, beaucoup de
much, (*adv.*) beaucoup, bien, fort, très
as much as, autant que
muck, fumier *m.*; saleté *f.*
mucous, (*adj.*) muqueux(-euse)
mud, boue *f.*; vase *f.*; limon *m.* (slime); -**guard,** pareboue *m.*
muddiness, état (*m.*) boueux
muddle, *v.t.* embrouiller; troubler
muddle, embrouillement *m.*

muddy, (*adj.*) boueux(-euse); bourbeux(-euse)
muff, manchon *m.*
muffle, *v.t.* emmitoufler; assourdir (sound)
mufti (in), *m.* en civil
mug, pot *m.*; gobelet *m.*; (*coll.*) poire *f.* (dupe); museau *m.* (face)
mulberry, mûre *f.*
mulberry (tree), mûrier *m.*
mule, mulet *m.*
muleteer, muletier *m.*
mulled, (*adj.*) chaud et épicé (wine)
mullet, mulet *m.*; rouget *m.* (red mullet)
multicoloured, (*adj.*) multicolore
multifarious, (*adj.*) divers
multiple, (*adj.*) multiple
multiply, *v.t.* multiplier
multitude, *f.* multitude
multitudinous, (*adj.*) très nombreux
mumble, *v.t.* marmotter; mâchonner
mummy, momie *f.*; maman *f.* (mamma)
mumps, oreillons *m. pl.*
munch, *v.t.* mâcher
mundane, (*adj.*) du monde, mondain
municipal, municipal
municipality, municipalité *f.*
munificence, munificence *f.*
munificent, généreux(-euse), libéral
munition, munition *f.*
murder, meurtre *m.*; homicide *m.*
murder, *v.t.* assassiner, tuer
murderer, assassin(e) *m.* (*f.*)
murmur, murmure *m.*
murmur, *v.i.* murmurer
muscatel, muscat *m.*; raisin (*m.*) muscat (grape)
muscle, muscle *m.*
muscular, (*adj.*) musculaire
muse, *v.i.* méditer, rêver
museum, musée *m.*
mushroom, champignon *m.*
music, musique *f.*
music-hall, café concert *m.*; music-hall *m.*

music-stand, pupitre (*m.*) à
musique
music-stool, tabouret (*m.*) à
musique
musical, (*adj.*) musical; har-
monieux(-euse)
musician, musicien(ne) *m.* (*f.*)
musk, musc *m.*
musketeer, mousquetaire *m.*
musketry, tir *m.*
muslin, mousseline *f.*
mussel, moule *f.*
must, *v.i.* falloir (*absolute oblig.*);
devoir (*moral oblig.*)
mustard, moutarde *f.*
mustard gas, gaz (*m.*) moutarde
mustard-pot, moutardier *m.*
muster, appel *m.*; rassemblement
m.
muster, *v.i.* s'assembler, se réunir
musty, (*adj.*) moisi
mutation, changement *m.*; mutation *f.*
mute, (*adj.*) muet(te) *f.*
mutilate, *v.t.* mutiler
mutilated, (*adj.*) mutilé
mutilation, mutilation *f.*
mutineer, rebelle *m.*; révolté *m.*;
mutin *m.*
mutiny, révolte *f.*; mutinerie *f.*
mutiny, *v.i.* se mutiner, se
révolter
mutter, *v.i.* and *v.t.* marmotter
muttering, marmottement *m.*
mutton, mouton *m.*
mutton-chop, côtelette (*f.*) de
mouton
leg of mutton, gigot (*m.*) de
mouton
saddle of mutton, selle (*f.*) de
mouton
mutual, (*adj.*) réciproque,
mutuel(le)
mutually, (*adv.*) réciproquement
muzzle, museau *m.*; muselière
f. (for dogs); gueule *f.* (of guns)
muzzle, *v.t.* museler
muzzle velocity, vitesse (*f.*) à la
bouche
my (*poss. adj.*) mon *m.*; ma *f.*;
mes *pl.*
myosotis, myosotis *m.*
myriad, myriade *f.*

myself, (*pron.*) moi-même; moi
mysterious, (*adj.*) mystérieux
(-euse)
mystery, mystère *m.*
mystic, (*adj.*) mystique
mystic, mystique *m.* and *f.*
mystification, mystification *f.*
mystical, (*adj.*) mystique
mystify, *v.t.* mystifier
myth, légende *f.*; mythe *m.*
mythology, mythologie *f.*

N

nab, *v.t.* saisir; (*fam.*) pincer
nacre, nacre *f.*
nag, bidet *m.*; *v.t.* and *v.i.*
quereller
nail, clou *m.* (*pl.* -s); ongle *m.* (of
finger)
nail, *v.t.* clouer
nail-brush, brosse (*f.*) à ongles
nail scissors, ciseaux (*m. pl.*) à
ongles
naïve, (*adj.*) naïf (naïve); ingénu
naked, (*adj.*) nu
nakedness, nudité *f.*
namby-pamby, maniéré; affecté
name, nom *m.*; réputation *f.*
Christian name, prénom *m.*
name, *v.t.* nommer, appeler
to be named, se nommer
nameless, (*adj.*) anonyme; inconnu
namely, (*adv.*) à savoir
namesake, homonyme *m.*
nankeen, nankin *m.*
nap, somme *m.* (sleep); sieste *f.*
nap, poil *m.* (fur); duvet *m.*
(plants)
nape (of neck), nuque *f.*
napery, lingerie (*f.*) de table
naphtha, naphte *m.*
napkin, serviette *f.*
napkin-ring, rond (*m.*) de serviette
narcissus, narcisse *m.*
narcotic, narcotique *m.*; stupé-
fiant *m.*; (*adj.*) narcotique
narrate, *v.t.* raconter
narration, narration *f.*; récit *m.*

narrative, récit *m.*

narrator, narrateur(-trice) *m.* (*f.*)

narrow, (*adj.*) étroit; resserré

narrow, *v.i.* se rétrécir; *v.t.* resserrer

narrow-minded, à l'esprit borné

narrowly, (*adv.*) étroitement

narrowness, étroitesse *f.*

narrows, (*geog.*) détroit *m.*

nasal, (*adj.*) nasal

nasturtium, capucine *f.*

nasty, (*adj.*) vilain; désagréable

natal, (*adj.*) natal

nation, nation *f.*

national, (*adj.*) national

nationalisation, nationalisation *f.*

nationalise, *v.t.* nationaliser

nationality, nationalité *f.*

native, (*adj.*) natif(-ive); indigène (du pays); naturel(le)

native, natif(-ive) *m.* (*f.*); indigène (plants, etc.) *m.* (*f.*)

nativity, nativité *f.*

natural, (*adj.*) naturel(le)

naturalise, *v.t.* naturaliser

naturalist, naturaliste *m.* (*f.*)

nature, nature *f.*; naturel *m.* (i.e. person's character, etc.)

naught, rien *m.*; zéro *m.*; néant *m.*

naughtiness, méchanceté *f.*

naughty, méchant; grivois (anecdote, etc.)

nausea, nausée *f.*; soulèvement (*m.*) de cœur

nauseate, *v.t.* dégoûter

nauseate, *v.i.* avoir du dégoût pour; avoir mal au cœur

nauseating, (*adj.*) nauséabond

nautical, (*adj.*) nautique

naval, (*adj.*) naval (*pl.* -als); maritime; de la marine

nave, nef (*f.*) (of church)

navel, nombril *m.*

navigable, (*adj.*) navigable

navigate, *v.i.* naviguer; *v.t.* gouverner

navigation, navigation *f.*

navvy, terrassier *m.*

navy, marine *f.*; marine (*f.*) de guerre

nay, non

neap-tide, morte-eau *f.*

near, (*adj.*) voisin, proche; parcimonieux(-euse) (stingy)

near, (*adv.*) près; (*prep.*) près de, auprès de

near, *v.i.* s'approcher de

near-sighted, myope

nearly, (*adv.*) presque

nearness, proximité *f.*; voisinage *m.*; parcimonie *f.*

neat, (*adj.*) net(te); soigné; bien rangé; propre

neatly, (*adv.*) proprement, nettement

neatness, propreté *f.*; netteté *f.*

nebula, nébuleuse *f.*

nebulous, (*adj.*) nébuleux(-euse)

necessaries, le nécessaire

necessarily, (*adv.*) nécessairement, forcément

necessary, (*adj.*) nécessaire

necessitous, nécessiteux(-euse)

necessity, nécessité *f.*; besoin *m.*

neck, cou *m.* (*pl.* -s); goulot *m.* (of bottles)

necklace, collier *m.*

necktie, cravate *f.*

nectarine, brugnon *m.*

need, besoin *m.*; nécessité *f.*

need, *v.t.* avoir besoin de

needful, (*adj.*) nécessaire

needle, aiguille *f.*

needless, (*adj.*) inutile

needy, (*adj.*) nécessiteux(-euse)

nefarious, (*adj.*) abominable

negation, négation *f.*

negative, (*adj.*) négatif(-ive); négatif *m.* (*phot.*); négative *f.* (*gram.*)

neglect, *v.t.* négliger; manquer à

neglect, négligence *f.*; manque (*m.*) d'égards

negligent, (*adj.*) négligent

negotiable, (*adj.*) négociable

negotiate, *v.t.* négocier

negotiation, négociation *f.*

negress, négresse *f.*

negro, nègre *m.*

neigh, *v.i.* hennir; hennissement *m.*

neighbour, voisin(e) *m.* (*f.*)

neighbour, *v.t.* avoisiner

neighbourhood, voisinage *m.*

neighbouring, (*adj.*) voisin, avoisinant

neither, (*adj.* and *pron.*) ni l'un ni l'autre

neither, (*conj.*) ni; non plus

neology, néologie *f.*

neophyte, néophyte *m.* (*f.*)

nephew, neveu *m.*

nepotism, népotisme *m.*

nerve, nerf *m.*; audace *f.* (courage); toupet *m.* (impudence)

nerveless, sans nerf

nervous, (*adj.*) nerveux(-euse) (highly strung or sinewy); timide

nervousness, inquiétude *f.*; timidité *f.*

nest, nid *m.*; nichée *f.* (brood of birds)

nest of tables, table (*f.*) gigogne

nest, *v.i.* nicher; faire un nid

nestle, *v.i.* se nicher, se blottir

nestling, petit oiseau *m.*

net, filet *m.*; réseau *m.* (of railways, roads)

nether, inférieur

nettle, ortie *f.*; *v.t.* irriter

neuralgia, névralgie *f.*

neuter, neutral, (*adj.*) neutre

neutrality, neutralité *f.*

never, (*adv.*) (ne)... jamais

never more, (*adv.*) (ne) jamais plus

nevertheless, néanmoins; toutefois

new, neuf (neuve) (unused); nouveau(x) (recent); frais (fraîche), récent

New Year's Day, jour (*m.*) de l'an

news, nouvelle *f.*; nouvelles *f. pl.*

newsagent, marchand (*m.*) de journaux

newspaper, journal *m.*

next (*adj.*) prochain; suivant

the next day, the morrow, le lendemain

nibble, *v.t.* ronger, mordiller

nice, (*adj.*) agréable; gentil(le); délicat, charmant, aimable, juste

niche, niche *f.*

nick, entaille *f.*

in the nick of time, à point nommé

nickname, sobriquet *m.*

nicotine, nicotine *f.*

niece, nièce *f.*

niggardly, (*adj.*) mesquin, ladre

nigger, nègre *m.*; moricaud *m.*

nigh, (*adv.*) presque; proche

night, nuit *f.*; soir *m.* (evening)

night-cap, bonnet (*m.*) de nuit

night-club, boîte (*f.*) de nuit

night-dress, chemise (*f.*) de nuit

nightfall, nuit tombante *f.*

nightmare, cauchemar *m.*

nightingale, rossignol *m.*

nimble, (*adj.*) agile, leste

nine, neuf *m.*

ninepins, jeu (*m.*) de quilles

nip, *v.t.* pincer

nippers, pincettes *f. pl.*

nipple, mamelon *m.*; bout (*m.*) de sein

nitrate, nitrate *m.*

nitre, nitre *m.*

nitric, (*adj.*) nitrique

nitrogen, azote *m.*

no, (*adj.*) and *adv.*) non, pas, ne... pas, ne... point, nul(le)

nobility, noblesse *f.*

noble, (*adj.*) noble; magnifique; noble *m.*

nobody, (*pron.*) personne *m.*; (ne...) personne

nocturnal, (*adj.*) nocturne

nod, *v.i.* faire un signe de tête

nod, signe (*m.*) de tête; inclination (*f.*) de tête

noise, bruit *m.*; tapage *m.*; vacarme *m.* (uproar)

noiseless, (*adj.*) sans bruit; silencieux(-euse)

noisily, (*adv.*) bruyamment

noisy, (*adj.*) bruyant; tapageur (-euse); turbulent (people)

nominal, (*adj.*) nominal

nominate, *v.t.* nommer; désigner

non, (*prefix*) non-

non-ability, incapacité *f.*

non-attendance, absence *f.*

non-commissioned (**officer**), sous-officier *m.*

nondescript, (*adj.*) indéfinissable

none, (*pron.*) nul(le) *m.* (*f.*); aucun(e) *m.* (*f.*); pas un, pas une; personne *m.*

nonentity, nullité *f.*

nonplus, *v.t.* embarrasser, interdire

nonsense, sottise *f.*; galimatias *m.* (rubbish); absurdité *f.*; (*exclam.*) allons donc!

nonsensical, (*adj.*) absurde

nook, coin *m.*

noon, midi *m.*

noose, nœud (*m.*) coulant; collet *m.*

nor, (*conj.*) ni; ni... ne

normal, (*adj.*) normal

north, nord *m.*

north, northern, northerly, (*adj.*) septentrional, nord (*invar.*)

north star, étoile (*f.*) polaire

northward, (*adv.*) vers le nord

Norwegian, (*adj.* and *subst.*) norvégien(ne)

nose, nez *m.*

nose-bag, musette (*f.*) mangeoire; musette *f.*

nose-dive, *v.i.* piquer du nez

flat-nosed, à nez plat; camus

nostalgia, nostalgie *f.*

nostril, narine *f.*

not, (*adv.*) non; ne... pas; ne... point

not at all, point du tout

notability, notabilité *f.*

notable, (*adj.*) notable

notary, notaire *m.*

notch, entaille *f.*; brèche *f.*

notch, *v.t.* entailler, ébrécher

notch (back sight of rifle), cran (*m.*) de mire

note, note *f.*; marque *f.*; lettre *f.*; billet *m.*; marque *f.* (distinction)

note-book, carnet *m.*; calepin *m.*

note-paper, papier (*m.*) à lettres

noted, distingué, remarquable

noteworthy, remarquable

nothing, rien *m.*; néant *m.*

nothing, (*adv.*) nullement, aucunement

nothingness, néant *m.*

notice, attention *f.*; avis *m.*; notice *f.* (article in newspaper); congé *m.* (to leave, or quit)

notice, *v.t.* prendre connaissance de; remarquer

to give notice, donner avis,

avertir; donner. congé (i.e. to leave)

noticeable, (*adj.*) perceptible

notification, notification *f.*; avis *m.*; avertissement *m.*

notify, *v.t.* notifier, faire savoir

notion, notion *f.*; idée *f.*

notoriety, notoriété *f.*

notorious, (*adj.*) notoire

notwithstanding, (*prep.*) malgré, nonobstant; (*adv.*) néanmoins

nought, rien *m.*; zéro *m.*

nourish, *v.t.* nourrir; entretenir

nourishment, nourriture, *f.*

novel, (*adj.*) nouveau(-elle); neuf(-ve) *m.* (*f.*)

novel, (book) roman *m.*

novelist, romancier *m.*

novelty, nouveauté *f.*

November, novembre *m.*

novice, novice *m.* and *f.*

novitiate, noviciat *m.*

now, (*adv.*) maintenant, à présent; or (in argument)

now and then, de temps en temps

nowadays, (*adv.*) de nos jours, aujourd'hui

nowhere, (*adv.*) nulle part

nowise, (*adv.*) nullement

noxious, (*adj.*) nuisible

nozzle, nez *m.*; bec *m.*; tuyau *m.*

nuclear, (*adj.*) nucléaire; **-power,** énergie atomique *f.*

nucleus, noyau *m.*

nude, (*adj.*) nu

nudge, *v.t.* donner un coup de coude

nudity, nudité *f.*

nugget, pépite *f.*

nuisance, peste *f.*; fléau *m.*; plaie *f.*; ennui *m.*; ordures (filth) *f. pl.*; dommage *m.* (*law*)

commit no nuisance, défense d'uriner

what a nuisance! comme c'est ennuyeux!

null, (*adj.*) nul(le)

nullify, *v.t.* annuler

numb, (*adj.*) engourdi

numb, *v.t.* engourdir .

number, nombre *m.*; numéro *m.*; chiffre *m.*; quantité *f.*

number, *v.t.* compter; numéroter (things in succession)
numbering, numérotage *m.*
numberless, (*adj.*) innombrable
numbness, engourdissement *m.*
numeral, numéral *m.*; chiffre *m.*
numerically, (*adv.*) numériquement
numeration, numération *f.*
numerous, (*adv.*) nombreux (-euse)
numismatics, numismatique *f.*
numskull, idiot(e) *m.* (*f.*)
nun, religieuse *f.*
nuncio, nonce *m.*
nunnery, couvent (*m.*) de religieuses
nuptial, (*adj.*) nuptial
nuptials, noces *f. pl.*
nurse, nourrice *f.* (wet-nurse); bonne *f.* (for children); garde-malade *m.* (*f.*) (for sick people); infirmier(-ère) *m.* (*f.*) (in hospitals)
nurse, *v.t.* soigner; nourrir (to feed); allaiter (to suckle)
nursery, chambre (*f.*) des enfants; pépinière *f.* (nursery garden)
nursery-maid, bonne (*f.*) d'enfant
nurseryman, pépiniériste *m.*
nut, noix *f.*; écrou *m.* (of metal)
nut-crackers, casse-noisettes *m.*
nut (tree), noisetier *m.*
nutmeg, muscade *f.*
nutriment, nourriture *f.*
nutrition, nutrition *f.*
nutritious, (*adj.*) nourrissant
nux-vomica, noix (*f.*) vomique
nymph, nymphe *f.*

O

oaf, sot(te) *m.* (*f.*); benêt *m.*
oak, chêne *m.*; bois (*m.*) de chêne
oak-apple, pomme (*f.*) de chêne
oaken, de chêne
oakum, étoupe *f.*
oar, rame *f.*
oarsman, rameur *m.*
oasis, oasis *f.*

oat(s), avoine *f.*
oath, serment *m.*; juron *m.* (swear word)
oatmeal, gruau (*m.*) d'avoine
obduracy, endurcissement *m.*; entêtement *m.*
obdurate, (*adj.*) obstiné; opiniâtre
obedience, obéissance *f.*; soumission *f.*
obedient, (*adj.*) obéissant
obeisance, révérence *f.*; salut *m.*
obelisk, obélisque *m.*
obese, (*adj.*) obèse, ventru
obesity, obésité *f.*; embonpoint *m.*
obey, *v.i.* and *v.t.* obéir (à)
obituary, (*adj.*) nécrologique
obituary notice, notice (*f.*) nécrologique
obituary, nécrologie *f.*
object, objet *m.*; chose *f.*
object, *v.t.* objecter (à); *v.i.* faire objection (à)
objection, objection *f.*
objectionable, répréhensible
objective, objectif *m.*; but *m.*
oblation, offrande *f.*
obligation, obligation *f.*; engagement *m.*
obligatory, (*adj.*) obligatoire
oblige, *v.t.* obliger; astreindre (compel); rendre service à (to help)
obliging, (*adj.*) obligeant; serviable
oblique, (*adj.*) oblique
obliquity, obliquité *f.*
obliterate, *v.t.* effacer
obliteration, rature *f.*; oblitération *f.*
oblivion, oubli *m.*
oblivious (of), oublieux(-euse) (de)
oblong, (*adj.*) oblong(-ue)
obloquy, opprobre *m.*
obnoxious, (*adj.*) odieux(-euse)
obscene, (*adj.*) obscène
obscenity, obscénité *f.*
obscuration, obscurcissement *m.*
obscure, (*adj.*) obscur; caché
obscure, *v.t.* obscurcir; voiler (light)
obscurity, obscurité *f.*

obsequies, obsèques *f. pl.*

obsequious, servile, obséquieux (-euse)

observable, remarquable, sensible, observable

observance, observance *f.*; pratique *f.* (*relig.*)

observant, (*adj.*) observateur (-trice); attentif(-ive)

observation, observation *f.*

observatory, observatoire *m.*

observe, *v.t.* observer, remarquer; faire remarquer (point out)

observer, observateur(-trice) *m.* (*f.*)

obsolete, (*adj.*) suranné, inusité

obstacle, obstacle *m.*; empêchement *m.*; difficulté *f.*

obstetrics, obstétrique *f.*

obstinacy, opiniâtreté *f.*; entêtement *m.*

obstinate, (*adj.*) opiniâtre, entêté

obstreperous, (*adj.*) turbulent, tapageur(-euse)

obstruct, *v.t.* obstruer; gêner, encombrer

obstruction, empêchement *m.*; obstacle *m.*

obtain, *v.t.* obtenir; gagner; *v.i.* prévaloir

obtainable, (*adj.*) qu'on peut obtenir

obtrude, *v.t.* importuner

obtrusion, importunité *f.*

obtuse, (*adj.*) obtus, émoussé

obviate, *v.t.* obvier (à)

obvious, (*adj.*) évident

obviously, (*adv.*) évidemment

occasion, occasion *f.*; cause *f.*; occurrence *f.*

occasion, *v.t.* occasionner

occasional, (*adj.*) occasionnel(le)

occasionally, (*adv.*) quelquefois; parfois; de temps en temps

occident, occident *m.*

occult, (*adj.*) occulte

occupancy, occupation *f.*

occupant, occupant(e) *m.* (*f.*); locataire *m.* (*f.*) (tenant)

occupation, occupation *f.*; emploi *m.*; métier *m.*

occupy, *v.t.* occuper; habiter

occur, *v.i.* venir à l'esprit (to the mind); avoir lieu, arriver (to happen)

occurrence, événement *m.*

ocean, océan *m.*

oceanic, (*adj.*) océanique

ochre, ocre *f.*

octagon, octogone *m.*

octagonal, (*adj.*) octogonal

octave, octave *f.*

octavo, in-octavo *m.*

October, octobre *m.*

octopus, poulpe *m.*

ocular, (*adj.*) oculaire

oculist, oculiste *m.*

odd, (*adj.*) impair (number); étrange; singulier(-ère); bizarre (queer)

oddity, bizarrerie *f.*; singularité *f.*

oddly, (*adv.*) bizarrement; étrangement

oddments, fins (*f.*) de série (in a shop)

odds, chances *f. pl.*

odious, (*adj.*) odieux(-euse)

odium, détestation *f.*; réprobation *f.*

odorous, (*adj.*) odorant; parfumé

odour, odeur *f.*; parfum *m.*

of, (*prep.*) de

off, (*adv.*) loin, au loin, à distance; rompu (broken off); fini (finished)

off-hand, (*adv.*) immédiatement; sans réflexion

off-hand, (*adj.*) brusque (in manner)

offal, restes *m. pl.*; viande (*f.*) de rebut; abats *m. pl.* (*cook.*)

offence, offence *f.*; outrage *m.*; contravention *f.*

to take offence at, se formaliser de

offend, *v.t.* offenser, choquer, blesser; violer (against the law)

offensive, (*adj.*) désagréable, offensant

offensive, offensive *f.*

offer, offre *f.*

offer, *v.t.* offrir; présenter; proposer à; *v.i.* s'offrir

offering, offre *f.*

offertory, quête *f.*

office, charge *f.*; emploi *m.*; fonctions *f. pl.*; bureau *m.*

officer, officier *m.*; fonctionnaire *m.* (of the government)

official, (*adj.*) officiel(le); public

official, employé *m.*; fonctionnaire *m.*

officiate, *v.i.* desservir; exercer les fonctions

officious, (*adj.*) officieux(-euse); importun

offing, large *m.*

offscouring, rebut *m.*

offshoot, rejeton *m.*

offspring, descendants *m. pl.*

often, (*adv.*) souvent

(how) often, combien de fois

too often, trop souvent

ogle, *v.t.* lancer des œillades à; lorgner

oil, huile *f.*

oil can, bidon (*m.*) à huile

oil, *v.t.* huiler, graisser

oil-painting, peinture (*f.*) à l'huile

oilcloth, toile (*f.*) cirée

oilskin, toile (*f.*) vernie

oil well, puits (*m.*) pétrolifère

oiliness, onctuosité, nature (*f.*) huileuse

oily, onctueux(-euse); huileux (-euse)

ointment, onguent *m.*

old, vieux, vieil (vieille), âgé, ancien(ne), antique

old man, vieillard *m.*; un vieux

old woman, vieille *f.* (femme)

how old are you? quel âge avez vous?

oldish, (*adj.*) vieillot(te)

oldness, vieillesse *f.*; ancienneté *f.*

oleander, laurier-rose *m.*

old-fashioned, (*adj.*) démodé

olive, olive *f.*

olive (tree), olivier *m.*

omelet, omelette *f.*

omen, augure *m.*

ominous, (*adj.*) de mauvais augure; sinistre, menaçant

omission, omission *f.*

omit, *v.t.* omettre; oublier

omnibus, omnibus *m.*

motor-bus, autobus *m.*

on, (*prep.*) sur; dessus; à; en;

dans; (*adv.*) en avant; (of tap) ouvert

on fire, en flammes

once, une fois, une seule fois; autre fois, jadis (formerly)

at once, sur-le-champ (immediately); à la fois (simultaneously)

one, un(e); seul; on (*indefinite pron.*)

it's all one to me, cela m'est égal

one another, l'un(e) l'autre

onion, oignon *m.*

onlooker, spectateur(-trice) *m.* (*f.*)

only, (*adj.*) seul, unique; (*adv.*) seulement, ne... que; (*conj.*) mais

onset, attaque *f.*

onward, (*adv.*) en avant

ooze, limon *m.*; vase *f.*

ooze, *v.i.* suinter

opal, opale *f.*

opaque, (*adj.*) opaque

open, *v.t.* ouvrir (door); déboucher (a bottle); entamer (conversation, etc.); défaire (a package)

open, (*adj.*) ouvert; découvert; à découvert, à nu; franc (franche)

open-mouthed, bouche-bée

tin-opener, ouvre-boîtes *m.*

opera, opéra *m.*

opera-glass, jumelles *f. pl.*

operate, *v.i.* opérer; agir; *v.t.* opérer; faire jouer

operation, opération *f.*

operative, ouvrier(-ère) *m.* (*f.*)

become operative, entrer en vigueur

operator, opérateur *m.*; sans-filiste *m.*, (wireless) radio *m.*; téléphoniste *f.* (at exchange)

opinion, opinion *f.*; avis *m.*

opium, opium *m.*

opponent, adversaire *m.*

opportune, (*adj.*) opportun

opportunity, occasion *f.*

oppose, *v.t.* s'opposer à, résister à

opposite, (*adj.*) opposé, contraire; vis-à-vis

opposition, opposition *f.*; résistance *f.*; concurrence *f.*

oppress, *v.t.* opprimer

oppression, oppression *f.*

oppressive, (*adj.*) oppressif(-ive); lourd

opprobrious, (*adj.*) injurieux (-euse)

optic(al), (*adj.*) optique

optician, opticien *m.*

optimism, optimisme *m.*

optimist, optimiste *m.*

optimistic, (*adj.*) optimiste

optional, (*adj.*) facultatif(-ive)

opulent, (*adj.*) opulent

or, (*conj.*) ou; ni (*negative*)

oracle, oracle *m.*

oral, (*adj.*) oral

orange, orange *f.*

orange (tree), oranger *m.*

oration, discours *m.*; oraison *f.* (funeral)

orator, orateur *m.*

orbit, orbe *m.*; orbite *f.* (of eye or star)

orchard, verger *m.*

orchestra, orchestre *m.*

orchid, orchidée *f.*

ordain, *v.t.* ordonner; décréter; établir

ordeal, épreuve *f.*

order, ordre *m.*; règlement *m.*; consigne *f.* (*mil.*); classe *f.*; rang *m.*; mandat *m.* (money-order, draft); commande *f.* (goods); ordres *m. pl.* (holy orders)

order, *v.t.* ordonner; donner l'ordre à; arranger (regulate); commander (goods, etc.)

(made to) order, fait sur commande

call to order, rappeler à l'ordre

in order to, afin de

order arms ! reposez (vos) armes !

orderliness, ordre *m.*; méthode *f.*

orderly, (*adj.*) en bon ordre; rangé

orderly, (*mil.*) planton *m.*; ordonnance *f.*

orderly officer, officier (*m.*) de service

orderly, (*adv.*) en ordre

ordinary, (*adj.*) ordinaire, normal

ordnance, artillerie *f.* (general term); ravitaillement *m.* (supplies)

ordnance map, carte (*f.*) du dépôt de la guerre; carte (*f.*) de l'état-major

ore, minerai *m.*

organ, organe *m.*; orgue *m.* (*mus.*)

organise, *v.t.* organiser

orgy, orgie *f.*

orient, orient *m.*

oriental (*adj.*) oriental

orifice, orifice *m.*; ouverture *f.*

origin, origine *f.*; source *f.*; provenance *f.*

original, (*adj.*) original; primitif (-ive)

originality, originalité *f.*

originate, *v.i.* provenir; *v.t.* donner naissance à

ornament, ornement *m.*

ornament, *v.t.* orner; décorer

ornate, (*adj.*) élégant; paré

orphan, orphelin(e) *m.* (*f.*)

orphanage, orphelinat *m.*

orthography, orthographe *f.*

oscillate, *v.i.* osciller; *v.t.* balancer

osier, osier *m.*

ostensible, (*adj.*) soi-disant

ostentatious, (*adj.*) pompeux (-euse); fastueux(-euse)

ostentation, faste *m.*

ostler, garçon (*m.*) d'écurie

ostrich, autruche *f.*

other, (*adj.*) autre; (*pron.*) autre

otherwise, (*adv.*) autrement

every other day, tous les deux jours

otter, loutre *f.*

ought, (*v. aux.*) devoir; falloir

ounce, once *f.* (*circa* 28 grammes)

our, (*adj. possess.*) notre (*pl.* nos)

ours, (*pron.*) le (la) nôtre (*pl.* les nôtres)

out, (*adv.*) hors; dehors; sorti (gone out); découvert (e.g. the secret is out); éteint (fire, etc.); épuisé; fini

outbid, *v.t.* enchérir sur

outbreak, éruption *f.*; émeute *f.* (riot); épidémie *f.* (of sickness); incendie *m.* (fire); ouverture *f.* (hostilities)

outcast, expulsé(e) *m.* (*f.*); exilé(e) *m.* (*f.*)

outcome, résultat *m.*
outcry, clameur *f.*
outdo, *v.t.* surpasser
outdoor, *(adj.)* en plein air
outdoors, *(adv.)* au dehors, hors de la maison
outer, *(adj.)* extérieur; hors zone (shooting)
outfit, équipement *m.*
outflank, *v.t.* déborder
outgoings, dépenses *f. pl.*
outgrow, *v.t.* devenir trop grand pour
outhouse, dépendance *f.*
outlaw, proscrit *m.*
outlay, dépense *f.*; débours *m. pl.*
outlet, sortie *f.*; débouché *m.*; voie (*f.*) d'écoulement
outline, contour *m.*; *v.t.* contourner; esquisser
outlive, *v.t.* survivre (à)
outpace, *v.t.* dépasser
outpost, avant-poste *m.*
outrage, *v.t.* outrager
outrage, outrage *m.*
outrageous, *(adj.)* outrageant; exagéré
outright, *(adv.)* sur le coup
outset, commencement *m.*; début *m.*
outshine, *v.t.* éclipser
outside, *(adv.)* dehors; en dehors; à l'extérieur
outside, *(prep.)* en dehors de; hors de
outside, *(adj.)* extérieur, externe
outsider, étranger(-ère) *m.* (*f.*); profane *m.*; (racing) cheval (*m.*) non classé parmi les favoris
outskirt, lisière *f.* (of a wood); faubourg *m.* (of a town)
outstrip, *v.t.* devancer, dépasser
outward, *(adj.)* extérieur, superficiel(le)
outwit, *v.t.* duper
oval, *(adj.)* ovale; ovale *m.*
oven, four *m.*
over, *(prep.)* sur; pardessus; au-dessus de; de l'autre côté de; au delà de
over, *(adv.)* de l'autre côté; pardessus; au-dessus; de l'un côté à l'autre; fini (finished)

all over, partout (everywhere)
over against, en face (de)
overall, blouse *f.*; sarrau *m.*
overbear, *v.t.* maîtriser, accabler
overburden, *v.t.* surcharger
overcast, *v.i.* obscurcir
overcharge, *v.t.* surcharger; faire payer trop cher
overcoat, pardessus *m.*
overcome, *v.t.* surmonter, vaincre
overdone, *(adj.)* trop cuit
overeat, *v.i.* manger trop
overflow, *v.i.* déborder
overflow, débordement *m.*; trop-plein *m.*
overgrow, *v.t.* couvrir
overhang, *v.t.* surplomber
overhasty, *(adj.)* trop pressé
overhaul, *v.t.* examiner, réviser
overhead, par-dessus la tête; en haut
overhead expenses, frais (*m. pl.*) généraux
overheat, *v.t.* surchauffer
overland, *(adv.)* par voie de terre
overlap, *v.t.* recouvrir
overlay, *v.t.* couvrir; étouffer
overlook, *v.t.* surveiller; négliger (neglect)
overmuch, trop *m.*
overpower, *v.t.* vaincre; accabler (de)
overproduction, surproduction *f.*
overrate, *v.t.* surestimer
overreach, *v.t.* duper; dépasser
override, *v.t.* surmener (horse); outrepasser
overrule, *v.t.* annuler (*legal*); gouverner
overrun, *v.t.* envahir
overseas, *(adj.)* d'outre-mer
oversee, *v.t.* surveiller
overseer, inspecteur(-trice) *m.* (*f.*); contremaître(-sse) *m.* (*f.*)
overset, *v.t.* renverser
overshadow, *v.t.* jeter dans l'ombre
overshoes, caoutchoucs *m. pl.*
overshoot, *v.t.* dépasser
oversight, oubli *m.*
oversleep (oneself), *v.i.* dormir trop longtemps

overspread, *v.t.* se répandre sur, couvrir.

overstep, *v.t.* dépasser

overstrain, *v.t.* forcer, (se) surmener

overt, (*adj.*) manifeste

overtax, *v.t.* surcharger, surtaxer

overthrow, chute *f.*; défaite *f.*; renversement *m.*

overthrow, *v.t.* renverser, bouleverser, détruire

overtime, heures supplémentaires *f. pl.*

overtop, *v.t.* surpasser, s'élever au-dessus de

overweening, présomptueux (-euse)

overweight, excédent (*m.*) de poids; surpoids *m.*

overwhelm, *v.t.* accabler

overwhelming, (*adj.*) accablant, écrasant

overwork, *v.t.* surcharger de travail, surmener

overwrought, (*adj.*) surmené

owe, *v.t.* devoir

owing, dû; à cause de

owl, hibou *m.* (*pl.* -x)

owlet, white owl, chouette *f.*

own, propre (à soi)

own, *v.t.* posséder, avouer (to own up to)

owner, propriétaire *m.* and *f.*

ox, bœuf *m.*

oxide, oxyde *m.*

oxidise, *v.t.* oxyder

oxygen, oxygène *m.*

oyster, huître *f.*

oyster-bed, banc (*m.*) d'huîtres

ozone, ozone *m.*

P

pabular, (*adj.*) alimentaire

pabulum, aliment *m.*; nourriture *f.*

pace, pas *m.*; allure *f.*

pace, *v.i.* aller au pas, marcher; *v.t.* arpenter

pachyderm, pachyderme *m.*

pacific, (*adj.*) pacifique

pacification, pacification *f.*

Pacific Ocean, Océan (*m.*) Pacifique; Pacifique *m.*

pacifist, pacifiste *m.* (*f.*)

pacify, *v.t.* pacifier, apaiser

pack, paquet *m.*; ballot *m.*; meute *f.* (hounds); sac *m.* (soldier's)

pack, *v.t.* emballer; empaqueter; *v.i.* s'attrouper (of people)

pack off, *v.i.* se débarrasser de; *v.t.* expédier

pack up, *v.t.* emballer; (*fig.*) décamper (go off)

pack-cloth, toile (*f.*) d'emballage

pack-thread, ficelle *f.*

package, colis *m.*

packing, emballage *m.*

packing case, caisse (*f.*) d'emballage

pact, pacte *m.*

pad, tampon *m.*; bourrelet *m.* (cushion)

pad, *v.i.* aller lentement (pad along slowly)

pad, *v.t.* ouater, rembourrer

paddle, pagaie *f.*; rame *f.*

paddle, *v.i.* pagayer, ramer

paddle-wheel, roue (*f.*) à aubes

paddock, enclos *m.*; pesage *m.*

padlock, cadenas *m.*

padre, aumônier *m.* (*mil.*)

pagan, (*adj.* and *subst.*) païen(ne)

paganism, paganisme *m.*

page, page *f.* (book); page *m.*, chasseur *m.* (page-boy)

pageant, spectacle *m.*; pompe *f.*

pageantry, parade *f.*; faste *m.*

paging, pagination *f.* (*print.*)

paid, (*adj.*) payé, acquitté (bill, etc.)

pail, seau *m.*

pain, douleur *f.*; peine *f.* (care)

to take pains to, se donner de la peine pour

pain, *v.t.* faire mal à; faire souffrir

painful, (*adj.*) douloureux(-euse); pénible

painless, (*adj.*) sans douleur

painstaking, (*adj.*) assidu

paint, couleur *f.*; peinture *f.*; fard *m.* (make up)

paint, *v.t.* peindre; farder (to make up face, etc.)

paint-brush, pinceau *m.*

painter, peintre *m.*; amarre *f.* (mooring rope)

painting, peinture *f.* (à l'huile, à l'aquarelle, etc.)

pair, paire *f.*; couple *m.*

pair, *v.i.* s'accoupler; *v.t.* assortir (to match)

pal, (*fam.*) copain *m.*, copine *f.*

palace, palais *m.*

palatable, (*adj.*) agréable au goût

palate, palais *m.*

palatinate, Palatinat *m.*

pale, (*adj.*) pâle; blême; blafard (light).

pale, *v.t.* faire pâlir

pale, *v.i.* s'éclipser, pâlir

paleness, pâleur *f.*

palette, palette *f.* (painter's)

paling, palissade *f.*

palish, (*adj.*) un peu pâle; pâlot(te)

pall, poêle *m.*; drap (*m.*) mortuaire

pall, *v.i.* devenir fade

pallet, grabat *m.*

palliate, *v.t.* pallier

palliation, palliation *f.*

palliative, palliatif *m.*; (*adj.*) palliatif(-ive)

pallid, (*adj.*) pâle; blême; blafard (light)

pallor, pâleur *f.*

palm, palmier *m.* (tree); palme *f.*; paume *f.* (of hand)

Palm Sunday, dimanche (*m.*) des Rameaux

palm-oil, huile (*f.*) de palme

palmated, (*adj.*) palmé

palmistry, chiromancie *f.*

palpable, (*adj.*) palpable

palpability, palpabilité *f.*

palpitate, *v.i.* palpiter

palpitation, palpitation *f.*

palsied, (*adj.*) paralysé

palsy, paralysie *f.*

paltriness, mesquinerie *f.*; pétitesse *f.*

paltry, mesquin; chétif(-ive)

pamper, *v.t.* choyer, gâter (spoil)

pamphlet, brochure *f.*; pamphlet *m.*

pamphleteer, auteur (*m.*) de brochures

pan, terrine *f.*; poêle *f.* (frying-pan); cuvette *f.*

panacea, panacée *f.*

pancake, crêpe *f.*; *v.i.* (of plane) descendre à plat, plaquer

pander, *v.i.* se prêter à

pane, carreau *m.*; vitre *f.*

panegyric, panégyrique *m.*

panel, panneau *m.*; liste *f.*

panelling, lambrissage *m.*

pang, angoisse *f.*; vive douleur *f.*

panic, terreur *f.*; panique *f.*

panic-stricken, (*adj.*) saisi d'une terreur panique

pannier, panier *m.*

pannikin, poêlon *m.*

pansy, pensée *f.*

pant, *v.i.* haleter, palpiter

pantaloons, pantalon *m.*

pantechnicon, voiture (*f.*) de déménagement

panther, panthère *f.*

panting, battement du cœur *m.*; souffle (*m.*) haletant

pantomime, pantomime *f.* (dumb show)

pantry, garde-manger *m.*

pants, pantalon *m.* (U.S.A.); caleçon *m.*

pap, bouillie *f.*

papa, papa *m.*; père *m.*

papacy, papauté *f.*

papal, (*adj.*) papal; du pape

paper, papier *m.*; journal *m.* (newspaper); valeurs *f. pl.* (bills, shares, etc.); étude *f.* (article); feuille de papier *f.*; composition *f.* (exam.)

paper, *v.t.* tapisser (to paper wall)

paper-fastener, attache-papier *f.*

paper-hanger, colleur *m.*

paper-knife, coupe-papier *m.*

paper-trade, papeterie *f.*

paper-weight, presse-papiers *m.*

papered, (*adj.*) tapissé

papist, papiste *m.* and *f.*

papistry, papauté *f.*

par (above), au-dessus du pair

par (at), au pair
par (below), au-dessous du pair
parable, parabole *f.*
parachute, parachute *m.*; *v.i.*
  descendre en parachute
parade, parade *f.*; étalage *m.*;
  faste *m.* (display); promenade *f.*;
  rassemblement *m.* (*mil.*)
parade, *v.t.* faire parade de; *v.i.*
  faire la parade, défiler (*mil.*)
paradise, paradis *m.*
paradox, paradoxe *m.*
paradoxical, (*adj.*) paradoxal
paraffin (oil), pétrole *m.*
paragon, modèle (*m.*), parangon *m.*
paragraph, paragraphe *m.*
paragraph, *v.t.* diviser en para-
  graphes
parallel, (*adj.*) parallèle; semblable, pareil(le)
parallel, parallèle *f.*
paralyse, *v.t.* paralyser
paralysis, paralysie *f.*
paralytic, (*adj.*) paralytique
paramount, (*adj.*) suprême,
  souverain
paramour, amant *m.*; maîtresse *f.*
parapet, parapet *m.*
parasite, parasite *m.*; pique-
  assiette *m.* (sponger)
parasol, ombrelle *f.*
parcel, colis *m.*; paquet *m.*; lot *m.*
parcel, *v.t.* diviser, partager,
  morceler
parcel post, service (*m.*) des colis
  postaux
parcels-delivery, service (*m.*) de
  messageries
parch, *v.t.* brûler; dessécher
parchment, parchemin *m.*
pardon, pardon *m.*; grâce *f.* (*legal*)
pardon, *v.t.* pardonner (à);
  gracier
pardonable, (*adj.*) pardonnable;
  excusable
pare, *v.t.* peler (fruit); rogner
  (nails)
parent, père *m.*; mère *f.*
parentage, parentage *m.*
parental, (*adj.*) des parents
parenthesis, parenthèse *f.*
parish, paroisse *f.* (*eccles.*);
  commune *f.* (*admin.*)

parishioner, paroissien(ne) *m.* (*f.*)
park, parc *m.*; *v.t.* parquer
" no parking," stationnement
  interdit
parley, pourparlers *m. pl.*
parley, *v.i.* parlementer (*mil.*)
parliament, parlement *m.*;
  l'assemblée nationale *f.* (in
  France)
parliamentary, (*adj.*) parlementaire
parlour, parloir *m.*; petit salon *m.*
parody, parodie *f.*
parody, *v.t.* parodier
parole, parole (*f.*) d'honneur
paroxysm, accès *m.*
parrot, perroquet *m.*; perruche *f.*
parry, *v.t.* parer; éviter
parse, *v.t.* analyser
parsimonious, parcimonieux
  (-euse)
parsley, persil *m.*
parson, curé *m.* (Catholic); pasteur *m.* (Protestant)
part, part *f.*; partie *f.*; portion *f.*;
  rôle *m.* (*theat.*); parti *m.* (side);
  région *f.*
part, *v.i.* se séparer de; se quitter
part, *v.t.* diviser; séparer
part with, *v.i.* se défaire de; se
  séparer de
partake, *v.i.* participer (à);
  prendre part (à)
partial, (*adj.*) partial (biassed);
  partiel(le) (in part)
partiality, partialité *f.*; prédilection *f.*
participate, *v.i.* participer (à)
participation, participation *f.*
participle, participe *m.*
particle, particule *f.*; molécule *f.*
particular, (*adj.*) particulier(-ère),
  spécial, déterminé
particular, détail *m.* (*pl.* -s);
  renseignements *m. pl.*; particularité *f.*
parting, (*adj.*) de séparation;
  d'adieu
parting, séparation *f.*; départ *m.*
partisan, partisan *m.*
partition, cloison *f.* (in room);
  partage *m.* (into portions)
partly, (*adv.*) en partie

partner, associé(e) *m.*; partenaire *m.* and *f.* (cards, etc.)
partnership, association *f.*
partridge, perdrix *f.*; perdreau *m.* (young partridge)
party, partie *f.* (pleasure); réunion *f.*; soirée *f.* (evening party); parti *m.* (*polit.*); individu *m.* (person)
pass, passage *m.*; défilé *m.*; gorge *f.*; col *m.* (mountain pass); permis *m.*; laissez-passer *m.* (*mil.*); sauf-conduit *m.* (safe-conduct); permission *f.* (leave pass)
pass, *v.i.* passer; s'écouler (time); être reçu (exam.)
pass, *v.t.* passer, passer par; faire passer; voter (a law); approuver (accounts)
free pass (theatre, etc.), billet (*m.*) de faveur
railway pass, carte (*f.*) de circulation
pass-key, passe-partout *m.* .
passage, passage *m.*; traversée *f.* .(sea trip, etc.); couloir *m.* (*arch.*); corridor *m.*
passenger, voyageur(-euse) *m.* (*f.*); passager(-ère) *m.* (*f.*) (on ship)
passenger train, train (*m.*) de voyageurs
passer-by, passant(e) *m.* (*f.*)
passing, (*adj.*) passager(-ère)
passion, passion *f.*; colère *f.* (anger)
Passion week, la semaine sainte (*f.*)
passionate, (*adj.*) passionné, ardent
passive, (*adj.*) passif(-ive); passif *m.*
Passover, Pâque *f.*
passport, passeport *m.*
pass-word, mot (*m.*) d'ordre
past, (*adj.*) passé, dernier(-ère)
past, passé *m.*
half-past (six), (six) heures et demie
paste, pâte *f.*; colle *f.* (for sticking)
paste, *v.t.* coller
paste up, *v.t.* afficher

paste-board, carton *m.*
pastime, passetemps *m.*
pastor, pasteur *m.*
pastry, pâtisserie *f.*
pasture, pâturage *m.*
pasture, *v.i.* paître; *v.t.* faire paître
pasty, pâté *m.*
pat, tape *f.* (blow); rond (*m.*) de beurre
pat, (*adj.*) à point (for answers)
pat, *v.t.* taper
patch, pièce *f.*; morceau *m.* (land)
patch, *v.t.* rapiécer, raccommoder
patent, (*adj.*) patent
patent, brevet *m.*; brevet (*m.*) d'invention
patent, *v.t.* breveter
patent leather, cuir (*m.*) verni
patentee, breveté *m.*
paternal, (*adj.*) paternel(le)
paternity, paternité *f.*
path, sentier *m.*; chemin *m.*; allée *f.* (in garden)
pathetic, (*adj.*) pathétique
pathway, chemin *m.*
patience, patience *f.*; (cards) réussite *f.*
patient, (*adj.*) patient
patient, (sick person) malade *m.* and *f.*
patrimony, patrimoine *m.*.
patriot, patriote *m.* and *f.*
patriotic, (*adj.*) patriotique
patron(-ess), protecteur(-trice) *m.* (*f.*)
patron saint, patron(ne) *m.*. (*f.*)
patronage, protection *f.*
patronise, *v.t.* protéger, favoriser
patter, boniment *m.* (of cheapjack); fouettement *m.* (of rain)
pattern, modèle *m.*; patron *m.* (of dress); échantillon *m.* (sample); dessin *m.* (design)
paucity, petite quantité *f.*
pauper, pauvre *m.* and *f.*; indigent(e) *m.* (*f.*)
pause, pause *f.*; moment (*m.*) de silence; intervalle *m.*
pause, *v.i.* faire une pause; s'arrêter; délibérer
pave, *v.t.* paver (de)

pavement, pavé *m.*; trottoir *m.* (sidewalk)

pavilion, pavillon *m.*; tente *f.*

paving-stone, pavé *m.*

paw, patte *f.*

paw, *v.t.* manier (to handle); griffer (to scratch)

pawn, pion *m.* (chess); gage *m.* (in pawn)

pawn, *v.t.* mettre en gage

pawnbroker, prêteur sur gage *m.*

pawnshop, mont-de-piété *m.*; crédit municipal *m.*

pay, solde *f.*; gages *m. pl.*; salaire *m.*; traitement *m.*

pay, *v.i.* payer; rapporter (of business) (bring in)

pay, *v.t.* acquitter (bills); payer; rendre (a visit)

payable, *(adj.)* payable

payment, payement *m.*; paiement *m.*

payment in full, pour solde de tout compte

payment on account, accompte *m.*

pea, pois *m.*

green peas, petits pois *m.*

pea-shooter, sarbacane *f.*

peace, paix *f.*

peaceful, *(adj.)* paisible

peacefulness, tranquillité *f.*

peach, pêche *f.*

peach (tree), pêcher *m.*

peacock, paon *m.*

peahen, paonne *f.*

peak, cime *f.* (of mountain); pic *m.*; sommet *m.*; visière *f.* (of cap); apogée *m.* (zenith)

peal, carillon *m.* (of bells); coup *m.*

peal, *v.t.* faire résonner

pear, poire *f.*

pear (tree), poirier *m.*

pearl, perle *f.*

mother-of-pearl, nacre *f.*

peasant, paysan(ne) *m.* *(f.)*

peasantry, paysans *m. pl.*; gens de campagne *m. pl.*

peat, tourbe *f.*

pebble, caillou *m.* *(pl.* -x)

pebbly, *(adj.)* caillouteux(-euse)

peck, picotin *m.* (measure); coup de bec *m.* (of bird)

peck, *v.t.* becqueter

pectoral, *(adj.)* pectoral

peculation, péculat *m.*

peculiar, *(adj.)* particulier(-ère); singulier(-ère); bizarre (queer)

peculiarity, particularité *f.*

pecuniary, *(adj.)* pécuniaire

pedal, pédale *f.*

pedal, *v.i.* pédaler

pedant(e), pédant *m.* *(f.)*

pedantic, *(adj.)* pédantesque

peddle, *v.t.* colporter

peddling, colportage *m.*

pedestrian, piéton *m.*

pedigree, généalogie *f.*

pedlar, colporteur *m.*

peel, pelure *f.*; écorce *f.* (oranges, etc.)

peel, *v.t.* éplucher, peler; *v.i.* s'écailler

peep, coup d'œil *m.*; point *m.* (of day)

peep, *v.i.* regarder à la dérobée

peer, *v.i.* scruter

peer, pair *m.*

peerage, pairie *f.*

peeress, pairesse *f.*

peerless, *(adj.)* incomparable

peevish, *(adj.)* maussade, grincheux(-euse)

peg, cheville *f.*; patère *f.* (for hats); piquet *m.* (tent)

pelican, pélican *m.*

pell-mell, *(adv.)* pêle-mêle

pelmet, lambrequin *m.*

pelt, peau *f.*

pelt, *v.i.* tomber à verse (of rain); *v.t.* lancer (to throw)

pen, plume *f.*; enclos *m.* (animals)

pen, *v.t.* parquer; écrire

penholder, porte-plume *m.*

penknife, canif *m.*

pen-wiper, essuie-plume *m.*

penmanship, calligraphie *f.*

penal, *(adj.)* pénal

penal servitude, travaux *(m.)* forcés

penalty, peine *f.*; amende *f.* (fine)

penance, pénitence *f.*

pencil, crayon *m.*; (propelling) porte-mine *(m.)* à vis

pencil-case, porte-crayon *m.*

pencil-sharpener, taille-crayon *m.*

pendant, pendant *m.*

pendulum, pendule *m.*; balancier *m.*

penetrate, *v.i.* and *v.t.* pénétrer (dans)

penetration, pénétration *f.*; (*fig.*) sagacité *f.*

peninsula, péninsule *f.*; presqu'île *f.*

penitent, (*adj.*) pénitent; contrit; pénitent(e) *m.* (*f.*)

pennant, banderole *f.*; flamme *f.* (*naval*)

penny, deux sous *m.* (*purely nominal*)

penny-a-liner, journaliste (*m.*) de faits divers

penny-in-the-slot machine, distributeur (*m.*) automatique

pension, pension *f.*; pension (*f.*) de retraite; retraite *f.* (officers, etc.)

pension off, *v.t.* mettre à la retraite

pensioner, pensionnaire *m.* (*f.*); invalide *m.* (*mil.*)

pensive, (*adj.*) pensif(-ive)

Pentecost, Pentecôte *f.*

penthouse, appentis *m.*

pent-up, (*adj.*) enfermé; (*fig.*) étouffé

penumbra, pénombre *f.*

penury, indigence *f.*; misère *f.*

people, peuple *m.*; nation *f.*; gens *m. pl.*; la foule *f.* (crowd); les personnes *f. pl.*; le monde *m.*

people, *v.t.* peupler

pepper, poivre *m.*; poivre (*m.*) de Cayenne

pepper, *v.t.* poivrer; (*fig.*) cribler de coups

pepper-caster, poivrière *f.*

peppermint, menthe poivrée *f.*; peppermint *m.*

peppery, (*adj.*) irritable; poivré

perambulate, *v.t.* parcourir

perambulator, voiture (*f.*) d'enfant

perceivable, (*adj.*) perceptible

perceive, *v.t.* apercevoir; s'apercevoir de

per cent., pour cent

percentage, pourcentage *m.*

perception, perception *f.*; sensibilité *f.*

perceptive, (*adj.*) perceptif(-ive)

perch, perche *f.* (fish); perchoir *m.* (for fowls)

perch, *v.i.* se percher, jucher

perchance, (*adv.*) par hasard

percolator, filtre *m.*

percussion, percussion *f.*

percussion fuse, fusée (*f.*) percutante

peremptory, (*adj.*) péremptoire

perfect, (*adj.*) parfait; complet (-ète), accompli

perfect, *v.t.* perfectionner; achever

perfection, perfection *f.*

perfidious, (*adj.*) perfide

perfidy, perfidie *f.*

perforate, *v.t.* perforer; percer

perform, *v.t.* exécuter; accomplir; effectuer; faire

performance, exécution; ouvrage *m.*; œuvre *f.*; représentation *f.* (*theat.*)

no performance, relâche

performer, acteur(-trice) *m.* (*f.*); exécutant *m.*; musicien(ne) *m.* (*f.*); artiste *m.* and *f.*

perfume, parfum *m.*

perfume, *v.t.* parfumer (de)

perfumer, parfumeur *m.*

perhaps, (*adv.*) peut-être

peril, péril *m.*; danger *m.*

perilous, (*adj.*) périlleux(-euse); dangereux(-euse)

period, période *f.*; durée *f.*; époque *f.*

periodical, (*adj.*) périodique

periodical, journal *m.*; périodique *m.*

perish, *v.i.* périr (de); dépérir

perishable, (*adj.*) périssable

periwig, perruque *f.*

perjure, *v.t.* parjurer

perjury, parjure *m.*; faux témoignage *m.*

permanent, (*adj.*) permanent

permanent wave, ondulation (*f.*) permanente

permanent way, voie (*f.*) ferrée

permission, permission *f.*; permis *m.*

permissible, *(adj.)* permissible

permit, permis *m.*; congé *m.*

permit, *v.t.* permettre

pernicious, *(adj.)* pernicieux (-euse)

perpendicular, *(adj.)* perpendiculaire; ligne perpendiculaire *f.*

perpetrate, *v.t.* commettre

perpetual, *(adj.)* perpétuel(le); continuel(le)

perplex, *v.t.* embarrasser

perquisite, émolument *m.*; pourboire *m.*

persecute, persécuter

persecution, persécution *f.*

perseverance, persévérance *f.*

persevere, *v.i.* persévérer

Persian, *(adj.)* persan(e) *(geog.)*; perse *(hist.)*

persist, *v.i.* persister (à)

persistence, persistance *f.*

person, personne *f.*; personnage *m.*; personnes *f. pl.*; gens *m. pl.*

personal, *(adj.)* personnel(-le)

personal property, biens mobiliers *m. pl.*

personify, *v.t.* personnifier

perspective, *(adj.)* perspectif (-ive)

perspective, perspective *f.*

perspicacious, *(adj.)* pénétrant; perspicace

perspiration, transpiration *f.*; sueur *f.*

perspire, *v.i.* transpirer

persuade, *v.t.* persuader

persuade from, *v.t.* dissuader

persuasion, persuasion *f.*; croyance *f.* (creed)

persuasive, *(adj.)* persuasif(-ive)

pert, *(adj.)* impertinent; insolent

perturb, *v.t.* troubler

perusal, lecture *f.*

peruse, *v.t.* lire attentivement; parcourir

pervade, *v.t.* s'infiltrer dans

perverse, *(adj.)* pervers, contraire

pervert, perverti(e) *m.* *(f.)*

pervert, *v.t.* pervertir

pervious, perméable; pénétrable

pestilence, pest, peste *f.*

pestilential, pestilentiel(le); contagieux(-euse)

pestle, pilon *m.*

pet, favori(-te) *m.* *(f.)*

pet, *(adj.)* favori(te)

pet aversion, bête noire *f.*

pet, *v.t.* choyer, dorloter

petal, pétale *m.*

petition, pétition *f.*; demande *f.*; prière *f.*

petitioner, pétitionnaire *m.* and *f.*

petrification, pétrification *f.*

petrify, *v.t.* pétrifier

petrol, essence *f.*

petroleum, pétrole *m.*

petticoat, jupon *m.*

pettifogging, *(adj.)* chicaneur (-euse)

petty, *(adj.)* mesquin, chétif(-ive)

pew, banc *(m.)* d'église

pewter, étain *m.*

phantom, fantôme *m.*

Pharisee, pharisien *m.*

pharmacy, pharmacie *f.*

phase, phase *f.*

pheasant, faisan *m.*

phenomenal, *(adj.)* phénoménal

phenomenon, phénomène *m.*

phial, fiole *f.*

philanthropic, *(adj.)* philanthropique

philanthropist, philanthrope *m.* and *f.*

philanthropy, philanthropie *f.*

philologist, philologue *m.*

philology, philologie *f.*

philosopher, philosophe *m.*; savant *m.*

philosophy, philosophie *f.*

phonetic, *(adj.)* phonétique

phosphorus, phosphore *m.*

photograph, photographie *f.*

photograph, *v.t.* photographier

photographer, photographe *m.*

photography, photographie *f.*

phrase, phrase *f.*; expression *f.*; locution *f.*

phthisis, phtisie *f.*

physic, *v.t.* médicamenter; droguer

physical, *(adj.)* physique

physician, médecin *m*

physic, médecine *f.*

physics, *pl.* physique *f.*
pianist, pianiste *m.* and *f.*
piano, piano *m.*
  cottage piano, piano droit
  grand piano, piano (*m.*) à queue
pick, pic *m.*; choix *m.* (choice)
pick, *v.t.* cueillir (gather); ôter
  (to pull off); ronger (pick a bone);
  chercher (pick a quarrel); crocheter (a lock); éplucher (clean);
  grignoter (nibble)
pick up, *v.t.* ramasser
picked, (*adj.*) d'élite; choisi
picket, jalon *m.*; petit poste;
  piquet *m.* (guard)
picket-boat, vedette *f.*
picking, épluchage *m.* (cleaning);
  choix *m.* (words)
pickings, épluchures *f. pl.*; petits
  profits *m. pl.*
pickle, marinade *f.*
pickle, *v.t.* mariner
pickles, conserves (*f. pl.*) au
  vinaigre
picklock, crochet *m.* (tool);
  crocheteur *m.* (person)
pickpocket, voleur *m.*; pickpocket *m.*
picnic, pique-nique *m.*
pictorial, illustré *m.* (paper)
picture, tableau *m.*; image *f.*;
  peinture *f.* (painting)
picture, *v.t.* dépeindre; représenter; s'imaginer
picture-book, livre d'images *m.*
picture-frame, cadre *m.*
picture-gallery, galerie (*f.*) de
  tableaux; musée (*m.*) de peintures
picture-palace, cinéma *m.*
picturesque, (*adj.*) pittoresque
pie, pâté *m.* (meat); tourte *f.*
  (fruit)
piece, pièce *f.*; morceau *m.*;
  fragment *m.*; bout *m.*
piece, *v.t.* rapiécer; mettre une
  pièce à
piece-goods, tissus (*m. pl.*) en
  pièce
piecemeal, (*adv.*) peu à peu
piece together, *v.t.* joindre
piecework, travail (*m.*) à la tâche
pier, jetée *f.*; embarcadère *m.*;
  pile *f.* (of a bridge)

pierce, *v.t.* percer, pénétrer;
  transpercer
piety, piété *f.*
pig, cochon *m.*; porc *m.*; pourceau *m.*
pigheaded, entêté
pig-iron, fer (*m.*) en gueuse
pigeon, pigeon *m.*
carrier-pigeon, pigeon voyageur
pigeon-hole, case *f.*
pigeon-house, pigeonnier *m.*
pike, pique *f.*; brochet *m.* (fish)
pile, tas *m.*; monceau *m.*; édifice
  m. (building); pilotis *m.* (foundations); pieu *m.* (post); faisceau
  m. (of arms)
pile, *v.t.* entasser, amasser
pilfer, *v.t.* chiper; voler
pilfering, petit vol *m.*
pilgrim, pèlerin(e) *m.* (*f.*)
pilgrimage, pèlerinage *m.*
pill, pillule *f.*
pill-box, boîte (*f.*) à pilules; (*mil.*)
  blockhaus *m.*
pillage, pillage *m.*
pillage, *v.t.* piller, saccager
pillar, pilier *m.*; colonne *f.*
pillar-box, boîte (*f.*) aux lettres
pillion (to ride), monter derrière
  (*cycle*)
pillow, oreiller *m.*
pillow-case, taie (*f.*) d'oreiller
pilot, pilote *m.*
pilot, *v.t.* piloter, servir de pilote;
  conduire
piloting, pilotage *m.*
pilule, dragée *f.*; pilule *f.*
pimp, maquereau *m.*
pimple, bouton *m.*; pustule *f.*
pin, épingle *f.*
safety-pin, épingle (*f.*) de sûreté
pin, *v.t.* attacher avec une épingle;
  épingler
pincers, pince *f.*; tenailles *f. pl.*
pinch, pincée *f.* (of salt, etc.);
  prise *f.* (snuff); (*fig.*) embarras
  m.; gêne *f.*
pinch, *v.i.* se gêner; se priver de
pinch, *v.t.* pincer; serrer; gêner
  (shoes, etc.); (*slang*) chiper
at a pinch, au besoin
pine (tree), pin *m.*
pine, *v.i.* languir

pineapple, ananas *m.*

pinion, aileron *m.*; pignon *m.* (*mech. engin.*)

pink, (*adj.*) rose; (flower) œillet *m.*

pinnace, pinasse *f.*; grand canot *m.*

pinnacle, pinacle *m.*; sommet *m.*

pint, demi-litre *m.*

pioneer, pionnier *m.*

pious, (*adj.*) pieux(-euse)

pipe, tuyau *m.*; conduit *m.* (gas, etc.); pipe *f.* (smoking)

pipe, *v.i.* siffler

piping, tuyautage *m.*; `baguette *f.* (on uniform)

piquant, (*adj.*) piquant

pirate, pirate *m.*

pistol, pistolet *m.*

piston, piston *m.*

piston-rod, tige (*f.*) de piston

pit, fosse *f.*; carrière *f.* (quarry); parterre *m.* (*theat.*); puits *m.* (mining); creux *m.* (of stomach)

pit against, *v.t.* opposer à

arm-pit, aisselle *f.*

coal-pit, mine (*f.*) de houille

pit-coal, charbon (*m.*) de terre; houille *f.*

pit-prop, poteau (*m.*) de mine

pitch, poix *f.* (tar); élévation *f.*; degré *m.* (slope); tangage *m.* (of ship)

pitch, *v.i.* tanguer (of ship); tomber (to fall); camper (to camp)

pitch, *v.t.* lancer, jeter; dresser (a tent)

pitcher, cruche *f.*; broc *m.*

pitchfork, fourche *f.*

piteous, pitiful (*adj.*) piteux (-euse), pitoyable

pitfall, piège *m.*; fosse *f.*

pitiful, (*adj.*) lamentable; compatissant

pity, pitié *f.*; compassion *f.*; dommage *m.* (regret)

pity, *v.t.* avoir pitié de, plaindre

placard, placard *m.*; affiche *f.* (notice on wall, etc.)

place, lieu *m.*; endroit *m.*; localité *f.*; place *f.* (situation); position *f.*; rang *m.* (rank); résidence *f.*; poste *m.*; maison *f.* (dwelling); emploi *m.* (work)

place, *v.t.* placer, mettre

take place, *v.i.* avoir lieu

plague, peste *f.*; tourment *m.*

plague, *v.t.* tourmenter

plain, (*adj.*) simple; plat; sans façon (simple); évident; clair; ordinaire

in plain clothes (i.e. mufti), en civil

plain, plaine *f.*

plain-speaking, franchise *f.*

plainness, simplicité *f.*; clarté *f.*

plaintiff, demandeur(-eresse) *m.* (*f.*); plaignant(e) *m.* (*f.*)

plaintive, (*adj.*) plaintif(-ive)

plait, tresse *f.* (of hair)

plait, *v.t.* tresser

plan, plan *m.*; projet *m.*

plan, *v.t.* projeter; faire le plan de

plane, *v.t.* raboter, aplanir (wood, etc.); *v.i.* descendre en vol plané (of aircraft)

plane, plan *m.*; rabot *m.* (tool); avion *m.* (aircraft)

plane (tree), platane *m.*

planet, planète *f.*

plank, planche *f.*

plant, plante (botanical) *f.*; matériel (industrial) *m.*; outillage *m.* (*tech.*); (*slang*) coup (*m.*) monté (swindle)

plant, *v.t.* planter

plaster, plâtre *m.* (building material); emplâtre *m.* (*med.*)

plaster, *v.t.* plâtrer

plasterer, plâtrier *m.*

plastic, (*adj.*) plastique

plate, assiette *f.*; plaque *f.*; argenterie *f* (silver plate); vaisselle d'or *f.* (gold plate); planche *f.* (engraving)

plate, *v.t.* plaquer; argenter, dorer (to plate with silver, or gold)

platform, plate-forme *f.*; estrade *f.*; quai *m.* (railway)

plating, placage *m.*; blindage *m.* (armour plating)

platinum, platine *m.*

platoon, section *f.*

plausible, (*adj.*) plausible

play, jeu *m.*; récréation *f.*; spectacle *m.* (theatre, etc.)

play, *v.i.* and *v.t.* jouer (*à* of games, *de* of instruments)
give free play to, donner libre cours à
playful, (*adj.*) badin
playground, cour (*f.*) de récréation; préau *m.*
play-hour, heure (*f.*) de récréation
playmate, camarade *m.* and *f.*
plaything, jouet *m.*
plea, procès (*m.*); cause *f.*
plead, *v.i.* and *v.t.* plaider; intercéder (pour)
pleading, plaidoirie *f.*
pleasant, (*adj.*) agréable; gai; charmant
please, *v.t.* plaire à; faire plaisir à; contenter
if you please, s'il vous plaît
pleased, (*adj.*) content; heureux (-euse); charmé
pleasing, (*adj.*) agréable, charmant
pleasure, plaisir *m.*; gré *m.*
pledge, gage *m.*; garantie *f.*; nantissement *m.*
pledge, *v.t.* engager; mettre en gage; boire à (to toast)
plenipotentiary, plénipotentiaire *m.*
plentiful, (*adj.*) abondant
plenty, abondance *f.*
pleurisy, pleurésie *f.*
pliable, pliant, (*adj.*) pliable, flexible
plight, état *m.*; condition *f.*
plight, *v.t.* engager
plod, *v.i.* marcher péniblement; piocher (i.e. to grind, to swot)
plot, morceau (*m.*) de terre; complot *m.*; conspiration *f.*
plot, *v.t.* comploter; relever (diagram, etc.)
plough, charrue *f.*
plough, *v.t.* labourer; sillonner; refuser (a candidate)
ploughman, laboureur *m.*
pluck, courage *m.*
pluck, *v.t.* arracher; cueillir (flowers, etc.)
plucky, courageux(-euse)
plug, tampon *m.*; bouchon *m.*;

prise (*f.*) de courant (electric); bougie (*f.*) d'allumage (sparking plug)
plum, prune *f.*
plum (tree), prunier *m.*
plumb-line, fil (*m.*) à plomb
plumbago, plombagine *f.*
plumber, plombier *m.*
plume, plume *f.*; panache *m.*
plump, (*adj.*) potelé, gras(se)
plunder, butin *m.*; pillage *m.*
plunder, *v.t.* piller
plunge, *v.i.* se plonger; se précipiter
plunge, *v.t.* plonger; précipiter
plunger, plongeur *m.* (*pump*)
plush, peluche *f.*
plush, (*adj.*) de peluche
ply, *v.i.* faire le service entre (ply between)
ply, *v.t.* exercer; employer
pneumatic, (*adj.*) pneumatique
pneumatic tyre, pneu *m.*
pneumonia, pneumonie *f.*
poach, *v.t.* pocher (eggs); braconner (steal)
poacher, braconnier *m.*
pocket, poche *f.*; (of waistcoat) gousset *m.*
pocket, *v.t.* empocher
pocket-book, carnet *m.*; portefeuille *m.*
pocket-handkerchief, mouchoir *m.*
pocket-knife, canif *m.*
pocket-money, argent (*m.*) de poche
pocketful, pleine poche *f.*
pod, cosse *f.*; gousse *f.*
poem, poème *m.*; poésie *f.*
poet, poète *m.*
poetical, (*adj.*) poétique
poetry, poésie *f.*
point, point *m.* (place); pointe *f.* (sharp end); aiguille *f.* (railway)
point, *v.t.* aiguiser
point (at *or* out), *v.t.* indiquer
point-blank, (*adv.*) à bout portant
pointed, (*adj.*) pointu; direct, mordant (remark or manner)
poison, poison *m.*
poison gas, gaz (*m.*) toxique

poison, *v.t.* empoisonner

poisonous, (*adj.*) vénéneux(-euse), venimeux(-euse) (snakes, etc.)

poke, coup *m.*; poche *f.* (i.e. pocket)

poke, *v.t.* pousser (du coude); tisonner (the fire)

poker, tisonnier *m.*; poker *m.* (cards)

polar, (*adj.*) polaire

pole, perche *f.* (measure); bâton *m.* (stick); poteau *m.*; pôle *m.* (geog.)

polemics, polémique *f.*

police, police *f.*; gendarmerie *f.* (mil.)

police-court, tribunal (*m.*) de simple police

policeman, agent de police *m.*; sergent de ville *m.*; gardien de la paix *m.*

police-station, commissariat (*m.*) de police

policy, politique *f.*; police *f.* (insurance)

Polish, polonais(e) (nationality)

polish, poli *m.*; vernis *m.*

shoe polish, cirage *m.*

polish, *v.t.* polir; vernir; cirer

polished, (*adj.*) poli (shoes)

polishing, polissage *m.*

polite, (*adj.*) poli, civil

political, (*adj.*) politique

politician, homme politique *m.*

politics, la politique *f.*

poll, liste électorale *f.*; scrutin *m.*

poll, *v.t.* voter

pollute, *v.t.* souiller

pollution, souillure *f.*

polyglot, (*adj.* and *subst.*) polyglotte *m.* and *f.*

polytechnic, (*adj.*) polytechnique

pomade, pommade *f.*

pommel, pommeau *m.*

pommel, *v.t.* rosser

pomp, pompe *f.*; éclat *m.*; faste *m.*

pompous, (*adj.*) pompeux(-euse); prétentieux(-euse)

pond, étang *m.*; vivier *m.* (fish-pond)

ponder, *v.i.* méditer

ponder, *v.t.* considérer; peser

ponderous, (*adj.*) lourd, pesant

poniard, poignard *m.*

pontiff, pontife *m.*

pontoon, ponton *m.*

pony, poney *m.*; petit cheval *m.*

poodle, caniche *m.* and *f.*

pool, étang *m.*; mare *f.*; (game) poule *f.*

poor, (*adj.*) pauvre, indigent; malheureux, triste (paltry, trifling)

the poor, les pauvres *m.* and *f.* *pl.*; les indigents *m.* *pl.*

poor-box, tronc (*m.*) des pauvres

poor-house, asile (*m.*) des indigents

poorly, (*adj.*) indisposé, souffrant

poorness, pauvreté *f.*; médiocrité *f.* (quality)

pop, *v.i.* éclater, crever

pope, pape *m.*

popery, papisme *m.*

poplar, peuplier *m.*

poppy, pavot *m.*; coquelicot *m.* (field poppy)

populace, populace *f.*

popular, (*adj.*) populaire; en vogue

populous, (*adj.*) populeux(-euse)

porcelain, porcelaine *f.*

porch, porche *m.*; portique *m.*

pore, pore *m.*

pore over, *v.i.* s'absorber dans

pork, porc *m.*

pork butcher, charcutier *m.*

pork chop, côtelette (*f.*) de porc

pornographic, (*adj.*) pornographique

porous, (*adj.*) poreux(-euse)

porpoise, marsouin *m.*

porridge, bouillie (*f.*) d'avoine

port, port *m.* (harbour); bâbord *m.* (naval); porto *m.* (wine)

port-hole, sabord *m.*

portable, portatif(-ive)

portal, portail *m.* (*pl.* -s)

portend, *v.t.* présager; augurer

porter, concierge *m.* (of flats); porteur *m.* (railway); commissionnaire *m.*; facteur *m.*

portfolio, portefeuille *m.*; serviette *f.*

portion, portion *f.*; partie *f.*; part *f.*

portion out, v.t. distribuer
portly, (adj.) corpulent
portrait, portrait m.
portray, v.t. peindre; décrire (describe)
pose, pose f.; affectation f.
pose, v.t. and v.i. poser
position, situation f.; position f.; état m.; condition f.
positive, (adj.) positif(-ive); absolu; sûr
possess, v.t. posséder; avoir; jouir de
possession, possession f.
possessor, possesseur(-euse) m.(f.)
possibility, possibilité f.; moyen m. (means)
possible, (adj.) possible
post, courrier m..(mail); poste m. (mil.); poteau m. (wooden post)
post, v.t. mettre à la poste; poster (a sentry)
by return of post, par retour du courrier
postcard, carte (f.) postale
postman, facteur m.
postmark, cachet (m.) de la poste
postmaster, directeur (m.) des postes
post-office, bureau m. (pl. -x) de(s) poste(s)
post-office order, mandat-poste m.
post-paid, affranchi
postage, affranchissement m.; port m.
postage stamp, timbre-poste m.
poster, affiche f.
posterior, postérieur m.; derrière m.
posterity, postérité f.
posthumous, (adj.) posthume
postpone, v.t. ajourner, différer, remettre·
postscript, postscriptum m.
posture, posture f.; position f.
pot, pot m.; marmite f.
pot, v.t. mettre en pot; tirer (to shoot)
potash, potasse f.
potato, pomme (f.) de terre; **boiled -,** à l'eau; **fried -,** frite(s)

potent, (adj.) puissant; fort
potential, (adj.) potentiel(le); potentiel m.
pothouse, cabaret m.; taverne f.
potter, potier m.
potter about, v.i. flâner, trottiner
pottery, poterie f.
pouch, poche f.; petit sac m.; blague f. (for tobacco); cartouchière f. (for cartridges)
pouch, v.t. empocher
poulterer, marchand (m.) dé volaille
poultry, volaille f.
pounce on, v.i. s'abattre sur
pound, livre f. (both for weight and sterling)
pound, v.t. piler, pilonner
pour, v.t. verser
pour, v.i. couler; pleuvoir à verse (raining)
pout, v.i. faire la moue
poverty, pauvreté f.; **to live in -,** vive dans la gêne
powder, poudre f.; poudre (f.) dentifrice (tooth); poudre à canon (gun)
powder, v.t. pulvériser; réduire en poudre; (se) poudrer (le visage)
powder factory (or **magazine**), poudrière f.
powdered, (adj.) pulverisé; en poudre; poudré
power, pouvoir m.; force f. (strength); puissance f. (might)
the Great Powers, les grandes puissances f. pl.
horse-power, puissance (f.) en chevaux
power-house, usine (f.) génératrice
powerful, (adj.) puissant
powerless, impuissant
pox, vérole f.; petite vérole (small pox)
practicable, (adj.) praticable
practical, (adj.) pratique
practice, pratique f.; habitude f.; usage m.; clientèle f. (of doctors, lawyers, etc.)
practise, v.t. exercer; pratiquer (a profession); mettre en pratique

practise, *v.i.* s'exercer (à)
practitioner, praticien(ne) *m.* (*f.*)
prairie, prairie *f.*
praise, louange *f.*; éloge *m.*
praise, *v.t.* louer; faire l'éloge de
praiseworthy, (*adj.*) louable
prank, escapade *f.*; tour *m.*
prattle, *v.i.* babiller; (*subst.*) babil *m.*
prawn, crevette *f.*
pray, *v.i.* and *v.t.* prier; supplier; implorer
prayer, prière *f.*; supplication *f.*
prayer-book, livre (*m.*) de prières
Lord's Prayer, oraison (*f.*) dominicale
preach, *v.t.* prêcher
preamble, préambule *m.*
precarious, (*adj.*) précaire
precaution, précaution *f.*
precede, *v.t.* précéder; avoir le pas sur
precedence, priorité *f.*; préséance *f.*
precedent, précédent *m.*
preceding, (*adj.*) précédent
precept, précepte *m.*
precious, (*adj.*) précieux(-euse)
precipice, précipice *m.*
precipitate, (*adj.*) précipité; précipité *m.* (*chem.*)
precipitate, *v.t.* précipiter
précis, précis *m.* (abstract)
precise, (*adj.*) précis; exact; pointilleux(-euse)
precision, précision *f.*; exactitude *f.*
preclude, *v.t.* exclure
precocious, (*adj.*) précoce
preconceived, (*adj.*) formé d'avance
precursor, avant-coureur *m.*
predatory, (*adj.*) rapace
predicament, prédicament *m.*; situation (*f.*) difficile
predict, *v.t.* prédire
prediction, prédiction *f.*
predilection, prédilection *f.*
predominant, prédominant
preface, préface *f.*; avant-propos *m.*
prefatory, (*adj.*) préliminaire

prefer, *v.t.* préférer; aimer mieux
preferable, (*adj.*) préférable
preference, préférence *f.*
preference shares, actions privilégiées
preferment, avancement *m.*
pregnant, (*adj.*) enceinte
prejudice, préjugé *m.*; tort *m.*; dommage *m.*
prejudice, *v.t.* prévenir (contre); nuire (à)
prelate, prélat *m.*
preliminary, (*adj.*) préliminaire
prelude, prélude *m.*
premature, (*adj.*) prématuré
premeditation, préméditation *f.*
premier, premier ministre *m.*; président (*m.*) du conseil; (*adj.*) premier(-ère)
premises, lieux *m. pl.*; local *m.*; prémisse *f.* (in logic)
on the premises, sur les lieux
premium, prime *f.*; récompense *f.*
premonition, prémonition *f.*
prepaid, (*adj.*) affranchi; franc de port
preparation, préparation *f.*; préparatifs *m. pl.*; heures (*f. pl.*) d'étude (scholastic)
preparatory, (*adj.*) préparatoire; (*as adv.*) préalablement
prepare, *v.i.* se préparer; s'apprêter à
prepare, *v.t.* préparer
prepay, *v.t.* payer d'avance; affranchir
prepossess, *v.t.* prévenir
prepossessing, (*adj.*) prévenant
preposterous, (*adj.*) absurde
presage, *v.t.* présager
presbyterian, presbytérien(ne) *m.* (*f.*)
presbytery, presbytère *m.*
prescribe, *v.t.* prescrire
prescription, ordonnance *f.*
presence, présence *f.*; air *m.*; mine *f.* (mien)
present, (*adj.*) présent; courant; actuel(le)
present, cadeau *m.*; don *m.*; présent *m.*
present, *v.t.* présenter; offrir

presentable, (adj.) présentable

presentation, présentation f.

presentiment, pressentiment m.

presently, tout à l'heure; bientôt

preservation, conservation f.

preservative, préservatif m.; (adj.) préservatif(-ive)

preserve, confiture f.; conserves f. pl.; chasse (f.) réservée (shooting)

preserve, v.t. préserver; conserver; confire

life preserver, matraque f.; casse-tête m.

preside, v.i. présider (à)

president, président m.; recteur (m.) (university)

press, la presse f.; armoire f. (cupboard); pressoir m. (fruit, wine, etc.)

press, v.i. presser; pousser (push); avancer (press forward)

press, v.t. presser; serrer (squeeze); étreindre; insister sur

press cutting, coupure (f.) de journal

pressman, journaliste m.; reporter m.

in the press, sous presse (publishing term)

pressing, (adj.) urgent

pressure, pression f.; charge f. (of water, etc.); poids m. (weight)

pressure gauge, manomètre m.

presumably, (adv.) probablement

presume, v.t. présumer

presumption, présomption f.

presumptuous, (adj.) présomptueux(-euse)

pretence, prétexte m.; feinte f.

false pretences, moyens frauduleux m. pl.

under pretence of, sous prétexte de

pretend, v.i. prétendre (à); feindre (de)

pretend, v.t. faire semblant de; prétendre

pretend ignorance, faire l'ignorant

pretended, (adj) prétendu, soidisant

pretension, prétention f.

pretentious, (adj.) prétentieux (-euse)

pretext, prétexte m.

prettily, (adv.) joliment; gentiment

prettiness, gentillesse f.; élégance f.

pretty, (adj.) joli, gentil(le)

pretty, (adv.) assez; passablement

prevail, v.i. prévaloir; l'emporter sur; dominer; - upon, décider qn. à

prevalent, (adj.) dominant; général

prevent, v.t. empêcher; prévenir

preventable, (adj.) évitable

prevention, empêchement m.

preventive, préservatif m.

preventive, (adj.) préventif(-ive)

previous, (adj.) préalable; antérieur

prey, proie f.

prey on, v.i. ronger; obséder (on mind)

fall a prey to, devenir la proie de

price, v.t. mettre un prix (à)

price, prix m.

at any price, coûte que coûte

cost price, prix de revient

half-price, à moitié prix

lowest price, dernier prix

reduced price, au rabais

price list, tarif m.

market price, cours du change (stock exchange)

priceless, sans prix; innappréciable; (slang) impayable

prick, piqûre f.

prick, v.t. piquer; dresser les oreilles (dog)

pride, orgueil m.; fierté f.

priest, prêtre m.

priggish, (adj.) suffisant

prim, (adj.) affecté, guindé

primary, (adj.) primaire; principal

primate, primat m.

prime, v.t. amorcer (a pump, etc.)

prime, (adj.) de première qualité; excellent

prime of life, fleur (f.) de l'âge

prime minister, premier ministre *m.*; président du conseil)
(France)
primeval, (*adj.*) primitif(-ive),
primordial
primrose, primevère *f.*
prince, prince *m.*
princess, princesse *f.*
principal, (*adj.*) principal; pre-
mier(-ère)
principal, directeur(-trice) *m.*
(*f.*), proviseur *m.* (of lycée)
principality, principauté *f.*
principle, principe *m.*
print, empreinte *f.* (mark); impression *f.*; imprimé *m.* (printed
matter); épreuve *f.* (*phot.*);
caractère *m.*; trace *f.*
print, *v.t.* imprimer; faire une
empreinte sur
printer, imprimeur *m.*
printing-office, imprimerie *f.*
prior, (*adj.*) antérieur
prior, prieur *m.*
priority, priorité *f.*
prism, prisme *m.*
prismatic, (*adj.*) prismatique
prison, prison *f.*
prisoner, prisonnier(-ère) *m.* (*f.*)
private, (*adj.*) particulier(-ère);
personnel(le); secret(-ète); con-
fidentiel(le)
private, (*mil.*) simple soldat *m.*
privacy, intimité *f.*
privation, privation *f.*
privilege, privilège *m.*
privilege, *v.t.* privilégier
privy, (*adj.*) privé, caché
privy council, conseil privé *m.*
prize, prix *m.*; lot *m.* (in lottery);
prise *f.* (capture)
prize, *v.t.* évaluer, estimer
prize-court, tribunal (*m.*) des
prises
prize-fighter, pugiliste *m.*; boxeur *m.*
prize-fighting, la boxe *f.*
prize-giving, distribution (*f.*)
des prix
prize-winner, médaillé *m.*; lau-
réat(e) *m.* (*f.*) (scholastic)
pro and con, pour et contre
probability, probabilité *f.*

probable, (*adj.*) probable
problem, problème *m.*
problematic, (*adj.*) problématique
procedure, procédé *m.*
proceed, *v.i.* procéder; avancer;
marcher; provenir (de); continuer; se mettre à (proceed to,
begin)
proceeding, procédé *m.*; manière
(*f.*) d'agir
proceedings, *pl.* compte rendu
m.; procès-verbal *m.* (*legal*)
process, procédé *m.*; procès *m.*
procession, cortège *m.*
proclaim, *v.t.* proclamer; déclarer
proclamation, proclamation *f.*;
déclaration *f.*
procrastinate, *v.i.* temporiser
procreate, *v.t.* procréer
procuration, procuration *f.*
procure, *v.t.* procurer; faire avoir
procuress, entremetteuse *f.*
prod, *v.t.* pousser, tâter
prodigal, (*adj.*) prodigue
prodigality, prodigalité *f.*
prodigious, prodigieux(-euse)
prodigy, prodige *m.*
produce, produit *m.*
produce, *v.t.* produire
producer, producteur *m.*;
(*theat.*) metteur (*m.*) en scène
product, production, produit
m.; production *f.*
productive, productif(-ive)
profane, (*adj.*) profane
profane, *v.t.* profaner
profanity, impiété *f.*
profess, *v.t.* déclarer; exercer (a
profession)
profession, profession *f.*; métier
m. (calling)
professional, (*adj.*) du métier;
professionnel(le)
professor, professeur *m.*
professorship, professorat *m.*
profile, profil *m.*
profit, profit *m.*; bénéfice *m.*;
rapport *m.*
profit, *v.i.* profiter (de)
profitable, profitable, avanta-
geux(-euse)
profligacy, libertinage *m.*

profligate, (*adj.*) débauché
profligate, libertin *m.*; mauvais sujet *m.*
profound, (*adj.*) profond
profuse, (*adj.*) abondant, excessif(-ive)
profusion, abondance *f.*; profusion *f.*; prodigalité *f.*
prognostic, pronostic *m.*
programme, programme *m.*
progress, progrès *m.*; cours *m.*; marche *f.*
progress, *v.i.* s'avancer, faire des progrès
prohibit, *v.t.* prohiber, défendre
prohibition, défense *f.*; interdiction *f.*
project, projet *m.*
project, *v.i.* être en saillie (to jut out)
project, *v.t.* projeter
projectile, projectile *m.*
projecting, (*adj.*) en saillie; saillant
proletarian, (*adj.*) prolétaire
proletariat, prolétariat *m.*
prolific, (*adj.*) fertile; fécond
prologue, prologue *m.*
prolongation, prolongement *m.*; prolongation *f.* (time)
prolong, *v.t.* prolonger
promenade, promenade *f.*; promenoir *m.* (indoor gallery)
prominence, proéminence *f.*; distinction *f.*
prominent, (*adj.*) proéminent; saillant; accentué; éminent
promiscuous, (*adj.*) sans ordre; confus
promiscuously, en commun; en promiscuité
promise, promesse *f.*; espérance *f.* (hope)
promise, *v.i.* and *v.t.* promettre
promissory note, billet (*m.*) à ordre
promontory, promontoire *m.*
promote, *v.t.* avancer; encourager
promoter, lanceur (*m.*) d'affaires (company promoter, etc.); fondateur *m.*
promotion, promotion *f.*; avancement *m.*

prompt, *v.t.* suggérer, pousser; souffler (*theat.*)
prompt, (*adj.*) empressé; prompt
prompter, souffleur *m.* (*theat.*)
promulgate, *v.t.* promulguer
prone, (*adj.*) incliné; étendu; disposé (prone to)
prong, fourchon *m.*
pronoun, pronom *m.*
pronounce, *v.t.* prononcer; annoncer, déclarer
pronunciation, prononciation *f.*; accent *m.*
pronounced, (*adj.*) prononcé
proof, preuve *f.*; épreuve *f.*
as a proof, en preuve
proof against, à l'épreuve de
put to the proof, *v.t.* mettre à l'épreuve
proof-reader, correcteur *m.*
proof-sheet, épreuve *f.*
prop, étai *m.* (stay); soutien *m.*; appui *m.*
prop, *v.t.* étayer (prop up); appuyer; soutenir
propagate, *v.t.* propager; répandre; enfanter (children)
propel, *v.t.* pousser en avant; faire marcher
propeller, hélice *f.* (of ship or plane)
propensity, penchant *m.*
proper, (*adj.*) propre, particulier (-ère); convenable; exact (time)
properly, (*adv.*) convenablement
property, propriété *f.* (estate); bien *m.*; biens *m. pl.*; accessoire *m.* (*theat.*)
personal property, effets (*m. pl.*) mobiliers
real property, biens (*m. pl.*) immeubles
prophecy, prophétie *f.*
prophecy, *v.t.* prédire
prophet, prophète *m.*
proportion, proportion *f.*; mesure *f.*
in proportion as, à mesure que
proportional, proportionnel(le); en proportion
proposal, proposition *f.*
propose, *v.t.* proposer; offrir
proposition, proposition *f.*

proprietor, propriétaire *m.* and *f.*

propriety, convenance *f.*; convenances *f. pl.*

prorogation, prorogation *f.*

prorogue, *v.t.* proroger

prosaic, (*adj.*) prosaïque

proscribe, *v.t.* proscrire

prose, prose *f.*

prose-writer, prosateur *m.*

prosecute, *v.t.* poursuivre; poursuivre en justice

prosecution, poursuite *f.*; poursuites (*f. pl.*) judiciaires

prospect, perspective *f.*; vue *f.*; coup d'œil *m.*; avenir *m.* (future)

prospecting, recherches *f. pl.*

prospective, (*adj.*) en perspective

prospectus, prospectus *m.*

prosper, *v.i.* prospérer; réussir

prosperity, prospérité *f.*

prosperous, (*adj.*) prospère; florissant

prostitute, prostituée *f.*

prostitute, *v.t.* prostituer

prostitution, prostitution *f.*

prostrate, (*adj.*) prosterné

prostrate, *v.t.* se prosterner devant

protect, *v.t.* protéger, défendre; sauvegarder (interests)

protection, protection *f.*; défense *f.*; garantie *f.*

protective, (*adj.*) protecteur (-trice)

protector, protecteur(-trice) *m.* (*f.*)

protectorate, protectorat *m.*

protest, protestation *f.*; protêt *m.* (*commer.*)

protest, *v.t.* protester; faire protester; *v.i.* protester

protestant, protestant(e) *m.* (*f.*)

protestation, protestation *f.*

protract, *v.t.* prolonger; faire traîner, différer (defer)

protrude, *v.i.* s'avancer, faire saillie

protrusion, saillie *f.*

protuberance, protubérance *f.*

proud, (*adj.*) fier (fière); orgueilleux(-euse)

to be proud of, être fier de; s'enorgueillir (de)

prove, *v.i.* se montrer

prove, *v.t.* prouver, démontrer; mettre à l'épreuve; éprouver; vérifier (will, etc.)

proved, (*adj.*) prouvé; reconnu

proverb, proverbe *m.*

proverbial, (*adj.*) proverbial

provide, *v.t.* pourvoir; fournir; stipuler

provide against, *v.i.* prendre des mesures contre

provide oneself with, se pourvoir de

provided that, pourvu que

providence, providence *f.*; prévoyance *f.*

provident, (*adj.*) prévoyant

providential, (*adj.*) providentiel (le)

province, province *f.*; département *m.*; ressort *m.*

provision, stipulation *f.*; disposition *f.* (*legal*)

provisions, vivres *m. pl.*; provisions *f. pl.*

to lay in provision, faire provision de

to make provision for, pourvoir; faire une pension à

provisional, (*adj.*) provisoire

proviso, clause *f.*; condition *f.*

with the proviso that, à condition que

provocation, provocation *f.*

provocative, (*adj.*) provocant

provoke, *v.t.* provoquer; inciter

prow, proue *f.*

prowess, bravoure *f.*; prouesse *f.*

proximity, proximité *f.*

proxy, procuration *f.*; délégué(e) *m.* (*f.*) (person)

prude, prude *f.*

prudence, prudence *f.*

prudent, (*adj.*) prudent, sage

prune, pruneau *m.*

prune, *v.t.* tailler, émonder

prurience, démangeaison *f.*; pensées (*f. pl.*) lascives

prurient, lascif(-ive)

Prussian, (*adj.* and *subst.*) prussien(ne)

psalm, psaume *m.*

psychologic(al), (*adj.*) psychologique

psychologist, psychologue *m.*

psychology, psychologie *f.*

public, (*adj.*) public (*f.* publique)

public, public *m.*; peuple *m.*

public house, café *m.*, bistrot *m.*; auberge *f.*

publican, patron de café (bistrot); aubergiste *m.*

publication, publication *f.*

publicist, publiciste *m.*

publish, *v.t.* publier; éditer

publisher, éditeur *m.*

pucker, ride *f.*; *v.t.* rider

pudding, pouding *m.*

puddle, flaque (*f.*) d'eau

puff, souffle *m.* (breath); bouffée *f.* (smoke, wind); houppe *f.* (powder-puff); réclame *f.* (advertisement)

puff, *v.i.* souffler; haleter

pug-nose, nez (*m.*) épaté

pugilist, boxeur *m.*

pull, traction *f.*; coup *m.*; avantage *m.*; (*slang*) piston *m.* (i.e. influence)

pull, *v.t.* tirer; arracher

pull back, *v.t.* faire reculer

pull down, *v.t.* faire tomber; abattre

pull off, *v.t.* arracher, enlever (clothes)

pull open, *v.t.* ouvrir

pull up, *v.i.* s'arrêter

pulley, poulie *f.*

pulmonary, (*adj.*) pulmonaire

pulp, pulpe *f.*

pulpit, chaire *f.*

pulse, pouls *m.*

feel the pulse, tâter le pouls

pulverise, *v.t.* pulvériser; réduire en poudre

pumice, pierre-ponce *f.*

pump, pompe *f.*; escarpin *m.* (shoe)

petrol pump, pompe à essence

pump, *v.t.* pomper; *v.i.* pomper

pumpkin, citrouille *f.*

pun, calembour *m.*

punch, coup (*m.*) de poing (blow); poinçon *m.* (for tickets, etc.)

punch, *v.t.* percer, poinçonner, donner un coup de poing

Punch, polichinelle *m.*; guignol *m.* (Punch and Judy)

punctilious, (*adj.*) pointilleux (-euse)

punctual, (*adj.*) ponctuel(le)

punctuality, ponctualité *f.*

punctuation, ponctuation *f.*

puncture, ponction *f* (*surg*); piqûre *f.*; crevaison *f.* (of tyre)

puncture, *v.t.* piquer; crever (of tyre)

pungency, aigreur *f.*; piquant *m.*

pungent, (*adj.*) âcre; piquant; mordant

punic, (*adj.*) punique

punish, *v.t.* punir; corriger

punishment, punition *f.*; peine *f.*; châtiment *m.*

punitive, (*adj.*) punitif(-ive)

punt, bachot *m.*; coup (*m.*) de volée (football)

punt, *v.i.* ponter (cards); parier (turf)

puny, (*adj.*) chétif(-ive)

pup, puppy, petit chien *m.*; freluquet *m.* (of person)

pupil, élève *m.* and *f.*; prunelle *f.* (of eye)

puppet, poupée *f.*; marionnette *f.*; pantin *m.*

puppet government, gouvernement (*m.*) fantoche

purblind, (*adj.*) myope

purchase, achat *m.*; emplette *f.*

purchase, *v.t.* acheter; faire des emplettes

pure, (*adj.*) pur

purgative, purgatif *m.*; (*adj.*) purgatif(-ive)

purgatory, purgatoire *m.*

purge, *v.t.* purger; purge *f.*

purification, purification *f.*; épuration *f.*

purify, *v.t.* purifier

purist, puriste *m.* and *f.*

puritan, (*adj.* and *subst.*) puritain(e) *m.* (*f.*)

purity, pureté *f.*

purlieu, alentours *m. pl.*

purloin, *v.t.* dérober; voler

purple, (*adj.*) pourpre; pourpre *m.*

purport, sens *m.*

purpose, but *m.*; objet *m.*; dessein *m.*; intention *f.*

purpose, *v.t.* se proposer; avoir l'intention de

to answer a purpose, remplir un but, servir

on purpose, exprès

to no purpose, en vain

to the purpose, à propos

purposely, exprès, à dessein

purr, *v.i.* ronronner

purring, ronron *m.*

purse, porte-monnaie *m.*; bourse *f.*

purse, *v.t.* plisser; froncer (eyebrows, etc.)

purser, commissaire *m.* (ship)

in pursuance of, conformément à

pursue, *v.t.* poursuivre; suivre

pursuit, poursuite *f.*

pursuit plane, chasseur *m.*

pursy, (*adj.*) poussif(-ive)

purulence, purulence *f.*

purulent, (*adj.*) purulent

purvey, *v.t.* fournir

purveyor, fournisseur *m.*

pus, pus *m.*

push, coup *m.*; poussée *f.*; impulsion *f.*

push, *v.t.* pousser; importuner

pushing, (*adj.*) entreprenant

pusillanimity, pusillanimité *f.*

pusillanimous, (*adj.*) pusillanime

puss(y), minet *m.*; minette *f.*

pustule, pustule *f.*

pustular, (*adj.*) pustuleux(-euse)

put, *v.t.*, mettre; poser; placer; poser (ask question, etc.)

put aside, *v.t.* mettre de côté

put away, *v.t.* ranger; écarter

put back, *v.t.* remettre

put down, *v.t.* déposer; supprimer

put forward, *v.t.* avancer (theory, etc.)

put in mind of, *v.t.* rappeler

put off, *v.t.* ôter; différer (defer)

put on, *v.t.* mettre (clothes); prendre (assume)

put out, *v.t.* mettre dehors (outside); éteindre (fire); déranger (trouble)

put up, *v.i.* descendre... chez (at a friend's house, or hotel)

put up with, *v.t.* endurer, supporter

putative, (*adj.*) putatif(-ive)

putrefaction, putréfaction *f.*

putrefy, *v.i.* se putréfier; pourrir

putrid, (*adj.*) putride

putt, *v.t.* (golf) poter

putty, mastic *m.*

puzzle, énigme *f.*; rébus *m.*

puzzle, *v.i.* and *v.t.* embarrasser; intriguer

pygmy, pygmée *m.* and *f.*

pyramid, pyramide *f.*

pyramidal, (*adj.*) pyramidal

pyre, bûcher *m.*

Pyrenees, Pyrénées *f. pl.*

pyrotechnic, (*adj.*) pyrotechnique

python, python *m.*; pythonisse *f.*

pyx, ciboire *m.*

Q

quack, charlatan *m.*; couin-couin *m.* (of duck)

quackery, charlatanerie *f.*

quadrangle, quadrangle *m.*; cour *f.*

quadrant, quart (*m.*) de cercle

quadrilateral, quadrilatère *m.*

quadrille, quadrille *m.*

quadroon, quarteron(ne) *m.* (*f.*)

quadruped, quadrupède *m.*

quadruple, (*adj.*) quadruple

quaff, *v.t.* boire à grands traits

quagmire, fondrière *f.*

quail, caille *f.*

quail, *v.i.* fléchir, trembler

quaint, (*adj.*) bizarre, original, singulier(-ère)

quaintness, singularité *f.*

quake, *v.i.* trembler

qualify, *v.t.* rendre capable de; modifier (one's opinion); *v.i.* être reçu (to qualify as)

qualification, titres *m pl.*; réserve *f.*

quality, qualité *f.*

qualm, scrupule *m.*; soulèvement (*m.*) de cœur
quantitative, (*adj.*) quantitatif (-ive)
quantity, quantité *f.*; portion *f.*; grand nombre *m.*
quarantine, quarantaine *f.*
quarrel, querelle *f.*; dispute *f.*
quarrel, *v.i.* se quereller
quarrelsome, (*adj.*) querelleur (-euse)
quarry, carrière *f.* (stone); proie *f.* (prey)
quart, litre *m.* (*approx.*)
quartan, fièvre quarte *f.*
quarter, quart (fraction) *m.*; quartier *m.* (district); trimestre *m.* (three months); terme *m.* (quarter-day); cantonnement *m.*; logement *m.* (of troops)
quarter, *v.t.* loger; diviser en quatre
quarter-deck, gaillard (*m.*) d'arrière
quarterly, (*adj.*) trimestriel(le)
quartermaster-general, intendant général *m.*
quartermaster-sergeant, maréchal (*m.*) des logis chef (cavalry and artillery); sergent-chef (*m.*) (infantry)
quartern, quart (*m.*) de pinte; pain (*m.*) de quatre livres
quartet, quatuor *m.*
quarto, in-quarto *m.*
quartz, quartz *m.*
quash, *v.t.* écraser; casser (a sentence, verdict)
quasi, (*adv.*) quasi
quatrain, quatrain *m.*
quaver, trille *m.*; croche *f.* (note in music)
quaver, *v.i.* triller; trembloter (in speaking)
quay, quai *m.*
quean, fille (*f.*) de mauvaise vie; donzelle *f.*
queen, reine *f.*; dame *f.* (*cards*)
queenly, (*adv.*) de reine
queer, (*adj.*) étrange; drôle
queerness, étrangeté *f.*
quell, *v.t.* dompter; réprimer
quench, *v.t.* éteindre; étancher

quenchless, inextinguible
querulous, plaintif(-ive)
querulousness, habitude (*f.*) de se plaindre
query, question *f.*
query, *v.t.* mettre en doute
quest, recherche *f.*
question, question *f.*; mise (*f.*) en doute
question, *v.t.* questionner; interroger; douter
the question is . . . ., il s'agit de...
questionable, (*adj.*) contestable, douteux
questioner, interrogateur(-trice) *m.* (*f.*)
quibble, chicane *f.*; jeu (*m.*) de mots
quibble, *v.i.* ergoter
quick, (*adj.*) rapide; prompt, agile; vif (vive) (alive); intelligent
quick(ly), (*adv.*) vite; rapidement
quicken, *v.i.* s'animer; *v.t.* stimuler, animer
quicklime, chaux-vive *f.*
quickness, vitesse *f.*; rapidité *f.*; vivacité *f.*
quicksand, sable (*m.*) mouvant
quicksilver, vif-argent *m.*; mercure *m.*
quick-tempered, vif, colérique
quick-witted, à l'esprit vif
quid, chique *f.*; (*slang*) livre *f.* (sterling)
quiet, (*adj.*) calme, tranquille; en repos; modeste
quiet, *v.t.* tranquilliser, calmer
quiet down, *v.i.* s'apaiser; se calmer
quietness, tranquillité *f.*; calme *m.*; repos *m.*
quietus, coup (*m.*) de grâce
quill, plume *f.*; plume (*f.*) d'oie
quilt, couvre-pieds *m.*
quince, coing *m.*
quince (tree), cognassier *m.*
quinine, quinine *f.*
quinquagesima, quinquagésime *f.*
quinquennial, (*adj.*) quinquennal
quinsy, esquinancie *f.*
quip, mot piquant *m.*; raillerie *f.*

quire (of paper), main *f.*
quirk, subtilité *f.*
quit, *v.t.* quitter, abandonner
quit-rent, redevance *f.*
quite, tout à fait; entièrement; complètement
quits, (*adj.*) quitte(s)
quittance, quittance *f.*; décharge *f.*
quiver, carquois *m.*
quiver, *v.i.* trembler, frémir
quixotic, (*adj.*) exalté, de Don Quichotte
quiz, *v.t.* railler, persifler
quiz, devinette *f.*; examen oral *m.*
quoit, palet *m.*
quondam, (*adj.*) ci-devant
quorum, nombre (*m.*) suffisant
quota, quote-part *f.*; contingent *m.*
quotation, citation *f.*; cote *f.* (*commer.*); cours *m.* (*Stock Exchange*)
quote, *v.t.* citer; coter (*commer.*)
quotient, quotient *m.*

R

rabbi, rabbin *m.*
rabbit, lapin(e) *m.* (*f.*)
rabbit-warren, garenne *f.* (à lapins)
rabble, canaille *f.*; cohue *f.*
rabid, (*adj.*) féroce, furieux (-euse); enragé (dogs)
rabies, hydrophobie *f.*; rage *f.*
race, race *f.* (breed); course *f.* (contest)
race, *v.i.* courir vite; *v.t.* lutter de vitesse avec
race-course, champ (*m.*) de courses
race-horse, cheval (*m.*) de course
race-meeting, concours (*m.*) hippique
racing, les courses *f. pl.*
rack, râtelier *m.* (in stable); porte-manteau; *m,* (hat); filet *m.* (for luggage)
racket, raquette *f.* (tennis); fracas *m.* (uproar); escroquerie *f.* (swindle)

racking, (*adj.*) atroce (pain)
racy, (*adj.*) piquant, vif
radial, (*adj.*) radial
radiance, éclat *m.*; rayonnement *m.*
radiant, (*adj.*) éclatant, radieux (-euse)
radiate, *v.i.* rayonner; *v.t.* émettre; diffuser (a wireless programme)
radiation, rayonnement *m.*
radiator, radiateur *m.*
radical, (*adj.*) radical
radicalism, radicalisme *m.*
radio (set), poste (*m.*) de T.S.F.
radio-operator, sansfiliste *m.*; radio *m.*
radish, radis *m.*
radius, rayon *m.*
raffle, loterie *f.*; tombola *f.*
raft, train (*m.*) de bois (lumber); radeau *m.*
rafter, poutre *f.*; chevron *m.*
rag, chiffon *m.*; canular *m.* (joke, etc.)
rag-picker, chiffonnier(-ère) *m.* (*f.*)
rage, rage *f.*; fureur *f.*; furie *f.*
rage, *v.i.* être furieux
ragged, en haillons
raging, (*adj.*) furieux(-euse)
raging, fureur *f.*
ragout, ragoût *m.*
raid, incursion *f.*; razzia *f.*; rafle *f.* (police raid); raid *m.*
raider, maraudeur *m.*
rail, barre *f.*; rampe *f.* (of staircase); balustrade *f.*; grille *f.*; garde-fou *m.*; chemin de fer *m.* (railway)
rail (at), *v.i.* dire des injures à
rail round, *v.t.* entourer d'une grille, griller
railing, grille *f.*; garde-fou *m.*
raillery, raillerie *f.*
railway, chemin de fer *m.*; voie (*f.*) ferrée
raiment, vêtements *m. pl.*
rain, pluie *f.*
rain, *v.i.* pleuvoir
rain cats and dogs, *v.i.* pleuvoir des hallebardes
rain hard, *v.i.* pleuvoir à verse
rainbow, arc-en-ciel *m.*

rainproof, (*adj.*) imperméable

rainy, pluvieux(-euse)

raise, *v.t.* lever; élever; hausser (prices); soulever (to lift); augmenter (increase); se procurer (money)

raisin, raisin sec *m.*

rake, râteau *m.* (tool); débauché *m.* (person)

rake, *v.t.* râteler

rake-off (*slang*), gratte *f.*

rakish, (*adj.*) dissolu, élancé (car, ship)

rally, *v.t.* rallier; rassembler; railler (jeer at); rallye *m.* (cars)

ram, bélier *m.*; mouton *m.*

ram, *v.t.* enfoncer, bourrer

ramble, excursion *f.*; promenade *f.*

ramble, *v.i.* errer, rôder; (*fig.*) divaguer (in speech)

ramification, ramification *f.*

ramp, rampe *f.*; affaire (*f.*) véreuse (swindle)

rampage, vacarme *m.*; désordre *m.*

rampageous, (*adj.*) fougueux (-euse)

rampant, (*a d j.*) rampant (*heraldry*); effréné

rampart, rempart *m.*

ramshackle, (*adj.*) délabré

rancid, (*adj.*) rance

rancorous, (*adj.*) rancunier(-ère); haineux(-euse)

rancour, rancune *f.*

random (at), au hasard

range, rang *m.* (row); rangée *f.*; portée *f.* (of gun); chaîne *f.* (of mountains); fourneau *m.* (kitchen)

rank, rang *m.*; ordre *m.*; grade *m.* (*mil.*)

rank, *v.t.* ranger, classer

rank, *v.i.* être classé

rankle, *v.i.* s'envenimer; s'enflammer

rankness, luxuriance *f.*; odeur forte *f.*

ransack, *v.t.* saccager; fouiller

ransom, rançon *f.*

ransom, *v.t.* rançonner, racheter

rant, *v.i.* déclamer avec vigueur

ranting, (*adj.*) extravagant

rap, coup *m.*

rap, *v.t.* frapper

rapacious, (*adj.*) rapace

rapacity, rapacité *f.*

rape, viol *m.*

rape, colza *m.* (oil and seed)

rape, *v.t.* violer

rapid, (*adj.*) rapide

rapidity, rapidité *f.*

rapier, rapière *f.*

rapine, rapine *f.*

rapt, (*adj.*) ravi; extasié

rapture, ravissement *m.*

rapturous, ravissant; enthousiaste

rare, (*adj.*) rare; fameux(-euse); (cooking) saignant, peu cuit

rarefy, *v.t.* raréfier

rareness, rarity, rareté *f.*

rascal, fripon *m.*; gredin *m.*; coquin *m.*

rascality, friponnerie *f.*

rase, raze, *v.t.* raser, effacer

rash, (*adj.*) téméraire, imprudent

rash, éruption *f.*

rashness, imprudence *f.*; témérité *f.*

rasp, râpe *f.*

rasp, *v.t.* râper, râcler

raspberry, framboise *f.*

rat, rat *m.*

to smell a rat, flairer un piège

rate, proportion *f.*; cours *m.*; taux *m* (exchange); vitesse *f.* (of speed); impôt *m.*

rate, *v.t.* évaluer; réprimander; classer

rateable, (*adj.*) imposable

ratepayer, contribuable *m.* and *f.*

rather, (*adv.*) plutôt; quelque peu (somewhat); assez (passably)

I would rather, j'aimerais mieux

ratification, ratification *f.*

ratify, *v.t.* ratifier

ratio, proportion *f.*

ration, *v.t.* rationner

ration, ration *f.*

rational, (*adj.*) raisonnable; rationnel(le)

rattle, *v.t.* faire sonner

rattle, cliquetis *m.* (of metals);

crépitement *m.* (musketry); hochet *m.* (toy)

rattle-snake, serpent (*m.*) à sonnettes

ravage, ravage *m.*

ravage, *v.t.* ravager

rave, *v.i.* être en délire; (*fig.*) divaguer

raven, corbeau *m.*

ravening, ravenous, (*adj.*) dévorant, vorace

ravine, ravin *m.*

raving, (*adj.*) délirant; furieux (-euse)

ravish, *v.t.* ravir; enlever de force

raw, (*adj.*) cru (meat, etc.); écorché (bare); sans expérience

ray, rayon *m.*; raie *f.* (fish)

razor, rasoir *m.*

safety-razor, rasoir de sûreté

razor-blade, lame (*f.*) de rasoir

reach, portée *f.*; étendue *f.* (extent)

out of reach, hors d'atteinte

reach, *v.t.* atteindre, toucher; parvenir à

reach, *v.i.* s'étendre (extend)

react, *v.i.* réagir

reactionary, réactionnaire *m.* and *f.* and (*adj.*)

read, *v.t.* lire, faire la lecture de, étudier

readable, (*adj.*) lisible

reader, lecteur(-trice) *m.* (*f.*); correcteur *m.* (of proofs, etc.)

readily, (*adv.*) volontiers; de bonne grâce; facilement

readiness, empressement *m.*; promptitude *f.*

reading, la lecture *f.*

reading lamp, lampe (*f.*) de travail

reading-room, salle (*f.*) de lecture

ready, (*adj.*) prêt; prompt, disposé (à)

ready-made, (*adj.*) tout fait.

real, (*adj.*) réel(le); véritable

realise, *v.t.* réaliser (a project); se rendre compte de (to understand)

realisation, réalisation *f.*

reality, réalité *f.*

really, (*adv.*) réellement, en effet; vraiment

realm, royaume *m.*; (*fig.*) domaine *m.*

ream, rame *f.* (of paper)

reap, *v.t.* moissonner; (*fig.*) recueillir

reaper, moissonneur *m.*

reaping, moisson *f.*

reaping-machine, moissonneuse *f.*

reappear, *v.i.* reparaître

rear, arrière-garde *f.*; derrière *m.* (of building)

rear-admiral, contre-amiral *m.*

rear-light, feu-arrière *m.*

rear wheel, roue (*f.*) d'arrière

rear, *v.t.* élever; se cabrer (of horse)

reason, raison *f.*

reason, *v.t.* and *v.i.* raisonner

reasonable, (*adj.*) raisonnable

reassemble, *v.t.* rassembler, remonter; *v.i.* se rassembler

reassure, *v.t.* rassurer

rebate, rabais *m.*

rebel, rebelle *m.* and *f.*

rebel, *v.i.* se révolter

rebellion, rébellion *f.*; révolte *f.*

rebind, *v.t.* relier de nouveau

rebound, *v.i.* rebondir

rebound, contre-coup *m.*; rebondissement *m.*

rebuff, échec *m.*

rebuke, réprimande *f.*

rebuke, *v.t.* réprimander

recalcitrant, (*adj.*) récalcitrant, réfractaire

recall, révocation *f.*; rappel *m.*

recall, *v.t.* rappeler; se rappeler (remember)

recapitulate, *v.t.* récapituler

receipt, reçu *m.*; quittance *f.*; acquit *m.*; recette *f.* (recipe); réception *f.*

receipts, recette *f.* (takings)

receivable, (*adj.*) à recevoir (*commer.*)

receive, *v.t.* recevoir; accepter; receler (stolen goods)

receiver, receveur *m.*; récepteur *m.* (of telephone)

recent, (*adj.*) récent

reception, réception *f.*

recess, rentrant *m.*; vacances *f.
pl.* (holidays)

recipe, recette *f.*

reciprocal, (*adj.*) réciproque

recital, récit *m.*; narration *f.*

recitation, récitation *f.*

recite, *v.t.* réciter

reckless, (*adj.*) insouciant; insensé

reckon, *v.t.* compter; calculer

reckon on, compter sur

reckoner, calculateur *m.*

ready-reckoner, barème *m.*

reckoning, compte *m.*; calcul *m.*

reclaim, *v.t.* corriger; assécher (land)

recline, *v.t.* reposer; *v.t.* s'appuyer

recognisable, (*adj.*) reconnaissable

recognise, *v.t.* reconnaître

recognition, reconnaissance *f.*

recoil, *v.i.* reculer; recul *m.*

recollect, *v.t.* se souvenir (de)

recollection, souvenir *m.*

recommence, *v.t.* and *v.i.* recommencer

recommend, *v.t.* recommander

recommendation, recommandation *f.*

recompense, récompense *f.*

recompense, *v.t.* récompenser

reconcile, *v.t.* réconcilier

reconciliation, réconciliation *f.*

reconnoitre, *v.t.* reconnaître

reconsider, *v.t.* considérer de nouveau

record, registre *m.*; archives *f.
pl.* (office and official records); disque *m.* (gramophone); record *m.* (sport, etc.)

record, *v.t.* enregistrer

recorder, enregistreur *m.*; archiviste *m.*; (tape) magnétophone *m.*

recover, *v.t.* retrouver, reprendre, réparer (a loss); *v.i.* se remettre, se rétablir (in health)

recovery, guérison *f.* (health); redressement *m.* (economic)

recreation, récréation *f.*

recruit, recrue *f.*

recruit, *v.t.* recruter

rectangle, rectangle *m.*

rectangular, (*adj.*) rectangulaire

rectify, *v.t.* rectifier

rector, curé *m.* (of a parish); recteur *m.* (of university)

recumbent (*adj.*) couché

recur, *v.i.* revenir; se reproduire

recuperate, *v.i.* se remettre

red, (*adj.*) rouge, roux (rousse) (of hair); vermeil(le) (bright red)

redbreast, rouge-gorge *m.*

red tape, paperasserie *f.*

redden, *v.t.* and *v.i.* rougir

reddish, (*adj.*) rougeâtre

redeem, *v.t.* racheter

Redeemer, Rédempteur *m.*

redemption, rédemption *f.*

redistribution, répartition *f.*

redouble, *v.t.* redoubler

redoubtable, (*adj.*) redoutable

redress, réparation *f.*

redress, *v.t.* réparer

reduce, *v.t.* réduire; diminuer

reduction, réduction *f.*

re-echo, *v.i.* retentir

reed, roseau *m.*; chalumeau *m*

reef, récif *m.*

reek, fumée *f.*; vapeur *f.*

reek, *v.i.* fumer

reel, bobine *f.*; dévidoir *m.* (winder)

reel, *v.i.* chanceler, trébucher; *v.t.* dévider

re-elect, *v.t.* réélire

re-election, réélection *f.*

refasten, *v.t.* rattacher

refectory, réfectoire *m.*

refer (to), *v.i.* s'en rapporter à; s'adresser à; faire allusion (à)

refer, *v.t.* remettre à la décision de

referee, arbitre *m.*

reference, allusion *f.*; renseignements *m. pl.* (of character); référence *f.*

refine, *v.t.* raffiner

refined, (*adj.*) raffiné, cultivé

refinement, raffinage *m.* (of sugar, etc.); délicatesse *f.*; affectation *f.* (generally used in contemptuous way)

refinery, raffinerie *f.*

reflect, *v.t.* réfléchir; refléter

reflect, *v.i.* réfléchir, faire réflexion

reflection, reflexion, réflexion *f.*; reflet *m.*; censure *f.*; blâme *m.*

reflector, réflecteur *m.*

reflex, réflexe *m.*

reform, réforme *f.*

reform, *v.t.* réformer; *v.i.* se réformer

re-form, *v.t.* reformer; *v.i.* se reformer

reformation, réformation *f.*

reformatory, maison (*f.*) de correction

refractory, (*adj.*) réfractaire

refrain, *v.i.* s'abstenir de; refrain *m.* (chorus)

refresh, *v.t.* rafraîchir

refreshment, rafraîchissement *m.*

refreshment-room, buffet *m.*

refrigerator, glacière *f.*

refuge, refuge *m.*

refugee, réfugié(e) *m.* (*f.*)

refund, *v.t.* rembourser

refusal, refus *m.*

refuse, *v.t.* refuser

refuse, rebut *m.* (rubbish)

refute, *v.t.* réfuter

regal, (*adj.*) royal

regale, *v.t.* régaler

regard, égard *m.*; considération *f.*; amitiés *f. pl.*

regard, *v.t.* regarder

regardless, peu soigneux (de); sans égard (pour)

regatta, régate *f.*

regency, régence *f.*

regent, régent(e) *m.* (*f.*)

regimen, régime *m.*

regiment, régiment *m.*

region, région *f.*

register, registre *m.*; liste (*f.*) électorale (of voters)

register, *v.t.* enregistrer; inscrire; recommander (a letter); *v.i.* s'inscrire sur le registre

registrar, archiviste *m.*; officier (*m.*) de l'état civil

regret, regret *m.*

regret, *v.t.* regretter.

regrettable, à regretter

regular, (*adj.*) régulier(-ère), ordinaire

regularity, régularité *f.*

regulate, *v.t.* régler; diriger

rehearsal, répétition *f.*

rehearse, *v.t.* répéter; réciter

reign, règne *m.*

reign, *v.i.* régner

reimburse, rembourser

rein, rêne *f.*

reindeer, renne *m.*

reinforce, *v.t.* renforcer; (of concrete) armer

reinsurance, réassurance *f.*

reinsure, *v.t.* réassurer

reissue, nouvelle émission *f.*

reject, *v.t.* rejeter, repousser

rejection, rejet *m.*; refus *m.*

rejoice, *v.i.* se réjouir (de)

rejoicing, réjouissance *f.*

rejoin, *v.t.* rejoindre; *v.i.* répliquer

rejoinder, réplique *f.*

relapse, rechute *f.*

relapse, *v.i.* retomber dans

relate, *v.t.* raconter; rapporter

related, parent de; allié à (by marriage)

relating, (*adj.*) relatif(-ive)

relationship, parenté *f.*

relative, (*adj.*) relatif(-ive); qui se rapporte à; parent(e) *m.* (*f.*)

relax, *v.t.* relâcher; détendre

relax, *v.i.* se distraire; se délasser

relaxation, relâchement *m.*; repos *m.* (rest)

release, *v.t.* lâcher; libérer; faire jouer (spring, etc.)

relent, *v.i.* s'adoucir, se laisser attendrir

relentless, (*adj.*) impitoyable, inflexible

reliable, (*adj.*) digne de confiance

reliance, confiance *f.*

relic, reste *m.*; relique *f.* (generally in connection with saints, etc.)

relief, soulagement *m.* (from pain, etc.); secours *m.* (assistance)

relieve, *v.t.* soulager; adoucir; secourir (help); aider; relever (a sentry)

religion, religion *f.*

religious, religieux(-euse)

relinquish, *v.t.* abandonner; renoncer (à)

relish, goût *m.*; saveur *f.*
relish, *v.t.* savourer
reluctance, répugnance *f.*
reluctant, (*adj.*) peu disposé (à)
reluctantly, à contre-cœur
rely (on), *v.i.* compter sur
remain, *v.i.* rester, demeurer
remainder, reste *m.*
remaining, (*adj.*) de reste, restant
remains, restes *m. pl.*
remark, remarque *f.*
remark, *v.t.* observer; remarquer
remarkable, (*adj.*) remarquable
remarry, *v.i.* se remarier
remedy, remède *m.*
remedy, *v.t.* remédier (à)
remember, *v.i.* se rappeler; se souvenir (de)
remembrance, souvenir *m.*; mémoire *f.*
remind, *v.t.* rappeler
reminder, mémento *m.*
reminiscence, réminiscence *f.*
remiss, (*adj.*) négligent
remit, *v.t.* remettre; envoyer
remittance, envoi (*m.*) de fonds
remnant, reste *m.*; coupon *m.* (of cloth, etc., in sale in shops)
remonstrance, remontrance *f.*
remonstrate (with), *v.i.* faire des remontrances (à)
remorse, remords *m.*
remorseful, (*adj.*) plein de remords
remorseless, (*adj.*) impitoyable
remote, (*adj.*) éloigné, reculé
removal, déplacement *m.*; révocation *f.* (from situation, etc.); déménagement *m.* (of furniture, etc.)
remove, *v.t.* déplacer; éloigner; transporter (convey); destituer (from office)
remove, *v.i.* se déplacer; changer de domicile
remunerate, *v.t.* rémunérer
remuneration, rémunération *f.*
remunerative, (*adj.*) rémunérateur(-trice)
renaissance, renaissance *f.*
rend, *v.t.* déchirer, fendre
render, *v.t.* rendre

rendezvous, rendez-vous *m.*
renegade, renégat *m.*
renew, *v.t.* renouveler
renewal, renouvellement *m.*; reprise *f.*
renounce, *v.t.* renoncer (à), renier
renovate, *v.t.* renouveler, mettre à neuf
renown, renommée *f.*; renom *m.*
renowned, (*adj.*) renommé; célèbre
rent, déchirure *f.* (in clothes); loyer *m.* (of houses, etc.)
rent, *v.t.* louer
reoccupy, *v.t.* réoccuper
reorganise, *v.t.* réorganiser
repair, *v.t.* réparer; raccommoder (clothes); *v.i.* aller (go)
repair, réparation *f.*; raccommodage *m.* (of clothes)
repay, *v.t.* rembourser, rendre
repayment, remboursement *m.*
repeat, *v.t.* répéter; réitérer
repeatedly, (*adv.*) à plusieurs reprises
repel, *v.t.* repousser
repellent, (*adj.*) répulsif(-ive)
repent, *v.i.* se repentir (de)
repentance, repentir *m.*
repentant, (*adj.*) repentant
repetition, répétition *f.*; reprise *f.*
replace, *v.t.* remettre; remplacer (substitute for)
replacement, remplacement *m.*; remise (*f.*) en place
replete, (*adj.*) rempli
reply, réponse *f.*; réplique *f.* (*legal*)
reply, *v.i.* répondre
report, *v.t.* rapporter; raconter; rendre compte de
report, *v.i.* faire un rapport (sur); se présenter (for duty)
report, rapport *m.*; exposé *m.*; bruit *m.* (rumour); détonation *f.*
reporter, journaliste *m.*; sténographe *m.* (shorthand writer); reporter *m.*
repose, *v.i.* se reposer
repose, repos *m.*
repository, dépôt *m.*
represent, *v.t.* représenter

representation, représentation f.

representative, (adj.) représentatif(-ive)

representative, représentant m.

repress, v.t. réprimer

repression, répression f.

reprieve, commutation f.; répit m.

reprimand, réprimande f.

reprimand, v.t. réprimander

reprisal, représaille f.

reproach, reproche m.

reproach, v.t. reprocher, faire un reproche à

reprobate, vaurien m.

reproduce, v.t. reproduire

reproduction, reproduction f.

reproof, réprimande f.

reprove, réprimander; blâmer

reptile, reptile m.

republic, république f.

republican, (adj.) républicain

repudiate, v.t. répudier

repudiation, répudiation f.

repugnance, répugnance f.

repugnant, (adj.) répugnant, contraire à

repulse, v.t. repousser; échec m.

repulsion, répulsion f.

repulsive, (adj.) repoussant

repurchase, v.t. racheter

reputable, (adj.) honorable

reputation, réputation f.

reputed, (adj.) réputé, supposé

request, demande f.; prière f. "stop by request," arrêt (m.) facultatif

request, v.t. demander (à); solliciter; prier

require, v.t. exiger, requérir, réclamer

requirement, exigence f.; nécessité f.; besoins m. pl.

requisite, (adj.) nécessaire, indispensable

requite, v.t. récompenser

rescind, v.t. annuler

rescue, délivrance f.; sauvetage m.; secours m.

rescue, v.t. sauver, délivrer

research, recherche f.

resemblance, ressemblance f.

resemble, v.t. ressembler (à)

resemble each other, se ressembler

resent, v.t. ressentir; s'offenser de

resentment, ressentiment m.

reservation, réserve f.; arrière-pensée f.; restriction f.

reserve, réserve f.; prudence f.

reserve, v.t. réserver; retenir (a seat)

reserved, (adj.) réservé

reservoir, réservoir m.

reside, v.i. demeurer, résider

residence, domicile m.; résidence f.; séjour m.

resident, habitant(e) m. (f.)

resident, (adj.) résidant, interne (serving in hospital, school, etc.)

residue, résidu m.

resign, v.t. résigner, donner sa démission, céder, renoncer (à)

resignation, résignation f.; démission f.

resin, résine f.

resist, v.t. résister (à); combattre

resistance, résistance f.

resolute, (adj.) résolu, déterminé

resoluteness, résolution f.; fermeté f.

resolution, résolution f.; décision f.

resolve, v.t. résoudre; v.i. se décider (à); se dissoudre (melt)

resort, ressource f.; lieu (m.) fréquenté (holiday); station climatique f. (health); last -, dernier ressort

resort (to), v.i. recourir (à); avoir recours à

resound, v.i. résonner, retentir

resource, ressource f.

respect, respect m.; égard m.; estime f.; hommages m. pl.

respect, v.t. respecter

respectable, (adj.) respectable

respectability, honorabilité f.

respectful, (adj.) respectueux (-euse)

respective, (adj.) respectif(-ive)

respecting, (prep.) à l'égard de

respite, répit m.; relâche m.; sursis m.

respite, v.t. accorder un sursis à

resplendent, (*adj.*) resplendissant
respond, *v.i.* répondre
responsibility, responsabilité *f.*
responsible, (*adj.*) responsable
rest, repos *m.*; reste *m.* (remainder); pause *f.* (*mus.*)
rest, *v.i.* se reposer; *v.t.* reposer, appuyer
restaurant, restaurant *m.*
restive, (*adj.*) rétif(-ive)
restless, inquiet (inquiète); agité
restoration, restauration *f.*
restore, *v.t.* restituer; rendre; rétablir (order); restaurer (building)
restrain, *v.t.* retenir, contenir, restreindre
restraint, contrainte *f.*; restriction *f.*
restrict, *v.t.* restreindre, limiter
restriction, restriction *f.*
result, résultat *m.*
as a result of ..., par suite de...
result, *v.i.* résulter
resume, *v.t.* reprendre
resurrection, résurrection *f.*
retail, vente (*f.*) au détail
retailer, détaillant *m.*; marchand (*m.*) au détail
retain, *v.t.* retenir, garder, conserver
retainer, serviteur *m.*
retake, *v.t.* reprendre
retaliate, *v.i.* user de représailles (envers)
retaliation, représailles *f. pl.*
retarded (mentally), arriéré(e)
reticent, (*adj.*) taciturne
retinue, suite *f.*; cortège *m.*
retire, *v.i.* se retirer; reculer (yield ground); prendre sa retraite (on pension)
retired, (*adj.*) retiré; retraité (of officer, etc.)
on retired list, en retraite
retirement, retraite *f.*
retiring, (*adj.*) réservé, timide
retort, réplique *f.*; cornue *f.* (*chem.*)
retort, *v.t.* répliquer, riposter
retrace, *v.t.* revenir sur
retract, *v.t.* rétracter
retreat, retraite *f.*

retreat, *v.i.* se retirer, battre en retraite (*mil.*)
retrench, *v.t.* retrancher (*mil.*); restreindre (expenses)
retrenchment, retranchement *m.*; réduction *f.*
retribution, récompense *f.*
retrieve, *v.t.* rétablir; réparer; recouvrer (regain)
retrospective, (*adj.*) rétrospectif (-ive)
return, retour *m.*
return, *v.i.* revenir (come back); retourner (go back); rentrer; répliquer (return answer); *v.t.* élire (return at election); rendre (give back)
return-ticket, billet (*m.*) d'aller et retour
reunion, réunion *f.*
reunite, *v.i.* se réunir; *v.t.* réunir
reveal, *v.t.* révéler
revel, orgie *f.*
revel, *v.i.* se réjouir, se divertir
revelation, révélation *f.*
revenge, vengeance *f.*
revenge, *v.t.* venger, se venger de
revengeful, vindicatif(-ive)
revenue, revenu *m.*; rentes *f. pl.*; fisc *m.* (state revenues)
reverberate, *v.i.* retentir; *v.t.* renvoyer, réverbérer
revere, *v.t.* révérer
reverence, révérence *f.*
reverend, (*adj.*) vénérable, révérend (of clergy)
reverent, (*adj.*) respectueux(-euse)
reverse, contraire *m.*; revers *m.*; (*adj.*) contraire, inverse
reverse, *v.t.* renverser
reverse the engine, faire machine arrière
reversion, réversion *f.*; succession *f.*
revert, *v.i.* revenir sur
review, revue *f.*; revision *f.*; critique *f.*
review, *v.t.* revoir, reviser, critiquer
reviewer, critique *m.*
revile, *v.t.* injurier
revisal, revision *f.*
revise, *v.t.* revoir, reviser

revision, revision *f.*

revisit, *v.t.* visiter de nouveau

revival, reprise *f.*; renaissance *f.* (art, etc.)

revive, *v.t.* faire revivre; ressusciter; *v.i.* se ranimer; reprendre connaissance

revocable, (*adj.*) révocable

revoke, *v.t.* révoquer; renoncer (cards generally)

revolt, révolte *f.*

revolt, *v.i.* se révolter, se soulever

revolution, révolution *f.*; tour *m.* (of wheel, etc.)

revolutionise, *v.t.* révolutionner

revolutionary, (*adj.*) révolutionnaire

revolve, *v.i.* tourner; *v.t.* faire tourner

revolver, revolver *m.*

reward, récompense *f.*; prix *m.*

reward, *v.t.* récompenser

rewrite, *v.t.* récrire

rhetoric, rhétorique *f.*; éloquence *f.*

rheumatism, rhumatisme *m.*

rhinoceros, rhinocéros *m.*

rhubarb, rhubarbe *f.*

rhyme, rime *f.*; vers *m. pl.*

rhyme, *v.i.* and *v.t.* rimer

rhythm, rhythme *m.*

rib, côte *f.*

ribald, (*adj.*) licencieux(-euse); obscène

ribbon, ruban *m.*

to tear to ribbons, mettre en lambeaux

rice, riz *m.*

rich, (*adj.*) riche; fécond (fertile)

riches, richesse *f.*

richness, richesse *f.*; fécondité *f.*

rick, meule *f.*

rickets, rachitisme *m.*

rickety, (*adj.*) rachitique; (*fig.*) bancal (of furniture, etc.)

rid, *v.t.* délivrer, débarrasser

riddle, énigme *f.*; crible *m.* (sieve)

riddle, *v.t.* cribler

ride, *v.i.* monter à cheval (bicyclette, etc.); se promener *or* aller à cheval *or* en voiture; *v.t.* monter un cheval

ride, promenade (*f.*) à cheval *or* en voiture; trajet *m.* (en autobus, etc.)

rider, cavalier *m.*; ajouté *m.*

ridge, sommet *m.* (top); chaîne *f.* (of mountains); cime *f.*

ridicule, *v.t.* tourner en ridicule

ridiculous, (*adj.*) ridicule, absurde

riding-master, maître (*m.*) d'équitation

riding-school, école (*f.*) d'équitation; manège *m.*

riding-whip, cravache *f*

rife, (*adj.*) répandu, général

rifle, fusil *m.*

rifle, *v.t.* piller, dévaliser; rayer (gun barrel)

rifle-shot, coup (*m.*) de fusil

rifleman, chasseur à pied *m.*

rigging, agrès *m. pl.* (tackle)

right, (*adj.*) droit; direct; vrai; convenable

to be right, avoir raison

right, (*adv.*) droit, tout droit; justement

right, droit *m.*

"keep to the right," tenez la droite

right off (at once), sur-le-champ

right or wrong, à tort ou à raison

right, *v.t.* rendre justice à; faire droit

right, *v.i.* se redresser; *v.t.* redresser (a boat or a wrong)

all right, c'est entendu

right-about, demi-tour (*m.*) à droite

right-handed, (*adj.*) droitier (-ère)

righteous, (*adj.*) juste, droit

righteousness, droiture *f.*

rightful, (*adj.*) légitime, véritable

rigid, (*adj.*) rigide, raide

rigorous, rigoureux(-euse)

rigour, rigueur *f.*

rim, bord *m.*; rebord *m.*; jante *f.* (of wheel)

rime, givre *m.*

ring *v.i.* (of bells) sonner, tinter; *v.t.* sonner

ring off, couper la communication

ring up (telephone), donner un coup de téléphone (à)

ring, anneau *m.*; bague *f.* (for finger); cercle *m.*; arène *f.*; ring *m.* (boxing); alliance *f.* (wedding); tintement *m.*; sonnerie *f.* (of bells)

ring-fence, enclos *m.*

ring-finger, annulaire *m.*

ring-leader, meneur *m.*

ringlet, boucle *f.*

rinse, *v.t.* rincer

rinsing, rinçage *m.*

riot, émeute *f.*; débauche *f.·*

rioter, émeutier *m.*; tapageur *m.*

riotous, tumultueux(-euse); séditieux(-euse)

riotousness, désordre *m.*

rip, *v.t.* fendre, déchirer

ripe, *(adj.)* mûr

ripen, *v.t.* and *v.i.* mûrir

ripeness, maturité *f.*

ripple, *v.i.* se rider; ride *f.*

rippling, murmure *m.*

rise, *v.i.* se lever (to get up); se relever (after a fall); s'élever, monter (ascend) (of mountains, etc.); se dresser; prendre de l'altitude (of aircraft).

rise, lever *m.* (of curtain or sun); montée *f.* (of tide); hausse *f.* (of barometer, prices, etc.)

rising, *(adj.)* levant; qui s'élève; montant

rising, soulèvement *m.* (of peoples); crue *f.* (of waters); hausse *f.* (of prices, etc.)

risk, risque *m.*

risk, *v.t.* risquer

risky, *(adj.)* hasardeux(-euse); risqué

rite, cérémonie *f.*

ritual, rituel *m.·; (adj.)* rituel(le)

rival, *(adj.* and *noun)* rival(e) *m.* *(f.)*

rival, *v.t.* rivaliser (avec)

rivalry, rivalité *f.*

river, rivière *f.*; fleuve *m.* (big river)

river-side, bord *(m.)* de la rivière; bord de l'eau *m.*

rivet, rivet *m.*

rivet, *v.t.* river

rivulet, ruisseau *m.*

road, route, *f.*; chemin *m.*; chaussée *f.* (roadway); rade *f.* (*naut.*)

road-making, construction *(f.)* de routes

road-map, carte *(f.)* routière

road-mender, cantonnier *m.*

roadside, bord *(m.)* de la route

roadstead, rade *f.*

roadway, chemin *m.*; chaussée *f.*; voie *f.* (of railway)

roadworthy, en état de marche

roam, *v.i.* rôder, errer

roan, *(adj.)* rouan

roar, *v.i.* mugir

roar, roaring, mugissement *m.*

roast, *v.t.* griller, rôtir

roast (beef, etc.), rôti *m.*

rob, *v.t.* voler; piller

robber, bandit *m.*; voleur(-euse) *m.* *(f.)*

robbery, vol *m.*

robe, robe *f.*

robust, *(adj.)* robuste, vigoureux (-euse)

rock, rocher *m.*; roche *f.* (*geol.*)

rock, *v.t.* balancer,. bercer; *v.i.* balancer

rocker, bascule *f.*

rocket, fusée volante *f.*

rocket (apparatus), porte-amarre *m.* (*naut.*)

rockiness (of soil), nature *(f.)* rocailleuse

rocking-chair, chaise *(f.)* à bascule

rocky, *(adj.)* rocheux(-euse); rocailleux(-euse)

rod, verge *f.*; tringle *f.* (curtain); canne *(f.)* à pêche (fishing)

rodent, *(adj.)* rongeur(-euse); rongeur *m.·*

roe, chevreuil *m.*

roe (of fish), œufs (*m. pl.*) de poisson; laitance *f.* (soft roe)

rogue, fripon *m.*; coquin *m.*

roguish, *(adj.)* coquin, fripon(ne); espiègle (joking)

roll, rouleau *m.*; roulement *m.* (rolling); roulis *m.* (of ship); petit pain *m.* (bread); liste *f.*

roll, *v.t.* rouler; laminer (metal)

roller, rouleau, *m.*; lame *f.* (wave)
roller-blind, store *m.*
rolling-stock, matériel (*m.*) roulant (railway)
romance, roman *m.*
romantic, (*adj.*) romanesque; romantique (scenery)
romp, *v.i.* folâtrer
romp, gamine *f.* (girl); jeu (*m.*) turbulent
roof, toit *m.*; impériale *f.* (of omnibus)
roof, *v.t.* couvrir d'un toit; (*fig.*) abriter (shelter)
rook, corneille *f.*
rook (somebody), (*slang*) *v.t.* filouter; rouler
rookery, colonie (*f.*) de corneilles
room, chambre *f.*; salle *f.*; pièce *f.*; place *f.*, espace *f.* (space)
roomy, (*adj.*) spacieux(-euse); vaste
root, racine *f.*
rope, corde *f.*; cordage *m.* (*naut.*)
rope, *v.t.* corder (parcel)
rosary, rosaire *m.*
rose, rose *f.*; rosace *f.* (*arch.*)
rose-bed, massif (*m.*) de rosiers
rosebud, bouton (*m.*) de rose
rose-colour, (*adj.*) rose
rose-garden, roseraie *f.*
rosemary, romarin *m.*
rosy, (*adj.*) rose
rot, pourriture *f.*; (*slang*) blague *f.*
rot, *v.i.* (se) pourrir; *v.t.* faire pourrir
rotary, (*adj.*) rotatoire
rotate, *v.i.* tourner
rotten, (*adj.*) pourri, corrompu
rotund, (*adj.*) rond, arrondi
rouge, rouge *m.*; fard *m.*
rouge, *v.t.* mettre du rouge
rough, (*adj.*) rude, raboteux (-euse) (roads); ébouriffé (ruffled); houleux(-euse) (of sea); orageux(-euse) (of weather); agité
round, (*adj.*) rond, circulaire
round, (*adv.*) en rond, tout autour
round, (*prep.*) autour de
round, rond *m.*; cercle *m.*
round, *v.t.* entourer, arrondir
round, *v.i.* s'arrondir

round-shouldered, (*adj.*) voûté
rouse, *v.t.* éveiller; (*fig.*) réveiller, exciter
rout, débandade *f.*; déroute *f.* (of army)
to rout, *v.t.* mettre en déroute
route, route *f.*; chemin *m.*
routine, routine *f.*
rove, *v.i.* rôder
roving, errant
row, rang *m.*; rangée *f.*; colonne *f.* (of figures); promenade (*f.*) sur l'eau
row, *v.i.* ramer
row (noise), tapage *m.*; vacarme *m.*; querelle *f.*
rowdy, (*adj.*) tapageur(-euse)
rowing, canotage *m.* (boating)
royal, (*adj.*) royal
royalist, royaliste *m.* and *f.*
royalty, royauté *f.*; droit. (*m.*) d'auteur (on books, etc.)
rub, *v.t.* frotter; frictionner; *v.i.* se frotter
rubber, frottoir *m.*
rubber (substance), caoutchouc *m.*; gomme (*f.*) à effacer (eraser)
rubbish, débris *m. pl.*; décombres *m. pl.*; rebut *m.* (worthless thing); (*exclam.*) Quelle blague!
rubbishy, (*adj.*) sans valeur
rubicund, (*adj.*) rubicond
rubric, rubrique *f.*
ruby, (*adj.*) vermeil(le)
ruby, rubis *m.*
rudder, gouvernail *m.*
ruddiness, fraîcheur (*f.*) du teint
ruddy, frais (fraîche); rougeâtre
rude, (*adj.*) grossier(-ère); impoli; insolent; rude
rudeness, insolence *f.*; grossièreté *f.*
rudiment, rudiment *m.*
rudimentary, (*adj.*) rudimentaire
rue, *v.t.* regretter
rueful, (*adj.*) triste; déplorable
ruff, fraise *f.* (collar)
ruffian, brigand *m.*; scélérat *m.*
ruffianly, (*adj.*) brutal
ruffle, manchette *f.*
ruffle, *v.t.* rider; froisser (rumple); (*fig.*) irriter (temper); ébouriffer (hair)

rug, descente (*f.*) de lit (bedside); couverture (*f.*) de voyage

rugged, (*adj.*) rude; raboteux (-euse)

ruggedness, rudesse *f.*

ruin, ruine *f.*; perte *f.* (loss)

ruin, *v.t.* ruiner

ruinous, ruineux(-euse)

rule, règle *f.*; règlement *m.*, pouvoir *m.*; gouvernement *m.*; ordonnance *f.*

rule, *v.t.* gouverner; diriger; régler; régner (sur)

ruler, règle *f.*; souverain(e) *m.* (*f.*)

ruling, (*adj.*) dominant

ruling, décision *f.* (*legal*); réglage *m.* (on paper)

rum, rhum *m.*

rumble, *v.i.* gronder, grouiller

rumbling, grondement *m.*; grouillement *m.*

ruminant, (*subst.*) ruminant *m.*; (*adj.*) ruminant(e)

ruminate, *v.i.* and *v.t.* ruminer

rummage, *v.t.* fouiller (dans)

rumour, rumeur *f.*

there is a rumour, le bruit court

rump, croupe *f.*; croupion *m.*

rumple, *v.t.* chiffonner, froisser

run, *v.i.* courir, accourir; se sauver (run away); couler (to flow); diriger (a business); rouler (to be on wheels); suppurer (of wounds, etc.)

run ashore, *v.i.* échouer

run in, *v.i.* entrer en courant; *v.t.* conduire au poste (criminal)

run into, entrer en collision avec

run into debt, *v.i.* faire des dettes

run off the rails, dérailler

run on, courir, continuer

run, *v.t.* courir, conduire, faire arriver (trains, etc.)

run down, *v.t.* décrier

run out, *v.i.* s'épuiser (exhaust)

run over, *v.t.* parcourir du regard; écraser (of vehicle)

runaway, fuyard *m.*

run short, *v.i.* faire défaut

run, course *f.* (running); vogue *f.* (success); trajet *m.* (journey)

runner, coureur *m.*

runway, piste (*f.*) d'envol

rupture, rupture *f.*; hernie *f.*

rural, (*adj.*) rural

rush, jonc *m.* (for plaiting)

rush, élan *m.*; mouvement (*m.*) précipité; ruée *f.*

rush, *v.i.* se précipiter; se ruer sur, *v.t.* prendre d'assaut (onomy position)

rushy, (*adj.*) couvert de joncs

rusk, biscotte *f.*

russet, (*adj.*) roussâtre

Russian, (*adj.* and *subst.*) russe

rust, rouille *f.*

rust, *v.i.* se rouiller; *v.t.* rouiller

rustic, (*adj.*) rustique

rustic, rustaud *m.*

rustication, vie (*f.*) champêtre

rusticity, rusticité *f.*

rustiness, rouille *f.*

rustle, *v.i.* bruire

rustle, rustling, bruissement *m.*

rusty, rouillé.

rut, ornière *f.* (of road)

rut, *v.i.* être en rut (of deer)

ruthless, (*adj.*) impitoyable

rye, seigle *m.*

rye-grass, ivraie *f.*

S

Sabbath, sabbat *m.*

sable, zibeline *f.*; sable *m.* (*heraldry*)

sable, (*adj.*) noir; de zibeline

sabotage, sabotage *m.*; *v.t.* saboter

sabre, sabre *m.*

sabre, *v.t.* sabrer

sacerdotal, (*adj.*) sacerdotal

sack, sac *m.*

sack, *v.t.* saccager; mettre à sac; congédier (dismiss)

sacking, saccagement *m.* (of town, etc.); toile (*f.*) à sac

sacrament, sacrement *m.*

sacramental, (*adj.*) sacramentel (-le)

sacred, (*adj.*) sacré; saint (of history, etc.); inviolable

sacrifice, sacrifice *m.*; victime

sacrifice, v.i. and v.t. sacrifier
to sell at a sacrifice, vendre au-dessous du cours
sad, (adj.) triste; déplorable
sadden, v.t. attrister
saddle, selle f.; v.t. seller
saddler, sellier m.
sadness, tristesse f.
safe, (adj.) sauf; en sûreté; hors de danger; à l'abri de
safe and sound, sain et sauf
safe, coffre-fort m. (money); garde-manger m. (food)
safe-conduct, sauf-conduit m.
safeguard, sauvegarde f.
safe-keeping, sûreté f.
safely, sans danger; en toute sécurité
safety, sûreté f.
safety-valve, soupape (f.) de sûreté
safety-catch, cran (m.) de sûreté
saffron, safran m.
sag, v.i. s'affaisser
sagacious, (adj.) sagace; intelligent (dog, etc.)
sagacity, sagacité f.
sage, (adj.) sage, prudent
sage, sauge f. (herb); sage m. (wise man)
sagging, affaissement m.
sago, sagou m.
sail, voile f.; aile f. (windmill)
sail, v.t. naviguer sur; voguer sur
sail-cloth, toile (f.) à voiles
sailing-boat, bateau (m.) à voiles
sailing-ship, navire (m.) à voiles
sailor, marin m.; matelot m.
to be a good sailor, avoir le pied marin
saint, saint(e) m. (f.)
saintly, (adj.) de saint
sake, cause f., égard m., amour m.
for God's sake, pour l'amour de Dieu
for pity's sake, par pitié
salad, salade f.
salad-bowl, saladier m.
salaried, (adj.) salarié
salary, appointements m. pl.; traitement m.; salaire m.
sale, vente f.; mise (f.) en vente; liquidation f.

sale by auction, vente (f.) aux enchères
for sale, à vendre
on sale, en vente
saleable, vendable
sale-room, salle (f.) de vente
salesman (-woman), vendeur (-euse) m. (f.)
salient, saillant m.; (adj.) saillant(e)
saline, (adj.) salin
saliva, salive f.
sallow, (adj.) blême; jaunâtre
sally, sortie f.
sally (to make a), faire une sortie
salmon, saumon m.
saloon, salon m.
dining-saloon, salle (f.) à manger
saloon car, voiture (f.) à conduite intérieure
saloon-passenger, voyageur (m.) de première classe
salt, sel m.
salts (Epsom), sulfate (m.) de magnésie
salt, (adj.) salé
salt, v.t. saler
salt-cellar, salière f.
saltish, (adj.) saumâtre
saltless, (adj.) sans sel, insipide
saltness, salure f.
saltpetre, salpêtre m.
salty, (adj.) salé
salubrious, (adj.) salubre
salutary, (adj.) salutaire
salute, salut m.; salutation f.
salute, v.t. saluer
salvage, sauvetage m.; sauver v.t.
salvation, salut m.
Salvation Army, armée (f.) du salut
salve, onguent m.
salver, plateau m.
salvo (artillery), rafale f.; salve f.
same, (adj.) le (la) même; (les) mêmes
it is all the same to me, cela m'est égal
sameness, identité f.; uniformité f.
sample, échantillon m.
sample, v.t. échantillonner

sampler, modèle (*m.*) de broderie
sampling, échantillonnage *m.*
sanctification, sanctification *f.*
sanctified, (*adj.*) sanctifié; saint
sanctify, *v.t.* sanctifier
sanctimonious, (*adj.*) hypocrite; (contempt.) béat
sanction, sanction *f.*
sanction, *v.t.* sanctionner ; autoriser
sanctuary, sanctuaire *m.*
sand, sable *m.*
sand, *v.t.* sabler
sand-bag, sac (*m.*) à terre
sandbank, banc (*m.*) de sable
sandhill, dune *f.*
sand-martin (bird), hirondelle (*f.*) de rivage
sandpaper, papier (*m.*) de verre
sand-pit, sablonnière *f.*
sandstone, grès *m.*
sandstorm, ouragan (*m.*) de sable
sanded, sablonneux(-euse), sablé
sandwich, sandwich *m.*
sandy, (*adj.*) sablonneux(-euse)
sane, (*adj.*) sain d'esprit
sanguinary, (*adj.*) sanguinaire
sanguine, (*adj.*) plein de confiance, sanguin
sanitary, (*adj.*) hygiénique, sanitaire
sanitation, assainissement *m.*; hygiène *f.*
sanity, état sain *m.*; jugement sain *m.*
sap, sève *f.*
sap, *v.t.* saper
sapient, (*adj.*) sage
sapless, (*adj.*) sans sève; desséché
sapling, jeune arbre *m.*
sapper, sapeur *m.*; **the Sappers,** le corps du génie *m.*
sapphire, saphir *m.*
sappy, (*adj.*) plein de sève
saracen, (*adj.* and *subst.*) sarrasin *m.*
sarcasm, sarcasme *m.*
sarcastic, (*adj.*) sarcastique
sarcophagus, sarcophage *m.*
sardine, sardine *f.*
sarsaparilla, salsepareille *f.*
sash, ceinture *f.*; écharpe *f.*; châssis *m.* (window)

sash-window, fenêtre (*f.*) à guillotine
satanic, (*adj.*) satanique
satchel, petit sac *m.*; cartable *m.*
sate, *v.t.* rassasier
satellite, satellite *m.*
satiate, *v.t.* rassasier
satiety, satiété *f.*
satin, satin *m.*
satire, satire *f.*
satirical, (*adj.*) satirique
satirist, satirique *m.*
satisfaction, satisfaction *f.*; contentement *m.*
satisfactory, (*adj.*) satisfaisant
satisfy, *v.t.* satisfaire; convaincre (convince); remplir (condition)
satisfying, (*adj.*) satisfaisant
saturate, *v.t.* saturer
Saturday, samedi *m.*
sauce, sauce *f.*; (*slang*) culot *m.* (impertinence)
saucepan, casserole *f.*
saucer, soucoupe *f.*
saucy, (*adj.*) impertinent, fripon(ne)
saunter, *v.i.* flâner
sausage, saucisse *f.*; saucisson *m.* (large sausage)
savage, (*adj.*) sauvage; féroce; farouche
savageness, férocité *f.*; brutalité *f.*
savagery, férocité *f.*; barbarie *f.*
save, *v.t.* sauver (de); épargner (spare); mettre de côté (put by); économiser
save, *v.i.* faire des économies
save, (*prep.*) sauf, excepté
savings, économies *f. pl.*; épargne *f.*
savings bank, caisse (*f.*) d'épargne
saviour, sauveur *m.*
savour, saveur *f.*; goût *m.*
savour, *v.i.* sentir
savoury, (*adj.*) savoureux(-euse)
saw, scie *f.*; dicton *m.*
saw, *v.t.* scier
sawdust, sciure (*f.*) de bois
saw-mill, scierie *f.*
sawyer, scieur *m.*; scieur (*m.*) de long

Saxon, (*adj.*) saxon(ne)
say, *v.t.* dire; parler; réciter
I say ! dites donc!
it is said, on dit
that is to say, c'est-à-dire
you don't say ! pas possible!
saying, mot *m.*; dicton *m.*
scabbard, fourreau *m.*
scabrous, (*adj.*) scabreux(-euse)
scaffold, échafaud *m.*
scald, brûlure *f.*
scald, *v.t.* échauder
scale, écaille *f.* (fish); échelle *f.* (map); gamme *f.* (*mus.*); plateau *m.* (of balance)
scales, balance *f.*
scale, *v.t.* escalader; *v.i.* peser (weight)
scamp, chenapan *m.*; mauvais sujet *m.*
scamp, *v.t.* bâcler
scamper (off), *v.i.* détaler
scandal, scandale *m.*
scandalous, scandaleux(-euse)
scanty, (*adj.*) peu abondant, insuffisant, mesquin
scapegoat, bouc (*m.*) émissaire
scapegrace, vaurien *m.*
scar, cicatrice *f.*; balafre *f.*
scar, *v.t.* cicatriser; balafrer
scarce, (*adj.*) rare
scarcely, à peine
scarcity, rareté *f.*
scare, panique *f.*
scare, *v.t.* effrayer; épouvanter; faire peur à
scarecrow, épouvantail *m.* (*pl.* -s.)
scarf, écharpe *f.*; fichu *m.* (woman's); cache-col *m.* (man's)
scarlet, écarlate
scarlet fever, fièvre (*f.*) scarlatine
scatter, *v.t.* disperser; dissiper; *v.i.* s'éparpiller
scavenger, boueur *m.*; balayeur *m.*
scene, scène *f.*; décor *m.* (theatrical " set ".)
scene painter, brosseur (*m.*) de décors
scenery, décors *m. pl.*, mise (*f.*) en scène (*theat.*); vue *f.*; paysage *m.* (landscape)
scenic, (*adj.*) scénique

scent, odeur *f.*; odorat *m.*; parfum *m.*; flair *m.* (dog); piste *f.* (track)
scent, *v.t.* parfumer; sentir; flairer (game)
scentless, (*adj.*) inodore; sans odeur
sceptic, sceptique *m.* (*f.*)
sceptre, sceptre *m.*
scheme, projet *m.*; plan *m.*; complot *m.*
scheme, *v.t.* projeter, faire des projets; intriguer (to plot)
scholar, écolier(-ère) *m.* (*f.*); savant *m.*
scholarly, (*adj.*) érudit
scholarship, bourse *f.* (at university, etc.); science *f.*
scholastic, (*adj.*) scolastique
school, école *f.*; pensionnat *m.*
elementary school, école primaire *f.*
grammar school, collège *m.*; lycée *m.*
schoolboy (-girl), écolier *m.*; écolière *f.*
schooling, instruction *f.*
schoolmaster, maître d'école *m.*; professeur *m.*
schoolmistress, institutrice *f.*
schooner, goélette *f.*
sciatic(a), (*adj.* and *subst.*) sciatique *f.*
science, science *f.*
scientific, (*adj.*) scientifique
scientist, savant *m.*; homme (*m.*) de science
scissors, ciseaux *m. pl.*
scoff (at), *v.i.* se moquer (de); railler
scoffer, moqueur(-euse) *m.* (*f.*)
scoffing, moquerie *f.*
scold, *v.i.* and *v.t.* gronder
scoop, *v.t.* écoper, excaver
scooter, (*aut.*) scooter *m.*
scope, étendue *f.*; champ *m.*
to give full scope to, donner libre essor à
scorch, *v.t.* brûler, griller, roussir
scorching, (*adj.*) brûlant
score, entaille *f.* (cut); compte *m.*; vingtaine *f.*

score, *v.t.* marquer

scorn, dédain *m.*; mépris *m.*

scorn, *v.t.* mépriser; dédaigner

scornful, *(adj.)* méprisant; dédaigneux(-euse)

Scotch (Scottish), *(adj.)* écossais(e)

scoundrel, coquin *m.*; scélérat *m.*

scour, *v.t.* écurer; nettoyer (clean); battre (country)

scourge, fouet *m.*; fléau *m.* (calamity)

scout, éclaireur *m.*; boy-scout *m.*

scowl, *v.i.* froncer les sourcils

scowling, *(adj.)* menaçant

scramble, *v.i.* grimper (à quatre pattes)

scrambled eggs, œufs brouillés *m. pl.*

scrap .morceau *m.*; fragment *m.*; fracas (fight) *m.*; restes *m. pl.* (i.e. what is left over)

scrape, *v.t.* râcler; ratisser *(cook.)*; décrotter (boots)

scrape, *(coll.)* mauvais pas *m.*

scraper, décrottoir *m.* (for shoes)

scraping, grattage *m.*; ramassis *m.* (things collected together)

scratch, égratignure *f.*; coup *(m.)* de griffe *or* d'ongle; rayure *f.* (on paint, etc.)

scratch, *v.t.* gratter, égratigner; rayer (paint, etc.)

scratching, grattage *m.*; égratignure *f.*

scrawl, griffonnage *m.*

scrawl, *v.t.* griffonner

scream, cri *m.*; cri perçant *m.*

scream, *v.i.* crier; pousser un cri perçant

screech, cri *(m.)* perçant

screech-owl, chouette *f.*

screen, écran *m.*; paravent *m.* (folding screen); pare-brise *m.* (windscreen of car); rideau *m.* (of trees, etc.)

screen, *v.t.* abriter contre; protéger; mettre à l'écran *(cin.)*

screw, vis *f.*; hélice *f.* (of steamer, etc.)

screw, *v.t.* visser; serrer (press)

screw-driver, tournevis *m.*

screw-wrench, clef *(f.)* anglaise

screwed, *(adj.)* à vis; gris (drunk)

scribble, griffonnage *m.*

scribble, *v.t.* griffonner

Scriptures, l'Écriture sainte

scrofula, scrofule *f.*

scrounge, *v.t.* chiper

scrub, broussailles *f. pl.* (undergrowth)

scrub, *v.t.* frotter fort; laver

scrubbing, frottage *m.*

scrubbing-brush, brosse *(f.)* dure

scruple, scrupule *m.*

scrupulous, *(adj.)* scrupuleux (-euse)

scrutinise, *v.t.* scruter, examiner

scrutiny, enquête *(f.)* rigoureuse; recherche *(f.)* minutieuse

sculptor, sculpteur *m.*

sculpture, sculpture *f.*

scum, écume *f.*; crasse *f.*; rebut *m.* (refuse); lie *f.* (dregs of the population)

scum, *v.t.* écumer

scurf, pellicules *f. pl.*

scurrilous, *(adj.)* injurieux (-euse)

scurvy, *(adj.)* vil; ladre (stingy)

scuttle, seau *(m.)* à charbon (for coal); *v.t.* saborder (a ship)

scythe, faux *f.*

sea, mer *f.*; océan *m.*

at sea, en mer; sur mer

beyond the seas, outre-mer

heavy sea, mer *(f.)* houleuse

sea-bathing, bains *(m. pl.)* de mer

sea-coast, côte *(f.)* de la mer; littoral *m.*

sea-gull, mouette *f.*

seaman, marin *m.*; matelot *m.*

seaside, bord *(m.)* de la mer

seaside resort, plage *f.*

sea-sickness, mal *(m.)* de mer

seaweed, algue *f.*

seaworthy, en bon état de navigabilité

seal, cachet *m.*; sceau *m.* (official); phoque *m.* (animal)

seal, *v.t.* cacheter; sceller (official)

sealing-wax, cire *(f.)* à cacheter

seam, couture *f.* (sewing); couche *f.* (mining); veine *f.* *(geol.)*

seamstress, couturière *f.*

search, recherche *f.*; perquisition *f.* (police, etc.); visite *f.* (customs)

search, *v.t.* visiter; examiner; faire une perquisition

search for, *v.t.* chercher

searchlight, projecteur *m.*

search warrant, mandat (*m.*) de perquisition

searching, (*adj.*) pénétrant, vif (vive)

season, saison *f.*; temps *m.*

out of season, hors de saison

season, *v.t.* assaisonner (food); modérer; acclimater; se sécher (timber)

season-ticket, carte (*f.*) d'abonnement

seasonable, (*adj.*) de saison

seasoned, (*adj.*) assaisonné (food); endurci; acclimaté; aguerri (of troops)

seasoning, assaisonnement *m.*

seat, siège *m.*; banc *m.*; place *f.* (train, etc.); château *m.* or maison (*f.*) de campagne; fond *m.* (of pants)

seat, *v.t.* asseoir; faire asseoir; placer

take your seats ! en voiture!

seated, (*adj.*) assis

(two-)seater, voiture (*f.*) à deux places (car); appareil (*m.*) biplace (*aviat.*)

secluded, (*adj.*) retiré, écarté

second, (*adj.*) second, deuxième; deux (of month)

second, seconde *f.* (time)

second, *v.t.* seconder, aider, appuyer (support)

second-hand, (*adj.*) d'occasion

second-rate, (*adj.*) inférieur

secondary, (*adj.*) secondaire; subordonné

secrecy, discrétion *f.*; secret *m.*

secret, secret *m.*; (*adj.*) secret (-ète)

keep a secret, garder un secret

open secret, secret (*m.*) de polichinelle

secretary, secrétaire *m.* and *f.*

Home Secretary, ministre (*f.*) de l'intérieur

secretaryship, secrétariat *m.*

secrete, *v.t.* cacher; sécréter (of glands)

secretly, (*adv.*) en secret

sect, secte *f.*

section, section *f.*

cross-section, coupe (*f.*) transversale

sector, secteur *m.*

secular, (*adj.*) séculier(-ère), séculaire

secularise, *v.t.* séculariser

secure, (*adj.*) sûr; assuré; à l'abri de

secure, *v.t.* mettre en sûreté; protéger; assurer (make certain); retenir

security, sécurité *f.*; sûreté *f.*; garantie *f.*

securities, titres *m. pl.*; valeurs *f. pl.*

securities (government), fonds (*m. pl.*) publics

sedate, (*adj.*) posé, calme

sedative, sédatif *m.*; (*adj.*) sédatif (-ive)

sedentary, (*adj.*) sédentaire

sediment, sédiment *m.*

sedition, sédition *f.*

seduce, *v.t.* séduire

seducing, (*adj.*) séduisant

seduction, séduction *f.*

see, siège (*m.*) épiscopal; évêché *m.*

see, *v.t.* voir; apercevoir; saisir

I see, je comprends

to see about, *v.t.* se charger de

to see into, pénétrer

to see over, visiter

to see about something, s'occuper de

to see through, pénétrer; mener à bonne fin

to see to, s'occuper de, veiller à

seed, semence *f.* (grain); graine *f.* (vegetables)

seed-time, semailles *f. pl.*

seedling, sauvageon *m.* (tree)

seedy, (*adj.*) râpé (clothes); souffrant (sick)

seeing, vue *f.*; vision *f.*

seeing, (*conj.*) vu que

seek, *v.t.* chercher; poursuivre

seek for, chercher; tâcher de trouver

seek from, demander à

seeking, recherche *f.*

seem, *v.i.* sembler; paraître; avoir l'air de

it seems to me, il me semble

seeming, *(adj.)* semblant

seemly, *(adj.)* convenable

see-saw, bascule *f.*; balançoire *f.*

seethe, *v.t.* bouillir, bouillonner

segment, segment *m.*

seize, *v.t.* saisir; s'emparer de; *v.i.* se caler (of engine)

seizing, saisie *f.* *(legal)*

seizure, saisie *f.*; attaque *f.* *(med.)*

seldom, *(adv.)* rarement

select, *v.t.* choisir

select, *(adj.)* d'élite

selection, choix *m.*; sélection *f.*

self, *(pron.)* même, soi-même; *(reflexive)* se

by one's self, tout seul

for myself, de ma part

self-centred, *(adj.)* égoïste, égocentrique

self-conceit, suffisance *f.*

self-confident, plein d'assurance

self-consciousness, gêne *f.*

self-defence, défense *(f.)* légitime; défense *(f.)* personnelle

self-denial, abnégation *f.*

self-made man, l'artisan de sa fortune, le fils de ses œuvres

self-praise, éloge *(m.)* de soi-même

self-propelled, *(adj.)* automoteur (-trice)

self-respect, amour-propre *m.*

self-respecting, *(adj.)* qui se respecte

self-same, *(adj.)* identique

self-satisfied, *(adj.)* content de soi

self-seeking, *(adj.)* intéressé, égoïste

self-starter, (auto)démarreur *(m.)*

self-willed, *(adj.)* obstiné, opiniâtre

selfish, *(adj.)* égoïste

selfishness, égoïsme *m.*

sell, *v.t.* vendre

seller, vendeur *m.*; vendeuse *f.*

best-seller, livre *(m.)* à succès

semblance, apparence *f.*

semi *(prefix)* demi, semi

senate, sénat *m.*

senator, sénateur *m.*

send, *v.t.* envoyer; expédier (goods)

send about his business, *v.t.* envoyer promener

send away, *v.t.* renvoyer, congédier

send for, *v.t.* envoyer chercher

send on (letters), *v.t.* faire suivre

sender, expéditeur(-trice) *m.* *(f.)*

senior, *(adj.)* aîné (age); supérieur (rank)

sensation, sensation *f.*

sensation (to make), faire sensation

sensational, *(adj.)* sensationnel(le)

sense, sens *m.*; bon sens *m.*; opinion *f.*; sentiment *m.*; sens commun *m.* (common sense)

senseless, *(adj.)* insensé; absurde; sans connaissance

sensibility, sensibilité *f.*

sensible, *(adj.)* sensé; raisonnable; reconnaissant de

sensitive, *(adj.)* sensible; impressionable

sensual, *(adj.)* sensuel(le)

sensualism, sensualisme *m.*

sensualist, sensualiste *m.*

sensuous, *(adj.)* voluptueux(-euse)

sentence, phrase *f.*; jugement *m.*; sentence *f.*

to pass sentence (of death), condamner (à mort)

sentiment, sentiment *m.*; opinion *f.*; pensée *f.* (thought)

sentimental, *(adj.)* sentimental

sentimentality, sensiblerie *f.*

sentinel, sentry, sentinelle *f.*; factionnaire *m.*

to be on sentry, être de faction

to relieve a sentry, relever une sentinelle

sentry-box, guérite *f.*

separate, *v.i.* se séparer; *v.t.* séparer, désunir

separate, *(adj.)* séparé; à part (distinct); détaché

separation, séparation *f.*; désunion *f.*
sepia, sépia *f.*
September, septembre *m.*
septuagenarian, septuagénaire *m.* and *f.*
sepulchre, sépulcre *m.*
sequel, suite *f.*; conséquence *f.*
sequence, suite *f.*; ordre *m.*; succession *f.*
seraglio, sérail *m.*
serene, (*adj.*) serein, calme
sergeant, sergent *m.* (infantry); maréchal (*m.*) des logis (mounted troops); brigadier *m.* (police)
serge, serge *f.*
serial (story), roman-feuilleton *m.*
series, série *f.*
serious, (*adj.*) sérieux(-euse), grave
seriousness, gravité *f.*
sermon, sermon *m.*
serpent, serpent *m.*
servant, serviteur *m.*; servante *f.*; domestique *m.* and *f.*; ordonnance *f.* (batman); bonne *f.*
serve, *v.t.* servir; être utile à
serve, *v.i.* servir, suffire (to suffice)
serve as, servir de
service, service *m.*; utilité *f.*; signification *f.* (writ)
at your service, à votre disposition
serviceable, (*adj.*) utile (of things); serviable (of persons)
servile, (*adj.*) servile
session, session *f.*; séance *f.*
set, collection *f.*; assortiment *m.*; garniture *f.*; parure *f.* (jewels); manche *f.* (tennis); poste *m.* (wireless)
set, *v.t.* mettre; poser; placer; planter (plant); ajuster; repasser (sharpen); sertir (jewels); régler (controls, fuses, etc.)
set about, *v.i.* se mettre à (faire, etc.)
setback, échec *m.*
set forth, *v.t.* exposer; *v.i.* partir (pour)
set free, *v.t.* libérer

set off, *v.t.* faire valoir
set out, *v.i.* partir, se mettre en route
set up, *v.i.* s'établir; *v.t.* établir, fonder, monter
settee, canapé *m.*
setter, chien (*m.*) d'arrêt
setting, mise *f.*; coucher *m.* (of the sun); repassage *m.* (razors, etc.)
settle, *v.t.* fixer, établir, déterminer, décider, arrêter (decide); coloniser, assigner (property); régler, résoudre (problem, question)
settle, *v.i.* s'établir; se remettre (weather)
to settle down to, s'appliquer à
to settle up, régler les comptes
settled, (*adj.*) établi, fixe
settlement, établissement *m.*; arrangement *m.*; règlement *m.*; rente *f.*; pension *f.*; contrat (*m.*) de mariage (marriage settlement); colonie *f.* (colony)
settler, colon *m.*
settling, tassement *m.* (building); règlement *m.*
settling day, jour (*m.*) de liquidation
seven, (*adj.*) sept
seventeen, (*adj.*) dix-sept
seventeenth, (*adj.*) dix-septième
sever, *v.i.* se séparer de; *v.t.* séparer, diviser
several, (*adj.*) plusieurs
severe, (*adj.*) sévère, rigoureux (-euse)
severity, sévérité *f.*; rigueur *f.*
sew, *v.t.* coudre
sewer (in town, etc.), égout *m.*
sewing machine, machine (*f.*) à coudre
sex, sexe *m.*
sexagenarian, sexagénaire *m.* and *f.*
sexton, sacristain *m.*; fossoyeur *m.*
sexual, (*adj.*) sexuel(le)
sexuality, sexualité *f.*
shabby, râpé (clothes); mesquin (petty); ignoble (conduct)
shade, ombre *f.*; ombrage *m.* (of

tree); abat-jour *m.* (of lamp); nuance *f.* (colour)

shade, *v.t.* ombrager; obscurcir; cacher; nuancer (*paint.*)

shadow, ombre *f.*

shadow, *v.t.* ombrager; filer (to spy on)

shadowy, (*adj.*) ombragé; ténébreux(-euse) (gloomy)

shady, ombragé; louche (suspect)

shaft, puits *m.* (of mine); souche *f.* (chimney stack); limon *m.* (of cart, etc.); arbre *m.* (machinery); trait *m.* (arrow)

shaggy, (*adj.*) poilu

shagreen, peau (*f.*) de chagrin

shake, secousse *f.*; poignée *f.* (of hand); ébranlement *m.*

shake, *v.t.* secouer, branler, agiter, serrer (of hand); faire trembler

shake, *v.i.* trembler (de)

shake hands, donner une poignée de main

shaken, (*adj.*) ébranlé, secoué

shaking, secousse *f.*; ebranlement *m.*

shallow, (*adj.*) peu profond; (*fig.*) superficiel(le)

sham, (*adj.*) simulé, faux (fausse)

sham, feinte *f.*

sham, *v.t.* feindre, simuler (illness)

shambles, boucherie *f.*; abattoir *m.*

shame, honte *f.*; ignominie *f.*

shame, *v.t.* faire honte à; déshonorer

shamefaced, (*adj.*) honteux (-euse); penaud

shameful, (*adj.*) honteux(-euse)

shameless, (*adj.*) effronté, impudent

shampoo, *v.t.* frictionner, faire un schampooing

shamrock, trèfle *m.*

shape, forme *f.*; figure *f.*; taille *f.* (of person); façon *f.*

shape, *v.t.* former, façonner

shapeless, (*adj.*) sans forme, informe

shapely, (*adj.*) bien fait

share, part *f.*; portion *f.*; action *f.* (*finan.*)

share, *v.t.* partager; avoir part à; *v.i.* participer (à)

shareholder, actionnaire *m.* and *f.*

shark, requin *m.* (fish); escroc *m.* (swindler)

sharp, (*adj.*) tranchant; pointu; aigu; intelligent; perçant (piercing); aigre (taste); rusé (sly)

sharpshooter, tirailleur *m.*

sharp-sighted, à la vue perçante

sharp-witted, éveillé

sharpen, *v.t.* aiguiser; tailler

sharper, filou *m.*; chevalier (*m.*) d'industrie

sharply, (*adv.*) vivement, avec âpreté

sharpness, tranchant *m.*; pointe *f.*; finesse *f.*

shave, *v.t.* se raser; faire la barbe à

to have a narrow shave, l'échapper belle

shaving, action (*f.*) de (se) raser; copeau *m.* (wood)

shaving-brush, blaireau *m.*

shaving-soap, savon (*m.*) à barbe

shawl, châle *m.*

she, (*pron.*) elle

sheaf, gerbe *f.*

shear, *v.t.* tondre

shearing, tondaison *f.*

shears, grands ciseaux *m. pl.*

sheath, fourreau *m.*; gaine *f.*

sheathe, *v.t.* mettre au fourreau

shed, hangar *m.*; appentis *m.*; atelier *m.*; hutte *f.* (hovel)

shed, *v.t.* répandre, faire couler, verser

sheep, mouton *m.*; brebis *f.* (ewe)

sheep-dog, chien (*m.*) de berger

sheep-fold, parc (*m.*) à moutons *m.*

sheep-shearing, tonte *f.*

sheepish, (*adj.*) niais; bête

sheer, (*adj.*) perpendiculaire, escarpé; pur

sheer nonsense, une pure sottise

sheet, drap (*m.*) de lit; feuille *f.* (of paper)

sheet-iron, tôle *f.*

sheet lead, plomb (*m.*) en feuilles

shelf, rayon *m.* (of book-case);

planche *f.* (cupboard); récif *m.* (reef); tablette *f.*

shell, coque *f.* (eggs); coquille *f.* (molluscs); écaille *f.* (oysters, etc.); obus *m.* (artillery)

shell, *v.t.* écosser (peas); bombarder (artillery)

shell-fire, bombardement *m.*

shell-fish, coquillages *m. pl.*

shell-hole, entonnoir *m.*

shell-shocked, (*adj.*) commotionné

shelling, écossage *m.*; bombardement *m.*

shelter, abri *m.*; asile *m.*

shelter, *v.t.* abriter; *v.i.* s'abriter

shepherd(-ess), berger(-ère) *m.* (*f.*)

sherry, vin de Xérès *m.*

shield, bouclier *m.*; écusson *m.* (*heraldry*)

shield, *v.t.* défendre, protéger

shift, changement *m.*; expédient *m.*; équipe *f.* (relay of workers)

shift, *v.t.* and *v.i.* changer de place

shifty, (*adj.*) sournois; retors

shilling, shilling *m.*

shin-bone, tibia *m.*

shine, éclat *m.*; lustre *m.*

shine, *v.i.* luire, briller, reluire

shingle, bardeau *m.* (roofing); galets *m. pl.* (on shore)

shining, (*adj.*) luisant, brillant

ship, navire *m.*; bâtiment *m.*; vaisseau *m.*

ship, *v.t.* embarquer; charger (load); expédier (goods); mettre à bord

merchant ship, navire (*m.*) marchand

warship, vaisseau (*m.*) de guerre

shipbuilding, construction (*f.*) de vaisseaux

ship-chandler, fournisseur (*m.*) de navires

shipowner, armateur *m.*

shipwreck, naufrage *m.*

shipwrecked, (*adj.*) naufragé

to be shipwrecked, faire naufrage

shipyard, chantier *m.*

shipper, expéditeur *m.*

shipping, navires *m. pl.*; marine *f.*; marine marchande *f.*

shipping agent, expéditeur *m.*

shire, comté *m.*

shirker, embusqué *m.*

shirt, chemise (*f.*) d'homme, chemise *f.*

dress-shirt, chemise empesée

shirt-sleeves, manches (*f. pl.*) de chemise

shirting, toile (*f.*) pour chemises

shiver, *v.i.* frissonner, grelotter (with cold); *v.t.* briser en éclats (to break)

shiver, frissonnement *m.*

shoal, banc *m.* (of fish); foule *f.* (of people); bas-fond *m.* (a shallow)

shock, choc *m.*; ébranlement *m.*; commotion *f.*; secousse *f.*

shock-troops, troupes (*f. pl.*) d'assaut

shock, *v.t.* choquer; offenser; blesser

shocking, choquant, affreux (-euse), blessant, révoltant, dégoûtant

shoe, soulier *m.*; chaussure *f.*; fer (*m.*) à cheval (horse)

shoe, *v.t.* chausser; ferrer (a horse)

shoe-black, décrotteur *m.*

shoemaker, cordonnier *m.*

shoeing-smith, maréchal (*m.*) ferrant

shoot, *v.t.* tirer; (at = sur) décharger; atteindre (to hit); fusiller; abattre (aircraft); faire passer par les armes (execute); lancer (a glance); marquer (a goal)

shoot, bourgeon *m.* (bud); plante *f.*; rejeton *m.* (offshoot)

shooting, chasse (*f.*) au tir; tir *m.* (firearms, etc.)

shooting-star, étoile (*f.*) filante

shop, boutique *f.* (small); magasin *m.* (store); atelier *m.* (workshop)

shop, *v.i.* faire des emplettes

shop-girl, demoiselle (*f.*) de magasin

shopkeeper, marchand(e) *m.* (*f.*); boutiquier(-ère) *m.* (*f.*)

shop-man, commis (*m.*) de magasin

shore, rivage *m.*; bord *m.*; plage *f.*

shore up, *v.t.* étayer

short, (*adj.*) court; bref (brève); de courte durée; petit (height)

short of (to be), manquer (de)

in short, bref, enfin

shortcoming, insuffisance *f.*

shorthand, sténographie *f.*

shorthand-typist, sténodactylographe *m.* (*f.*)

short-sighted, (*adj.*) myope (sight); peu prévoyant

shortage, déficit *m.*; disette *f.*

shorten, *v.t.* raccourcir (clothes, step); abréger (speech, etc.)

shortening, raccourcissement *m.*

shortly, (*adv.*) bientôt, sous peu; brièvement

shortness, courte durée *f.*; petitesse *f.* (height)

shot, coup de fusil *m.*; coup de feu *m.*; balle *f.* (rifle bullet); portée *f.* (range)

shoulder, épaule *f.*

shoulder, *v.t.* endosser; porter (rifle); se frayer un chemin (one's way)

shoulder-blade, omoplate *f.*

shout, cri *m.*

shout, *v.i.* pousser des cris

shove, *v.t.* pousser; fourrer (to stuff into)

shovel, pelle *f.*; *v.t.* pelleter (coal, etc.)

show, spectacle *m.*; exposition *f.* (exhibition); étalage *m.* (show-window)

show, *v.t.* montrer; faire voir; exposer; manifester; démontrer (prove); indiquer; expliquer (explain)

show, *v.i.* se montrer; se faire remarquer

show in, *v.t.* faire entrer

show off, *v.i.* poser; *v.t.* faire valoir

shower, ondée *f.* (slight); averse *f.* (heavy); volée *f.* (blows, etc.)

shower, *v.i.* pleuvoir; *v.t.* verser

shower-bath, douche *f.*

showery, (*adj.*) pluvieux(-euse)

showiness, ostentation *f.*

showy, (*adj.*) voyant, fastueux (-euse)

shrapnel, obus (*m.*) à balles

shred, lambeau *m.*

shrew, mégère *f.*

shrewd, (*adj.*) rusé, sagace

shrewdness, finesse *f.*

shriek, cri perçant *m.*

shriek, *v.i.* crier

shrill, (*adj.*) aigu, perçant

shrimp, crevette *f.*

shrine, châsse *f.*; sanctuaire *m.*

shrink, *v.i.* (se) rétrécir; reculer de (from); se rapetisser (in stature)

shrinkage, shrinking, rétrécissement *m.*; contraction *f.*

shrivel, *v.i.* se ratatiner; *v.t.* ratatiner, rider

shroud, linceul *m.*

shroud, *v.t.* envelopper

Shrove Tuesday, mardi gras *m.*

shrub, arbuste *m.*; arbrisseau *m.*

shrubbery, bosquet *m.*; plantation (*f.*) d'arbrisseaux

shrug, haussement (*m.*) d'épaules

shrug, *v.t.* hausser les épaules

shudder, frisson *m.*

shudder, *v.i.* frissonner

shuffle, battement *m.* (cards); subterfuge *m.*

shuffle, *v.t.* traîner (feet); battre (cards); *v.i.* tergiverser (of conduct)

shuffling, (*adj.*) évasif(-ive); traînant (walk)

shun, *v.t.* éviter

shunt, *v.t.* garer (railway)

shunting, manœuvres (*f. pl.*) de triage

shut, *v.t.* fermer, enfermer (shut in); refermer

shut off, *v.t.* couper (steam, light)

shut out, *v.t.* exclure

shut up, *v.t.* fermer, enfermer; emprisonner

shut up! tais-toi! taisez-vous!

shutter, volet *m.*; obturateur *m.* (camera); contrevent *m.* (outside)

shuttle, navette *f.*

shuttle service, (faire) la navette (entre)

shy, (adj.) timide; réservé; farouche (animals)
shy, v.i. broncher (of horse)
shyness, timidité f.
sick, (adj.) malade
sick leave, congé (m.) de convalescence
sick nurse, garde-malade m. and f.
sick room, chambre (f.) de malade
sick ward, infirmerie f.
sicken, v.t. rendre malade; dégoûter; v.i. tomber malade de; écœurer
sickening, (adj.) écœurant
sickle, faucille f.
sickly, (adj.) maladif(-ive)
sickness, maladie f.; mal (m.) au cœur
side, côté m.; bord m.; versant m. (of mountain)
side, (adj.) de côté; latéral
sideboard, buffet m.
side-face, profil m.
sidelong, (adj.) oblique
side-path, sentier (m.) détourné
side-walk, trottoir m.
sideways, (adv.) de côté
siding, voie (f.) de garage
sidle, v.i. marcher de côté
siege, siège m.
sieve, tamis m.; crible m. (large)
sift, v.t. tamiser, cribler; examiner scrupuleusement (evidence, etc.)
sigh, soupir m.
sigh, v.i. soupirer
sight, vue f.; vision f.; yeux m. pl.; spectacle m.; guidon m. (foresight of rifle); hausse f. (backsight)
lose sight of, v.t. perdre de vue
sight, v.t. apercevoir; viser
at sight, à vue
out of sight, hors de vue
sighted, en vue
sightseer, curieux(-euse) m. (f.)
sightless, (adj.) aveugle
sign, signe m.; enseigne f. (signboard)
sign, v.t. signer; v.i. sign on (of workmen), s'embaucher
sign-post, poteau m.; poteau indicateur m.

signal, signal m.
signal-box, cabine (f.) à signaux
signal, v.t. signaler; (adj.) insigne (i.e. noteworthy)
signaller, signaleur m.
signatory, signataire m.
signature, signature f.; marque f.
signet, sceau m.; cachet m.
signification, significance, signification f.; sens m.
significant, (adj.) significatif (-ive)
signify, v.t. signifier; vouloir dire; faire connaître
silence, silence m.; taciturnité f.
silence, v.t. réduire au silence; faire taire
silent, (adj.) silencieux(-euse); taciturne
silk, soie f.
silk fabrics, soieries f. pl.
silkworm, ver (m.) à soie
silky, (adj.) soyeux(-euse)
sill, appui m. (of window)
silly, (adj.) sot (sotte); niais(se); simple
to be silly, faire la bête
silt, v.t. envaser; vase f.
silver, argent m.; argenterie f (plate)
silver, (adj.) d'argent
silver(-plate), v.t. argenter; étamer (mirror)
similar, (adj.) semblable; pareil(le)
similarity, ressemblance f.
simper, v.i. minauder
simple, (adj.) simple; ingénu, naïf (naïve)
simpleton, nigaud(e) m. (f.)
simplicity, simplicité f.
simplify, v.t. simplifier
simultaneous, (adj.) simultané
sin, péché m.
sin, v.i. pécher
since, (conj.) puisque; depuis que
since, (adv.) depuis
sincere, (adj.) sincère
sincerity, bonne foi f.; sincérité f.
sinecure, sinécure f.

sinew, nerf *m.*; tendon *m.*

sinful, (*adj.*) criminel(le)

sing, *v.i.* chanter

singe, *v.t.* flamber, roussir (clothes); brûler légèrement

singer, chanteur *m.*; chanteuse *f.*; cantatrice *f.* (opera)

single, (*adj.*) seul, unique; individuel(le); célibataire (unmarried), simple *m.* (tennis)

singular, (*adj.*) singulier(-ère)

singularity, singularité *f.*

sink, évier *m.*

sink, *v.i.* couler à fond; sombrer; couler bas (ship); s'affaiblir (decline); baisser (prices)

sink, *v.t.* couler bas (ship); diminuer; faire baisser; foncer (shaft, etc.)

sinking, tassement *m.* (foundations); foncement *m.* (shafts, etc.); défaillance *f.* (weakening)

sinking-fund, fonds (*m.*) d'amortissement

sinner, pécheur *m.*; pécheresse *f.*

sinuosity, sinuosité *f.*

sip, gorgée *f.*

sip, *v.t.* and *v.i.* boire à petits coups

siphon, siphon *m.*

sir, monsieur *m.*

sire, sire *m.*; père *m.*

siren, sirène *f.*

sirloin, aloyau *m.*

sister, sœur *f.*; surveillante *f.* (hospital)

sister-in-law, belle-sœur *f.*

sit, *v.i.* s'asseoir; être assis (be seated); couver (birds)

to be sitting, siéger (parliament, judges, etc.)

to sit down, s'asseoir

to sit up, veiller (to stay awake)

to make someone sit up, épater quelqu'un (to surprise)

site, site *m.*; emplacement *m.* (for house)

sitting, séance *f.* (parliament, law-courts, etc.)

situated, (*adj.*) situé

situation, situation *f.*; emploi *m.*; place *f.* (job)

size, grandeur *f.*; taille *f.* (height); grosseur *f.*; pointure *f.* (shoes); volume *m.* (bulk); format *m.* (book, paper); encolure *f.* (shirts)

size up, *v.t.* jauger, juger

skate, patin *m.*; raie *f.* (fish)

skate, *v.i.* patiner

skeleton, squelette *m.*

sketch, esquisse *f.*; croquis *m.*

sketch, *v.t.* esquisser, faire le croquis de

skewer, brochette *f.*

ski, ski *m.*; *v.i.* faire du ski

skid, dérapage *m.* (of car)

skid, *v.i.* déraper (of car, etc.)

skilful, skilled, (*adj.*) adroit, habile

skill, habileté *f.*; adresse *f.*

skim, *v.t.* écumer; écrémer (milk)

skim, écume *f.*

skin, peau *f.*; pelure *f.* (banana)

skin, *v.t.* écorcher; peler, éplucher (fruit)

skip, saut *m.*

skip, *v.i.* sautiller, sauter

skipper, patron *m.* (of ship)

skirmish, escarmouche *f.*

skirt, jupe *f.* (dress); bord *m.* (forest, etc.); basque *m.* (overcoat)

skirt, *v.t.* contourner

skittle, quille *f.*

skull, crâne *m.*

sky, ciel *m.* (*pl.* cieux); firmament *m.*

sky-blue, (*adj.*) bleu de ciel

skylight, châssis vitré *m.*

sky-scraper, gratte-ciel *m.*

slab, dalle *f.*; plaque *f.*

slack, (*adj.*) lâche; faible; mou (molle); négligent

slacken, *v.i.* se relâcher; tomber (to flag)

slacken, *v.t.* relâcher, ralentir (pace)

slam, *v.t.* fermer avec violence

slander, médisance *f.*; calomnie *f.*; diffamation *f.*

slander, *v.t.* calomnier; diffamer (*legal*)

slanderous, (*adj.*) calomnieux (-euse)

slanderer, calomniateur(-trice) *m.* (*f.*)

slang, argot *m.*; *v.t.* injurier

slant, *v.i.* être en pente; *v.t.* mettre en pente.
slanting, (*adj.*) oblique
slap, claque *f.*; gifle *f.*
slap, *v.t.* taper, souffleter
slate, ardoise *f.*; réprimander *v.t.*
slating, toiture (*f.*) en ardoise
slaughter, tuerie *f.*; boucherie *f.*
slaughter, *v.t.* massacrer; abattre (animals)
slaughter-house, abattoir *m.*
slave, esclave *m.* and *f.*
slavery, esclavage *m.*
slay, *v.t.* tuer
slayer, tueur *m.*; assassin *m.*
slaying, tuerie *f.*
sledge, traîneau *m.*
sleek, (*adj.*) lisse; poli
sleep, sommeil *m.*
sleep, *v.i.* dormir; reposer
sleeper, (**railway**) wagon-lit *m.*; traverse *f.* (cross-piece on railway line)
sleeping-berth, couchette *f.*
sleeping-car, wagon-lit *m.*
sleeping-partner (**business**), associé (*m.*) commanditaire
sleepiness, somnolence *f.*
sleepless, (*adj.*) sans sommeil
sleepless night, nuit blanche
sleeplessness, insomnie *f.*
sleepy, (*adj.*) endormi; somnolent; cotonneux(-euse) (fruit)
to go to sleep, *v.i.* s'endormir
sleet, grésil *m.*
sleet, *v.i.* grésiller
sleeve, manche *f.*; manchon *m.* (of mechanism)
sleigh, traîneau *m.*
slender, (*adj.*) svelte, mince, élancé (tree, etc.); maigre (means)
slice, tranche *f.*
slice, *v.t.* découper en tranches
slide, glissade *f.*; coulisse *f.* (groove)
slide, *v.i.* (se) glisser; *v.t.* glisser
to let slide, laisser aller
slight, (*adj.*) mince, léger(-ère); peu considérable
slight, manque (*m.*) d'égards; affront *m.*; dédain *m.*

slight, *v.t.* manquer d'égards (envers)
slim, (*adj.*) mince, svelte
slime, vase *f.*; limon *m.*
slimy, (*adj.*) vaseux(-euse); visqueux(-euse)
sling, écharpe *f.* (*surg.*); fronde *f.*
sling, *v.t.* lancer; suspendre
slip, glissade *f.*; erreur *f.*; faux pas *m.*; combinaison *f.* (cost.)
slip, *v.i.* and *v.t.* glisser
slip away, s'esquiver (person); s'écouler (time)
slip on (of clothes), enfiler
slipper, pantoufle *f.*
slippery, (*adj.*) glissant; difficile à tenir; peu sûr
slippery (**customer**), rusé (compère) *m.*
slipshod, (*adj.*) négligé; désordonné
slit, fente *f.*
slit, *v.t.* fendre; *v.i.* se fendre
slither, *v.i.* glisser
sloop, sloop *m.*; chaloupe *f.*
slope, pente *f.*; talus *m.*
slope, *v.i.* pencher; être en pente
sloping, (*adj.*) en pente, en talus
slot, rainure *f.* (groove)
slot machine, distributeur (*m.*) automatique
slow, (*adj.*) lent, tardif(-ive); lourd (dull); en retard (of watches)
slow down, *v.i.* ralentir (speed)
sluggard, paresseux(-euse) *m.* (*f.*)
sluggish, (*adj.*) indolent, lourd
sluice, écluse *f.*
sluice-gate, vanne *f.*
slum, taudis *m.*; bas quartier *m.*
slumber, sommeil *m.*
slumber, *v.i.* sommeiller
slump, effondrement *m.*; crise (*f.*) économique
sly, (*adj.*) rusé, sournois
smack, claque *f.* (slap); gifle *f.* (in face); goût *m.* (taste); bateau (*m.*) pêcheur (fishing)
small, (*adj.*) petit; menu; faible (weak); fin; peu considérable; modeste
smallness, petitesse *f.*
smallpox, petite (*f.*) vérole

smart, (*adj.*) piquant, cuisant, douloureux(-euse); éveillé (alive); beau (belle); pimpant (natty); chic (spruce); (*fam.*) snob

smart, vive douleur *f.*

smart, *v.i.* cuire, brûler

smartness, élégance *f.*

smash, fracas *m.*; faillite *f* (*finan.*); catastrophe *f.*

smash, *v.t.* briser, écraser, ruiner

go smash, faire faillite

smattering, connaissance (*f.*) superficielle

smear, tache *f.*

smear, *v.t.* barbouiller de

smell, odeur *f.*; odorat *m.* (sense); flair *m.* (of dogs)

smell, *v.t.* sentir; flairer; *v.i.* sentir

smelt, éperlan *m.* (fish)

smelt, *v.t.* fondre

smelting, fonte *f.*

smelting furnace, haut fourneau *m.*

smile, sourire *m.*

smile, *v.i.* sourire

smirk, *v.i.* minauder

smite, *v.t.* frapper

smith, forgeron *m.*

smithy, forge *f.*

smock, blouse *f.*; sarrau *m.* (school child)

smoke, fumée *f.*

smoke, *v.i.* fumer

smoker, fumeur *m.*; (railway) compartiment (*m.*) pour fumeurs

smoky, (*adj.*) enfumé

smooth, (*adj.*) uni; lisse; égal (even)

smooth(e), *v.t.* adoucir (calm); lisser (hair); faciliter (make easy); caresser (an animal)

smoothness, égalité *f.*; calme *m.* (of sea)

smother, *v.t.* étouffer, suffoquer

smoulder, *v.i.* brûler sans flamme; brûler lentement; (*fig.*) couver (anger, etc.)

smudge, *v.t.* tacher d'encre; souiller

smuggle, *v.t.* passer en contre-bande

smuggler, contrebandier *m.*

snack, casse-croûte *m.*

snail, limaçon *m.*

snake, serpent *m.*

snap, *v.t.* happer (of dog); claquer (of whip); *v.i.* se casser (in two)

snapshot, instantané *m.*

snare, piège *m.*

snarl, *v.i.* grogner

snarling, (*adj.*) hargneux

snatch, *v.t.* saisir

snatch at, *v.t.* se raccrocher à; chercher à saisir

sneak, mouchard *m.* (tell-tale)

sneak, *v.i.* s'en aller furtivement; moucharder

sneer, ricanement *m.*

sneer, *v.i.* ricaner

sneeze, *v.i.* éternuer

sneezing, éternuement *m.*

sniff, *v.i.* and *v.t.* renifler

snip, coup (*m.*) de ciseaux; coupure *f.*; (*fam.*) bonne affaire *f.*

snipe, bécassine *f.*

sniper, canardeur *m.*; franc-tireur *m.* (military)

snivel, *v.i.* pleurnicher

snivelling, (*adj.*) pleurnicheur (-euse)

snob, poseur *m.*; prétentieux (-euse) (*adj.*)

snore, *v.i.* ronfler

snore, snoring, ronflement *m.*

snout, museau *m.*

snow, neige *f.*

snow, *v.i.* neiger, tomber de la neige

snub, avanie *f.* [neige

snub-nose, nez camus *m.*; (*adj.*) (au nez) camus

snuff, tabac (*m.*) à priser

snuffle, *v.i.* nasiller, renifler

snug, (*adj.*) commode (house)

so, (*adv.*) ainsi; de cette manière; comme ça; si; tellement; tant (degree); à peu près (about)

and so on, et ainsi de suite

so that, (*conj.*) de sorte que; si bien que

soak, *v.t.* tremper

soaking, trempée *f.* (rain)

soap, savon *m.*

cake of soap, (pain de) savon *m.*

soar, *v.i.* prendre l'essor, monter

sob, sanglot *m.*

sob, *v.t.* sangloter
sober, *(adj.)* sobre; modéré
sociability, sociabilité *f.*
sociable, *(adj.)* sociable
social, *(adj.)* social
socialism, socialisme *m.*
socialist, socialiste *m.* and *f.*
society, société *f.*; la société *f.*; le monde *m.*
sock, chaussette *f.*
socket, orbite *f.* (eye); douille *f.* (machinery); cavité *f.*
sod, gazon *m.*; motte *f.*
soda, soude *f.*
soda-water, eau (*f.*) de seltz
sodden, *(adj.)* détrempé
sodium, sodium *m.*
sofa, canapé *m.*; sofa *m.*
soft, *(adj.)* mou (molle); doux (douce); tendre
soften, *v.t.* amollir; adoucir; attendrir (heart); *v.i.* s'amollir, s'attendrir
softening, amollissement *m.*; attendrissement *m.*
softness, mollesse *f.*; douceur *f.*
soil, sol *m.* (earth); terre *f.*
soil, *v.t.* salir; souiller
sojourn, séjour *m.*
sojourn, *v.i.* séjourner
solace, consolation *f.*; soulagement *m.*
solar, *(adj.)* solaire
solder, soudure *f.*
solder, *v.t.* souder
soldier, soldat *m.*; militaire *m.*
soldierly, *(adj.)* martial; militaire
sole, semelle *f.* (shoe); plante *f.* (of foot); sole *f.* (fish)
sole, *(adj.)* seul, unique
sole, *v.t.* ressemeler (shoe)
solely, *(adv.)* uniquement
solemn, *(adj.)* solennel(le); grave; sérieux(-euse)
solemnity, solennité *f.*; gravité *f.*
solicit, *v.t.* solliciter
soliciting, raccolage *m.* (touting, etc.)
solicitor, avoué *m.* (*legal*)
solicitude, sollicitude *f.*
solid, *(adj.)* solide, massif(-ive)

solidarity, solidarité *f.*
solidify, *v.i.* solidifier
solitary, *(adj.)* solitaire
solstice, solstice *m.*
solution, solution *f.*; dissolution *f.*
solve, *v.t.* résoudre
solvency, solvabilité *f.* (of person)
solvent, *(adj.)* solvable
sombre, *(adj.)* sombre
some, *(adj.)* quelque, quelques; quelques-uns (-unes); un certain; un peu de; du, de la, des
somebody, quelqu'un *m.*; quelqu'une *f.*
somehow, *(adv.)* de façon ou d'autre; d'une façon quelconque
someone, *(pron.)* quelqu'un, quelqu'une
something, *(pron.)* quelque chose
sometime, *(adv.)* autrefois
sometimes, *(adv.)* quelquefois; parfois
somewhat, *(adv.)* quelque peu, un peu
somewhere, *(adv.)* quelque part
somewhere else, *(adv.)* ailleurs
somnambulism, somnambulisme *m.*
somnolent, *(adj.)* somnolent
son, fils *m.*
son-in-law, gendre *m.*
god-son, filleul *m.*
sonata, sonate *f.*
song, chanson *f.*; chant *m.*; cantique *m.* (hymn)
songster, chanteur *m.*
sonnet, sonnet *m.*
sonorous, *(adj.)* sonore
soon, *(adv.)* bientôt
as soon as, aussitôt que
too soon, trop tôt
very soon, dans très peu de temps
sooner, plutôt (rather); plus tôt (of time)
soonest, le plus tôt
soot, suie *f.*
soothe, *v.t.* apaiser; calmer
soothsayer, devin *m.*; devineresse *f.*
sooty, *(adv.)* couvert de suie
sop, morceau trempé *m.*; (*fig.*) douceur *f.* (gratuity)

sorcerer(-ess), sorcier(-ère) *m.* (*f.*)

sorcery, sorcellerie *f.*

sordid, (*adj.*) sordide; vil

sore, plaie *f.*

sore, (*adj.*) douloureux(-euse), endolori, sensible (tender)

sorrel, oseille *f.*

sorrow, chagrin *m.*; peine *f.*; tristesse *f.*

sorry, (*adj.*) fâché (de); triste; méchant (unimpressive)

sort, sorte *f.*; genre *m.*; espèce *f.*

sort, *v.t.* trier (letters, etc.); classer

soul, âme *f.*; être *m.* (being)

sound, (*adj.*) en bon état; sain (healthy); solide

sound, son *m.*; bruit *m.*; détroit *m.* (*geog.*); sonde *f.* (*surg.*)

sound, *v.t.* sonner; *v.i.* retentir; *v.t.* sonder (fathom or probe)

soup, soupe *f.*; potage *m.*

clear soup, consommé *m.*

sour, (*adj.*) aigre, acide, tourné (milk)

source, source *f.*

south, (*adj.*) du sud; méridional

south, sud *m.*; midi *m.*

southerly, (*adj.*) du sud

southern, (*adj.*) méridional

southwards, (*adv.*) vers le sud

sovereign, souverain *m.*; (*adj.*) souverain(e)

sow, truie *f.*

sow, *v.t.* semer; ensemencer

space, espace *m.*; étendue *f.*

spacious, (*adj.*) spacieux(-euse)

spaceship (craft), astronef *m.*

spade, bêche *f.*

span, *v.t.* franchir, enjamber; envergure *f.* (wingspread of bird or plane)

Spanish, (*adj.*) espagnol

spanner, clef (*f.*) anglaise

spare, (*adj.*) maigre; sec (sèche) (lean); disponible (time)

spare parts, pièces (*f.*) de rechange

spare, *v.t.* se passer de (do without); ménager; céder (let have)

spare-room, chambre (*f.*) d'ami

sparing, (*adj.*) parcimonieux (-euse); économe, frugal

spark, étincelle *f.*

sparking-plug, bougie (*f.*) d'allumage

sparkle, (*subst.*) étincellement *m.*; *v.i.* étinceler

sparkling, (*adj.*) étincelant; mousseux (wine)

sparrow, moineau *m.*

sparse, (*adj.*) épars; éparpillé

spasm, spasme *m.*

spawn, frai *m.*

spawn, *v.i.* frayer; (*fig.*) engendrer

speak, *v.t.* parler, causer avec; faire un discours; prendre la parole

speaker, orateur *m.*; président *m.* (parliament)

loud-speaker, haut-parleur *m.* (wireless)

spear, lance *f.*; harpon *m.*

special, (*adj.*) spécial; exprès; particulier(-ère)

speciality, spécialité *f.*

specie, espèces *f. pl.* (monetary)

species, espèce *f.*; genre *m.*; sorte *f.*

specimen, spécimen *m.*; exemple *m.*

specification, mémoire (*m.*) descriptif; spécification *f.*

speck, tache *f.*

spectacle, spectacle *m.*

spectacles, lunettes *f. pl.*

spectacular, spectaculaire

spectator, spectateur(-trice) *m.* (*f.*)

spectre, spectre *m.*; fantôme *m.*

spectrum, spectre solaire *m.*

speculate, *v.i.* spéculer (*finan.*); méditer (think over)

speech, discours *m.*; parole *f.* (faculty of speech)

figure of speech, figure (*f.*) de rhétorique

speech-day, distribution (*f.*) des prix

speechless, (*adj.*) muet(te); interdit

speed, hâte *f.*; vitesse *f.*; célérité *f.*; promptitude *f.*

speed, *v.i.* se hâter

speedy, (*adj.*) prompt, rapide

spell, charme *m.*; période *f.* (time)

spell, *v.t.* épeler; orthographier (in writing)

spelling, orthographe *f.*

spend, *v.t.* dépenser (money); passer (time)

spendthrift, prodigue *m.*; (*adj.* and *subst.*) dépensier(-ère) *m.* (*f.*)

sphere, sphère *f.*

sphinx, sphinx *m.*

spice, épice *f.*

spice, *v.t.* épicer

spicy, (*adj.*) épicé, aromatique

spider, araignée *f.*

spider's web, toile (*f.*) d'araignée

spigot, fausset *m.* (faucet); robinet *m.*

spike, pointe *f.* (de fer); cheville *f.* (of wood)

spill, culbute *f.* (upset); allumette (*f.*) en papier

spill, *v.t.* répandre; renverser (upset)

spin, *v.t.* filer; *v.i.* tourner

spinach, épinards *m. pl.*

spinner, fileur(-euse) *m.* (*f.*); filateur *m.*

spinning, filature *f.*

spinning-wheel, rouet (*m.*) à filer

spinster, fille (*f.*) non mariée; (*contempt.*) vieille fille

spiral, (*adj.*) spiral

spiral, spirale *f.*

spire, flèche *f.*

spirit, esprit *m.*; âme *f.*; verve *f.*; élan *m.*; moral *m.* (of troops); spectre *m.*

spirit, liqueur alcoolique *f.*

spirits, les spiritueux *m.*

spirit, *v.t.* animer

spirit away, *v.t.* faire disparaître

spirited, (*adj.*) animé; plein de verve; ardent (horses)

spiritual, (*adj.*) spirituel(le)

spiritualism, spiritualisme *m.*; spiritisme *m.*

spirituous, (*adj.*) spiritueux (-euse)

spit, broche *f.* (*cook*)

spit, *v.i.* cracher

spite, dépit *m.*; rancune *f.*

in spite of, malgré, en dépit de

out of spite, par dépit

spiteful, (*adj.*) rancunier(-ère); vindicatif(-ive); méchant (animal)

spittle, salive *f.* [mals]

splash, éclaboussure *f.*; clapotis *m.* (of waves)

splash, *v.t.* éclabousser; *v.i.* clapoter

spleen, rate *f.* (internal organ); humeur (*f.*) noire

splendid, (*adj.*) resplendissant; magnifique; splendide

splendour, splendeur *f.*

splint (*surg.*), éclisse *f.*

splinter, éclat *m.*; éclat de bois (d'obus); esquille *f.* (*surg.*)

splinter, *v.i.* voler en éclats; *v.t.* briser en éclats

split, fente *f.*; fissure *f.*; rupture *f.*

split, *v.t.* fendre; diviser (divide); *v.i.* se fendre

splutter, bredouillement *m.*

splutter, *v.t.* bredouiller

spoil, butin *m.*; pillage *m.*

spoil, gâter (a child, etc.); abîmer (damage); ravager (plunder)

spoke, rais *m.* (of wheel)

to put a spoke in the wheels, mettre des bâtons dans les roues

spokesman, orateur *m.*; porte-parole *m.* (of deputation, etc.)

sponge, *f.* éponge

sponge, *v.t.* éponger

spongy, (*adj.*) spongieux(-euse)

sponsor, répondant(e)

spontaneous, (*adj.*) spontané

spoon, cuiller *f.*

spoonful, cuillerée *f.*

sport, jeu *m.*; divertissement; sport *m.*; raillerie *f.* (mockery); le sport (racing, etc.)

sport, *v.i.* (se) divertir

sporting, (*adj.*) sportif(-ive)

sportsman, chasseur *m.*; sports-man *m.*; amateur (*m.*) de sport

spot, tache *f.* (stain); souillure *f.* (on character); endroit *m.*, lieu *m.* (place).

spot, *v.t.* tacher, souiller; (*fig.*) reconnaître

spotless, (*adj.*) sans taches; pur

spouse, époux *m*.; épouse *f*.

spout, tuyau *m*.; tuyau de décharge *m*.

spout, *v.i.* jaillir

sprain, foulure *f*.; entorse *f*.

sprain, *v.t.* se fouler

sprat, sprat *m*.

sprawl, *v.i.* s'étaler, s'étendre

spray, écume *f*. (from waves); embrun *m*. (of sea, etc.); branche *f*.

spray, *v.t.* arroser

spread, étendue *f*.; expansion *f*.; envergure *f*. (of wings, etc.)

spread, *v.t.* étendre; répandre; propager (propagate); *v.i.* s'étendre, se répandre

spreading, propagation *f*.; extension *f*.

sprightly, (*adj.*) vif (vive), animé

spring, saut *m*. (jump); bond *m*. (leap); ressort *m*. (of bed, etc.); source *f*. (water); printemps *m*. (season)

spring, *v.i.* bondir, s'élancer, jaillir (gush forth); descendre (spring from); provenir

springboard, tremplin *m*.

springtide, grande marée *f*.

springtime, printemps *m*.

springiness, élasticité *f*.

springlike, (*adj.*) printanier(-ère)

sprinkle, *v.t.* asperger, arroser

sprout, pousse *f*.; rejeton *m*.

sprouts (Brussels), choux (*m. pl.*) de Bruxelles

sprout, *v.i.* pousser, germer

spruce, (*adj.*) pimpant; sapin *m*. (tree)

spruce, *v.t.* se faire beau (belle)

spunk, amadou *m*.; (*fig.*) courage *m*.

spur, éperon *m*.; stimulant *m*. (urge)

spur, *v.t.* éperonner; stimuler, inciter

spurious, (*adj.*) faux (fausse); contrefait

spurn, *v.t.* mépriser; (*fig.*) repousser du pied

spurt, effort soudain *m*.; jaillissement *m*.

spurt, *v.t.* jaillir; s'élancer

sputter, *v.i.* cracher (of pen); bredouiller (of speech)

spy, espion *m*.; espionne *f*.

spy, *v.i.* espionner; *v.t.* remarquer

spy-system, espionnage *m*.

squabble, querelle *f*.; chamaillerie *f*.

squabble, *v.i.* se chamailler

squadron, escadre *f*. (ships); escadrille *f*. (aeroplanes); escadron *m*. (cavalry)

squalid, (*adj.*) malpropre; misérable

squall, cri *m*. (cry); rafale *f*. (wind)

squall, *v.i.* crier, brailler

squally, à rafales (weather)

squander, *v.t.* dissiper; gaspiller

squanderer, gaspilleur(-euse) *m*. (*f*.); prodigue *m*.

square, (*adj.*) carré

square, carré *m*.; place (*f*.) publique; square *m*. (place); équerre *f*. (rule)

square, *v.t.* carrer; balancer (accounts)

square up, régler ses comptes

squash, *v.t.* écraser

squash, foule (*f*.) serrée (crowd)

squat, (*adj.*) ramassé, trapu (thick-set)

squat, *v.i.* s'accroupir

squeak (squeal), cri (*m*.) aigu

squeak (squeal), *v.i.* pousser des cris aigus

squeamish, (*adj.*) trop délicat

squeeze, *v.t.* presser, serrer

squib, pétard *m*.

squint, louchement *m*.

squint, *v.i.* loucher

squire, écuyer; châtelain *m*. (country squire, owner of country property)

squirrel, écureuil *m*.

stab, coup (*m*.) de poignard

stab, *v.t.* poignarder

stability, stabilité *f*.

stable, (*adj.*) stable, fixe, solide; constant

stable, écurie *f*. (horses); étable *f*. (cattle)

stable-boy or man, garçon (*m*.) d'écurie

stack, meule *f.* (hay); pile *f.* (of wood); souche *f.* (chimney)

stack, *v.t.* mettre en meule; empiler (wood)

staff, bâton *m.*; état-major *m.* (*mil.*); personnel *m.* (school, hotel, etc.)

staff-college, école (*f.*) supérieure de guerre

staff-officer, officier (*m.*) d'état major

stag, cerf *m.*

stage, estrade *f.* (platform); échafaudage *m.* (scaffolding); scène *f.* (*theat.*); théâtre *m.* (profession); étape *f.* (journey)

stage-coach, diligence *f.*

stage-fright, trac *m.*

stage-manager, régisseur *m.*

stagger, *v.i.* chanceler, fléchir; (*fig.*) étonner

staggering blow, coup (*m.*) foudroyant

stagnancy, stagnation *f.*

stagnant, (*adj.*) stagnant

staid, (*adj.*) posé; grave

stain, tache *f.*; (*fig.*) honte *f.*; souillure *f.* (on character)

stain, *v.t.* tacher; (*fig.*) souiller

stained, (*adj.*) taché

stainless, sans tache; inoxydable (steel)

stair, marche *f.*; degré *m.*; (*pl.*) les escaliers

to be downstairs, être en bas

to be upstairs, être en haut

staircase, escalier *m.*

stake, pieu *m.*; poteau *m.*; jalon *m.* (*mil.*); enjeu *m.* (cards, etc.); mise *f.*; bûcher *m.* (i.e. burning at stake)

stake, *v.t.* parier (bet); mettre en jeu, miser; hasarder (to risk)

stake out, *v.t.* jalonner

stale, (*adj.*) rassis (bread); vieux; usé, passé

stalk, tige *f.*; quéue *f.* (flower); trognon *m.* (cabbage)

stalk, *v.i.* marcher fièrement; chasser à l'affût (shooting)

stall, stalle *f.*; échoppe *f.*; baraque *f.* (stall at fair, etc.); fauteuil *m.* (theatre)

stallion, étalon *m.*

stalwart, (*adj.*) robuste

stamina, vigueur *f.*

stammer, *v.i.* bégayer, balbutier (hesitate)

stamp, timbre *m.* (postage); poinçon *m.* (punch); empreinte *f.* (impression); timbre *m.* (on documents); estampille *f.* (on goods); trempe *f.* (character); cachet *m.* (seal)

stamp, *v.t.* marquer (de); imprimer; timbrer (documents, letters); estampiller (goods); poinçonner (tickets)

stamp-collector, philatéliste *m.* and *f.*

stamp-duty, impôt (*m.*) du timbre

stampede, débandade *f.*

stanch, *v.t.* étancher

stand, station *f.*; halte *f.*; poste *m.*; estrade *f.* (platform); pied *m.* (furniture); porte-parapluie *m.* (umbrellas, etc.); pupitre *m.* (*mus.*); (*fig.*) résistance *f.*

stand, *v.i.* se tenir debout; se placer (place oneself); se soutenir (keep on one's legs); *v.t.* souffrir, supporter

stand aside, *v.i.* se tenir à l'écart

stand back, *v.i.* se tenir en arrière

stand by, *v.t.* soutenir, défendre

stand close, se serrer

stand fast (firm), tenir bon

standard, étendard *m.*; drapeau *m.*; étalon *m.* (weights, etc.); degré *m.*; modèle *m.*

standard, (*adj.*) classique

standing, (*adj.*) établi; stagnant (water)

standing, pose *f.*; place *f.*; position *f.*; rang *m.* (rank); date *f.*; durée *f.*

long standing, de longue date

staple, (*adj.*) principal

staple product, produit (*m.*) principal; denrée *f.*; crampon *m.* (wire staple)

star, étoile *f.*; astre *m.*; vedette *f.* (cinema)

star, *v.t.* étoiler
starboard, tribord *m.*
starch, amidon *m.*
starch, *v.t.* empeser
stare, *v.i.* regarder fixement;
(*subst.*) regard (*m.*) fixe
starling, sansonnet *m.*
starry, (*adj.*) étoilé
start, tressaillement *m.*; saut *m.*;
départ *m.*
start, *v.i.* tressaillir; partir; se
mettre en route; débuter; faire
un bond
starting-point, point (*m.*) de
départ
startle, *v.t.* faire tressaillir,
effrayer
startling, (*adj.*) étonnant, foudroyant; saisissant
starvation, inanition *f.*; faim *f.*
starve, *v.i.* mourir de faim; *v.t.*
faire mourir de faim
starving, (*adj.*) affamé, mourant
de faim
state, état *m.*; pompe *f.*; condition *f.*
state, *v.t.* déclarer, énoncer,
affirmer, constater
stately, (*adj.*) imposant; majest-
ueux(-euse); noble
statement, exposé *m.*; rapport
m.; relevé *m.* (accounts)
statesman, homme (*m.*) d'état
station, gare *f.* (railway); station
f.; poste *m.*; condition *f.* (in life);
position sociale *f.*
station, *v.t.* placer, ranger
stationary, (*adj.*) stationnaire
stationer, papetier *m.*; libraire
m.
stationery, papeterie *f.*
stationmaster, chef (*m.*) de gare
statistical, (*adj.*) statistique
statistics, statistique *f.*
statuary, statuaire *f.*
statue, statue *f.*
stature, taille *f.*
status, condition *f.*; rang *m.*
statute, statut *m.*; loi *f.*
staunchness, dévotion *f.*; fermeté
f.
stay, support *m.*; *v.t.* étayer
stay, séjour *m.*; sursis *m.* (*legal*)

stay, *v.i.* rester; demeurer (sojourn); descendre (at hotel, etc.)
stay at, *v.i.* rester (à); demeurer à
stay-at-home, (*adj.* and *subst.*)
casanier(-ère) *m.* (*f.*)
stay away, *v.i.* s'absenter
stay in, *v.i.* rester à la maison
stay up, *v.i.* veiller
stays, corset *m.*
stead, lieu *m.*
steadfast, (*adj.*) ferme
steady, (*adj.*) ferme; sûr; posé,
sérieux(-euse)
steady, *v.t.* raffermir; *v.i.* se
raffermir
steak, bifteck *m.*
steal, *v.t.* voler; dérober; soustraire quelque chose
steal away, *v.i.* se dérober; se
glisser furtivement
by stealth, à la dérobée
steam, vapeur *f.*
steam, *v.i.* jeter de la vapeur;
fumer
steam, *v.t.* passer à la vapeur
steam-engine, machine (*f.*) à
vapeur
steamship, steamer, bateau
(*m.*) à vapeur, vapeur *m.*
steam-tug, remorqueur *m.*
steaming, (*adj.*) fumant
steed, coursier *m.*
steel, acier *m.*
steel, (*adj.*) en acier
steel, *v.i.* (*fig.*) s'endurcir contre;
v.t. acérer (of metal)
steel-works, aciérie *f.*
steep, (*adj.*) raide, escarpé
steep, *v.t.* tremper; infuser
steeple, clocher *m.*
steeplechase, course (*f.*) à
obstacles
steer, *v.t.* gouverner, diriger,
conduire
steer, (jeune) bœuf *m.*
steering-gear, timonerie *f.*
steering-wheel, roue (*f.*) du
gouvernail (ship); volant *m.*
(car)
stem, tige *f.*; queue *f.* (flower);
tronc *m.* (of tree)
stem, *v.t.* refouler (a flood);
contenir

from stem to stern, de l'avant à l'arrière

stench, puanteur *f.*

stenographer, sténographe *m.* and *f.*

stenography, sténographie *f.*

step, pas *m.* (pace); degré *m.*; marche *f.* (of stairs); échelon *m.* (ladder); marchepied *m.* (of car, etc.)

steps, échelle *f.* (ladder); perron *m.* (flight of steps)

step, *v.i.* faire un pas; marcher; monter (into); descendre (down from)

step aside, *v.i.* s'écarter

step forward, *v.i.* s'avancer

step in, *v.i.* entrer; (*fig.*) intervenir

step into, *v.i.* entrer (dans)

step on, *v.i.* mettre le pied sur

step over, franchir, enjamber

a good step, un bon bout de chemin

step in the right direction, une bonne démarche

step by step, pas à pas

step-brother, beau-frère *m.*; demi-frère *m.*

step-daughter, belle-fille *f.*

step-father, beau-père *m.*

step-mother, belle-mère *f.*

step-sister, belle-sœur *f.*: demi-sœur *f.*

step-son, beau-fils *m.*

stereotype, cliché *m.*

sterile, (*adj.*) stérile

sterility, stérilité *f.*

sterilise, *v.t.* stériliser

sterling, livre (*f.*) sterling (pound) (*fig.*) vrai, de bon aloi

stern, (*adj.*) sévère, dur

stern, poupe *f.*; arrière *m.*

sternness, sévérité *f.*

stew, ragoût *m.* (meat); compote *f.* (fruit)

stew, *v.t.* faire cuire à la casserole

steward, économe *m.*; intendant *m.*; steward *m.* (ship)

stick, bâton *m.*; canne *f.*

stick, *v.t.* coller (paste); enfoncer (into); afficher (posters)

stick, *v.i.* se coller, se fixer, s'attacher; rester (remain)

sticky, (*adj.*) gluant, collant

stiff, (*adj.*) raide; rigide; opiniâtre (resistance, etc.); gêné (constrained)

stiffen, *v.t.* raidir, renforcer

stifle, *v.t.* étouffer

stigma, stigmate *m.*; tache *f.*

stigmatise, *v.t.* stigmatiser

still, (*adj.*) immobile; tranquille, calme, paisible

still, (*adv.*) encore, cependant, néanmoins (nevertheless)

still, *v.t.* calmer, tranquilliser

stilt, échasse *f.*

stimulant, stimulant *m.*

stimulate, *v.t.* stimuler, encourager

stimulating, (*adj.*) stimulant

sting, aiguillon *m.* (incentive, etc.); piqûre *f.*; dard *m.* (of nettle, wasp, etc.)

sting, *v.t.* piquer; *v.i.* cuire (i.e. to smart)

stingy, (*adj.*) avare, ladre

stink, puanteur *f.*

stink, *v.i.* puer

stipend, traitement *m.*

stipulate, *v.i.* and *v.t.* stipuler

stir, *v.t.* remuer; (*fig.*) agiter, exciter (stir up)

stir, mouvement *m.*; (*fig.*) bruit *m.* (i.e. make a stir)

stirrup, étrier *m.*

stitch, point *m.*; maille *f.* (knitting)

stitch, *v.t.* coudre, piquer; suturer (*surg.*)

stitched, (*adj.*) piqué

stock, souche *f.* (of tree, family); race *f.*; bétail *m.*; manche *m.* (handle); provision *f.*

stocks, fonds *m. pl.*; fonds publics *m. pl.*; actions *f. pl.*

stock, *v.t.* pourvoir (de); meubler (farm, etc.); garnir (shop)

stockbroker, agent (*m.*) de change

stock exchange, bourse *f.*

stockholder, actionnaire *m.* and *f.*

stock-in-trade, marchandises (*f. pl.*) disponibles

stock-raising, l'élevage *m.*

stock-taking, inventaire *m.*

stock-yard, parc (*m.*) à bétail

stocking, bas *m.*

stocky, (*adj.*) trapu

stoical, (*adj.*) stoïque

stoker, chauffeur *m.*

stoking, chauffage *m.*

stomach, estomac *m.*; appétit *m.*

stomach, *v.t.* tolérer

stomach-ache, mal (*m.*) à l'estomac

stone, pierre *f.*; caillou *m.*; pépin *m.* (grapes); noyau *m.* (fruit); grès *m.* (stoneware); meule *f.* (mill)

stone, (*adj.*) de pierre; en pierre; de grès

stone, *v.t.* lapider

stone cutting, taille (*f.*) de pierres

stone-mason, maçon *m.*

stone-pit, quarry, carrière *f.*

stony, (*adj.*) pierreux(-euse)

stool, tabouret *m.*; selle *f.* (*med.*)

stoop, *v.i.* se baisser; se pencher; se voûter (person)

stooping, (*adj.*) courbé, voûté

stop, halte *f.*; pause *f.*; interruption *f.*; obstacle *m.*; empêchement *m.*; arrêt *m.* (of trains, etc.); point (full stop)

stop, *v.t.* arrêter, empêcher, cesser (payment); retenir (wages, etc.); plomber (tooth); *v.i.* s'arrêter

stoppage, interruption *f.*; arrêt *m.*; suspension *f.* (of payment)

stopper, bouchon *m.*

stopping, arrêt *m.*; plombage *m.* (teeth)

storage, emmagasinage *m.*

store, magasin *m.* (big shop); provision *f.*; réserve *f.*; approvisionnement *m.*

store, *v.t.* approvisionner (de); mettre en dépôt

stores, provisions *f. pl.*; matériel (*m.*) de guerre; vivres *m. pl.*

store up, *v.t.* amasser

store-house, dépôt *m.*; entrepôt *m.*

stork, cigogne *f.*

storm, orage *m.*; tempête *f.*

storm, *v.t.* prendre d'assaut

stormy, orageux(-euse)

story, histoire *f.*; récit *m.*; conte *m.*; mensonge *m.* (lie); étage *m.* (floor)

stout, (*adj.*) fort, robuste; corpulent, gros(se)

stout, bière (*f.*) noire forte

stout-hearted, courageux(-euse)

stoutness, embonpoint *m.*; corpulence *f.*

stove, poêle *m.*; fourneau *m.* (cook.)

stow, *v.t.* mettre en place, serrer

stowage, arrimage *m.* (*naut.*)

straggler, traînard *m.* (*mil.*)

straight, (*adj.*) droit; (*fig.*) juste

straight, (*adv.*) droit, tout droit

straight away, sur-le-champ, immédiatement

straighten, *v.t.* rendre droit; redresser; mettre en ordre

straightforward, (*adj.*) direct; juste; franc(he)

straightforwardness, honnêteté *f.*; franchise *f.*

strain, grand effort *m.*; tension *f.*; entorse *f.* (*med.*)

strain, *v.t.* tendre (ear); filtrer (liquids); fouler (ankle); forcer (heart)

strain, *v.i.* s'efforcer; faire de grands efforts

strait, (*adj.*) étroit; rigide; rigoureux(-euse)

strait, détroit *m.* (*geog.*); pas (*m.*) de Calais (of Dover)

strait-waistcoat, camisole (*f.*) de force

strand, cordon *m.* (rope); plage *f.* (beach); côte *f.* (coast)

strand, *v.i.* échouer

stranded, échoué; (*fig.*) à bout de ressources

strange, (*adj.*) étrange, singulier (-ère); bizarre; inconnu (unknown); extraordinaire

strangeness, étrangeté *f.*

stranger, étranger(-ère) *m.* (*f.*): inconnu(e) *m.* (*f.*)

strangle, *v.t.* étrangler

strap, (*subst.*) courroie *f.*; *v.t.* lier avec une courroie

stratagem, stratagème *m.*

strategical, (adj.) stratégique
strategy, stratégie f.
stratum, couche f.
straw, paille f.; fétu m. (wisp)
last straw, c'est le comble!
straw-mattress, paillasse f.
not worth a straw, ne pas valoir un fétu
strawberry, fraise f.
strawberry plant, fraisier m.
stray, v.i. s'égarer, errer
stray(ed), (adj.) égaré; (of bullet) perdu
streak, raie f.; trait m. (light)
streak, v.t. rayer
streaky, (adj.) rayé; entrelardé (bacon)
stream, courant m.; fleuve m.; ruisseau m. (brook); jet m. (light); torrent m. (words); flot m. (people)
stream, v.i. couler; ruisseler; rayonner (light)
stream-lined, (adj.) aérodynamique
street, rue f.
street-lamp, réverbère m.
street-sweeper (machine), balayeuse f.
strength, force f.; résistance f. (metals); effectif m. (mil.)
strengthen, v.i. se fortifier
strengthen, v.t. fortifier; renforcer (mil.)
strenuous, (adj.) énergique
stress, force f.; violence f. (weather); accent m. (gram.)
lay stress on, v.t. appuyer sur
stretch, étendue f.; extension f.; effort m.
stretch, v.i. s'étendre
stretch, v.t. tendre; étendre
stretch a point, faire une exception en faveur
stretcher, brancard m.
stretcher-bearer, brancardier m.
strew, v.t. répandre, semer
strict, (adj.) exact, strict, sévère
strictly speaking, à vrai dire
strictness, rigueur f.
stride, grand pas m.; enjambée f.
stride, v.i. marcher à grands pas
strife, lutte f.

strike, grève f. (industrial); coup m. (blow)
strike, v.t. frapper, battre, cogner, porter un coup à; sonner (the hour); faire grève (go on strike)
striker, gréviste m.
striking, (adj.) frappant; saisissant; remarquable
string, corde f.; ficelle f.
string, v.t. garnir de cordes; enfiler (beads)
strip, bande f.; ruban m.
strip, v.t. dévaliser (rob); déshabiller (undress); dépouiller de (strip of); v.i. se dévêtir
stripe, raie f.; barre f.; (mil.) galon m.
stripe, v.t. rayer, barrer
strive, v.i. s'efforcer (de); tâcher de
stroke, coup m. (blow); coup (m.) de pinceau (of brush); trait (m.) de plume (pen); coup (m.) de sang (paralytic); brassée f. (swimming)
stroke, v.t. caresser
stroll, promenade f.; tour m.
stroll, v.i. flâner
strong, fort; solide; vigoureux (-euse)
stronghold, forteresse f.
strong-room, cave (f.) des coffres-forts
strop, cuir (m.) à rasoir
strop, v.t. repasser
structural, de construction
structure, édifice m.; bâtiment m.
struggle, lutte f.
struggle, v.i. lutter (contre); être aux prises (avec)
strumpet, prostituée f.
strut, v.i. se pavaner
strychnine, strychnine f.
stub, bout m. (pencil or cigarette); souche f. (of counterfoils)
stubble, chaume m.
stubborn, opiniâtre
stucco, stuc m.
stud, bouton (m.) de chemise; clou m.; haras m. (breeding establishment)
stud, v.t. garnir de clous
student, étudiant(e) m. (f.)

studied, étudié; calculé

studio, atelier *m.*; studio *m.*

studious, studieux(-euse); appliqué

study, étude *f.*; attention *f.*; application *f.*; cabinet (*m.*) de travail

study, *v.t.* étudier; s'occuper de; faire ses études

stuff, étoffe *f.*; tissu *m.*; drap *m.*

stuff, *v.t.* rembourrer, remplir; farcir (*cook.*); empailler (taxidermy)

stuffing, farce *f.* (*cook.*); empaillage *m.*; rembourrage *m.*

stuffy, (*adj.*) qui sent le renfermé (room)

stumble, faux pas *m.*

stumble, *v.i.* trébucher

stumbling-block, pierre (*f.*) d'achoppement

stump, tronçon *m.*

stump, *v.i.* marcher en clopinant

stun, *v.t.* étourdir; foudroyer; assommer

stupefaction, stupéfaction *f.*

stupefy, stupéfier, engourdir

stupendous, (*adj.*) prodigieux (-euse)

stupid, (*adj.*) stupide, sot(te), bête

stupidity, stupidité *f.*

stupor, stupeur *f.*

sturdy, (*adj.*) vigoureux(-euse), fort

sturgeon, esturgeon *m.*

stutter, *v.i.* and *v.t.* bégayer

sty, étable (*f.*) à cochons; orgelet *m.* (on eye)

style, style *m.*; genre *m.*; manière *f.*; raison sociale *f.* (of firm)

style, *v.t.* appeler, qualifier de

stylish, (*adj.*) élégant, chic

subaltern, (*adj.*) subalterne; subalterne *m.*

subdivide, *v.t.* subdiviser

subdue, *v.t.* subjuguer; adoucir (sound)

subject, (*adj.*) soumis, sujet(te) (à)

subject, sujet(te) *m.* (*f.*); matière *f.*

subject, *v.t.* soumettre; exposer à

subjection, soumission *f.*

subjoin, *v.t.* adjoindre

subjugate, *v.t.* subjuguer

sublet, *v.t.* sous-louer

sublime, (*adj.*) sublime, élevé

submarine, (*adj.*) sous-marin; sous-marin *m.*

submerge, *v.t.* submerger; *v.i.* plonger (of submarine)

submission, soumission *f.*

submit, *v.i.* se soumettre

submit, *v.t.* soumettre

subordinate, (*adj.*) subordonné, inférieur

subscribe, *v.t.* souscrire à; se cotiser; s'abonner à (a newspaper, etc.)

subscription, souscription *f.*; abonnement *m.*

subsequent, (*adj.*) subséquent

subside, *v.i.* s'affaisser (sink); s'apaiser (abate)

subsidise, *v.t.* subventionner

subsidy, subvention *f.*

subsist, *v.i.* subsister, exister

subsistence, subsistance *f.*

substance, substance *f.*; fond *m.* (meaning); biens *m. pl.* (goods); avoir *m.*

substantial, (*adj.*) substantiel(le); solide; matériel(le)

substitute, remplaçant(e) *m.* (*f.*); substitut *m.*

substitute, *v.t.* substituer

subterfuge, faux-fuyant *m.*; subterfuge *m.*

subterranean, (*adj.*) souterrain

subtle, (*adj.*) subtil, fin, rusé

subtlety, subtilité *f.*

subtract, *v.t.* soustraire

subtraction, soustraction *f.*

suburb, faubourg *m.*; banlieue *f.*

suburban, (*adj.*) de faubourg, de la banlieue

subversion, renversement *m.*; subversion *f.*

subversive, (*adj.*) subversif(-ive)

subway, passage souterrain *m.*

succeed, *v.i.* succéder à (throne); parvenir à, réussir (à) (be successful)

succeeding, (*adj.*) suivant; futur

success, succès *m.*; réussite *f.*; chance *f.* (luck)

successful, (*adj.*) heureux(-euse); victorieux(-euse)

succession, succession *f.*; suite *f.*; postérité *f.* (lineage)

successive, (*adj.*) successif(-ive)

successor, successeur *m.*

succour, secours *m.*

succour, *v.t.* secourir

succulence, succulence *f.*

succulent, (*adj.*) succulent

succumb, *v.i.* succomber

such, (*adj.*) tel (telle); pareil(le); semblable

such, (*pron.*) tel; telle; de tels *m. pl.*; de telles *f. pl.*; ceux *m. pl.*; celles *f. pl.*

such a man, un tel homme

such is not the case, il n'en est pas ainsi

at such a time, à un tel moment

no such thing, rien de semblable

suck, *v.t.* sucer; téter (child)

sucker, suceur(-euse) *m. (f.)*; suçoir *m.* (*entom.*)

suckle, *v.t.* allaiter

suction, succion *f.*; aspiration *f.*

suction pump, pompe (*f.*) aspirante

sudden, subit; soudain; inattendu

suddenly, soudain, tout à coup

suds, eau (*f.*) de savon

sue, *v.t.* poursuivre (*legal*); (*fig.*) demander

sue for, solliciter, implorer

suet, graisse (de rognon) *f.*

suffer, *v.t.* souffrir; supporter; endurer; subir (undergo); permettre (permit); *v.i.* souffrir

sufferable, (*adj.*) supportable; tolérable

sufferance, tolérance *f.*

sufferer, victime *f.*

suffering, souffrance *f.*

suffice, *v.t.* suffire (à); *v.i.* suffire

sufficiency, suffisance *f.*

sufficient, (*adj.*) suffisant, assez

suffocate, *v.t.* suffoquer; étouffer

suffrage, suffrage *m.*

sugar, sucre *m.*

sugar, *v.t.* sucrer

barley sugar, sucre (*m.*) d'orge

brown sugar, cassonade *f.*

castor sugar, sucre (*m.*) en poudre

sugar basin, sucrier *m.*

sugar-refinery, raffinerie (*f.*) de sucre

sugar-tongs, pincettes (*f. pl.*) à sucre

sugary, (*adj.*) sucré

suggest, *v.t.* suggérer; inspirer

suggestion, suggestion *f.*

suicide, suicide *m.*

suicide (commit), *v.i.* se suicider

suit, pétition *f.*; requête *f.* (petition); couleur *f.* (cards); complet *m.* (clothes); procès *m.* (*legal*)

suit, *v.t.* adapter; aller à; plaire à (please); convenir à (suitable to)

suit-case, valise *f.*

suitable, (*adj.*) convenable

suite, suite *f.*; (of furniture) mobilier *m.*

suitor, prétendant *m.* (in love); plaideur(-euse) *m.* (*f.*) (*legal*)

sulky, (*adj.*) boudeur(-euse)

sullen, (*adj.*) maussade; morose

sully, *v.t.* souiller

sulphate, sulfate *m.*

sulphur, soufre *m.*

sultan, sultan *m.*

sultana, sultane *f.* (sultan's wife); sultana *m.* (fruit)

sultry, (*adj.*) étouffant; d'une chaleur étouffante

sum, somme *f.* (money); calcul *m.* (*arith.*); montant *m.* (total)

sum up, *v.t.* résumer; (a person) classer

summarily, (*adv.*) sommairement

summary, sommaire *m.*; précis *m.*; résumé *m.*

summer, été *m.*

summer, (*adj.*) d'été, estival

summer-house, pavillon *m.*

summer-time, heure (*f.*) d'été (i.e. not Greenwich time)

summing-up, résumé *m.*

summit, sommet *m.*; cime *f.*; comble *m.* (height of)

summon, *v.t.* appeler; convoquer; poursuivre (*law*); citer en justice; sommer (to call on)

summons, convocation *f.*; sommation *f.* (to surrender); mandat (*m.*) de comparution

sumptuous, somptueux(-euse)

sun, soleil *m.*
sunbeam, rayon (*m.*) de soleil
sunburn, hâle *m.*
sunburnt, (*adj.*) basané, hâlé
Sunday, dimanche *m.*
sundial, cadran (*m.*) solaire
sunflower, tournesol *m.*
sunlight, lumière (*f.*) du soleil
sunset, coucher (*m.*) du soleil
sunshine, soleil *m.*
sunstroke, coup (*m.*) de soleil
sundries, frais divers *m. pl.*; articles divers *m. pl.*
sundry, (*adj.*) divers
sunny, (*adj.*) ensoleillé
sup, gorgée *f.*
sup, *v.i.* souper
superannuated, (*adj.*) suranné; retraité
superb, (*adj.*) superbe; magnifique
supercharger, compresseur *m.*
supercilious, (*adj.*) dédaigneux (-euse)
superficial, (*adj.*) superficiel(le); peu profond
superfluous, (*adj.*) superflu, inutile
superhuman, (*adj.*) surhumain
superintend, *v.t.* surveiller; diriger
superintendence, surveillance *f.*; direction *f.*
superintendent, chef *m.*; directeur(-trice) *m.* (*f.*); commissaire *m.*
superior, (*adj.*) supérieur
superiority, supériorité *f.*
superlative, (*adj.*) suprême; superlatif (*gram.*)
superman, surhomme *m.*
supernatural, (*adj.*) surnaturel (-le)
superscription, inscription *f.*; adresse *f.*
superstition, superstition *f.*
superstitious, (*adj.*) superstitieux(-euse)
supper, souper *m.*
the Lord's Supper, la Sainte Cène
supplant, *v.t.* supplanter
supplement, supplément *m.*

supplementary, (*adj.*) supplémentaire
supply, fourniture *f.*; approvisionnement *m.*; vivres *m. pl.* (*mil.*); ravitaillement *m.* (*mil.*)
supply, *v.t.* fournir, pourvoir (de); remplacer (supply in place of)
supply-teacher, remplaçant(e) d'un professeur
support, appui *m.*; soutien *m.*
support, *v.t.* soutenir; supporter (to bear); faire vivre; appuyer (to second)
supportable, (*adj.*) supportable, tolérable
suppose, *v.t.* supposer; s'imaginer; penser
supposition, supposition *f.*; hypothèse *f.*
suppress, *v.t.* supprimer; réprimer
suppression, suppression *f.*; répression *f.*
suppurate, *v.i.* suppurer
supreme, (*adj.*) suprême; souverain
supremacy, ascendant *m.*; suprématie *f.*
sure, (*adj.*) sûr; certain; infaillible
surely, (*adv.*) sûrement, assurément
sureness, certitude *f.*
surety, garant *m.* (*legal*)
surf, les brisants *m. pl.*
surface, surface *f.*; étendue *f.* (area)
surgeon, chirurgien(ne) *m.* (*f.*)
army surgeon, médecin (*m.*) militaire
surgery, chirurgie *f.* (practice); cabinet (*m.*) de consultation (place)
surgical, (*adj.*) chirurgical
surly, (*adj.*) morose, maussade, hargneux (dogs)
surmise, soupçon *m.*; conjecture *f.*
surmise, *v.t.* soupçonner; conjecturer
surmount, *v.t.* surmonter
surpass, *v.t.* surpasser; dépasser
surplice, surplis *m.*

surplus, (*adj.*) de surplus; surplus *m.*

surplus, excédent *m.*; surplus *m.*

surprise, surprise *f.*; étonnement *m.*; coup (*m.*) de main (*mil.*)

surprise, *v.t.* surprendre; étonner

surrender, reddition *f.*; capitulation *f.*

surrender, *v.i.* se rendre

surrender, *v.t.* abandonner, rendre

surreptitious, (*adj.*) clandestin

surround, *v.t.* entourer; environner

surroundings, alentours *m. pl.*; environs *m. pl.*

survey, coup (*m.*) d'œil; inspection *f.*; examen *m.*; levé *m.* (land)

survey, *v.t.* examiner; contempler; arpenter (land); lever le plan de (ordnance)

surveying, arpentage *m.*

surveyor, inspecteur *m.*; contrôleur *m.* (taxes); arpenteur *m.* (land); ingénieur (mil. or nav.)

survival, survivance *f.*

survive, *v.i.* and *v.t.* survivre (à)

susceptibility, susceptibilité *f.*

susceptible, (*adj.*) susceptible; (*fig.*) sensible (à)

suspect, *v.t.* soupçonner, se douter (de)

suspect, suspect(e) *m.* (*f.*)

suspend, *v.t.* suspendre

suspenders, bretelles *f. pl.* (U.S.A.); jarretelles *f. pl.* (stockings); fixe-chaussettes *m.* (socks)

suspense, suspens *m.*

suspension, suspension *f.* (of payments, etc.)

suspension bridge, pont (*m.*) suspendu

suspensor, suspensoir *m*

suspicion, soupçon *m.*

suspicious, (*adj.*) soupçonneux (-euse); suspect

sustain, *v.t.* soutenir, supporter; essuyer (losses)

sustaining, (*adj.*) fortifiant, nourrissant

sustenance, aliments *m. pl.*; nourriture *f.*   ,

suture, suture *f.*

swab, torchon *m.*; faubert *m.* (*naut.*)

swab, *v.t.* nettoyer; fauberter

swagger, *v.i.* faire le fanfaron; plastronner

swallow, hirondelle *f.* (bird); gosier *m.* (gullet)

swallow, *v.t.* avaler; engloutir (engulf)

swamp, marais *m.*

swamp, *v.t.* faire chavirer; inonder

swampy, marécageux(-euse)

swan, cygne *m.*

swap, *v.t.* échanger, troquer

sward, gazon *m.*

swarm, essaim *m.* (bees, etc.); nuée *f.* (crowd)

swarm, *v.i.* essaimer (of bees); grouiller (of people)

swarthiness, teint (*m.*) basané

swarthy, (*adj.*) basané

swashbuckler, fanfaron *m.*

swathe, *v.t.* emmailloter

sway, domination *f.*; pouvoir *m.*; oscillation *f.*

sway, *v.i.* ballotter (to and fro); *v.t.* influencer; balancer

swear, *v.i.* jurer; prêter serment

swearing, prestation (*f.*) de serment; juron *m.*

sweat, sueur *f.*; transpiration *f.*

sweat, *v.i.* suer, transpirer

Swedish, (*adj.*) suédois(e)

sweep, *v.t.* balayer (carpet); ramoner (chimney)

sweeper, balayeur(-euse) *m.* (*f.*); ramoneur *m.* (chimney)

sweepings, balayures *f. pl.*; ordures *f. pl.*

sweepstake, poule *f.*

sweet, (*adj.*) doux (douce); sucré; parfumé; gentil(le) (nice)

sweetbread, ris (*m.*) de veau

sweetbrier, églantier *m.*

sweeten, *v.t.* sucrer; purifier (air)

sweetening, sucrage *m.*; adoucissement *m.*

sweetheart, amoureux(-euse) *m.* (*f.*)

sweetness, douceur *f.*; fraîcheur *f.*

sweet-pea, pois (*m.*) de senteur

sweets, bonbons *m. pl.*

sweetshop, confiserie *f.*

swell, houle *f.* (sea); renflement *m.* (sound)

swell, *v.i.* enfler; gonfler; augmenter (increase); *v.t.* gonfler

swell, (*adj.*) épatant (U.S.A.); élégant

swelling, enflure *f.*; gonflement *m.*; crue *f.* (rivers)

swelter, *v.i.* étouffer de chaleur; griller

swerve, *v.i.* s'écarter; faire une embardée (car)

swift, (*adj.*) rapide; prompt; léger(-ère); vite; martinet *m.*

swiftness, rapidité *f.*; vitesse *f.*; promptitude *f.*

swill, *v.t.* laver; rincer; (*coll.*) boire avidement

swim, *v.i.* nager; tourner (of head)

swim, *v.t.* traverser à la nage

swimmer, nageur(-euse) *m.* (*f.*)

swimming, natation *f.* (art of); nage *f.* (act of)

swimming-bath, piscine *f.*

swimmingly, (*adv.*) comme sur des roulettes

swindle, *v.t.* escroquer; voler

swindle, escroquerie *f.*

swindler, escroc *m.*; chevalier (*m.*) d'industrie

swine, cochon *m.*; porc *m.*

swing, balançoire *f.* (for recreation); branle *m.*; balancement *m.*; va-et-vient *m.*

to be in full swing, battre son plein

swing, *v.i.* se balancer; osciller

swing, *v.t.* faire tourner; brandir (brandish); agiter (wave)

swinish, (*adj.*) bestial; de cochon; grossier(-ère)

swirl, *v.i.* tourbillonner

swish, *v.i.* bruire (sound); *v.t.* fouetter (whip)

Swiss, (*adj.*) suisse

switch, aiguille *f.* (railway); badine *f.* (cane); interrupteur *m.* (electric)

switch, *v.t.* aiguiller; cingler (whip)

switch off, *v.t.* couper (light, etc.)

switch on, *v.t.* ouvrir (light, etc.)

switch-man, aiguilleur *m.*

swivel, pivot *m.*

swivel-gun, canon (*m.*) à pivot

swoon, évanouissement *m.*

swoon, *v.i.* s'évanouir

swoop, *v.i.* s'abattre

sword, épée *f.*; sabre *m.*

sword-belt, baudrier *m.*; ceinturon *m.*

sword-edge, tranchant (*m.*) d'épée

sword-fish, espadon *m.*

sword-stick, canne (*f.*) à épée

sword-thrust, coup (*m.*) d'épée

sworn, (*adj.*) juré; assermenté (*legal*)

to be sworn in, être assermenté; prêter serment

sybarite, sybarite *m.* (*f.*)

sycamore (tree), sycomore *m.*

sycophant, adulateur(-trice) *m.*

syllable, syllabe *f.*

syllabus, sommaire *m.*; programme *m.* [(*f.*)

sylph, sylphe *m.*

symbol, symbole *m.*

symbolical, (*adj.*) symbolique

symmetrical, (*adj.*) symétrique

symmetry, symétrie *f.*

sympathetic, (*adj.*) sympathique

sympathise, *v.i.* sympathiser (avec)

sympathy, sympathie *f.*

symphony, symphonie *f.*

symptom, symptôme *m.*

synagogue, synagogue *f.*

syncope, syncope *f.*

syndic, syndic *m.*

syndicate, syndicat *m.*; *v.t.* syndiquer

synod, synode *m.*

synonym, synonyme *m.*

synonymous, (*adj.*) synonyme

synopsis, résumé *m.*

syntax, syntaxe *f.*

synthesis, synthèse *f.*

synthetic, (*adj.*) synthétique

syphilis, syphilis *f.*

syphilitic, (*adj.*) syphilitique
syringa, seringa *m.*
syringe, seringue *f.*
syringe, *v.t.* seringuer
syrup, sirop *m.*
system, système *m.*; régime *m.*; méthode *f.*: réseau *m.* (railway network)
systematic, (*adj.*) systématique
systole, systole *f.*

T

table, table *f.*; tableau *m.* (list); guéridon *m.* (occasional table); table gigogne (nest of -s)
tablecloth, nappe *f.*
table-cover, tapis (*m.*) de table
tablespoon, cuiller (*f.*) à bouche
table-wine, vin (*m.*) ordinaire
tablet, plaque *f.*; comprimé *m.* (*med.*); pain *m.* (soap)
taboo, tabou *m.*
taboo, *v.t.* interdire, tabouer
tabular, (*adj.*) tabulaire
tacit, (*adj.*) tacite
taciturn, (*adj.*) taciturne
tack, petit clou *m.* (nail)
tack, *v.t.* clouer; *v.i.* louvoyer (ship)
tack on, *v.t.* ajouter
tacking, virement (*m.*) de bord (*naut.*)
tackle, attirail *m.*; cordages *m. pl.*
tackle, *v.t.* saisir; aborder (a difficulty)
tact, savoir faire *m.*; tact *m.*
tactful, (*adj.*) discret(-ète)
tactics, tactique *f.*
tactician, tacticien *m.*
tadpole, têtard *m.*
taffeta, taffetas *m.*
tag, attache *f.*
tag-rag, canaille *f.*
tail, queue *f.*; derrière *m.*; pan *m.* (of shirt)
tail-end, extrémité *f.*
tail-lamp, feu (*m.*) d'arrière
tailed, à queue
tailless, sans queue
tailor, tailleur *m.*

tailor-made, (*adj.*) tailleur; tailleur *m.*
tailoring, métier (*m.*) de tailleur
taint, tache *f.* (blemish); corruption *f.*
taint, *v.t.* corrompre, gâter, infecter
take, *v.t.* prendre; mener (lead); porter (carry); s'emparer (seize); accepter; recevoir; faire (a walk); prendre d'assaut (by storm); se garer (cover)
take away, *v.t.* enlever, emporter
take in, *v.t.* duper; comprendre (include)
take off, *v.t.* ôter, enlever; imiter; *v.i.* décoller (of plane)
take place, *v.i.* avoir lieu
taker, preneur(-euse) *m.* (*f.*)
taking, prise *f.*; (*pl.*) recette *f.* (money)
taking, (*adj.*) attrayant, séduisant
tale, conte *m.*; récit *m.*; histoire *f.*
tale-bearer, rapporteur(-euse) *m.* (*f.*)
talent, talent *m.*
talk, *v.i.* parler, causer, bavarder
talk, entretien *m.*; conversation *f.*; causerie *f.* (chat); bavardage *m.*
talkative, (*adj.*) bavard, loquace
talking, conversation *f.*; causerie *f.*; (picture) film (*m.*) parlant
tall, (*adj.*) grand (of persons); haut (of things)
tallness, hauteur *f*
tallow, suif *m.*
tally, *v.i.* s'accorder (avec)
tally, *v.t.* marquer sur la taille (in discharging cargo)
talon, serre *f.*
tamable, apprivoisable
tame, (*adj.*) apprivoisé
tame, *v.t.* dompter (wild beasts, etc.); apprivoiser (birds, etc.)
tameness, insipidité *f.*; soumission *f.*
tamer, dompteur(-euse) *m.* (*f.*) (of lions, etc.)
tamper, *v.i.* falsifier; suborner (a witness); fausser (a lock, etc.)
tan, tan *m.*; hâle *m.* (sunburn)
tan, *v.t.* tanner; basaner (sunburn); *v.i.* se basaner

tandem, tandem *m.*.

tangent, tangente *f.*

tangible, (*adj.*) tangible

tangle, embrouillement *m.*; embarras *m.*

tangle, *v.t.* embrouiller, emmêler

tank, citerne *f.*; réservoir *m.*; tank *m.*; char (*m.*) d'assaut (*mil.*)

tanker, bateau-citerne *m.*

tanner, tanneur *m.*

tannery, tannerie *f.*

tantalise, *v.t.* tantaliser

tantamount, (*adj.*) équivalent

tantrum, mauvaise humeur *f.*

tap, petit coup *m.* (knock at door); robinet *m.* (gas, water); tape *f.* (a rap, blow)

tap, *v.t.* taper; frapper doucement; inciser (a tree)

tape, ruban (*m.*) de fil; (insulating) ruban (*m.*) isolant

taper, bougie *f.*; cierge *m.*

taper, *v.i.* s'effiler

tapering, (*adj.*) effilé (nails, etc.)

tapestry, tapisserie *f.*

tapeworm, ver (*m.*) solitaire

tar, goudron *m.*

tar, *v.t.* goudronner

tardily, (*adv.*) tardivement

tardiness, lenteur *f.*

tardy, (*adj.*) tardif(-ive); en retard

tare, tare *f.*

target, cible *f.*; but *m.*

tariff, tarif *m.*; tableau *m.*

tarnish, *v.i.* se ternir; *v.t.* ternir

tarpaulin, toile (*f.*) goudronnée

tarragon, estragon *m.*

tart, tarte *f.*; tourte *f.*

tart, (*adj.*) piquant

task, tâche *f.*; besogne *f.*; travail *m.*; devoir *m.* (lesson)

tassel, gland *m.* (de soie, etc.)

taste, goût *m.*; prédilection *f.*; (sugar) **to taste,** (du sucre) à volonté

taste, *v.t.* goûter, savourer; *v.i.* avoir un goût (de)

tasteful, (*adj.*) de bon goût

tasteless, (*adj.*) insipide, fade

tasting, dégustation *f.*

tasty, (*adj.*) savoureux(-euse)

tatters, lambeaux *m. pl.*; haillons *m. pl.*

tattle, *v.i.* jaser, bavarder

tattle, bavardage *m.*; babil *m.*

tattoo, *v.t.* tatouer; (*subst.*) tatouage *m.*; retraite *f.* (*mil.*)

taunt, reproche amer *m.*

taunt, *v.t.* dire des injures à; insulter

taut, tendu

tavern, cabaret *m.*; taverne *f.*

tawdry, (*adj.*) de mauvais goût, clinquant

tax, *v.t.* taxer; frapper d'un impôt

tax, impôt *m.*; taxe *f.*; contributions *f. pl.*

taxation, impôts *m. pl.*

tax-collector, percepteur (*m.*) des contributions

tax-payer, contribuable *m.* and *f.*

taxable, (*adj.*) imposable

taxi-cab, taxi *m.*

tea, thé *m.*

tea-caddy, boîte (*f.*) à thé

tea-cup, tasse (*f.*) à thé

tea-kettle, bouilloire *f.*

tea-party, un thé *m.*

teaspoon, cuiller (*f.*) à thé

tea-pot, théière *f.*

tea-things, service (*m.*) à thé

teach, *v.t.* enseigner; instruire

teacher, maître *m.*; maîtresse *f.*; instituteur *m.*; institutrice *f.*; professeur *m.*

teaching, enseignement *m.*

teak, te(c)k *m.*

team, attelage *m.* (of horses); équipe *f.* (games)

tear, larme *f.*; **to burst into tears,** fondre en larmes

tearful, (*adj.*) tout en larmes

tearfully, (*adv.*) les larmes aux yeux

tear (rent), déchirure *f.*

tear, *v.t.* déchirer; **tear down, away,** etc., arracher; *v.i.* **to tear along,** aller à toute vitesse

tease, *v.t.* tourmenter, taquiner; (wool) carder

tease, taquin(e) *m.* (*f.*)

teat, téton *m.*; tétin *m.* (of woman)

technical, (*adj.*) technique

technician, technicien *m.*

technology, technologie *f.*

tedious, (*adj.*) ennuyeux(-euse), fatigant

teem (with), *v.i.* fourmiller (de), regorger (de)

teenager, adolescent(e) *m.* (*f.*)

teethe, *v.i.* faire ses dents

teething, dentition *f.*

teetotaler, buveur(-euse) *m.* (*f.*) d'eau

telegram, télégramme *m.*; dépêche *f.*

telegraph, *v.i.* and *v.t.* télégraphier; télégraphe *m.*

telegraph-operator, télégraphiste *m.* (*f.*)

telegraph-post, poteau (*m.*) télégraphique

telegraph-wire, fil (*m.*) télégraphique

telephone, téléphone *m.*

telephone, *v.i.* and *v.t.* téléphoner

telephone-box, cabine (*f.*) téléphonique

telephone-call, coup (*m.*) de téléphone

telephonic, (*adj.*) téléphonique

telescope, téléscope *m.*; longue vue *f.*

television, télévision *f.*

tell, *v.t.* dire; exprimer; raconter; avouer (confess); reconnaître (recognise)

teller, receveur *m.*; comptable *m.* (in banks, etc.); raconteur (-euse) *m.* (*f.*)

telling, (*adj.*) frappant; efficace

temerity, témérité *f.*

temper, tempérament *m.*; disposition *f.*; humeur *f.* (humour); colère *f.* (anger); trempe *f.* (of steel)

temper, *v.t.* modérer; tremper (steel)

temperament, tempérament *m.*

temperance, tempérance *f.*; sobriété *f.*

temperate, (*adj.*) modéré; tempéré (climate, heat, etc.)

temperature, température *f.*

tempest, tempête *f.* (sea); orage *m.* (land)

tempestuous, (*adj.*) orageux (-euse); tempétueux(-euse)

temple, temple *m.*

temporal, temporel(le)

temporary, (*adj.*) temporaire

tempt, *v.t.* tenter

temptation, tentation *f.*

tempting, (*adj.*) tentant, séduisant

ten, (*adj.*) dix

about ten, une dizaine *f.*

tenacious, (*adj.*) tenace

tenancy, location *f.*

tenant, locataire *m.* and *f.* (of house); fermier *m.*

tend, *v.t.* soigner; *v.i.* tendre

tendency, tendance *f.*; disposition *f.*

tender, (*adj.*) tendre

tender, offre *f.*; soumission *f.* (for contracts); tender *m.* (railway)

tenderness, tendresse *f.*

tenement (house), local *m.*; logement *m.*

tennis, tennis *m.*

tense, temps *m.*

tense, (*adj.*) tendu, raide

tension, tension *f.*

tent, tente *f.*

to pitch (a tent), dresser (une tente)

tepid, (*adj.*) tiède

term, terme *m.* (expression); trimestre *m.* (school); session *f.* (*legal*); condition *f.* (of contract)

term, *v.t.* nommer

terms, conditions *f. pl.*; prix *m. pl.*

come to terms, *v.i.* s'arranger, s'accorder avec

terminate, *v.t.* terminer, achever

termination, terminaison *f.*; conclusion *f.*

terminus, tête (*f.*) de ligne; terminus *m.*

terrace, terrasse *f.*

terrible, (*adj.*) terrible, formidable

terrific, (*adj.*) épouvantable

terrify, *v.t.* effrayer

territorial, (*adj.*) territorial

territory, territoire *m.*

terror, terreur *f.*; effroi *m.*; épouvante *f.*

terse, (*adj.*) net(te), concis

test, épreuve *f.*; essai *m.*; examen *m.*

test, *v.t.* éprouver. essayer

testament, testament *m.*

testamentary, (*adj.*) testamen-taire

testator(-trix), testateur(-trice) *m.* (*f.*)

testify, *v.i.* témoigner (de); *v.t.* témoigner, déposer

testimonial, témoignage *m.*; certificat *m.*

testimony, témoignage *f.*; dé-position *f.*

testy, (*adj.*) maussade, irritable

teuton(ic), (*adj.*) teuton(ne), teutonique

text, texte *m.*; écriture *f.*

text-book, manuel *m.*

textile, (*adj.*) textile; textile *m.*

than, (*conj.*) que; de (before numerals)

thank, *v.t.* remercier

thanks, remerciements *m. pl.*

to give thanks to, rendre grâces à

thankful; (*adj.*) reconnaissant (de)

thankfulness, gratitude *f.*

thankless, (*adj.*) ingrat

thanksgiving, action (*f.*) de grâces

that, (*adj. demonst.*) ce, cet (cette), ces

that, (*pron. demonst.*) celui-là (celle-là)

that, (*pron. relat.*) qui, lequel (laquelle)

that, (*conj.*) que, afin que, pour que

thatch, chaume *m.*

thatch, *v.t.* couvrir de chaume

thaw, dégel *m.*

thaw, *v.i.* dégeler; *v.t.* dégeler

theatre, théâtre *m.*; salle (*f.*) d'opération (*surg.*)

theatrical, (*adj.*) théâtral

theft, vol. *m.*; larcin *m.*

their, (*adj. possess.*) leur, (*pl.*) leurs; (*pron.*) le (la, les), leur(s)

them, (*pron.*) eux *m. pl.*, elles *f. pl.*; les (object.); leur (dat.)

theme, thème *m.*; sujet *m.*

themselves, (*pron.*) eux-mêmes *m. pl.*; elles-mêmes *f. pl.*; reflex. (se)

then, (*adv.*) alors; ensuite (after-wards); puis; donc (therefore); en ce cas (in that case)

then, (*conj.*) donc

thence, (*adv.*) de là

theologian, théologien *m.*

theology, théologie *f.*

theorem, théorème *m.*

theoretic(al), (*adj.*) théorique

theory, théorie *f.*

there, (*adv.*) là, y; (*interj.*) voilà!

thereabouts, par là;. à peu près (approximately)

thereby, par ce moyen

therefore, (*adv.*) par conséquent; donc

thereupon, sur cela, là-dessus

thermal, (*adj.*) thermal

thermometer, thermomètre *m.*

thermos flask, bouteille (*f.*) isolante

thick, (*adj.*) épais(sc); gros(se); fort

thicken, *v.t.* épaissir

thicket, taillis *m.*

thickheaded, (*adj.*) stupide

thickness, épaisseur *f.*

thickset, (*adj.*) trapu

thief, voleur(-euse) *m.* (*f.*)

thieve, *v.t.* voler

thieving, vol *m.*

thigh, cuisse *f.*

thigh-bone, fémur *m.*

thimble, dé *m.*

thin, (*adj.*) mince, maigre, rare

thin, *v.i.* amincir, réduire, diminuer

thing, chose *f.*; objet *m.*; affaires *f. pl.* (one's " things ")

think, *v.t.* and *v.i.* penser, croire, songer, réfléchir

thinker, penseur(-euse) *m.* (*f.*)

thinking, pensée *f.*

to my way of thinking, à mon avis

third, (*adj.*) troisième

third (part), tiers *m.*

thirst, soif *f.*

thirst, *y.i.* avoir soif

thirstily, (*adv.*) avidement

thirsty, (*adj.*) qui a soif, altéré

thirteen, (*adj.*) treize

thirteenth, (*adj.*) treizième

thirtieth, (*adj.*) trentième

thirty, (*adj.*) trente

this, (*adj.*) ce, cet, cette

this, (*pron.*) celui-ci, celle-ci, ceci

thistle, chardon *m.*

thither, (*adv.*) là, y

thong, courroie *f.*

thorn, épine *f.*

thorny, (*adj.*) épineux(-euse)

thorough, (*adj.*) profond; parfait

thoroughbred, (*adj. and subst.*) pur sang *m.* (of horses)

thoroughfare, rue *f.*; voie (*f.*) publique; (main thoroughfare) artère *f.*

" no thoroughfare," " passage interdit "

those, (*adj.*) ces

those, (*pron.*) ceux *m. pl.*; celles *f. pl.*; ceux-là *m. pl.*; celles-là *f. pl.*

though, (*conj.*) bien que, quoique (both used with subj.); quand même (even if); cependant (nevertheless)

thought, pensée *f.*

thoughtful, (*adj.*) pensif (pensive); plein d'égards (considerate)

thoughtfulness, méditation *f.*; égards *m. pl.*

thoughtless, (*adj.*) insouciant, étourdi

thoughtlessness, insouciance *f.*, étourderie *f.*

thrash, *v.t.* battre; rosser (to drub)

thrashing, battage *m.* (= threshing); correction *f.*

thrashing-machine, batteuse *f.*

thread, fil *m.*

thread, *v.t.* enfiler

threadbare, (*adj.*) usé (argument); râpé (clothes)

threat, menace *f.*

threaten, *v.t.* menacer

three, (*adj.*) trois

three-cornered, (*adj.*) triangulaire; (of hat) tricorne

threefold, (*adj.*) triple

thresh, *v.t.* battre

threshing-machine, batteuse *f.*

threshold, seuil *m.*

thrice, (*adv.*) trois fois

thrift, économie *f.*; frugalité *f.*

thriftiness, économie *f.*; épargne *f.*

thrifty, (*adj.*) économe, ménager (-ère)

thrill, *v.t.* faire tressaillir (de)

thrill, tressaillement *m.*

thrilling, (*adj.*) saisissant, sensationnel(le)

thrive, *v.i.* prospérer; réussir

thriving, (*adj.*) florissant; qui prospère

throat, gorge *f.*; gosier *m.* (gullet)

throb, *v.t.* palpiter

throbbing, battement *m.*; palpitation *f.*

throne, trône *m.*

throng, foule *f.*; multitude *f.*

throng, *v.i.* se presser; *v.t.* encombrer

throttle, *v.t.* étrangler

throttle (of engine), papillon *m.*

through, (*prep.*) à travers; par

through, (*adv.*) d'un bout à l'autre; à travers

through, (*adj.*) direct (of tickets, trains)

throughout, (*prep.*) partout dans

throw, *v.t.* jeter; lancer, renverser (upset)

throw away, rejeter; laisser passer (opportunity)

throw, jet *m.*; coup (*m.*) de dé (dice)

thrush, grive *f.* (bird)

thrust, *v.t.* pousser, enfoncer, fourrer

thrust, coup *m.*; poussée *f.*

thumb, pouce *m.*

thump, *v.t. and v.i.* cogner; battre (of heart)

thump, coup (*m.*) de poing

thunder, tonnerre *m.*

thunder, *v.i.* tonner

thunderbolt, foudre *f.*

thunderclap, coup (*m.*) de tonnerre

thunderstorm, orage *m.*
thunderstruck, foudroyé
Thursday, jeudi *m.*
thus, (*adv.*) ainsi
thwart, *v.i.* contrarier
tiara, tiare *f.*
ticket, billet *m.*; étiquette *f.* (label)
return ticket, billet (*m.*) d'aller et retour
single ticket, billet (*m.*) simple
ticket-collector, contrôleur *m.*
ticket-office, bureau des billets *m.*; guichet *m.*
tickle, *v.t.* chatouiller
tickling, chatouillement *m.*
ticklish, (*adj.*) chatouilleux (-euse); difficile
tidal, (*adj.*) de marée
tide, marée *f.*; courant *m.*
tidings, nouvelles *f. pl.*
tidy, (*adj.*) propre, rangé
tidy, *v.t.* mettre en ordre
tie, *v.t.* lier; attacher; nouer
tie, lien *m.* (bond); cravate *f.* (round neck)
to tie (draw) at sport, faire match nul, être à égalité avec
tier, rang *m.*
in tiers, étagé
tiger, tigre *m.*
tigress, tigresse *f.*
tight, serré; tendu; étroit; gris (drunk)
tighten, *v.t.* serrer; tendre
tile, tuile *f.*
till, (*prep.*) jusqu'à; (*conj.*) jusqu'à ce que (+ subj.)
till, caisse *f.* (of shop)
till, *v.t.* labourer
tilling, labourage *m.*
tilt, *v.t.* incliner; *v.i.* s'incliner
full tilt, tête baissée
timber, bois (*m.*) de charpente
timber-merchant, marchand (*m.*) de bois de construction
timber-yard, chantier *m.*
time, temps *m.*; époque *f.*; saison *f.* (time of year); heure *f.* (of day or night); moment *m.*; fois *f.* (occasion); mesure *f.* (*mus.*)
at such a time, à un tel moment

at that time, alors, à cette époque
at the same time, en même temps
behind time, en retard
every time, chaque fois
high time, il était grand temps
in time, à temps, avec le temps
once upon a time, une fois
time-piece, pendule *f.*
time-sheet, feuille (*f.*) de présence
time-table, indicateur *m.* (railway); horaire *m.*
timely, (*adj.*) opportun
timid, (*adj.*) timide, craintif(-ive), peureux(-euse)
timidity, timidité *f.*
tin, étain *m.*; fer-blanc *m.*; boîte *f.* (preserved goods, etc.); bidon *m.* (for petrol)
tin, *v.t.* étamer
tin, (*adj.*) d'étain, en fer-blanc
tinfoil, feuille (*f.*) d'étain
tin-opener, ouvre-boîtes *m*
tinplate, fer-blanc *m.*
tinsmith, ferblantier *m.*
tin-ware, ferblanterie *f.*
tincture, teinture *f.*
tinder, amadou *m.*
tinge, teinte *f.*; nuance *f.*
tingle, *v.i.* vibrer, tinter
tinker, rétameur *m.*
tint, teinte *f.*
tint, *v.t.* nuancer, teinter
tiny, (*adj.*) tout petit, minuscule
tip, bout *m*; pointe *f.*; pourboire *m.* (to waiter, etc.); tuyau *m* (sporting)
tip, *v.t.* donner un pourboire à; graisser la patte à; tuyauter (sporting)
tip over, *v.t.* renverser; *v.i.* se renverser
tip-toe, pointe (*f.*) du pied
tip-top, de premier rang
tire, *v.t.* fatiguer, lasser; *v.i.* se fatiguer
tired, fatigué, las(se)
tissue, tissu *m.*
tissue paper, papier (*m.*) de soie
tit (bird), mésange *f.*
tit-bit, morceau (*m.*) friand
title, titre *m.*; (*fig.*) document *m.*

title-deed, titre (m.) de propriété
titled, (adj.) titré.
titter, petit rire m.
to, (prep.) à; de; pour
toad, crapaud m.
toast, pain (m.) grillé; toast m. (health); santé f. (health)
toast, v.t. griller; porter un toast à (drink the health of)
tobacco, tabac m.
tobacco pouch, blague f.
tobacconist, marchand de tabac m.; (shop) débit (m.) de tabac
to-day, aujourd'hui m. (also m. and adv.)
toe, doigt (m.) de pied; orteil m.
together, (adv.) ensemble; à la fois; en même temps que
toil, peine f.; labeur m.
toil, v.i. travailler fort; peiner
toilet, toilette f.
toilet-case, nécessaire (m.) de toilette m.
toilet-paper, papier (m.) hygiénique
token, marque f.; gage m.
tolerable, (adj.) tolérable, passable
tolerate, v.t. tolérer
toleration, tolérance f.
toll, péage m. (tax); tintement m. (bell)
toll, v.t. and v.i. sonner (the bell)
tomato, tomate f.
tomb, tombe f.; tombeau m.
tombstone, pierre (f.) tombale
to-morrow, demain (m. and adv.)
day after to-morrow, après-demain
ton, tonneau m.; tonne f. (weight)
tone; ton m.; accent m.; timbre (of voice)
tone down, v.t. adoucir; v.i. s'adoucir
toneless, (adj.) peu harmonieux (-euse); atone
tongs, pincettes f. pl.
tongue, langue f.; languette f. (of shoe)
hold one's tongue, v.i. se taire
tonic, (adj.) tonique; tonique m.

to-night, (adv.) ce soir; cette nuit
tonnage, tonnage m.
too, (adv.) trop, aussi (also); de même (likewise)
tool, outil m.; ustensile m.
toot (of motor-horn), coup (m.) de klaxon; v.i. corner
tooth, dent f.
toothache, mal (m.) de dents
toothbrush, brosse (f.) à dents
toothpick, cure-dents m.
toothpaste or **powder**, dentifrice m.
top, haut m.; sommet m.; toupie f. (toy); cime f. (of mountain, tree)
top, v.t. surpasser; dépasser; couronner
top hat, chapeau (m.) haut de forme
top-heavy, (adj.) trop lourd du haut
topic, sujet m.
topical, (adj.) topique; d'actualité
topmost, (adj.) le plus haut; le plus élevé
topple, v.i. s'écrouler; v.t. faire tomber
topsy-turvy, sens (m.) dessus dessous
torch, torche f.; flambeau m.; torche électrique
torchlight procession, retraite (f.) aux flambeaux
torment, v.t. tourmenter; faire souffrir
torment, tourment m.; supplice m.
torpedo, torpille f.
torpedo-boat, torpilleur m.
torpedo-boat destroyer, contre-torpilleur m.
torpid, (adj.) torpide, engourdi
torpor, torpeur f.; engourdissement m.
torrent, torrent m.
torrential, (adj.) torrentiel(le)
tortoise, tortue f.
tortuous, (adj.) tortueux(-euse); sinueux(-euse)
torture, v.t. torturer, mettre à la torture; (fig.) tourmenter
torture, torture f.; tourment m.

torturer, bourreau *m.*

toss, *v.t.* jeter; lancer; secouer (the head)

total, total *m.*; montant *m.*; (*adj.*) total, global

total, *v.i.* se monter (à)

totter, *v.i.* chanceler

touch, toucher *m.* (sense); coup *m.*; contact *m.* (in touch with, etc.)

touch, *v.t.* toucher; atteindre (to reach); regarder (concern); faire jouer (to touch off a mine, etc.)

toucher, *v.i.* se toucher

touchiness, irascibilité *f.*

touchy, (*adj.*) irritable, susceptible

tough, (*adj.*) dur, tenace

toughen, *v.t.* durcir; *v.i.* s'endurcir (of person)

tour, tour *m.*; voyage *m.*

touring, le tourisme *m.*

tourist, touriste *m.* and *f.*

tournament, tournoi *m.*

tout, racoleur *m.*

tow, *v.t.* remorquer (a boat, etc.)

tow, étoupe *f.* (hemp)

tow (rope *or* process), remorque. *f.*

tow-boat, remorqueur *m.*

towards, (*prep.*) vers (of place); du côté de; à l'égard de; envers (of feelings)

towel, essuie-main(s) *m.*; serviette *f.*

bath-towel, drap (*m.*) de bains

tower, tour *f.*

tower, *v.i.* s'élever, dominer

town, ville *f.*

town clerk, greffier (*m.*) municipal

town council, conseil (*m.*) municipal

town hall, hôtel (*m.*) de ville (big town); mairie *f.*

townsman, bourgeois *m.*

townspeople, habitants (*m. pl.*) de la ville; citadins

toy, jouet *m.*; joujou *m.* (*pl.* -x)

toy, *v.i.* jouer; s'amuser avec

trace, trace *f.*; tracé *m.* (a tracing of plan, etc.); trait *m.* (of harness)

trace, *v.t.* tracer, traquer (get on the track of)

tracer-bullet, balle (*f.*) traceuse

track, piste *f.*; sentier *m.* (path); voie *f.* (railway)

tract, contrée *f.*; région *f.*; brochure *f.* (booklet)

trade, commerce *m.*; trafic *m.*; métier *m.* (calling, etc.); industrie *f.* (manufacture)

trade (in), *v.i.* trafiquer (en); faire le commerce (de)

trade-mark, marque (*f.*) de fabrique

tradesman, marchand *m.*; fournisseur *m.*

trade-union, association (*f.*) ouvrière; (in France) confédération générale du travail (C.G.T.)

trade-winds, vents (*m. pl.*) alizés

trader, négociant(e) *m.* (*f.*)

tradition, tradition *f.*

traditional, (*adj.*) traditionnel(le)

traffic, trafic *m.*; circulation *f.* (in streets, etc.)

traffic-lights, feux (*m. pl.*) de circulation

tragedy, tragédie *f.*

tragic(al), (*adj.*) tragique

trail, traînée *f.* (of smoke, etc.); trace *f.*; piste *f.*

trail, *v.i.* traîner; *v.t.* traquer; *v.i.* se traîner (trail along)

trailer, remorque *f.*; baladeuse *f.* (attached to car)

train, train *m.* (railway); suite *f.* (cortège); queue *f.* (of dress); série *f.* (of events)

train, *v.t.* instruire, dresser (animals); pointer (a gun); *v.i.* s'exercer; s'entraîner (of athlete)

trainer, dresseur *m.* (animals); entraîneur *m.* (sporting)

training-aeroplane, avion-école *m.*

traitor, traître *m.*

traitorous, (*adj.*) traître(-sse)

tram (way), tramway *m.*

tramp, *v.i.* aller à pied; rôder

tramp, bruit (*m.*) de pas; chemineau *m.* (person)

trample, *v.t.* fouler aux pieds; *v.i.* piétiner

trance, extase *f.*

tranquil, (*adj.*) tranquille

transact business, *v.t.* faire des affaires

transaction, affaire *f.*; opération *f.* (business)

transatlantic, *(adj.)* transatlantique

transcribe, *v.t.* copier

transfer, *v.t.* transférer *(law)*; transporter (from one place to another)

transfer, transfert *m.* (shares); déplacement *m.* (of an official)

transferable, *(adj.)* transférable, transportable

transform, *v.t.* transformer, convertir

transformer, transformateur *m.* (electric)

transgress, *v.t.* transgresser; contrevenir à

transgression, violation *f.*

transit, transit *m.*; passage *m.*

transition, transition *f.*

transitory, *(adj.)* passager(-ère)

translatable, *(adj.)* traduisible

translate, *v.t.* traduire

translation, traduction *f.*

translator, traducteur *m.*

transmit, *v.t.* transmettre

transmitter, transmetteur *m.*

transmitting station, poste *(m.)* émetteur

transparency, transparence *f.*

transparent, *(adj.)* transparent, clair

transpire, *v.i.* transpirer

transplant, *v.t.* transplanter

transport, transport *m.* (ship or joy)

transport, *v.t.* transporter

trap, *v.t.* prendre au piège

trap, piège *m.* (snare); trappe *f.* (pitfall or trap-door); cabriolet *m.* (vehicle)

trapeze, trapèze *m.*

trapper, trappeur *m.*

trash, rebut *m.*; camelote *f.*

travel, *v.i.* voyager; être en voyage; *v.t.* parcourir (un pays)

traveller, voyageur(-euse) *m.* *(f.)*; *(commer.)* commis voyageur *m.*

travelling, voyage *m.*; voyages *m. pl.*

travelling expenses, frais *(m. pl.)* de voyage

traverse, traverse *f.*; (in trenches) pare-éclats *m.*

traverse, *v.t.* traverser

travesty, parodie *f.*

trawler, chalutier *m.*

tray, plateau *m.*

ash-tray, cendrier *m.*

treacherous, *(adj.)* traître, perfide

treachery, trahison *f.*

treacle, mélasse *f.*

tread, *v.i.* mettre le pied, marcher sur; *v.t.* écraser du pied (tread underfoot)

tread, pas *m.*; giron *m.* (of stair)

treason, trahison *f.*

treasonable, *(adj.)* séditieux (-euse)

treasure, trésor *m.*

treasure, *v.t.* garder précieusement; priser

treasurer, trésorier(-ère) *m.* *(f.)*

treasury, trésor public *m.*; finances *f. pl.*

the treasury, le ministère des finances

treat, *v.t.* traiter (deal with); traiter (patient, subject)

treat, régal *m.*; festin *m.*

treatise, treaty, traité *m.*

treatment, traitement *m.*

treble, *v.t.* tripler

treble, *(adj.)* triple

treble, soprano *m.* *(mus.)*

tree, arbre *m.*

trellis, treillis *m.*

tremble, *v.i.* trembler

trembling, tremblement *m.*

tremendous, terrible, épouvantable, énorme

tremor, tremblement *m.*

tremulous, *(adj.)* tremblant; *(fig.)* timide

trench, tranchée *f.*

trench, *v.t.* creuser (une tranchée)

communication-trench, boyau *m.*

fire-trench, tranchée *(f.)* de tir

trench-mortar, crapouillot *m.*; lance-bombes *m.*

trenchant, (*adj.*) tranchant
trespass, *v.i.* violer une propriété; empiéter (sur); (*fig.*)
transgresser
trespass, violation (*f.*) de propriété; offense *f.* (*Biblical*)
tress, tresse *f.* (de cheveux)
trestle, tréteau *m.*; chevalet *m.*
trial, procès *m.* (*legal*); épreuve *f.*
(test)
trial shot, coup (*m.*) d'essai
triangle, triangle *m.*
triangular, (*adj.*) triangulaire
tribe, tribu *f.*
tribunal, tribunal *m.*
tributary, (*adj.*) tributaire
tributary, affluent *m.* (river)
tribute, tribut *m.*
trice (in a), en un clin d'œil
trick, tour *m.*; ruse *f.*; levée *f.* (at
bridge, etc.)
the whole bag of tricks, tout le
tremblement
trick, *v.t.* duper; tricher (cheat)
trickle, *v.i.* dégoutter, couler;
filet *m.*
trickster, fourbe *m.*
tricky, (*adj.*) rusé; (*fig.*) incertain
tricolour, (*adj.*) tricolore
tricolour, drapeau tricolore *m.*
trifle, bagatelle *f.*; *v.i.* jouer (avec);
(cookery) diplomate *m.*
trifling, (*adj.*) insignifiant
trigger, détente *f.*
trim, arranger; mettre en ordre;
tailler (hedge)
trimmed with, orné de, garni de
trim, propre; soigné
trimming, garniture *f.*
trinket, breloque *f.*
trip, excursion *f.*; tour *m.*; faux
pas *m.*
trip, *v.i.* trébucher, faire un faux
pas
tripe, tripes *f. pl.*
triple, (*adj.*) triple
tripod, trépied *m.*
trite, (*adj.*) usé, banal.
triumph, triomphe *m*
triumph (over), *v.i.* triompher
(de)
trivial, (*adj.*) insignifiant

trolley, trolley *m.*; (porter's)
diable *m.*
troop, troupe *f.*
troops, les troupes *f. pl.*
storm, shock troops, troupes
d'assaut
troop, *v.i.* s'attrouper
trooper, cavalier *m.*
troopship, transport *m.*
trophy, trophée *m.*
tropic, tropique *m.*
tropical, (*adj.*) tropical
trot, trot *m.*
trot, *v.i.* trotter; *v.t.* faire trotter
trouble, trouble *m.*; peine *f.* (work);
affliction *f.*; ennui *m.* (annoyance)
trouble, *v.t.* affliger, troubler,
déranger (disturb); importuner
(annoy, pester); *v.i.* s'inquiéter
de (trouble about, worry over)
troublesome, (*adj.*) ennuyeux
(-euse)
trough, auge *f.*; pétrin *m.*
(kneading trough); abreuvoir *m.*
(drinking); creux *m.* (of wave)
trousers, pantalon *m.*
trout, truite *f.*
trowel, truelle *f.*
truant (to play), faire l'école
buissonnière
truce, trêve *f.*
truck, camion *m.*; wagon *m.*
(railway); charrette *f.*
to have no truck with, n'avoir
rien à faire avec
truculence, truculence *f.*
trudge, *v.i.* marcher péniblement
true, (*adj.*) réel(le); véritable;
vrai; fidèle; loyal
truffle, truffe *f.*
trump, atout *m.* (cards); (*slang*)
bon type *m.*
trumpery, (*adj.*) de camelote
trumpet, trompette *f.*
trumpeter, trompette *m.*
trumpet, *v.t.* proclamer; *v.i.*
sonner de la trompette; barrir
(elephant)
truncheon, bâton *m.*
trundle, *v.i.* rouler; *v.t.* faire rouler
trunk, tronc *m.* (tree, etc.);
malle *f.* (luggage); trompe *f.*
(elephant)

trunk-call, appel (*m.*) à longue distance; appel (*m.*) interurbain

truss, bandage (*m.*) herniaire (*surg.*); botte *f.* (straw)

trustee, dépositaire *m.*; administrateur *m.*

trust, confiance *f.*; garde *f.* (care); crédit *m.* (of goods on trust); cartel *m.* (industrial)

trust, *v.t.* and *v.i.* se fier à; *v.t.* espérer (hope, trust)

trustworthy, (*adj.*) digne de confiance

trusty, sûr, fidèle

truth, vérité *f.*; le vrai *m.*

in truth, en vérité

truthful, (*adj.*) véridique, vrai

try, *v.i.* essayer (de); tâcher (de) (attempt); *v.t.* essayer

try, *v.t.* éprouver; faire l'épreuve de (test); juger (an accused, a case)

try, essai *m.*

trying, (*adj.*) difficile, pénible

trying-on, essayage *m.* (clothes, etc.)

tub, baquet *m.*

tube, tube *m.*; conduit *m.*; métro *m.* (underground railway)

inner tube, chambre (*f.*) à air (of tyre)

tubercle, tubercule *m.*

tubercular, (*adj.*) tuberculeux (-euse)

tuberculosis, tuberculose *f.*

tubular, (*adj.*) tubulaire

tuck, pli *m.*; plissé *m.*

tuck, *v.t.* faire des plis à; serrer

Tuesday, mardi *m.*

tuft, touffe *f.*; huppe *f.* (in bird)

tufted, (*adj.*) touffu

tug, *v.t.* and *v.i.* tirer; *v.t.* remorquer (to tow)

tug, remorqueur *m.*; traction *f.*

tuition, instruction *f.*

private tuition, leçons (*f. pl.*) particulières

tulip, tulipe *f.*

tumble, *v.i.* tomber; faire des culbutes (of acrobats); *v.t.* renverser

tumbledown, (*adj.*) délabré

tumbler, verre *m.* (glass)

tumbril, tombereau *m.*

tumour, tumeur *f.*

tumult, tumulte *m.*

tumultuous, (*adj.*) tumultueux (-euse)

tun, tonneau *m.*

tune, air *m.*; ton *m.*; harmonie *f.*

tune, *v.t.* accorder; mettre en accord

tuneful, (*adj.*) harmonieux(-euse)

tuneless, (*adj.*) discordant

tuning, accord *m.*

tuning up, mise (*f.*) au point (engines)

tuner, accordeur *m.*

tunic, tunique *f.*

tuning-fork, diapason *m.*

tunnel, tunnel *m.*; souterrain *m.*

tunnel, *v.t.* percer

tunny fish, thon *m.*

turban, turban *m.*

turbid, (*adj.*) trouble

turbine, turbine *f.*

turbulence, turbulence *f.*

turbulent, (*adj.*) turbulent

tureen, soupière *f.*

turf, gazon *m.*; tourbe *f.* (peat); turf *m.* (racing)

turfing, gazonnement *m.*

turgid, (*adj.*) gonflé, ampoulé

turkey, dindon *m.*; dinde *f.*

Turkish, (*adj.*) turc (turque)

turmoil, trouble *m.*; vacarme *m.*

turn, tour *m.*; tournure *f.* (of phrase); virage *m.* (motor-car)

turn, *v.t.* tourner, changer, (change); diriger; *v.i.* **turn back,** rebrousser chemin; **turn round,** se retourner

turn aside or away, *v.i.* se détourner

turn off, *v.t.* fermer, couper (gas, etc.)

turncoat, renégat *m.*

turner, tourneur *m.*

turning, tour *m.*; tournant *m.* (in road)

turnpike, barrière *f.*

turnscrew, tournevis *m.*

turnspit, tournebroche *m.*

turnstile, tourniquet *m.*

turning-point, moment (*m.*) critique

turnip, navet *m.*
turpentine, térébenthine *f.*
turpitude, turpitude *f.*
turquoise, turquoise *f.*
turret, tourelle *f.*
turtle, tortue *f.*
turn turtle, *v.i.* capoter
tusk, défense *f.*
tussle, lutte *f.*; bagarre *f.*
tutelage, tutelle *f.*
tutelary, (*adj.*) tutélaire
tutor, précepteur *m.*; répétiteur *m.*
twang, son (*m.*) nasillard
tweak, *v.t.* pincer
tweezers, pincettes *f. pl.*
Twelfth Night, jour des Rois *m.*
twentieth, (*adj.*) vingtième; le vingt (of a month)
twenty, (*adj.*) vingt
twice, (*adv.*) deux fois
twig, petite branche *f.*
twilight, crépuscule *m.*
twill, étoffe (*f.*) croisée
twin, jumeau *m.*; jumelle *f.*
twin-beds, lits jumeaux; **twin-engined,** bimoteur
twine, ficelle *f.*
twine, *v.i.* s'entrelacer, se tordre
twine, *v.t.* entrelacer, tordre
twinge, élancement *m.*
twinge, *v.i.* élancer
twinkle, *v.i.* étinceler; scintiller; clignoter (of eye)
twinkling, scintillement *m.*; clignotement *m.* (of eyes)
twirl, *v.i.* tournoyer rapidement; *v.t.* faire tournoyer, pirouetter (of dancer)
twist, *v.t.* tordre; entortiller; enlacer (wind round); *v.i.* (of road) faire des lacets
twist, cordon *m.*
twit, *v.t.* reprocher
twitch, mouvement (*m.*) convulsif; tic *m.*
twitch, *v.i.* se contracter, se crisper
twitter, *v.i.* gazouiller
two, (*adj.*) deux
twofold, (*adj.*) double
two-seater, voiture (*f.*) à deux places

tympanum, tympan *m.*
type, type (*m.*), caractère *m.* (*print.*)
type, *v.t.* dactylographier; écrire à la machine
typewriter, machine (*f.*) à écrire
typhoid, typhoïde *f.*
typhoon, typhon *m.*
typhus, typhus *m.*
typical, (*adj.*) typique; caractéristique
typist, dactylographe *m.* and *f.*
typographer, typographe *m.*
tyrannical, (*adj.*) tyrannique
tyrannise, *v.i.* faire le tyran
tyranny, tyrannie *f.*
tyrant, tyran *m.*
tyre, pneu *m.*
balloon tyre, pneu ballon *m.*

U

ubiquitous, (*adj.*) qui se trouve partout
U-boat, sous-marin (*m.*) allemand
udder, mamelle *f.*
ugliness, laideur *f.*
ugly, (*adj.*) laid, vilain
ulcer, ulcère *m.*
ulcerate, *v.i.* s'ulcérer; *v.t.* ulcérer
ulceration, ulcération *f.*
ulcerous, (*adj.*) ulcéreux(-euse)
ulterior, (*adj.*) ultérieur
ultimate, (*adj.*) dernier(-ère) final; ultime
ultimatum, ultimatum *m.*
ultimo, (*adj.*) du mois dernier
ultra, ultra *m.*
ultra, (*adj.*) extrême
ultramarine, (*adj.*) d'outremer
umbrage, ombrage *m.*
umbrella, parapluie *m.*
umbrella-stand, porte-parapluie *m.*
umpire, arbitre *m.*
un, (*prefix*) non; in; dé; pas; peu; mal
unabashed, (*adj.*) sans vergogne; sans être déconcerté
unabated, (*adj.*) sans diminution

unable, *(adj.)* incapable (de)

unaccented, *(adj.)* non-accentué

unacceptable, *(adj.)* inacceptable

unacclimatised, *(adj.)* inacclimaté

unaccommodating, *(adj.)* peu accommodant

unaccompanied, *(adj.)* non accompagné; seul

unaccomplished, *(adj.)* inachevé

unaccountable, *(adj.)* inexplicable

unaccustomed, *(adj.)* inaccoutumé

unacknowledged, *(adj.)* non reconnu; sans réponse (of letters)

unadjusted, *(adj.)* mal ajusté

unadorned, *(adj.)* simple, naturel(le)

unadulterated, *(adj.)* pur

unadvisable, *(adj.)* peu sage

unadvised, *(adj.)* imprudent, indiscret(-ète)

unaffected, *(adj.)* sans affectation; insensible (à)

unaided, *(adj.)* sans aide

unalloyed, *(adj.)* pur

unambitious, *(adj.)* sans ambition

unanimity, unanimité *f.*

unanimous, *(adj.)* unanime

unanimously, *(adv.)* à l'unanimité

unanswerable, *(adj.)* incontestable; sans réplique

unanswered, *(adj.)* sans réponse

unappeasable, *(adj.)* implacable

unappeased, *(adj.)* non apaisé

unappreciated, *(adj.)* peu estimé

unapproachable, *(adj.)* inabordable, inaccessible

unapproved, *(adj.)* inapprouvé

unarmed, *(adj.)* sans armes

unassailable, *(adj.)* inattaquable

unassisted, *(adj.)* sans aide

unassorted, *(adj.)* non assorti

unassuming, modeste

unassured, non assuré

unattached, *(adj.)* sans être attaché à; en disponibilité *(mil.,* etc.)

unattainable, *(adj.)* inaccessible

unavailing, *(adj.)* inutile

unavoidable, *(adj.)* inévitable

unaware, (adj.) ignorant

unbalanced, *(adj.)* instable; dérangé (of mind)

unbearable, *(adj.)* insupportable

unbecoming, *(adj.)* peu convenable

unbefitting, *(adj.)* peu propre

unbelief, incrédulité *f.*

unbelieving, *(adj.)* incrédule

unbend, *v.t.* détendre, relâcher; *v.i.* se détendre

unbind, *v.t.* délier

unbleached, *(adj.)* écru

unblushing, *(adj.)* éhonté

unbound, *(adj.)* délié

unbounded, *(adj.)* illimité; sans bornes

unbreakable, *(adj.)* incassable

unbuckle, *v.t.* déboucler

unburden, *v.t.* décharger; soulager (one's feelings)

unbusinesslike, *(adj.)* peu pratique

unbutton, *v.t.* déboutonner

uncanny, *(adj.)* surnaturel(le)

unceasing, *(adj.)* incessant

unceasingly, *(adv.)* sans cesse

unceremonious, *(adj.)* peu cérémonieux(-euse); sans façon

uncertain, *(adj.)* incertain, irrésolu, peu sûr

uncertainty, incertitude *f.*

unchangeable, *(adj.)* immuable, invariable

uncharitable, *(adj.)* peu charitable

uncivil, *(adj.)* impoli

uncivilised, *(adj.)* incivilisé

uncle, oncle *m.*

unclean, *(adj.)* malpropre; sale

uncomfortable, *(adj.)* mal à l'aise (of persons); incommode; peu confortable

uncommon, *(adj.)* rare; peu commun; extraordinaire

uncompleted, *(adj.)* inachevé, incomplet

unconcern, insouciance *f.*, indifférence *f.*

unconcerned, *(adj.)* indifférent, insouciant

uncongenial, (adj.) peu sympathique

unconquerable, (adj.) invincible

unconscionable, (adj.) déraisonnable, exorbitant

unconscious, (adj.) sans connaissance, inconscient

unconsciously, (adv.) sans le savoir, à son insu

unconstitutional, (adj.) anti-constitutionnel(le)

uncontested, (adj.) incontesté

uncork, v.t. déboucher

uncouth, (adj.) grossier(-ère); rude

uncover, v.t. découvrir

unction, onction f.

undamaged, (adj.) indemne

undaunted, (adj.) intrépide

undeceive, v.t. détromper

undecided, (adj.) indécis, irrésolu

undemonstrative, (adj.) peu démonstratif(-ive)

undeniable, (adj.) incontestable

under, (prep.) sous, au-dessous de

under, (adv.) dessous, au-dessous

under, (adj.) inférieur, subordonné (rank); subalterne

under, (prefix) sous, sub

underbred, (adj.) mal élevé

underclothes, vêtements (m. pl.) de dessous

undercut, filet m. (joint); v.t. vendre moins cher que (prices)

underdone, (adj.) pas assez cuit, pas trop cuit, saignant

undergo, v.t. subir, supporter

undergraduate, étudiant(e) m. (f.)

underground, (adj.) souterrain, clandestin; (railway) le métro m.

undergrowth, broussailles f. pl.

underhand, (adj.) clandestin, sournois

underlet, v.t. sous-louer

underline, v.t. souligner

underlinen, linge (m.) de corps (de dessous)

underlying, (adj.) fondamental

undermine, v.t. miner

undermost, (adj.) le plus bas; inférieur

underneath, (adv.) au-dessous de, sous

underrate, v.t. sous-estimer

undersigned, (adj. and subst.) sous-signé(e)

understand, v.t. comprendre, entendre, entendre dire

understandable, intelligible

understanding, intelligence f.; compréhension f.; entente f. (agreement); accord m.

understudy, v.t. doubler; doublure f.; suppléant m.

undertake, v.t. entreprendre; se charger de

undertaker, entrepreneur (m.) de pompes funèbres

undertaking, entreprise f.

undervalue, v.t. sous-estimer

underwood, broussailles f. pl.

underwrite, v.t. assurer (insurance); souscrire

underwriter, assureur m.

undeserved, (adj.) non mérité

undeserving, (adj.) indigne de

undesirable, (adj.) peu désirable

undetermined, (adj.) indécis, incertain

undeveloped, (adj.) non développé, inexploité

undies, (fam.) lingerie (f.) de femme

undigested, (adj.) indigéré

undisguised, (adj.) non dissimulé, franc(he)

undisturbed, (adj.) calme, tranquille

undo, v.t. défaire (clothes); ruiner; réparer (damage caused)

undoubted, (adj.) indubitable

undress, v.t. déshabiller

undress, v.i. se déshabiller

undrinkable, (adj.) qui n'est pas potable

undue, excessif(-ive); outré (excessive); indu (improper)

undulate, v.t. and v.i. onduler

undulating, (adj.) ondoyant; accidenté (of land)

undulation, ondulation f.

undying, (adj.) immortel(le)

unearthly, (adj.) surnaturel(le); qui n'est pas de ce monde

UNE 476 UNL

uneasiness, inquiétude *f.*
uneasy, (*adj.*) inquiet(-ète), mal à son aise
unemployed, (*adj.*) sans travail; sans emploi
unemployed, (*adj.*) (collective) les chômeurs
unemployment, chômage *m.*
unenterprising, (*adj.*) peu entreprenant
unequal, (*adj.*) inégal
unequalled, (*adj.*) sans égal
unequivocal, (*adj.*) clair, sans équivoque
unerring, (*adj.*) infaillible
uneven, (*adj.*) inégal; raboteux (-euse) (rough); impair (of numbers)
unexampled, (*adj.*) sans exemple, sans pareil
unexceptionable, irréprochable; sans défaut
unexpected, (*adj.*) inattendu
unfailing, (*adj.*) infaillible, inépuisable (inexhaustible)
unfair, (*adj.*) injuste; peu équitable
unfairness, injustice *f.*
unfaithful, (*adj.*) infidèle
unfashionable, (*adj.*) démodé
unfasten, *v.t.* ouvrir (open); défaire (parcel, etc.); détacher
unfathomable, (*adj.*) sans fond; impénétrable
unfavourable, (*adj.*) défavorable
unfeeling, (*adj.*) insensible
unfeigned, (*adj.*) sincère
unfit, (*adj.*) peu propre (à); inapte (for military service)
unfold, *v.t.* révéler (reveal); exposer (plan); déplier (newspaper)
unforeseen, (*adj.*) imprévu
unforgiving, (*adj.*) implacable
unfortunate, (*adj.*) infortuné; malheureux(-euse); fâcheux (-euse)
unfounded, (*adj.*) sans fondement
unfriendly, (*adj.*) peu amical
unfurnished, (*adj.*) non meublé
ungainly, (*adj.*) maladroit, gauche
ungentlemanly, (*adj.*) indélicat; pas comme il faut

ungraceful, (*adj.*) peu gracieux (-euse)
ungrateful, (*adj.*) ingrat
ungratefulness, ingratitude *f.*
unhappiness, malheur *m.*; chagrin *m.*
unhappy, (*adj.*) malheureux (-euse)
unhealthy, (*adj.*) maladif(-ive) (of persons); malsain (of places, etc.)
unheard of, (*adj.*) inouï
unhoped for, (*adj.*) inespéré
unhorse, *v.t.* désarçonner
unidentified, (*adj.*) non reconnu
uniform, (*adj.*) uniforme
uniform, tenue *f.*; uniforme *m.*
unify, *v.t.* unifier
unimaginable, (*adj.*) inimaginable
uninhabited, (*adj.*) inhabité
unintelligible, (*adj.*) inintelligible
unintentional, (*adj.*) fait sans intention; involontaire
uninterested, (*adj.*) indifférent
uninterrupted, (*adj.*) ininterrompu
union, union *f.*
union jack, pavillon (*m.*) britannique
unique, (*adj.*) unique
unison, unisson *m.*
unit, unité *f.*
unite, *v.t.* unir; joindre; *v.i.* s'unir
unity, concorde *f.*; harmonie *f.*; unité *f.*
universal, (*adj.*) universel(le)
universe, univers *m.*
university, université *f.*
unjust, (*adj.*) injuste
unjustifiable, (*adj.*) inexcusable
unkind, (*adj.*) dur; peu aimable
unknown, (*adj.*) *m.* (*f.*) inconnu(e)
unladylike, indigne d'une femme bien élevée
unlawful, (*adj.*) illégal, illicite
unless, à moins que...ne
unlettered, (*adj.*) illettré
unlike, (*adj.*) différent (de), peu ressemblant

unlikely, (adj.) peu probable, invraisemblable
unlimited, (adj.) illimité
unload, v.t. décharger
unlock, v.t. ouvrir
unlooked for, (adj.) imprévu
unloose(n), v.t. délier
unlucky, (adj.) malheureux(-euse)
unmanly, (adj.) indigne d'un homme, efféminé
unmarried, (adj.) non marié, célibataire
unmask, v.t. démasquer; v.i. se démasquer
unmerciful, (adj.) sans pitié
unmindful, (adj.) oublieux(-euse); peu soucieux(-euse) (de)
unmistakable, (adj.) évident
unnatural, (adj.) dénaturé (persons); contre la nature
unnoticed, (adj.) inaperçu
unoccupied, (adj.) inoccupé, libre
unoffending, (adj.) inoffensif(-ive)
unopposed, (adj.) sans opposition
unpack, v.t. défaire; déballer; dépaqueter
unpaid, (adj.) non payé; non affranchi (letters, etc.)
unparalleled, (adj.) sans pareil
unpardonable, (adj.) impardonnable
unpleasant, (adj.) désagréable, déplaisant
unpopular, (adj.) impopulaire
unprecedented, (adj.) sans précédent
unprejudiced, (adj.) impartial
unpretentious, (adj.) modeste
unprincipled, (adj.) sans principes
unpublished, (adj.) inédit
unpunctual, (adj.) inexact
unpunished, (adj.) impuni
unqualified, (adj.) incompétent
unquestionable, (adj.) incontestable
unreadable, (adj.) illisible
unreasonable, (adj.) déraisonnable, extravagant
unrelenting, (adj.) inexorable
unremarked, (adj.) inaperçu

unremitting, (adj.) sans cesse, soutenu
unreserved, (adj.) sans réserve; non réservé (of seats)
unripe, vert; pas mûr
unrivalled, (adj.) sans rival; sans égal
unruly, (adj.) turbulent, insoumis
unsafe, peu sûr, dangereux(-euse)
unsatisfactory, (adj.) peu satisfaisant
unscrew, v.t. dévisser
unscrupulous, (adj.) peu scrupuleux(-euse)
unseal, v.t. décacheter
unseemly, (adj.) inconvenant, indécent
unselfish, (adj.) désintéressé
unsettled, (adj.) mal établi; incertain; variable (weather); irrésolu
unship, v.t. débarquer; décharger (cargo)
unsightly, (adj.) laid, vilain
unsound, (adj.) malsain; non solide; défectueux(-euse)
unsparing, (adj.) prodigue; impitoyable (merciless)
unspeakable, (adj.) inexprimable; indicible
unsteady, (adj.) inconstant; chancelant (walking); incertain; irrégulier (conduct)
unsuccessful, (adj.) sans succès; manqué
untamable, (adj.) indomptable
untaught, (adj.) illettré
unthinking, (adj.) irréfléchi; étourdi
untidiness, désordre m.
untidy, (adj.) en désordre, négligé
untie, v.t. délier, dénouer
until, (prep.) jusqu'à; avant
until, (conj.) jusqu'à ce que; avant que
untimely, (adj.) prématuré; mal à propos
untiring, (adj.) infatigable
untold, (adj.) non exprimé; immense; énorme
untrue, (adj.) faux (fausse); inexact; infidèle

untruth, mensonge *m.*

untruthful, *(adj.)* mensonger (-ère); menteur(-euse)

unusual, *(adj.)* extraordinaire

unutterable, *(adj.)* inexprimable

unveil, *v.t.* dévoiler

unwarrantable, *(adj)* inexcusable; injustifiable

unwary, *(adj.)* imprudent

unwavering, *(adj.)* ferme, résolu

unwelcome, *(adj.)* mal venu; mal vu; déplaisant

unwell, *(adj.)* indisposé, malade

unwholesome, *(adj.)* malsain; *(fig.)* pernicieux(-euse)

unwieldy, *(adj.)* lourd, pesant

unwilling, *(adj.)* peu disposé (à); de mauvaise volonté

unwillingly, *(adv.)* à contre-cœur

unwind, *v.t.* dérouler, dévider

unworthy, *(adj.)* indigne

unyielding, *(adj.)* inflexible

up, *(adv.)* en haut, en l'air; sur pied (out of bed); debout (on one's legs); fini (over); à court d'argent (hard up)

up, *(prep.)* en haut de; au haut de

up, haut *m.*

ups and downs, le haut et le bas

up to..., à la hauteur de...; jusqu'à...

upbraid, *v.t.* reprocher

uphill, *(adj)* montant; pénible

uphold, *v.t.* soutenir, maintenir

upholsterer, tapissier *m.*

upholstery, tapisserie *f.*

upkeep, maintien *m.*

uplift, *v.t.* élever, soulever

upon, *(prep.)* sur

upper, *(adj.)* supérieur, de dessus

uppermost, *(adj.)* le plus élevé; le plus haut

upraise, *v.t.* élever

upright, *(adj.)* droit, debout; *(fig.)* honnête

uprightness, droiture *f.*; intégrité *f.*

uproar, tapage *m.*; vacarme *m.*; tumulte *m.*

uproarious, *(adj.)* bruyant, tumultueux(-euse)

uproot, *v.t.* déraciner

upset, *v.t.* renverser; troubler

upshot, issue *f.*; fin *f.*

upside-down, sens dessus dessous

upstairs, *(adv.)* en haut

upstart, parvenu(e) *m. (f.)*

up-to-date, *(adj.)* moderne; à la mode; à la page

upward, *(adv.)* en haut; en montant

urban, *(adj.)* urbain

urbane, *(adj.)* poli

urbanity, urbanité *f.*

urchin, gamin *m.*; polisson *m*; galopin *m.*

sea urchin, oursin *m.*.

urethra, urètre *m.*

urge, *v.t.* presser, pousser, exciter

urgency, urgence *f.*; besoin *(m.)* pressant

urgent, *(adj.)* urgent, pressant

urinal, urinoir *m.*

urine, urine *f.*

urn, urne *f.*

us, *(pron.)* nous

usage, usage *m.*; traitement *m.*; emploi *m.*

use, emploi *m.*; usage *m.*; utilité *f.*; profit *m.* (advantage);' coutume *f.*

use, *v.t.* se servir de; employer; utiliser

use, *v.i.* avoir l'habitude (de)

useful, *(adj.)* utile

usefulness, utilité *f.*

useless, *(adj.)* inutile

usher, huissier *m.* (in court of law); pion *m.* (in schools)

usual, *(adj.)* ordinaire, habituel(le)

usurer, usurier *m.*

usurious, *(adj.)* exorbitant, usuraire

usurp, *v.t.* usurper

usurper, usurpateur *m*

usury, usure *f.*

utensil, ustensile *m.*

uterine, *(adj.)* utérin

utilise *v.t.* utiliser

utility, utilité *f.*

utmost, *(adj.)* extrême; le dernier; le plus grand

Utopia, l'utopie *f.*

utopian, *(adj.)* utopique

utter, *v.t.* pousser (a cry); pro-férer; prononcer

utter, (*adj.*) total; complet(-ète)

utterance, énonciation *f.*; parole *f.*

utterly, (*adv.*) complètement; tout à fait

uvula, uvule *f.*; luette *f.*

uxorious, (*adj.*) esclave de sa femme; uxorieux(-euse)

V

vacancy, poste vacant *m.*; vide *m.*

vacant, (*adj.*) vacant, libre

vacate, *v.t.* vider; quitter

vacation, vacances *f. pl.*

vaccinate, *v.t.* vacciner

vaccination, vaccination *f.*

vaccine, vaccin *m.*

vacillate, *v.i.* vaciller

vacillation, vacillation *f.*

vacuity, vacuité *f.*; vide *m.*

vacuous, (*adj.*) vide, niais

vacuum, vide *m.*

vacuum-cleaner, aspirateur (*m.*) électrique

vagabond, vagabond(e) *m.* (*f.*) (*subst.* and *adj.*)

vagary, caprice *m.*; lubie *f.*

vagina, vagin *m.*

vagrancy, vagabondage *m.*

vagrant, vagabond(e) *m.* (*f.*) (*subst.* and *adj.*)

vague, (*adj.*) vague; indéterminé

vagueness, vague *m.*

vain, (*adj.*) vain; vaniteux(-euse); orgueilleux(-euse)

in vain, en vain

vainglorious, (*adj.*) vaniteux (-euse)

vainglory, vaine gloire *f.*

vale, vallon *m.*

valerian, valériane *f.*

valet, valet *m.*; valet de chambre

valetudinarian, valétudinaire *m.* and *f.*; malade imaginaire *m.* and *f.*

valiant, (*adj.*) vaillant

valid, (*adj.*) valable, bon(ne)

validity, validité *f.*

valise, valise *f.*; mallette *f.*

valley, vallée *f.*

valorous, (*adj.*) valeureux(-euse)

valour, vaillance *f.*

valuable, (*adj.*) précieux(-euse); de grande valeur *f.*

value, valeur *f.*; prix *m.*

value, *v.t.* estimer; évaluer

valueless, (*adj.*) sans valeur

valve, soupape *f.*; (wireless) lampe *f.*

vampire, vampire *m.*

van, voiture (*f.*) de déménage-ment (removal); camion *m.* (lorry); fourgon *m.* (luggage van); avant-garde *f.* (vanguard)

vandal, vandale *m.*

vandalism, vandalisme *m.*

vane, girouette *f.*; ailette *f.*

vanilla, vanille *f.*

vanish, *v.i.* s'évanouir; dis-paraître

vanity, vanité *f.*

vanquish, *v.t.* vaincre

vanquished, (*adj.*) vaincu

vanquisher, vainqueur *m.*

vantage, avantage *m.*

vapid, (*adj.*) fade; insipide

vaporise, *v.t.* vaporiser; *v.i.* se vaporiser

vaporous, (*adj.*) vaporeux(-euse)

vapour, vapeur *f.*

variability, variabilité *f.*

variable, (*adj.*) variable

variance, désaccord *m.*

varicose vein, varice *f.*

variegate, *v.t.* varier; bigarrer

variety, variété *f.*; diversité *f.*

various, (*adj.*) divers

varnish, vernis *m.*

varnish, *v.t.* vernir

vary, *v.i.* changer; *v.t.* varier

vase, vase *m.*

vassal, vassal *m.*

vast, (*adj.*) vaste

vat, cuve *f.*

vault, voûte *f.*; cave *f.*; saut *m.* (leap)

vaunt, *v.i.* se vanter (de)

veal, veau *m.*

veal cutlet, côtelette (*f.*) de veau

veer, *v.i.* tourner; virer

vegetable, (*adj.*) végétal

vegetable, légume *m.* (*food*); (early) primeurs *f. pl.*

vehemence, véhémence *f.*; ardeur *f.*

vehicle, véhicule *m.*

veil, *v.t.* voiler; (*subst.*) voile *m.*

vein, veine *f.*

velocity, vitesse *f.*

velvet, velours *m.*

velvety, (*adj.*) velouté

venal, (*adj.*) vénal

venality, vénalité *f.*

vendor, vendeur(-euse) *m.* (*f.*)

veneer, *v.t.* plaquer

veneer, placage *m.*; (*fig.*) apparence *f.*

venerable, (*adj.*) vénérable

venerate, *v.t.* vénérer

veneration, vénération *f.*

venereal, (*adj.*) vénérien(ne)

Venetian, (*adj.*) vénitien(ne)

venetian blind, jalousie *f.*

vengeance, vengeance *f.*

venial, (*adj.*) véniel(le)

venison, venaison *f.*

venom, venin *m.*

venomous, (*adj.*) venimeux (-euse); empoisonné

vent (give vent to), donner libre cours à

vent, trou *m.*; passage *m.*

ventilate, *v.t.* ventiler; aérer

ventilator, ventilateur *m.*; soupirail *m.* (*pl.* -aux)

ventriloquist, ventriloque *m.* and *f.*

venture, *v.t.* oser; *v.i.* s'aventurer (venture into)

venture, aventure *f.*; entreprise *f.*

veracious, (*adj.*) véridique

veracity, véracité *f.*

veranda(h), véranda *f.*

verb, verbe *m.*

verbal, (*adj.*) verbal, oral

verdant, (*adj.*) verdoyant

verdict, verdict *m.*

verdigris, vert-de-gris *m.*

verge, bord *m.*; bordure *f.*

verger, bedeau *m.*

verify, *v.t.* vérifier

verily, (*adv.*) en vérité

vermicelli, vermicelle *m.*

vermifuge, vermifuge (*m.* and *adj.*)

vermin, vermine *f.*

vermin-killer, poudre (*f.*) insecticide

verminous, (*adj.*) vermineux (-euse)

verse, vers *m.*; poésie *f.*; verset *m.* (Bible)

versed (in), versé (dans)

version, version *f.*

vertical, (*adj.*) vertical

vertical dive, une descente piquée

vertigo, vertige *m.*

very (*adj.*) vrai, même, véritable

very, (*adv.*) très, fort, bien

vespers, vêpres *f. pl.*

vessel, vase *m.*; vaisseau *m.*; bâtiment *m.* (ship)

vest, gilet *m.*

vest, *v.t.* investir (de); revêtir

vestige, trace *f.*

vestry, sacristie *f.*

veteran, (*adj.*) expérimenté; aguerri

veteran, vétéran *m.*; ancien *m.*

veterinary surgeon, vétérinaire *m.*

veto, veto *m.*

veto, *v.t.* mettre son veto à

vex, *v.t.* fâcher; vexer; ennuyer, contrarier

vexation, vexation *f.*; contrariété *f.*

vexatious, (*adj.*) fâcheux(-euse)

viaduct, viaduc *m.*

vial, fiole *f.*

viands, aliments *m. pl.*

viaticum, viatique *m.*

vibrate, *v.i.* vibrer; *v.t.* faire vibrer

vicar, ministre *m.*; curé *m.*

vicarage, presbytère *m.*

vice, vice *m.*; (tool) étau *m.*

viceroy, vice-roi *m.*

vicinity, voisinage *m.*

vicious, (*adj.*) vicieux(-euse)

vicissitude, vicissitude *f.*

victim, victime *f.*

victor, vainqueur *m.*

victorious, (*adj.*) victorieux (-euse)

victory, victoire *f.*
victuals, vivres *m. pl.*
videlicet, (*adv.*) c'est-à-dire; savoir
vie, *v.i.* rivaliser (avec)
view, vue *f.*; perspective *f.*; coup d'œil *m.*; opinion *f.*
view, *v.t.* voir, regarder, contempler, inspecter
vigilance, vigilance *f.*
vigorous, (*adj.*) vigoureux(-euse)
vigour, vigueur *f.*
vile, (*adj.*) vil; bas(se)
vilify, *v.t.* diffamer
villa, villa *f.*
village, village *m.*
villager, villageois(e) *m.* (*f.*)
villain, gredin *m.*; scélérat *m.*
vindicate, *v.t.* justifier, défendre
vindication, défense *f.*; apologie *f.*
vindictive, vindicatif(-ive)
vine, vigne *f.*
vine-grower, viticulteur *m.*; vigneron *m.*
vinegar, vinaigre *m.*
vineyard, vigne *f.*; clos (*m.*) de vigne
vintage, récolte *f.*; vendanges *f. pl.*
vintage wine, vin (*m.*) de marque
violate, *v.t.* violer
violence, violence *f.*
violent, (*adj.*) violent
violet, (*adj.*) violet(te); (colour) violet *m.*; (flower) violette *f.*
violin, violon *m.*
violinist, violoniste *m.* and *f.*
viper, vipère *f.*
virago, mégère *f.*
virgin, vierge *f.*; (*adj.*) virginal, de vierge
virginity, virginité *f.*
virile, (*adj.*) viril, mâle
virtual, (*adj.*) virtuel(le); de fait
virtue, vertu *f.*
virtuous, (*adj.*) vertueux(-euse)
viscid (viscous), visqueux (-euse)
viscount(-ess), vicomte(sse) *m.* (*f.*)
visibility, visibilité *f.*
visible, (*adj.*) visible
vision, vision *f.*; vue *f.*

visit, visite *f.*
visit, *v.t.* rendre visite; visiter (officially or medically)
visitor, visiteur(-euse) *m.* (*f.*)
vista, perspective *f.*; éclaircie *f.*
visual, (*adj.*) visuel(le); optique
vital, (*adj.*) vital; essentiel(le)
vitality, vitalité *f*
vitamin, vitamine *f.*
vitiate, *v.t.* vicier
vitriol, vitriol *m.*
vituperation, invectives *f. pl.*
vivacious, (*adj.*) vif (vive); animé
vivacity, vivacité *f.*; animation *f.*
vivid, (*adj.*) vif (vive), vivant
vivify, *v.t.* animer
vixen, renarde *f.*; mégère *f.* (shrew)
vocabulary, vocabulaire *m.*
vocal, (*adj.*) vocal; bruyant
vocation, vocation *f.*
vociferate, *v.i.* vociférer
vociferous, (*adj.*) vociférant, bruyant
vogue, mode *f.*
voice, voix *f.*
voice, *v.t.* exprimer
void, (*adj.*) vide; nul(le); dépourvu de (devoid of)
volatile, (*adj.*) volatil
volatilise, *v.t.* volatiliser; *v.i.* se volatiliser
volcanic, (*adj.*) volcanique
volcano, volcan *m.*
volley, volée *f.*; bordée *f.*; salve *f.*
volt, volt *m.*
voltage, voltage *m.*; tension (*f.*) en volts
volubility, volubilité *f.*
volume, volume *m.*; livre *m.*; tome *m.* (large book)
voluminous, (*adj.*) volumineux (-euse)
voluntary, (*adj.*) volontaire, spontané
volunteer, volontaire *m.* and *f.*
volunteer, *v.i.* s'offrir (spontanément); (*mil.*) s'engager comme volontaire
voluptuous, (*adj.*) voluptueux (-euse)
voluptuousness, sensualité *f.*

vomit, v.t. and v.i. vomir
voracious, (adj.) vorace
voracity, voracité f.
vortex, tourbillon m.
vote, vote m.; scrutin m.; motion f.; voix f.
vote, v.i. and v.t. voter
voter, électeur(-trice) m. (f.); votant(e) m. (f.)
vouch (for), v.i. répondre (de)
voucher, fiche f. (commer.); bon m. (for cash); pièce (f.) justificative
vow, vœu m.; serment m.
vow, v.t. vouer, jurer
vowel, voyelle f.
voyage, voyage (m.) sur mer; v.i. naviguer
voyager (on sea), passager(-ère) m. (f.)
vulcanite, vulcanite f.
vulcanise, v.t. vulcaniser
vulgar, (adj.) vulgaire, commun
vulgarise, v.t. vulgariser
vulgarity, vulgarité f.
vulnerability, vulnérabilité f.
vulnerable, (adj.) vulnérable
vulture, vautour m.

W

wad, tampon m.
wad (to), v.t. ouater
wadding, ouate f.
waddle (to), v.i. se dandiner
wade, v.i. marcher (dans l'eau, etc.); v.t. passer à gué (i.e. to ford)
wafer, pain (m.) à cacheter; gaufrette f. (biscuit); hostie f. (consecrated)
waffle, gaufrè f.
waft (to), v.t. transporter; faire flotter
wag, farceur m.; mouvement m. (of tail)
wag (to), v.t. remuer, agiter
wage war, v.t. faire la guerre
wager, pari m.; gageure f.
wager (to), v.t. gager, parier
wages, gages m. pl.; salaire m.

waggish, (adj.) espiègle, facétieux (-euse)
waggon, **wagon**, charrette f.; chariot m.; wagon m.
waggoner, charretier m.
wagtail, bergeronnette f.
wail, lamentation f.; plainte f.
wail, v.i. lamenter; pleurer
wainscot, boiserie f.
wainscot, v.t. lambrisser
waist, taille f.; ceinture f.
waistcoat, gilet m.
wait (to), v.i. attendre, servir (à table); v.t. attendre
to lie in wait, se tenir en embuscade; être à l'affût
waiter, garçon m.
waiting, attente f.; service m.
waiting-room, salle (f.) d'attente
waitress, fille (f.) de salle
waive, v.t. renoncer (à)
wake, v.t. éveiller, réveiller; v.i. s'éveiller; se réveiller
wale, marque f.
walk, promenade f.; marche f.; tour m.
to go for a walk, faire une promenade
walk, v.i. marcher; aller à pied; se promener
walk away, v.i. s'en aller
walk in, v.i. entrer
walk (into), entrer dans
walk on, v.i. continuer de marcher
walker, promeneur(-euse) m. (f.); piéton m.
wall, mur m.; muraille f.; paroi f.
wall in, v.i. entourer de murailles
wallflower, giroflée f.
wall-fruit, fruit (m.) d'espalier
wall-paper, papier (m.) peint
wallet, sac m.; bissac m.; portefeuille m.
wallow, v.i. se vautrer, se rouler
walnut, noix f.
walnut (tree, wood), noyer m.
walrus, morse m.
waltz, valse f.
waltz, v.i. valser
wan, (adj.) pâle; blême
wand, baguette f.

wander, *v.i.* errer; délirer (delirium)

wane, déclin *m.*

wane, *v.i.* décroître; s'affaiblir; décliner

want (need), besoin *m.*; manque *m.*; indigence *f.*; misère *f.*; défaut *m.* (lack of)

for want of, faute de

want, *v.t.* avoir besoin de; manquer de; vouloir; désirer (wish for)

wanton, (*adj.*) libertin, licencieux (-euse)

wantonness, libertinage *m.*

war, guerre *f.*; *v.i.* **to war against,** lutter contre

war minister, ministre (*m.*) de la guerre

war office, ministère (*m.*) de la guerre

war-like, (*adj.*) belliqueux(-euse)

warble, *v.i.* gazouiller

warbler, chanteur *m.*; fauvette *f.*

ward, pupille *m.* (*f.*)

ward (hospital), salle (*f.*) d'hôpital

ward off, *v.t.* parer, écarter

warden, gardien *m.*; recteur *m.* (of university)

warder, gardien(ne) *m.* (*f.*)

wardrobe, garde-robe *f.*; armoire *f.*

warehouse, magasin *m.*; entrepôt *m.*

warehouseman, garde-magasin *m.*

wares, marchandises *f. pl.*

warfare, guerre *f.*

warm, (*adj.*) chaud; chaleureux (-euse) (welcome, etc.); ardent (affection)

warm, *v.t.* chauffer; réchauffer

warm, *v.i.* se chauffer; se réchauffer

warming, chauffage *m.*

warmly, (*adv.*) chaudement; chaleureusement

warmth, chaleur *f.*; ardeur *f.*

warn *v.t.* avertir, prévenir

warning, avertissement *m.*; avis *m.*; congé *m.* (dismissal)

warp, chaîne *f.* (for weaving)

warp, *v.t.* faire déjeter (wood); haler (ship)

warrant, autorisation *f.*; ordre *m.*; mandat *m.*; mandat d'arrêt (arrest); garantie *f.*

warrant, *v.t.* garantir, autoriser

warranty, garantie *f.*; autorisation *f.*

warren, garenne *f.*

warrior, guerrier *m.*

wart, verrue *f.*

wary, (*adj.*) prudent; avisé

wash, blanchissage *m.* (linen); lessive *f.* (of clothes); lotion *f.* (med.); lavis *m.* (of paint); remous *m.* (in wake of ship)

wash, *v.t.* blanchir (linen); laver (paint, etc.)

wash, *v.i.* se laver (wash oneself); se baigner

washer, rondelle *f.* (on tap)

washer-up, plongeur(-euse) de vaisselle (in restaurant)

washer-woman, blanchisseuse *f.*

washing, blanchissage *m.*, lessive *f.*

wash-hand basin, cuvette *f.*

wash-house, lavoir *m.*

wash-leather, peau (*f.*) de chamois

wash-stand, lavabo *m.*

wasp, guêpe *f.*

waspish, (*adj.*) irascible, acariâtre

waste, perte *f.* (loss); déchet *m.* (for cleaning); gaspillage *m.*; dépense (*f.*) inutile; terre inculte *f.*; rebut *m.* (refuse)

waste, *v.t.* gaspiller; dissiper

waste paper, papier (*m.*) de rebut

waste-paper basket, corbeille (*f.*) à papier

waste pipe, tuyau (*m.*) de dégagement

wasted, (*adj.*) gaspillé, perdu (trouble); amaigri (of persons)

wasteful, (*adj.*) gaspilleur(-euse); prodigue

wastefulness, prodigalité *f.*; gaspillage *m.*

watch, montre *f.* (time); garde *f.*;
  vigilance *f.*; surveillance *f.*
watch, *v.t.* veiller, surveiller,
  garder; *v.i.* veiller
watch-dog, chien (*m.*) de garde
watchmaker, horloger *m.*
watch-making, horlogerie *f.*
watchman, gardien *m.*; veilleur
  (*m.*) de nuit (night-watchman)
water, eau *f.*
water, *v.t.* arroser; donner à boire
  à (animals); mettre de l'eau
  dans; couper (to mix water
  with)
fresh water, eau douce *f.*
high water, haute marée *f.*
holy water, eau bénite
low water, marée basse
water bottle, carafe *f.*
water closet, cabinet (*m.*) (d'aisances)
water colour, aquarelle *f.*
waterfall, cascade *f.*
water fowl, oiseau aquatique
  m.
waterproof, imperméable *m.*
waterspout, trombe (*f.*) d'eau
  (natural); descente (*f.*) d'eau
  (plumbing)
water supply, distribution (*f.*)
  des eaux
water tank, citerne *f.*
water-tight, (*adj.*) étanche (à
  l'eau) (bulkhead, etc.)
watering, arrosage *m.*
watering place, abreuvoir *m.*;
  (seaside resort) bains (*m. pl.*)
  de mer, plage *f.*
watering pot, arrosoir *m.*
watery, (*adj.*) aqueux(-euse)
wattle, claie (*f.*) d'osier
wave, vague *f.* (of sea, etc.); flot
  m.; signe *m.* (of hand)
wave, *v.i.* onduler, flotter, s'agiter
wave, *v.t.* agiter, onduler (hair);
  faire signe de
waving, ondulation (hair) *f.*;
  ondoiement *m.*
wavy, (*adj.*) ondulé, onduleux
  (-euse)
wax, cire *f.*
sealing wax, cire à cacheter
wax, *v.t.* cirer

wax, *v.i.* (grow) croître; (to
  become) devenir
waxwork, figure (*f.*) de cire
way, chemin *m.*; voie *f.*; route *f.*;
  direction *f.*; manière *f.*; façon *f.*;
  état *m.* (condition); distance *f.*
by the way, en passant; à propos
in the family way, enceinte
find a way to, trouver moyen de
find one's way, trouver son
  chemin
give way, céder
lose one's way, s'égarer
make way, faire place
this way, par ici
wayfarer, voyageur(-euse) *m.* (*f.*)
waylay, *v.t.* guetter
wayward, (*adj.*) fantasque, têtu
we, (*pron.*) nous; (*indef.*) on
weak, (*adj.*) faible, infirme
weaken, *v.t.* affaiblir; atténuer;
  v.i. s'affaiblir
weak-headed, (*adj.*) faible d'esprit
weak-hearted, (*adj.*) pusillanime
weakness, faiblesse *f.*
weal, bien *m.*; contusion *f.* (on
  skin)
wealth, richesse *f.*; richesses *f. pl.*;
  abondance *f.*
wealthy, (*adj.*) riche, opulent
wean, *v.t.* sevrer
weapon, arme *f.*
wear, *v.t.* porter (clothes); user
wear out, *v.i.* s'user (clothes); *v.t*
  épuiser (exhaust)
weariness, fatigue *f.*; lassitude *f.*
wearing, usage *m.*; usure *f.*
  (wearing out)
wearing well, durable; d'un bon
  usage
wearisome, (*adj.*) ennuyeux
  (-euse)
weary, *v.t.* lasser, fatiguer; ennuyer (to bore); *v.i.* se lasser
weasel, belette *f.*
weather, temps *m.*
weather-cock, girouette *f.*
weather forecast, prévisions (*f.
  pl.*) du temps
weather-glass, baromètre *m.*
weave, *v.t.* tisser
weaver, tisserand *m.*

web, tissu *m* ; (of spider) toile (*f*) d'araignée
webbed, (*adj.*) palmé
webbing, sangles *f. pl*
web-footed, (*adj*) aux pieds palmés
wed, *v.t* épouser se marier avec
wedding, noce *f* ; noces *f pl.*; mariage *m*
wedding-ring, alliance *f.*
wedding tour, voyage (*m.*) de noces
wedlock, mariage *m.*
Wednesday, mercredi *m.*
Ash Wednesday, mercredi (*m.*) des cendres
wee, (*adj.*) tout petit, mignon(ne)
weed, mauvaise herbe *f.*
weed, *v.t.* arracher les mauvaises herbes, sarcler
weeding, sarclage *m.*
weedy, (*adj.*) plein de mauvaises herbes
weedy, (*adj.*) (sickly), chétif(-ive)
week, semaine *f.*
a week ago, il y a huit jours
every week, tous les huit jours
Holy Week, la semaine sainte *f.*
Passion Week, la semaine de la Passion *f*
to-day week, d'aujourd'hui en huit jours
week-end, fin (*f.*) de semaine ; week-end *m.*
weep, *v.i.* pleurer ; verser des larmes
weeping willow, saule (*m.*) pleureur
weevil, charançon *m.*
weft, trame *f.*; tissu *m.*
weigh, *v.i.* peser ; avoir un poids de ; *v.t* peser ; considérer
weigh-bridge, bascule *f*
weighing, pesage *m.*
weight, poids *m.*; pesanteur *f.*
weightiness, pesanteur *f.*; gravité *f.*; importance *f.*
weighty, (*adj.*) lourd ; grave
weir, barrage *m.*
weird, (*adj.*) fantastique, étrange
welcome, (*adj.*) bienvenu ; acceptable
welcome, bienvenue *f.*

welcome, *v.t.* souhaiter la bienvenue (à) ; faire bon accueil (à)
weld, *v.t.* souder
welfare, bien-être *m.*; bonheur *m.*
Welfare State, l'État Providence
well, (*adj.*) bien ; en bonne santé
well, puits *m.*
well-spring, source *f.*
well-being, bien-être *m.*
well-off, (*adj.*) à son aise, aisé
well-tried, (*adj.*) bien éprouvé
Welsh, (*adj.*) gallois(e)
wench, donzelle *f.*; fille *f.*
west, (*adj.*) occidental, de l'ouest
west, ouest *m.*; occident *m.*
western, (*adj.*) occidental
westward, (*adv.*) à (vers) l'ouest
wet, (*adj.*) mouillé, humide ; pluvieux(-euse) (rainy)
wet, *v.t.* mouiller ; humecter
wet-nurse, nourrice *f.*
wether, mouton *m.*
whale, baleine *f.*
wharf, quai *m.*; embarcadère *m.*; débarcadère *m.*
what, (*rel. pron.*) ce qui ; ce que ; que
what ? (*inter. pron.*) qu'est-ce qui ? ; qu'est-ce que ? ; que ?
what, (*adj.*) quel ; quelle ; *pl.* quels, quelles
what for ? quoi ? pourquoi ?
whatever, (*pron. and adj.*) quoi que ce soit ; quel(le) que soit...
wheat, blé *m.*; froment *m.*
wheedle, *v.t.* cajoler, enjôler
wheel, roue *f.*
driving wheel, roue motrice *f.*
flywheel, volant *m.*
steering wheel, volant *m.*
wheel, *v.t.* rouler ; faire tourner ; pédaler ; *v.i.* tourner (en rond)
wheelbarrow, brouette *f.*
wheel-chair, voiture (*f.*) de malade
when, (*adv.*) quand ; lorsque ; que ; où
whence, (*adv.*) d'où
whenever, (*adv.*) toutes les fois que
where, (*adv.*) où
anywhere, (*adv.*) n'importe où

whereas, (*adv.*) tandis que ; vu que

wherefore, (*adv.*) donc ; pourquoi

wherever, (*adv.*) partout où ; n'importe où

whereupon, (*adv.*) sur quoi

wherry, bachot *m.* ; canot *m.*

whet, *v.t.* aiguiser

whether, (*conj.*) soit que ; si

whether... or, soit... soit

whetstone, pierre (*f.*) à aiguiser

whey, petit lait *m.*

which, (*adj.*) quel, quelle, quels, quelles, (*pron.*) lequel, laquelle, lesquels, lesquelles

which, (*rel. pron.*) qui, que ; lequel, laquelle, lesquels, lesquelles ; ce qui, ce que (**that which**)

while, (*conj.*) pendant que ; tandis que ; tout en...

while, temps *m.*

a little while, peu de temps

while (away), *v.t.* faire passer (le temps)

worth while (to be), valoir la peine

whim, caprice *m.*

whimper, *v.i.* pleurnicher

whimsical, (*adj.*) fantasque capricieux(-euse)

whine, *v.i.* geindre, se plaindre, gémir

whining, plaintes *f. pl.*

whip, fouet *m.* ; cravache *f.*

whip, *v.t.* fouetter

whip-hand (to have), avoir le dessus

whirl, *v.t.* faire tourner ; *v.i.* tournoyer

whirlpool *or* **whirlwind,** tourbillon *m.*

whirr, vrombissement *m.* ; *v.i.* vrombir

whisk (cream, etc.), *v.t.* fouetter

whiskers, favoris *m. pl.*

whisky, whisk(e)y *m.*

whisper, chuchotement *m.* ; murmure *m.* ; bruit (*m.*) qui court

in a whisper, tout bas

whisper, *v.i.* chuchoter, parler bas

whistle, sifflet *m.* ; sifflement *m.* (of wind)

whistle, *v.i.* and *v.t.* siffler

whit, iota *m.*

white, (*adj.*) blanc (blanche) ; blanc *m.*

whitebait, blanchaille *f.*

white-livered, (*adj.*) lâche

whitewash, blanc (*m.*) de chaux

whitewash, *v.t.* badigeonner (en blanc)

whitewashing, badigeonnage *m.* (en blanc)

whiten, *v.t.* and *v.i.* blanchir ; *v.i.* pâlir

whither, (*adv.*) où, par où

whiting, merlan *m.*

Whitsun(tide), Pentecôte *f.*

whizz, *v.t.* siffler

who, (*pron.*) qui

whoever, (*pron.*) quiconque

whole, (*adj.*) tout(e) ; entier(-ère) ; complet(-ète)

whole, tout(e) *m.* (*f.*) ; total *m.* ; somme *f.*

wholesale, totalité *f.* ; vente (*f.*) en gros

wholesome, (*adj.*) sain

whoop, *v.i.* and *v.t.* huer

whom, (*pron.*) que ; qui (*indirect and direct object of persons ; interrogative*) lequel, laquelle, lesquels, lesquelles ; **of whom,** de qui, dont, desquels, desquelles

whomsoever, qui que ce soit

whore, prostituée *f.* ; putain *f.*

whose, de qui ; dont ; duquel, de laquelle, desquels, desquelles

whosoever, qui que soit ; qui

why, (*adv.*) pourquoi

wick, mèche *f.*

wicked, (*adj.*) méchant ; mauvais

wickedness, méchanceté *f.*

wicker, osier *m.*

wicker, (*adj.*) en osier

wicket, guichet *m.*

wide, (*adj.*) large ; ample ; vaste ; répandu

wide awake, (*adj.*) bien éveillé

wide-open, (*adj.*) grand-ouvert

wide-spreading, (*adj.*) répandu

widen, *v.i.* s'élargir ; *v.t.* élargir, étendre

widow, veuve *f.*

widower, veuf *m.*

widowhood, veuvage *m.*

width, largeur *f.*; étendue *f.*

wield, *v.t.* manier; exercer

wife, femme *f.*; épouse *f.*

wig, perruque *f.*

wild, *(adj.)* sauvage; farouche; fou (folle)

wilderness, désert *m.*

wilful, *(adj.)* opiniâtre; volontaire; prémedité

wilfully, *(adv.)* avec intention

wilfulness, entêtement *m.*; obstination *f.*

will, volonté *f.*; vouloir *m.*; gré *m.* (pleasure); testament *m.* (document)

goodwill, bonne volonté *f.* (*commer.*); clientèle *f.*

will, *v.t.* vouloir

willing, *(adj.)* bien disposé

willingly, *(adv.)* volontiers

willow, saule *m.*

wily, *(adj.)* rusé

win, *v.t.* and *v.i.* gagner; remporter (victory, etc.)

win back, *v.t.* regagner

win through, *v.i.* venir à bout (de)

wind, vent *m.*; souffle *m.*; respiration *f.* (breathing); haleine *f.* (breath)

breath of wind, souffle (*m.*) de vent

high wind, grand vent

wind, *v.t.* faire perdre haleine à

windfall, fruit (*m.*) abattu par le vent; bonne aubaine *f.* (lucky chance)

wind gauge, anémomètre *m.*

windmill, moulin à vent *m.*

wind-pipe, trachée-artère *f.*

wind, *v.t.* enrouler (coil); dévider (silk, etc.); remonter (clock or watch); conclure ou liquider (*commer.*); *v.i.* tourner, serpenter

windlass, cabestan *m.*

window, fenêtre *f.*; croisée *f.*; étalage *m.* (of shop); vitrine *f.* (show-case); vitrail *m.* (*pl.* -aux) (of church).

window-blind, store *m.*

window-box, caisse (*f.*) à fleurs

window-pane, carreau *m.*

window-sill, appui *m.* (de fenêtre)

windward, (adv.) au vent

windy, (adj.) venteux(-euse)

wine, vin *m.*

wine-cask, fût *m.*

wine-cellar, cave *f.*

wine-cooler, glacière (*f.*) à vin; seau (*m.*) à frapper

wine-glass, verre (*m.*) à vin

wine-growing, viticulture *f.*

wine list, carte (*f.*) des vins

wine-shop, débit (*m.*) de vins

wing, aile *f.*

wings, (*theat.*) coulisses *f. pl.*

wing (on the), au vol

wink, clin (*m.*) d'œil

to have forty winks, faire un petit somme

wink, *v.i.* cligner de l'œil

not to have a wink of sleep, ne pas fermer l'œil (de toute la nuit)

winner, gagnant(e) *m.* (*f.*); vainqueur *m.*

winning, (adj.) gagnant; séduisant (manner)

winter, hiver *m.*

winter, *v.i.* hiverner; passer l'hiver

wintering, hivernage *m.*

wintry, (adj.) d'hiver, hivernal

wipe, coup (*m.*) d'éponge (de mouchoir)

wipe, *v.t.* essuyer

wiper, (cloth) torchon *m.*; essuie-glace *m.* (on windscreen)

wire, fil *m.*; fil de fer *m.*; barreau *m.* (of cage); dépêche *f.* (telegram)

wire, *v.t.* lier avec du fil de fer; télégraphier; canaliser (with electricity)

barbed wire, fil de fer barbelé

wire netting, grillage *m.*; treillage *m.* (en fil de fer)

wire-puller, intrigant(e) *m.* (*f.*)

wire-work, grillage métallique *m.*

wireless, (adj.) sans fil

wireless set, poste (*m.*) de T.S.F.

wireless telegraphy, télégraphie (*f.*) sans fil, T.S.F.

wiry, (*adj.*) nerveux(-euse) (*physical*)

wisdom, sagesse *f.*; prudence *f.*

wise, (*adj.*) sage; prudent

wise (**in no**), d'aucune façon

wish, souhait *m.*; désir *m.*; envie *f.*; vœu *m.*; intention *f.*

wish, *v.i.* and *v.t.* souhaiter, désirer, vouloir

wishful, désireux(-euse) (de)

wishy-washy, (*adj.*) faible, fade

wisp, bouchon (*m.*) de paille (straw); touffe *f.* (of grass)

wistful, (*adj.*) désireux(-euse); pensif(-ive)

wit, esprit *m.* (quality); bel esprit *m.* (person)

to wit, c'est-à-dire

witch, sorcière *f.*

witchcraft, sorcellerie *f.*; magie *f.*

with, (*prep.*) avec; de; par (by means of); chez; parmi (among)

withal, (*adv.*) en outre

withdraw, *v.i.* se retirer, s'éloigner de

withdraw, *v.t.* retirer, rappeler

withdrawal, retraite *f.*

withdrawing, rappel *m.*

wither, *v.i.* se dessécher; languir

wither, *v.t.* flétrir; dessécher

withhold, *v.t.* retenir

within, (*adv.*) en dedans; à l'intérieur; chez soi

within, (*prep.*) dans, en

without, (*adv.*) en dehors; au dehors; à l'extérieur

without, (*conj.*) à moins que (unless)

without, (*prep.*) sans (not having); hors de; en dehors de

withstand, *v.t.* résister (à); combattre

witness, témoin *m.* (person); témoignage *m.* (testimony)

witness, *v.t.* attester; assister à (an event)

witness, *v.i.* porter témoignage, témoigner (de)

witted (**half-**), (*adj.*) niais

witted (**quick-**), (*adj.*) à l'esprit vif

witticism, bon mot *m.*

witty, (*adj.*) spirituel(le)

wizard, sorcier *m.*; magicien *m.*

wobble (**to**), *v.i.* vaciller, chanceler

wobbling, (*adj.*) chancelant

woe, peine *f.*; douleur *f.*

woeful, (*adj.*) triste

wolf, loup *m.*; louve *f.*

wolfish, (*adj.*) rapace, vorace

woman, femme *f.*

womanhood, état (*m.*) de femme

womanly, (*adj.*) de femme; féminin

wonder, étonnement *m.*; surprise *f.*; merveille *f.*; miracle *m.*

wonder, *v.i.* s'étonner (de); se demander (whether)

wonderful, (*adj.*) étonnant; merveilleux(-euse)

wonted, (*adj.*) accoutumé

woo, *v.t.* faire la cour à; rechercher en mariage; (*fig.*) solliciter

wood, bois *m.*

wooded, (*adj.*) boisé

wood(en), (*adj.*) de bois; en bois

woodbine, chèvrefeuille *m.*

woodcock, bécasse *f.*

woodcut, gravure (*f.*) sur bois

wood-cutter, bûcheron *m.*

woodpecker, pivert *m.*

wooer, prétendant *m.*

wool, laine *f.*

woollen, de laine

woollens, lainages *m. pl.*

woolly, (*adj.*) laineux(-euse)

word, mot *m.*; parole *f.*; promesse *f.* (promise)

by word of mouth, verbalement

send word to, faire savoir

work, travail *m.*; ouvrage *m.*; besogne *f.*; œuvre *f.* (of charity, art, etc.)

works, usine *f.* (factory); mécanisme *m.* (engine); mouvement *m.* (watch, etc.)

work, *v.i.* travailler; fonctionner (function); opérer; avoir de l'effet (operate)

work, *v.t.* travailler; façonner; faire marcher

workable, (*adj.*) faisable, réalisable

worker, ouvrier(-ère) *m.* (*f.*); employé(e) *m.* (*f.*); travailleur (-euse) *m.* (*f.*)

workhouse, asile (*m.*) des pauvres
working, fonctionnement *m.*; jeu *m.* (of machines); exploitation *f.* (of mines, etc.)
working class, classe (*f.*) ouvrière
working day, jour (*m.*) ouvrable
workmanlike, (*adj.*) bien travaillé
workshop, atelier *m.*
world, monde *m.*; l'univers *m.*
world-wide, (*adj.*) universel(le)
worldliness, mondanité *f.*
worldly, (*adj.*) mondain
worm, ver *m.*
worm-eaten, (*adj.*) vermoulu; rongé des vers
worm (one's way), *v.t.* s'insinuer; se glisser
wormwood, absinthe *f.*
worry, souci *m.*; ennui *m.*; inquiétude *f.*
worry, *v.t.* tourmenter, tracasser; *v.i.* se tracasser
worse, (*adj.*) pire; plus mauvais, plus mal (health)
worse, (*adv.*) pis; plus mal
worship, culte *m.*; adoration *f.*; honneur *m.* (title only)
worship, *v.t.* adorer
worst, (*adj.*) le pire; le plus mauvais
worst, (*adv.*) le pis; le plus mal
worst, le pire *m.*; désavantage *m.*
worst, *v.t.* battre
worsted, laine (*f.*) filée
worth, valeur *f.*; prix *m.*
worth, (*adj.*) qui vaut; valant; qui mérite
worthless, (*adj.*) sans valeur; méprisable (contemptible)
worthy, (*adj.*) digne
would-be, (*adj.*) soi-disant
wound, blessure *f.*; plaie *f.*
wound, *v.t.* blesser
wrack, varech *m.*; débris *m.*
wrangle, dispute *f.*; querelle *f.*
wrangle, *v.i.* se disputer; se chamailler; se quereller
wrangle, dispute *f.*; querelle *f.*
wrap, *v.t.* envelopper; rouler

wrap, wrapper, châle *f.*; robe (*f.*) de chambre; peignoir *m.*; manteau *m.*
wrapping, couverture *f.*
wrapping paper, papier (*m.*) d'emballage
wrath, colère *f.*; courroux *m.*
wrathful, (*adj.*) furieux(-euse); en colère
wreak vengeance on, se venger de
wreath, guirlande *f.*; couronne *f.*
wreathe, *v.t.* entortiller; couronner
wreck, naufrage *m.*; épave *f.*; (*fig.*) ruine *f.*
wreck, *v.t.* faire faire naufrage à; (*fig.*) ruiner
wreckage, débris *m. pl.*; épaves *f. pl.*
wrecked, (*adj.*) naufragé
to be wrecked, faire naufrage
wren, roitelet *m.*
wrench, torsion *f.*; arrachement *m.*; foulure *f.* (sprain); clef *f.* (tool)
wrench, *v.t.* arracher (à *or* de); se fouler (to sprain)
wrest, *v.t.* arracher (à)
wrestle, *v.i.* lutter
wrestler, lutteur *m.*
wrestling, lutte *f.*
wretch, malheureux(-euse) *m.* (*f.*); infortuné(e) *m.* (*f.*)
wretched, (*adj.*) misérable
wretchedness, misère *f.*
wriggle, *v.i.* se tortiller; frétiller; s'agiter
wright, artisan *m.*; constructeur *m.*
wring, *v.t.* tordre
wrinkle, ride *f.* (of face); pli *m.* (in clothes); tuyau *m.* (hint)
wrinkle, *v.i.* se rider; *v.t.* rider
wrist (wristband), poignet *m.*
wrist-watch, montre-bracelet *f.*
writ, mandat *m.*; assignation *f.*
write, *v.t.* écrire
write in full, écrire en toutes lettres
writer, écrivain *m.*; auteur *m.*
writhe, *v.i.* se tordre
writing, écriture *f.*

the **writings of,** les écrits (*m. pl.*) de

in writing, par écrit

writing-book, cahier (*m.*) d'écriture

writing-desk, pupitre *m.*; bureau *m.*

writing-pad, sous-main *m.*; buvard *m.*

writing paper, papier (*m.*) à écrire

writing table, bureau *m.*; table (*f.*) à écrire

wrong, (*adj.*) faux (fausse); inexact; mal, mauvais

wrong, (*adv.*) mal

wrong, (*subst.*) mal *m.*; tort *m.*; injustice *f.*; dommage *m.*

wrong, *v.t.* faire (du) tort à; faire injure à

wrongful, (*adj.*) injuste; nuisible

wroth, (*adj.*) en colère

wrought, (*adj.*) travaillé, façonné

wrought-iron, fer (*m.*) forgé

wry, (*adj.*) de travers; tordu

wry-neck, torticolis *m.*; torcol *m.* (bird)

X

xebec, chébec *m.*

Xmas, Noël *m.*; la fête de Noël

X-rays, rayons x (*m. pl.*)

X-ray, *v.t.* radiographier

xylographer, xylographe *m.*

xylography, xylographie *f.*

Y

yacht, yacht *m.*; *v.i.* faire du yachting

yam, igname *f.*

Yankee, Américain *m.*, yankee *m.*

yap, *v.i.* japper

yard, cour *f.*; chantier *m.* (work-yard)

yard, (measure) mètre *m.* (yard = ·914 metres)

yard, (nautical) vergue *f.*

yarn, fil *m.*; laine filée *f.*; récit *m.* (story)

yarrow, mille-feuilles *f.*

yawl, yole *f.*

yawn, bâillement *m.*

yawn, *v.i.* bâiller

year, an *m.* (unit of time); année *f.* (particular year)

by the year, par an, à l'année

every year, tous les ans

half-year, semestre *m.*

next year, l'an prochain; l'année prochaine

year-book, annuaire *m.*

yearling, âgé d'un an

yearly, annuel(le); chaque année *f.*

yearn, *v.i.* soupirer après; avoir bien envie de

yearning, envie *f.*

yeast, levure *f.*

yell(ing), hurlement *m.*

yell, *v.i.* and *v.t.* hurler

yellow, jaune *m.*

yellow, (*adj.*) jaune

yellowish, (*adj.*) jaunâtre

yellowness, teint (*m.*) jaune

to become yellow, *v.i.* jaunir

yelp, *v.i.* glapir

yelping, glapissement *m.*

yeoman, fermier-propriétaire *m.*

yes, (*adv.*) oui; si

yesterday, (*adv.* and *m.*) hier

day before yesterday, avanthier

yet, (*conj.*) pourtant; cependant; toutefois

yet, (*adv.*) encore

as yet, jusqu'ici; jusqu'à présent

not yet, pas encore

yew, if *m.*

yield, rendement *m.*; produit *m.*; rapport *m.*

yield, *v.t.* produire; donner, rapporter; *v.i.* céder; se rendre

yielding, (*adj.*) mou (molle); complaisant

yielding, soumission *f.*; consentement *m.*

yoke, joug *m.*

yoke, *v.t.* atteler; réduire à l'esclavage

yokel, rustre *m.*

yolk, jaune (*m.*) d'œuf

yonder, (*adv.*) là, là-bas

yore, (*adv.*) autrefois; jadis

you, (*pers. pron.*) vous; (*indef.*) on

young, (*adj.*) jeune; inexpérimenté (inexperienced)

young (**grow**), *v.i.* rajeunir

younger, (*adj.*) plus jeune; cadet(te)

youngish, (*adj.*) assez jeune

youngster, jeune homme *m.*; gamin *m.*; blanc bec *m.*

your, (*adj.*) votre (*pl.* vos)

yours, (*pron.*) le vôtre, la vôtre, les vôtres

youth, jeunesse *f.*; adolescence *f.*; jeune homme *m.*

youthful, (*adj.*) jeune

youthfulness, jeunesse *f.*

yule-log, bûche (*f.*) de Noël

yuletide, Noël *m.*; la saison de Noël

Z

zany, bouffon *m.*

zeal, zèle *m.*

zealot, zélateur(-trice) *m.* (*f.*)

zealous, (*adj.*) zélé

zebra, zèbre *m.*

zenith, zénith *m.*; apogée *m.*

zephyr, zéphire *m.*

zero, zéro *m.*; rien *m.*

zest, goût *m.*; élan *m.*

zigzag, (*adj.*) en zigzag

zigzag, *v.i.* aller en zigzag; zigzaguer

zinc, zinc *m*

zinc, *v.t.* zinguer

zinc-roofing, toiture (*f.*) de zinc

zinc-worker, zingueur *m.*

zip-fastener, fermeture (*f.*) éclair

zodiac, zodiaque *m.*

zone, zone *f.*; ceinture *f.*

zoological, (*adj.*) zoologique

zoological gardens, jardin (*m.*) zoologique

zoologist, zoologiste *m.* and *f.*

zoology, zoologie *f.*

zoophyte, zoophyte *m*

zounds! (*interj.*) sapristi! morbleu!

Zulu, Zoulou *m.*

zymotic(al), (*adj.*) zymotique

LANGUAGES IN TEACH YOURSELF BOOKS

☐ 05771 8	**Arabic** A. S. Tritton	£1·00
☐ 05774 2	**Arabic, Colloquial** T. F. Mitchell	75p
☐ 05772 6	**Bengali** D. F. Hudson	40p
☐ 05936 2	**Cantonese** R. Bruce	95p
☐ 05773 4	**Chinese** H. R. Williamson	£1·30
☐ 05776 9	**Czech** W. R. & Z. Lee	60p
☐ 05777 7	**Danish** H. A. Koefoed	75p
☐ 05778 5	**Dutch** H. Koolhoven	60p
☐ 05779 3	**Dutch Dictionary** P. & M. King	95p
☐ 05780 7	**English for Swahili Speaking People** D. V. Perrot	40p

□ 05828 5   **Turkish**
               G. L. Lewis   60p

□ 05740 8   **Urdu**
               T. Grahame Bailey   60p

□ 05829 3   **Welsh**
               T. Bowen & T. J. Rhys Jones   60p

□ 05995 8   **Yoruba**
               E. C. Rowlands   60p

All these books are available at your local bookshop or newsagent, or can be ordered direct from the publisher. Just tick the titles you want and fill in the form below.

Prices and availability subject to change without notice.

TEACH YOURSELF BOOKS, P.O. Box 11, Falmouth, Cornwall.

Please send cheque or postal order, and allow the following for postage and packing:

U.K.– One book 19p plus 9p per copy for each additional book ordered, up to a maximum of 73p.

B.F.P.O. and EIRE – 19p for the first book plus 9p per copy for the next 6 books, thereafter 3p per book.

OTHER OVERSEAS CUSTOMERS – 20p for the first book and 10p per copy for each additional book.

Name ....

Address ....

....